Higher Education Law

in America

5th Edition

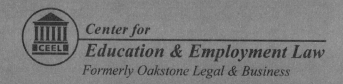

Center for

Education & Employment Law

Formerly Oakstone Legal & Business

Center for Education & Employment Law
P.O. Box 3008
Malvern, PA 19355

"This publication is designed to provide accurate and authoritative information in regard to the subject matter covered. It is sold with the understanding that the publisher is not engaged in rendering legal, accounting or other professional services. If legal advice or other expert assistance is required, the service of a competent professional person should be sought." -from a Declaration of Principles jointly adopted by a Committee of the American Bar Association and a Committee of Publishers and associations.

Library of Congress Cataloging-in Publication Data

Higher Education Law in America.

    p. cm.

Includes index.

ISBN 1-933043-02-4 (pbk.)

1. Universities and colleges--Law and legislation--United States. I. Center for Education & Employment Law.

KF4225 .H54 2000

378.73--dc21

KF
4225
.H54
2004

00-055074

ISBN 1-933043-02-4

TABLE OF CONTENTS

TABLE OF CONTENTS

TABLE OF CONTENTS

CHAPTER FIVE
Employment

CHAPTER SIX
  Employment Discrimination

TABLE OF CONTENTS

TABLE OF CONTENTS

INTRODUCTION

Higher Education Law in America provides an encyclopedic compilation of federal and state court decisions in the area of college and university law. We have reviewed hundreds of federal and state court decisions involving higher education law and have included the most important ones in this deskbook. The chapters have been arranged topically, and the cases have been presented in an easy-to-use manner.

Each chapter contains explanatory passages at the beginning of each section to help you develop an overall understanding of the legal issues in that particular area. The case summaries have been written in everyday language, and at the start of each case is a brief note highlighting the holding or the significant issues discussed within. Further, the case summaries themselves contain boldface type to emphasize important facts, issues and holdings.

We feel that *Higher Education Law in America* will help you understand your rights and responsibilities under state and federal law. It has been designed with professional educators in mind, but also has tremendous value for lawyers. We hope you will use this book to protect yourself and to gain greater wisdom and understanding. Hopefully, we have succeeded in making the law accessible to you regardless of your level of understanding of the legal system.

Jim Roth, Esq.
Senior Legal Editor
Center for Education & Employment Law

ABOUT THE EDITORS

James A. Roth is Senior Editor of *Special Education Law Update* and *Legal Notes for Education*. He is also a co-author of the deskbook *Students with Disabilities and Special Education*. He is a graduate of the University of Minnesota and William Mitchell College of Law. Mr. Roth is admitted to the Minnesota Bar and is an adjunct program associate professor at St. Mary's University of Minnesota — Twin Cities Campus.

Steve McEllistrem is Senior Legal Editor of Center for Education & Employment Law. He co-authored the deskbook *Statutes, Regulations and Case Law Protecting Individuals with Disabilities* and is editor of *Special Education Law Update*. He graduated *cum laude* from William Mitchell College of Law and received his undergraduate degree from the University of Minnesota. Mr. McEllistrem is admitted to the Minnesota Bar.

Curt J. Brown is the Group Publisher of the Center for Education and Employment Law. Prior to assuming his present position, he gained extensive experience in business-to-business publishing, including management of well-known publications such as *What's Working in Human Resources, What's New in Benefits & Compensation, Keep Up to Date with Payroll, Supervisors Legal Update,* and *Facility Manager's Alert.* Mr. Brown graduated from Villanova University School of Law and graduated magna cum laude from Bloomsburg University with a B.S. in Business Administration. He is admitted to the Pennsylvania Bar.

Carol S. Weinman is the editor of the monthly newsletters *Private Education Law Report* and *Higher Education Legal Alert.* She graduated from Temple University's School of Law and received her undergraduate degree from Temple University's School of Communications and Theater. Previously, she wrote for *The Philadelphia Business Journal, The Legal Intelligencer,* and *Healthink & Vitality Communications, Inc.* Ms. Weinman was also a Philadelphia Assistant District Attorney, an arbitrator and an instructor at Pennsylvania State University. She is admitted to the Pennsylvania and New Jersey bars.

How to Use Your Deskbook

We have designed *Higher Education Law in America* in an accessible format for both professional educators and attorneys to use as a research and reference tool toward prevention of legal problems.

Research Tool

As a research tool, our deskbook allows you to conduct your research on two different levels — by topics or cases.

Topic Research

◆ If you have a general interest in a particular **topic** area, our **table of contents** provides descriptive chapter headings containing detailed subheadings from each chapter.

 ➢ For your convenience, we also include the chapter table of contents at the beginning of each chapter.

> **Example:**
> For more information on liability, the table of contents indicates that a discussion of teacher misconduct takes place in Chapter Eight, under Intentional Conduct, on page 408:
>
> CHAPTER EIGHT
> School Liability
>

How to Use Your Deskbook

◆ If you have a specific interest in a particular **issue**, our comprehensive **index** collects all of the relevant page references to particular issues.

> **Example:**
> For more information on student activities, the index provides references to all of the cases dealing with student activities instead of only those cases dealing with fraternities and sororities:
>
> Statewide testing, 58, 361-363
> → Student activities
>   Facilities and services, 136-138
>   Fraternities and sororities 140-143
>   Hazing, 146-150
>   Injuries, 143-146
>   Operation and school supervision, 138-140
>   Organizational liability, 141-143
>   Freedom of expression, 134-136
> Student activity fees, 177, 187-190

Case Research

◆ If you know the **name** of a particular case, our **table of cases** will allow you to quickly reference the location of the case.

> **Example:**
> If someone mentioned a case named *Gonzaga Univ. v. Doe,* looking in the table of cases, which has been arranged alphabetically, the case would be listed under section "G" and would be found on p. 53 of the text.
>
> **G**
>
> Girsky v. Touro College, Fuchsberg Law
>   Center, 40
> Glenn v. Univ. of Southern California, 417
> Godinez v. Siena College, 413
> Gomes v. University of Maine, 20
> Gonyo v. Drake Univ., 125
> → Gonzaga Univ. v. Doe, 53
> Gonzalez v. National Bd. of Medical Examiners, 81
> Goodreau v. Rector and Visitors of Univ.
>   of Virginia, 27

✓ Each of the cases summarized in the deskbook also contains the case citation, which will allow you to access the full text of the case if you would like to learn more about it. *See How to Read a Case Citation, p. 515.*

◆ If your interest lies in cases from a **particular state**, our **table of cases by state** will identify the cases from your state and direct you to their page numbers.

Example:
If cases from California were of interest, the table of cases by state, arranged alphabetically, would list all of the case summaries contained in the deskbook from that state.

CALIFORNIA

→ Barnhart v. Cabrillo Community College, 400
Bauer v. Sampson, 157
Bessard v. California Community Colleges, 163
Brown v. Li, 179
Brown-Alkire v. Univ. of LaVerne, 391
California Cosmetology Coalition v. Riley, 16

✓ Remember, the judicial system has two court systems — state and federal court — which generally function independently from each other. *See The Judicial System, p. 511.* We have included the federal court cases in the table of cases by state according to the state in which the court resides. However, federal court decisions often impact other federal courts within that particular circuit. Therefore, it may be helpful to review cases from all of the states contained in a particular circuit.

Reference Tool

As a reference tool, we have highlighted important resources which provide the framework for many legal issues.

◆ If you would like to see specific wording of the **U.S. Constitution**, refer to **Appendix A**, which includes relevant provisions of the U.S. Constitution such as the First Amendment (freedom of speech and religion) and the Fourteenth Amendment (which contains the Equal Protection Clause and the Due Process Clause).

How to Use Your Deskbook

◆ If you would like to review **U.S. Supreme Court decisions** in a particular subject matter area, our topical list of U.S. Supreme Court case citations located in **Appendix B** will be helpful.

The book also contains a glossary, which provides definitions of legal terms and certain statutes. The glossary can be found on p. 517.

We hope you benefit from the use of *Higher Education Law in America.* If you have any questions about how to use the deskbook, please contact James Roth at jroth@pbp.com.

TABLE OF CASES

TABLE OF CASES

TABLE OF CASES

TABLE OF CASES

TABLE OF CASES

TABLE OF CASES BY STATE

TABLE OF CASES BY STATE

TABLE OF CASES BY STATE

TABLE OF CASES BY STATE

WYOMING

CHAPTER ONE

Student Rights

I. THE CONTRACTUAL RELATIONSHIP

The relationship between students and colleges or universities is generally a contractual one, and the terms of the contract define the duties of both parties. Generally, when a contract has been breached, extra-contractual damages (like punitive damages) are not available. Only when there has been some egregious behavior, like fraud, will such damages be recoverable.

A. Breach of Contract

Courts generally hold that a valid educational contract is created upon acceptance of a student for admission. The contract terms exist in the tuition agreement, college catalogues or brochures and student handbooks. Both the institution and the student have obligations under the contract, and failure of either party to fulfill its obligations may result in a breach of contract claim.

◆ *The U.S. Supreme Court held that the doctrine of substantial performance–which allows a party who has substantially performed her promise under a contract to expect the other party to perform–applied to contracts in an academic setting. Moreover, the Court found that the doctrine applied even though one of the parties was a private educational institution.*

An overweight Rhode Island college student joined a nursing program in her sophomore year. During her junior year, the school began to pressure her to lose weight. The college tried to get her to sign a contract in which she would attend Weight Watchers. She refused to sign the contract, but attended Weight Watchers regularly without losing any significant weight. She obtained a failing grade in a clinical nursing course for reasons related to her weight and not her performance. Although expulsion was generally required for failing a clinical course, the school offered her another contract that required her to lose at least two pounds per week in order to remain in the program. She signed the contract but failed to lose two pounds per week, and was asked to voluntarily withdraw from the nursing program. She withdrew and transferred to another nursing program, which caused her nursing education to last five years instead of the usual four. She sued the college in federal court and was awarded damages for breach of contract. The school appealed to the U.S. Court of Appeals, First Circuit, which noted that the student-college relationship is essentially a contractual one, and that **as long as the student maintained good grades, paid tuition and abided by the disciplinary rules, the college was required to provide her with an education**. When the school forced her to withdraw because she was overweight and for no other reason, the school breached the contract.

The U.S. Supreme Court then heard the case and concluded that the court of appeals should have reviewed the case *de novo* (as if hearing it for the first time). It remanded the case with an order to review the district court's application of the substantial performance doctrine to the contract at issue. *Salve Regina College v. Russell*, 499 U.S. 225, 111 S.Ct. 1217, 113 L.Ed.2d 190 (1991). The doctrine of substantial performance allows a party who has substantially performed her promise under a contract to expect the other party to perform its promise. On remand, a jury found that **the student had substantially performed, and that the school had breached the contract** by not rendering its part of the exchange. The issue on appeal was whether the doctrine should have been applied to a contract in an academic setting. The college argued that the doctrine's application was limited and urged certification to the Rhode Island Supreme Court to determine two issues: 1) whether a school can refuse enrollment in a course where the student has not met mutually established weight loss requirements, and 2) whether the doctrine of substantial performance applies to a dispute between a student and a private college. The court denied the school's request as inappropriate and unnecessary. It explained that **the doctrine was not precluded simply because one of the parties was a private educational institution**, and stated that "the instant case simply **does not implicate concerns of a school's academic integrity**." The award of damages for the student was affirmed. *Russell v. Salve Regina College*, 938 F.2d 315 (1st Cir. 1991). [RI]

◆ *A Connecticut court held a university course catalogue was not an enforceable contract for educational services.*

A post-graduate student became dissatisfied with his clinical rotation and the credentials of his instructors. He withdrew from a course when he had problems with it. The student could not graduate in four years because of his light course load. He took a leave of absence and sued the university in a state superior court for breach of contract, claiming the university program did not live up to what was represented in its course catalogue. The court stated a contractual relationship exists between private universities and their students. **A university may not be held liable for breach of contract unless its program fundamentally fails to satisfy a specific contractual promise.** See *Gupta v. New Britain General Hospital*, 239 Conn. 574, 687 A.2d 111 (1996). The student did not show the university program failed in any fundamental way in its educational offerings. "Fundamental" items included the number of days or hours of instruction and other objective criteria. As the student did not offer any concrete evidence of a fundamental failure that made it impossible for him to obtain a medical degree, there was no support for his breach of contract claim. The student did not show the university broke a particular contract promise. The catalogue was not a contract and the court awarded summary judgment to the university. *Cullen v. University of Bridgeport*, No. CV-020396010, 2003 WL 23112678 (Conn. Super. 12/10/03). [CT]

◆ *An Illinois private university had a rational basis for expelling a student who failed to earn credits for two consecutive semesters.*

The student failed two required field work assignments for her master's in social work program. The student accused the university of failing to offer her a remediation plan as described in the university handbook. The university claimed she did not qualify for remediation and expelled her from the program under a handbook policy requiring dismissal of any student failing to earn credit in consecutive semesters. She sued the university in a state court for breach of contract and other claims. The court held the university handbook created a contract and found the university breached the contract by not creating a remediation plan. It ordered the university to refund her tuition.

The university appealed to the Appellate Court of Illinois, which found the university adequately documented the student's problems. It held the relationship between a student and private university is not purely contractual. Courts are generally unwilling to interfere with private university student regulations. **A student may prevail on a contract claim against a private university only if an adverse academic decision is arbitrary, capricious or in bad faith.** A student must show a dismissal was without any discernable rational basis. As there was no such showing in this case, the court reversed the judgment. *Raethz v. Aurora Univ.*, 805 N.E.2d 696 (Ill. App. 2d Dist. 2004). [IL]

◆ *A student's lawsuit for breach of contract should not have been dismissed where questions of fact existed.*

A Georgia high school student applied for a scholarship at a Mississippi university pursuant to a 1997 catalog and application. Under those terms, the university waived the out-of-state tuition rate, and the student was to receive

$1,000 per year. When the student attended the orientation, he was given a 1998 catalog, which listed the scholarship amount at $500 per year, and was informed that he no longer qualified for the nonresident tuition waiver. He sued for breach of contract. A federal court dismissed his lawsuit, but the Mississippi Court of Appeals reversed. Here, although the 1998 catalog was the one to be used for determining the contractual relationship of the parties, that catalog allowed for a waiver of nonresident tuition. As a result, the student was entitled to the waiver. However, the scholarship amount would be $500 per year. On further appeal, the Supreme Court of Mississippi reversed and remanded the case. **Neither party received a fair evaluation as to whether a contract for a scholarship existed between the student and the university based on the terms of the school catalog**. The trial court improperly dismissed the case, and the court of appeals improperly refused to allow the university to present a defense. *Aronson v. University of Mississippi*, 828 So.2d 752 (Miss. 2002). [MS]

◆ *A promise to grant "many credits" for classes taken at a Russian university was not precise enough to be the basis for a breach of contract action.*

An immigrant with a master's degree in engineering from a Russian university enrolled in an 18-month nursing program at a Connecticut university. After her poor academic and clinical performance, she was dismissed from the program. She sued the university for breach of contract, among other claims, asserting that the university had promised to give her "many credits" for her Russian education. She claimed that because she had to take 11 additional liberal arts courses, she was unable to complete the nursing program in a timely manner, which resulted in her dismissal. A trial court ruled for the university, and the Connecticut Appellate Court affirmed. Here, **the student's claim regarding transfer credits was too imprecise to allow for a breach of contract action**. Also, since all her other claims grew out of the breach of contract action, those claims could not proceed either. *Faigel v. Fairfield Univ.*, 815 A.2d 140 (Conn. App. 2003). [CT]

◆ *A university breached its contract with a student by arbitrarily and capriciously removing her from the nursing program.*

An Ohio nursing student struggled academically. First, she withdrew from a class because her father-in-law passed away. Later, she received several D grades and had to retake some classes. After obtaining permission to retake a class, a new dean took over the nursing program. She notified the student that she could not take the final class needed to complete her degree because she was no longer in the nursing program. This was because she could not complete the program within the required time period.

The student sued the university in an Ohio court, asserting that it breached its contract with her by removing her from the program. The court ruled in favor of the student, and the Ohio Court of Appeals affirmed. Because the previous dean had readmitted the student to the nursing program so that she could retake the class she "failed," **it was not reasonable for the new dean to disallow her to take the final class she needed**. Although the student was not entitled to money damages, she should have been allowed back into the program to complete the last class. *Stratton v. Kent State Univ.*, No. 02AP-887, 2003 WL 1227570 (Ohio App. 10th Dist. 3/18/03). [OH]

◆ *An Illinois student's breach-of-contract action against a college was allowed to proceed in part.*

A student transferred to the Illinois Institute of Technology after he was allegedly lured there with the promise of a scholarship and credit for past courses at other schools. However, his pre-registration was canceled for failure to pay tuition. He attended classes anyway and completed 10 courses over a two-year period. Eventually, the institute offered him a payment plan and informed him of his outstanding balance. He made two payments to the institute and was granted a conditional reinstatement, but he was not given credit for courses he had taken when he was not formally registered. He then sued the institute for breach of contract in an Illinois federal court, and the institute sought to dismiss the suit. The court refused to dismiss the action, finding that an implied contract existed between students and colleges. Here, issues of fact remained as to **whether the student had performed under the terms of the implied contract such that the institute should have awarded him course credits and a degree**. However, because the institute had offered the student a payment plan to discharge his debt, that part of the student's lawsuit had to be dismissed. *Imam v. Illinois Institute of Technology*, No. 2002 WL 88566 (N.D. Ill. 1/23/02). [IL]

◆ *A nursing student was unable to establish that New York University breached its implied contract with her when it terminated her from its master's nursing program for poor academic performance.*

A student of NYU's School of Education's Master of Arts Program in Nursing Care: Infants, Children and Adolescents alleged that the preceptor to whom she was assigned "abused her incessantly … [and] tormented her." She requested a different preceptor, but received no response from the university. **Based on her poor clinical performance, the school terminated her enrollment.** More than three years later, she sued NYU and its nursing division for breach of contract, promissory estoppel and fraudulent misrepresentations. A federal court dismissed her lawsuit. She presented no evidence that NYU acted arbitrarily and capriciously in terminating her enrollment. The court deferred to the school's decision regarding academic matters. It found no "circumstantial evidence of conscious misbehavior or recklessness" by the university. *Ward v. New York Univ.*, 2000 WL 1448641 (S.D.N.Y. 9/28/00). [NY]

◆ *A Texas student's breach of contract claim could not succeed where she failed a required course.*

A nursing student at a Texas university passed the academic portion of a required nursing leadership/management course, but failed the clinical component when she was ordered off the hospital floor for compromising the safety of a patient. The university allowed her to complete the clinical component through an independent assessment, but she failed that as well. She sued the university and a number of officials for breach of contract, among other claims. A trial court ruled for the university, and the student appealed. The Texas Court of Appeals noted that a contractual relationship need not necessarily be inferred between a student and a public school. However, where, as here, the school was private, an implied contract existed. Nevertheless, **the student could not succeed on her breach of contract claim because she did not satisfy her obligations under the contract. She failed the clinical portion of a required class, and the court refused to second-guess the university's grading process.** *Southwell v. University of the Incarnate Word,* 974 S.W.2d 351 (Tex. App.–San Antonio 1998). [TX]

◆   *By changing its procedure for selecting medical students from a university program, the school breached its contracts with the students.*

An Illinois university traditionally gave serious consideration to its applied physiology program students for entrance to its medical school where the students achieved a GPA of at least 3.0. However, **the university changed its policy to allow no more than 50 students from the physiology program into the medical school. It notified students of the change after they showed up for orientation even though it knew of the change two weeks earlier** and could have notified them before they sent their deposits to reserve their places. When a number of students who achieved a GPA of 3.0 or greater did not get into the medical school because of the 50-student limitation, they sued for breach of contract and fraud. A trial court found that because the purpose of the program was to allow students to get into medical school, the university had breached an implied contract with the students, but that it had not committed actionable fraud. The Appellate Court of Illinois affirmed. It stated that the school's unilateral change of the contract's terms amounted to a breach. However, the students failed to show actionable fraud under either the consumer protection act or the common law. *Brody v. Finch Univ. of Health Sciences,* 698 N.E.2d 257 (Ill. App. 2d Dist. 1998). [IL]

◆   *The First Circuit found that a student's breach of contract claim failed because he did not have a signed written offer of admission, which the school's graduate school catalog indicated was required to make an offer binding.*

A student applied for admission to a private university's graduate school, and was admitted as a probationary special student, which allowed the taking of graduate level courses but would not lead to a master's degree. An associate dean met with the student and explained to him that his admission was probationary because he lacked the requisite academic background or coursework in computer science. She told him that to be admitted to the degree program, he would need to successfully complete coursework in the computer science department and obtain a faculty advisor. However, **the university's graduate school catalog specifically provided that offers of admissions had binding force only when made by the school in writing**. The student obtained a letter from a professor that stated that he would be working under the professor's supervision for his master's project. Subsequently, the university informed the student that his special student status was discontinued and that he had not been admitted into the master's program. The student sued the university for breach of contract in a Rhode Island federal district court, and the judge granted judgment as a matter of law to the university.

The student appealed to the U.S. Court of Appeals, First Circuit, asserting that the district court judge had improperly taken the case from the jury. He asserted that he reasonably expected that if he satisfactorily performed his coursework and obtained a sponsor for his master's project, he would be admitted as a master's degree candidate based on the statement of the associate dean. The court, however, noted that **the graduate school catalog divested faculty members of any authority** to promise admission or to determine the necessary prerequisites for admissions. **Even if the associate dean had the authority to offer admission to the student, she could not do so except by a signed writing.** Further, the letter from the student's advisor did not qualify as a faculty recommendation. Accordingly, the student's breach of contract claim failed. The district court's decision was affirmed. *Mangla v. Brown Univ.*, 135 F.3d 80 (1st Cir. 1998). [RI]

◆   *When an individual is induced to enroll in a college based upon an award for certain life experience credits, the institution may not thereafter revoke those credits.*

A detective enrolled in a master's degree program at a private college in Pennsylvania. He claimed that upon admission he was to be awarded certain **life experience credits**. In order to fulfill the requirements for his degree, the detective enrolled in a one-week course entitled "Gender Stereotyping." As part of a classroom exercise, the instructor directed a classmate, whom the detective alleged to be a "known homosexual," to make physical advances toward the detective. The classmate complied by telling the detective he was attracted to him and by touching the detective above the knee. The detective rejected these advances, and the instructor assigned that same classmate to act as a "facilitator" to deal with the detective's anger. The detective voiced his objections suggesting that the exercise was improper. The instructor then allegedly became openly critical of the detective's attitude and performance, and awarded him a "C" grade for the course. Thereafter, the instructor allegedly had himself appointed as the detective's academic adviser, and revoked and persuaded other instructors to revoke certain preapproved credits that had been granted upon admission. The detective filed suit claiming, among other things, breach of contract. The claims were dismissed by the trial court, and the detective appealed to the Superior Court of Pennsylvania.

The appellate court began by reversing the trial court's order striking the detective's breach of contract claim. The court rejected the trial court's holding that the college was entitled to revoke credits previously granted for work performed out of school. The court noted that **an institution is not free to make a contractual obligation to a student and then later ignore it**. When an individual is induced to enroll in a college based upon an award for certain life experience credits, the institution may not thereafter revoke those credits. *Britt v. Chestnut Hill College*, 632 A.2d 557 (Pa.Super. 1993). [PA]

◆   *A New Jersey court found the closure of a college did not constitute a breach of contract because the university acted fairly and in good faith.*

A private university maintained a dental college in Hackensack, New

Jersey. The university published an annual Graduate Studies Bulletin that detailed the programs offered, the curriculum, and the terms of acceptance, admission and continuation. **The bulletin contained a reservation of rights provision that allowed the university to eliminate a college, subject only to giving adequate notification to its students.** The dental college learned it would receive no state aid after the 1989-90 school year, and that aid would be reduced by 25% in that year. The president recommended to the board of trustees that the dental college be closed. The college set up a transfer program for its students and linked it with a tuition subsidy package funded by the New Jersey Department of Health and Education. Various dental students then brought suit against the board of trustees asserting that the university had breached a contract between the students and itself by closing the dental school.

The students argued that by paying their first year's tuition, they had entered into a complete and binding contract for the entire educational program. The board asserted the court was required to give deference to university autonomy in academic decision making, and that its administrative decision to close the college was within the autonomous area. The board further claimed that there was no contract with the students, and that, even if there was such a contract, the university had reserved the right to close the college upon adequate notice. The Superior Court of New Jersey determined the "true" university-student "contract" was one of mutual obligations implied by law. Having decided that, it then became necessary to ascertain whether the university had acted in good faith and dealt fairly with its students. The court found that the **trustees had acted promptly and forthrightly as soon as they learned of the change in their financial circumstances**. Accordingly, the court ruled in favor of the board of trustees. *Beukas v. Board of Trustees of Fairleigh Dickinson Univ.*, 605 A.2d 776 (N.J. Super. Law Div. 1991). [NJ]

The students then appealed to the Superior Court of New Jersey, Appellate Division, which affirmed the trial court's decision for substantially the same reasons as expressed by the trial court judge. However, the appellate court also noted that **even if an enforceable contract existed, the reservation of rights clause worked to defeat the students' claim because the university acted fairly and in good faith when it exercised its rights**. *Beukas v. Board of Trustees of Fairleigh Dickenson Univ.*, 605 A.2d 708 (N.J. Super. A.D. 1992). [NJ]

◆   *Although courts generally reject breach of contract claims based on the quality of a school's "educational experience," the Supreme Court of Colorado found that a breach of contract may occur where a school has failed to provide specifically promised educational services.*

Several Colorado residents enrolled in a private college that provided training for technical jobs in medical and dental careers. The students cited a variety of deficiencies, which allegedly breached their enrollment agreements. Specifically, the students alleged that the college promised in their enrollment agreements and in the college catalogue to provide up-to-date equipment, qualified faculty, computer training, English language instruction and the ability to repeat courses with no additional fees. The students filed breach of contract claims in a Colorado district court. The district court held for the school, and the students appealed to the Court of Appeals of Colorado. The court of appeals reversed with respect to the breach of contract claim.

The school appealed to the Supreme Court of Colorado, which noted **breach of contract claims that attack the quality of a school's "educational experience" are generally rejected**. These are essentially repackaged educational malpractice claims, and raise questions that must be answered by reference to principles of duty, standards of care, and reasonable conduct—things associated with the law of torts, not contract. However, **a breach of contract may occur where a school has failed to provide specifically promised educational services**. Here, the college allegedly failed to provide up-to-date equipment, qualified faculty, computer training and English language instruction. Thus, the students stated breach of contract claims to the extent that the alleged obligations to the students were educational services for which the students already had paid. The holding of the court of appeals was affirmed. *Cencor, Inc. v. Tolman*, 868 P.2d 396 (Colo. 1994). [CO]

◆ *Students could not sue for breach of contract when a state closed a university campus.*

When the South Dakota legislature passed a law converting a university campus to a minimum security prison, it allowed students to complete the academic year and included other provisions to help the students acquire their degrees. A number of students sued the board of regents, asserting breach of contract, violations of their civil rights under 42 U.S.C. § 1983, and that the law was unconstitutional. A trial court granted pretrial judgment to the defendants, and the Supreme Court of South Dakota affirmed. It noted that **the students had no enforceable contract rights because their contract with the school was for the current term only**. It also held that the board of regents was not a person under § 1983, and that none of the students' constitutional rights were invaded by the closing of the school. *Aase v. State*, 400 N.W.2d 269 (S.D. 1987). [SD]

◆ *An implied contract arises between a student and a school where the school promises to grant a degree upon completion of the terms outlined.*

Based on an advertisement published by the Teachers College of Columbia University, an undergraduate student with 60 credits became interested in the "Accel-A-Year" program offered by the college that would grant him a combined Bachelor of Science and Master of Arts degree. The combined degree could be obtained after an additional two years of study, thereby saving him one year toward the graduate degree. The student received an advisory statement from the college that referred to the prospective granting of his combined degree in this manner: "Application is in process to Albany for approval of this program as a *combined* degree program of B.S./M.A." The student checked the box marked "Master of Arts Degree" on his application for admission, and the letter of acceptance from the college referred to his admission to a program leading to a Master of Arts degree. Oral statements by a college representative also indicated that the program would lead to a Master of Arts degree but that the application for the combined degree program had not yet been approved. When the student was notified that the application would not be approved in time for him to receive the combined degree he resumed his studies and received a Master of Arts degree in 1982 after three years of graduate study. The student sued the college for breach of contract and fraud in a New York trial court, which ruled for the college.

The student appealed to the New York Supreme Court, Appellate Division. It observed an **implied contract** arises between a student and a school which states that if a student complies with the terms outlined by the school, the student will obtain the degree. **The rights and obligations of the parties outlined in the college's bulletins, circulars and regulations become a part of the contract.** Because these documents merely stated that he was entering a program that would lead to a Master of Arts degree, the lower court properly dismissed his breach of contract claim. The student's fraud claim was rejected because he could not have justifiably relied on statements in the advertisements and advisory statement to the effect that the program would result in a one-year saving in schooling. Any oral statements that the application was expected to be granted were merely predictions and were not misrepresentations. The trial court's decision was affirmed. *Vought v. Teachers College, Columbia Univ.*, 511 N.Y.S.2d 880 (A.D. 2d Dept. 1987). [NY]

B. Fraudulent Misrepresentation

Claims for fraudulent misrepresentation often accompany breach of contract claims. The claims usually involve the failure to provide promised services including qualified teachers and equipment or misrepresentations regarding enrollment and admissions.

◆ *Two university employees could be sued for fraud where they allegedly misled a student about a music media program.*

A student enrolled at an Alabama university because its catalogue indicated it had a music media major and "state of the art" equipment. However, the student encountered problems when he tried to take classes in music media. His academic advisor first required him to take the university's core-requirement courses, then told him the university was seeking an instructor to teach music media classes. When the student was finally placed in a "basic recording" course, the instructor missed the first four classes. Another instructor later showed him the university's outdated recording studio, in which some of the equipment did not work. He informed the student that he was not qualified to teach basic recording. The student withdrew from school and sued the university, its board, a number of officials and his advisor for breach of contract and fraud. A state court dismissed his claims, but the Supreme Court of Alabama reinstated fraud claims against the advisor and a vice president of academic affairs. **There was evidence that they made misrepresentations to the student with the intent to deceive him, and that he relied on those misrepresentations.** *Byrd v. Lamar*, 846 So.2d 334 (Ala. 2002). [AL]

◆ *Although educational malpractice claims cannot succeed in most states, including Minnesota, claims alleging consumer fraud or deceptive trade practices can be used where a school fails to perform specific promises.*

A group of students filed a lawsuit against a for-profit, proprietary trade school, claiming fraud, misrepresentation, breach of contract and violation of the Minnesota consumer fraud and deceptive trade practices statutes in connection with a computer program offered by the school. A trial court characterized the students' claims as educational malpractice claims and granted the school's motion for pretrial judgment. The trial court further determined that neither the consumer fraud nor the deceptive trade practices statutes applied, and that neither of these statutes allowed damages.

The state court of appeals noted that **while educational malpractice claims were barred by public policy, claims for breach of contract, fraud or other intentional torts alleging the failure to provide promised educational services were actionable**. Under this analysis, the trial court correctly granted pretrial judgment to the school on the claims challenging the instructors and quality of education provided. The claims arising from the alleged failure to fulfill certain representations and promises were actionable; therefore, the trial court erred in granting pretrial judgment to the school on those claims. They were remanded to the trial court along with the claims based on the state consumer fraud statute (which allowed the recovery of money damages) and the state deceptive trade practices statute (which did not allow the recovery of money damages, but did allow for injunctive relief). *Alsides v. Brown Institute, Ltd.*, 592 N.W.2d 468 (Minn. App. 1999). [MN]

◆ *A college was potentially liable for fraud and breach of contract where questions existed about representations it had made to incoming students.*

A college established a satellite campus in Alabama after acquiring the facilities of a psychotherapy institute. Four students enrolled in the college, but it experienced financial difficulties and had to close before they could complete their degrees. One of the reasons for its failure was its inability to get licensure for former students of the institute. This resulted in fewer students enrolling and less tuition revenue. The students sued the college for breach of contract and fraud, among other claims. An Alabama trial court granted pretrial judgment to the college, and the students appealed.

The Court of Civil Appeals of Alabama found factual issues existed as to whether the college had breached the contract or committed fraud. The contract with the students was ambiguous, being made up of different documents and oral representations. There were questions as to whether the college had promised to do more than simply provide an education for each semester in exchange for tuition. The students stated a potential fraud claim. In Alabama, a party can be liable for fraud even where a misrepresentation is "made by mistake and innocently," if another party acted on the misrepresentation and suffered harm. Because the college was potentially liable, the court reversed and remanded the case for a trial. *Craig v. Forest Institute of Professional Psychology*, 713 So.2d 967 (Ala. Civ. App. 1997). [AL]

◆ *A federal district court held that recruiting vulnerable students and failing to provide promised services could support a fraud claim. However, New York law does not provide a cause of action based on negligent misrepresentation in the educational context.*

A New York corporation directing private business and data processing schools throughout the United States allegedly used unlicensed recruiters to entice persons with little or no education or income to enroll at the school. For example, the recruiters persuaded several persons without a high school diploma and who were dependent on public assistance to incur several thousand dollars in student loan debt to enroll in various programs. The school's published catalogue promised a high quality education provided by certified teachers. Instead, the students alleged that the teachers were frequently absent, unqualified or unlicensed and that the school failed to provide the specific courses promised in the catalogue. It also allegedly exaggerated the available curricula, instructional equipment, and placement services. The students filed suit in the U.S. District Court for the Eastern District of New York, alleging fraud, breach of contract, mail and wire fraud, and violations of the Higher Education Resources and Assistance Act (HEA).

The court held the allegations that the school had recruited vulnerable students and that it had failed to provide promised services pleaded fraud with adequate particularity. Because **the misrepresentations would influence a reasonable person's decision to attend the school**, they were "material" as required for pleading a fraud claim. Further, **the school had both a motive and a clear opportunity to commit fraud**. Government loans were readily available to vulnerable, uneducated persons from which the school stood to gain financially. The court noted that the students had adequately pleaded a cause of action for mail and wire fraud also, under the Civil Racketeer Influenced and Corrupt Organizations Act. However, New York law did not provide a cause of action based on negligent misrepresentation in the educational context. Nor did the HEA create a fiduciary duty between school and students sufficient to state a breach of fiduciary duty claim. *Moy v. Adelphi Institute, Inc.*, 866 F.Supp. 696 (E.D.N.Y. 1994). [NY]

◆   *When a student possesses a right to cancel her contract, the student's misrepresentation claim may be based on postcontract-formation representations made during the cancellation period.*

After seeing several television commercials and newspaper advertisements, a prospective student contacted a business college to inquire about its program of study. She met with a representative of the school and signed an enrollment contract that called for a $500 down payment. The college catalogue was read aloud by the student to her mother that same evening. The catalogue made representations concerning the quality of its teachers, equipment, and training aids. It also stated that any student could cancel his or her contract within 72 hours of signing, and would receive a complete refund of the down payment. The student declined to cancel, but was greatly disappointed with the quality of education she received before eventually withdrawing. She contended that the college did not live up to the representations made in its catalogue and sued the school for violations of the Texas Deceptive Trade Practices Act. A jury awarded the student $28,000, and the school appealed to the Court of Appeals of Texas.

The court held that **when a student possesses a right to cancel, the student's misrepresentation claim may be based on postcontract-formation representations made during the cancellation period**. The representative from the school, with whom the student originally spoke, gave testimony affirming that the catalogue had misrepresented the quality of teachers, equipment, and training aids. The court upheld the jury's findings that the student had suffered mental anguish as a result of the misrepresentations. However, it disagreed with the amount of attorney's fees that had been awarded. The decision was affirmed as modified. *American Commercial Colleges, Inc. v. Davis*, 821 S.W.2d 450 (Tex. App.–Eastland 1991). [TX]

◆ *A Washington college was not liable for a teacher's representations about the content of a course.*

Under a Washington law, persons must satisfy education and experience requirements to become a licensed real estate appraiser. A technical college developed a real estate appraising program and although the course fulfilled the educational requirements of the statute, the college made no statements that the course was designed to fulfill the licensure requirements. The course instructor represented to students that realistic training and experience would be provided, and that this would count toward the licensing requirements. However, the instructor was fired, and the new instructor stated that the program would not meet the experience requirements for licensure. All the students finished the course. They filed suit against the college in state court, alleging breach of contract and violation of the state Consumer Protection Act (CPA). The court found for the college, and the students appealed to the Court of Appeals of Washington.

The students argued that they would not have taken the course had they known that it would not provide any work experience hours. The court of appeals noted that to show the existence of a contract, the students had to prove mutual assent between the contracting parties. **The court held that in all of the written materials regarding the program, the college stated that the course objective was to qualify students for entry-level employment in the appraising industry. It never stated that the program would meet the state licensure requirements.** The students argued that their first instructor was an agent of the college and that he orally represented that the program would provide work experience hours. **The court found no authority stating that an instructor could create a contract between students and a school through oral representations.** The students also failed to show that the instructor had the authority to legally bind the school. Finally, the court held that the CPA did not apply to the college. Finding no contract between the students and the school, the court affirmed the trial court's decision. *Ottgen v. Clover Park Technical College*, 928 P.2d 1119 (Wash. App. 2d Div. 1996). [WA]

C. Tuition Issues

Courts generally enforce tuition contracts based on enrollment agreements, school handbooks or bulletins. Where a private school has breached its contractual obligations, courts will often award tuition refunds.

In addition to general contract considerations, post-secondary institutions have additional requirements under the Higher Education Act (HEA) and its amendments addressing the refunding of unearned tuition. Generally, the HEA requires schools to develop "fair and equitable" policies for refunding unearned tuition in the event the student fails to complete the enrollment period. Some of the regulations specify the order for reimbursement, while other regulations govern the calculation of the appropriate amount of the student's refund.

◆ *The Court of Appeals of Maryland held state universities were not liable to students who claimed unreasonable mid-year tuition increases.*

When the state board of university regents learned it was about to lose funding, it approved tuition increases of up to five percent during a semester. Several students sued the board in a state circuit court for breach of contract and related claims. The court granted the Board's motion for summary judgment and dismissed the case. The students appealed the contract issue to the Court of Appeals of Maryland. It held the board was protected by sovereign immunity against the contract claim because the students did not establish they had a written contract. The legal relationship between the students and universities was characterized as a "quasi-contract." Under a quasi-contract theory, the board could make unilateral changes within the parties' reasonable expectations. The court held the board qualified for sovereign immunity as an arm of the state government. Since the state code provided for a sovereign immunity waiver only in tuition cases that involve a refund, waiver did not apply. The court affirmed the judgment for the board. *Stern v. Board of Regents, Univ. System of Maryland*, 836 A.2d 996 (Md. 2004). [MD]

◆ *A Virginia court held a student did not qualify for in-state tuition just because she lived in the state at the time she attended school.*

A student moved from New York to attend Virginia Commonwealth University. She met Virginia requirements for residency including continuous residence in the state for one year, filing and paying state income tax and possessing a state driver's license. She also registered as a Virginia voter, had a job in the state and owned property there. However, **to be eligible for in-state tuition, a student arriving from another state must show the intention of living in Virginia for the long-term and not merely to attend school**.

A university residency appeals committee found the student's primary reason for moving to Virginia was to attend the university and denied her request for in-state tuition. The student appealed to a state circuit court, which noted the Virginia Code limited its powers of review to whether the committee's decision was arbitrary, capricious or otherwise contrary to law. The court reviewed evidence that the student had applied to school in South Carolina as well as Virginia. She did not move to Virginia until after she was accepted to the university. For these reasons, the committee's decision was not arbitrary, capricious or contrary to law, and the court denied the student's appeal. *Gauthier v. Virginia Cmwlth. Univ.*, No. CH03-1896-1, 2004 WL 1386321 (Va.Cir. 2004). [VA]

◆ *A Massachusetts student was no longer entitled to reduced tuition after her mother resigned from her job with the university.*

A Boston University student received tuition remission because her mother worked for the university. At the start of her junior year, the university sent her a "projected tuition remission" for the year. However, during the fall semester, the student's mother resigned. The university notified the student that she was no longer entitled to tuition remission benefits as of the spring semester, and the student sued. A trial court ruled for the university, and the Appeals Court of Massachusetts affirmed. **The projected tuition remission was not an unconditional offer of financial aid** for one year but rather was conditioned on the student's mother continuing her employment with the university. When the mother resigned, the university's obligation to offer remission benefits ended. *Lindley v. Boston Univ.*, 778 N.E.2d 31 (Mass. App. 2002). [MA]

◆ *Where the Texas community college system improperly raised student services fees, it had to reimburse students who paid too much.*

A Texas community college district, composed of seven junior colleges, decided to adopt a sliding scale fee schedule for student services, which included a technology fee. Five students brought a class action lawsuit against the district, arguing that the fee increase violated the Texas Education Code and that the technology fee was unlawful. A court and a jury ruled in favor of the class, and the Court of Appeals of Texas affirmed in part. Here, the district failed to comply with the statutory guidelines when it imposed the technology fee because it did not set forth a proposal in a resolution that was approved by the state attorney general. Also, **the increase in the student services fee was unlawful because the district imposed the increase without a majority vote of the students or the student governments** at the seven junior colleges. Moreover, the fees were paid under implied duress because if the students refused to pay, the district could prevent them from registering for classes and/or deny them academic credit. The court affirmed the award to the class of over $15 million in damages for the improperly collected fees. *Dallas County Community College Dist. v. Bolton*, 89 S.W.3d 707 (Tex. App. 2002). [TX]

◆ *Under U.S. Department of Education regulations, institutions with cohort default rates of more than 25 percent for any of the three most recent fiscal years are disqualified from participation in Title IV programs.*

The Higher Education Act (HEA) requires educational institutions to develop "fair and equitable" policies for refunding unearned tuition. One provision states that refunds must be credited first to reimburse federal government programs, then other sources of aid, and last to the student. Formerly, institutions were not required to consider the student's scheduled, but not yet paid, cash payments in making their refund calculations. A new regulation required that after calculating the refund, the school subtract the student's unpaid charges from the amount it would otherwise retain. The HEA also provided that institutions with cohort default rates equal to or greater than 25 percent for each of the three most recent fiscal years were not eligible to participate in Title IV programs. The U.S. Department of Education (DOE) passed regulations that disqualified institutions with cohort default rates of more than 25 percent for any of the three most recent fiscal years. Several institutions filed a lawsuit challenging the regulations, alleging they violated the HEA. A federal district court granted pretrial judgment to the DOE, and the institutions appealed.

The U.S. Court of Appeals, District of Columbia Circuit, rejected an argument by the institutions that the refund regulations impermissibly modified the definition of a "fair and equitable refund policy" as defined in the HEA. It held the failure to include the unpaid amount had the effect of constructively refunding the amount to the student. This came at the expense of the federal government. **The present regulations properly put the risk of the student's default on the institution.** Because the DOE was expressly authorized to define administrative capability, the court held that it properly modified the 25 percent default rate criterion. *Career College Ass'n v. Riley*, 74 F.3d 1265 (D.C. Cir. 1996). [DC]

◆ *The Ninth Circuit enjoined implementation of a U.S. Department of Education regulation that effectively increased the required refund a school had to pay above the amount resulting from the statutory calculations.*

The Higher Education Amendments (HEA) of 1992 require post-secondary institutions that participate in Title IV programs to develop refund policies for students who do not complete the period of enrollment. The amendments require the institutions to refund the largest of the amounts provided under: 1) applicable state law, 2) the refund requirements of the institution's nationally recognized accrediting agency, or 3) the amount required under the *pro rata* refund calculation described in the HEA. In the present case, the largest of the statutory calculations would result under the *pro rata* or state regulations. The DOE published a regulation requiring institutions to exclude "any unpaid amount of a scheduled cash payment" from the amount of earned institutional charges the school could retain. The regulation increased the required refund a school had to pay above the amount resulting from the statutory calculations. An association of cosmetology schools brought an action in a federal district court, seeking to enjoin implementation of the regulatory scheme.

The association contended that the payment of additional refunds pursuant to the regulation promulgated by the DOE violated the HEA. The court agreed and granted the association's motion for a preliminary injunction, ruling that the association established a strong likelihood of success on the merits. **The regulation arguably violated the enabling statute by requiring institutions to refund more money than the HEA deemed "fair and equitable."** Further, the mandated increase in refund payments could drive some small schools out of business and could saddle students with unexpected additional debt. Consequently, the court held the association established the requisite likelihood of irreparable harm so as to justify injunctive relief. *California Cosmetology Coalition v. Riley*, 871 F.Supp. 1263 (C.D. Cal. 1994).

The Ninth Circuit granted the association pretrial judgment and issued a permanent injunction to enjoin implementation of the regulation. *California Cosmetology Coalition v. Riley*, 110 F.3d 1454 (9th Cir. 1997). [CA]

D. Educational Malpractice

Claims for educational malpractice usually stem from accusations that a school has failed to evaluate and properly place a student, or failed to provide the educational services necessary to educate the student. However, courts have generally been extremely reluctant to recognize lawsuits based upon educational malpractice. In particular, claims for educational malpractice lack readily acceptable standards of care, cause or injury. The cause and nature of any damages to the student also are uncertain. Public policy considerations, such as an increase in litigation and embroiling courts in the day-to-day operations of schools, provide additional bases for denying an educational malpractice claim.

◆ *A student could not avoid the bar against educational malpractice claims by suing a school for constructive discharge.*

A dental student claimed to have witnessed rampant cheating that school officials refused to address. She asserted that this devalued her education and breached the university's promise to abide by its code of conduct. She also asserted that she had been constructively discharged from the dental program due to mistreatment by a faculty member. The faculty member in question had flunked her in a class, and she had subsequently failed the exam twice more. In her lawsuit against the university, a federal district court ruled in favor of the school. **It noted that her breach of contract claim was in essence a claim for educational malpractice, and that such a claim could not survive. The student failed to present specific promises that the school had breached.** Rather, she was asserting that the school had failed to provide an effective education. Further, the court refused to create a new cause of action for constructive discharge from a university. Doing so would undermine the public policy of leaving to professional educators decisions related to education, and would allow students to avoid the bar against educational malpractice claims. *Gally v. Columbia Univ.*, 22 F.Supp.2d 199 (S.D.N.Y. 1998). [NY]

◆ *New York courts have declined to consider actions of educational malpractice because they require courts to make decisions as to the validity of broad educational policies such as the appropriateness of a textbook.*

Two New York residents registered for a Pascal computer programming course at an area private university. Prior to registration, they read the university's catalogue, which encouraged students without a computer programming background to attend. They also read the class schedule, which noted that there were no prerequisites for the Pascal course. Their advisor assured them that the course did not require an advanced math background and that their rudimentary high school math skills would suffice. They paid $855.00 to the university under its installment plan. The professor assigned readings from a course textbook designed for computer science majors, scientists and engineers. He also assigned problems requiring an extensive math background. The students' advisor instructed them to keep working on the admittedly difficult problems. The professor attempted unsuccessfully to explain the problems during the first five class periods. The students then withdrew from the class in frustration. They were unable to contact their advisor for nearly three weeks, at which time they were no longer eligible for any type of tuition refund. The students filed suit against the school in a New York city court, seeking relief for breach of contract, rescission, breach of fiduciary duty, educational malpractice, and unfair and deceptive business practices.

The court held that the professor's use of an unsuitable textbook coupled with his inappropriate classroom examples intentionally drawn from math and science constituted breach of the college's educational contract with the students. Rescission of the contract was justified because it was unconscionable and because the students were induced to enter into the contract in reliance upon the college's gross misrepresentations. Further, the college assumed the obligations of a fiduciary when it assigned the students an advisor who made misrepresentations on which the students relied to their detriment. The court also held that the college was liable for educational malpractice, ruling that use of the improper textbook was a *per se* example of negligence, incompetence and malpractice. The school's actions also violated a New York law prohibiting deceptive business practices. The court ordered the school to reimburse the students and imposed punitive damages against it. *Andre v. Pace Univ.*, 618 N.Y.S.2d 975 (N.Y. City Ct. 1994). [NY]

The university appealed to the New York Supreme Court, Appellate Term, which noted that, as a matter of public policy, New York courts have declined to consider actions of educational malpractice because they require courts to make decisions as to the validity of broad educational policies. It noted that the claims asserted in this case entailed **an evaluation of the adequacy and quality of the textbook and the effectiveness of the teaching methods. These are determinations best left to the educational community**, and the trial court erred by making them. The court also found that the trial court erroneously dismissed the university's counterclaim for the remainder of the tuition owed. The students were aware of the university's policy and did not present any evidence showing that their delay in requesting a refund was caused by the university. Thus, they were liable for the full tuition. The court reversed the trial court's decision and entered judgment for the university. *Andre v. Pace Univ.*, 655 N.Y.S.2d 777 (N.Y. Sup. 1996). [NY]

◆   *In rejecting an educational malpractice claim, the Seventh Circuit noted that the claim lacked a satisfactory standard of care, involved uncertainties about damages, created the potential for a flood of litigation, and embroiled courts in the day-to-day operations of schools.*

A Kansas high school basketball star was recruited by a private university in Nebraska to play on its team. The student was unprepared for a university education, but was assured that he would receive sufficient tutoring so that he would receive a meaningful education. During the student's four years at the university, his language and reading skills never rose to even a high school level. The university then made arrangements with an Illinois preparatory school to provide him a year of remedial education. Afterward, the student attended another university in Chicago, but had to withdraw for lack of funds. Following a depressive and destructive episode, the student sued the Nebraska university for negligence and breach of contract. The negligence claims were based on educational malpractice and negligent admission. A federal district court granted the university's motion to dismiss the case. *Ross v. Creighton Univ.*, 740 F.Supp. 1319 (N.D. Ill. 1990). [IL]

The student appealed to the U.S. Court of Appeals, Seventh Circuit, which noted that courts in at least 11 states have considered and rejected educational malpractice claims. The main reasons for doing so included: 1) the **lack of a satisfactory standard of care** by which to evaluate an educator, 2) the inherent **uncertainties about the cause and nature of damages**, 3) the **potential for a flood of litigation** against schools, and 4) the threat of **embroiling courts in the day-to-day operations of schools**. With respect to the negligent admission complaint, the court applied many of the same reasons to reject the claim. On the breach of contract claim, the court found that a student would have to show more than that the education provided by the university was not good enough. This would be nothing more than a repackaging of an educational malpractice claim. Instead, the student "must point to an identifiable contractual promise that the [university] failed to honor." Here, the student had alleged a breach of promise with respect to certain services, which effectively cut him off from *any* participation in and benefit from the university's academic program. The court affirmed in part the dismissal of the student's complaint, but allowed the breach of contract claim to proceed. *Ross v. Creighton Univ.*, 957 F.2d 410 (7th Cir. 1992). [IL]

II. DISCIPLINARY ACTIONS

A. Due Process

1. Procedural Safeguards

Due process includes the notion of fundamental fairness and the provision of notice and an opportunity to be heard at some point during disciplinary procedures. A federal district court explained that informal procedures may minimize the risk of lawsuits in higher education disciplinary cases. These include: 1) use of an impartial decisionmaker; 2) providing notice of the charges and the evidence against the student; 3) an opportunity for the student to appear before the decisionmaker; 4) an opportunity for the student to suggest witnesses; 5) avoiding the imposition of sanctions against witnesses; and 6) permitting the student to either voluntary accept discipline or the ruling of the decisionmaker. See A. v. C. College, 863 F.Supp. 156 (S.D.N.Y. 1994).

◆ *A federal district court denied the University of Maine's motion to dismiss a due process lawsuit involving the discipline of two football players. There was evidence it did not conduct their hearing with fundamental fairness.*

The football players were accused of sexually assaulting a female student at her off-campus apartment. Police investigated, but did not file criminal charges against them. The players asserted the sex was consensual, but the university charged them with violating the student conduct code. After a hearing, a panel found the players guilty of sexual assault, and they were suspended from school and thrown off the football team. They also lost their scholarships. The players sued the university and school officials in a federal district court for due process and contract violations. They claimed the university failed to provide them with copies of witness and evidence lists, the victim's statement to the police, and a third party's statement regarding her credibility. The players asserted their attorney could not effectively cross-examine the victim because she remained behind a partition at the hearing.

The court noted that education is not a fundamental right or liberty interest. The university's motion to dismiss their substantive due process claim was granted. Regarding the procedural due process claim, the court explained that **colleges and universities must inform a student facing discipline of the charges and the nature of the evidence, and provide the student an opportunity to respond. A student may only be punished based on substantial evidence**. The court found that the student conduct code required the university to conduct disciplinary hearings with fundamental fairness. The code was considered a contract between the players and university. The players' procedural due process allegations raised sufficient questions as to whether the university complied with its contractual promise of fundamental fairness. While they could proceed with their procedural due process and contract claims, their remaining claims were dismissed. *Gomes v. University of Maine*, No. CIV. 03-123-B-W, 2004 WL 343511 (D. Me. 2004). [ME]

◆   *A South Carolina court held a student who was recently dismissed from his academic program remained a "student" at the time university police issued him a parking citation. The court affirmed his expulsion from the university.*

The University of South Carolina dismissed the student for academic reasons. While his dismissal was on appeal, he agreed to be placed on conduct probation for 15 months in settlement of an earlier non-academic incident. The student signed a form acknowledging the board had explained his rights to him. He later argued with a university police officer over a parking citation. The officer issued him a notice of policy violation for harassing him. The university then denied the student's academic dismissal appeal. He failed to attend a campus judicial board hearing on the parking citation and the board expelled him. The student appealed his expulsion, arguing he was not a student at the time of the citation incident and did not have to adhere to university policies.

The university denied the student's appeal and he sued it in a state court. The court granted the university's motion for summary judgment and the student appealed to the Court of Appeals of South Carolina. The court noted the student had settled his disciplinary appeal by agreeing to conduct probation for 15 months. He clearly considered he would be a student in the future. The court found no change in his student status between the date he signed the agreement and the parking violation. The court rejected the student's contention that the university handbook definition of "continuing student relationship" was vague. The academic appellate process was still taking place at the time of the parking violation and the dismissal became final long after the incident. The student held himself out to be a student, and continued his student relationship with the school. The court affirmed the decision for the university. *Carter v. University of South Carolina*, No. 3832, 2004 WL 1441927 (S.C. App. 2004). [SC]

◆   *A federal district court refused to dismiss an action by a student expelled by a Florida law school for threatening and disruptive behavior, based on claims that the school did not provide him with the procedural safeguards specified in the school's code of academic integrity.*

The student allegedly threatened to blow up an office at the school and frightened three students with intimidating behavior. A school counselor called him "the most volatile and frightening student she had encountered." The school dean issued the student an expulsion letter based on "serious threats" and "physically intimidating conduct." The student claimed he did not receive any notice of the charges and was not provided with a hearing. He sued the school and several of its officials in a federal district court for negligence, defamation and breach of contract. The school and officials moved to dismiss the case for failure to state a claim upon which relief could be granted.

The court agreed to dismiss the negligence claim. Under Florida law, a student may be suspended or expelled for breaching a university's code of conduct. Even if school officials were mistaken in issuing the notice, they were not liable unless they acted with malice. As there was no finding of malice in this case, the negligence claim was dismissed. There could also be no liability for defamation. The dean's statements were privileged because they were based on the school's interest or duty to investigate and resolve the case. The court held a contract existed between the student and school, which was governed by the terms of the student handbook. **The law school's code of academic integrity specified that students would receive procedural protections before any expulsion decision**. The court denied the school's motion to dismiss this claim, as it had apparently breached these contract terms. The court dismissed the remaining claims. *Jarzynka v. St. Thomas Univ. School of Law*, 310 F.Supp.2d 1256 (S.D. Fla. 2004). [FL]

◆ *A university could consider evidence of a student's off-campus misconduct during a hearing regarding his on-campus misconduct.*

The University of Minnesota charged the student with violating its student conduct code for on-campus misconduct. He challenged the charge at a hearing before the campus committee on student behavior, which permitted evidence of his off-campus sexual encounters and past assaults at the hearing. They were deemed relevant to his on-campus behavior. The committee recommended a two-year suspension, but a review panel advised the president of the university not to accept the recommendation. The president personally reviewed the record, then accepted the recommended suspension.

The student appealed to the Minnesota Court of Appeals, which upheld the president's decision. Although **the university would have to be careful to avoid unduly prejudicial testimony at future disciplinary hearings**, the student was issued written notices of the charges against him, received an opportunity to confront his accusers, and was represented by an advocate. Thus, the off-campus evidence did not taint the proceeding so as to render it unfair. The student would have to serve the suspension. *R.T. v. University of Minnesota*, No. C9-01-1596, 2002 WL 1275663 (Minn. App. 6/11/02). [MN]

◆ *Academic dismissals require less procedural protection than disciplinary dismissals; however, even an academic dismissal requires adequate notice.*

A graduate student at the University of Alaska Anchorage applied for and was accepted to an advanced practicum in special education. He worked with a host teacher at the school district to which he was assigned and was supervised by a university professor. After the host teacher notified the professor of problems with the student, the professor met with the student and attempted to rectify the problem. However, the school's principal later told the professor that things were worse than they had appeared at the previous meeting. The professor met with the principal and the host teacher before determining that the student should be removed from the practicum. The student was notified of his removal from the practicum and was subsequently notified that he was being removed from the special education program. He appealed under the university's procedures, and the case ultimately reached the Supreme Court of Alaska. There, the court held that **the university had complied with its internal guidelines for dismissing a student from the practicum. However, an issue remained as to whether the student had been given proper notice that he was at risk of being removed from the special education program.** The court remanded the case. *Nickerson v. University of Alaska Anchorage*, 975 P.2d 46 (Alaska 1999). [AK]

Private schools have broad discretion to establish disciplinary rules and procedures through their contractual relationships with students. Generally, private school students are only entitled to receive the procedural safeguards specifically provided for by the institution in its enrollment agreement, student handbook or catalogue.

◆   *The Supreme Court of Kentucky held a state licensing statute did not create a duty for a private college to provide due process procedures as a condition of being licensed.*

College officials searched the student's dormitory room after others reported he threatened to harm a classmate. The search yielded three pocket knives and a large Army survival knife with a blade over five inches long. The college's student handbook prohibited dangerous weapons and included dismissal as a sanction for weapons possession. College officials met with the student and told him of the accusation of threats and the discovery of the knives. The student did not deny the threats and admitted he owned the knives. An official handed him a dismissal letter, but told him he could be readmitted if he agreed to psychiatric treatment and evaluation. The student instead sued the college and its officials in a state court for due process violations. The court granted the college's motion for summary judgment, finding the handbook clearly warned students that weapons possession could result in dismissal. The state court of appeals reversed the judgment, finding that state licensing regulations imposed due process requirements upon private colleges.

The Supreme Court of Kentucky explained that the main purpose of the licensing statute was to "protect the Commonwealth's citizens from fraudulent or substandard educational institutions." **The appeals court erroneously held that state law authorized recovery for a violation of the licensing statute. The statute did not impose due process obligations on private colleges.** According to the court, a private college "does not necessarily subject itself to the entire panoply of due process requirements that would be applicable at a state-sponsored education institution." The college had great flexibility with regard to its due process obligations. While a contract had been formed between the parties, the court found the handbook did not guarantee due process rights. The handbook stated that under "unusual circumstances," due process procedures would not be followed. **Since the student breached college rules by possessing weapons on campus, the college was not obligated to perform under the contract. His admission of misconduct justified immediate dismissal and nullified any reason for a hearing.** The supreme court reinstated the judgment for the college. *Centre College v. Trzop*, 127 S.W.3d 562 (Ky. 2003). [KY]

◆ *The U.S. Court of Appeals, Fifth Circuit, held private religious university campus police had probable cause to arrest a student who tried to register for classes after he was suspended from school.*

The school suspended the student for violating the student code of conduct by stalking two female students. When the student appeared at school to register for a summer session, campus police arrested him for criminal trespass and turned him over to county police. Although the student was charged with criminal trespass, the district attorney's office later dropped the charges. The student sued the university, campus police and a university dean in a federal district court for false arrest, false imprisonment and malicious prosecution, among other claims. The school, campus police, and dean requested summary judgment and dismissal of the charges, as the student did not offer facts to show they acted with malice. The district court agreed and dismissed the action. The student appealed to the Fifth Circuit, which found the university and its officials had probable cause to arrest and prosecute the student. For this reason, it affirmed the district court judgment. *Barnes v. Johnson*, No. 03-51012, 99 Fed. Appx. 534, 2004 WL 1161875 (5th Cir. 2004). [TX]

◆ *Brandeis University did not violate its obligations in conducting an investigation and disciplinary proceeding against a student accused of rape.*

In March 1996, a female student filed a complaint with the Brandeis student judicial system, alleging that a male student had engaged in intercourse with her without her consent. Following a hearing, the university board on student conduct determined that the male student engaged in unwanted sexual activity and created a hostile environment. As a penalty, he was suspended for the four-month summer term and was placed on disciplinary probation until he graduated. The male student filed a complaint against Brandeis listing various tort, civil rights and contractual claims. He argued that he was unfairly disciplined and sought injunctive relief and compensatory damages. The trial court dismissed the complaint, but the court of appeals reversed on the breach of contract claim. The student sought further review.

The Massachusetts Supreme Judicial Court ruled that Brandeis did not breach its contractual relationship with the student. Although a contractual relationship existed, the student failed to establish that the school did not meet his reasonable expectations. The student cited to several sections under "Rights and Responsibilities" in the student handbook in support of his claim that the university breached its disciplinary procedures. Specifically, he contended that Brandeis: (1) did not interview him at the investigatory stage; (2) did not apply the "clear and convincing evidence" standard of proof to its decision; (3)

excluded his expert's testimony; and (4) failed to make a complete record of the proceedings. In rejecting the student's allegations, **the court strictly construed the language of the handbook in favor of Brandeis**. As to the first assertion, the court determined that the section at issue did not apply to investigations of student misconduct, but to invasion of privacy claims in connection with room inspections. **The court also found nothing in the handbook that required the university to interview the student or to seek evidence from him at the investigatory stage.** Next, the court found "ample evidence" to conclude that the board reached its decision based on clear and convincing evidence. Third, the handbook did not mention the admission of witness testimony. As to the student's fourth allegation, the court acknowledged that the 12-line report of the disciplinary proceeding was brief, but concluded that the handbook did not require the report to be of a specific length. Accordingly, the student failed to state a claim upon which relief could be granted, and the judgment of the trial court was affirmed. *Schaer v. Brandeis Univ.*, 432 Mass. 474, 735 N.E.2d 373 (Mass. 2000). [MA]

◆   *Where a school substantially followed its published rules and regulations for academic dismissal, the student was without recourse.*

A third-year dental student received one F and two Ds. The student academic performance committee recommended his dismissal from the program, but the student was allowed to remediate his grades during a summer program. He was then promoted to his fourth year. However, the student performed even worse. He took an F in one course, unsatisfactory in three others, and had an unsatisfactory performance in four clinical departments. The committee again recommended his dismissal. Two administrative appeals by the student were unsuccessful, and he was dismissed from the school. He sued, claiming that the student handbook created a contract that set forth pupil performance procedures and that the school had breached the contract. However, he did not specify how the school had breached the contract. The case reached the Superior Court of New Jersey, Appellate Division, which ruled in favor of the school. **The court refused to apply rigid contractual principles to university-student conflicts involving academic performance. It then noted that no evidence had been presented that the school had deviated from its published rules and regulations in some significant way.** The breach of contract claim could not succeed. *Mittra v. University of Medicine & Dentistry of New Jersey*, 719 A.2d 693 (N.J. Super. A.D. 1998). [NJ]

◆   *A federal district court found that a private college student was not entitled to procedures that were not found in the college's regulations.*

A student at a private, New York college received messages on his answering machine threatening him with physical violence because of his homosexuality. The student reported the incident, and the college began an investigation. It played a tape of the messages throughout the campus and, allegedly, a number of students stated that they thought another male student was one of the callers. The official conducting the investigation supposedly told others that she also thought that the student had made the calls. The student was later charged with harassment, and a formal hearing was held. The student requested a voice analysis of the tapes, but the college denied the request. Witnesses testified both for and against him and, in the end, the hearing panel was unable to reach a conclusion on the charge. It stated that it found the student neither guilty nor innocent and that if the victimized student obtained any new evidence, the hearing would resume. However, the charged student would not be allowed to reopen the hearing with new evidence in his defense. He soon withdrew from the college, claiming mental and physical exhaustion from the experience and filed suit against the college in the U.S. District Court for the Southern District of New York. The college filed a motion to dismiss.

The student argued the disciplinary proceedings against him were not conducted in accordance with the college's established rules. The college argued that because the student had not been expelled or suspended as a result of the proceeding, he could not assert this cause of action. The student responded that he had been constructively discharged since the school had made it impossible for him to continue there, but the court found no evidence of such conduct. The student also argued that the college violated its own procedures by denying his request for a voice analysis, by not preserving his confidentiality during the investigation, by not allowing all of his character witnesses to testify, by allowing the investigating official to testify, and by not declaring him innocent once the hearing panel failed to find him guilty. The court found that none of these criteria were contained in the college's regulations as required procedures and that after the hearing no sanctions had been imposed on the student. Because the student failed to show that the college did not follow its established procedures, the motion to dismiss was granted. *Fraad-Wolff v. Vassar College*, 932 F.Supp. 88 (S.D.N.Y. 1996). [NY]

◆ *Because a college breached its contractual obligations to provide a student with notice of the nature of the charges against him, he was entitled to have the case reheard.*

A female student at a Vermont private college accused a male student of rape. After conducting an investigation, the county declined to prosecute the male student, but the college pursued disciplinary steps against him as prescribed in the college handbook. The handbook provided that the student be given notice of the charges with "sufficient particularity to permit [him] to prepare to meet the charges." When asked to clarify the charges against him, the dean allegedly told the student to "concentrate on the issue of rape." The student was found not guilty of rape but guilty of engaging in inappropriate sexual activity with the female student. The College's Judicial Review Board upheld the ruling, and the student appealed to a federal district court.

The court held that **colleges are contractually bound to provide students with promised procedural safeguards**. However, the unique relationship between college and student with respect to disciplinary proceedings precluded rigid application of contract law. Here, the college had improperly deviated from its procedural obligations when it failed to notify the student prior to the hearing that there were two charges pending against him. He was never told that even if he was able to rebut the rape charge, he still could be found guilty of another charge. **Because the college did not state the nature of the charges with sufficient particularity to permit the student to meet them, the**

hearing had been fundamentally unfair. However, since the inadequate notice provided the student was the only breach of the student-college contract, his case could be reheard after proper notice was given. *Fellheimer v. Middlebury College*, 869 F.Supp. 238 (D. Vt. 1994). [VT]

2. Hearings

◆ *Students who were given notice and an opportunity to be heard before discipline was imposed could not show their due process rights were violated.*

Five fraternity brothers on their way home from a convenience store encountered another student on campus. Four of them got into a fight with the student. The other fraternity brother went back to their house before the situation escalated. After the injured student filed a student disciplinary complaint with the university's Judiciary Committee, a hearing was conducted. However, the three fraternity brothers still involved at that point believed that their request for a postponement had been granted, and they failed to show for the hearing (the fourth fraternity brother accepted other punishment).

The committee recommended expelling the fraternity brothers, but the university vice president instead created a panel to review the case. The brothers presented their story. After the review, the panel recommended suspensions, which the university president increased. Two of the fraternity brothers then sued the school for violating their due process rights under 42 U.S.C. § 1983. A Virginia federal court granted pretrial judgment to the university, and the Fourth Circuit affirmed. **The earlier expulsion recommendation did not violate the bothers' due process rights because they were never expelled.** Since they had an opportunity to present evidence and confront witnesses before the review panel, they could not succeed on the § 1983 claim. *Tigrett v. Rector and Visitors of Univ. of Virginia*, 290 F.3d 620 (4th Cir. 2002). [VA]

◆ *A former student's claims that the University of Virginia breached its contract and violated due process requirements in the process leading up to the revocation of his degree were sufficient to prevent pretrial judgment.*

The student was admitted as a transfer student and was a participant in the university's Honor System. Pursuant to the terms of the Honor System, a student's breach of the Honor Code would result in "permanent dismissal." During his senior year, the student defrauded the university of $1,500 by submitting forged or false reimbursement vouchers. When the fraud was discovered, university police investigated and the student was charged with felony embezzlement. He later pled guilty to a reduced charge, and the Honor Committee initiated a case against him. The student was notified of the committee's investigation and his right to a hearing. A committee member sent him two certified letters. Both were returned. Eventually, in his absence, the university revoked his degree.

The student sued the university and various employees, asserting breach of contract, Fourteenth Amendment due process violations by individuals, and violations of his rights under the Family Educational Rights and Privacy Act. A federal court **rejected the university's claims of qualified immunity and the**

"prior bad acts" defense. The school's actions during its various administrative proceedings, as alleged by the student, could establish that it violated his Fourteenth Amendment due process rights to notice and hearing. The court also found the university's "prior bad acts" defense failed because the issue was not embezzlement, but they manner in which the university conducted the proceedings. The student raised genuine issues of fact regarding the university's awareness of problems with the Honor Committee and improper training of committee members. The university's motion for pretrial judgment was denied in part. *Goodreau v. Rector and Visitors of Univ. of Virginia*, 116 F.Supp.2d 694 (W.D. Va. 2000). [VA]

◆   *Where a student received notice and an opportunity to be heard, he could not claim due process violations.*

After spending 12 years as an engineer, a native of Iran enrolled in the College of Dentistry at the University of Tennessee. He took exception to a policy promulgated by two of his professors—namely, that first-year students were not allowed to sit in the last row of their classrooms. He claimed that he could see and hear better in the last row of the room. However, his professors refused to let him do so. One day, when there was a guest lecturer, the student refused to leave the last row and left the classroom rather than move up one row. The academic standing committee convened a hearing to determine whether his behavior warranted discipline. The student was given notice of the hearing and an opportunity to be heard. He said the dispute over the last-row rule was really a power struggle between him and his professors and indicated he did not intend to comply with the rule. The committee found the student guilty of misconduct and ordered a reprimand. It also ordered him to apologize, placed him on disciplinary probation, and warned him he would be dismissed for any other academic infractions.

After losing an appeal, the student voluntarily withdrew from the college and sued it in a federal district court. The student maintained he was discriminated against on the basis of national origin and disability, and asserted numerous other claims, including violations of his free speech, due process and equal protection rights under the Constitution. A federal district court granted pretrial judgment to the defendants, and the student appealed to the Sixth Circuit Court of Appeals. The court of appeals affirmed the decision against the student. **He presented no factual evidence of discrimination, and he was given notice and an opportunity to respond to the charges against him. Further, the pursuit of a power struggle against two professors did not amount to free speech under the First Amendment**. Accordingly, the student failed to show a constitutional violation. *Salehpour v. University of Tennessee*, 159 F.3d 199 (6th Cir. 1998). [TN]

◆   *Where numerous instances of dishonesty and failure to demonstrate professional responsibility were presented at a hearing, the decision to dismiss a student from medical school was upheld.*

A student was accepted into a Wisconsin medical school. She deferred her enrollment for one year, then withdrew during her first semester, and enrolled in and withdrew from another medical college. She reapplied and was accepted again but had a number of problems with taking examinations, and took a couple of leaves from the school. After several semesters, the academic standing committee warned her that she would have to take and pass the NBME to avoid dismissal. However, when the exam was stolen, the NBME was cancelled for everyone. The school then notified all students who had been scheduled to take the examination that it would be offered three months later. The student failed to take the NBME at that time. After a review of the student's status, **the academic standing committee voted to conduct a dismissal hearing and notified the student. She appeared at the hearing, at which evidence was presented of dishonesty on her part.** Also, the hearing committee was presented with evidence of her failure to demonstrate the expected level of professional responsibility by failing to take certain examinations, and evidence of her unwillingness to accept responsibility for her actions. The academic standing committee then voted to dismiss her.

The student sued the school in a state trial court, which granted pretrial judgment to the school. She appealed to the Court of Appeals of Wisconsin. The court affirmed the decision, finding **the school did not breach a contract with the student because it followed the procedures and policies in place prior to dismissing her. It granted her a hearing before making its decision.** Further, none of the school officials' actions was such as could support a claim for intentional infliction of emotional distress. Their actions were not so extreme or outrageous that an average member of the community would find them to be a complete denial of her dignity. The court also held that the school's dismissal of the student was not arbitrary and capricious. Finally, the other claims against the school also had been properly dismissed. *Fernandez v. Medical College of Wisconsin*, 549 N.W.2d 792 (Wis. App. 1996). [WI]

◆ *Noting that private institutions have broad discretion in making rules and setting up procedures, an Ohio court held a private college properly conducted a disciplinary hearing for a student's off-campus misconduct.*

A female student claimed that a fellow student physically and sexually assaulted her at his off-campus apartment. She filed a complaint with college authorities alleging that he violated the student code of conduct. According to school policy, a hearing was held before a judicial board to decide whether the student had violated the student code and to recommend appropriate sanctions. The board received evidence and found that the charges were justified. It recommended that the student be indefinitely suspended and ineligible for readmission for four years. The student appealed the decision, and an appellate board upheld the findings but reduced the suspension to just under two years. The student filed suit against the college in state court, seeking to be reinstated as a student. The college filed a motion to dismiss, which the court granted. The student appealed to the Court of Appeals of Ohio.

On appeal, the student argued that the college violated a contractual obligation to provide him with a fair disciplinary hearing. He first stated that the college could not discipline him for an act that occurred off-campus. The court of appeals disagreed, finding that the college could discipline conduct that adversely affected its interests. The student also argued that members of the judicial board were inadequately trained and had conflicts of interest. The trial court found that **the board's actions were not arbitrary or capricious** and therefore upheld its decision. The court of appeals agreed with its findings, noting that private institutions have broad discretion in making rules and setting up procedures. Furthermore, **private schools must be allowed to meet their educational and doctrinal responsibilities**. Absent a clear abuse of discretion by the judicial board, the court could not interfere with its decision. Because the college's action was not an abuse of discretion, the trial court's decision was upheld. *Ray v. Wilmington College*, 667 N.E.2d 39 (Ohio App. 12th Dist. 1995). [OH]

◆ *A private university can formulate its own rules and implement its own punishment as applied to its students, staff and faculty subject to judicial review for arbitrary or capricious decisions.*

Two freshmen students (male and female) at a Louisiana private university left a local bar extremely inebriated. When the couple returned to the male student's dormitory, the female student told security that they had engaged in sex, that it was consensual, and that she did not need assistance. The security officer observed that she appeared coherent. The following morning, the female student filed a complaint with the campus police alleging that she had not consented to the intercourse. After two hearings and an appeal, the male student was convicted of "causing harm or a reasonable apprehension of physical harm," in violation of the university's code of student conduct. The vice president of student affairs suspended him without academic credit for one semester, required him to attend a rape awareness program, and required him to write a letter to the female student.

A Louisiana trial court enjoined the university from implementing the sanctions and ordered the university to reconsider the charges. The university appealed to the Court of Appeal of Louisiana, Fourth Circuit. The university contended that private schools could properly administer their own internal remedies. The court of appeal agreed. It first noted that **a private university could formulate its own rules and implement its own punishment as applied to its students, staff and faculty**. A trial court could only review a decision by a private university if it was deemed "arbitrary or capricious." As the university exceeded the process due even for public universities, the court reversed the trial court decision. *Ahlum v. Administrators of Tulane Educ. Fund*, 617 So.2d 96 (La. App. 4th Cir. 1993). [LA]

◆ *Although a medical school's student handbook provided for a formal hearing before expulsion, it did not apply to a student who misrepresented his previous academic background to gain admission into the school.*

A New York medical school expelled a student based on his misrepresentations regarding the grades he previously received at another school. The student sought a formal hearing pursuant to a provision in the student handbook, but the college denied his request on the ground that the handbook was inapplicable to his situation. The student appealed to a New York trial court. The trial court directed the college to conduct a hearing concerning the student's alleged misrepresentations, and the college appealed to the New York Supreme Court, Appellate Division. The appellate division reversed, ruling that the college's decision was neither arbitrary nor capricious so as to warrant judicial intervention. **The handbook was aimed at misconduct committed by an individual while a student at the medical school, not to fraudulent acts committed prior to admission to the school.** Because the settled policy and practice of the school was to summarily dismiss any student who engaged in such misrepresentations, the school properly denied the student a formal hearing. The holding of the trial court was reversed. *Mitchell v. New York Medical College*, 617 N.Y.S.2d 894 (A.D. 2d Dept. 1994). [NY]

3. Search and Seizure

◆ *The pre-eminent search and seizure case in the public school context is New Jersey v. TLO. Although it involved a high school student, the principles used to decide the case apply to colleges and universities. In TLO, the Supreme Court stated that a search by school officials need only be reasonable at its inception, and its scope may not exceed that which is necessary under the circumstances.*

A New Jersey high school teacher found two girls smoking in the lavatory in violation of school rules. She brought them to the assistant vice principal's office where one of the girls admitted smoking in the lavatory. The other denied even being a smoker. The assistant vice principal then asked the latter girl to come to his private office where he opened her purse and found a pack of cigarettes. As he reached for them he noticed rolling papers and decided to thoroughly search the entire purse. He found marijuana, a pipe, empty plastic bags, a substantial number of one dollar bills and a list of "people who owe me money." He then turned her over to the police. A juvenile court hearing was held, and the girl was found delinquent. She appealed the juvenile court's determination, contending that her constitutional rights had been violated by the search of her purse. She argued that the evidence against her obtained in the search should have been excluded from the juvenile court proceeding.

The U.S. Supreme Court held that the search did not violate the Fourth Amendment prohibition against unreasonable search and seizure. **When police conduct a search, they have to meet the probable cause standard. However, school officials are held to a lower standard: reasonable suspicion.** Two considerations are relevant in determining the reasonableness of a search. First, the search must be justified initially by reasonable suspicion. Second, the scope and conduct of the search must be reasonably related to the circumstances that gave rise to the search, and school officials must take into account the student's age, sex and the nature of the offense. **The Court upheld the search of the student in this case because the initial search for cigarettes was supported by reasonable suspicion.** The discovery of the rolling papers then justified the further searching of the purse since such papers are commonly used to roll marijuana cigarettes. The "reasonableness" standard was met by school officials in these circumstances and thus the evidence against the girl was properly obtained. *New Jersey v. T.L.O.*, 469 U.S. 325, 105 S.Ct. 733, 83 L.Ed.2d 720 (1985). [NJ]

◆ *College security officers did not need probable cause before searching a student's dorm room.*

College safety and security officers entered a student's dorm room and found marijuana. State authorities then charged the student with possession. The student filed a motion to suppress the evidence, asserting that the search of his room was unconstitutional under the Fourth and Fourteenth Amendments and the New Hampshire Constitution. A state court suppressed the evidence, but the Supreme Court of New Hampshire reversed. Here, the student did not have the same constitutional rights he would have had if the police had searched his room. **The campus security officers were not acting as agents of the police; therefore, there was no governmental action so as to justify increased constitutional protection.** The marijuana confiscated during the search could be used against the student in the criminal proceeding. *State v. Nemser*, 807 A.2d 1289 (N.H. 2002). [NH]

◆ *University police officers did not make an unconstitutional seizure of a student who failed to respond to the officers.*

While driving through campus, an Indiana student lapsed into diabetic shock. His vehicle ended up on a sidewalk. When university police arrived on the scene, the student was unresponsive. The police officers forcibly removed him from his car and handcuffed him until an ambulance arrived, even though they had noticed his medical alert bracelet. The student sued the university and officers under 42 U.S.C. § 1983 for violating his Fourth Amendment rights. A federal court ruled in favor of the university and the officers. **The forcible removal and the detainment were justified by the student's unresponsiveness.** The Seventh Circuit Court of Appeals affirmed the decision. The student's failure to respond added an element of unpredictability to the situation, and the police reasonably believed he was an intoxicated driver. Also, the police did not use excessive force in removing the student from his car. *Smith v. Ball State Univ.*, 295 F.3d 763 (7th Cir. 2002). [IN]

◆ *Although the relationship between private colleges and local police may sometimes require application of Fourth Amendment protections, the Supreme Court of Tennessee found that a dormitory director's search of a student's room did not implicate the Fourth Amendment.*

A student at a private Tennessee college lived in a dormitory located on campus. As a condition to living in the dormitory, students had to consent to unannounced entries into their rooms for the purpose of maintaining order with respect to school policy. This policy was stated in the student handbook and was included in the housing contracts executed by the students. The contracts also prohibited the use of illegal substances in the dormitories. When the director of the dormitory received information that illegal drugs were located in the student's room, he went to the room, knocked on the door and, when no one answered, used his master key to get in. He found scales and a box containing a white, powdery substance. He called a police officer who acted as a liaison between the college and the police. The student was later arrested and convicted of possession of cocaine with intent to sell. The court of appeals affirmed, and the student appealed to the Supreme Court of Tennessee.

The student argued that the director acted as an agent of the state by searching his room without a warrant, and therefore violated Fourth Amendment protections against unreasonable searches and seizures. The court noted that the Fourth Amendment only limits governmental activities. **Evidence found by private persons (and, perhaps, by illegal means) need not be excluded from trial.** Two factors must be considered when determining whether a private person has acted as an agent or instrument of the state. The first factor is the government's knowledge and acquiescence to the search and the second factor is the intent of the party performing the search. Here, the court found that it was not the dormitory director's intent to act as an agent of the state. In searching the room, he was acting in furtherance of established school policy, not state policy. The court noted that sometimes the relationship between private colleges and local police can establish a sufficient link to create state action but it found that such a link was not present here. Because **the director was not acting as an agent of the state when he searched the student's room**, the search did not violate the Fourth Amendment. *State v. Burroughs*, 926 S.W.2d 243 (Tenn. 1996). [TN]

◆   *A student who was searched because of a belief she was cheating had no recompense against the officials involved.*

A first-year veterinary student in Virginia fell below the grade point average necessary to continue her studies. She claimed that "test anxiety" caused her poor grades and was allowed to retake her first-year classes. She again experienced academic difficulties in her third-year studies and, after failing a urology class, obtained permission to re-take the test. During the exam, she went to the lavatory. Because she was gone for a while, her professor sent a secretary to check up on her. The secretary saw notes arrayed on the floor and heard paper rustling when the student left one of the stalls. She reported this to the professor, who accused the student of cheating.

The professor and a dean directed the student to submit to a strip search by two female employees. No notes were found on the student; however, notes were found in the lavatory and in the room where the student was taking the exam. She was not allowed to finish the test. The student honor board found her guilty of cheating and suspended her for six weeks. She was then dismissed from the program because of her failing grade in urology. She sued various university officials in federal court, seeking damages for the strip search, and reinstatement. The court granted pretrial judgment to the officials, and the Fourth Circuit Court of Appeals affirmed. **The officials had reasonably believed that the student was cheating, and her ready acquiescence to the strip search led them to believe that she had impliedly consented to it.** *Carboni v. Meldrum*, 103 F.3d 116 (4th Cir. 1996). [VA]

◆   *A regulation authorizing warrantless searches of dorm rooms was struck down in the following case.*

A student at Southern University was arrested when 12 bags of marijuana were found in his room during a dormitory sweep. The sweep was authorized by the campus housing agreement, which the student signed. After the student was expelled, he sued the university for unconstitutionally searching his dorm room. A state trial court held that **the regulation authorizing warrantless searches of rooms by university officials and police officers violated the Fourth Amendment**. The Court of Appeal of Louisiana affirmed. It differentiated this case from *State v. Hunter*, 831 P.2d 1033 (Utah App.1992), where a Utah State University regulation authorizing warrantless searches was upheld. In that case, university officials did not conduct their searches at the request of police officers or with the assistance of the police. Further, the stated purposes of the inspections at issue in *Hunter* were to maintain university property, the health and safety of students, and to preserve discipline in an educational atmosphere. However, the regulation at issue here allowed entry of dorm rooms accompanied by police without any stated purpose. **The court rejected the university's argument that its interest in eliminating weapons and drugs from the educational environment made its regulation constitutionally permissible.** Society shared that interest, yet was compelled to abide by the Fourth Amendment. The regulation was unconstitutional. *Devers v. Southern Univ.*, 712 So.2d 199 (La. App. 1st Cir. 1998). [LA]

◆ *All evidence obtained from an illegal search has to be suppressed in criminal proceedings.*

A maintenance worker at a state college in Massachusetts heard a cat inside a dormitory suite. He reported the noise to college officials who posted notices on the four bedrooms of the suite, informing the students of a possible violation of college policy, and alerting them that a "door to door check" would be conducted by 10 p.m. to ensure that the cat had been removed. When the officials inspected the individual bedrooms, they noticed a light behind one closet door. Fearing a fire hazard, they opened the door and found marijuana plants. **They summoned campus police who conducted a search and confiscated the plants without obtaining a warrant. In the criminal action that followed, the district court suppressed the evidence,** and the Supreme Judicial Court of Massachusetts affirmed. Although the initial search by the college officials was proper, the subsequent search and seizure by the campus police violated the Fourth Amendment. As a result, all evidence obtained from the illegal search had to be suppressed. *Commonwealth v. Neilson*, 666 N.E.2d 984 (Mass. 1996). [MA]

B. Academic Dismissals

Courts generally distinguish between academic and nonacademic dismissals. In particular, courts usually grant schools greater deference regarding dismissal decisions based on academic deficiencies. Thus, so long as notice is provided, a hearing is not necessary, whereas for nonacademic dismissals, both notice and a hearing are required.

1. Poor Performance

◆ *Schools and universities are generally given a great deal of latitude by courts in making academic decisions. Their choices, however, must have some rational basis and not be arbitrary. The Supreme Court upheld a university's decision to dismiss a student from an advanced academic program based on poor performance.*

A student was enrolled in the University of Michigan's "Inteflex" program, which is a special six-year course of study leading to both an undergraduate and medical degree. The student struggled with the curriculum for six years, completing only four years' worth of study and barely achieving minimal competence. Because he was given a grade of "incomplete" in several important classes and was forced to delay taking his examinations, he was placed on an irregular program. Finally, he completed the four years of basic study necessary to take the NBME Part I, a test administered by the National Board of Medical Examiners which is a prerequisite to the final two years of study under the Inteflex program. Unfortunately, the student failed the exam, receiving the lowest score ever in the brief history of the Inteflex program.

The university's medical school executive board reviewed the student's academic career, decided to drop him from registration in the program, and denied his request to retake NBME Part I. The executive board was not swayed by arguments that his failure on the exam was due to his mother's heart attack 18 months previously, the excessive amount of time he had spent on an essay contest that he had entered, and his breakup with his girlfriend. The student brought suit in federal court claiming breach of contract under state law and also alleging a violation of his due process rights under the U.S. Constitution.

At trial, the evidence showed that **the university had established a practice of allowing students who had failed the NBME Part I to retake the test one, two, three, or even four times. The student here was the only person ever refused permission to retake the test.** The district court ruled against him on the contract claim and further held that his dismissal was not violative of the Due Process Clause. The U.S. Court of Appeals, Sixth Circuit, reversed and held that the student had possessed a property interest in his continued participation in the Inteflex program, and that the university had arbitrarily deprived him of that property interest by singling him out as the only student ever denied permission to retake the NBME Part I.

The U.S. Supreme Court unanimously reversed the court of appeals' decision and reinstated the district court's ruling against the student. **The Due Process Clause was not offended because the university's liberal retesting custom gave rise to no state law entitlement to retake NBME Part I.** Furthermore, the university had based its decision to dismiss the student upon careful, clear and conscientious deliberation, which took his entire academic career into account. The university had acted in good faith. The Supreme Court further observed that the discretion to determine, on academic grounds, who may be admitted to study is one of the "four essential freedoms" of a university. The Court thus held that the Due Process Clause was not violated by the student's dismissal. *Regents of Univ. of Michigan v. Ewing*, 474 U.S. 214, 106 S.Ct. 507, 88 L.Ed.2d 523 (1985). [MI]

◆ *Unlike dismissals for disciplinary reasons, dismissals for academic reasons do not require the procedural requirements of* Goss v. Lopez, *419 U.S. 565 (1975) a public high school case involving suspensions of students for misconduct. In disciplinary cases, school officials must give a student notice of the charges and an opportunity to respond to them. School officials have a broader discretion in dealing with academic expulsions and suspensions than in disciplinary actions involving misconduct.*

The academic performance of students at the University of Missouri-Kansas City Medical School was assessed periodically by the Council of Evaluation, a faculty-student body with the power to recommend probation or dismissal subject to approval by a faculty committee and the Dean. Several faculty members expressed dissatisfaction with the performance of a medical student. As a result, the Council of Evaluation recommended that she be advanced to her final year on a probationary status. Faculty complaints continued, and the Council warned the student that absent "radical improvement," she would be dismissed. She was allowed to take a set of oral and practical examinations as an "appeal" from the Council's decision.

The student spent a substantial portion of time with seven practicing physicians who supervised the examinations. Two recommended that she be allowed to graduate. Two recommended that she be dropped immediately from the school. The remaining three recommended that she not be allowed to graduate in June and be continued on probation pending further reports of her progress. Subsequent reports regarding the student were negative, and she was dropped from the program following the Council's recommendation. The student sued, alleging that she had not been accorded due process prior to her dismissal. The district court determined that the student had been afforded due process. The U.S. Court of Appeals, Eighth Circuit, reversed.

On appeal, the U.S. Supreme Court held that **the student had been given due process as guaranteed by the Fourteenth Amendment**. The procedures leading to the student's dismissal, under which the student was fully informed of faculty dissatisfaction with her progress, and the consequent threat to the student's graduation and continued enrollment did not violate the Fourteenth Amendment. **Dismissals for academic reasons do not necessitate a hearing before the school's decision-making body.** *Board of Curators v. Horowitz*, 435 U.S. 78, 98 S.Ct. 948, 55 L.Ed.2d 124 (1978). [MO]

◆ *The Supreme Court of Alaska held a university did not violate a student's due process rights by dismissing him and denying him readmission.*

The student did not get along with a field instructor who supervised his field course work toward a social work degree. Although the field instructor did not recommend a failing grade, a faculty liaison professor assigned him an incomplete grade that was later changed to failure. An academic review panel upheld the grade and the university later denied his reapplication. The student sued the university in the state court system, alleging due process violations for allegedly not following its own rules and failing to provide him with proper notice and an opportunity to be heard. The student added discrimination claims based on his gender and a disability. The court held the professor gave the student adequate notice of his academic deficiencies. She warned him several times about on-going lateness and inferior work. The court awarded judgment to the university, and the student appealed. The state supreme court affirmed the decision, agreeing that the university had provided the student with due process. **A person has no due process interest in admission to a professional**

school in the absence of dishonesty or publication of the reason for denying admission. *Hermosillo v. University of Alaska, Anchorage*, No. S-10563, 2004 WL 362384 (Alaska 2004). [AK]

◆ *A California law school did not have to re-admit a student during his lawsuit challenging his academic dismissal.*

The student did poorly in his first semester and was notified that he was not in good academic standing. His performance improved in his second semester, but by the end of his fourth semester, his GPA in required courses plummeted to 1.96 (the mandatory minimum GPA in required courses was 2.05). The law school dismissed him, and the academic standards committee upheld the dismissal. The student then sued for breach of contract, among other claims, and sought an injunction ordering the school to reinstate him while the lawsuit was pending. A court refused to issue the injunction, and the California Court of Appeal affirmed that decision. To be entitled to injunctive relief, the student would have to show he was likely to succeed on his claims at trial, and he would suffer more harm than the law school if he was not reinstated. Because he failed to show a reasonable likelihood of success on the merits, the law school did not have to re-enroll him. *Rosenberg v. Golden Gate Univ.*, No. A097304, 2002 WL 31439753 (Cal. App. 1st Dist. 10/31/02). [CA]

◆ *An Alaska university student could be removed from a program where he failed a competency exam.*

The student applied for admission to the elementary education program and was accepted on the condition that he pass the Praxis exam, which measures teacher competency. He failed the reading and writing portions of the exam, and school officials notified him that if he failed again, he would be removed from the program. When he failed a second time, he was removed. He appealed his removal internally, but the academic appeals committee upheld the decision. The case reached the Alaska Supreme Court, which also ruled against the student. Here, even though the university, at the time, did not require all elementary education students to pass the Praxis exam, **its decision was not arbitrary because the student showed a real weakness in his reading and writing skills when he applied for admission**. The university could have rejected him on that basis alone. Further, since passing the Praxis exam was a requirement for obtaining a teaching license, the decision to require the student to pass the test was reasonable. *Hunt v. University of Alaska, Fairbanks*, 52 P.3d 739 (Alaska 2002). [AK]

◆ *A Tennessee state university medical student suspended for academic reasons did not have to be provided a formal hearing.*

The student was informed of his academic deficiencies and unprofessional conduct by a dean toward the end of his second year. Although he eventually passed all his second-year courses, he failed the USMLE Step 1 the following summer. Early in his third year, after a negative report to the student promotion committee, a recommendation was made that the student be suspended, and the suspension was upheld. The student appealed internally without success, then sued the state under 42 U.S.C. § 1983 for violating his Fourteenth Amendment due process rights. A federal court ruled in his favor, but the Sixth Circuit reversed, noting that academic decision, unlike disciplinary decisions, do not require a formal hearing to satisfy the Fourteenth Amendment's procedural due process requirements. **The medical school reached a careful and deliberate decision** based on an evaluation of the student's medical knowledge, ethical conduct and interpersonal skills. This adhered to its internal procedures and provided the student with sufficient procedural due process. *Ku v. State of Tennessee*, 322 F.3d 431 (6th Cir. 2003). [TN]

◆ *Where a failing student received notice and an opportunity to respond, she was appropriately dismissed from school.*

A graduate student in a nurse anesthesiology program began receiving poor grades. Counselors advised her on how to improve her performance, but she continued to miss program goals and was placed on probation. After her third failing term, a clinical education committee unanimously recommended her dismissal. She received notice of the committee's decision and requested a due process hearing, but her dismissal was upheld. She sued the university trustees for breach of contract and intentional infliction of emotional distress. A state court ruled in favor of the trustees, and the Michigan Court of Appeals affirmed. Even though there was an implied contract between the student and the university, it required only that dismissal not be arbitrary. Here, **the university followed all appropriate procedures when dismissing the student**, and she received proper due process. The trial court was correct in deferring to the university's judgment that her academic performance warranted dismissal. *Carlton v. Trustees of Univ. of Detroit Mercy*, 2002 WL 533885 (Mich. App. 4/9/02). [MI]

◆ *The University of New Mexico was justified in dismissing a student despite her claim that the dismissal was in retaliation for protected activities and her outspoken views on race relations at the university.*

A graduate student wrote a letter protesting the denial of tenure to a professor. In the letter, she praised the professor's support of "underrepresented students of color." During that semester, she also participated in a panel discussion about racism on campus. The student took several classes with another professor, including a field practicum class that required her to serve in a supervised counseling position in the community and to participate in weekly classroom sessions on campus. She complained to another faculty member that the practicum professor had graded her unfairly and had made an inappropriate remark about Hispanics. The student completed the internship class and received credit, but the practicum professor reported several concerns about her. The coordinator of the counseling program dismissed the student for antagonistic behavior that was disruptive to the academic enterprise. The student challenged the decision and presented her case personally at a faculty meeting. The faculty denied the appeal but appointed a special committee to address the issue of how she could complete the internship requirements. The student sued, claiming her First Amendment and due process rights were violated. A federal court determined that the dismissal was unrelated to her protected activities.

In affirming, the Tenth Circuit found the student's retaliation theory was "unable to account for the significant delay–from March 1996 until January 1997–between the protected activity of writing a letter in support of tenure for a professor and the allegedly retaliatory action." The student provided evidence that she and the practicum professor did not get along. However, **the university presented convincing evidence in support of the decision to dismiss the student–conflicts with professors and the quality of her class performance**. The court noted that she was removed from only one class and was ultimately allowed to finish her internship and receive her degree. The court also found that the university's appointment of a special committee to assist her in completing the internship class and her opportunity to argue her case at the faculty meeting satisfied the Due Process Clause. *Ornelas v. Regents of Univ. of New Mexico,* 229 F.3d 1164 (10th Cir. 2000). [NM]

◆   *The Gonzaga University School of Law was not negligent in the process it followed to increase its minimum cumulative grade point average requirement and was justified in dismissing a student for having a sub-standard GPA.*

Gonzaga Law School required students to maintain both a semester and a cumulative GPA of 2.2. If they did not, they would be placed on academic probation for one semester. If their grades did not improve, Gonzaga dismissed them. In Fall 1994, the school revised its academic standing rule to eliminate probation and base dismissal solely on failure to achieve a 2.2 cumulative GPA after the first year. It also required students with a low-semester or cumulative GPA to negotiate and establish an individual academic plan with their faculty advisor. The new rule was distributed to all students, but was not implemented until the following year, after a task force of students and faculty reviewed the changes. In the beginning of the Fall 1995 semester, Gonzaga distributed the new handbook and implemented the revised rule, notifying all students through a memorandum placed in their mailboxes. A student began his second year of law school in the Fall of 1995 in good standing. During that semester, however, he earned a GPA of 1.7 and his cumulative GPA fell to 2.047. As a result, he was dismissed. The student sued, claiming he was notified of the change in academic rules seven weeks into the Fall 1995 semester. He also claimed that by enrolling in the law school, he had formed a contract with Gonzaga, one term of which was the academic standing rule, and that the university had breached the contract by changing the rule without adequate notice to him.

A Washington trial court ruled for Gonzaga, and the student appealed. The state court of appeals held that while the relationship between a student and a university is "primarily contractual in nature," contract law cannot be rigidly applied when addressing student-university relationships. The court concluded that **Gonzaga did not act arbitrarily and capriciously by changing the academic standard rule.** Therefore, the trial court's ruling in Gonzaga's favor was correct. **Gonzaga's administration, faculty and students worked for more than a year on the rule before it was implemented.** As to timely notification, the student admitted he received the memo and the Law Student Handbook, which contained a copy of the disputed academic policy. *Ishibashi v. Gonzaga Univ. School of Law,* 101 Wash. App. 1078 (Wash. App. 2000). [WA]

◆ *Where a student received numerous warnings about her performance, and where the school's decision to dismiss her was not irrational or taken in bad faith, there was no due process violation.*

A graduate student in dentistry at a Nebraska university received evaluations that were substantially below those of the other students. Eight deficiencies were listed, and she was warned that she was in danger of dismissal from the program. She engaged in remediation efforts, but continued to have problems with her technical skills. Eventually, she was dismissed from the program. She sued the university in federal court, asserting that it had violated her due process rights and that it had discriminated against her on the basis of disability. The court found that, with respect to her disability (a vision problem), she never informed anyone at the university of it, other than to say that she had a depth perception problem, and she never asked for an accommodation. **With respect to her due process claims, the court found that she was given repeated warnings of the faculty's dissatisfaction. Further, there was no evidence that university officials had acted irrationally or in bad faith in dismissing the student.** The court ruled in favor of the university. *Rossomando v. Board of Regents of the Univ. of Nebraska*, 2 F.Supp.2d 1223 (D. Neb. 1998). [NE]

◆ *A New York appellate court held that a school can expel a student for academic reasons in the exercise of its discretion as long as it does not act in an arbitrary or capricious manner or violate its rules and regulations.*

A student at a New York medical school had attended the school for four years but had not yet completed the second-year requirements and failed to pass the only class he was taking in his current school year. An academic committee recommended his dismissal, and he appealed to a faculty committee. He reached an agreement with the committee under which he was to pass the first step of the national medical licensing examination on his first attempt or withdraw from the college. When he failed to pass the first step of the exam, the college dismissed him. He filed suit against the college in state court to annul the college's decision. The trial court dismissed his petition, and he appealed to the New York Supreme Court, Appellate Division. The appellate court noted that there are strong policy considerations against the intervention of courts in disputes relating to a school's judgment of a student's academic performance. **Absent any arbitrary behavior, a school can expel a student in the exercise of its discretion.** Since the student did not present any evidence that the college's decision was arbitrary or capricious, or in violation of its rules and regulations, the trial court's decision was affirmed. *McDermott v. New York Medical College*, 644 N.Y.S.2d 834 (A.D. 3d Dept. 1996). [NY]

◆ *Academic dismissals made by educational institutions must be upheld unless arbitrary and capricious, irrational, made in bad faith, unconstitutional or contrary to statute.*

A student attending a New York private law school failed Civil Procedure in his first semester. The school informed him that it was dissatisfied with his progress. After he failed Constitutional Law and performed lower than average or failed to complete his other courses, he was dismissed for academic deficiency because his cumulative grade point average fell below 2.0. The school's Academic Policy Committee denied his request for probation in lieu of dismissal, and he appealed to a New York trial court. The trial court ordered the school to hold another hearing on the issue, and the school appealed to the New York Supreme Court, Appellate Division. The court noted that terminations made by educational institutions must be upheld unless arbitrary and capricious, irrational, made in bad faith, unconstitutional or contrary to statute. The trial court had improperly vacated the school's decision. **The committee, as an expert evaluator of the cumulative information relating to the student's performance, was in a better position to determine whether or not he demonstrated a strong probability of future compliance with the school's academic standards.** The trial court's ruling was reversed, and the case was dismissed. *Girsky v. Touro College, Fuchsberg Law Center*, 621 N.Y.S.2d 85 (A.D. 2d Dept. 1994). [NY]

◆ *An Illinois appellate court found that a Ph.D. candidate had no right to receive an additional two years to complete her dissertation. The university had properly enforced reasonable academic requirements, which were designed to ensure that the university students would safely serve the public as health care providers, in dismissing her.*

A candidate for a Ph.D. degree in speech and language pathology at Northwestern University was required to prepare a prospectus, undertake creative research, complete a written dissertation, and pass an oral examination prior to graduation. Against the advice of her director, the candidate began working on a prospectus on apraxia. The director allegedly asked her out and told her that they should "be together." He and several other faculty members evaluated three different drafts of her prospectus and each time concluded that they were unacceptable for a variety of reasons. She began to work on a new topic, but several professors again determined that it was not academically acceptable. The candidate alleged that the director had "usurped her ideas and surreptitiously utilized much of the information researched." She failed to complete her dissertation within the required five-year time frame. The university declined to grant the candidate a two-year extension, stating that she was unlikely to be able to research, prepare and defend a dissertation within a reasonable time. She sued the university and the director in an Illinois trial court, alleging breach of contract and tortious interference with contract. The court issued an injunction to allow her an additional two years of study in which to complete her dissertation. The student appealed.

The Appellate Court of Illinois reversed, holding the trial court improperly granted injunctive relief absent a clearly ascertainable right to the two-year extension, a showing of irreparable harm or the inadequacy of legal remedies. The **college had properly enforced reasonable academic requirements** that were designed to ensure that the university students would safely serve the public as health care providers. Although the candidate had worked hard toward obtaining a degree at Northwestern, **the school's decision did not preclude her obtaining a degree at another institution**. Consequently, the harm was not irreparable. Further, Illinois law recognized the availability of monetary damages: an alternative legal remedy. Finally, **the candidate failed to establish evidence that the university's determination was arbitrary and capricious**. Rather, the professors' explanations showed a discernible rational basis for the university's decision. The injunction was reversed, and the case remanded for further proceedings. *Bilut v. Northwestern Univ.*, 645 N.E.2d 536 (Ill. App. 1st Dist. 1994). [IL]

◆ *Where a school had properly based its expulsion decision on the totality of the evidence, the dismissal was neither arbitrary nor capricious and did not constitute a breach of contract.*

A phlebotomy student at an Illinois medical technology school received low scores on all but one of five examinations. As a result, she was placed on probation and notified that in order to graduate she would have to pass another exam, show marked improvement, better consider patient needs, handle patients more gently, and listen more closely to the instructor. She failed to achieve a passing score on the examination. **Her supervisor then described her treatment of patients as "brutal,"** noting instances where she: 1) failed to use proper procedures, 2) left an open dirty needle on top of a hazard box, and 3) left a urinal in a patient's bed. She also asked a patient who had undergone a double mastectomy "why she was in the hospital if she had just recently had a baby." The school expelled the student based on her performance, and she appealed to the U.S. District Court for the Northern District of Illinois.

The court employed a two-step analysis to determine whether the school had committed a breach of contract: 1) whether it breached a promise made either explicitly or through its academic bulletins or application forms; and 2) whether it acted arbitrarily, capriciously, and in bad faith. Because the school properly based its expulsion decision on the totality of the evidence, the dismissal was neither arbitrary nor capricious and did not constitute breach of contract. The student had failed to achieve the requisite score on her exam, had failed to improve her phlebotomy and communication skills, had failed to improve her handling of patients, and had failed to improve her ability to listen and to take constructive criticism. Even if the second term of her probation agreement obligated the instructor to review her performance, **her failure to achieve the other probationary conditions justified the expulsion.** *Haynes v. Hinsdale Hospital*, 872 F.Supp. 542 (N.D. Ill. 1995). [IL]

◆ *Courts may review a grading policy that is arbitrary and capricious, irrational, made in bad faith or contrary to federal or state law.*

A New York Law School student performed below a 2.0, or "C," cumulative average. The law school rules required students to maintain a 2.0 or better, or be subject to academic dismissal by the Academic Status Committee. The student appeared before the committee to state her case, but the committee failed to be persuaded by the student's excuses and voted unanimously to dismiss her. The student asked the committee to reconsider its decision. When the committee declined, the student filed suit in a New York trial court challenging the committee's decision and the grades she received in three of her classes. The trial court dismissed all of the claims, but the appellate division reversed and remanded with respect to the student's grade in one of her classes to determine if the grade was a rational exercise of discretion.

Both parties appealed to the Court of Appeals of New York. The student claimed that when she met with the professor he indicated she had received a zero on an essay question, worth 30 percent of her grade, because she had analyzed the problem under Delaware and New York law when only Delaware law was asked for. The student explained she analyzed the problem under New York law to get extra credit. **Courts have traditionally left grading policies to the special expertise of educators**, but may review a grading policy that is arbitrary and capricious, irrational, made in bad faith or contrary to federal or state law. The court determined **the student failed to meet this standard of review because the allegations went to the heart of the professor's evaluation of her academic performance**. The court dismissed the claim in its entirety. *Susan M. v. New York Law School*, 556 N.E.2d 1104 (N.Y. 1990). [NY]

2. Cheating and Plagiarism

◆   *The Appeals Court of Massachusetts held a university fully complied with its disciplinary procedures in finding a student guilty of plagiarism.*

A Brandeis University professor noticed a second term senior student did not properly attribute four secondary sources in a paper. She filed a student judicial system referral report, accusing him of verbatim plagiarism. The university's board of student conduct unanimously found the student guilty of plagiarism, and he unsuccessfully challenged the finding through the university appeal process. The student sued Brandeis in a Massachusetts trial court for breach of contract and breach of fiduciary duty. The court granted Brandeis's motion for summary judgment, and the student appealed. **The state court of appeals explained the university was expected to conduct hearings with basic fairness**. In reviewing the record, the court found Brandeis satisfied that expectation by providing the student all of the process he was due under the terms of the handbook, from notification of the charge through the hearing process. **The handbook clearly warned him that violation of academic honesty policies could lead to serious penalties**. Moreover, the sanction was consistent with those imposed on other upper-classmen for similar infractions. The trial court did not err in granting summary judgment to the university. *Morris v. Brandeis Univ.*, 804 N.E.2d 961 (Mass. App. 2004). [MA]

◆   *A state court upheld the academic suspensions of two Texas university students after they were disciplined for making "strikingly similar" answers on an organic chemistry examination.*

The students were a husband-wife couple who created suspicion because they gave incorrect answers to questions despite "millions of possible incorrect solutions." The were tested together in a hotel room while attending an off-campus conference. Their incorrect answers led to charges of violation of the school honor code. The university honor council held a hearing and found the students violated the code. The students were assigned F grades for the course and suspended for two months. The students failed to appear at a second hearing they requested. They then sought a state court order to remove their academic suspensions and the F grades from their transcripts. The court rejected the students' argument that the university blue book created a contract. They appealed to the Court of Appeals of Texas, which noted the record of their suspensions would only appear on internal school records. Since the students would not suffer any irreparable harm in the absence of a court order, the court affirmed the decision. *Law v. Rice Univ.*, 123 S.W.3d 786 (Tex. App. 2003). [TX]

◆ *The Court of Appeal of California held a law school provided a student with due process before suspending him for one semester for plagiarism.*

A second-year law student at the UCLA Law School submitted a 49-page paper to a professor who discovered "substantial portions" of it had been copied from a book without acknowledgment. The school's assistant dean and law school librarian agreed that the student had committed plagiarism. During an informal meeting, the student admitted his work was "fast and loose," but he denied any intent to commit plagiarism. The school allowed the student's request to postpone a disciplinary meeting so he could take a final examination. He then attended the disciplinary meeting, where he was represented by counsel. After reviewing the evidence, the school dean found he had committed plagiarism in violation of the Student Conduct Code. The school retroactively suspended the student and required him to complete 300 hours of community service. After unsuccessfully appealing his suspension, he complied with the disciplinary terms. Following his graduation, the student filed a state court action to set aside his suspension on the basis that he did not receive procedural due process. The court granted UCLA's summary judgment motion.

The student appealed to the Court of Appeal of California. The court noted that before any disciplinary action was initiated, the student's paper was reviewed by several school officials and even fellow students. All of these individuals concluded he had plagiarized the book. **The student received notice of the accusation against him and was informed of the definition of plagiarism in the Student Conduct Code**. The school provided him with an explanation of disciplinary procedures, and it was his obligation to learn UCLA's disciplinary procedures. Moreover, the student admitted the plagiarism. For this reason, he was not entitled to a hearing before the student conduct committee. **UCLA had provided the student with several opportunities to explain his actions.** Even had he received a hearing, it was unlikely he could have presented any new evidence to change the conclusion that he committed plagiarism, especially since he had admitted this conduct. The judgment for UCLA was affirmed. *Viriyapanthu v. Regents of the Univ. of California*, No. B157836, 2003 WL 22120968 (Cal. App. 2d Dist. 2003). [CA]

◆ *A North Carolina state university was immune from a lawsuit brought by an expelled law student.*

A state university law school student attempted to obtain the answers a study group had prepared for previous exams used in a particular course. She was unable to do so. On the day of the exam, she went to the emergency room complaining of stomach problems, and missed the test. After the test, she called a fellow student and asked for the answers, claiming she already had taken the test and wanted the answers to prepare for the bar exam. When a dean learned of her dishonesty, she refused to let the student take a makeup exam. Disciplinary proceedings were initiated, and the student was eventually expelled. She sued the university in a federal court under 42 U.S.C. § 1983 and also asserted a negligence claim. The court dismissed her lawsuit on Eleventh Amendment immunity grounds because she could not show that an exception applied to permit her suit to continue. **North Carolina never waived its immunity, and § 1983 did not eliminate states' immunity in such situations either.** *Pfouts v. North Carolina Central Univ.*, No. 1:02CV00016, 2003 WL 1562412 (M.D.N.C. 3/24/03). [NC]

◆ *Union University's Albany College of Pharmacy could not expel or fail three students for cheating where the college relied on statistical evidence showing that they had given the same incorrect answers on various exams.*

All three students were in their fourth year at the college when several professors accused them of cheating on tests in various courses over a two-year period. The Student Honor Code Committee found the students guilty based on evidence that they gave the same incorrect answers on various exams, similarly calculated answers to questions (although the students had arrived at the answers through different methods), and two anonymous notes questioning whether the students were cheating. Two of the students were found guilty of cheating in six courses and were expelled. The other student was charged with cheating in one course and received a failing grade for the class. The students appealed the committee's decision to a state trial court, which upheld the committee's decision as rational.

On appeal, the New York Supreme Court, Appellate Division, reviewed whether the committee's decision was arbitrary or capricious. It noted that the committee relied on a compilation of statistics showing the similarities in the students' answers, but **the statistical evidence only gave rise to a suspicion of cheating**. The court pointed to an affidavit from an expert statistician who said the statistics were not valid because they lacked "randomness," specifically that the students had no knowledge of the subject matter on the tests, and that there was "independence," in that the students had not studied together. The court also found the notes used as evidence by the committee to be inadmissible hearsay. Overall, **the court found the committee's decision irrational because it found the students guilty of cheating based merely on a statistical compilation of information, even though the students had taken the exams in separate rooms, and the exam proctors discerned no evidence of cheating**. The court annulled the committee's determination. *Basile v. Albany College of Pharmacy of Union Univ.*, 719 N.Y.S.2d 199 (A.D. 2001). [NY]

◆ *A Texas university student accused of plagiarism lost his appeal claiming the school's decision to expel him was an act of racial discrimination.*

The matter arose after the student turned in his final project to his theater professor. The project was a script titled "Return to Live," which the student submitted as his own original writing. Upon receiving a B for the project, he complained to an administrator in the College of Arts and Sciences, that he deserved a higher grade. Suspicious of the script's originality, the professor researched similar plays in the public library and discovered that the student's script replicated another work called "Resurrection" almost word-for-word. As a result, the student failed the theater course and was expelled. The student sued for discrimination, among other claims, but his lawsuit was dismissed.

The student appealed to the Texas Court of Appeals, claiming he had told his professor he would be using an existing work for his project and therefore did not plagiarize. He cited testimony by the administrator that finding the allegedly plagiarized play in the library would be like finding a "needle in a haystack." The student noted that the professor would therefore not be aware of the previously published play unless he himself had told her. The court determined the administrator's "needle in a haystack" reference referred to trying to find a play before limiting the search to a particular category. The professor explained that she limited her search to Afro-American dramas, a much smaller collection to search than all of the plays in the library. **The court rejected the student's argument that his expulsion constituted racial discrimination. A white student who was caught plagiarizing but denied the charge also was expelled.** The district court decision was affirmed in full. *Ntreh v. University of Texas at Dallas*, 2000 WL 1093233 (Tex. App. 8/7/00). [TX]

◆ *An African-American student failed to demonstrate that his discharge for cheating was racially motivated.*

A Virginia university economics professor, concerned about cheating, drafted two different exams, making only slight changes to the questions. He alternated the tests in a pile that a teaching assistant handed out in class. A student incorrectly answered several questions on his exam, but his answers were accurate responses to the corresponding questions in the other version of the exam. At his honor trial, the student jury found him guilty. The honor committee's appeal panel upheld the student jury's verdict. The student then sued the university in the U.S. District Court for the Western District of Virginia. Most of the claims were dismissed, except those alleging denial of equal protection of the laws, procedural due process violations and defamation.

To prove denial of equal protection, **the student used raw statistics to show that more minority students were prosecuted in similar situations compared to non-minority students, but the court found the actual evidence showed race was not a factor**. The court stated that statistics, standing alone, did not create a constitutional violation. In addition, three other students were charged with honor violations on the same exam. The case against the other African-American student was dropped for insufficient evidence, one of the white students was found not guilty, and the other white student left the university after being formally accused. **The student's procedural due process claim also failed** because even though his honor advisor did not contact him until the following semester, the delay should not have resulted in his inability to recreate the seating arrangement on the test day, record the mental processes he used to come up with the answers he devised, and preserve the other students' papers and the honor committee files before they were destroyed. While having an honor advisor assigned during the pre-trial process may be beneficial, the due process clause does not *require* such assistance. The student's claim of defamation also failed because a letter that was circulated among persons within the university only went to persons who had a duty and interest in the subject matter. The university's motion for pretrial judgment was granted. *Cobb v. Rector and Visitors of Univ. of Virginia*, 84 F.Supp.2d 740 (W.D. Va. 2000). [VA]

◆   *Where Texas professors did not take allegations of cheating into account when grading a student, a federal court held he had no cause of action against them for being dismissed from the university.*

A graduate student in psychology received two grades of C that subjected him to possible expulsion. A number of his professors also knew of allegations against him for cheating. However, they asserted they did not take the allegations into account when grading him. After the student's second C, he was placed in a remediation program. He then received two more Cs and failed two oral comprehensive examinations. A second, more demanding remediation plan was then drafted, calling for the student to enroll in a specific class. When he failed to do so, he was dismissed from the program because of his failure to comply with program academic requirements. He sued, claiming that the decision to dismiss him was tainted by the allegations of cheating and that he was not given a chance to address those allegations.

A federal district court ruled in favor of the university, and the Fifth Circuit Court of Appeals affirmed. **The dismissal had been for academic reasons, not disciplinary reasons. The protections available to the student were not as great. Even if the dismissal had been for disciplinary reasons, the student had essentially been given a hearing** when he went over the remediation plans with school personnel. It was only after he failed to meet the requirements of the second remediation plan that he was dismissed from the program. *Wheeler v. Miller*, 168 F.3d 241 (5th Cir. 1999). [TX]

◆   *A loss of credit for two classes in which a student was found to have violated a university honor code was fair punishment.*

The University of Tennessee Board of Trustees' honor code created a violation for failure to report the giving or receiving of unauthorized aid on an examination. Four students reported observing a group of other students who apparently gave or received aid during several examinations. One of the accused students was charged with cheating on five examinations under the honor code. An administrative law judge found the student not guilty on three charges and guilty on two others. He imposed as a punishment one year of probation and the loss of credit for the two classes in which she was held in violation of the honor code. The student appealed the decision to a Tennessee trial court, stating that a 19-day delay by the administrative law judge in issuing his opinion caused her to delay retaking the two courses. The student nonetheless graduated. The court held for the university, and the student appealed to the Court of Appeals of Tennessee. **The court of appeals found ample evidence in the record that the student had violated the honor code. There was evidence that the student had been looking at another person's examination papers.** The administrative law judge's delay did not violate state law, and the court affirmed the trial court's judgment for the university. *Daley v. University of Tennessee at Memphis*, 880 S.W.2d 693 (Tenn. App. 1994). [TN]

◆ *A student who was dismissed for cheating was given due process because she received notice and an opportunity to be heard.*

An Indiana medical school student was observed copying another student's paper during a final examination. Two professors who monitored the test submitted the papers of both students to a statistician who determined that there was a significant probability of cheating based upon matching wrong answers. The professors assigned the student accused of cheating a failing grade and, **because she had received a prior failing grade, an informal conference was held to determine whether she should be dismissed from the school**. The decision to assign a failing grade was affirmed, and a formal dismissal hearing was held before an academic committee at which the student was represented by an attorney. The dean of the medical school adopted the committee's recommendation to dismiss the student, and she filed a lawsuit against school officials to challenge the action in an Indiana trial court. The court denied the student's motion for a preliminary order preventing dismissal, and she appealed to the Court of Appeals of Indiana.

The court rejected the student's claim that the medical school's procedures had violated her due process rights. In cases of academic dismissals, only minimal procedural protections are required. Where dismissal occurs for disciplinary reasons, due process requires only notice and an opportunity to be heard. **The student had received a hearing in this case, which satisfied due process requirements under the standards for both academic and disciplinary dismissals.** She was not entitled to formally cross-examine the professors as she claimed. There also was no merit to her argument that the school's rules had violated her rights by allowing her dismissal for the "appearance of cheating." In this case, there was substantial evidence of cheating, and the court affirmed the trial court order. *Reilly v. Daly*, 666 N.E.2d 439 (Ind. App. 1996). [IN]

C. Nonacademic Dismissals

Sometimes cheating is determined to be an academic dismissal. Other times it is considered a "nonacademic dismissal." Educational institutions should follow reasonable procedures and provide students facing discipline with appropriate notice and an opportunity to be heard.

◆ *A federal appeals court found no merit to a student's claim that a Texas university maintained a "zero tolerance" drug policy.*

A Southwest Texas State University student claimed the university's drug policy, as written in the student handbook, mandated automatic dismissal if a student was found guilty of the possession, use or distribution of illegal drugs. In protest of what he deemed a "zero tolerance drug policy," he lit a marijuana cigarette at an on-campus rally. The university suspended him for two semesters. He sued the university and various officials in a federal district court, alleging the policy violated his Equal Protection rights. The court granted summary judgment to the university, and the student appealed.

The U.S. Court of Appeals, Fifth Circuit, found that although the handbook had some conflicting language, there was no evidence it contained a "zero tolerance" drug policy. The court found the policy provided disciplinary options to impose suspensions or dismissals, undermining the "zero tolerance" policy argument. Student code penalty provisions were not automatic. Moreover, students were entitled to a hearing before a disciplinary committee with the discretion to consider mitigating factors and reduce suspensions to probation. The court held the student's Equal Protection claim lacked merit, and it affirmed the judgment. *Anderson v. Southwest Texas State Univ.*, No. 02-51141, 73 Fed. Appx. 775, 2003 WL 22100831 (5th Cir. 2003). [TX].

◆ *A Georgia dental college properly expelled a student for drug use and falsifying documents.*

The student performed well academically, but was suspected of trafficking in narcotics. After university police searched his apartment and found controlled substances, he admitted using drugs. He was granted a medical leave to enter a rehabilitation program. Subsequently, the university learned that he had let his insurance coverage lapse in violation of school policy. After a hearing, he was dismissed from school. When he applied for readmission six months later, the university denied his application based on additional charges of possessing a loaded weapon and falsifying his financial aid application. He sued, and a federal court ruled in favor of the university. First, the court determined that he was not disabled under § 504 because he was considered a current drug user. Only two months passed between his admittance to the treatment program and his dismissal. Second, **there was no due process violation**. Not only is attendance at a dental school not a fundamental right, but **the student had been given notice and an opportunity to be heard during the proceedings** against him. *Federov v. Board of Regents for the Univ. of Georgia*, 194 F.Supp.2d 1378 (S.D. Ga. 2002). [GA]

◆ *A university could expel a student for murdering a classmate even though he had completed all his degree requirements.*

A student enrolled at Johns Hopkins University and completed his degree requirements in three and a half years. However, because the university held its graduation ceremonies only once a year at the end of the spring semester, he had to wait to receive his diploma. During the spring semester, the dean of students contacted him about complaints of harassment filed by another student, and told him that he would have to notify her and campus security when he intended to be on campus. He informed the dean that he would be on campus on a particular date to attend a student organization meeting. As promised, he attended the meeting, where he got into a confrontation with the student who had accused him of harassment. He shot and killed the student, then pled guilty to murder. When the dean informed him that the university had expelled him and that he was not going to receive his diploma, he sued.

A state trial court dismissed his action, and the Court of Special Appeals of Maryland affirmed. It did not matter that the student would have already received his diploma had the university conducted a fall graduation ceremony. What mattered was that the student had not yet been awarded his degree, and that he remained subject to the student handbook rules. **Since the student handbook required him to not only complete his coursework, but also to**

comply with the university's conduct code, and since murder was a violation of that code, the university was justified in expelling the student despite his completion of all degree requirements. The student was not entitled to a diploma. *Harwood v. Johns Hopkins Univ.*, 747 A.2d 205 (Md. App. 2000). [MD]

◆ *An Arkansas community college nursing student who tried to get drugs with a fraudulent prescription could be expelled.*

The student was arrested for attempting to obtain a controlled substance with a fraudulent prescription. She was suspended pending the police charges against her and pleaded no contest to a misdemeanor offense. The college then expelled her from school. It later conducted a new hearing to give the student another opportunity to review all the evidence and participate in the hearing with the help of counsel. The college again upheld the decision to expel the student. She sued the college in a federal court under 42 U.S.C. § 1983, asserting that the college had violated her constitutionally protected due process rights. The court dismissed her lawsuit.

The Eighth Circuit affirmed the ruling for the college. First, **the college's Standards of Conduct were not void for vagueness.** They required students to obey all rules and regulations formulated by the college as well as all federal, state and local laws. This was sufficient to notify the student that criminal conduct was not acceptable. Second, the student had been provided with adequate notice of the charges against her and an opportunity to present her side of the story. As a result, her claim against the college could not succeed. *Woodis v. Westark Community College*, 160 F.3d 435 (8th Cir. 1998). [AR]

◆ *Courts are required to show great respect for the judgment of college faculty members and cannot override their decisions unless there is a showing of a substantial departure from accepted academic norms.*

An Iowa medical student attending an osteopathic medical college achieved superior grades on his examinations, but exhibited eccentric behavior, strong psychopathic tendencies and socially unacceptable behavior. Because of his unkempt appearance and lack of interpersonal skills, he failed his clinical assignment and was asked to withdraw from the college. He threatened to drive his car off a bridge and was briefly placed in a psychiatric ward. When he refused to withdraw from the program, the college dismissed him, and he filed an unsuccessful appeal through the college.

An Iowa trial court held the dismissal violated the college's written procedures concerning the evaluation and remediation of clinical students and that college officials failed to exercise appropriate professional judgment. The college appealed the trial court's order to reinstate the student and to offer him an opportunity to repeat the clinic. The Supreme Court of Iowa determined that the trial court had applied an incorrect legal standard. **Courts were required to show great respect for the judgment of college faculty members and could not override their decisions unless there was a showing of a substantial departure from accepted academic norms.** The court rejected the student's characterization of the dismissal as "nonacademic." It also found that, contrary to the student's arguments, the school administration had shown great concern for him. The court reversed and remanded the judgment of the district court, dismissing the student's claims. *Lekutis v. University of Osteopathic Medicine and Health Sciences*, 524 N.W.2d 410 (Iowa 1994). [IA]

◆ *Schools generally receive greater deference with respect to dismissals involving academic deficiency than for those involving nonacademic reasons.*

A student at a private college of osteopathic medicine failed several courses during his first year. He also failed his spring clinical rotations and a neurobiology class during his third year. However, he later passed the classes after retaking them. During his fourth year, the student refused the college's request to return from an internship in Minneapolis after problems arose there. He finally returned, was placed on probation, and then assigned to do his clinical rotations in Des Moines. After serious attendance problems, two alleged incidents of unauthorized practice of medicine, and one alleged incident of forgery, the student was dismissed following a series of notices and hearings. The student challenged his dismissal in an Iowa trial court.

The court held that the dismissal was arbitrary and capricious, but it denied reinstatement and awarded him the equivalent of four years' tuition. Both parties appealed their adverse rulings to the Supreme Court of Iowa. The court stated that **schools generally are accorded greater deference with respect to dismissals involving academic deficiency** than for those involving nonacademic reasons. Here, the school's admission at trial established that the student's dismissal was nonacademic. **Although professional training violations were academic matters, they also were considered nonacademic disciplinary violations.** However, even under the stricter burden applied to nonacademic disciplinary actions, the court held that the two incidents of unauthorized practice of medicine coupled with the events that led to his probation justified his dismissal. The holding of the district court was reversed. *Pflepsen v. University of Osteopathic Medicine*, 519 N.W.2d 390 (Iowa 1994). [IA]

◆ *The Eighth Circuit upheld a school's refusal to reinstate a student who pled guilty to a criminal offense, even though the charge was eventually dismissed.*

A law school student was arrested after attempting to use a stolen credit card. When authorities formally charged the student, he had only two semesters to complete before graduating. The student moved the court for a continuance until after his expected graduation date. Meanwhile, the law school faculty reviewed his criminal file and passed a resolution suspending any student indicted or charged with criminal conduct while the matter was pending in court. The faculty also suspended the student and notified him by letter. He then sued the school in an Iowa state court for an injunction that would compel the school to reinstate him the following semester. The court ruled against the student, who then pled guilty and was sentenced in the criminal case.

A year later, the student completed probation, the charge was dismissed, and his criminal record cleared. He then petitioned the school for reinstatement. The school rejected the petition. The student sued the school in an Iowa federal district court alleging violations of his constitutional rights and breach of contract. The court ruled for the school and the U.S. Court of Appeals, Eighth Circuit, affirmed. The court had not been in error when it ruled that the **school's**

honor code, student handbook, and reservation of rights clause had formed a contract between the school and the student. **Because the jury had not found that the school had breached the contract in any respect, the student could not now challenge the verdict** as a matter of law. *Warren v. Drake Univ.*, 886 F.2d 200 (8th Cir. 1989). [IA]

◆ *An Illinois university followed its standards and procedures for disciplinary violations and properly expelled a student for violation of its harassment policy.*

An Illinois university disciplinary committee expelled a graduate student for violating the university's harassment policy. He appealed the committee's decision to a university review board arguing that the penalty was too harsh. When the board affirmed the committee's decision, the student brought a breach of contract action in federal court. He claimed the university had expelled him arbitrarily, capriciously, and in bad faith, thus breaching the contract between himself and the university. He sought an injunction compelling the university to rescind his expulsion and to award him an M.B.A. retroactively. He also sought monetary damages for humiliation and financial losses. After a bench trial, the court determined that the relationship between the university and its students was a contractual one and was governed by the terms set forth in the university's catalogs and manuals.

The court held the university was obligated to follow its published standards and procedures when disciplining its students. However, the student also was obligated to abide by university rules of conduct. The court held that **the committee's determination that the student engaged in a "systematic, prolonged and premeditated pattern of harassment" against a fellow student was rationally based on the evidence**. The student argued that the faculty members on the disciplinary committee were biased against him because of professional and social contacts with the victim and her brother. However, he failed to offer any credible evidence. The faculty committee was entitled to a presumption of impartiality. Also, the student had failed to establish that the school had breached its contractual obligations in conducting its disciplinary proceedings. The court entered judgment for the university. *Holert v. University of Chicago*, 751 F.Supp. 1294 (N.D. Ill. 1990). [IL]

◆ *A Pennsylvania court found that courts should not interfere with internal disciplinary matters unless the process has been found to be biased, prejudicial or lacking in due process.*

A student attending a private school operated by a Pennsylvania charitable foundation was suspended for one year after he repeatedly photographed and accosted visitors and scholars of the foundation. He was suspended for an additional two-year period after impersonating a foundation employee on three occasions in order to gain access to an area containing unique and priceless art. The student filed a lawsuit in a Pennsylvania trial court seeking a decree rescinding his suspension from the school. The trial court dismissed the lawsuit for lack of jurisdiction, and the student appealed to the Superior Court of Pennsylvania. The superior court held that because the student's lawsuit sounded in equity, the trial court had improperly declined to assert jurisdiction.

However, pursuant to *Schulman v. Franklin & Marshall College*, 371 Pa. Super. 345, 538 A.2d 49 (1988), **courts should not interfere with internal disciplinary matters unless the process has been found to be biased, prejudicial or lacking in due process**. Here, the court held that the school reasonably suspended the student for his harassing behavior and unauthorized entries into areas containing priceless art. *In re Barnes Foundation*, 661 A.2d 889 (Pa. Super. 1995). [PA]

III. STUDENT PRIVACY RIGHTS

Federal laws and the common law of most states provide for the protection of students' privacy interests, particularly in students' academic records. The laws provide guidelines as to the maintenance and disclosure of records as well as procedures for challenging the contents of the records.

A. The Family Educational Rights and Privacy Act

The Family Educational Rights and Privacy Act (FERPA) of 1974 [20 U.S.C. § 1232(g)], also called the Buckley Amendment, applies to any educational institution receiving federal funds. The act, along with U.S. Department of Education regulations at 34 CFR Part 99, contains extremely detailed requirements regarding the maintaining and disclosing of student records. These requirements become applicable only upon a student's attendance at the school.

FERPA [at 20 U.S.C. § 1232g(d)] requires schools to allow college students the right to inspect and review their education records. When students request access to their education records, schools must grant that access within a reasonable time, not to exceed 45 days. Students also must be given the opportunity for a hearing to challenge the content of their education records, to ensure that the records are not inaccurate, misleading, or otherwise in violation of their privacy or other rights.

Education records include those records, files, documents and other materials that contain information directly related to a student and that are maintained by the school or by an agent of the school. Records maintained by a law enforcement agency of a school (for the purpose of law enforcement) do not constitute education records for purposes of FERPA. Schools cannot release, or provide access to, any personally identifiable information in education other than directory information without the parents' written consent. Violating FERPA results in a loss of federal funds.

At times, FERPA seems to come into conflict with other laws, like the 1990 Student Right-to-Know and Campus Security Act, 20 U.S.C. § 1092(f), which requires all institutions of higher education that participate in federal funding programs to prepare, publish and distribute to all current students and employees an annual campus security report. Because colleges and universities sometimes deal with student crime through disciplinary boards, rather than through campus police, there can be pressure to seal student disciplinary records (under FERPA) that would otherwise be public under the Campus Security Act.

Further, FERPA provides that a college or university can include in the education record of any student "appropriate information ... concerning disciplinary action taken against such student for conduct that posed a significant risk to the safety or well-being of that student, other students, or other members of the school community." [20 U.S.C. § 1232g(h).] Since schools often benefit more from designating a particular act a violation of the student code (and being able to keep the information private) rather than designating it a crime (and having to release the information to the public), reports on campus security are not always accurate.

◆ *A student who claimed that a university violated FERPA could not sue under 42 U.S.C. § 1983 to enforce his "rights" under the act.*

A student attended a private university in Washington, intending to teach in the state's public school system after his graduation. At the time, the state required new teachers to obtain an affidavit of good moral character from the dean of their college or university. When the university's teacher certification specialist overheard a conversation implicating the student in sexual misconduct with a classmate, she commenced an investigation of the student and reported the allegations against him to the state teacher certification agency. She later informed the student that the university would not provide him with the affidavit of good moral character required for certification as a Washington teacher. The student sued the university and the specialist under state law and under 42 U.S.C. § 1983, alleging a violation of FERPA. A jury awarded him over $1 million in damages, and the case reached the U.S. Supreme Court, which ruled that **FERPA creates no personal rights that can be enforced under § 1983**. Congress enacted FERPA to force schools to respect students' privacy with respect to educational records. It did not confer upon students enforceable rights. As a result, the Court reversed and remanded the case for further proceedings. *Gonzaga Univ. v. Doe*, 536 U.S. 273, 122 S.Ct. 2268, 153 L.Ed.2d 309 (2002). [WA]

◆ *Using students to correct other students' work and call out the grades in class did not violate FERPA.*

An Oklahoma parent sued a school district and various administrators under FERPA after learning that students sometimes graded other students' assignments and called out the results in class. A federal court held this practice did not violate FERPA because calling out grades did not involve "education records" within the meaning of the statute. The Tenth Circuit reversed, but the U.S. Supreme Court noted that **student papers are not "maintained" within the meaning of FERPA when students correct them and call out grades**. Moreover, correcting a student's work can be as much a part of the assignment as taking the test itself. The momentary handling of assignments by students was not equivalent to the storing of information in a records room or a school's permanent secure database. *Owasso Independent School Dist. No. I-011 v. Falvo*, 534 U.S. 426, 122 S.Ct. 934, 151 L.Ed.2d 896 (2002). [OK]

◆ *An Illinois student's defamation and invasion of privacy claims were barred because they arose from remarks made by a professor that were deemed to be within the scope of his employment.*

An Illinois political science professor suspected a colleague of having a sexual relationship with a graduate student. He informed the department chair about their behavior and discussed the matter with four other professors. He also informed the student's boyfriend of his suspicions. During this time, other students complained that the colleague was generally unavailable and did not keep his office hours. The student filed a grievance against the professor, charging him with sexual harassment and violating her privacy, and made a charge against him with the Illinois Department of Human Rights. The professor sued the student in a federal district court, alleging deprivation of his First Amendment speech rights and retaliation. The student counterclaimed for defamation, intentional infliction of emotional distress and invasion of her privacy rights. The court awarded summary judgment to the professor.

The Seventh Circuit held the professor showed his comments were made within the scope of his employment. Evidence indicated the university was concerned about inappropriate professor-student relationships and encouraged professors to report suspicious relationships. The professor communicated his concerns during the academic year within normal office hours. The court rejected the student's characterization of his remarks as gossip. The professor spoke to other professors about the colleague's lack of professionalism and his observations were motivated, at least in part, by an intent to serve the university. **The court rejected the FERPA claim based on *Gonzaga Univ. v. Doe*, above, in which the Supreme Court held there is no private cause of action for FERPA violations under 42 U.S.C. § 1983.** *Shockley v. Svoboda*, 342 F.3d 736 (7th Cir. 2003). [IL]

◆ *University disciplinary records were held to be "education records" under FERPA and thus could not be disclosed to the press.*

A student newspaper at an Ohio university sought student disciplinary records from the University Disciplinary Board for an article about crime trends on campus. After a lawsuit, the Ohio Supreme Court held that student disciplinary records were not "education records" as defined by the Family Educational Rights and Privacy Act. As a result, the university had to hand over the records, redacting only name, Social Security number and student identification number. As a result of the student editors' success, another newspaper requested disciplinary records from two Ohio universities.

The U.S. Department of Education then brought a federal court action seeking declaratory and injunctive relief to prevent the universities from disclosing the disciplinary records. The court agreed with the DOE that disciplinary records are "education records" under FERPA, and issued an injunction to prevent the release of the information. The Sixth Circuit Court of Appeals affirmed, noting that **because the disciplinary records related to students and were kept by the universities, they were education records**

under FERPA. Since university disciplinary proceedings are not like criminal trials, which have been traditionally open to the press and the public, an injunction preventing release of the information was appropriate. *U.S. v. Miami Univ.*, 294 F.3d 797 (6th Cir. 2002). [OH]

◆   *Student applicant information was not protected by FERPA where it was not personally identifiable.*

The University of Wisconsin System received a request for records of applicants applying for admission to the system's 11 undergraduate campuses, its law school and its medical school over a six-year period. The system partially complied with the request, but withheld information on standardized test scores, race and gender because it believed the information was protected by FERPA and because it believed the release of such information would require it to create new records. The case reached the Supreme Court of Wisconsin, which held that **FERPA did not prevent disclosure of the requested data because it was not personally identifiable information**. Even though it might be possible for the data to create a list of identifying characteristics, the court concluded that the information was not personally identifiable. Also, the court noted that the system would not have to create new records to comply with the request. It merely would have to redact personally identifiable information from records it already maintained. Doing so would be burdensome; however, the system could charge a fee for photocopying records to alleviate its costs. The system had to provide the requested information. *Osborn v. Board of Regents of Univ. of Wisconsin System*, 647 N.W.2d 158 (Wis. 2002). [WI]

◆   *A state university was immune to suit where it negligently disseminated confidential student records.*

A freshman basketball player at a Texas university was suspended from the team when he failed to maintain good academic standing. Various newspapers reported the story. The day after the suspension, a fax containing a portion of his educational records was sent from the men's basketball office to two local radio stations. The stations broadcasted that information. The student sued the university and several officials for negligence under the state tort claims act and for violating the Family Educational Rights and Privacy Act. A state court dismissed the lawsuit on the grounds that the university had immunity, and the Texas Court of Appeals affirmed. Here, **there was no tangible personal property that led to his injury so as to bring his claim within the exception to immunity under the tort claims act**. The fax machine used to disseminate his confidential information did not cause his injury. Also, he conceded on appeal that the FERPA claim could not survive. *Axtell v. University of Texas at Austin*, 69 S.W.3d 261 (Tex. App. 2002). [TX]

◆   *An action against a Virginia medical school was dismissed because it raised the same issues from a previous case, in which a court held FERPA does not create a right to challenge the accuracy of an academic evaluation.*

The matter arose out of an Eastern Virginia Medical School student's 1991 pharmacology examination score. The exam was designed to determine students' competency in pharmacology if they took a course in that subject area at another school. After failing the exam by a small margin, the student claimed that two correct answers were marked incorrectly. He requested that EVMS reconsider his score, but the school denied reconsideration. In 1993, the student was dismissed from the school for poor academic performance, including his pharmacology exam score. The student requested unabridged tape recordings of the Student Progress Committee hearing where members recommended his expulsion. EVMS provided him with abridged recordings. The school also rejected the student's application for readmission.

The student sued EVMS in federal court, alleging he was denied due process. He also asserted violations of FERPA and § 504 of the Rehabilitation Act. The court found that EVMS did not violate the student's due process rights because the school's decision to dismiss him was academic, and courts only overrule academic decisions in rare circumstances. The court rejected the § 504 claim because the school's decision to dismiss the student was not based on a perceived disability. In examining the student's assertion that EVMS violated FERPA by failing to provide him with an adequate hearing to challenge the exam score, the court ruled that **FERPA did not establish a right for students to challenge an academic evaluation through a private lawsuit**.

The student then brought several common law claims in state court and also re-asserted the FERPA claims. EVMS removed the action to federal court. Under 42 U.S.C. § 1983, the student argued, EVMS violated FERPA by interfering with his efforts to obtain a complete recording of the committee hearing. He also sought relief under 42 U.S.C. § 1985, alleging that the medical school and various EVMS officials violated FERPA by conspiring to withhold the complete recording from him in retaliation for his challenge to their academic authority. The court dismissed the § 1983 claims because they already had been rejected. Since the student did not present any new causes of action or legal theories, the suit was barred under the doctrine of *res judicata*. The § 1985 conspiracy claim failed under the doctrine of intra-corporate immunity. **The student also failed to state a claim because he did not demonstrate that the medical school's failure to provide the unabridged recording caused him any cognizable injury**. *Lewin v. Cooke*, 95 F.Supp.2d 513 (E.D. Va. 2000). [VA]

◆   *The owner of off-campus housing, who succeeded in having a list of incoming freshmen released, was unable to obtain an award for attorneys' fees incurred in obtaining the list, because the student lists were not records of clearly significant interest to the general public.*

Owners of off-campus residential buildings approved by Southern Illinois University for student housing were given lists of the names and addresses of incoming freshmen so that they could directly contact students about housing arrangements. According to the school's housing policy, unmarried freshmen under the age of 21 who did not reside with their parents were required to live either in dormitories or in privately owned, university-approved, off-campus housing. As a result of declining enrollment, the university stopped releasing this information. In April 1993, the owner of an off-campus residential building sent a letter demanding "a complete listing of any and all records relating to freshman housing inquiries, made for the 1993-94 school year...." The university president responded that the Illinois Freedom of Information Act did not require disclosure of the information and that the requested information was exempt from disclosure under federal law. Pursuant to the IFOIA, the owner sued the university. A state court found that the university was not obligated to release this information for a commercial enterprise. However, the Illinois Supreme Court held that there was "no valid basis" for withholding the information. The owner then sought attorneys' fees under Section 11(i) of the IFOIA. The court denied them.

The Appellate Court of Illinois affirmed. In order to succeed on this motion, **the owner had to establish that: (1) he substantially prevailed; (2) the information was "of clearly significant interest to the general public"; and (3) there was no reasonable basis for withholding the information.** The court pointed out that an award of attorneys' fees is discretionary under the IFOIA. Here, the owner was unable to establish that the student information was important to the general public. Generally, courts are reluctant to award attorneys' fees where the success of the suit benefits only a few or is incidental to the public interest. In light of this reasoning, the appellate court concluded that the denial of a fee award to the owner was not an abuse of discretion. *Lieber v. Board. of Trustees of Southern Illinois Univ.*, 316 Ill.App.3d 266, 736 N.E.2d 213 (Ill. App. 2000). [IL]

◆ *Two universities violated FERPA by releasing disciplinary records containing personally identifiable information without the prior consent of the named students or their parents.*

In 1996, Miami University, Ohio, released copies of various disciplinary records to the school newspaper with the accused students' names, ages and sex excluded, as well as the date, time and location of the incidents. Dissatisfied with the amount of information provided in the redacted records, the newspaper requested full copies of the records with only the students' names and social security numbers deleted. The paper claimed it was entitled to full copies of the disciplinary records under the Ohio Public Records Act. The university maintained that the records it provided were in compliance with FERPA, which protects students' privacy interest in their educational records and generally prohibits the nonconsensual disclosure of personally identifiable information.

In 1997, the Ohio Supreme Court held that student disciplinary records were not "educational records" subject to FERPA because they "do not contain educationally related information, such as grades or other academic data, and are unrelated to academic performance, financial aid, or scholastic performance." *The Chronicle of Higher Education* requested disciplinary records from the university. The school notified the Federal Department of Education that, due to the Ohio Public Records Act, it might be unable to comply with FERPA. The department responded that FERPA is applicable to disciplinary records. After the U.S. Supreme Court refused to review the state supreme court's decision, Miami University provided *The Chronicle* with full copies of its disciplinary records, less the students' names and social security numbers. The newspaper also obtained disciplinary records from Ohio State University. The Department of Education sued to prevent the universities from providing *The Chronicle* with disciplinary records without the prior consent of the students or their parents. After finding that the department had standing to bring the action, the court held that university disciplinary records fell within the definition of "education records" under FERPA. **The court differentiated between disciplinary records and law enforcement records, which were not covered by FERPA. It granted the department's motion for pretrial judgment and permanently enjoined the universities from releasing student disciplinary records with personally identifiable information.** *United States v. Miami Univ.*, 91 F.Supp.2d 1132 (S.D. Ohio 2000) *affirmed*, 2002 WL 1378233 (6th Cir. 6/27/02). [OH]

◆ *Parts of a statewide test that were owned by the state were public records and had to be disclosed to a student.*

The Ohio Department of Education (ODE) administers the Ohio Proficiency Test to high school seniors to ensure that they have requisite knowledge in selected academic areas. Ohio State University also administered a statewide test to high school students that was developed to accelerate the modernization of vocational education in the state. Part of that test was developed and owned by a private entity. Both tests used a new format each time a test was administered and the tests were owned in part by the state agencies that administered, them. An Ohio student who had taken both examinations requested access to the tests after they had been administered. The ODE refused to release test information for review unless the student signed a nondisclosure agreement. The family refused to sign the agreement and instead sued to compel state education officials to release relevant portions of both tests pursuant to the state Public Records Act.

The Supreme Court of Ohio ruled **the state-owned parts of both tests were public records within the meaning of state law**. Further, none of the exceptions to the state law presumption in favor of public disclosure applied. The student sought release of the information for educational purposes and did not seek to use it for a commercial purpose. A state law that prohibits assisting a student in cheating on proficiency tests was not applicable to this case. The student was entitled to an order for disclosure of the requested information. However, the portion of the test devised by the private entity was not a public record and was not subject to release. *State ex rel. Rea v. Ohio Dep't of Educ.*, 81 Ohio St.3d 527, 692 N.E.2d 596 (1998). [OH]

◆ *Some student disciplinary records had to be disclosed to a university student newspaper because the records were not education records as defined by FERPA.*

An Ohio university student newspaper editor asked the university's student disciplinary board for certain student disciplinary records to develop a database and monitor crime on campus. The university denied the request, citing the state public records act. The editor made a written request for the records, requesting release of the data without identification such as names, social security numbers and student numbers. The university released copies of disciplinary board records and deleted not only personal information such as identity, sex and age, but other data sought by the editors including the times and locations of the incidents leading to discipline. The editors petitioned the Supreme Court of Ohio for an order requiring the release of the information.

The university argued that it had deleted the information in compliance with the confidentiality provisions of FERPA, which provides for sanctions against education institutions that do not comply with its confidentiality requirements for education records. The court found that university disciplinary board records involved violations of student rules and regulations and some criminal matters. **Because the board's proceedings were not academic in nature, they contained no education-related information and were not education records as defined in FERPA.** The deletion of the general location of the violation, type of punishment and other relevant data deprived the public of important information that might compromise public safety. The court granted the order requested by the editors. *State ex rel. The Miami Student v. Miami Univ.*, 79 Ohio St.3d 168, 680 N.E.2d 956 (1997). [OH]

◆   *Neither FERPA nor school policy provide a means by which a student may obtain information on how a particular grade was assigned.*

A Texas university student received a grade of C in a physics class. He was disappointed with the grade and sought to challenge the assignment of the grade in a federal district court, or in the alternative to strike it from the record. The university and the teacher moved to dismiss the case. FERPA provides that no federal funds shall be made available to any educational agency or institution unless the parents of a student who has been in attendance at such institution are provided an opportunity for a hearing for the purpose of ensuring that the content of the student's education records are not inaccurate, misleading, or otherwise in violation of the privacy rights of the student. Neither FERPA nor school policy provide a means by which a student may obtain information on how a particular grade was assigned. The court ruled that **at most, the student was only entitled to know whether the assigned grade was recorded accurately** in the records. Therefore, the court granted the defendants' motion to dismiss the case. *Tarka v. Cunningham*, 741 F.Supp. 1281 (W.D. Tex. 1990). [TX]

◆   *A student newspaper had to be allowed to attend student Organization Court meetings and had to be granted access to the court's records.*

After the student newspaper at the University of Georgia was denied access to Organization Court records and proceedings involving hazing at fraternities, the newspaper sued, seeking access to records and disciplinary proceedings of the student Organization Court. The university claimed that FERPA required it to keep confidential those records and proceedings. However, the Supreme Court of Georgia disagreed. It noted that even if FERPA could be construed as prohibiting the release of education records, **the access being sought here was not access to "education records." What the newspaper was seeking was documentation of hazing charges against fraternities.** The court determined that the newspaper was entitled to the records of proceedings as well as to Organization Court proceedings under the state's Open Meetings Act. *Red & Black Publishing Co. v. Board of Regents*, 427 S.E.2d 257 (Ga. 1993). [GA]

B. Implied Contractual Privacy Rights

Many states also recognize state or common law privacy claims based on contractual rights established through the student's enrollment contract with the private institution.

◆   *A Colorado student could sue a college for ordering an HIV test without his permission.*

A student in a medical assistant training program told his instructor that he had tested positive for HIV in an anonymous blood test. He asked the instructor to keep that information confidential. Shortly thereafter, the instructor informed the class that all students were required to be tested for rubella. **The student consented to the test with the understanding that his sample would be tested for rubella only. However, the instructor contacted the lab doing the testing and asked that the student's sample be tested for HIV.** She did not request such testing for any other student. After the sample tested positive, the lab reported the student's name, address and HIV status to the state department of health (as required by law) and informed the college of the results. The student sued the college for invasion of privacy, asserting the college unreasonably disclosed private facts and intruded upon his seclusion.

A court dismissed the intrusion upon seclusion claim, but a jury found that the student was entitled to damages for the college's unreasonable disclosure of private facts. On appeal, the Colorado Court of Appeals held in his favor. **The claim for intrusion upon seclusion involved the college's authorization of a test that the student had not authorized, which was the improper appropriation of confidential information. The claim for unreasonable disclosure of private facts involved the dissemination of that information.** That the student suffered harm because of the disclosure of information did not mean he could not have suffered harm because of the improper appropriation of the information. The court reversed and remanded the case. *Doe v. High-Tech Institute, Inc.*, 972 P.2d 1060 (Colo. App. 1998). [CO]

◆   *An Ohio court found that a university's maintenance of a student's summer law program grades with his undergraduate grades was reasonable.*

A student enrolled in Ohio Northern University's summer law school qualification program. The program was designed for students who were not qualified for admission under regular criteria. Those who achieved a "B-" average would be admitted to the law school. The student failed to maintain the required grade point average and thus was not enrolled in the law school. Prior to enrollment in the summer program, the student had received an undergraduate engineering degree from the university. He sued the university in state court claiming that on at least two occasions it released his undergraduate transcript containing a record of his performance in the law school summer program. He sought a court order prohibiting the university from maintaining a record of his performance in the summer program and asking for money damages. An Ohio court ruled against him, and he appealed. The Court of Appeals of Ohio held **the student failed to show that the maintaining of his summer law program grades together with his**

undergraduate record was unreasonable, arbitrary, or in violation of any federal or state law. Further, the court held that whether the student had been "admitted" to the law school or had merely been "participating" in the summer program was irrelevant. The important fact was that the student had attended courses at the law school. Accordingly, the university was entitled to maintain records of his law school attendance. The student's lawsuit against the university was dismissed. *Smith v. Ohio Northern Univ.*, 514 N.E.2d 142 (Ohio App. 3d Dist. 1986). [OH]

◆ *An implied contract between the student and school exists that prevents a school from maliciously or in bad faith refusing to award a degree to a student who has fulfilled its requirements.*

A student attended an Illinois Christian College from September 1976 to March 1981. During his last semester the dean of students was told by another student that he might be gay. In reliance upon the college's assurances that he would graduate if he sought counseling the student repeatedly traveled out of town to obtain counseling, and revealed many personal facts about his homosexuality. When the counselor reported the student's tendencies to the dean of students, the dean informed the student that the college would hold a hearing where he would be required to defend himself against the rumor that he was a homosexual. Afraid that the accusation of homosexuality on his transcript would destroy his career prospects, the student withdrew from the college. The hearing was held anyway and subsequently the dean informed the student's mother that her son was being dismissed because he was a homosexual. In November 1984, the student sued the college and the counselor in an Illinois circuit court. When the circuit court granted motions to dismiss the student's complaint, he appealed to the Appellate Court of Illinois.

The appellate court observed that the implied contract between a college and a student is legally enforceable. Because **a college cannot act maliciously or refuse in bad faith to award a degree to a student who fulfills its degree requirements**, the court concluded that the student's complaint stated a valid legal basis for breach of an implied contract. The court also ruled that if the student was later able to prove his factual allegations, the college would be judged to have violated **the Illinois Confidentiality Act**. It then concluded that the lower court was wrong in dismissing the student's claim that the college tortiously interfered with his contract with the counselor and that the counselor's disclosure of confidential information tortiously interfered with his contract with the college. These matters were remanded to the circuit court for further proceedings. *Johnson v. Lincoln Christian College*, 501 N.E.2d 1380 (Ill. App. 4th Dist. 1986). [IL]

C. Computer Privacy

◆ *A student who allegedly saved child pornography on university computer lab computers was not entitled to privacy under the Fourth Amendment.*

A student at the Lewiston-Auburn College of the University of Maine left an image on a university computer screen that a university employee considered pedophilic. University authorities investigated the incident and discovered similar images on the hard drives of other computer-lab computers. The university contacted the police, and the student was indicted for receiving child pornography in violation of 18 U.S.C. § 2252A(a)(2). The prosecution obtained two hard drives from the university that allegedly contained illegal images, as well as the university's computer usage logs, which indicated when the student used the computers. The student filed a motion to have the hard drives and logs suppressed as the product of searches that violated his Fourth Amendment right against unreasonable searches and seizures.

A federal court judge ruled the student had no right to privacy in this matter and denied the motion to suppress. **To assert a right under the Fourth Amendment, a defendant must show that he believes he had a right to privacy and that society would find his expectation objectively reasonable.** Because the usage logs were maintained for the benefit of the university, they could not be suppressed. The judge cited the U.S. Supreme Court's decision in *Smith v. Maryland*, 442 U.S. 735 (1970), in which the high court ruled that a telephone customer had no legitimate expectation of privacy in telephone numbers he had dialed because, in dialing, he voluntarily conveyed the information to the telephone company and assumed the risk that the information could be disclosed. As for the hard drives, the judge found the student pointed to no computer privacy policies at the university, no statements made to him about the use of the computer lab, no practices concerning access to and retention of the contents of the hard drives or even password requirements. As such, **the student was simply using university computers under circumstances where images on the monitor were visible to others**. *U.S. v. Butler*, 151 F.Supp.2d 82 (D. Me. 2001). [ME]

◆   *Companies that hosted Web sites selling videotapes of college student-athletes taken without their knowledge or consent were immune from suit under Section 230 of the Communications Decency Act. Immunity under Section 230 –traditionally applied to online service providers–extends to Web hosting activities as well, according to the following decision.*

Numerous Illinois State University student-athletes were videotaped in various states of undress in restrooms, showers or locker rooms. The tapes–made without their knowledge or consent–were then displayed and sold on Web sites. The athletes sued the Web sites' host companies. A federal court dismissed the athletes' complaint for "intrusion upon seclusion," finding that the defendants were immune from suit under Section 230, which states that online service providers are not to be treated as publishers of information provided by third-party "information content providers." The athletes amended their complaint to name the defendants in their capacity as hosts of the offending Web sites rather than as online service providers. The athletes also added several claims, including a "third-party benefit" claim based on the contracts between the defendants and the owners of the Web sites, and a claim for eavesdropping under the Electronic Communications Privacy Act, 18 U.S.C. § 2511(a), which is not preempted by the Communications Decency Act. The Web site hosts again moved to dismiss under Sec. 230.

The district court rejected the athletes' contention that the defendants' roles as Web hosts should alter the previous ruling. "**The [Communications**

Decency Act] creates federal immunity against any state law cause of action that would hold computer service providers liable for information originating from a third party....," the court wrote. The athletes' new characterization of two of the defendants' activities as Web hosts did not alter this finding. Mere involvement in Web hosting activities does not transform an entity into an information content provider. The court next rejected the third-party beneficiary claim because the athletes were not intended beneficiaries under the contracts between the defendants and their customers. Finally, the athletes failed to establish a claim under the Electronic Communications Privacy Act. The host companies did not post any of the offending communications themselves, but merely served as conduits. *Doe v. Franco Productions*, 2000 WL 816779 (N.D. Ill. 6/22/00). [IL]

IV. GRADING AND CURRICULUM

◆ *A student who waited more than two years to challenge an "incomplete" grade had her lawsuit dismissed.*

A disabled Georgia college student began a student-teaching assignment during the spring quarter of 1994. She alleged that the classroom teacher discriminated against her because of her disability. In May 1994, the teacher issued the student a grade of "Unsatisfactory." On May 31, **college faculty changed her grade to an "Incomplete," which allowed her to repeat the student-teaching program the next year.** On June 6, the student received a letter from the same faculty members informing her that the May 31 decision would stand. On June 6, 1996, the student sued the college in the U.S. District Court for the Northern District of Georgia alleging violations of Title II of the Americans with Disabilities Act (ADA) and the Rehabilitation Act. The college moved to dismiss her claims as time barred by a two-year state statute of limitations. The district court granted the motion for dismissal, and the student appealed to the U.S. Court of Appeals, Eleventh Circuit.

When a federal statute does not contain a limitations period, the courts should look to the most analogous state statute of limitations. Because Georgia had not passed a state law identical to the Rehabilitation Act, the trial court properly applied the state's two-year personal injury statute of limitations; civil rights actions are essentially personal injury claims. Because discrimination claims accrue when the plaintiff is informed of the discriminatory act, the court held that **the date the student first learned she would receive an "Incomplete," was when her claim began to accrue**. The letter of June 6, 1994 merely confirmed the faculty's May 31 decision, and at most only failed to undo prior discriminatory acts. Failure to remedy a prior discriminatory act does not constitute a new discriminatory act for the purpose of determining whether a claim is time barred. The lower court's judgment was affirmed. *Everett v. Cobb County School Dist.*, 138 F.3d 1407 (11th Cir. 1998). [GA]

For additional cases involving disability discrimination against students, see Chapter Two, Section I.

◆   *A temporary grade reduction did not sufficiently injure a student such that he was entitled to damages.*

A Texas community college teacher responded to a tardiness problem in an 8:00 a.m. English class by stating that attendance would be taken and that those not present at the beginning of class would be counted absent. The department's attendance policy stated that students who were absent six days from a class were subject to a failing grade. However, when a student reached his sixth absence for the class, the teacher lowered his grade from an A to a B rather than issuing a failing grade. The student waited for one year to challenge the grade and filed a complaint with the dean of the department. The teacher agreed to change the grade to an A, but the student filed a lawsuit against the college and some of its employees in the U.S. District Court for the Northern District of Texas. The court dismissed the complaint, and the student appealed to the U.S. Court of Appeals, Fifth Circuit.

The court found that the only injury claimed by the student was the reduction of the grade for approximately 12 months, which allegedly denied him an opportunity to compete for academic scholarships. **The student had failed to state that he actually applied for scholarships and thus failed to show that he was injured because of the grade reduction.** Any injury he suffered was purely speculative. Accordingly, the claim was frivolous and insufficient to invoke the jurisdiction of a federal court. The court affirmed the order to dismiss the lawsuit. *Dilworth v. Dallas County Community College Dist.*, 81 F.3d 616 (5th Cir. 1996). [TX]

◆   *A grading complaint at a community college was deemed to be of an academic nature. Thus, the dean had final decisionmaking power in the area.*

Nursing students attending a Missouri community college complained that testing procedures in a required course caused them to fail the class. The claims included typographical errors, testing on materials not covered in classes and inability to review quizzes after grading. One of the students who failed the class met with the college dean to discuss retaking the final test, but her request was denied. The students complained to the state board of nursing, which conducted an investigation. The college responded by submitting a compliance proposal and offered the course again to the students. One of the failing students who subsequently retook and passed the class sued the college and some of its officials in a Missouri federal court under 42 U.S.C. § 1983, alleging civil rights violations. The court granted pretrial judgment to the college and administrators, and the student appealed to the Eighth Circuit.

The student claimed she had suffered procedural due process violations when the college failed to follow its handbook grievance procedure for resolving grading disputes and that administrators used arbitrary and capricious administrative methods. She also complained of substantive due process violations in the college curriculum requirements and claimed that college administrators were motivated by bad faith. The court held the complaint was related to an academic matter for which the dean held final decisionmaking power. It rejected the student's assertion that her complaint was a procedural and not an academic matter. **The alleged procedural irregularities did not rise to the level of a constitutional violation** or bring the question of grading outside the realm of academics. The administrators had appropriately rescheduled the course. The court affirmed the district court decision. *Disesa v. St. Louis Community College*, 79 F.3d 92 (8th Cir. 1996). [MO]

◆   *Academic freedom could be used as a defense to a claim brought under the Establishment Clause.*

A New York resident audited a community college course entitled "Family Life and Human Sexuality" and claimed that it promoted eastern religions and disparaged traditional Jewish and Christian teachings on marriage, procreation and adultery. He reenrolled in the course the following semester and joined a number of New York taxpayers in filing a lawsuit against the community college, its administrators and board in the U.S. District Court for the Eastern District of New York, seeking declaratory and injunctive relief that the course offering violated the state and federal constitutions and New York law. The court considered several preliminary motions by the parties.

The court rejected the college and officials' dismissal motion based upon their claim that their right to academic freedom barred the plaintiffs from challenging college policies, activities and course materials. **Although the principles of academic freedom could provide a defense to the claims, they did not bar the claims altogether.** The individual taking the course did not have a viable claim because the class would have ended before the litigation did. Taxpayer status alone was insufficient to confer standing to allow a free exercise claim, and these claims were dismissed. The court was unable to construe a New York law requiring course offerings in college catalogues to be plainly disclosed, and this claim was dismissed. It also was unwilling to grant the requested order prohibiting the college from offering the course the following semester. However, **the court denied pretrial dismissal of the remaining taxpayers' claim that the course offering violated the Establishment Clause of the Constitution or the New York Constitution**. It dismissed the other claims. *Mincone v. Nassau County Community College*, 923 F.Supp. 398 (E.D.N.Y. 1996). [NY]

For additional cases involving academic freedom, please see Chapter Four, Section I, Part D.

◆   *A grade of F was properly assigned where a South Dakota student turned in his assignments late.*

After being dismissed for academic reasons, a student was readmitted to a medical school in South Dakota. He then received a grade of F in internal medicine and was again dismissed from the school. He sued in federal court, asserting that the grade he received should have been I (incomplete), because although he failed to do all the requisite work before the end of the semester, he did complete the work shortly after the next semester began. He maintained that the professor had stated that incompletes would be given where a student failed to get all the work done on time, and he allegedly relied on that statement. He asserted that the grade of F in place of I was arbitrary and capricious conduct in violation of his substantive due process rights. A federal court granted pretrial judgment to the school, and the student appealed. The

Eighth Circuit Court of Appeals held that there was no genuine issue of material fact as to whether the grade of F was arbitrary. **The student had failed the final written examination, failed to properly present patients during rounds, and failed to turn in required work on time. Thus, the grade was justified.** There had been no substantive due process violation, and the student had been properly dismissed from the school. The lower court's decision was affirmed. *Hines v. Rinker*, 667 F.2d 699 (8th Cir. 1981). [SD]

V. HOUSING

◆   *A medical school may have violated the New York City Human Rights Law by denying two lesbian couples the right to seek campus housing in the same manner as a married couple.*

Yeshiva University's Albert Einstein College of Medicine, a private institution, owns a number of apartments near its campus and offers them at discounted rates to its students on a first-come, first-serve basis. Priority is given to married couples. Two lesbian students requested housing for themselves and their life partners, but the university did not given them priority because they could not produce proof of marriage. The American Civil Liberties Union filed suit on behalf of the students, claiming the university violated the state's human rights law, the Roommate Law (Real Property Law § 235-f) and the New York City Human Rights Law by discriminating against them based on marital status. The complaint further alleged the housing policy had a disparate impact on lesbians and gay men and therefore discriminated on the basis of sexual orientation.

A trial court dismissed the complaint, finding no cause of action for marital-status discrimination. The court also ruled that the Roommate Law did not apply to temporary college housing. Finally, it ruled that the disparate impact theory held no weight because the students were able to obtain student housing without their partners. The Supreme Court, Appellate Division, affirmed, noting Yeshiva's policy impacted all unmarried students, whether homosexual or heterosexual, and therefore was not discriminatory.

The ACLU appealed to the New York Court of Appeals, arguing the policy had an adverse impact on gay and lesbian students and discriminated based on sexual orientation. New York Human Rights Law § 8-107(17) creates a cause of action for plaintiffs who can demonstrate that a seemingly neutral policy has a disparate impact on a protected group. It specifically prohibits discrimination based on sexual orientation. **The court held that the lower courts erred by comparing gay and lesbian students only to other nonmarried students without including married students in its comparison of how the policy affects potential housing residents.** To determine whether the housing policy had a disparate impact on the basis of sexual orientation, "there must be a comparison that includes consideration of the full composition of the class actually benefited under the changed policy." The disparate impact claim was wrongly dismissed, and the case was remanded for further proceedings. *Levin v. Yeshiva Univ.*, 96 N.Y.2d 484 (N.Y. 2001). [NY]

◆ *The Second Circuit dismissed a challenge to Yale University's rule requiring unmarried freshmen and sophomores to live in co-ed dormitories.*

A group of Orthodox Jewish students claimed Yale's housing rule violated their religious beliefs. They asserted constitutional violations against the university under 42 U.S.C. § 1983. A federal district court granted Yale's motion to dismiss, finding the university was not a state actor or instrumentality subject to § 1983. The court rejected the students' claims that the university's mandatory on-campus housing requirement is an attempt to monopolize the local housing market and violates the Fair Housing Act by denying students of certain religions the right to live in a single-sex dormitory. The students appealed to the Second Circuit.

The Second Circuit noted that only two of Yale's 19 board members were appointed by the state. Therefore, **Yale was not considered a state actor, and the § 1983 claims were invalid.** The court rejected the claim that Yale's underclass dormitory policy was an attempt to monopolize the local student housing market in violation of the Sherman Antitrust Act, 15 U.S.C. §§ 1-2, because Yale forced students to live in its housing facilities. The Second Circuit rejected this argument because students could receive an equally beneficial education at other universities around the nation. Also, Yale's refusal to exempt certain religious observers from co-educational housing did not violate the Fair Housing Act. The decision of the district court was affirmed. *Hack v. President and Fellows of Yale College*, 237 F.3d 81 (2d Cir. 2000). [CT]

◆ *A college's insurer could not sue a student to recover for fire damage to a dorm room.*

When a college student negligently caused a fire that damaged his dorm room, the college's insurer paid for the damage. It then sought to recover the amounts paid from the student. The Massachusetts Superior Court ruled that it could not do so. Here, the dorm agreement was not explicit enough to put the student on notice that he would be liable for fire damage. Also, the college did not require students to obtain fire insurance on their dorm rooms. As a result, **the student was an implied co-insured under the policy,** and the insurer could not recover from him under subrogation (standing in the shoes of the college). *Endicott College v. Mahoney*, No. 00-589C, 2001 WL 1173303 (Mass. Super. 10/3/01). [MA]

CHAPTER TWO

Discrimination Against Students

I. DISABILITY DISCRIMINATION

The Americans with Disabilities Act of 1990 (ADA), 42 U.S.C. § 12101 et seq., *states that no qualified individual with a disability shall, by reason of such disability, be excluded from participation in or be denied the benefit of services, programs, or activities of a public entity, place of public accommodation or other covered entity. The ADA is based on the anti-discrimination principles of § 504 of the Rehabilitation Act of 1973, 29 U.S.C. § 794.*

Colleges and universities are also subject to state anti-discrimination statutes, many of which use the same or similar language as the ADA and § 504. The ADA defines "disability" as a physical or mental impairment that substantially limits one or more major life activities; a record of such impairment; or being regarded as having such an impairment.

A. Colleges and Universities

◆ *The U.S. Supreme Court held that a school can only be required to make minor curricular modifications to accommodate a disability. This means that schools do not have to make accommodations that fundamentally alter the nature of the programs offered.*

A nursing school applicant with severe hearing impairments claimed the school's denial of her admission violated § 504, which states that an "otherwise qualified individual with a disability" may not be excluded from a federally funded program "solely by reason of her or his disability." The school explained the hearing disability made it unsafe for the applicant to practice as a registered nurse. The school pointed out that even with a hearing aid, she had to rely on her lip-reading skills, and that patient safety demanded the ability to understand speech without reliance on lip-reading.

Agreeing with the school, the Supreme Court held the term "otherwise qualified individual with a disability" meant an individual who is qualified in spite of his or her disability. The applicant's contention that her disability should be disregarded for purposes of determining whether she was otherwise qualified was rejected, as was her contention that § 504 imposed an obligation on the school to undertake affirmative action to modify its curriculum to accommodate her disability. **While a school may be required in certain cases to make minor curricular modifications to accommodate a disability, the applicant here was physically able to take only academic courses. No accommodations were required since clinical study would be foreclosed due to patient safety concerns.** The Court held that § 504 did not require a major curricular modification such as allowing the applicant to bypass clinical study. The school's denial of admission was upheld. *Southeastern Community College v. Davis*, 442 U.S. 397, 99 S.Ct. 2361, 60 L.Ed.2d 980 (1979). [NC]

◆   *The Supreme Court determined that a lower court had failed to consider a public university's argument that it should not have to pay for a handicapped student's special educational requirements in a case filed under § 504.*

A deaf graduate student at a Texas university requested a sign language interpreter. The university refused to pay for an interpreter because he did not meet university financial assistance guidelines. The student sued the university in a federal district court under § 504. He sought an order requiring the appointment of an interpreter at the university's expense for as long as he remained there. The court granted his request for a preliminary order requiring the university to pay for the interpreter. However, the court stayed further consideration of the case pending a final administrative ruling.

The university appealed to the U.S. Court of Appeals, Fifth Circuit, which affirmed the preliminary order, but vacated the stay pending administrative action. The university complied with the order by paying for the interpreter. The student completed his graduate program. The U.S. Supreme Court granted review to address the university's argument that the lower courts should make a final ruling on who was to pay for the interpreter. The student argued that the case was now moot in view of his graduation. The Court vacated the appeals court's decision and remanded the case for a trial on the merits to allow the university a full opportunity to argue for recoupment of its payments for the interpreter. *University of Texas v. Camenisch*, 451 U.S. 390, 101 S.Ct. 1830, 68 L.Ed.2d 175 (1981). [TX]

◆   *Congress exceeded its authority by allowing monetary damage awards against the states in Americans with Disabilities Act cases.*

The U.S. Supreme Court held Congress did not identify a history and pattern of irrational employment discrimination against individuals with disabilities by the states when it enacted the ADA, and therefore, states were entitled to Eleventh Amendment immunity from such claims. As a result, **two** state employees were unsuccessful in their attempt to recover money damages under the ADA from their state employer for disability discrimination. *Board of Trustees of Univ. of Alabama v. Garrett*, 531 U.S. 356, 121 S.Ct. 955, 148 L.Ed.2d 866 (2001). [AL]

◆ *The Court of Appeals of Minnesota held a community college did not discriminate against a student with a sleep disorder. He did not tell the college he needed accommodations and rejected some that were offered.*

The student had narcolepsy and had to repeat certain coursework to gain readmittance to the college nursing school. He did not contact the college Office for Students with Disabilities (OSD) to request accommodations. A teacher accused the student of falling asleep in class. The day before a final examination, an instructor advised him to meet with the OSD. The student brought a doctor's letter that did not mention the need for any accommodations. He declared he did not want to be treated differently than other students and rejected an offer for a private testing room and more time. The student failed his examination and sued the college in a state court for violating the ADA and state law. He claimed violation of his equal protection rights because the college allowed another student who failed the exam to take the next course.

The court found the two students were not similarly situated. The ADA claim was barred by sovereign immunity and the college was entitled to judgment on the state law claim. The student appealed to the state court of appeals, which found **the student did not show he was "disabled" because he did not show narcolepsy limited a major life activity. He also failed to tell the college about his disability and rejected accommodations because he did not want different treatment.** The court affirmed the judgment for the college. *Redden v. Minneapolis Community and Technical College*, No. A03-1202, 2004 WL 835768 (Minn. App. 2004). [MN]

◆ *Ohio State University was entitled to sovereign immunity in a discrimination suit by a student who claimed intentional discrimination.*

The student had attention deficit hyperactivity disorder and advised his instructors of his disability and the need for accommodations. He claimed his Latin professors discriminated against him by increasing the course workload and administering a three-hour final exam instead of a two-hour one. He failed a Latin class he needed to complete a degree in physics and sued the university, two Latin professors and other school officials in a federal district court. The court dismissed the claims, and the student appealed. **The Sixth Circuit held the university and officials were entitled to Eleventh Amendment immunity under the ADA. The professors were not liable for the § 504 claims, as § 504 does not provide for individual liability.** The court affirmed the judgment for the university and officials. *Bevington v. Ohio State Univ.*, No. 03-4031, 93 Fed. Appx. 748, 2004 WL 551479 (6th Cir. 2004). [OH]

◆ *The University of Connecticut did not violate federal disability law by dismissing a student after multiple failures on part of a medical licensing exam.*

The student failed her first year course requirements, then completed one of the courses with the help of a tutor. She was promoted to second year, but again failed her course requirements. The student failed Step I of the medical licensing exam twice. Step I was a prerequisite to the third year of medical school. The university provided the student with two years of free tutoring to help her satisfy her third year requirements, and conditionally promoted her to the third year if she passed Step I. The student failed Step I twice more, despite additional tutoring assistance from the university. The university initiated dismissal proceedings. A university neuropsychologist reported the student's academic problems were caused by dyslexia, attention deficit disorder anxiety and depression. The National Board of Medical Examiners declined the student's request for accommodations on Step I, stating she was not disabled.

The student sued the board and university in a federal district court for refusing to provide her requests for accommodation. The court held for the board and university, and the student appealed. The Second Circuit explained that qualified disabled individuals are entitled to reasonable accommodations under the ADA and § 504 for access to and participation in public services and accommodations. **To establish a violation, the student had to show she was a "qualified individual" with a disability. The court held she never proved she was a qualified individual with a disability or was otherwise eligible to continue her medical studies.** School records showed she was an average student throughout her academic career. The court found the school in no way discriminated against the student and actually went the extra mile to support her. The board did not discriminate against her by refusing to accommodate her, as she did not show she was disabled. The judgment was affirmed. *Powell v. National Bd. of Medical Examiners*, 364 F.3d 79 (2nd Cir. 2004). [CT]

◆ *A Massachusetts law school student with learning disabilities and carpal tunnel syndrome did not show she was disabled under the ADA.*

A Massachusetts law school student had previously worked for 15 years as a paralegal. She received permission to reduce her class load because of a medical condition. The student was then treated for anxiety and depression. She later fell below the school's academic standards and the school notified her she could no longer remain there. The student met with the director of student disability services and submitted ADA documentation. The school readmitted her and allowed her to use a note-taker, tape recorder and a word processor. The student was also allowed 15 minutes of rest time for each exam hour. The law school again dismissed her for failing to satisfy its academic standards. The student sued the school in a federal district court for violating the ADA.

The court stated that to prevail, the student had to show her impairments substantially limited one or more of her major life activities and show her disabilities were recognized as "impairments" under the ADA. She also had to demonstrate that her disability affected her ability to work and learn. **The court stated carpal tunnel syndrome is not a disability under the ADA. The student was not substantially impaired in the major life activity of working.** She had worked for 15 years as a paralegal before entering law school. **The inability to satisfy the academic requirements of one law school did not indicate she could not succeed at another. The student was not substantially limited in the major life activity of learning.** The law school's decision to accommodate her disabilities was not evidence that it "regarded her as having a disability." As the student was not disabled under the ADA, the law school was entitled to judgment. *Marlon v. Western New England College,* No. Civ. A. 01-12199DPW, 2003 WL 22914304 (D. Mass. 2003). [MA]

◆ *A disabled graduate student who could not meet a school's academic requirements even with a reasonable accommodation was not entitled to be reinstated to the program after his dismissal.*

A student in an M.D./Ph.D. program at a Massachusetts school suffered from bipolar disorder. After failing three courses in the M.D. program, he continued in the Ph.D. program with the accommodation of extra time to complete his written examinations. He was later dismissed from that program because of the generally poor quality of his research and because he failed to make sufficient progress in lab experiments that were basic program requirements for his thesis. He sued the school under Title III of the ADA and § 504 of the Rehabilitation Act, seeking reinstatement to the programs. A federal court ruled against him, noting that he was not an "otherwise qualified" person with a disability due to academic failure, disruptive behavior and insufficient progress in required lab experiments. **It was his lack of scientific aptitude and not a lack of time that caused his academic failure.** *El Kouni v. Trustees of Boston Univ.,* 169 F.Supp.2d 1 (D. Mass. 2001). [MA]

◆ *A student with multiple personality disorder was not protected by the ADA or the Rehabilitation Act.*

The student had 17 distinct personalities and enrolled in a North Carolina university's teacher certification program. However, she was suspected of plagiarism on one assignment and began exhibiting aggressive behavior. She also became hysterical after picking up a final exam when she could not find "Michael," one of her personalities. After she was removed from the program, she sued under the ADA and § 504, asserting that she had been dismissed because of her disability. A federal court ruled against her, and the Fourth Circuit affirmed. It found that **she was not substantially limited in a major life activity as a result of her multiple personalities**. She was simply unable to obtain a teaching certificate. Thus, she was not entitled to the protections of either act. *Davis v. University of North Carolina,* 263 F.3d 95 (4th Cir. 2001). [NC]

◆ *A Michigan community college did not fail to accommodate a student.*

The student had dyslexia and attention deficit disorder, and was allowed to take exams outside the classroom and check her spelling on a computer. For one test, however, she had a substitute teacher who was not familiar with her disabilities. The teacher refused to allow her these accommodations. Later, the student was involved in a verbal altercation with an instructor and was suspended from the program. She sued under the state civil rights act, but the Michigan Court of Appeals ruled against her. **A single incident of non-accommodation was not enough to prove that the community college had violated her rights under the civil rights law.** Here, the suspension was properly based on her verbal misconduct. *Detroyer v. Oakland Community College,* 2001 WL 965523 (Mich. App. 8/24/01). [MI]

◆ *An Iowa student failed to demonstrate a medical school violated § 504 by offering him different accommodations than those he suggested.*

Prior to being admitted to the University of Osteopathic Medicine and Health Services, a student informed the school that he had dyslexia. After he was admitted, he told the school that his disability hindered his ability to take multiple choice tests. He requested the accommodation of substituting essay tests or oral testing for the multiple choice tests the school used. The university denied the student the specific accommodations he requested. Instead, the student was administered the same multiple choice exams given to other students, but was given extra time, a separate room and allowed to have the questions read to him on audio tape. Eventually, the student failed too many multiple choice tests and was dismissed. He sued the school in a district federal court for failing to adequately accommodate his dyslexia.

The court ruled for the university, finding that the student failed to prove the school's accommodations were not sufficient. On appeal, the U.S. Court of Appeals for the Eighth Circuit affirmed, noting that **universities are not required to fundamentally alter their programs to accommodate disabled students, nor are they required to offer them preferred accommodations**. Universities also are not required to offer accommodations that constitute an undue burden. The university was only obligated to offer the student a reasonable accommodation. The student failed to demonstrate that the accommodations violated § 504. *Stern v. University of Osteopathic Medicine and Health Sciences*, 220 F.3d 906 (8th Cir. 2000). [IA]

◆ *A private university's refusal to allow course substitutions for its foreign language requirement as an accommodation for learning disabled students did not violate the ADA or § 504.*

Several learning disabled students at a private Massachusetts university initiated a class action suit against the university in a federal district court, alleging that its policies violated the ADA, § 504, and state law. The university had a policy under which learning disabled students were not allowed to make course substitutions for the foreign language requirement. The court held **the university did not violate the ADA or § 504.** The university committee that decided whether course substitutions would be acceptable was comprised of eminent members of the college faculty who deliberated the issue over a two-month period. The committee had vigorous discussions of the "unique qualities" of the foreign language requirement and its importance to the liberal arts curriculum. Finally, the committee's meeting minutes indicated that alternatives were discussed and the conclusion reached that **no content course taught in English could serve as a substitution**. The college had existing accommodations for learning disabled students and offered all students a variety of programs to assist in fulfilling the language requirement. *Guckenberger v. Boston Univ.*, 8 F.Supp.2d 82 (D. Mass. 1998). [MA]

◆ *Where a student refused to be tested for a learning disability, a West Virginia college could not be held liable for failing to reasonably accommodate him.*

A student was enrolled in a physician assistant program at a private West Virginia college, which maintained a written policy outlining the process by which a learning disabled student could obtain academic accommodations. The policy required a student to take a specific intelligence test and to be evaluated by a professional. The student alleged that he suffered from a learning disability but refused to take the required test, so evaluators were not able to diagnose a specific learning disability. The college allowed the student to continue his studies with certain accommodations, but eventually suspended him from the program. He sued the college in a West Virginia federal court, asserting that it failed to reasonably accommodate him in violation of the ADA, § 504 of the Rehabilitation Act and a state statute, and that it breached its agreement to provide certain accommodations. The college filed a motion to dismiss.

The court noted that under the ADA and § 504, a disability is defined as a physical or mental impairment that includes any mental or psychological disorder such as "specific learning disabilities." Here, **the student was never diagnosed with a specific learning disability and refused to take the test to determine if he had such a disability**. Also, the accommodations granted to the student were not rescinded; rather, he failed to take full advantage of them. He did not speak to his instructors at the beginning of the semester to arrange accommodations but waited until he already had missed assignments or had failed a test. The court held that **to provide further accommodations in these situations would result in the lowering of the standards of the program**. It granted the college's motion to dismiss the case. *Dubois v. Alderson-Broaddus College,* 950 F.Supp. 754 (N.D. W.Va. 1997). [WV]

◆ *A student was not entitled to the protections of the ADA and § 504 because he was not qualified to meet a Virginia medical school's requirements.*

The student was accepted into a medical school program designed for economically disadvantaged and minority students. He failed to meet program grading requirements and was tested for a learning disability. Although the student was not diagnosed with a specific impairment, the evaluation center recommended allowing him double the usual time to take his examinations. Although his grades improved with this accommodation, he still failed to achieve the GPA required to remain in the program, and the faculty committee rescinded its offer of admission. He was offered admission for the following year on different terms, but instead sued the university in a federal district court under the ADA and § 504. He requested preliminary and permanent injunctive relief, requiring the university to reinstate him.

The court noted that a one-year delay in obtaining admission to medical school does not usually warrant injunctive relief absent extraordinary circumstances. The student most likely had a disability based on the evaluation center's findings and the accommodations granted by the university. Also, he was **denied admission because of his poor performance**, which resulted from his learning problems. However, the student was not qualified to meet the subjective requirements and the court stated that it was not qualified to evaluate his performance. Finding **the university did not act with the purpose of denying education to disabled individuals**, the court denied the student's motion for preliminary injunctive relief. *Betts v. Rector & Visitors of Univ. of Virginia,* 939 F.Supp. 461 (W.D. Va. 1996). [VA]

◆ *An Ohio medical school could deny admission to a blind applicant.*
Allowing her to enroll would require the school to waive its requirements and
fundamentally alter the program.

A student became blind during her third year at a university. With
accommodation, she was able to complete her academic program and graduate,
cum laude, with a degree in chemistry. Although she was academically
qualified, the university's medical school denied her application. This decision
was in part based on standards issued by a medical association stating that
candidates must be able to accurately observe patients. Faculty members also
stated that she would not be able to look through a microscope, perform a
visual diagnosis or insert an I.V.; all requirements for graduation. The
university considered the experience of another blind student who received his
medical degree at a different school a number of years earlier. His success,
however, depended on the efforts of the faculty and other students to spend
extra time with him. The student filed a complaint with the Ohio Civil Rights
Commission (OCRC), which conducted a hearing. The examiner held the
university did not discriminate against her, but the OCRC ordered the
university to admit her. The state court of appeals reversed the order.

The Supreme Court of Ohio noted that the issue here was whether the
student was otherwise qualified to participate in the program. The student
needed to show that she could safely and substantially perform the program's
essential requirements with reasonable accommodation. **An accommodation
is not reasonable if it requires fundamental alterations in the essential
nature of the program or imposes an undue financial or administrative
burden.** Despite the experience of the other blind student, the evidence did not
demonstrate the student in this case would be able to perform the requirements
of this program. The decision to deny the application was an academic decision
the court was ill-equipped to evaluate. Acceptance would require a waiver of
the university's requirements and fundamentally alter the program. The court of
appeals' decision was affirmed. *Ohio Civil Rights Comm'n v. Case Western
Reserve Univ.*, 666 N.E.2d 1376 (Ohio 1996). [OH]

◆ *An educational institution is not required to provide any student with*
accommodations that will lower its academic standards.

A student at a California medical school had difficulty in her classes and
was referred for testing for a learning disability. When the test came back
positive, the student was offered a number of accommodations: double time on
exams, note-taking services, textbooks on audio cassettes, the option of
retaking courses, and the option for a decelerated schedule. However, she
continued to have trouble with her classes. Eventually, she completed the pre-
clinical portion of her schooling and took the USMLE, Part 1, which she failed.
She then retested and passed. She again had trouble in school, this time with
her clinical work. After being placed on academic probation, she was dismissed
from the program. The student sued the school under the ADA and § 504. A
federal district court ruled in the school's favor, and the student appealed. The
Ninth Circuit affirmed, finding **the school had offered her reasonable
accommodations. To accommodate her any further would have required
the school to fundamentally alter the nature of its program and lower its**

academic standards. Neither the ADA nor § 504 required this. *Zukle v. Regents of the Univ. of California*, 166 F.3d 1041 (9th Cir. 1999). [CA]

◆ *An Ohio college that offered accommodations to a learning disabled student had the right to dismiss her after she failed program requirements.*

A student in a college of podiatric medicine suspected she had a learning disability and notified an academic counselor of her belief. The counselor referred her for testing, where it was determined she did not have a learning disability but that she should be given some assistance with study skills. However, the student did not seek any accommodations from the college until after she had failed two courses and was dismissed from the program. At that time, she obtained reports from two psychologists who concluded that she had a learning disorder and listed 11 recommended accommodations for her. The college reinstated the student to its five-year program for students with special needs and offered her nine of the 11 recommended accommodations. She again failed biochemistry and was again dismissed from the program.

The student sued the college under § 504, the ADA and the Ohio Civil Rights Act, alleging disability discrimination. A federal district court granted pretrial judgment to the college, and the student appealed. The U.S. Court of Appeals, Sixth Circuit, held the college did not discriminate against the student. **Educational institutions are not required to lower or effect substantial modifications of standards to accommodate persons with disabilities.** Here, the college had provided almost all the recommended accommodations and its decision not to lower its standards was entitled to deference. *Kaltenberger v. Ohio College of Podiatric Medicine*, 162 F.3d 432 (6th Cir. 1998). [OH]

◆ *A New Mexico medical school student with test anxieties in two subjects was not considered disabled under the ADA.*

The student suffered from "chemistry and mathematics anxiety." However, he overcame this in undergraduate and graduate programs. The student informed his basic biochemistry professor of his anxiety, but stated that he needed no test-taking accommodations. After receiving marginal grades in two first-year courses, he was notified that he would have to repeat the first year. Instead, he sued the medical school for disability discrimination under the ADA. The court granted pretrial judgment to the school, and the student appealed. The U.S. Court of Appeals, Tenth Circuit, affirmed the lower court's decision. Here, **the student failed to show that his math and chemistry anxiety substantially limited him in the major life activity of learning. As a result, he was not a disabled person within the meaning of the ADA.** Further, even if he was, he could not demand an unreasonable accommodation from the school. Requiring the school to advance the student to the next level would require an unreasonable accommodation. *McGuinness v. University of New Mexico School of Medicine*, 170 F.3d 974 (10th Cir. 1998). [NM]

◆ *The inability to turn in work that has not been plagiarized is a valid reason for expelling a student with a disability.*

A graduate student at Virginia Commonwealth University suffered from dysgraphia and/or other broad written language disabilities. He was charged with cheating and plagiarism–both violations of the student honor code–and was expelled. He sued the university under the ADA and § 504, asserting that his disability affected and impaired his ability to reproduce or transcribe written language, and that the university failed to reasonably accommodate him. A federal district court granted pretrial judgment to the university. **It found that fulfilling the terms of the university's honor code was an essential function of being a graduate student, and that the student could not meet this requirement even with a reasonable accommodation.** Accordingly, the university did not violate the ADA or § 504 by expelling the student. *Childress v. Clement*, 5 F.Supp.2d 384 (E.D. Va. 1998). [VA]

◆   *Students with attention deficit hyperactivity disorder were not substantially limited in the major life activity of learning.*

Three students completed two years of medical school and were required to pass Step I of the U.S. Medical Licensing Examination, administered by the National Board of Medical Examiners. Each of the students was diagnosed with attention deficient hyperactivity disorder (ADHD), and two of the three students were diagnosed with specific learning disabilities. **The students sent applications to the board requesting additional time in private rooms while taking the examination.** The board submitted their applications to experts in the fields of ADHD and learning disabilities, but later denied the request and asserted that the students' alleged impairments did not significantly restrict one or more of their major life activities. The students sued the board in a West Virginia federal court, seeking to compel it to grant their request.

The students and the board both agreed that ADHD and specific learning disabilities were mental impairments for purposes of the ADA and also agreed that these disorders affect the major life activity of learning. However, the parties disagreed on whether the students' alleged disorders "substantially limited" their ability to learn. **A learning disability does not always qualify as a disability under the ADA.** None of the students exhibited a pattern of substantial academic difficulties. They were all able to graduate from high school and undergraduate school without any accommodations. Further, each of the students had an average or greater than average ability to learn. Because the students' disabilities did not substantially limit their ability to learn in comparison with most people, the court denied their requests. *Price v. National Bd. of Medical Examiners*, 966 F.Supp. 419 (S.D. W.Va. 1997). [WV]

◆   *A student with a disability could sue his school for breach of the implied duty of good faith and fair dealing.*

An incomplete paraplegic attended a Wyoming technical institute, but later withdrew, alleging his disability was not accommodated. He asserted the institute did not provide him with sufficient handicapped parking, accessible restrooms, or the equipment necessary to safely perform his assigned tasks. As a result, he suffered various injuries while in attendance there. He sued the institute for breach of an implied duty of good faith and fair dealing, arguing that his enrollment at the institute formed a contract between the parties that contained an implied covenant to act in fairness and good faith. The court found that **a cause of action for breach of an implied duty of good faith and fair**

dealing existed in every contract in which a special relationship of trust and reliance existed between the parties. The court found a special relationship existed because the student had a statutory right under § 504 and the ADA not to be discriminated against or unlawfully precluded from participation in the institute's programs based on his disability. Because a statutory right established the requisite special relationship between a student and a school, the duty of good faith and fair dealing gave rise to tort liability. While the actual determination of whether the institute had failed to act in good faith was an issue for the jury to decide, the court refused to dismiss the case. *Powers v. MJB Acquisition Corp.*, 993 F.Supp. 861 (D. Wyo. 1998). [WY]

B. Outside Entities

◆ *The U.S. Supreme Court determined that a Veterans' Administration regulation defining alcoholism was not invalid under the Rehabilitation Act.*

Two honorably discharged veterans who were recovering alcoholics sought an extension of the 10-year Veterans' Administration (VA) limitation for receipt of educational assistance under the G.I. Bill. The 10-year limitation on educational benefits can be extended by the VA if the veteran can show he was prevented from using his benefits earlier because of "physical or mental disability which was not the result of ... [his] own willful misconduct." VA regulations state that the deliberate drinking of alcohol is considered willful misconduct. **The VA denied their requests, stating that their alcoholism had been willful misconduct.** One veteran sued the VA in a New York federal court. The other veteran sought review in a D.C. federal court.

The New York court held for the VA, but its decision was reversed by the Second Circuit Court of Appeals. The D.C. court ruled that the VA regulation was contrary to § 504, but the D.C. Court of Appeals reversed that decision. Noting the disagreement between the two federal appeals courts, the U.S. Supreme Court granted review and heard the cases together. It held § 504 did not preclude an action against the VA. The Court noted that Congress had changed the time limit for benefits several times, most recently in 1977. The Rehabilitation Act of 1978 did not repeal the "willful misconduct" provision of the 1977 regulations. Accordingly, **Congress had the right to establish the allocation priorities for veterans' benefits.** The DC Court of Appeals decision was affirmed, and the Second Circuit Court of Appeals decision was reversed. The VA prevailed in both matters. *Traynor v. Turnage*, 485 U.S. 535, 108 S.Ct. 1372, 99 L.Ed.2d 618 (1988). [DC, NY]

◆ *In a § 504 lawsuit brought by a former student against the U.S. Merchant Marine Academy, the Supreme Court held Congress did not waive sovereign immunity for monetary damages awards for violations of § 504(a).*

A first-year student at the U.S. Merchant Marine Academy was diagnosed with diabetes. He was separated from the Academy on the grounds that his diabetes was a disqualifying condition. He filed suit in a federal district court against the Secretary of the Department of Transportation and others, alleging that they violated § 504(a) of the Rehabilitation Act. He requested reinstatement, compensatory damages, attorney's fees and costs. The district court granted the student summary judgment, finding that his separation from the Academy violated the Act, and ordered him reinstated.

The government disputed the compensatory damages award, contending that it was protected by sovereign immunity. The court disagreed and found that the student was entitled to damages. Soon after, the U.S. Court of Appeals, District of Columbia Circuit, held in another case that the government had not waived its immunity against monetary damages for violations of § 504(a). The court then vacated part of its prior decision and denied compensatory damages. The student appealed, and the D.C. Circuit Court of Appeals granted the government's motion for summary judgment. The U.S. Supreme Court granted review to determine **whether Congress has waived the government's sovereign immunity against monetary damage awards for § 504(a) violations**. It held a waiver of sovereign immunity must be clearly expressed in the statutory text. The Court found no such language in § 504(a). It also held the Department of Transportation is not a provider of financial assistance to the Academy because it manages the Academy. **As there was no clear expression of the government's intent to waive its sovereign immunity, the Court held monetary damage awards were not allowed under § 504(a) of the Act.** *Lane v. Pena*, 518 U.S. 187, 116 S.Ct. 2092, 135 L.Ed.2d 486 (1996). [DC]

◆ *A law school graduate with dyslexia would have to be given reasonable accommodations when she took the New York bar exam if she was ultimately determined to be disabled.*

The graduate asked for accommodations for the state bar examination. Because she had missed the deadline for requesting accommodations, her request was denied. She took and failed four consecutive bar exams. She sued the State Board of Law Examiners and its members in a federal district court under the ADA and § 504. The applicant claimed she was impaired in the major life activities of learning, reading and working. The court found she was substantially limited in the major life activity of working. It noted the relevant comparison group was the average person having comparable training, skills and abilities. When compared to the average law school student, her reading skills were well below normal. Therefore, her inability to read and take the bar examination as compared to other law school graduates had the effect of impeding her entry into a "class of jobs." The court held the applicant was excluded from performing any and all jobs that comprised the practice of law. Because she was disabled and was denied reasonable accommodations in taking the bar examination, her rights under the ADA and § 504 were violated. The court awarded her compensatory damages of $12,500 and ordered that she receive several accommodations should she decide to retake the examination.

On appeal, **the Second Circuit Court of Appeals agreed that the applicant was disabled, but found that she was substantially limited in the major life activities of reading and learning.** It also affirmed that the applicant was entitled to compensatory damages for the discrimination against her, but remanded the case for a determination of the proper amount. She was only entitled to be reimbursed for those exams she had taken where she had sought a reasonable accommodation and been denied one. *Bartlett v. New York State Bd. of Law Examiners*, 156 F.3d 321 (2d Cir. 1998). [NY]

On further appeal, the U.S. Supreme Court vacated and remanded the case for consideration in light of *Sutton v. United Air Lines, Inc.*, 527 U.S. 471 (1999), *Murphy v. UPS*, 527 U.S. 516 (1999), and *Albertsons, Inc. v. Kirkingburg*, 527 U.S. 555 (1999), in which the Court held that **mitigating measures must be taken into account in determining whether a person is disabled**. Because the applicant had a history of self-accommodation that allowed her to achieve roughly average reading skills (on some measures) when compared to the general population, there was a question as to whether she was disabled under the ADA. *New York State Bd. of Law Examiners v. Bartlett*, 527 U.S. 1031, 119 S.Ct. 2388, 144 L.Ed.2d 790 (1999).

The district court then determined that the applicant was entitled to reasonable accommodations when taking the bar exam because she was substantially limited in the major life activity of reading. Here, **the applicant's attempts to compensate for her learning disabilities did not correct her disability the way that glasses or medications can correct or compensate for similar physical disabilities**. After a close analysis of the coping strategies used by the applicant, the court concluded that these were not true mitigating measures, because they merely helped her function and did not affect her ability to read. As relief, the district court ordered the board of bar examiners to accommodate the applicant, awarded $7,500 in damages, and granted injunctive relief. *Bartlett v. New York State Bd. of Law Examiners*, 2001 WL 930792 (S.D.N.Y. 8/15/01). [NY]

◆ *A student's lawsuit against the National Board of Medical Examiners failed because he was unable to show that he was disabled under the ADA.*

A student at a Michigan medical school passed his first two years, then took the NBME Step 1 exam. He claimed to have a learning disability and asked for more time to take the exam as an accommodation from the National Board of Medical Examiners. The board denied his request, and he failed the exam twice. He then sued the board under Title III of the ADA, seeking a preliminary injunction that would force it to allow him twice the allotted time to take the exam. The question before the court was **whether the student's learning disability (slowness in language processing) amounted to a disability under the ADA. The court found that it did not. Even though some of the tests administered to the student indicated that he scored on the lower range of average, his verbal IQ was within the average range.** Further, his performance IQ was in the high average to superior range. As compared to the general population, the student's scores were overwhelmingly average to superior. Thus, he failed to demonstrate that he suffered from an ADA-defined disability that substantially limited him in a major life activity. The court ruled in favor of the board. *Gonzalez v. National Bd. of Medical Examiners*, 60 F.Supp.2d 703 (E.D. Mich. 1999). [MI]

◆ *A bar applicant's request to average out exam scores was held not to be a reasonable accommodation.*

A Florida bar applicant with attention deficit disorder requested and was granted an accommodation of 25 percent more time on all portions of the bar exam. With this accommodation, the applicant had taken the bar exam several times, but had been unable to earn a passing score. The applicant then petitioned the Board of Bar Examiners for admission to the bar by requesting, as a reasonable accommodation of her disability, that her scores on parts A and B, taken at separate administrations, be averaged. The board denied her request, and the applicant petitioned the Florida Supreme Court for relief. Assuming that the applicant was disabled under the Americans with Disabilities Act, the court found that the board had reasonably accommodated her by allowing her more time on the bar exam. However, **the applicant's request to average her exam scores was not an accommodation in the administration of the exam, but an accommodation in the scoring of the exam. This was not a reasonable accommodation.** A modification in the scoring of the exam would fundamentally alter the measurement of skills or knowledge the exam is intended to test. The court rejected the applicant's contention that averaging the score of her exam as though she took parts A and B at the same time would put her on equal footing with nondisabled applicants. This would give her an unfair advantage. The court denied her petition for relief. *Florida Bd. of Bar Examiners Re S.G.*, 707 So.2d 323 (Fla. 1998). [FL]

◆ *Inquiries made into applicants' mental health by a state board of bar examiners violated Title II of the ADA.*

Four women who applied to be admitted to the Florida bar claimed that certain questions on the application violated the ADA. Specifically, there were questions on the application asking whether an applicant had ever sought treatment for nervous, mental, or emotional conditions, had ever been diagnosed as having such a condition, or had ever taken any psychotropic drugs. The application also contained a consent form that released any of the applicant's mental health records to the Board of Bar Examiners. They sued under Title II of the Act, and the board sought to dismiss the lawsuit. A federal court denied the motion to dismiss, noting that regulations issued under Title II made clear that **the inquiries here discriminated against the applicants by subjecting them to additional burdens based on their disabilities**. *Ellen S. v. Florida Bd. of Bar Examiners*, 859 F.Supp. 1489 (S.D. Fla. 1994). [FL]

◆ *A student denied tuition assistance to attend law school could not sue the school under Title I of the Rehabilitation Act.*

A disabled Wisconsin student attended college under **Title I of the Rehabilitation Act** and received book and tuition assistance for classes through the Wisconsin Division of Vocational Rehabilitation (DVR). When he requested assistance under the Act to attend law school, the DVR declined to provide further tuition assistance and closed his file. He sued the DVR in the U.S. District Court for the Eastern District of Wisconsin under the Act. The DVR moved for pretrial judgment, which was granted by the court.

The student appealed to the U.S. Court of Appeals for the Seventh Circuit. The purpose of Title I is to provide disabled individuals with certain benefits and rights that will enable such persons to become gainfully employed. To this end, the person and a vocational counselor develop a written plan to which both agree. The Act provides specific administrative processes to address grievances but no private rights of action in a court. Because Congress only provided administrative remedies, the court determined **Congress neither intended to create nor expressly implied a private cause of action under § 504. Nor did § 504 guarantee an individual the right to tuition assistance at an institution of higher education.** The court affirmed the judgment. *Mallett v. Wisconsin Division of Vocational Rehabilitation*, 130 F.3d 1245 (7th Cir. 1997) [WI]

◆ *A student was not entitled to receive a full ride to law school under § 504 because the Act does not require the maximizing of people's abilities.*

A profoundly deaf Florida student sought educational assistance from the state Division of Vocational Rehabilitation (DVR) so that he could attend college. The DVR certified the student as disabled and developed an individualized written rehabilitation plan, which called for him to obtain a psychology degree. It then funded the student's attendance at several universities. After graduating, the student asked the DVR to pay for him to attend law school. The DVR refused to do so. The student sued it in a federal district court, asserting it had discriminated against him in violation of § 504. A magistrate judge ruled in favor of the DVR, and the student appealed.

The U.S. Court of Appeals, Eleventh Circuit, held that **the student's claim failed. He was unable to show that he had been treated differently than anyone else when he was denied a full scholarship to law school. Section 504 is not designed to maximize abilities, but rather to maximize "meaningful" employment.** By paying for the student's college degree and offering him a job as a counselor for the deaf, the DVR had assisted the student in obtaining meaningful employment. It was not required to do more. *Berg v. Florida Dep't of Labor and Employment Security, Division of Vocational Rehabilitation*, 163 F.3d 1251 (11th Cir. 1998). [FL]

II. SEX DISCRIMINATION AND HARASSMENT

College and university students have federally protected rights to be free from sex discrimination and sexual harassment. Title IX of the Education Amendments of 1972 prohibits recipients of federal funding from denying any person educational participation or benefits on the basis of gender.

A. Discrimination

◆ *The U.S. Supreme Court held the categorical exclusion of women from the Virginia Military Institute (VMI) denied equal protection to women.*

The U.S. Attorney General's office filed a complaint against the state of Virginia and VMI on behalf of a female high school student seeking admission to the state-affiliated, male-only college. A federal court found that because single gender education conferred substantial benefits on students and preserved the unique military training offered at VMI, the exclusion of women did not violate the Equal Protection Clause. The U.S. Court of Appeals, Fourth Circuit, vacated the judgment, ruling that Virginia had failed to state an adequate policy justifying the male-only program. On remand, the district court found that the institution of coeducational methods at VMI would materially affect its program. It approved the state's plan for instituting a parallel program for women even though the program differed substantially from VMI's in its academic offerings, educational methods and financial resources. The court of appeals affirmed, and the U.S. Supreme Court agreed to review the case.

The Court stated that parties seeking to defend gender-based government action must demonstrate an exceedingly persuasive justification that is genuine and not invented as a response to litigation. Virginia had failed to show an exceedingly persuasive justification for excluding women from VMI. There was evidence that some women would be able to participate at VMI, and the lower courts had improperly found that most women would not gain from the adversative method employed by the college. **The remedy proposed by Virginia left its exclusionary policy intact and afforded women no opportunity to experience the rigorous military training offered at VMI.** The parallel women's program was substantially limited in its course offerings, and participants would not gain the benefits of association with VMI's faculty, stature, funding, prestige and alumni support. The proposal did not remedy the constitutional violation, and the Court reversed and remanded the case. *U.S. v. Virginia*, 518 U.S. 515, 116 S.Ct. 2264, 135 L.Ed.2d 735 (1996). [VA]

◆   *While Title IX clearly prohibits sex discrimination, it was not clear whether Congress intended to allow private citizens to bring lawsuits for Title IX violations until the Supreme Court upheld a private cause of action in 1979.*

After being denied admission to two private Illinois medical schools, a woman sued the schools in a federal district court, alleging exclusion on the basis of her gender. The dismissed the case, since Title IX did not expressly authorize a private right of action by a person injured by a violation of § 901. The court also held that no private remedy should be inferred. The U.S. Court of Appeals for the Seventh Circuit agreed. The court of appeals concluded that Congress intended the remedy of § 902, which allowed termination of federal funding, to be the exclusive means of enforcement, and that Title VI of the Civil Rights Act of 1964 did not include an implied private cause of action.

On appeal, **the U.S. Supreme Court reversed, holding that the woman could maintain her lawsuit despite the lack of any express authorization in Title IX.** The Court stated that **Title IX expressly conferred a benefit on those discriminated against on the basis of sex, and the woman clearly fell into that class.** Title IX was patterned after Title VI of the Civil Rights Act of 1964, which had been construed to create a private remedy. Implying a private remedy was consistent with the legislative scheme since it provided better protection against discrimination. Since the Civil War, the federal government has been the primary protector of citizens from discrimination. *Cannon v. University of Chicago*, 441 U.S. 677, 99 S.Ct. 1946, 60 L.Ed.2d 560 (1979). [IL]

◆   *Gender-based distinctions in academic fields generally will not withstand constitutional scrutiny. The Supreme Court held that a university for women could not justify a policy that denied men the opportunity to enroll for credit.*

The policy of the Mississippi University for Women, a state-supported university, was to limit its enrollment to women. The university denied otherwise qualified males the right to enroll for credit in its School of Nursing. One male, who was denied admission, sued in federal court claiming that the university's policy violated the Fourteenth Amendment's Equal Protection Clause. The lower federal courts agreed, and the school appealed to the U.S. Supreme Court. The Court held **the university's discriminatory admission policy against men was not substantially and directly related to an important governmental objective**. The school argued that women enrolled in its School of Nursing would be adversely affected by the presence of men. However, the record showed that the nursing school allowed men to attend classes in the school as auditors, thus fatally undermining the school's claim that admission of men would adversely affect women students. The Court held that the policy of the university, which limited enrollment to women, violated the Equal Protection Clause. *Mississippi Univ. for Women v. Hogan*, 458 U.S. 718, 102 S.Ct. 3331, 73 L.Ed.2d 1090 (1982). [MS]

◆   *The Sixth Circuit affirmed a district court's ruling that a university did not violate Title IX by expelling a male student for committing a sexual assault.*

Two Ohio University students celebrated a birthday by drinking at an off-campus bar. They eventually left the bar together and had sexual contact in a dormitory room. The university investigated the incident and later charged the male student with sexual assault under its student code. Following a hearing, a university disciplinary board recommended his expulsion, which was upheld by the university president. The student sued the university and officials in a federal district court for sex discrimination under Title IX. The court granted summary judgment to the university, and he appealed to the Sixth Circuit.

The court relied on the Second Circuit's decision in *Yusuf v. Vassar College*, 35 F.3d 709 (2d Cir. 1994), below, to analyze the Title IX claim. The Second Circuit decision distinguished between "erroneous outcome" claims and "selective enforcement" claims. Under the erroneous outcome analysis, the student produced no evidence that the expulsion was discriminatory or motivated by a "chauvinistic view of the sexes." Under the selective enforcement theory, he did not establish the university treated similarly situated females more favorably. The court acknowledged that both students were intoxicated. However, the female could not remember what happened that night. This evidence did not show the university took action against the student based on his sex. Accordingly, the judgment for the university was affirmed. *Mallory v. Ohio Univ.*, No. 01-4111, 2003 WL 22146132 (6th Cir. 2003). [OH]

◆   *Title IX protected a biological male who was subjected to discriminatory conduct while being perceived as being a female.*

A transsexual student brought suit in federal court against a New York university for violations of Title IX. The student, a biological male, had undergone hormone treatments for breast augmentation but had not yet had sex-reassignment surgery. The student lodged a written complaint against a professor, alleging that he made unwelcome sexual advances. The university served a written reprimand on the professor, but permitted him to continue teaching at the graduate and undergraduate levels. The student also claimed hostile treatment by professors and administrators after the formal grievance proceedings. The student left the doctoral program and sued the university for violating Title IX. The court held Title IX protected a biological male who was subjected to discriminatory conduct while perceived as being a female. **It rejected the university's argument that the student was not among the class of persons whom Title IX was intended to protect and** denied the university's motion for summary judgment. *Miles v. New York Univ.*, 979 F.Supp. 248 (S.D.N.Y. 1997). [NY]

A Title IX exemption for private undergraduate institutions allows them to discriminate on the basis of sex in admissions (20 U.S.C. § 1681 (a)(1)). While private professional schools affiliated with a single-sex undergraduate institution may exclude students based upon sex, graduate institutions may not.

◆   *A private religious college policy against premarital sex did not constitute sex discrimination despite the potential for a disparate impact on women.*

A Tennessee woman attended a private college associated with the Church of God. According to the student handbook, students were prohibited from engaging in premarital sex. Violation of this policy would result in suspension or expulsion. However, if suspended, a student could apply for readmission the following semester. An unmarried student attending the college became pregnant and gave birth to a child. The college took no action against her. One year later, the student became pregnant again. This time the college suspended her. She was not allowed to finish the semester, but following the birth of her child, she reentered the college and later graduated. She then sued the college in a Tennessee federal court, alleging gender discrimination.

The court found that on its face, the college policy was not discriminatory. It applied to both sexes and evidence was presented that it had been equally enforced against both males and females. The court also found that it was a longstanding policy resulting from the college's religious beliefs and that women whose pregnancies resulted from rape had been allowed to stay in school. The court acknowledged that in practice, the policy might have a disparate impact on women since their violation of the policy could become known through pregnancy while a man's violation could remain secret. However, since no evidence was presented on this issue, the court held that the policy was not discriminatory. The court also noted that **no evidence was presented that the college took action against women because of pregnancy rather than because of their violation of the policy**. It found that the pregnant students who were allowed to remain in school were not treated any differently than other students. Finding **no evidence of pregnancy discrimination**, the court held in favor of the college. *Hall v. Lee College*, 932 F.Supp. 1027 (E.D. Tenn. 1996). [TN]

◆   *A private college student presented facts that sex discrimination tainted the outcome of his school disciplinary proceeding.*

A student from Bangladesh enrolled at a New York private college. His Caucasian roommate allegedly attacked him, causing physical injuries. The roommate was arrested by the local police department and was given a "suspended suspension" by college officials. He was permitted to remain in school until he graduated the following semester. The roommate's girlfriend then filed sexual harassment charges against the student, allegedly in retaliation for his pursuit of criminal prosecution against the roommate. Following a hearing, the student was found guilty of sexual harassment. Among other penalties, he was suspended from May 20, 1992 until the spring of 1993. The Dean of Student Life affirmed the decision, and the student filed a Title IX gender and race discrimination lawsuit against the college in a New York federal court. The court dismissed both claims, and the student appealed.

The U.S. Court of Appeals, Second Circuit, reversed, noting that **the student had alleged facts suggesting that gender bias was a motivating factor behind the finding of harassment**. Specifically, he alleged that: 1) a false and stale sexual harassment charge was made in retaliation for his criminal prosecution, 2) he was on good terms with the complainant until this time, 3) actions of the disciplinary tribunal prevented him from fully defending himself, and 4) males were systematically found guilty of sexual harassment without an evidentiary basis. A jury would have to determine whether gender discrimination tainted the outcome of the disciplinary proceeding. *Yusuf v. Vassar College*, 35 F.3d 709 (2d Cir. 1994). [NY]

◆ *New York could not use SAT scores only in awarding certain scholarships where doing so discriminated against female students.*

Ten New York high school students sued the state department of education under Title IX and the Equal Protection Clause of the Fourteenth Amendment, asserting the state's exclusive reliance on SAT scores to determine eligibility for prestigious Empire and Regents scholarships discriminated against female students. They sought a preliminary injunction to stop the practice, alleging that although the policy of using only SAT scores was neutral on its face, it had a discriminatory impact on female students. A federal court agreed. It rejected the state's argument that the policy satisfied an educational necessity. In fact, the state could not even show a rational relationship between the policy and its purpose of recognizing and rewarding academic achievement in high school. **The students had offered a much better alternative for awarding scholarships–a combination of grade point averages and SAT scores. The court ordered the state to stop using SAT scores as the sole determinant in awarding scholarships.** *Sharif v. New York State Educ. Dep't*, 709 F.Supp. 345 (S.D.N.Y. 1989). [NY]

B. Harassment

1. Sexual Harassment by Employees

In Franklin v. Gwinnett County Public Schools, *503 U.S. 60, 112 S.Ct. 1028, 117 L.Ed.2d 208 (1992), a high school student who was harassed and sexually abused by a teacher sued her school under Title IX. The case reached the U.S. Supreme Court, which held she could recover monetary damages under Title IX for the teacher's harassment.*

The liability standards from the Supreme Court's decisions in Franklin, Gebser v. Lago Vista School Dist., *524 U.S. 274, 118 S.Ct. 1989, 141 L.Ed.2d*

277 (1998), and Davis v. Monroe County Bd. of Educ., *526 U.S. 629, 119 S.Ct. 1661, 143 L.Ed.2d 839 (1999) apply in the higher education setting. When a sexual harassment claim is based on the conduct of an employee, the student must prove a school official with authority to take corrective action actually knew of the conduct, but remained deliberately indifferent to it to prevail under Title IX. The student must also show the harassment was so severe, pervasive and objectively offensive that it caused a deprivation of educational benefits.*

◆ *The U.S. Supreme Court found that an award of damages would be inappropriate in a Title IX case unless an official with the authority to address the discrimination failed to act despite actual knowledge of it, in a manner amounting to deliberate indifference to discrimination.*

The Supreme Court examined the potential liability of a Texas school district in a case involving a student who had a sexual relationship with a teacher. The Court rejected the liability standard advocated by the student and by the U.S. government, which resembled *respondeat superior* liability under Title VII. Title IX contains an administrative enforcement mechanism that assumes actual notice has been provided to officials prior to the imposition of enforcement remedies. An award of damages would be inappropriate in a Title IX case unless an official with the authority to address the discrimination failed to act despite actual knowledge of it, in a manner amounting to deliberate indifference to discrimination. Here, **there was insufficient evidence that a school official should have known about the relationship so as to impose liability on the school district.** *Gebser v. Lago Vista Independent School Dist.,* 524 U.S. 274, 118 S.Ct. 1989, 141 L.Ed.2d 277 (1998). [TX]

◆ *To prevail in a Title IX action alleging harassment by an employee, the student must prove a school official with authority to take corrective action actually knew of the conduct, yet remained deliberately indifferent to it.*

An Illinois university music student was hired as an office assistant to her voice teacher. The student claimed the teacher asked her if she loved him and he ask to rub her shoulders, tickle her and have her hug him. She told a female teacher and a counselor what happened, but neither of them reported the teacher's behavior. Two years earlier, a school dean had investigated sexual harassment charges against the voice teacher by faculty members. The investigation revealed the voice teacher made advances to three other female students who never filed complaints and to a fourth student who did file a complaint. The student transferred from the university, then filed a complaint about the voice teacher's conduct. The school ordered the teacher to take training in the proper behavior towards female students and placed a letter in his personnel file.

The student sued the university under Title IX for sexual harassment, and added a sexual harassment claim against the teacher under Title IX and 42 U.S.C. § 1983. A federal district court granted summary judgment to the university and teacher, and the student appealed to the Seventh Circuit. **The court held a student seeking to hold a university liable for Title IX violations must prove a school official with authority to take corrective measures against the harasser actually knew of the behavior, but was**

deliberately indifferent to it. The court found the university had no actual notice of the teacher's misconduct and affirmed the judgment in its favor. **The student's § 1983 claim against the teacher was not foreclosed by Title IX.** The court reinstated her action against him and remanded it to the district court. *Delgado v. Stegall*, 367 F.3d 668 (7th Cir. 2004). [IL]

◆ *The Second Circuit reversed a decision against a student on her sexual harassment claim against a former professor, but affirmed the judgment on her Title IX claim for the state university that had employed him.*

A New York student accused a tenured professor of referring to her as "Monica," based upon her physical resemblance to Monica Lewinsky. She did not report his conduct until meeting with the department chair midway through the academic year. At least five officials met to discuss his conduct, and the student delivered a handwritten complaint to the chair. The professor admitted making the comments, but insisted they were jokes or punishment for classroom disruptions. Within three months, he resigned. The student stopped attending her classes and received all failing grades. She sued the professor in a federal district court for violating her equal protection rights under 42 U.S.C. § 1983. She also claimed university officials violated Title IX. The court awarded judgment to the professor and university, and the student appealed.

The U.S. Court of Appeals, Second Circuit, held **a professor employed by a state university is a state actor under § 1983**, based on the authority position held by professors over student educational and advancement opportunities. **There was evidence that the professor's remarks may have been pervasive enough to create a hostile environment.** The district court had improperly used a rigid, mathematical methodology to calculate the number of instances of misconduct to determine "pervasiveness." The court vacated the judgment for the professor and remanded the claim against him for additional proceedings. **University officials could not be held liable for his conduct, as the record indicated they adequately responded to the student's complaint.** The court affirmed the judgment for the university. *Hayut v. State Univ. of New York*, 352 F.3d 733 (2d Cir. 2003). [NY]

◆ *A Tennessee court upheld a decision that a tenured professor engaged in sexual harassment and created a hostile educational environment in class.*

A 17-year-old state community college student accused a tenured computer programming instructor of making remarks about adultery, massaging students in class and making sexual comments and advances to her in his office. She withdrew from the class and filed a formal sexual harassment complaint against the instructor. The college affirmative action officer investigated and found sufficient evidence to justify a one year, unpaid suspension. The instructor challenged the suspension at a hearing, where he admitted making some remarks but denied the inappropriate advances. He admitted touching students, but accused the student of using this as an excuse for her poor performance. The affirmative action officer testified she had previously admonished the instructor for touching students several years earlier, and that he had been cautioned by his supervisor not to touch students.

An administrative law judge (ALJ) found the conduct was sexual harassment that created a hostile educational environment. The ALJ reduced the suspension to one semester. A state trial court upheld the ALJ's decision and the college appealed to the Court of Appeals of Tennessee. It reversed and remanded the case to the trial court. The trial court reinstated the ALJ's decision, and the case returned to the appeals court, which explained that **to determine if an environment is hostile or abusive, courts review the "totality of the circumstances."** In this case, several incidents created a hostile environment. The ALJ did not abuse her discretion by crediting the student's testimony instead of the instructor's. The record established that five years before the student filed her complaint, college officials had warned the instructor about his inappropriate conduct. Accordingly, the court affirmed the judgment. *Stephens v. Roane State Community College*, No. M2001-03155-COA-R3-CV, 2003 WL 21918758 (Tenn. App. 2003). [TN]

◆ *A California court awarded judgment to an arts institute, dismissing a student's contract and negligence claims arising from alleged harassment.*

A musical arts student claimed a professor subjected her to unwanted sexual advances. She filed a sexual harassment complaint with the institute that was investigated, but reached an inconclusive result. The institute reprimanded the professor and instructed him not to retaliate against the student. She sued the institute and various school officials in the state court system, alleging claims for breach of contract and negligence. A trial court granted the institute summary judgment and the student appealed.

The Court of Appeal of California rejected the student's breach of contract claim, finding the institute complied with its handbook and other school literature describing it as a "safe and secure environment free from harassment, retaliation, and abuse." **The institute complied with its contractual obligations by investigating the student's complaint and reminding the professor of the sexual harassment policy.** After this action, the student made no additional harassment allegations. The court rejected her retaliation claim. This had been based on her assertion that the institute negligently allowed the student body to retaliate against her for the possible cancellation of an African music program. **School officials testified they had no knowledge of harassment by other students, and they had no duty to protect her from the actions of other students.** *Sandra V. v. California Institute of the Arts*, No. B155508, 2003 WL 21766253 (Cal. App. 2d Dist. 2003). [CA]

◆ *A student in a consensual sexual relationship with a professor could not succeed in a lawsuit against the university for sexual harassment.*

A student at a Minnesota university took a class from a professor, then enrolled in an independent study course with him. However, she failed to complete her work by the deadline and did not receive a grade. Some time later, the professor asked her out, and the two of them engaged in a consensual sexual relationship that lasted for nine months. After it ended, the student filed a sexual harassment complaint with the university, then sued it under 42 U.S.C. § 1983 for violating her "equal protection right to an education free of sexual harassment." A federal court ruled for the university, and the Eighth Circuit Court of Appeals affirmed. Here, **not only was the relationship consensual,**

but even if it wasn't, the student was not actually a "student" at the time of the alleged harassment. Despite being technically enrolled, she either failed or withdrew from her classes. Thus, she could not establish a connection between the professor in his role as teacher and the violation of her rights as a student. *Waters v. Metropolitan State Univ.*, 52 Fed. Appx. 1 (8th Cir. 2002). [MN]

◆ *A university was not liable under Title IX where it took appropriate action to allegations of harassment by a professor.*

A Louisiana university student claimed that her art professor made inappropriate sexual comments to her that continued from the fall semester into the spring. She complained to the department chair, who passed the information on to the university provost the same day. The school ordered an investigation into the matter and one week later informed the student of her right to be transferred out of the professor's class. The university concluded the professor did not harass the student, but reprimanded him for the appearance of impropriety and warned him about the consequences of future allegations of misconduct. The student then sued the university and the professor under Title IX, alleging that the university allowed the professor to harass her. A federal court ruled against her, finding no evidence that the university was "deliberately indifferent" to her complaint. Here, **the university took prompt and reasonable remedial action after an official with authority to correct the problem learned of the allegations**. *Owens v. Dillard Univ.*, 2002 WL 1822932 (E.D. La. 8/8/02). [LA]

◆ *A university could not be held liable under Title IX where a jury found no sexual harassment committed by an assistant coach.*

A student at Ohio State University participated on the track and cross-country teams. After her eligibility expired, an assistant coach allegedly offered to let her continue to train with the team and become a volunteer assistant coach. He then asked her out on two occasions. She refused to date him and allegedly was unable to continue training with the teams as a result of her refusal. She sued the university, the assistant coach and the athletic director under Title IX and 42 U.S.C. § 1983. The defendants moved to dismiss the lawsuit. The U.S. District Court for the Southern District of Ohio dismissed the case against the university, finding that **once the student informed school officials of the assistant coach's actions, they took prompt action to ensure that the "harassing" behavior, which had already ceased, would not recur**. However, the court found that a genuine issue of fact remained as to whether the assistant coach's actions in asking the student out amounted to a request for sexual favors. Accordingly, the case against the assistant coach could not be dismissed. A jury then ruled that the assistant coach had not sexually harassed the student by demanding sexual favors in return for coaching her. Nor had he created a sexually hostile environment. When the student appealed the ruling in favor of the university to the Sixth Circuit, the court of appeals held that it could not be liable under Title IX where there had been no underlying discrimination on the part of the assistant coach. *Klemencic v. Ohio State Univ.*, 263 F.3d 504 (6th Cir. 2001). [OH]

◆ *A New York student was allowed to proceed with his Title IX claim against a university.*

A graduate student began a consensual sexual relationship with the director of the doctoral program and later ended the affair. He alleged that she then retaliated against him by insisting that he withdraw his dissertation proposal and by preventing him from obtaining approval for a new dissertation topic. After he was terminated from the doctoral program, he sued the university, the dean and the director under Title IX, and the defendants sought to dismiss the action. A New York federal court held that the Title IX claim against the university could proceed. Here, **the student had established a *prima facie* case of *quid pro quo* sexual harassment in an educational setting**. However, because Title IX claims cannot be asserted against faculty members or other school employees, the court dismissed the dean and the director from the lawsuit. *Kraft v. Yeshiva Univ.*, 2001 WL 1191003 (S.D.N.Y. 10/5/01). [NY]

◆ *The slow resolution of a student's sexual harassment complaint did not create liability for a college where it immediately began the proceedings.*

A student at Northern Marianas College claimed that she was sexually harassed by a professor, who grabbed and touched her inappropriately and stuck his tongue in her mouth. With the help of a school counselor, she filed a complaint against the professor, then dropped his class. She received additional assistance in presenting her complaint before the college's committee on sexual harassment. Approximately one year after the harassment occurred, the committee issued its findings in favor of the student, and the college then disciplined the professor. The student sued the college, various school officials and the professor under Title IX. A federal court granted pretrial judgment to all the defendants except the professor, and a jury then awarded her $10,000 in compensatory damages and $30,000 in punitive damages. The student appealed the dismissal of the college, but the Ninth Circuit affirmed. Here, **the one-year delay in processing the complaint was due to bureaucratic sluggishness and the fact that the student had moved** to New Mexico, not to deliberate indifference by school officials. The college began proceedings immediately upon being notified of the harassment. *Oden v. Northern Marianas College*, 284 F.3d 1058 (9th Cir. 2002). [N. Mariana Islands]

◆ *A Virginia student could proceed with her Title IX claim against a university alleging faculty members retaliated against her for charging a professor with sexual harassment.*

The worked as the professor's research assistant until he began to harass her. The university ordered the professor to leave the student alone, but refused to investigate the matter further. The student alleged that the engineering faculty responded to her sexual harassment complaint by refusing to interact with her and locking her out of the computer lab. As a result, she sent suggestive and hostile e-mails to certain faculty members, resulting in two professors filing sexual harassment charges against her. The University Judicial Board found the student guilty of sexual harassment, and she was dismissed. The student then sued the university in a federal district court for sexual harassment and retaliation under Title IX.

The court dismissed the student's sexual harassment claim because she failed to show the university had actual knowledge of the harassment and was deliberately indifferent to it. The university received actual knowledge of the professor's conduct when the student's complaint was filed with the Equity Office, and it was not deliberately indifferent because it ordered the professor to stay away from her. In analyzing the student's Title IX retaliation claim, the court noted she was required to prove that the university intentionally discriminated against her. **A plaintiff must prove intentional discrimination in a Title IX retaliation claim in the same manner as a sexual harassment claim** by showing an official had actual knowledge of harassment, but acted with deliberate indifference to it. The university conceded it had actual notice of the alleged retaliation and did not investigate it, but it maintained it did not have to investigate because the student did not file an official written complaint, as required by school policy. The court held the student's verbal complaints of retaliation required a jury trial and refused to dismiss the retaliation claim. *Litman v. George Mason Univ.*, 131 F.Supp.2d 795 (E.D. Va. 2001). [VA]

◆ *Where a school allegedly conducted a "sham" investigation into charges of sexual harassment by a coach, there was an issue as to whether school officials had shown deliberate indifference to misconduct.*

Two former members of the Syracuse University women's tennis team, together with their parents, sued their former coach under Title IX for sexually harassing them over a three-year period. They also sued the university and several of its employees and agents, alleging they had concocted a "sham" investigatory proceeding to conceal the extent of the coach's misconduct, which they claimed went back more than 20 years. A New York federal court held that under *Gebser v. Lago Vista Independent School Dist.*, 524 U.S. 274 (1998), where a school official has actual knowledge of sexual harassment against a student and is deliberately indifferent to that misconduct, the student can sue the school under Title IX. **Here, there were issues of fact to be resolved as to whether the defendants had been deliberately indifferent to the alleged misconduct.** The defendants' motion to dismiss the case was denied. *Erickson v. Syracuse Univ.*, 35 F.Supp.2d 326 (S.D.N.Y. 1999). [NY]

◆ *A federal court allowed a claim of retaliation under Title IX to proceed.*

A student brought discrimination charges against a private university before the U.S. Department of Education, Office for Civil Rights. She alleged that she then suffered adverse action by being evaluated and treated unfairly. She also maintained that the university denied her access to instructors who could serve as references for jobs and denied her the opportunity to pursue a graduate degree. **The U.S. District Court of the Northern District of Illinois found an implied right of action for retaliation in Section 106.1 of the Title IX regulations.** Section 106.1 prohibits retaliation against "any individual who has made a complaint, testified, or participated in any manner in an investigation into alleged noncompliance with Title IX."

The court also found that the pleading standard for retaliation in a Title IX suit is the same as under Title VII. To state a claim of retaliation under Title VII, a claimant must allege that (1) she engaged in a statutorily protected activity;

(2) she suffered an adverse action; and (3) there was a causal link between the protected activity and the adverse action. Here, because the student's complaint properly alleged retaliation by the university, the court refused to dismiss the case. *Adams v. Lewis Univ.*, No. 97 C 7636, 1999 WL 162762 (N.D. Ill. 1999). [IL]

◆ *Allegations of a number of harassment incidents prevented a university from having a Title IX suit dismissed.*

A tenured professor at an Indiana university allegedly harassed a female graduate student, attempting to enter into a sexual relationship with her. The university issued the professor a written reprimand, warning him that another incident could lead to his firing. He then allegedly touched a visiting high school student on the buttocks. The university then referred the professor to a psychiatrist, but after learning that he had visited the doctor, did not follow up to determine the results of his counseling. The professor's supervisor, however, allegedly knew that a number of female students were uncomfortable in the professor's presence.

Approximately five years later, the professor allegedly made inappropriate remarks to another student and put his arm around her a few times. The director of student services allegedly knew about this incident but did nothing other than warn the professor to "clean up his act." Two years later, the professor allegedly groped and kissed a student against her will.

The university instituted proceedings against the professor, who resigned with full benefits. When the student sued the university for harassment under Title IX, the university sought to dismiss the lawsuit. The court denied the motion. It noted that **a reasonable jury could find that the university had been deliberately indifferent to the professor's misconduct**. Rather than firing him after the second incident, the university had only required counseling and had not followed up to determine its effectiveness. Further, it had done nothing after the third incident. Thus, **factual issues existed as to whether the university was liable under Title IX because of deliberate indifference to harassment**. *Chontos v. Rhea*, 29 F.Supp.2d 931 (N.D. Ind. 1998). [IN]

◆ *In a sexual harassment case under Title IX, a student must show actual notice of the harassment and deliberate indifference by school officials.*

Two days before graduating from a private college, a student filed a sexual harassment complaint against one of her professors. Her complaint was processed and, less than two months later, she signed off on an informal grievance procedure notifying the professor that his conduct amounted to sexual harassment. Two years later, she sued the college under Title IX. An Ohio federal court ruled in favor of the college, finding that the student could not show that the college had been deliberately indifferent to her situation after receiving actual notice of her complaint. **The U.S. Supreme Court has held that both deliberate indifference and actual notice are required for liability to attach under Title IX.** Pretrial judgment in favor of the college was granted. *Burtner v. Hiram College*, 9 F.Supp.2d 852 (N.D. Ohio 1998). [OH]

◆ *A federal court held that Title IX does not authorize a cause of action against individuals.*

A 28-year-old female student-employee at a Pennsylvania university accused her supervisor, an administrative level employee, of sexually harassing her on several different occasions. The university suspended the administrator, and he allegedly retaliated against the student by defaming her and by filing a civil complaint against her. The student filed a Title IX sexual harassment lawsuit against the administrator in the U.S. District Court for the Eastern District of Pennsylvania. The court dismissed the claim, holding that Title IX does not authorize a cause of action against individuals. A 1986 amendment to Title IX bolstered this conclusion since only remedies against "public or private entities" were mentioned. The court also noted that the full body of regulations promulgated under Title IX, found at 28 C.F.R. Part 106, suggested that **only "owners or operators" of independent educational programs or activities, rather than individual employees of the operator, were subject to Title IX lawsuits.** *Nelson v. Temple Univ.*, 920 F.Supp. 633 (E.D. Pa. 1996). [PA]

2. Sexual Harassment by Peers

◆ *The U.S. Supreme Court held schools may be held liable for incidents of peer sexual harassment under Title IX.*

The case involved a fifth-grade Georgia student who claimed that a classmate subjected her to unwanted sexual comments, physical abuse and ongoing harassment for about five months. She complained to her teacher and the school's principal, but claimed that they did nothing in response. When the case reached the Supreme Court, it held that **a recipient of federal funds may be held liable for student-on-student sexual harassment under Title IX where the funding recipient is deliberately indifferent to known student sexual harassment and the harasser is under the recipient's disciplinary authority**. The Court additionally held that in order to make a finding of deliberate indifference, the recipient's response to harassment must be clearly unreasonable in light of the known circumstances. **In order to create Title IX liability, the harassment must be so severe, pervasive and objectively offensive that it deprives the victim of access to the funding recipient's educational opportunities or benefits**. *Davis v. Monroe County Bd. of Educ.*, 526 U.S. 629, 119 S.Ct. 1661, 143 L.Ed.2d 839 (1999). [GA]

◆ *The Supreme Court held Congress exceeded its authority when enacting the civil remedies portion of the Violence Against Women Act (VAWA).*

A Virginia university student alleged she was raped by two members of the school football team. Based on her report, a university judicial committee obtained a confession by one of the perpetrators at a hearing and suspended him for two semesters. Officials advised the student another hearing would be held based on their belief that the perpetrator who admitted guilt had been charged under a new student handbook policy that had not yet been widely disseminated to students. A second hearing was held, after which officials deferred the perpetrator's suspension until after his graduation. The officials did not notify the victim of the altered discipline, and the perpetrator kept his full athletic scholarship. The victim quit school after reading a newspaper report of the reduced discipline. She filed a federal district court action against the university and perpetrators under Title IX and the VAWA, a federal law creating a cause of action for victims of violent crimes motivated by gender.

The court dismissed the action, and the U.S. Court of Appeals, Fourth Circuit, affirmed the judgment. It held that although the alleged conduct came within the act's language, the VAWA violated the Commerce Clause because Congress lacked the authority to enact the civil remedy provisions of the VAWA [42 U.S.C. § 13981]. The U.S. Supreme Court affirmed. It noted that **Congress could not regulate noneconomic, violent criminal conduct based solely on the conduct's aggregate effect on interstate commerce. Section 13981 could not be justified by the enforcement provision of the Fourteenth Amendment because the Fourteenth Amendment prohibits only state conduct, not private conduct.** The Court stated that the victim's remedy had to be provided by state courts under state law. *U.S. (Brzonkala) v. Morrison,* 529 U.S. 598, 120 S.Ct. 1740, 146 L.Ed.2d 658 (2000). [VA]

◆   *An educational institution may be held liable for Title IX violations under standards similar to those applied in cases under Title VII where an employer is culpable because it "knew or should have known of the conduct."*

A second-year New York university student was allegedly harassed by a clinic patient who made unwanted advances, continually stared at her, and repeatedly followed her to her apartment. The chief of the dental clinic warned the patient to cease the offensive behavior after another student filed a complaint about him. The chief's admonitions were unavailing, and after further harassment, the student asked a clinic doctor for assistance with the patient. He told her to "grow up" and deal with the problem herself.

The student failed six classes and received incomplete grades in four of them. The academic standing committee recommended that she repeat the second-year curriculum. Her appeal, based on the harassment that allegedly caused her poor academic performance, was dismissed. The student filed a Title IX gender discrimination lawsuit against the university in a U.S. district court. The court granted the university's motion to dismiss, and the student appealed

The U.S. Court of Appeals, Second Circuit, noted that in a Title IX lawsuit for gender discrimination based on sexual harassment of a student, an educational institution may be held liable under standards similar to those applied in cases under Title VII. An employer is culpable under Title VII where it "knew or should have known of the conduct." However, even under this standard, which the court declined to apply in the present case, **the student's complaint failed to allege that the university's agents "should have known" about the continued harassment.** The student never informed the clinic chief that the harassing behavior continued following the chief's warning to the patient nor did she inform the doctor that the "problem" involved ongoing sexual harassment. The court also noted that **the university had not selectively enforced its academic standards** and the academic committee's decision had been made before the student informed them of the harassment. *Murray v. New York Univ. College of Dentistry,* 57 F.3d 243 (2d Cir. 1995). [NY]

◆ *A federal district court dismissed a student's sexual harassment lawsuit against two Louisiana law schools.*

The student claimed two female classmates talked to him about sexually deviant topics and one of them sexually harassed him while he was at Louisiana State University (LSU) Law School. He transferred to Loyola University Law School, where he claimed female students made sexual overtures to him. He also claimed a professor rubbed him and sexually harassed him. The school dean called the student to his office after receiving numerous complaints that he had sent inappropriate and offensive e-mails. The student agreed to take a medical leave from school, then sued both law schools for sexual harassment in violation of Title IX. The student added a claim against LSU for defamation based on his assertion of a rumor about his raping and impregnating another student. LSU and Loyola moved to dismiss the case.

The court stated that **to impose liability under Title IX, the student had to show sexual harassment that was known to a school official with authority to address the alleged discrimination, but failed to take corrective measures despite this knowledge.** As the student did not show Loyola officials had actual knowledge of the professor's actions, the court dismissed the harassment claims against Loyola. It also dismissed the claims against LSU, which were time-barred under state law. *Menard v. Board of Trustees of Loyola Univ. of New Orleans,* 2004 WL 856641 (E.D. La. 2004). [LA]

◆ *A Colorado university was not entitled to discovery of a student's diary entries that were unrelated to the sexual harassment claim she was litigating.*

The student alleged the university knew about repeated sexual harassment by varsity football players and recruits, but failed to take any corrective action. She asserted the harassment had a devastating effect on her life and her education and that she suffered severe emotional distress and mental anguish. The student sued the university in a federal district court for Title IX violations. The university argued her allegations did not establish the school was deliberately indifferent, and asked the court to order her to produce copies of her diary. It contended the diary entries could identify stress or trauma in her life and thus related to her emotional distress claim. The student submitted her diary to the court for it to review privately. The court found only the entries related to the harassment incidents were relevant or likely to lead to admissible evidence. It denied the school's request to produce the entire diary. *Simpson v. University of Colorado,* 220 F.R.D. 354 (D. Colo. 2004). [CO]

III. RACE AND NATIONAL ORIGIN DISCRIMINATION

A. Affirmative Action

◆ *While achieving a diverse student body may be a worthy goal, the means to achieve that goal must comply with the Equal Protection Clause. The U.S. Supreme Court allowed race to be used as a "plus" factor in admissions.*

The University of Michigan had an admissions policy for its law school that used race as a "plus" factor for underrepresented minorities. The policy was flexible, utilized an individualized assessment system, and did not create quotas. When the policy was challenged as unconstitutional by white students who were not accepted for enrollment, the case reached the U.S. Supreme Court, which upheld the policy. The Court first noted that the goal of achieving diversity in the student body was a compelling governmental interest. As a result, the policy would not be violative of the Equal Protection Clause if it was narrowly tailored to achieving that goal. Since the law school's policy did not set impermissible quotas, and since **it utilized an individualized assessment system by using race/ethnicity as a "plus" factor when evaluating individual applicants for admission**, it was constitutional. The Court also noted that race-conscious admissions policies should be limited in time so that racial preferences would be ended as soon as practicable. *Grutter v. Bollinger,* 539 U.S. 306, 123 S.Ct. 2325, 156 L.E.2d 304 (2003). [MI]

◆ *The Supreme Court found unconstitutional the University of Michigan's undergraduate admissions policy, which awarded applicants in underrepresented minority groups 20 points out of 100 needed for admission.*

Applying the same strict scrutiny analysis it used in *Grutter*, above, the Court held the undergraduate policy was not narrowly tailored to achieve the compelling governmental interest in a diverse student body. **The undergraduate admissions policy did not assess points on an individualized basis**, but rather awarded them to all minority applicants. The failure to review each applicant individually doomed the policy under the Equal Protection Clause. *Gratz v. Bollinger,* 539 U.S. 244, 123 S.Ct. 2411, 156 L.Ed.2d 257 (2003). [MI]

◆ *In 1978, the Supreme Court held a special admissions program at a California medical school that reserved close to one-sixth of the school's openings each year for minority students violated the Equal Protection Clause.*

The Medical School of the University of California at Davis had two admission programs for its entering class of 100 students. Under the regular procedure, candidates whose overall undergraduate grade point averages fell below 2.5 on a scale of 4.0 were summarily rejected. The special admissions policy, designed to assist minority or other disadvantaged applicants, reserved 16 of the 100 openings each year for medical school admission based upon criteria other than that used in the general admissions program. Special admission applicants did not need to meet the 2.5 or better grade point average of the general admission group nor were their Medical College Admission Test scores measured against general admission candidates.

A white male brought suit to compel his admission to medical school after he was twice rejected for admission even though candidates with lower grade point averages and lower test score results were being admitted under the special admissions program. The plaintiff alleged that **the special admissions excluded him from medical school on the basis of his race** in violation of the Equal Protection Clause of the Fourteenth Amendment, the California Constitution, and Title VI of the 1964 Civil Rights Act. Title VI of the Civil Rights Act provides that no person shall on the ground of race or color be excluded from participating in any program receiving federal financial assistance. The Equal Protection Clause states that no state shall deny to any person within its jurisdiction the equal protection of the law. The California Supreme Court concluded that the special admissions program was not the least intrusive means of achieving the state's goals of integrating the medical profession under a strict scrutiny standard.

On appeal, the U.S. Supreme Court held that **while the goal of achieving a diverse student body is sufficiently compelling to justify considerations of race in admissions decisions under some circumstances, the special admissions program, which foreclosed consideration to persons such as the plaintiff, was unnecessary to achieve this compelling goal and was therefore invalid under the Equal Protection Clause**. Since the school could not prove that the plaintiff would not have been admitted even if there had been no special admissions program, the Court ordered that he be admitted to the medical school. *Regents of the Univ. of California v. Bakke*, 438 U.S. 265, 98 S.Ct. 2733, 57 L.Ed.2d 750 (1978). [CA]

◆ *The Supreme Court held that a university could avoid liability for a race-based admission policy if it could show that the applicant would have been denied admission absent the policy.*

An African immigrant of Caucasian descent applied for admission to the Ph.D. program in counseling psychology at a Texas public university. The university considered the race of its applicants at some stage of the review process and denied admission to the applicant. He sued for money damages and injunctive relief, asserting that the race-conscious admission policy violated the Equal Protection Clause. The university moved for summary judgment, arguing that even if it had not used race-based criteria, it would not have admitted the applicant because of his GPA and his GRE score. A federal court granted summary judgment to the university, but the Fifth Circuit Court of Appeals reversed. The case reached the U.S. Supreme Court, which noted that its decision in *Mt. Healthy City Bd. of Educ. v. Doyle*, 429 U.S. 274, 97 S.Ct. 568, 50 L.Ed.2d 471 (1977), made clear that **if the government has considered an impermissible criterion in making an adverse decision to the plaintiff, it can nevertheless avoid liability by demonstrating that it would have made the same decision absent the forbidden consideration**. Therefore, if the state could show that it would have made the decision to deny admission to the applicant absent the race-based policy, it would be entitled to summary judgment on the claim for damages. With respect to the claim for injunctive relief, it appeared that the university had stopped using a race-based admissions policy. However, that issue had to be decided on remand. *Texas v. Lesage*, 528 U.S. 18, 120 S.Ct. 467, 145 L.Ed.2d 347 (1999). [TX]

◆ *The Florida Supreme Court held the NAACP had associational standing to challenge an executive order abolishing the use of race and gender preferences for admission to Florida state institutions of higher learning.*

The state board of regents amended three sections of the state administrative code in response to Executive Order 99-281, which asked the board to immediately prohibit racial or gender set-asides, preferences, or quotas in admissions to all Florida institutions of higher education. The

NAACP and its members brought a rule challenge under state law. An administrative law judge denied a motion for dismissal by the board of regents and the state board of education, finding the NAACP had "associational standing" because its members included students in middle school, high school and college. The Florida District Court of Appeal reversed and remanded the case. It held the NAACP could not establish associational standing because it failed to show how its members would suffer a real and immediate injury.

The Supreme Court of Florida held an association that challenges a state rule must demonstrate a substantial number of its members are substantially affected by the rule. The rule's subject matter must be within the association's general scope of interest and activity, and the relief requested must be of the type appropriate for a trade association representing its members. The record indicated some NAACP members were prospective state university candidates and were minorities who would be affected by these changes. The appellate decision required the NAACP to prove actual harm to gain associational standing. State law did not impose this requirement. As the NAACP showed the amendments would have a sufficient impact on its membership, it satisfied the requirement of "substantial impact" for "associational standing." The court quashed the appellate decision, and remanded the case. *NAACP v. Florida Bd. of Regents*, 863 So.2d 294 (Fla. 2003). [FL]

◆   *The University of Georgia's admissions policy, which offered additional points to minority applicants, was held unconstitutional because it restricted the use of other factors in violation of the Equal Protection Clause.*

In 1995, the University of Georgia developed a three-stage admissions process. The initial stage evaluated the applicant based on objective academic criteria without regard to race or gender. At stage two, UGA assessed the applicant's total student index. Candidates were awarded points based on a variety of factors including race, extracurricular activities, state residency and academic achievement. At this stage of the admissions process, candidates with a TSI score of 4.93 were automatically accepted; applicants with a TSI score below 4.66 were automatically rejected. The candidates whose scores fell between 4.66 and 4.92 moved to the third stage. At the "edge read" stage (ER stage), all applicants start with a score of zero and race is not a factor. Three white female applicants were denied admission to the UGA 1999 freshman class. One of the applicants would have automatically been admitted if she received gender and minority credit; the other two women would have qualified for consideration at the ER stage. The women sued for race discrimination in violation of the Equal Protection Clause and Title VI, and gender discrimination in violation of the Equal Protection Clause and Title IX. The court concluded that UGA's admissions policy violated Title VI, and by extension the Equal Protection Clause, because striving for a diverse student body was not a compelling interest able to withstand strict scrutiny. The court held for the women. UGA appealed.

The Eleventh Circuit affirmed, but on different grounds. The court of appeals ruled that regardless of whether diversity is a compelling interest, UGA's admissions policy, which restricted the use of other factors relevant to diversity, could not satisfy strict scrutiny and therefore violated the Equal

Protection Clause. First, **UGA's policy lacked flexibility; it "mechanically" assigned bonus points for race without conducting individual evaluations of each candidate** and limited the factors at the TSI stage to only 12. Second, the policy failed to fully consider race-neutral factors, such as income level and language skills. Third, the value assigned to race was "arbitrary." In addition, only an SAT score between 1200 and 1600 was accorded more value than a race factor and, **among the non-academic factors, no factor was worth more than the race.** Finally, UGA did not show that before adopting its race-conscious admissions policy, it had considered race-neutral factors and rejected them as inadequate. For these reasons, UGA's admissions policy violated the Equal Protection Clause. *Johnson v. Board of Regents of Univ. of Georgia*, 263 F.3d 1234 (11th Cir. 2001). [GA]

◆ *A class action alleging the University of Washington Law School discriminated in its admissions policy by favoring minorities was held moot.*

Students who were denied admission to the law school sued the school in a federal district court in 1997, alleging it illegally discriminated against white applicants based on their race. The school used race as a factor in its admissions policy from 1994 till November 1998, when Washington voters passed Initiative Measure 200 (I-200). The measure prevented the state from discrimination or giving preferential treatment based on race, sex or ethnicity in the operation of public employment, public education or public contract. Because of I-200, the university moved to dismiss the suit as moot. The court dismissed the case, and the students appealed to the Ninth Circuit.

The court rejected the plaintiffs' claim that their action was not moot after the passage of I-200. Although the school voluntarily opted to change its admissions policy, the school's decision to change its admissions policy was not fully voluntary since it was prompted by I-200. As a result, there was no reason to believe the school would violate the measure in the future. Therefore, **the district court had properly decertified the class because the matter was moot.** The Ninth Circuit also examined whether race can be used as a factor at all in educational admissions decisions and concluded that, at the very least, a majority of the *Bakke* court would have allowed for some race-based considerations in educational institutions, both under Title VI and under the Fourteenth Amendment. **The court refused to interpret *Bakke* further and held that the University of Washington Law School's admissions policy was constitutional.** *Smith v. University of Washington Law School*, 233 F.3d 1188 (9th Cir. 2000), *cert. denied*, 121 S.Ct. 2192 (2001). [WA]

◆ *Although a university's use of racial preferences for admissions to law school was unconstitutional, four students failed to show that they would have been admitted to the school absent the discrimination.*

Four white students applied for admission to the University of Texas School of Law. After they were denied admission, they sued under Title VI of the Civil Rights Act of 1964 and 42 U.S.C. §§ 1981 and 1983, asserting that the law school's use of racial preferences for the purpose of achieving a diverse student body violated those laws. A federal court found that although the government had a compelling interest in achieving a diverse student body, and a compelling interest in overcoming the present effects of past race discrimination, the law school's use of separate admissions procedures for minority and nonminority students was not narrowly tailored to achieve those compelling interests. The court then held that the students had the ultimate burden to prove that they would have been admitted to the law school absent the unconstitutional procedures used by the university. It found that they failed to meet that burden. On appeal, the Fifth Circuit held that **the law school's use of racial preferences served no compelling state interests** and that the burden should have been on the law school to show that under a constitutional admissions procedure, the students would not have been admitted. On remand, the district court held that **the university had shown that the students would not have been admitted even if its procedures had been constitutional**. They all fell within the discretionary screening zone and were just four of 3,500 applicants, including 1,500 Texas residents, who were denied admission to the school. The university had to have the freedom to make the necessary difficult choices about who should be admitted to its law school. *Hopwood v. Texas*, 999 F.Supp. 872 (W.D. Tex. 1998). [TX]

On second appeal to the Fifth Circuit, the court upheld the district court's determination that the students would not have been admitted to the law school even if the admissions policy was constitutional. *Hopwood v. Texas*, 236 F.3d 256 (5th Cir. 2000). [TX]

B. Discrimination and Equal Protection

◆   *The U.S. Supreme Court held individuals cannot sue colleges, schools and states for policies that unintentionally discriminate against minorities under Title VI. They may still sue entities for acts of intentional discrimination.*

Alabama amended its constitution in 1990 to declare English its official language. It began administering driver's license exams only in English, and a federal court agreed with a class of individuals that the state violated a Title VI regulation published by the U.S. Department of Justice. Title VI is one of the principal federal laws preventing discrimination on the basis of race, color or national origin. It prohibits recipients of federal funding, including states and educational institutions, from practicing discrimination in any covered program or activity and is commonly cited in education cases alleging discrimination on those grounds. The case reached the U.S. Supreme Court, which noted that Title VI prohibits only intentional discrimination and cannot be used to enforce a disparate-impact action. **Because disparate-impact regulations of the kind at issue in this case did not apply to Title VI, the private right of action under § 601 did not include a private right to enforce disparate-impact regulations**. The lower court judgments were reversed. *Alexander v. Sandoval*, 532 U.S. 275, 121 S.Ct. 1511, 149 L.Ed.2d 517 (2001). [AL]

◆   *A Nebraska college did not discriminate against a student by rejecting her applications for a post-graduate program.*

The student applied to the college's post-graduate physician's assistant program. After being rejected for the third time, she sued the college in a federal district court for race discrimination. The court dismissed the case, based on evidence that the student failed many classes, had a poor attendance record and did not hand in her assignments. She failed to rebut the college's legitimate, non-discriminatory reasons for denying her application.

The student appealed to the Eighth Circuit, where she asserted a college academic advisor coerced her into taking three challenging science courses at one time rather than sequentially, as a college policy required. She failed two of those courses and got a D in the other. The student also said interviewers asked her inappropriate questions and gave her a low interview score because of race discrimination. The court held that even if it disregarded the three courses she took because of alleged coercion, the nine courses she needed to retake were ample evidence of her academic ineptitude. She offered no evidence that the interview process was unfair or the calculation of her initial grade average was ill-motivated. As the student could not disprove the college's legitimate, non-discriminatory reasons for denying her admission, the court affirmed the judgment. *Baker v. Union College*, 95 Fed. Appx. 844, 2004 WL 886323 (8th Cir. 2004). [NE]

◆   *Four black students could sue a private university for civil rights violations after security officers had them arrested while letting white students go free.*

A group of students were socializing in the lobby of a private university's library when a university security officer instructed them to disperse. He confiscated a black student's ID card, then called other security officers and the local police department. Four black male students were arrested and jailed overnight as a result, but no white students were arrested. After the charges were dismissed, the black students sued the university under 42 U.S.C. § 1981, alleging that they were deprived of the "full and equal benefit of all laws and proceedings…as is enjoyed by white citizens." A federal district court dismissed the action on the grounds that there was no state action. The Second Circuit vacated and remanded the case. **The students did not have to show state action; they only had to show a nexus to state laws or proceedings**. They did this by showing the security officers attempted to trigger a legal proceeding against them, but not against the white students. The case required a trial. *Phillip v. University of Rochester*, 316 F.3d 291 (2d Cir. 2003). [NY]

◆   *A university may have discriminated against a black student by expelling him but not three white students.*

A black student lived with a white student in a mobile home on the campus of a Missouri university. One night, they had a party with two white female students and several non-students. Everyone but the black student drank alcohol. When campus police entered the home, the black student cooperated with them. However, since the university did not allow students who lived on campus to possess alcohol or have visitors of the opposite sex, the black student and the other three students were expelled. Shortly thereafter, the three white students were readmitted, but the black student was not. He sued the university under 42 U.S.C. § 1981 for race discrimination. A federal court granted pretrial judgment to the university, but the Eighth Circuit reversed. The court held that **the black student had presented sufficient evidence of intentional discrimination to warrant a trial**. He was the only student at the party not drinking, and he cooperated the most with campus police. Further, he presented evidence that students expelled for violating the alcohol and/or visitation rules were always readmitted. Finally, he alleged that university officials made repeated references to his race during the investigation. As a result, the case should not have been dismissed. *Williams v. Lindenwood Univ.*, 288 F.3d 349 (8th Cir. 2002). [MO]

◆   *The NCAA was not liable for Title VI claims alleging Proposition 16 had a disparate impact on African-American students.*

A number of African-American high school student athletes graduated with GPAs that exceeded the NCAA's requirements. However, they all scored lower than the minimum SAT score required for participation in Division I collegiate athletics as freshmen. They sued the NCAA, asserting that the minimum SAT score requirement of Proposition 16 had a disparate impact on African-American athletes in violation of Title VI. They claimed Proposition 16 was neutral on its face, but its impact discriminated against African-American students. They also claimed the NCAA was a program or activity that received federal financial assistance and that, under Title VI, it could not discriminate on the basis of race. The NCAA maintained it was not subject to Title VI because it did not receive direct financial assistance, but rather received money from colleges and universities that received federal financial assistance. A Pennsylvania federal court found that the NCAA was subject to suit under Title VI, and that Proposition 16 had a disparate impact on African-Americans.

The NCAA appealed, and the Third Circuit Court of Appeals reversed. It assumed without deciding that the NCAA received federal financial assistance. However, it then stated that **Title VI was intended to be program specific. In other words, it only prohibited discrimination in programs or activities that received federal funds.** Further, even though Congress had enacted the Civil Rights Restoration Act to broaden the protections of Title VI and Title IX, the Department of Education had not yet enacted regulations to implement that statute. Further, it was unclear whether those regulations could prohibit neutral actions that had a discriminatory effect (disparate impact discrimination) or whether they could only prohibit intentional (disparate treatment) discrimination. As a result, **the NCAA did not come under the umbrella of Title VI. It was not a direct recipient of federal funds and did not exert sufficient authority over its member institutions to make it liable under Title VI.** *Cureton v. NCAA*, 198 F.3d 107 (3d Cir. 1999). [PA]

In response to the Third Circuit's decision, attorneys for the plaintiffs filed a motion in district court seeking to amend their original complaint with a claim alleging intentional discrimination. The judge denied the motion, finding the plaintiffs had waited too long to amend the complaint, that allowing the amendment would result in impermissible prejudice to the NCAA, and that the amendment would be futile. On appeal, the Third Circuit upheld the district court decision, agreeing that the amended complaint was filed too late. According to the circuit court, allowing the plaintiffs to proceed under the amended complaint would be burdensome to the NCAA. *Cureton v. NCAA*, 252 F.3d 267 (3d Cir. 2001). [PA]

◆ *A Ph.D. candidate was unable to show that discrimination resulted in her inability to pass qualifying examinations.*

An African-American Ph.D. candidate received a fellowship for minority students in the University of Maryland's applied mathematics program. Only 40 to 50 percent of students enrolled in the program eventually received a Ph.D. Doctoral candidates were required to pass qualifying exams in three subject areas. The African-American candidate failed qualifying examinations nine times and was dismissed from the program. She filed a federal district court action against the university and certain university officials, claiming race and sex discrimination in violation of federal laws including Title IX of the Education Amendments of 1972, Title VI of the Civil Rights Act of 1964 and 42 U.S.C. §§ 1981 and 1983. The court considered summary judgment motions by the university and officials.

The candidate claimed that a teaching assistant and a professor had made racially biased remarks concerning the academic ability of African-American students and had established more difficult testing conditions than those experienced by male students. **The court found that there was no link between these incidents and the candidate's failure to pass the qualifying examinations. It is impermissible to base a lawsuit brought under federal antidiscrimination laws on speculation** and belief, especially where the incidents are unrelated to a central issue, such as failure to pass qualifying tests. Because the candidate had failed to demonstrate that she was qualified to continue in the program, the court granted summary judgment to the university and officials. *Middlebrooks v. University of Maryland at College Park*, 980 F.Supp. 824 (D.Md. 1997). [MD]

C. National Origin

◆ *A federal district court held that the rights-creating provision of Title VI allowed a private right of action for a retaliation.*

The case involved a student who was an American citizen of East Indian descent. His advanced biochemistry instructor reported him to the university honor council for suspected plagiarism. The council found the student violated the honor code and recommended a one-semester suspension. He challenged the result and obtained another hearing. However, a different hearing board recommended the same penalty. The student sued the university in a federal district court for retaliation and discrimination based on his national origin in violation of Title VI. The court considered the university's dismissal motion.

The student argued the honor council treated him differently than "similarly situated white students" by failing to produce a definition of plagiarism or considering mitigating circumstances. The court rejected his discrimination claim. Council documents indicated a definition of plagiarism was introduced during the disciplinary hearing, and listed several examples of plagiarism. The council was not required to consider mitigating circumstances, such as a family crisis. The suspension was not unduly and unusually harsh. The national origin discrimination claim was dismissed. **The court held there is a private right of action for retaliation under Title VI, § 601. To establish retaliation, the student had to show the university knew he was challenging**

protected activity. His complaint failed this standard, as it merely stated he thought he was being treated unfairly or differently than others. The court dismissed the case in its entirety. *Chandamuri v. Georgetown Univ.*, 274 F.Supp.2d 71 (D.D.C. 2003). [DC]

◆   *Five individuals were denied permission to remain anonymous in a federal district court case challenging state-supported Virginia colleges and universities for denying admission to illegal aliens.*

In 2002, the Virginia Attorney General advised state-supported colleges and universities to deny admission to illegal aliens and to report all individuals suspected of undocumented status to the Attorney General's office and the U.S. government. Five unnamed individuals and an association representing their interests brought a federal district court action against seven state-operated institutions. Some of the individuals had legal status in the U.S., but at least one stood to be deported. They claimed the use of their immigration status for denial of admission into state-supported institutions of higher learning violated the Supremacy Clause and sought declaratory and injunctive relief.

The court denied the individuals' request to proceed with the action anonymously. Their status as illegal aliens was not a personal matter requiring confidentiality. Two of the individuals had obtained legal status and lacked standing to challenge the policy. The court believed it was unlikely they would be discouraged from proceeding with their case even if their identities were revealed. Finally, barring these plaintiffs from proceeding anonymously was not likely to dissuade all other illegal aliens in the state from filing a similar suit. The court denied the individuals' motion to proceed using fictitious names. *Doe v. Merten*, 219 F.R.D. 387 (E.D.Va. 2004). [VA]

IV. AGE DISCRIMINATION

In addition to state laws, the Age Discrimination Act of 1975 (42 U.S.C. § 6101, et seq.) provides the basis for claims of age discrimination by students. Similar to Title IX claims, however, the Age Discrimination Act applies only to programs or activities receiving federal funding. Since the Age Discrimination in Employment Act (ADEA) is a broader statute (albeit only in employment), the Age Discrimination Act is not used very often, but its protections should be noted.

◆   *The Age Discrimination Act applies only to recipients of federal funding.*

In February 1983, a man sued Yale University alleging that Yale had discriminated against him on the basis of both handicap and age. Yale had dismissed him as a student in the graduate English department in 1967 and denied him readmission in 1975 and 1981. The issue before a U.S. district court was whether Yale discriminated against the man in violation of the Rehabilitation Act of 1973 and the Age Discrimination Act of 1975 when it denied him readmission.

The court observed that a July 1986 evidentiary hearing revealed that the Yale English department received no federal funding, which would trigger the application of the Acts. **The fact that a few of the English department's**

professors participated in Yale's summer program, which was federally funded, did not trigger the application of the acts since the seminars did not involve Yale graduate students. The summer program office administered the federal grants relating to the English department professors. The man could not meet his threshold burden that the specific program that allegedly discriminated against him, in this case the English department, received federal financial assistance. The man was not protected by the acts, and therefore his case was dismissed. *Stephanidis v. Yale Univ.*, 652 F.Supp. 110 (D. Conn. 1986). [CT]

◆ *An older student's claim of age discrimination failed where he could not show that he was qualified for entrance into a medical school's class.*

A 53-year-old psychologist applied to be a member of a first-year medical class at the Albert Einstein College of Medicine. The psychologist was called for an interview, and recommended for acceptance by the interviewer. However, the psychologist was not accepted. He alleged age discrimination in violation of New York Education Law and filed suit in a state court. The complaint alleged that faculty members indicated that the problem was not with the psychologist's qualifications, but with his age. The school contended that the psychologist's qualifications clearly precluded him, and that it had followed its established and published admittance regulations. The school was granted a dismissal, and the psychologist appealed to the state appellate division.

The issue in this case was whether the psychologist was otherwise qualified for admittance, ignoring his age. A court's review of a school's policies is limited to determining whether it acted in good faith or irrationally and arbitrarily. The school showed that the psychologist's grades, in both science classes and overall grade point average, were clearly unacceptable. It also alleged that his Medical College Aptitude Test score was lower than any student accepted. The psychologist pointed out that he was called for an interview and not summarily dismissed. He also noted his accomplishments in his current field, which included having hosted a weekly television show on mental health. The court ruled that **the psychologist was trying to create his own entrance standards, which the court had no power to allow**. The dismissal of claims was affirmed. *Brown v. Albert Einstein College of Medicine*, 568 N.Y.S.2d 61 (A.D. 1st Dept. 1991). [NY]

◆ *A student's Age Discrimination Act claim failed where he was unable to show that his age had anything to do with the denial of his readmission to medical school.*

A student at Thomas Jefferson University Medical School who also was a practicing attorney sued the school for age discrimination after he was denied readmission to the school. Asserting a claim under the Age Discrimination Act (among other claims), **the student averred that he was treated differently because he was older than his classmates**. He maintained that he was improperly failed in Family Medicine, that he was given less than average evaluations in Pediatrics, that his request for transfer of his Internal Medicine clerkship was denied, and that his application for readmission to the school was denied after his withdrawal. He further claimed that he had been fraudulently induced to sign an agreement withdrawing from the school and that he had signed the agreement under duress. He also contended that the school's attorney induced him to sign the agreement by stating that he had received a failing grade in his Family Medicine written examination when in fact the exam had not yet been graded. However, the student had drafted the agreement himself. It specified that if he were allowed to resign from the school in good standing, he would agree to withdraw an age discrimination complaint he had filed with the U.S. Department of Health and Human Services.

A Pennsylvania federal court noted that the student was an experienced attorney. **It rejected his age discrimination claim, noting that younger students also had failed courses under similar circumstances and had received evaluations based on the same criteria as were used to evaluate him.** Since he was the one who had drafted the agreement, and since the agreement had been drafted before the conversation with the school's attorney took place, the student could not show that the school's attorney fraudulently induced him to sign the agreement. The court further held that the school did not have to make extraordinary efforts to enable the student to practice law and study medicine at the same time. The court ruled for the school. *Petock v. Thomas Jefferson Univ.*, 630 F.Supp. 187 (E.D. Pa. 1986). [PA]

CHAPTER THREE

Athletics and Student Activities

I. ATHLETIC PROGRAMS

This section focuses on student legal issues, including personal injury claims. For additional cases involving school liability, see Chapter Eight.

◆ *An assistant athletic director did not have to grant special access to a Web site owner.*

The owner of a nonprofit Web site providing information on University of Colorado athletics sued the assistant athletic director and the university. He charged that the assistant AD interfered with his site by denying him access to coaches and practices by detaining him and ticketing him for trespassing in a university hallway, and by denying him resources from the assistant AD's office. A federal court dismissed the lawsuit, holding that the assistant AD did not violate the owner's constitutional rights. The Tenth Circuit Court of Appeals affirmed. As for the false arrest claim (related to the trespassing detention), the owner was not detained, restrained or confined for a substantial period of time. As for the free speech claim, **the assistant AD did not prevent the owner from maintaining a private Web site or from speaking freely about the university's athletic programs**. The assistant AD also did not have to grant special access to the owner as a member of the media. The court left it to the discretion of the assistant AD as to when to allow access. *Smith v. Plati*, 258 F.3d 1167 (10th Cir. 2001). [CO]

A. Eligibility of Participants

◆ *In a secondary school case, the U.S. Supreme Court noted that students have a lesser expectation of privacy than the general populace, and that student-athletes have an even lower expectation of privacy in the locker room.* **The Court upheld a random drug testing program imposed by an Oregon school district because the insignificant invasion of student privacy was outweighed by the school's interest in addressing drug use by students who risked physical harm while playing sports.** Similarly, drug testing programs applicable to private schools have been upheld under the notion that student athletes have a lower expectation of privacy. *Vernonia School Dist. 47J v. Acton,* 515 U.S. 646, 115 S.Ct. 2386, 132 L.Ed.2d 564 (1995). [OR]

◆ *Student athletes have a lower expectation of privacy than the general student population, and the NCAA has an interest in protecting the health and safety of student athletes involved in NCAA-regulated competition.*

In 1986, the NCAA instituted a drug testing program for six categories of banned drugs including steroids and street drugs. Under the program, the drug tests took place at championship competitions. In order to participate, all students had to sign a consent form at the start of each school year allowing the drug tests. Two Stanford athletes instituted an action in a California trial court, alleging that the drug testing program violated their right to privacy. The court granted a preliminary injunction prohibiting the NCAA from enforcing its drug testing program against Stanford or its students, except in football and men's basketball. After a full trial, the court permanently enjoined the NCAA from enforcing any aspect of its drug-testing program against Stanford or its students, including those involved in football and basketball. The Court of Appeal of California affirmed the judgment.

The NCAA appealed to the Supreme Court of California, which reversed the decisions of the lower courts, noting that student athletes had a lower expectation of privacy than the general student population. Observation of urination obviously implicated privacy interests. However, by its nature, participation in highly competitive post-season championship events involved close regulation and scrutiny of the physical fitness and bodily condition of student athletes. **Required physical examinations (including urinalysis) and the special regulation of sleep habits, diet, fitness and other activities that intrude significantly on privacy interests are routine aspects of a college athlete's life not shared by other students or the population at large.** Further, the court noted that drug testing programs involving student athletes have routinely survived Fourth Amendment privacy challenges. The court concluded that the NCAA had an interest in protecting the health and safety of student athletes involved in NCAA-regulated competition. *Hill v. NCAA,* 26 Cal.Rptr.2d 834 (Cal. 1994). [CA]

◆ *A drug testing program was struck down where it was not voluntary, and where the college athletes did not have a diminished expectation of privacy.*

The University of Colorado conducted a drug testing program for intercollegiate athletes that entailed a urine test at each annual physical with random tests thereafter. A program amendment substituted random rapid eye examinations for urinalysis, and the university prohibited any athlete refusing to consent to the testing from participating in intercollegiate athletics. The program called for progressive sanctions ranging from required participation in rehabilitation programs to permanent suspension from athletics. A group of athletes filed a class action suit against the university in a Colorado trial court seeking declaratory and injunctive relief. The court ruled for the athletes.

The Colorado Court of Appeals affirmed this decision, and the university appealed to the Supreme Court of Colorado. The court observed that the program did not ensure confidentiality and was mandatory, inasmuch as refusal to participate disqualified students from participating in university athletic programs. **The university was unable to articulate an important governmental interest for the program. Unlike cases involving high school athletes, college students did not have a diminished expectation of privacy under the Fourth Amendment that justified government searches in the absence of an important governmental interest.** Random, suspicionless urinalysis was unconstitutional. University student athletes did not consent to participation in the program because there could be no voluntary consent where the failure to consent resulted in denial of a governmental benefit. The court affirmed the decision for the athletes. *University of Colorado v. Derdeyn*, 863 P.2d 929 (Colo. 1993). [CO]

◆ *The U.S. Supreme Court held that the NCAA is not a state actor for purposes of liability under 42 U.S.C. § 1983.*

Following a lengthy investigation of allegedly improper recruiting practices by the University of Nevada, Las Vegas (UNLV), the NCAA found 38 violations, including 10 by the school's head basketball coach. The NCAA proposed a number of sanctions and threatened to impose more if the coach was not suspended. Facing an enormous pay cut, the coach sued the NCAA under 42 U.S.C. § 1983 for violating his due process rights. The Nevada Supreme Court held the NCAA's conduct constituted state action for constitutional purposes. It upheld a state trial court's dismissal of the suspension and an award of attorney's fees.

The NCAA appealed to **the U.S. Supreme Court, which held that the NCAA's participation in the events that led to the suspension did not constitute state action within the meaning of § 1983. The NCAA was not a state actor** on the theory that it misused the power it possessed under state law. UNLV's decision to suspend the coach in compliance with the NCAA's rules and recommendations did not turn the NCAA's conduct into state action. This was because UNLV retained the power to withdraw from the NCAA and establish its own standards. The NCAA could not directly discipline the coach, but could threaten to impose additional sanctions against the school. It was the school's decision and not the NCAA's to suspend the coach. *NCAA v. Tarkanian*, 488 U.S. 179, 109 S.Ct. 454, 102 L.Ed.2d 469 (1988). [NV]

◆ *A soccer player who was subject to sanctions after transferring from USC to UCLA failed to demonstrate that an athletic conference transfer rule violated federal antitrust laws.*

The player decided to attend the University of Southern California. USC athletic officials purportedly told her that she would be free to transfer to another school without penalty as long as she finished her freshman year at USC and met all academic requirements. After allegedly learning that USC athletes received fraudulent academic credit, the player transferred to the University of California, Los Angeles. Both USC and UCLA are members of the Pacific Ten collegiate athletic association. USC opposed the transfer and sought sanctions against the player pursuant to the Pac-10's transfer rule, which would not allow her to play soccer for UCLA during her first year there. As a result, the player sued USC, the USC officials who recruited her and the Pac-10. She alleged that USC had enforced Pac-10 sanctions only against her and never against other transferring athletes because she participated in an investigation into possible academic fraud at USC. She asserted that the transfer rule conflicted with the federal Sherman Act, 15 U.S.C. § 1, which prohibits contracts or conspiracies that restrain trade or commerce. A federal court dismissed her complaint, finding the Pac-10 transfer rule was out of reach of the Sherman Act. The player appealed to the Ninth Circuit.

The student claimed violated the Sherman Act under the rule-of-reason analysis. A restraint such as the transfer rule violates the rule of reason if its harm to interstate competition outweighs its competitive benefits. The player had to prove that the transfer rule produced significant anti-competitive effects in relevant geographic and product markets. A geographic market is an area where consumers can obtain a product from more than one source. A product market is the group of competing goods. The player claimed the relevant geographic market in this case was the Los Angeles area, and the relevant product market was the UCLA women's soccer program. The Ninth Circuit rejected this interpretation. First, it noted that schools outside the Los Angeles area attempted to recruit the player for similar soccer programs, so the relevant geographic market should extend to the national market of women's collegiate soccer programs. Similarly, her contention that the UCLA program was the relevant product market was rejected because it was interchangeable with many programs across the country. Even if the player had correctly asserted that the relevant market was national in scope, her suit would have failed because she objected to a Pac-10 transfer rule, which only applies to member schools and not the entire national market of college soccer programs. Finally, **because the player admitted she was the only USC athlete to suffer sanctions under the transfer rule, she conceded that the transfer rule does not affect all relevant consumers, thereby foiling her antitrust claim**. *Tanaka v. University of Southern California*, 252 F.3d 1059 (9th Cir. 2001). [CA]

◆ *A wrestler who transferred from the University of Nebraska to Brown University had to sit out for one year because he was not in good academic standing.*

The student, a talented wrestler, failed a course during his first semester at Nebraska and did not repeat the course before transferring to Brown. The NCAA notified him he would be prohibited from wrestling the next academic year because he had not successfully repeated the course. The student sued the NCAA in a federal district court, seeking an injunction to restrain the NCAA from preventing him from wrestling. The court denied the injunction. **NCAA** regulations prevent athletic participation for one year after transfer. There is an exception to this rule for students in good academic standing that would have been eligible to participate had they remained at their previous institution. Since he had failed the course, he would have been ineligible at Nebraska, so he was also ineligible at Brown. In addition, the student could not bring constitutional claims since the NCAA is a private actor, not a state agent. *Collier v. NCAA*, 783 F.Supp. 1576 (D.R.I. 1992). [RI]

◆ *The Massachusetts Civil Rights Act did not prohibit a drug testing policy that required varsity student athletes to sign a drug testing consent form.*

A private Massachusetts university required its varsity athletes to sign an NCAA student-athlete statement, which included a drug testing consent form. The university also required its athletes to sign a university drug testing consent form as a condition for participating in varsity athletics. The university's program required student athletes to be tested once each year for specific drugs and also authorized random testing throughout the year. Testing was required for all athletes before NCAA post-season competition. In practice, the university only tested its athletes prior to post-season competition. Students had the right to appeal to the university's review board at any time. A student who had participated in the university's track and field and cross-country teams signed the consent forms. Later he revoked them by letter and refused to sign either the university or NCAA drug testing consent forms. The university declared the student ineligible for varsity sports. The student was otherwise eligible to participate. Claiming that the university's program violated the Massachusetts Civil Rights Act, the student sued the university in a Massachusetts trial court. The court ruled in favor of the student, and the university appealed to the Massachusetts Supreme Judicial Court.

The court ruled that in order to prove a case under the state civil rights act, the complaining party must prove that a right guaranteed by the Constitution or laws of the U.S. or Massachusetts had been interfered with by threats, intimidation or coercion. The civil rights act was intended to provide a remedy for victims of racial harassment. According to the court, the state legislature did not intend to create a vast constitutional tort. **The act's application was limited to situations in which actual threats, intimidation or coercion were present.** The student had not proven that these conditions were present in the university's program. The court reversed the trial court's decision in favor of the student. *Bally v. Northeastern Univ.*, 532 N.E.2d 49 (Mass. 1989). [MA]

B. Students with Disabilities

◆ *A potential student athlete's challenge to the NCAA's core course requirement was allowed to proceed in the following case.*

A student with a learning disability who was deemed ineligible to play Division I football during his freshman year sued the NCAA, two universities that stopped recruiting him once he was declared ineligible, and the ACT/Clearinghouse, claiming the NCAA "core course" requirement violated Rehabilitation Act § 504 and the Americans with Disabilities Act (ADA). The **court denied the NCAA's motion for summary judgment, finding evidence** that its blanket exclusion of all courses taught "below the high school's regular instructional level (e.g., remedial, special education or compensatory)" from consideration as core courses was not facially neutral and was premised on a specified level of academic achievement that persons with disabilities were less capable of meeting. The court determined that the student should receive a trial to determine whether the NCAA was liable for monetary damages and should be granted full athletic eligibility. The court held that his claim based on the alleged deprivation of a chance to play professional football was too speculative to survive pre-trial dismissal. Further, it held he was without legal standing to challenge NCAA initial eligibility rules because he would never again be subject to them.

The NCAA moved the court for reargument, noting that the court had presumed that the student could never regain his full allotment of four years of athletic eligibility. The NCAA argued that its rules had been changed as the consequence of a 1998 consent decree between it and the U.S. Department of Justice. Under current NCAA regulations, partial and nonqualifying student athletes eventually could gain a fourth year of athletic eligibility. Since the student had not lost any athletic eligibility, the NCAA argued that his claim for injunctive relief was now moot. It further alleged that the student lacked standing to seek injunctive relief because he could not prove that he lost any years of eligibility due to its discriminatory conduct. The court agreed with the NCAA that the prior order had presumed that the student had forever lost a year of eligibility under pre-1998 NCAA rules. Under the current rules, he could regain a fourth year of athletic eligibility. The court held the student no longer had standing to seek injunctive relief against the NCAA. It amended its order to dismiss the claims seeking injunctive relief under the ADA and § 504. **The student was otherwise entitled to proceed with his ADA claims against the universities, and his § 504 claims against the universities and NCAA**. *Bowers v. NCAA*, 130 F.Supp.2d 610 (D.N.J. 2001). [NJ]

When Temple University sought an order requiring the University of Memphis (which also had recruited the student) to contribute to any potential damage award, the University of Memphis claimed sovereign immunity, but the court ruled that **Congress had validly eliminated immunity under Title II of the ADA**, and that the acceptance of Rehabilitation Act funds amounted to a waiver under that act. *Bowers v. NCAA*, 171 F.Supp.2d 389 (D.N.J. 2001). [NJ]

◆ *The performance of a specific activity, such as playing basketball, did not constitute a major life activity, and the student was not a qualified individual entitled to protection under § 504 of the Rehabilitation Act.*

A high school student suffered sudden cardiac death while playing basketball. He was resuscitated and a defibrillator was implanted in his body to restart his heart in case it stopped again. He had been recruited to play basketball by an Illinois university that stated it would honor his scholarship despite his medical condition. He was later found medically ineligible to play and, although he maintained his scholarship and his place on the team, he could not compete or practice. He filed sued the university in federal district court, alleging a violation of § 504 and requesting an injunction allowing him to play. The court found that playing basketball was a major life activity for the student and by not allowing him to play, the university violated § 504. The court granted the injunction. The university appealed.

The U.S. Court of Appeals, Seventh Circuit, held that **participating in intercollegiate athletics is not a major life activity.** In the regulations interpreting § 504, a major life activity is defined as a basic life function such as caring for one's self, walking, breathing or speaking. The court held that performing a specific activity, such as playing basketball, does not fit in with this list. It also held that the student's impairment did not prevent him from obtaining an adequate education and therefore did not limit his major life activity of learning. The court then found that as a matter of law, **the student was not a qualified individual.** To be qualified to play college basketball, the student had to meet all of the university's technical and physical requirements. The court found that the student's risk of potential injury was too great. Although some level of risk is inherent in all athletic activities, the student in this case faced the possibility of death. Because the university rationally and reasonably reviewed all of the medical evidence before making its decision, the court held that it had the right to find the student ineligible to play. The court reversed the district court's decision and denied the injunction. *Knapp v. Northwestern Univ.*, 101 F.3d 473 (7th Cir. 1996). [IL]

♦ *A college football player with a disability could be prohibited from continuing to play without violating § 504 of the Rehabilitation Act.*

A University of Kansas student who was on a football scholarship experienced an episode of transient quadriplegia during a scrimmage. The team physician discovered that the student had a congenital condition that put him at an extremely high risk for suffering severe and potentially permanent neurological injuries, including quadriplegia. **The university disqualified the student from participating in intercollegiate football.** Although he obtained opinions from three other doctors stating that his risk of injury was no greater than any other player's, the university denied his request to rejoin the football team. He filed a lawsuit against the university in a federal district court, claiming it had violated § 504, which prohibits discrimination by recipients of federal funding against individuals on the basis of disability, if the individual is otherwise qualified to participate in the recipient's programs or activities. The court denied the university's motion to dismiss the lawsuit, and the student filed a motion for a preliminary order to allow his reinstatement to the football team.

Because § 504's definition of a person with a disability involves a consideration of whether the individual is impaired in some major life activity, the court considered whether intercollegiate athletic participation was a major life activity. The university argued that it was not, because the general population cannot participate in college athletics. The student argued that his grades improved, and he gained many other opportunities for personal development by playing on the team. **The court agreed that playing football was related to the major life activity of learning, but held that his disqualification was not a substantial limitation on his continuing ability to learn.** The university had not revoked the student's athletic scholarship, and he retained the opportunity to participate in the football program in a role other than player. The court accepted the conclusion of the university's physicians that there was a reasonable basis for his exclusion from the team that did not violate § 504. The court denied the student's motion. *Pahulu v. University of Kansas*, 897 F.Supp. 1387 (D. Kan. 1995). [KS]

C. Academic Restrictions

The National Collegiate Athletic Association (NCAA) imposes academic requirements on collegiate student athletes. The academic requirements may include specific course requirements or designated grade point averages.

◆ *A former college baseball player, who alleged that he was denied an opportunity to participate on the baseball team during his senior year because he was given improper academic advice by the school's athletic academic counselor, was allowed to proceed with his suit for damages.*

For the first three years of his athletic eligibility, the player attended St. Leo College, a Division II school in Florida, on a partial scholarship. After three years, he decided to transfer to Division I Clemson University. He contacted one of Clemson's academic advisors about enrolling in classes. His main objective was to remain eligible to play baseball. Clemson did not offer the player's major, so the advisor suggested that he declare a different major. Under the NCAA's 50-percent rule, student-athletes must complete at least half of the course requirements of their degree programs to be eligible to compete during the fourth year of school. The advisor gave the player erroneous advice about what classes to take. Realizing the mistake, Clemson sought a waiver of the 50-percent rule. The NCAA denied the waiver, and the student did not play. The next year, the player returned to St. Leo College, completed his degree and played baseball for a final season. He then sued Clemson in a South Carolina court for negligence, breach of fiduciary duty and breach of contract.

The court granted Clemson's motion for pretrial judgment, holding that the player did not advance any tort theory under the South Carolina Tort Claims Act because the university's course of action did not constitute gross negligence. On appeal, the court agreed with the player that the trial court should not have decided the issue of gross negligence. **There were issues of fact as to whether the advisor committed gross negligence.** Although the advisor realized her mistake not even two weeks into the semester, she did not contact the athletic department supervisor or the NCAA compliance director, which was standard procedure. The appeals court also agreed that there may have been a breach of fiduciary duty and a breach of contract on the part of the university. The court remanded the case for reconsideration. *Hendricks v. Clemson Univ.*, 339 S.C. 552, 529 S.E.2d 293 (S.C. App. 2000). [SC]

◆ *A non-qualifying student whose scholarship was withdrawn could not sue Kansas State University (KSU) because of the Eleventh Amendment.*

A student was offered an NCAA-approved track scholarship at KSU that covered her tuition, fees, room, board and books. However, after she enrolled, KSU withdrew the scholarship when it learned **the NCAA Initial-Eligibility Clearinghouse had failed to certify the student because she was a "nonqualifier,"** having failed two high school classes. The clearinghouse report was not produced until after the student had enrolled. When KSU sought to recover tuition and other expenses for the fall semester, the student and her father sued KSU for breach of contract and fraud, also suing several KSU officials, including the track coach. A federal district court held KSU was immune to suit under the Eleventh Amendment,which prohibits a suit by an individual against a state in federal court. Since KSU had not consented to be sued, the student and her father could not maintain their action against it. Further, the officials had been acting in their official capacities; thus, they also were entitled to Eleventh Amendment immunity. *Adams v. Kansas State Univ.*, 27 F.Supp.2d 469 (S.D.N.Y. 1998). [NY]

◆   *An Illinois court held a student's religious courses and computer classes were not "core courses" under the NCAA academic eligibility requirements.*

The NCAA sets eligibility requirements for Division I competition, which mandate that students take at least 13 high school "core courses" and that students achieve a specified minimum grade point average in those courses, as well as a specified minimum score on either the SAT or ACT. The higher a student's test score, the lower the required GPA needed. An 18-year-old black student who excelled at basketball graduated from a private, Catholic high school. He was heavily recruited by colleges and universities, and selected a private Illinois university. The NCAA ruled the student was not qualified to compete in Division I play during his freshman season, and he sued the NCAA in a federal district court for an order allowing him to play in his freshman year.

The student asserted that the NCAA had improperly found him to be ineligible by excluding from the "core course" requirements two religion and two computer classes. The court determined the religion courses **were taught from a particular religious point of view—based on a Christian ideology**. The court also determined that, based on the syllabi **for the computer classes, at least 50 percent of the course instruction included keyboarding or word processing,** which took the classes outside core status. As a result, the student did not have even a negligible chance of success on the merits of his claim, and he was not entitled to injunctive relief. Further, the student's claims of breach of contract and misrepresentation likewise had a very slim chance of success. The court refused to overrule the NCAA's eligibility determination, and the student was not allowed to play basketball during his freshman season. *Hall v. NCAA*, 985 F.Supp. 782 (N.D. Ill. 1997). [IL]

◆   *Although the NCAA denied a student academic eligibility waiver arbitrarily, bad faith required a finding of a dishonest purpose.*

A high school senior intended to attend a private university under a basketball scholarship. However, the NCAA held he failed to complete the minimum of 13 "core courses" required under its eligibility standards. It notified the student that he was ineligible under NCAA guidelines to play college basketball for or receive financial aid from the university. The university sought a waiver of the eligibility requirements, which the NCAA denied on the ground that there were neither exceptional circumstances present nor independent evidence of the student's academic qualifications that warranted granting relief. The student sought a preliminary injunction from the U.S. District Court for the

District of Connecticut to prevent the NCAA from further interfering with his opportunity to attend the university and play basketball for its team. The district court granted the motion for an injunction, reasoning that the student would suffer irreparable harm if the injunction were denied, and that he was likely to prevail on his argument that the NCAA breached its duty to the student by arbitrarily refusing to grant him a waiver of its eligibility requirements. The NCAA appealed to the U.S. Court of Appeals, Second Circuit.

The court first determined that the injunction in this case was prohibitory in nature rather than mandatory. Accordingly, its terms would preserve the status quo by restraining the NCAA from acting to interfere with the university's decision to award the student a scholarship and to allow him to play basketball. As a result, the student and the university did not have to meet a heightened standard to obtain injunctive relief. However, the court then held that the district court had erred in finding that the NCAA had exhibited bad faith simply by acting arbitrarily. Under Connecticut law, bad faith means more than mere negligence; it involves a dishonest purpose. Here, **despite determining that the NCAA had arbitrarily refused to grant the student a waiver because it had granted waivers in similar cases in the past, the court failed to make a factual finding of bad intent**. The court remanded the case and left the injunction intact. However, it conditioned the maintenance of the injunction upon commencement of a trial on the merits within four months. *Phillip v. Fairfield Univ.*, 118 F.3d 131 (2d Cir. 1997). [CT]

D. Eligibility of Schools

◆   *The Fifth Circuit found that the NCAA's suspension of all athletic programs at a private university did not violate any property interests.*

An alumnus of Southern Methodist University (SMU) sued the NCAA in a federal district court on behalf of SMU, other SMU graduates, current SMU students, football team members and cheerleaders. The action challenged the NCAA's suspension of all 1987 SMU athletic programs and alleged that the NCAA had violated federal antitrust laws by restricting compensation to college football players. This allegedly violated price-fixing restraints under the Sherman Anti-Trust Act. The SMU suspension allegedly constituted a "group boycott" by NCAA members. The complaint also contained civil rights claims, which alleged that the suspension destroyed the careers of SMU football players and caused the cheerleaders emotional distress. The NCAA allegedly imposed these penalties on SMU repeatedly in a manner that violated due process of law. The lawsuit requested an order preventing the suspension as well as the payment of monetary damages in excess of $200 million.

The dismissed the lawsuit. The alumnus appealed to the U.S. Court of Appeals, Fifth Circuit, which noted that SMU had failed to represent itself in the lawsuit. The alumnus could not properly bring a suit on SMU's behalf, and the complaint failed to state any legal grounds. **No property interests were violated by the NCAA suspension and the damages were insufficient to support an antitrust lawsuit.** According to the court, **NCAA eligibility rules were reasonable and did not constitute price fixing**. They were an appropriate means to integrate athletics with academics. Enforcement of the rules did not constitute an illegal group boycott. The district court had properly dismissed the civil rights claims. State participation in a private entity such as the NCAA does not make the entity a state actor unless the entity enforces state laws. Because no state action existed in the enforcement of NCAA rules, there was no basis for the federal civil rights complaint. *McCormack v. NCAA*, 845 F.2d 1338 (5th Cir. 1988). [TX]

◆ *Although a private university was prevented from participating in NCAA championship playoffs, a federal court refused to grant an injunction to allow its participation since the other schools would have suffered harm if displaced by the university.*

Howard University's football team compiled a regular season record of nine wins and one loss in 1987. This was one of the best records for all National Collegiate Athletic Association (NCAA) Division I-AA schools. Howard won the championship of its conference, the Mid-Eastern Athletic Conference (MEAC). All of the MEAC schools including Howard are known as traditionally black institutions. Despite its fine season, Howard was excluded from the Division 1-AA championship. Howard brought an antitrust action in a federal district court, seeking to prevent the NCAA from holding its championship playoffs until a decision by the district court was issued.

The court noted that in order to obtain an injunction, Howard would have to show that it was likely to prevail in its case, that it would be irreparably harmed without the injunction, that other parties would not suffer substantial harm, and that the public interest would be served. While noting that Howard's low ranking by the committee ran contrary to logic, the possibility that Howard would suffer irreparable harm was balanced by the potential that any of the other 16 teams already in the playoffs would suffer equal harm if displaced by Howard. Because **the playoff games were already set and scheduled with television arrangements**, the district court was unwilling to delay the playoff schedule. **Any delay of the playoff games would be disruptive and cause severe hardships to the teams already selected.** Howard's interest was outweighed by that of the general public, and the games would commence as scheduled. *Howard Univ. v. NCAA*, 675 F.Supp. 652 (D.D.C. 1987). [DC]

E. Discrimination

Title IX of the Education Amendments of 1972 (20 U.S.C. § 1681 et seq.) addresses sex discrimination in school athletics. It applies only to athletic programs that receive federal financial assistance. One of the most important Title IX implementing regulations provides as follows:

A recipient that operates or sponsors interscholastic, intercollegiate, club or intramural athletics shall provide equal athletic opportunity for members of both sexes. In determining whether equal opportunities are available the Director will consider, among other factors:
(1) Whether the selection of sports and levels of competition effectively accommodate the interests and abilities of members of both sexes;
(2) The provision of equipment and supplies;

(3) Scheduling of games and practice time;
(4) Travel and per diem allowance;
(5) Opportunity to receive coaching and academic tutoring;
(6) Assignment and compensation of coaches and tutors;
(7) Provision of locker rooms, practice and competitive facilities;
(8) Provision of medical and training facilities and services;
(9) Provision of housing and dining facilities and services;
(10) Publicity.

Unequal aggregate expenditures for members of each sex or unequal expenditures for male and female teams if a recipient operates or sponsors separate teams will not constitute noncompliance with this section, but the Assistant Secretary may consider the failure to provide necessary funds for teams for one sex in assessing equality of opportunity for members of each sex. [34 CFR § 106.41(c).]

◆   *The U.S. Supreme Court has held that the NCAA is not a recipient of federal funds and is therefore not subject to suit under Title IX.*

The case was filed by a college graduate who had played two years of intercollegiate volleyball at a private college before enrolling in postgraduate programs at two other colleges. Because she had exhausted only two years of her athletic eligibility, she sought a waiver from the NCAA's Postbaccalaureate Bylaw, which allows postgraduate student-athletes to compete in intercollegiate sports only at the institution where they received an undergraduate degree. The student sued the NCAA in a Pennsylvania federal court after it denied her requests for a waiver. She claimed that the NCAA discriminated against her on the basis of gender in violation of Title IX. The complaint asserted that the NCAA granted more waivers to male postgraduate students than it did to females. The case reached the U.S. Supreme Court, which noted that Title IX covers entities that receive federal financial assistance—whether direct or indirect—whereas those entities that only benefit economically from federal financial assistance are not covered. **Because the NCAA only benefited economically from institutions that received federal financial assistance, it could not be sued under Title IX.** *NCAA v. Smith,* 525 U.S. 459, 119 S.Ct. 924, 142 L.Ed.2d 929 (1999). [PA]

◆   *A university could eliminate three men's teams to come into compliance with Title IX.*

An Ohio university with a history of disproportionately few women athletes determined that the best way to achieve gender equity under Title IX was to eliminate three men's teams. It eliminated men's soccer, tennis and wrestling. In the lawsuit that followed, the men's teams asserted that the decision to cut their teams violated Title IX and the Equal Protection Clause. A federal court ruled in favor of the university, and the Sixth Circuit affirmed. The policy interpretation of Title IX allowed the elimination of men's sports to comply with the law, and the men's teams were not challenging the constitutionality of either Title IX or its regulations. Moreover, **participation in collegiate athletics is not a constitutional right. Nor does Title IX grant rights to male athletes.** The court determined that there was no equal protection violation in the elimination of the teams. *Miami Univ. Wrestling Club v. Miami Univ.*, 302 F.3d 608 (6th Cir. 2002). [OH]

◆ *A university could cut men's wrestling to comply with Title IX.*

The University of North Dakota issued a report on gender equity in athletics in 1995, recommending that women's golf, tennis and soccer be added in the next few years to increase female athletic participation and decrease the difference between male and female athletic participation at the university. The report did not recommend any changes in men's athletics. Three years later, the university faced a budget crunch and eliminated the men's wrestling program in an effort to cut $95,000 from the athletic department's budget. The move also was made to comply with the dictates of Title IX. When wrestlers and recruits sued the university, claiming that the program elimination actually violated Title IX by discriminating against them on the basis of gender, a federal court ruled in favor of the university. The Eighth Circuit Court of Appeals affirmed. It noted that **the elimination of men's teams is a permissible means of complying with Title IX**. By eliminating wrestling, the university was following the "substantially proportionate" standard set forth in the regulations interpreting Title IX. The U.S. Department of Education has allowed universities to cut men's programs as a way to provide substantially proportionate participation opportunities for both male and female students. *Chalenor v. University of North Dakota*, 291 F.3d 1042 (8th Cir. 2002). [ND]

◆ *Four student-athletes were allowed to bring a class action Title IX lawsuit against a New Mexico university.*

Four female student-athletes at a New Mexico university filed a proposed class action lawsuit against the university under Title IX and the state constitution, seeking compensatory and equitable relief. While the judge deliberated on whether to grant class certification, a trial ensued and **a jury ruled in favor of the student-athletes, awarding them compensatory damages**. When the judge denied class certification, the athletes' request for declaratory and injunctive relief was denied. The athletes appealed to the Tenth Circuit Court of Appeals, which reversed the denial of class status. Here, the evidence indicated that one of the students was on the soccer team at the time the suit was filed. As a result, the lower court should not have ruled that the plaintiffs were not entitled to class status. The court also reversed the order denying injunctive and declaratory relief. *Paton v. New Mexico Highlands Univ.*, 275 F.3d 1274 (10th Cir. 2002). [NM]

◆ *A female place kicker who was dropped from the Duke University football team because of her sex was not entitled to punitive damages under Title IX.*

A female student who made the Duke University football team but was later dropped from it sued the university in a federal district court. She alleged discrimination in violation of Title IX when the football coach refused to allow her to participate in summer camps, games, and practices, and made offensive comments to her regarding her attempts to participate in the football program. After the case was initially dismissed, the Fourth Circuit concluded that once the student was allowed to try out for football, the university could not discriminate against her based on her sex. Although Title IX regulations made a distinction between contact and non-contact sports operated for members of one sex, the court concluded that this distinction vanished once a member of the opposite sex was allowed to try out for a single-sex contact sport team. Since the student was a member of the university's male football team at one point, her allegations of discrimination under Title IX stated a cause of action.

At trial, the student was awarded $1 in compensatory damages and $2 million in punitive damages from a jury. Duke sought to set aside the punitive damages award, arguing that even if the evidence supported the judgment, there is no clear-cut legal authority stating that punitive damages are allowable under Title IX. The Fourth Circuit again heard the case and agreed that the student was not entitled to punitive damages under Title IX. **Since Title IX is modeled after Title VI, and since the Supreme Court has held that punitive damages are not available in private actions brought under Title VI** [*see Barnes v. Gorman*, 536 U.S. 181 (2002)], **the court concluded that they are not available under Title IX either.** The court remanded the case for a determination of whether the student was entitled to her attorneys' fees. *Mercer v. Duke Univ.*, 50 Fed. Appx. 643 (4th Cir. 2002). [NC]

◆ *Two black student athletes could pursue their race discrimination lawsuit against the NCAA under Proposition 16.*

The NCAA uses Proposition 16 to determine which first-year college students can play Division I and II sports. The rule uses a combination of high-school grades in NCAA-approved "core courses" and scores on such standardized tests as the SAT and the ACT to determine eligibility. Two black students who signed national letters of intent to play sports at Division I schools failed to meet the NCAA's test score requirements. They were not allowed to play intercollegiate athletics their freshman year. The students sued the NCAA in a federal district court, alleging the NCAA intentionally discriminated against them on the basis of race in violation of Title VI of the Civil Rights Act of 1964 and 42 U.S.C. § 1981, and violated the Americans with Disabilities Act (ADA) and § 504 regarding one of the athletes.

In evaluating the ADA and § 504 claims, the court noted one athlete had suffered an injury by being denied athletic eligibility. She proved causation by claiming the design of Proposition 16 discriminated against her because of a disability. However, these claims failed because an NCAA rule change allows student-athletes who do not qualify for their initial year of eligibility to recoup that lost year with good grades. As a result, **the athlete was not denied a year of eligibility by failing to meet the initial qualifying requirements, and lacked standing to bring her ADA and § 504 claims.** The court then dismissed the race discrimination claims brought under Title VI and § 1981. On appeal, the Third Circuit reversed in part, noting **the students sufficiently alleged race discrimination** under § 1981 to survive pretrial dismissal. Their claim that the NCAA considered race when it adopted Proposition 16 could proceed further. However, the Title VI, ADA, and § 504 claims were properly dismissed. *Pryor v. NCAA*, 288 F.3d 548 (3d Cir. 2002). [PA]

◆ *The NCAA could not be sued under Title VI on the grounds that Proposition 16 had a disparate impact on African-American students.*

A number of African-American high school student athletes graduated with GPAs that exceeded the NCAA's requirements. However, they all scored lower than the minimum SAT score required for participation in Division I collegiate athletics as freshmen. They sued the NCAA, asserting that the minimum SAT score requirement of Proposition 16 had a disparate impact on African-American athletes in violation of Title VI. The NCAA maintained that it was not subject to Title VI because it did not receive direct financial assistance. A Pennsylvania federal court found that the NCAA was subject to suit under Title VI, and that Proposition 16 had a disparate impact on African-Americans.

The NCAA appealed, and the Third Circuit Court of Appeals reversed. It assumed without deciding that the NCAA received federal financial assistance. However, it then stated that **Title VI was intended to be program specific. In other words, it only prohibited discrimination in the programs or activities that received federal funds.** Further, even though Congress had enacted the Civil Rights Restoration Act to broaden the protections of Title VI and Title IX, the U.S. Department of Education had not yet enacted regulations to implement that statute. It was unclear whether those regulations could prohibit neutral actions that had a discriminatory effect (disparate impact discrimination) or whether they could only prohibit intentional (disparate treatment) discrimination. As a result, **the NCAA did not come under the umbrella of Title VI. It was not a direct recipient of federal funds and did not exert sufficient authority over its member institutions to make it liable under Title VI.** *Cureton v. NCAA*, 198 F.3d 107 (3d Cir. 1999). [PA]

◆ *The Fifth Circuit held that discrimination under Title IX was intentional even where it was motivated by chauvinistic notions rather than by enmity.*

A number of female undergraduate students at Louisiana State University brought separate lawsuits under Title IX, alleging that the university discriminated against women in the provision of facilities and teams for intercollegiate athletic competition. A federal district court held that LSU had violated and continued to violate Title IX, but determined that it had not intentionally violated the statute. As a result, the female students were not entitled to monetary damages. On appeal, the Fifth Circuit Court of Appeals determined that LSU had intentionally violated Title IX. The court stated that paternalism and stereotypical assumptions about female students' abilities and interests led to the decision not to provide equal facilities and teams for female students. **It did not matter that LSU had no intention to discriminate against women. What mattered was that it intended to treat women differently. By holding onto archaic assumptions about women in sports, LSU perpetuated a grossly discriminatory athletics system.** The court reversed the district court's decision, finding that LSU intentionally discriminated against female students in violation of Title IX. *Pederson v. Louisiana State Univ.*, 213 F.3d 858 (5th Cir. 2000). [LA]

◆   *The Ninth Circuit held that a university could reduce athletic opportunities for male students in order to come into compliance with Title IX.*

A California university with a high percentage of female students, but low participation rates in female interscholastic athletics, attempted to comply with Title IX by capping the roster of the men's wrestling team at 25. After team members sued, the Ninth Circuit held that a university could reduce athletic opportunities for male students to comply with Title IX. Later, the university eliminated the men's wrestling team. This helped the university meet the proportionality standard of Title IX's regulations. Team members again sued for gender discrimination under Title IX. The case again reached the Ninth Circuit, which upheld the university's action. Congress enacted Title IX with the understanding that male athletes had an enormous head start over female athletes for athletic resources. The intent of the act was to level the playing field and encourage female athletic participation. **Title IX permits universities to reduce athletic opportunities for male athletes** in order to bring participation into line with lower opportunities available for females. *Neal v. Board of Trustees of California State Universities*, 51 Fed. Appx. 736 (9th Cir. 2002). [CA]

◆   *Like the court in the case above, the Seventh Circuit held that eliminating athletic opportunities for men was not a violation of Title IX.*

Illinois State University responded to disproportionate athletic participation rates and budget concerns by dropping men's wrestling and soccer programs, adjusting men's team rosters, adding a women's soccer program and adjusting grants in aid for both sexes. Male enrollment at Illinois State was only 45 percent, but the athletic participation rate for males was 66 percent. The university decided to focus on the goal of substantial proportionality in athletic participation as a means of complying with Title IX. After making the adjustments, female athletic participation rose to almost 52 percent, while the male rate slipped to 48 percent. Former members of the men's soccer and wrestling team sued the university in a federal district court for Title IX and Equal Protection Clause violations.

The case reached the Seventh Circuit, which rejected arguments that the university could not eliminate male programs when the decision was motivated by sex-based considerations. Office for Civil Rights policy interpretations clearly stated that Title IX compliance may be shown where there is proof that female athletic participation is substantially proportionate to female enrollment. The court noted that **male athletic participation remained within three percentage points of male enrollment**. This did not violate the Equal Protection Clause. *Boulahanis v. Board of Regents, Illinois State Univ.*, 198 F.3d 633 (7th Cir. 1999). [IL]

◆   *An Iowa university was allowed to spend more money on scholarships for female athletes, even though male athletes represented the majority of athletes at the university, in order to meet its requirements under Title IX regulations.*

A strategic planning commission for the university recommended that the school terminate its wrestling program based on budgetary constraints. The director of athletics was not informed of this decision and told newly recruited wrestlers about the school's "total commitment" to the program. The undergraduate student body during the 1992-1993 school year was 57.2 percent female and 42.8 percent male but 75.3 percent of the athletes were men. The school spent 47 percent of its total athletic scholarship budget on male athletes and 53 percent on females. Male wrestlers sued the university in a federal district court for Title IX and constitutional violations.

The court noted a Title IX regulation, 34 C.F.R. § 106.37(c)(1), required universities to award scholarships "in proportion to the number of students of each sex participating in ... athletics." However, another regulation, 34 C.F.R. § 106.41(c)(1), required universities to provide "equal athletic opportunity for members of both sexes." The wrestlers argued that compliance with § 106.37 did not preclude liability under § 106.41. The court disagreed, ruling that such a holding might lock scholarships in at the current participation ratio and perpetuate the under-representation of women in university athletics. **Restricting universities from eliminating men's scholarship sports under 34 C.F.R. § 106.37 while requiring them to expand athletics under § 106.41 would improperly restrain their spending decisions**. Because § 106.37 served the remedial purposes of Title IX more effectively than § 106.41, the court granted summary judgment to the university on this claim. It dismissed the Equal Protection Clause challenge to Title IX as applied to the wrestlers, ruling that mere disadvantage to males did not support such a constitutional challenge. Since no state action was involved, the court dismissed their constitutional claim against the university based on 42 U.S.C. § 1983. *Gonyo v. Drake Univ.*, 879 F.Supp. 1000 (S.D. Iowa 1995). [IA]

◆   *Title IX liability requires a showing of underrepresentation, ineffective accommodations and lack of responsiveness to the underrepresented gender.*

A Rhode Island private university reduced its women's gymnastics and volleyball teams to intercollegiate club status. The teams lost university funding, admissions preferences, recruiting budgets and coaching salaries. They were permitted to participate in intercollegiate competition provided they raised their operating funds from private sources. Female athletes sued the university in a U.S. district court for Title IX violations. At the time of the lawsuit, the university had 63 percent male athletes and 37 percent female athletes despite a student population of 52 percent males and 48 percent females. The court granted the athletes' motion for a preliminary injunction, reinstating the women's gymnastics and volleyball teams to full varsity status.

The First Circuit Court of Appeals affirmed decision and remanded the case for a trial. The district court applied a U.S. Department of Education Title IX policy interpretation, and held **the university's athletic program did not comply with Title IX gender equity guidelines**. Because far more male athletes than female athletes were university funded, the program violated Title IX regulations. Consequently, the court ordered the university to balance its program to provide equal opportunities for both sexes but left the means of such Title IX compliance to the discretion of the university. *Cohen v. Brown Univ.*, 879 F.Supp. 185 (D.R.I. 1995). [RI]

The district court later held that the subsequently proposed plan failed to comply with Title IX, and ordered specific relief in place of the compliance plan. The university appealed. The First Circuit **rejected the university's** argument that the disparity in athletic opportunities for women was the result of a lack of interest on the part of its female students. However, the district court erred by substituting the order of specific relief in place of the university's compliance plan. Although the plan was ineffective and did not meet the requirements of Title IX, in accordance with academic freedom, places of higher education must be given as much freedom as possible in conducting their own affairs. The university was given another opportunity to submit a plan in compliance with Title IX, and the case was affirmed in part, reversed in part and remanded for further proceedings. *Cohen v. Brown Univ.*, 101 F.3d 155 (1st Cir. 1996). [RI]

◆ *Although a private cause of action to redress violations of Title IX exists, Title IX cannot be applied to school administrators and employees.*

The women's basketball coach at a private Texas university complained about the disparate allocation of resources among the men's and women's athletic programs. She noted inequities between the terms of her employment contract and those of the men's basketball coach. She was discharged three years later, allegedly for violations of NCAA and Southwest Conference rules. She filed a complaint with the U.S. Department of Education's Office of Civil Rights and was reinstated on the same terms under which she had been previously employed. Because she failed to achieve a winning record as required by the contract, her employment was again terminated.

The coach filed a Title IX lawsuit against the university and various officials in a U.S. district court, alleging gender discrimination in its allocation of funds to university athletic programs. The university and officials moved to dismiss the suit. The coach contended that **an employee of a private school that receives federal funds has a private cause of action against that school for damages under Title IX**. The court agreed, noting that the U.S. Supreme Court has created such an implied cause of action with respect to monetary damages for students who are sexually harassed in public schools. It also has held that those directly benefiting from federal grants, loans or contracts clearly fall within Title IX. Although the court found that there is a private cause of action to redress violations of Title IX, **Title IX could not be applied to individuals**, and the lawsuit against the school administrators and employees was dismissed. The lawsuit against the university was allowed to continue. *Bowers v. Baylor Univ.*, 862 F.Supp. 142 (W.D. Tex. 1994). [TX]

◆ *A university could eliminate a men's sports program without eliminating a women's program in order to comply with Title IX.*

The University of Illinois eliminated four varsity athletic programs, including men's swimming, in response to a $600,000 budget shortfall. The decision was in part motivated by the need to comply with Title IX. Participation in women's intercollegiate athletics at the university was disproportionate to female undergraduate enrollment; therefore, the university did not eliminate the women's swimming program. Members of the men's swim team sued the university and its board of trustees in an Illinois federal court, alleging violations of Title IX and their equal protection rights. The case reached the U.S. Court of Appeals, Seventh Circuit, which observed that

elimination of the women's swimming program could have exposed the university to further Title IX violations because of the great disparity between female enrollment and women's sports participation. The university's response to budget constraints had been reasonable and Title IX did not require parallel teams to ensure compliance. *Kelley v. Board of Trustees, Univ. of Illinois,* 35 F.3d 265 (7th Cir. 1994). [IL]

◆ *A university violated Title IX by eliminating women's gymnastics and field hockey, and it could not come into compliance by substituting women's soccer for gymnastics.*

A Pennsylvania university with an undergraduate population that was 56 percent female fielded an equal number of male and female varsity athletic teams. However, male teams had more athletes and were better funded. The university cut men's tennis and soccer and women's gymnastics and field hockey teams because of budget problems. Three female athletes sued the university under Title IX, seeking to force the university to reduce the disparity between men's and women's varsity athletics, and to reinstate women's gymnastics and field hockey. The court granted a preliminary injunction and certified a class. **It then held that the university was not in compliance with Title IX regulations and ordered reinstatement of the gymnastics and field hockey programs.** The university filed a motion to modify the injunction to allow replacement of the gymnastics team with a women's soccer team.

The court refused to modify the injunction, and the university appealed to the U.S. Court of Appeals, Third Circuit. The court observed that modification of an injunction is appropriate only when there has been a change of circumstances making the original order inequitable. There was no such change in circumstances in this case. The district court had not abused its discretion in ordering the temporary preservation of athletic programs. The university's proposal for a women's soccer program as a replacement for the women's gymnastic team would result in a net reduction in funding for women's athletics that was in contravention of Title IX goals. *Favia v. Indiana Univ. of Pennsylvania,* 7 F.3d 332 (3d Cir. 1993). [PA]

◆ *A federal district court determined that limited university resources had to be reallocated more equitably between men's and women's athletic programs requiring "equal opportunity" but not necessarily "equal funding."*

A private New York university had a competitive men's varsity ice hockey team. Hockey was an "emphasized sport" and received special support. Conversely, women's ice hockey was run as an informal club team. The women's requests for varsity status were repeatedly denied by the university's Committee on Athletics. Members of the women's hockey team sued the university under Title IX. The court stated that the women had provided ample evidence indicating unequal treatment. Foremost was the extreme disparity in the university's allocation of funds between the men and women. The men's funding was 50 times that of the women. The court then rejected the university's argument that there was insufficient interest in women's hockey and that there were too few female high school hockey players to justify recruitment efforts. On the contrary, thousands of girls in both the United

States and Canada played hockey on high school teams. Also, many women had shown interest in the university club team. The court also rejected the university's contention that the women lacked the ability expected of a varsity level team. Given the lack of university support, **the women had a sufficiently solid foundation to justify varsity status**. Finally, the court noted that despite the expense of funding a varsity women's hockey program, **"financial concerns alone could not justify gender discrimination."** Limited university resources had to be reallocated more equitably between men's and women's athletic programs. The court ordered the university to grant the women varsity status with "equal opportunity" but not necessarily "equal funding." *Cook v. Colgate Univ.*, 802 F.Supp. 737 (N.D.N.Y. 1992). [NY]

F. Injuries

Under common law, student-athletes were held to assume the risks inherent in participating in school athletics. Consequently, most lawsuits by injured individuals were unsuccessful. However, many courts have replaced the doctrine of assumption of risk with comparative negligence principles that allow at least partial recovery of damages upon proof of negligence.

◆   *An Indiana university was not liable to a varsity baseball player for injuries he suffered while practicing with the team.*

The injury occurred during a baseball team practice inside a university gym. During a practice drill, the student was struck in the eye by a ball thrown by a teammate, causing severe and permanent injury. The student sued the university, coaching staff and teammate in a state court for negligence. The court dismissed the case, and the student appealed.

The Court of Appeals of Indiana stated that while the Indiana Supreme Court has held secondary schools owe their students a duty to exercise ordinary and reasonable care, it has never imposed this duty on colleges or universities. The student argued the trend is for courts to find a "special" relationship between colleges or universities and their student-athletes. The court disagreed, stating the reasonable care standard was created to guide people in their everyday lives, not for athletes who choose to participate in sports. The court found being hit by a ball during team practice is an inherent and foreseeable danger of athletic participation. **Athletes assume the risk of a certain amount of foreseeable and inherent danger.** The court held that avoiding reckless or malicious behavior or intentional injury should be the standard of care for sporting events and practices. **Athletes should not recover in negligence cases unless they prove malicious, reckless or intentional conduct**. Since the university, coaches and teammate did not owe a duty of care to the student, the court affirmed the judgment. *Geiersbach v. Frieje*, 807 N.E. 2d 114 (Ind. App. 2004). [IN]

◆   *The Court of Appeals of Massachusetts dismissed a Boston College season ticket holder's challenge to the loss of his season tickets, finding Boston College had the right to revoke his ticket privileges due to his disorderly conduct.*

A group of spectators who were tailgating during a Boston College football game got into a fight with college police. The college revoked one spectator's season tickets for disorderly conduct and barred him from entering the campus. The spectator sued the college in a state court for "unlawful trespass warning," revocation of his season tickets, and intentional infliction of emotional distress. The court granted Boston College's motion for summary judgment and the spectator appealed to the Court of Appeals of Massachusetts.

The court noted each season ticket issued by Boston College clearly indicated it was a "revocable license." Consequently, **the college had the right to revoke the ticket privileges at any time and for any non-discriminatory reason. With regard to his trespass claim, the court stated that as a private college, Boston College could bar the spectator from its campus, regardless of his guilt or innocence**. The evidence did not support the intentional infliction of emotional distress claim. The actions of the college police were not "so extreme and outrageous as to be beyond all bounds of decency." The court upheld the trial court's decision to dismiss the case. *Dischino v. Boston College*, 799 N.E.2d 605 (Mass. App. 2003). [MA]

◆ *A freak weightlifting injury entitled a wrestler to an award of $50,000.*

A wrestler at the University of North Carolina was lifting weights in the student recreation center when a cable came loose on a weight machine. This resulted in a head injury to the wrestler. Although he was able to continue wrestling for the rest of the year, he had to give it up after suffering a second concussive injury. He entered medical school, suffered continuing problems, and sued UNC under the North Carolina Tort Claims Act, alleging that the machine that caused his injury had been negligently maintained by the university. An Industrial Commission deputy commissioner ordered UNC to pay the wrestler $500,000, but the full commission **reduced the award to $50,000**. The North Carolina Court of Appeals upheld the award of $50,000. Although the student continued to be affected by his injuries, he did not present sufficient evidence that he was permanently injured or that his future earning capacity had been negatively impacted so as to justify the larger award. However, he was entitled to the $50,000 because he lost one wrestling season, endured many headaches, and had his normal activities restricted for at least six months. *Hummel v. University of North Carolina*, 576 S.E.2d 124 (N.C. App. 2003). [NC]

◆ *Universities have an affirmative duty of care toward student-athletes who participate on school-sponsored, intercollegiate teams.*

A University of North Carolina cheerleader was injured in 1985 while the JV cheerleading squad was warming up before a women's basketball game. The squad did not use mats during the warm-up. While practicing a pyramid, the cheerleader fell off the top, and spotters were unable to prevent her head and shoulders from hitting the hardwood floor. The cheerleader suffered permanent brain damage. UNC did not provide a coach for the JV cheerleading squad during the 1984–1985 school year, but the varsity squad had a faculty supervisor who oversaw their stunts. A part-time UNC employee was the "administrative supervisor" for the JV team. The supervisor arranged travel plans and performed other managerial duties, but did not supervise the team's stunts, training or safety during games and practice. The JV cheerleaders essentially coached themselves, deciding how and when to perform stunts. The

North Carolina Industrial Commission initially determined the cheerleader could not sue UNC because the university did not have a duty to ensure her safety by providing a coach or faculty supervisor to monitor the school's cheerleading squad or by barring certain cheerleading stunts.

The cheerleader appealed to the North Carolina Court of Appeals, which found that UNC owed her a duty of care because she had a "special relationship" with the university. UNC depended on the JV cheerleading team to act as school representatives at athletic events. The university also provided the squad with uniforms and transportation, as well as the use of school facilities for practice. Cheerleading also satisfied one credit hour of UNC's physical education requirement. Additional evidence of a special relationship included the fact that UNC exerts a considerable degree of control over its cheerleaders. They must maintain a certain GPA and refrain from drinking alcohol in public. The court further ruled that **UNC not only had an affirmative duty of care, but also voluntarily undertook a separate duty of care by assuming certain responsibilities with regard to teaching the varsity cheerleaders about safety**, which made it legally obligated to educate the JV squad about safety. The court reversed and remanded the Industrial Commission's decision, leaving the commission to determine whether UNC breached its duty to the cheerleader. *Davidson v. University of North Carolina at Chapel Hill*, 543 S.E.2d 920 (N.C. App. 2001). [NC]

◆ *A university could not be held liable for injuries a student suffered when he was punched in the face during an intramural soccer game.*

A student at a California university was punched in the face by a member of the opposing team while playing in an intramural soccer game. He sued the university for negligent supervision. The university asserted that it had no duty to the student and that, even if had, it fulfilled that duty by providing referees for the game. It also asserted that a statute immunized it from liability because the student had engaged in a hazardous recreational activity. A trial court found that the university had no duty to the student and dismissed the case. The California Court of Appeal affirmed, noting that **the university had no general duty of care toward the student** by virtue of *in loco parentis* (a doctrine that places an entity in the place of the parents) because the student was not a child. Further, there existed no special relationship between the student and the university such that the university had to protect the student from the criminal act of a third party. Finally, **because soccer is an intensely physical game, fraught with risk of serious injury, the student's participation in the game amounted to a "hazardous recreational activity" for purposes of the immunizing statute**. *Ochoa v. California State Univ., Sacramento*, 85 Cal.Rptr.2d 768 (Cal. App. 3d Dist. 1999). [CA]

◆ *A student injured while playing rugby could not recover from the state of New York where he assumed the risk of injury.*

A student at a New York public university was a member of the school's rugby club, which was not a varsity sport. The club received funding from the student association, but did not receive state money. It did have a faculty advisor. On the day of the first practice, the student, who had been playing the sport for three years as a fullback and wingman, volunteered to play the hooker position, at which he was generally inexperienced. During the second scrumdown, the scrums moved prior to the call to engage, and the student's head became lodged against the opposing hooker's body. As the student's scrum moved to the low side of the field, he was lifted off the ground. Although he yelled, Stop!", before the players complied, the upward force of the players behind him broke his neck, rendering him a quadriplegic.

The student sued the state for failing to properly supervise the practice, for furnishing an unsafe field and for negligence in training and instructing the rugby players. The court of claims dismissed his action, and the New York Supreme Court, Appellate Division, affirmed. Here, **the student had assumed the risk of injury by participating in a sport that carried the potential for serious injuries. He had previously played rugby on the same field and under the same conditions; thus, he was aware of the dangers of the sport.** He also was unable to show that the slope of the field was a legal cause of his injury. Accordingly, the state could not be held liable. *Regan v. State of New York*, 654 N.Y.S.2d 488 (A.D. 3d Dept. 1997). [NY]

◆ *A Georgia court held a student presented sufficient facts demonstrating that the college's gross negligence caused his injuries and that his waiver did not encompass assumption of the risk.*

A member of a private college's men's varsity team was injured when he was struck in the back by another boat operated by members of the women's varsity team. The usual traffic pattern for boats on the river was the right-hand rule. However, on the day of the injury, the traffic pattern was changed to a left-hand rule to enable boats to practice on the actual course. The coach of the men's team, who also was the supervisor of the entire rowing program, notified the team that the left-hand rule was in effect. However, it was uncertain whether the coach of the women's team informed his team of the changed traffic pattern, or whether he was aware of the change on that day. After the accident, the injured rower sued the college and the coaches, among others, asserting that their gross negligence caused his injuries. The college and coaches maintained that at worst they were negligent and that, because the rower had signed a release document releasing all participants from any claims except those arising out of gross negligence, the case should not even go to the jury. The court denied their motion for a directed verdict, and the jury returned a verdict in favor of the rower. The college and coaches appealed to the Court of Appeals of Georgia.

The court of appeals noted that **there were sufficient facts presented to the jury to show gross negligence.** The jury could have concluded that the coach of the women's team was grossly negligent in failing to advise the team of the change in the traffic pattern, in failing to be aware of the change himself, and in failing to be on the water supervising his team at the time of the accident. The jury also could have concluded that the men's coach was grossly negligent in failing to stop the men's boat when he became aware of the women's boat on the course, and in failing to ensure that the women's team was advised of the traffic pattern change. The question had therefore been properly given to the jury, and it had concluded, within reason, that the defendants were grossly negligent. **With respect to the release form, even though the rower was**

aware of and assumed the general risks inherent in rowing, it could not be said that he had assumed the particular risk to which he was subjected as a result of the defendants' gross negligence. The court upheld the verdict. *Trustees of Trinity College v. Ferris*, 491 S.E.2d 909 (Ga. App. 1997). [GA]

◆ *It is only the risk that results in the harm that must be reasonably foreseeable, not the precise manner of the accident or the extent of the harm.*

A senior at the Massachusetts Institute of Technology (MIT) majored in aeronautical engineering and also was a member of the men's track and field team. He had been pole vaulting since his freshman year. While practicing under his coach's direct supervision, the student was injured after vaulting when he fell backward and struck his head on the hard track surface. Although the NCAA recommended a length of 16 feet for the pole-vaulting pit, the pit at MIT was only 13 feet in length. The coach had witnessed, or was at least aware of, a vaulter bouncing off the pit mattress, resulting in second-impact injuries. On the day of the accident, there were no pads at the back or sides of the pit. After noticing that the student was running too fast, the coach failed to instruct him to slow down or abort his vault. The student was later diagnosed as having a skull fracture with associated contusions to the brain. He sued the university and two of its track and field coaches for injuries.

The court entered judgment upon the jury verdict for the student. The defendants appealed to the Appeals Court of Massachusetts. On appeal, they argued there was no evidence to support a finding that they should have reasonably foreseen the student would land beyond the back of the pit and hit his head on the track surface. However, the court held **it is only the risk that results in the harm that must be reasonably foreseeable, not the precise manner of the accident or the extent of the harm**. The court held that from the evidence, the student's accident was reasonably foreseeable. The length of the landing pit and its location near a hard surface did not provide a safe environment for pole-vaulters. Accordingly, the lower court decision was affirmed. *Moose v. Massachusetts Institute of Technology*, 683 N.E.2d 706 (Mass. App. 1997). [MA]

◆ *Although some risks are inherent to activities like weightlifting, the risk of a spotter intentionally failing to provide necessary assistance is not.*

A scholarship player on an Ohio university basketball team was required by the university to lift weights to improve as a player. While lifting weights at the university's gym, the student attempted to bench-press a 365-pound weight. The weight fell on the student, injuring him. He claimed that a university employee agreed to act as a spotter for him, though the employee claimed that he had not done so. The student sued the employee and the university for his injuries, claiming that the employee's reckless and wanton misconduct had caused his injuries. The trial court held that the employee was at most negligent and granted pretrial dismissal to the defendants.

The Court of Appeals of Ohio noted that **where individuals are engaged in recreational or sports activities, they assume the ordinary risks of the activities and cannot recover for any injury unless they can show that their injury resulted from reckless or intentional conduct**. Here, it was undisputed that the student was engaged in a recreational activity at the time he was injured. However, there was a dispute over whether the employee had agreed to perform as a spotter for the student. As a result, the action should have gone to trial. The court reversed and remanded the case. *Sicard v. University of Dayton*, 660 N.E.2d 1241 (Ohio App. 1995). [OH]

◆ *A college was found to have a duty to provide prompt medical attention to all students participating in sports that presented a risk of severe injury.*

A Pennsylvania college student wished to play lacrosse and was examined by his family physician and the college's doctor, who both determined he was healthy and able to participate in physical activity. During an off-season lacrosse practice, the student collapsed. All attempts to resuscitate him were unsuccessful. He died of a cardiac arrest. Post-mortem examinations could not detect the reason for the student's fatal arrythmia. His parents sued the college in a federal district court, asserting its negligence caused their son's death. The court granted the college summary judgment, and the parents appealed to the U.S. Court of Appeals, Third Circuit.

Both parties disputed the amount of time lapse between the dispatch of the students and the arrival of medical aid. The parents contended that the college had a duty to take preventive measures that would assure that student-athletes who engaged in intercollegiate athletics received prompt medical attention for their injuries. The court of appeals agreed. **The college had a special relationship with the student and therefore a duty of care toward him.** Other student-athletes had died while competing in athletics and lacrosse was considered a relatively dangerous contact sport. Consequently, not having qualified trainers at the practice site posed a risk that was both foreseeable and unreasonable. **Although no athlete had previously suffered a cardiac arrest, the injury was one of a "broadly definable class of events."** The presence of foreseeability and consequent duty to care for the student was not "dependent on the foreseeability of a specific event." Therefore, the college had a duty to provide prompt medical attention to all students participating in sports that presented a risk of severe injury. The court of appeals reversed the holding of the district court on this issue. It remanded the case for a determination of whether prompt emergency medical service was actually given to the student. *Kleinknecht v. Gettysburg College*, 989 F.2d 1360 (3d Cir. 1993). [PA]

◆ *The doctrine of express assumption of the risk did not bar a student's claim, rather a jury had to determine the comparative fault of the student and the school.*

A cheerleader for a Florida private university severely injured her foot during practice after the coach failed to provide adequate spotters for a stunt. She filed a negligence lawsuit against the university in a Florida circuit court, alleging that the coach had failed to adequately supervise the students. The trial court held for the cheerleader, and the university appealed to the District Court of Appeal of Florida, Fourth District. The university contended that the doctrine of express assumption of risk barred the cheerleader's negligence claim. The court of appeal disagreed, ruling that although the cheerleader may have been foolish to attempt the stunt without spotters, her unreasonable conduct did not absolve the university from liability. The case was correctly submitted to a jury on comparative fault principles. It was the **jury's duty to weigh the reasonableness of her activity against the school's negligence**. Thus, the doctrine of express assumption of risk did not bar the cheerleader's claim. Finally, the court determined that the trial court had correctly denied the university's motion for a continuance until the cheerleader's foot was healed. Sufficient expert testimony existed from which a determination of future damages could be made. The holding of the trial court was affirmed. *Nova Univ. v. Katz*, 636 So.2d 729 (Fla. App. 4th Dist. 1993). [FL]

II. STUDENT ACTIVITIES

Colleges and universities must respect individual rights to free religious exercise and association as well as state and federal civil rights laws. However, schools may limit official recognition of particular organizations and impose restrictions on them. Liability for student organizations also becomes a concern for schools, particularly in relation to fraternities and sororities.

A. Student Associations and Activities

1. Freedom of Expression

◆   *The U.S. Supreme Court held that because a state university had opened a limited public forum by paying other third-party contractors on behalf of student groups, it could not deny a religious group's claim for funds on the basis of its viewpoint.*

A group of students who published a Christian publication sought financing from a state university student activity fund. Their request was denied by the student council and two university tribunals. Although political and religious organizations could qualify as approved student groups, they could not receive student activity funds. The student group filed a lawsuit in the U.S. District Court for the Western District of Virginia. The court granted summary judgment to the university, and the students appealed to the U.S. Court of Appeals, Fourth Circuit. The court of appeals affirmed, and the students appealed to the U.S. Supreme Court.

The Supreme Court held that because the university had opened a limited public forum by paying other third-party contractors on behalf of student groups, it could not deny the religious group's claim for funds on the basis of its viewpoint. Allowing the payment of the group's printing costs amounted to a policy of government neutrality for different viewpoints. The Court reversed the lower court decisions, ruling that access to public school facilities on a neutral basis does not violate the Establishment Clause of the First Amendment. *Rosenberger v. Rector and Visitors of Univ. of Virginia*, 515 U.S. 819, 115 S.Ct. 2510, 132 L.Ed.2d 700 (1995). [VA]

◆ *A Pennsylvania student who opposed a university play depicting Jesus Christ as a homosexual was entitled to a trial on his First Amendment rights.*

Temple University put on a play depicting Jesus Christ and his disciples as homosexuals who engaged in sexual acts with one another. The student asked the university to prohibit the production on campus and planned an alternative event to portray Jesus according to the student's beliefs. A university vice president assured the student a stage would be provided for an alternative event. However, university trustees met and decided not to provide a stage or any assistance for the student's planned event. The student became upset at the meeting and had to be restrained. The vice president ordered campus police to handcuff the student and take him to a hospital for a psychiatric evaluation. A university official applied for a warrant to involuntarily commit the student for an emergency psychiatric evaluation, but doctors released him.

The student sued the university and its officials in a federal district court for First Amendment violations and other claims. **He alleged the university violated his First Amendment rights by involuntarily committing him and refusing to assist him in retaliation for exercising his religious beliefs and speech rights.** The university conceded the student was engaged in protected activity, but argued his conduct was not a substantial factor in the decision to involuntarily commit him. **The court held that a hearing was necessary to determine whether the university acted in retaliation for the student's protected activity.** It denied summary judgment and ordered a trial on the First Amendment claims. *Marcavage v. Board of Trustees of Temple Univ.,* No. Civ.A. 00-5362 (PBT), 2004 WL 1151835 (E.D. Pa. 2004). [PA]

◆ *A theater student was allowed to continue with his production of a play alleged to be anti-Christian after a Seventh Circuit panel ruled that the play's production at a public university did not violate the Establishment Clause.*

The dispute arose after a theater student at an Indiana university chose to produce the play "Corpus Christi" for his senior performance project. The play depicts a homosexual Christ-like character who engages in sex with his apostles. A group of individuals, including taxpayers, members of the state General Assembly, and members of the Board of Trustees of Purdue University objected to the production of the play. In a lawsuit, they alleged that the publicly funded university would be violating the Establishment Clause by allowing the performance. The plaintiffs further asserted that if production of "Corpus Christi" were permitted, it would give the impression that the university endorsed the play's allegedly anti-Christian ideals. The plaintiffs filed a motion for a preliminary injunction to stop production until a federal district court could resolve the case.

The district court refused to grant the injunction, finding the theater was a limited public forum because it allowed students and community members to stage performances. **Because the theater was a limited public forum, the university could not discriminate against the viewpoint of those who stage performances.** The university was conducting itself in a viewpoint-neutral manner by allowing opponents of the play to hand out literature at the performance, holding an assembly to air both sides of the dispute and including a disclaimer in the playbill stating the university did not endorse the viewpoints presented within the play. On appeal, the U.S. Court of Appeals for the Seventh Circuit upheld the district court decision. The court found the plaintiffs' assertion that the First Amendment prevents state universities from providing venues for un-Christian ideas "absurd." There was no evidence the university was hostile to Christianity because it did not tell the student to produce the play, nor was there any indication that the play would have been prohibited if it were antagonistic toward other religions. *Linnemeir v. Board of Trustees of Purdue Univ.*, 260 F.3d 757 (7th Cir. 2001). [IN]

◆ *A university's funding system created a limited public forum under which it could not discriminate against speech on the basis of its viewpoint.*

The University of South Alabama encouraged a wide variety of activities through the establishment of student organizations that were eligible for certain benefits, including the use of campus banking services and funding from the student government association. A gay and lesbian group was denied the banking privileges and certain funding by the university because it believed such action would violate a state statute. The statute prohibited any college or university from using public funds or facilities to support any organization that promoted a lifestyle that was prohibited by the state sexual misconduct laws. The student group filed suit against the state attorney general and university officials in federal district court, alleging that the statute constituted impermissible viewpoint discrimination in violation of the First Amendment and that it was invalid on its face. The court found for the student group, and the attorney general appealed to the U.S. Court of Appeals, Eleventh Circuit.

The attorney general argued that the speech covered by the statute was not protected speech because it advocated the violation of sexual misconduct laws. The court disagreed, noting that the First Amendment protects advocacy to violate a law. The only exception is when such advocacy is directed to incite imminent lawless action and is likely to produce such action. The court then noted that the university's funding system created a limited public forum under which it could not discriminate against speech on the basis of its viewpoint. **Because the university funded groups that advocated compliance with the sexual misconduct laws, it could not discriminate on the basis of viewpoint and refuse to fund groups that advocated the violation of these laws.** The court then held that facial invalidation is a drastic remedy and should only be used when the statute's interpretation cannot be narrowed to make it constitutionally permissible. Finding that the statute here was overbroad and not susceptible to a narrowing interpretation, the court found it facially invalid and affirmed the district court's decision. *Gay Lesbian Bisexual Alliance v. Pryor*, 110 F.3d 1543 (11th Cir. 1997). [AL]

2. Facilities and Services

◆ *Although a university's Free Exercise Clause rights would be burdened to some extent by being forced to provide facilities and services to gay student groups, that burden was outweighed by the government's important goal of eradicating discrimination based upon sexual orientation.*

Georgetown University, a Jesuit-controlled Roman Catholic institution, was sued in a District of Columbia superior court by two gay rights groups when it refused to extend full university recognition to the groups as student organizations. The gay student groups claimed that the university's refusal to recognize them violated the District of Columbia Human Rights Act. The Act provided in part that educational institutions could not deny access to their "facilities and services" on the basis of sexual orientation. The university countered that the First Amendment's Free Exercise Clause protected it from violating the tenets of its religious heritage by recognizing student groups whose goals were at odds with the university's religious affiliation. The superior court upheld Georgetown's free exercise defense and ruled that it did not have to recognize the gay student groups. The gay student groups appealed. A three-judge panel of the District of Columbia Court of Appeals reversed the panel's ruling, and the case was held over for consideration by the entire court.

Modifying the three-judge panel's decision, **the court held the university had to provide the gay student groups with all the "facilities and services" afforded to groups that had attained university recognition**. However, the university was not required to endorse the gay student groups' goals by officially recognizing them. Although the university's Free Exercise Clause rights would be burdened to some extent by being forced to provide facilities and services to the gay student groups, that burden was outweighed by the government's important goal of eradicating discrimination based upon sexual orientation. **The university was ordered to provide the groups with facilities and services but was not required to actually recognize the groups.** *Gay Rights Coalition v. Georgetown Univ.*, 536 A.2d 1 (D.C. App. 1987). [DC]

◆   *A state commission on human relations could not prevent a university from making its placement service available to the military for recruitment even though it discriminated on the basis of sexual orientation.*

The Temple University School of Law operated a placement service that arranged interviews between employers and students. One of the potential employers was the Judge Advocate General (JAG) Corps of the U.S. Army, Navy and Marines. These branches did not employ homosexuals. After being notified of the practice, the Pennsylvania Commission on Human Relations issued a complaint against the law school, alleging that it had violated the Philadelphia Fair Practices Ordinance in permitting the JAG Corps to interview at the law school. The commission claimed that the law school had violated the ordinance when referring persons to the JAG Corps knowing that it was discriminatory in its hiring practices. A U.S. district court ruled in favor of the law school, and the commission appealed.

The U.S. Court of Appeals, Third Circuit, observed that all parties were in agreement that the commission could not directly keep the military from recruiting persons on whatever terms it deemed appropriate. However, the parties sharply disagreed as to whether the commission could prevent the school from making its placement service available to the JAG Corps for recruitment when it discriminated on the basis of sexual orientation. In ruling in favor of the JAG Corps and the law school, the court of appeals referred to the Federal Department of Defense Authorization Act of 1973, in which Congress declared that access to college and university employment facilities was of paramount importance. The court observed that in the above-mentioned act (and others similar to it) the government had shown **that recruitment on a variety of campuses is essential to having a broad scope of skilled personnel in the U.S. military.** The court ruled that to uphold the commission's complaint would potentially frustrate effective military recruiting in the area. The Philadelphia Fair Practices Ordinance was in direct conflict with federal legislative policy, and the court ruled that federal law took precedence. The local ordinance therefore could not be enforced against the law school. *U.S. v. City of Philadelphia*, 798 F.2d 81 (3d Cir. 1986). [PA]

B. Fraternities and Sororities

1. Operation and School Supervision

◆ *A college could use money from a fund-raising campaign to eliminate single-sex fraternities and sororities.*

A New Hampshire college initiated a five-year fund-raising campaign that raised about $568 million from alumni. Several years later, the board of trustees announced that it was going to use some of the money raised to eliminate single-sex fraternities and sororities. A group of alumni who had contributed to the campaign sued the college to prevent it from using the funds for that purpose. They asserted that the college had engaged in misrepresentation in violation of the state Consumer Protection Act, and that the board of trustees had withheld information about its intent to eliminate traditional fraternities and sororities. They also alleged that the board was in a fiduciary relationship to the alumni because there were alums on the board. A state court dismissed their lawsuit, and the Supreme Court of New Hampshire affirmed. First, the board of trustees did not owe a fiduciary duty to the alumni despite the existence of alums on the board. Second, **the alumni failed to show that the board engaged in intentional, fraudulent nondisclosure.** And third, since the fund-raising campaign was not commerce (the transactions were in the nature of a gift), there was no violation of the Consumer Protection Act. *Brzica v. Trustees of Dartmouth College*, 791 A.2d 990 (N.H. 2002). [NH]

◆ *A fraternity's First Amendment freedom of association rights were not violated when the University of Pittsburgh stripped the house of its status as a recognized student organization following the arrest of several members.*

Pi Lambda Phi had a local chapter at the University of Pittsburgh. On April 30, 1996, city police raided the fraternity house, finding drugs and drug paraphernalia. Four members were arrested and charged with possession of controlled substances. One of these members was the fraternity's "risk manager" and another was the president of the university's Interfraternity Council. A fourth was later convicted of possession and distribution of controlled substances and expelled. As a result, the university suspended the fraternity's campus chapter, pending an investigation. The university's vice chancellor later decided to revoke the fraternity's chapter for one year. In addition, he prohibited Pi Lambda Phi from participating in school-sponsored Greek activities and from recruiting new members. When the Interfraternity Council subsequently voted not to recertify Pi Lambda Phi, the fraternity sued the university in federal court, alleging violations of its members' rights of freedom of association under the First Amendment. The court determined that the fraternity was not protected by the First Amendment.

The Third Circuit affirmed. First, it described the two types of constitutionally protected associations. Intimate associations generally are seen as family relationships or other private relationships involving a relatively small group of people. Pi Lambda Phi did not satisfy this definition. Expressive associations are more broadly defined, and while political expression is not necessary to meet the definition of expressive organizations, there must be some public activity that involves an issue of political, social or cultural importance in order for the association to gain constitutional protection. Here, the fraternity raised $350 for charity and helped run a haunted house for the Pittsburgh School for the Blind. These "few minor charitable acts" were insufficient to meet the definition of expressive associations. Moreover, the university's actions did not significantly affect the group's ability to advocate its views. **The school's action in decertifying the fraternity had more to do with its involvement with drugs, which has no protected expressive element and which was unrelated to any expressive activity.** *Pi Lambda Phi Fraternity v. University of Pittsburgh*, 229 F.3d 435 (3d Cir. 2000). [PA]

◆ *A university's residential policy, which required all students to live in college-owned facilities, may constitute a violation of the Sherman Act.*

A New York private college announced a policy requiring all students to live in college-owned facilities and to purchase college-sponsored meal plans. Four college fraternities sued the college and its president, alleging that the residential policy violated the Sherman Act by unlawfully monopolizing the market for residential services in the city where the college was located. The court held the policy was not "trade or commerce" as it lacked a substantial connection to interstate commerce. The court dismissed the complaint, and the fraternities appealed to the U.S. Court of Appeals, Second Circuit, arguing that the residential plan had the commercial purpose of eliminating competition in the provision of residential services in order to raise revenues.

The college maintained that its purpose was to create an academic environment that was more appealing to female applicants who were unable to enjoy the privileges of fraternity life. The court noted the Sherman Act would apply only if the residential policy constituted trade or commerce. It then stated that in determining whether particular conduct was commerce, the principal focus had to be on the nature of the activity, rather than the form or objectives of the organization. Here, **the fraternities had provided facts to support a connection between the residential policy and interstate commerce.** The college collected approximately $4 million in room and board fees from students who came from outside New York State. Further, **the fraternities and other private landlords in the city would lose approximately $1 million per year as a result of the new policy**, a substantial portion of which would have been collected from out-of-state residents. Because the allegations were sufficient to survive dismissal, the court reversed and remanded the case. *Hamilton Chapter of Alpha Delta Phi v. Hamilton College*, 128 F.3d 59 (2d Cir. 1997). [NY]

◆ *A court's role was limited to determining whether a private university had substantially complied with its own disciplinary guidelines.*

A fraternity at a private university was burglarized, and records of the fraternity's activities were stolen. Portions of these records later appeared in the university's newspapers and were mailed to the university's officials. The published records alleged violations of the school's anti-hazing policy as well as other infractions. The dean of the university then conducted an investigation of the fraternity, which resulted in several penalties. The fraternity brought suit against the school in a state court and alleged that its members' Fourteenth Amendment due process rights had been violated. A New York trial court dismissed the claim, and the fraternity appealed to the Supreme Court, Appellate Division. **Private school students cannot allege violations of constitutionally protected due process rights absent a showing of state involvement in the university activity.** Here, no such state involvement was shown. A court's role in due process actions concerning a private institution, absent state involvement, is limited to determining whether the school had substantially complied with its own disciplinary guidelines. The court reviewed the record concerning the university's regulations and actions, and affirmed the dismissal of the claim. *Mu Chapter Delta Kappa Epsilon v. Colgate*, 578 N.Y.S.2d 713 (A.D. 3d Dept. 1992). [NY]

◆ *A college's decision to withdraw recognition from all fraternities was a legitimate exercise of the college's supervisory authority.*

A Maine private college decided to withdraw recognition from all fraternities on the campus in 1984. A Memorandum of Agreement executed in 1951 between a realty company and the college stated that the college could cancel the agreement only in the following circumstances: "In the event the ZETA PSI Fraternity ceases to have a chapter at Colby College, or in the event the Chapter is suspended or expelled for reason either by the College or the National Fraternity...." The realty company, on behalf of a fraternity, sued the college for breach of contract in a state superior court. The court ruled in favor of the college, and the realty company appealed.

The Supreme Judicial Court of Maine held the college rationally justified its decision to oust all fraternities from the campus as a move to more fully "integrate the housing units into the academic program of the college." It observed that **the president and trustees of the college had the right and responsibility to periodically evaluate and change policies for the purpose of achieving certain educational goals.** The court ruled that the 1984 decision by the college president and trustees to eliminate fraternity chapters at the college was a legitimate exercise of supervisory authority. The college, therefore, properly ended its relationship with the realtor and fraternity under the 1951 lease agreement. The decision of the superior court was affirmed. *Chi Realty Corp. v. Colby College*, 513 A.2d 866 (Me. 1986). [ME]

2. Organizational Liability

◆ *A Texas fraternity and its members was not liable to a student for allegedly defamatory statements that resulted in the termination his pledge invitation.*

A student who had pledged to join the Phi Gamma Delta Fraternity was accused of sexual misconduct. He denied the allegations, claiming they were part of an extortion scheme to gain money. Phi Gamma withdrew its pledge invitation. A year later, the student pledged to join a chapter of the same fraternity at a different Texas university campus. He was denied admittance based on information communicated between fraternity members at the different chapters. The student sued the fraternity and various fraternity members in the state court system for damaging his reputation and subjecting him to increased hazing based on the allegations of sexual misconduct. The court awarded summary judgment to the fraternities and their members.

The student appealed, arguing that Phi Gamma owed him a duty of care because its members made statements in the course and scope of their fraternity membership. The Court of Appeals of Texas rejected his arguments. There was no evidence indicating the fraternity was incorporated in the state. **As an unincorporated entity, the fraternity did not owe the student any duty of care**. Moreover, he was unable to show a member's remarks were made in the course of his official duties as a fraternity historian. **There was no evidence these comments were communicated to other fraternities at the University of Texas**. The court agreed with the trial court that the hazing claim was untimely filed under a two-year state statute of limitation. The entry of summary judgment was affirmed. *Waddill v. Phi Gamma Delta Fraternity Lambda Tau Chapter, Texas Tech Univ.*, 114 S.W.3d 136 (Tex. App. 2003). [TX]

◆ *A Kansas fraternity pledge could not sue the fraternity or its members when he passed out after drinking too much.*

A student attended a Pledge Dad night at a fraternity at the University of Kansas. While there, he consumed a large amount of alcoholic beverages. At 1 a.m., his pledge dad found him passed out in the living room of the fraternity house and took him to a local hospital emergency room, where his blood alcohol level was measured at .294. The student later sued the national fraternity, the local chapter and five individual members for negligence, and the company that owned the property for premises liability. The court ruled in favor of all the defendants, and the Kansas Supreme Court affirmed. **The local chapter was not a legal entity and therefore could not be sued**. Further, the individual members could not be liable because **they did not breach any duty they owed him; he voluntarily drank alcohol** that night. As far as the national fraternity was concerned, there was no special relationship between the student and the fraternity so as to give rise to liability. Finally, the company that owned the property could not be held liable for conditions on the premises at a fraternity party. *Prime v. Beta Gamma Chapter of Pi Kappa Alpha*, 47 P.3d 402 (Kan. 2002). [KS]

◆ *A national fraternity could not be held liable for a student's injuries because it was not in a position to control the actions of its chapters on a day-to-day basis and had no knowledge of any hazing activity.*

A student at a private university in Louisiana was accepted into a fraternity. During the intake process, he was physically beaten and abused by several members of the fraternity while they were conducting hazing activities. The student and his parents filed suit against the national fraternity, among others, to recover damages for the injuries sustained as a result of the hazing.

A state court granted summary judgment to the national fraternity, and the student and his parents appealed to the Court of Appeal of Louisiana. They argued the national fraternity should be liable for the actions of its chapter members because it had a duty to prevent injury to new members. They also asserted that the national fraternity's action in forbidding hazing activities showed a clear knowledge and former approval of those activities. The court, however, noted that the national executive director of the fraternity had stated by affidavit that he had no knowledge of any hazing activity at the local chapter and that the **national fraternity took numerous steps to inform local chapters and members that hazing activities were clearly prohibited**. Further, deposition testimony by several local chapter members indicated that **any hazing activity that occurred was purposely hidden from the national fraternity**. Because the national fraternity was not in a position to control the actions of its chapters on a day-to-day basis, and because it had no knowledge of any hazing activity, it could not be held liable for the student's injuries. The trial court decision was affirmed. *Walker v. Phi Beta Sigma Fraternity (RHO Chapter)*, 706 So.2d 525 (La. App. 1st Cir. 1997). [LA]

◆   *A student's negligence claim against a fraternity as a result of a member's alleged assault and rape of her failed, in part, because the fraternity never assumed a duty to provide security to the student.*

A college student in Ohio alleged that she was assaulted and raped by a fraternity member. After the fraternity member was arrested and charged with rape, the student filed a civil complaint against the fraternity for negligence as well as intentional and negligent infliction of emotional distress. She alleged that the fraternity breached its duty to provide security for guests and members and that it decided to wage a campaign against her by ostracizing her as revenge for her decision to file rape charges against one of its members.

The trial court granted summary judgment to the fraternity, and the student appealed to the Court of Appeals of Ohio, Sixth District. On appeal, the court noted that the **fraternity never assumed a duty to provide security to the student**. Nor could the student demonstrate that she had relied on the fraternity's security program (which had been set up to provide members with transportation home from local bars) to protect her. Accordingly, the negligence claim failed. The court noted that the student's assertion that the fraternity's members had called her names and otherwise harassed her did not amount to extreme and outrageous conduct so as to make the fraternity liable for intentional infliction of emotional distress. Further, the student presented no admissible evidence to show that the fraternity ordered its members to engage in such conduct. The court also stated that the negligent infliction of emotional distress claim failed because the student had not shown that she was in fear of real physical danger from the fraternity members as a result of their actions— a necessary element of such a cause of action in Ohio. Accordingly, the lower court's grant of summary judgment to the fraternity was affirmed. *Rine v. Sabo*, 680 N.E.2d 647 (Ohio App. 6th Dist. 1996). [OH]

◆ *Although the university had a substantial interest in maintaining an appropriate learning environment, it would have to do so without restricting expression based upon its content.*

Fraternity members who attended a Virginia university staged an **"ugly woman contest,"** which was objected to by other university students as racist and sexist. The university determined that the behavior created a hostile learning environment for women and blacks, which was incompatible with the university's mission. It suspended the fraternity from many school activities, and the fraternity filed a civil rights lawsuit in a federal district court.

The U.S. Court of Appeals, Fourth Circuit, affirmed the district court's summary judgment motion for the fraternity, ruling that **the contest was protected by the First Amendment**. This was because the contest was expressive conduct intended to convey a message. Although the university had a substantial interest in maintaining an appropriate learning environment, it would have to do so without restricting expression based upon its content. *IOTA XI Chapter of Sigma Chi Fraternity v. George Mason Univ.*, 993 F.2d 386 (4th Cir. 1993). [VA]

3. Injuries

◆ *A fraternity could not be held responsible for the deaths of six Texas students who were struck by a pickup truck on their way to a fraternity party.*

After a football game, a fraternity threw a party. Nine students drove to the party and parked on the road, after which they walked to the fraternity. Three of the students walked on the grass; the other six walked on the paved shoulder with their backs to oncoming traffic. Another student was driving a pickup truck along the road at that time and fell asleep at the wheel. The truck collided with some of the vehicles parked on the road and fatally injured the six students walking on the shoulder. **Their estates sued the fraternity for negligence, alleging that it engaged in "dangerous conduct" and that it created a foreseeable risk of harm.** A trial court ruled for the fraternity, and the Texas Court of Appeals affirmed. Here, there were two causes of the accident: the student driver falling asleep, and the six students walking on the shoulder with their backs to oncoming traffic. As a result, the fraternity could not be held liable for negligence. *Calp v. Tau Kappa Epsilon Fraternity*, 75 S.W.3d 641 (Tex. App. 2002). [TX]

◆ *A Missouri student could pursue his claims against a college and a fraternity after he was shot.*

A student enrolled in a college and moved into a fraternity house. During a party, he got into a heated telephone conversation with a man who was not a student at the college. He then tried to lock the front door of the fraternity but was unable to do so because the lock was broken. When the man appeared later and shot him, he sued the college and the fraternity for negligently failing to maintain the premises. A state court granted pretrial judgment to the defendants, but the Supreme Court of Missouri reversed and remanded the case. Here, there were material issues of fact concerning who was a landlord and who was a tenant such that a trial had to be conducted. **Without knowing** the status of the parties, the court could not determine the respective duties of the college, the fraternity and the student. *Letsinger v. Drury College*, 68 S.W.3d 408 (Mo. 2002). [MO]

◆ *Fraternity sponsors of a "paint ball" game could be liable for a player's injuries if their actions were negligent. They were not entitled to assert that the game was inherently dangerous.*

A prospective pledge at a fraternity participated in a "war game," wherein players shot paint balls at each other. During the game, the student's goggles were snagged by a tree limb and lifted away from his eyes. When he stood and fired another round without replacing them, a paint ball hit him, permanently blinding him in one eye. He sued the fraternity, the chapter that had sponsored the war game, and the chapter president, alleging that they had sponsored an unreasonably dangerous activity, that they had provided inadequate supervision and equipment, and failed to train him properly. A state trial court granted summary judgment to the defendants, finding that the student had engaged in a competitive contact sport, thereby assuming the risk of injury.

The student appealed to the Texas Court of Appeals, contending that **sponsors of an event cannot assert the "competitive contact sports" doctrine because they are not participants**. The court agreed. Participants in a competitive contact sport are judged under the intentional or reckless conduct standard because they are caught up in the spirit of the contest. Sponsors, however, have the benefit of time to reflect before they act. Thus, they are to be judged by concepts of ordinary negligence. The court reversed and remanded the case for further proceedings. *Moore v. Phi Delta Theta Co.*, 976 S.W.2d 738 (Tex. App.–Houston 1998). [TX]

◆ *A New York university had no legal duty to shield its students from their own dangerous activities.*

A student at a private New York university was a member of a fraternity. He lived at the fraternity house and his room had a window that was centered over a portico that covered the front entrance of the house. Although the student had no recollection of a fall and there were no witnesses to his actions, he was found one morning lying on the ground near the entrance of the house, unconscious and bleeding profusely. His blood alcohol level was .18 percent. He filed suit in state court against the university, the fraternity and the owner of the house, seeking to recover damages for his personal injuries. The defendants filed a motion to dismiss. The court granted the motion with regard to the university and the fraternity and partially granted the motion with regard to the owner of the house. The student appealed to the state appellate division.

The student argued that the university assumed the duty to control the conduct of students in fraternity houses when it stated in the student handbook that all roofs and porticos were off limits and that underage drinking was prohibited. He argued that the university knew or should have known that students at fraternity houses routinely violated these provisions, and therefore its failure to enforce its own rules should result in liability for his injuries. The appellate court disagreed, finding that **colleges have no legal duty to shield their students from their own dangerous activities. Despite the handbook**

provisions, the college did not assume any duty to take affirmative steps to supervise students and to prevent them from engaging in prohibited conduct. Also, since the university did not own or control the fraternity house, it was not required to install safety features to prevent the prohibited activity. The court affirmed the dismissal of the complaint against the university but held that an issue of fact existed as to whether the owner of the house maintained it in a reasonably safe condition. *Rothbard v. Colgate Univ.*, 652 N.Y.S.2d 146 (A.D. 3d Dept. 1997). [NY]

◆   *A college and national fraternity did not owe students a special duty of care to prevent underage drinking, which violated the college's alcohol policy.*

A minor freshman student in Pennsylvania was socializing at a fraternity house early in the afternoon prior to a large homecoming party scheduled for that evening. Kegs of beer arrived shortly after noon, and the students decided to tap them earlier than allowed by school policy. While the minor student socialized at the fraternity house, he sat in a hot tub provided for the party and drank beer. The student left the house hours later on his motorcycle, which had a dim or burnt out headlight. While driving down a local highway, he attempted to pass a car in front of him. A fatal head-on collision resulted and a subsequent analysis revealed that the minor was legally intoxicated at the time he was killed. The administratrix of the minor's estate filed suit against the college and the national fraternity. She alleged that the college's alcohol policy and lack of adult supervision impliedly sanctioned underage drinking on campus, that the college was negligent for these reasons, and that the college's policies and inaction were a direct cause of the minor's fatal collision. The administratrix also alleged that the national fraternity was responsible for control of the actions of its members.

A Pennsylvania trial court granted summary judgment in favor of both the college and the fraternity and the administratrix appealed to the Superior Court of Pennsylvania. On appeal, the court noted that **both the college and the national fraternity counseled against the use of alcohol, and neither defendant owed the student a special duty of care, which had been breached**. The holding in favor of both defendants was affirmed. *Cooperstein v. Liberty Mutual*, 611 A.2d 721 (Pa. Super. 1992). [PA]

◆   *An Illinois university had no duty to protect a student from fraternity members who had been drinking.*

A student at a private university was in her dormitory room when a fraternity member called her to the lobby. When she arrived, the fraternity member grabbed her, then threw her over his shoulder and ran out of the building. The student asserted that as the fraternity member ran, he fell, crushing her underneath him on the sidewalk. She claimed that as a result of a head injury she received in the fall she completely lost her sense of smell and also suffered hearing loss. The student filed a lawsuit against the fraternity member, the fraternity and the private university seeking monetary damages for doctors' bills, surgical treatments, medicine and nursing care. She also sought compensatory damages for a reduction in her earning capacity. The student claimed that the fraternity member had gone to the dormitory after a fraternity party at which members of the fraternity drank alcohol.

The student claimed that the university had failed to control the on-campus activities of the fraternity and its members. The student also asserted that by installing safety devices in the dormitory the university assumed the duty of protecting dormitory residents and that this duty was breached. The university sought a dismissal of the case before trial. An Illinois appellate court noted that although college students were once considered minors subject to control by colleges and universities, they are now generally considered adults. **Universities are educational rather than custodial institutions, and requiring the university to baby-sit each student would be inappropriate.** The university had no duty to protect the student from fraternity members who had been drinking. *Rabel v. Illinois Wesleyan Univ.*, 514 N.E.2d 552 (Ill. App. 4th Dist. 1987). [IL]

4. Hazing

◆   *Although a fraternity had a duty to a Pennsylvania student, it did not breach that duty when local chapter members hazed him.*

A University of Pittsburgh student applied to the Beta Epsilon chapter of the Kappa Alpha Psi fraternity after Kappa lifted a restriction on inducting new members that had been imposed when a Kappa pledge died in Missouri. The student attended a fraternity gathering and was paddled more than 200 times by four fraternity brothers. He went to the hospital the next day and remained there for three weeks with renal failure, seizures and hypertension.

He later sued Kappa, the local chapter, the chapter advisor and a number of others for negligence. A Pennsylvania trial court ruled in favor of the defendants, and an appellate court largely affirmed. Here, even though Kappa owed a duty of care to the student, the student failed to show that it breached that duty. For example, he failed to show that the two-year moratorium on new members was merely a symbolic gesture and not a sincere attempt to curb hazing. However, **he was allowed to proceed with his lawsuit against the chapter advisor**. The evidence indicated that the chapter advisor failed to discuss hazing with local chapter members and did not advise them to read the executive orders that imposed sanctions for hazing. *Kenner v. Kappa Alpha Psi Fraternity,* 2002 WL 1334739 (Pa. Super. 6/19/02). [PA]

◆   *Corps of Cadets officials at Texas A&M were entitled to immunity in the following hazing case.*

The Texas A&M Corps of Cadets is a voluntary student military training organization consisting of approximately 2,000 students (about 5 percent of the student population). Members of the Corps live together, drill together, stand for inspections and physically train on a daily basis. A freshman student enrolled as a member of the Corps and joined a precision rifle drill team. **During "hell week," he was allegedly subjected to numerous hazing incidents by the drill team advisors, including having his head taped like a mummy, and enduring several beatings.** He also was allegedly beaten after the drill team lost a competition to another school's team. He never reported the incidents to school authorities; however, he did tell his parents, who then informed school authorities that hazing was occurring. When asked about hazing by the faculty advisor, the student downplayed the seriousness of it. Near the end of his first year, he went to a "hound interview" (seeking to become an advisor to the drill team) where he was beaten and forced to cut himself with a knife. He and his parents then met with the Commandant of the Corps, who took them to the university police to file criminal charges. All the drill team advisors were then expelled or suspended for hazing.

He sued a number of Corps officials under 42 U.S.C. § 1983 and Texas' hazing statute, alleging that the officials' failure to supervise the Corps' activities demonstrated a deliberate indifference to his constitutional rights. The U.S. District Court for the Southern District of Texas held that **the actions of the Corps officials in educating students about the illegality of hazing were reasonable**. They disseminated brochures and other materials to students what hazing was and how to prevent it. They met with students and their parents to discuss hazing and to encourage parents to report it if they saw evidence of it, and they reasonably believed that their efforts were sufficient to prevent constitutional violations. **As a result, the court found that the officials were entitled to qualified immunity from suit.** On appeal, the Fifth Circuit Court of Appeals affirmed the grant of immunity to the officials. The student failed to show that the officials were deliberately indifferent to his constitutional rights. *Alton v. Hopgood*, 168 F.3d 196 (5th Cir. 1999). [TX]

◆ *A university could not be held liable for a student's hazing where it had no reason to know that hazing was going on.*

A student transferred to Cornell University after spending his first two years at other institutions. He was accepted to pledge a fraternity, the national organization of which prohibited hazing, as did Cornell. After allegedly enduring beatings and torture, psychological coercion, and embarrassment, the student sued Cornell for negligent supervision, premises liability and breach of an implied contract to protect him. The U.S. District Court for the Northern District of New York dismissed the action, finding that there was no special relationship between the university and the student, and that the university published information about the dangers of hazing and its prohibition on campus. **Further, the university did not have sufficient reason to believe that hazing activities were going on; and once it became aware of the hazing, it took disciplinary action against the perpetrators.** Finally, the court could find no evidence of any specific promises by the university that could be deemed part of an implied contract. The university was not liable for the hazing of the student. *Lloyd v. Alpha Phi Alpha Fraternity*, 1999 U.S. Dist. LEXIS 906 (N.D.N.Y. 1/26/99). [NY]

◆ *Fraternity members could be sued for negligence and for violating an anti-hazing statute in the following case.*

A 17-year-old college freshman was invited to pledge a fraternity and died after consuming excessive amounts of alcohol during a hazing ritual. His parents sued several members of the fraternity for negligence and also asserted claims under two New York statutes. The fraternity members sought to have two of the causes of action against them dismissed, and the case reached the Supreme Court, Appellate Division. The court held the fraternity members were not entitled to dismissal. **The parents had alleged their son's intoxication was not entirely voluntary and that careless acts by the fraternity members went beyond the mere furnishing of intoxicants.** Accordingly, the action against the fraternity members could proceed. *Oja v. Grand Chapter of Theta Chi Fraternity*, 684 N.Y.S.2d 344 (A.D. 1999). [NY]

◆   *A university that knew about prior instances of hazing had a duty to protect a student from such behavior.*

Four or five members of a fraternity at a Nebraska university kidnapped a pledge, handcuffed him to a radiator and gave him a large quantity of alcohol. After the pledge became ill from his intoxication, he was taken to a third-floor restroom where he was handcuffed to a toilet pipe. The pledge escaped from the handcuffs and attempted to escape by exiting a restroom window and sliding down a drainpipe. However, he fell and suffered severe injuries. He sued the university, claiming that it had acted negligently in failing to enforce prohibitions against acts of hazing, the consumption of alcohol, and acts of physical abuse, when it knew or should have known that the fraternity was in violation of those prohibitions. The university moved for a pretrial judgment, asserting that it owed the pledge no duty to supervise the fraternity and protect the pledge from harm. The court granted the university's motion, and appeal was taken to the Supreme Court of Nebraska.

The supreme court held **the university could be liable to the pledge as an invitee on its property**. Because the university knew of two prior instances of hazing at fraternities on campus, and because it was aware of several incidents involving members of that fraternity, the acts taken against the pledge were reasonably foreseeable. The university had a duty to protect the pledge. Whether it breached that duty was a question of fact that had to be decided at trial. The court reversed the pretrial judgment in favor of the university. *Knoll v. Board of Regents of the Univ. of Nebraska*, 601 N.W.2d 757 (Neb. 1999). [NE]

◆   *Where the consumption of alcohol is coerced by social pressure or otherwise, it may not be voluntary, and liability may result.*

A Missouri university student was invited to become a member of a campus organization that was responsible for organizing the annual St. Pat's festivities. To gain membership to the organization, the student had to undergo an initiation that allegedly consisted of the coerced chugging and excessive consumption of alcohol, as well as other physical and verbal abuse. Members of the organization allegedly forced the student to consume a heated preparation of grain alcohol and green peas until he became unconscious, then left him unattended despite knowing that a participant in the initiation had died three years earlier. The student died two days later, and his parents filed a wrongful death lawsuit against the organization and the individual members who had conducted the initiation, as well as the fraternities on whose property the initiation took place. The trial court dismissed the action, and the parents appealed to the Court of Appeals of Missouri.

The court of appeals reversed and remanded the case. **Here, despite the apparently voluntary consumption of alcohol by the student, there may have been great social pressure to drink.** That coercion may have overcome any decision the student might have made about whether he should consume alcohol and, if so, how much he should consume. The case should not have been dismissed. *Nisbet v. Bucher*, 949 S.W.2d 111 (Mo. App. 1997). [MO]

◆ *A university was liable to a student for hazing injuries where it knew or should have known that hazing was going on.*

After receiving a full football scholarship, a student at the University of Delaware decided to join a fraternity and began his pledge period. The university prohibited hazing, as did the national organization. However, hazing continued. At the end of the pledge period—on "hell night"—the student was subjected to physical and emotional abuse as part of the hazing process. The night culminated with a lye-based liquid oven cleaner being poured over his back and neck. He suffered first and second-degree chemical burns, withdrew from the university and relinquished his scholarship. The national organization revoked the local fraternity's charter, but the university, due to a lack of cooperation, was unable to discipline students after the incident. The student sued the university, the fraternity and the perpetrator who poured the lye on him, and a jury awarded him $30,000, apportioning 93 percent of the liability against the university and 7 percent against the perpetrating student. The court then overturned the jury verdict against the university.

On appeal to the Supreme Court of Delaware, the court held that the student could be deemed an invitee of the university. Accordingly, once the university knew or had reason to know that a third party's actions could cause harm to the student, it had a duty to protect him. **The court found that there was sufficient evidence before the university that hazing activities still were taking place, and that the university thus had a duty to protect the student.** Further, the university's anti-hazing and security regulations indicated that the university had control over the premises sufficient to justify the award of damages against it. The court reversed the lower court's decision to overturn the jury verdict. *Furek v. University of Delaware*, 594 A.2d 506 (Del. 1991). [DE]

◆ *A fraternity member was convicted under a hazing statute after the death of a pledge. His challenge to the constitutionality of the statute failed.*

A fraternity member at a university in Missouri subjected pledges to repeated physical abuse, including kicks, punches, caning of the soles of the feet, and other forms of beating. As a result of the abuse, one of the pledges blacked out. He never regained consciousness and died the following afternoon. An autopsy revealed that he had broken ribs, a lacerated kidney, a lacerated liver, upper body bruises and a subdural hematoma of the brain, which proved fatal. The fraternity member was charged with five counts of hazing and, after his conviction, was sentenced to six months imprisonment for each count. He appealed to the Supreme Court of Missouri, asserting that the hazing statute violated the First Amendment's right to associate, as well as the Fifth and Fourteenth Amendments' rights to due process and equal protection.

The supreme court found that **the hazing statute did not prevent fraternity members from meeting at any time and place they might choose**. Further, the statute did not infringe upon constitutional rights once the fraternity members met. It merely prohibited recklessly endangering the mental or physical health or safety of a prospective member as a condition of admission into or preservation of membership in the fraternity. Accordingly, the statute was constitutional, and the fraternity member's conviction was affirmed. *State v. Allen*, 905 S.W.2d 874 (Mo. 1995). [MO]

CHAPTER FOUR

Freedom of Speech and Religion

I. EMPLOYEES

The First Amendment guarantees freedom of speech by prohibiting the government from abridging that freedom. This does not mean that the freedom to speak is absolute. Certain kinds of speech are entitled to more protections than others. For example, the Supreme Court has held that obscenity is not protected by the First Amendment.

Where speech addresses a matter of public concern, rather than a purely private matter, courts balance the interests of the individual whose speech is being curtailed against the interests of the government in prohibiting that speech. Where the governmental interests outweigh the individual's interests, the right to speak is lost. Where the individual's right to speak prevails, the speech is protected by the First Amendment.

The First Amendment generally prohibits only governmental action against an individual's right to speak. Where the entity infringing on speech rights is private, the First Amendment does not protect against censorship. Thus, free speech issues are much more prevalent in the context of public college and university law.

Prior restraint–prohibiting a person from speaking before they can do so–is especially frowned upon. Courts presume that prior restraint is constitutionally invalid. Thus, the government must meet a very heavy burden to show that such restraint is necessary. The government's interest must be compelling and there must be no less restrictive means of achieving that governmental interest.

The balancing test utilized in First Amendment cases involving public employees comes from U.S. Supreme Court cases including Pickering v. Board of Educ. *and* Mt. Healthy City School Dist. v. Doyle, *below. In* Connick v. Myers, *461 U.S. 138, 103 S.Ct. 1684, 75 L.Ed.2d 708 (1983), the Court held* ***a public employee's speech upon matters of purely personal interest is not afforded constitutional protection.*** *In* Rankin v. McPherson, *483 U.S. 378, 107 S.Ct. 2891, 97 L.Ed.2d 315 (1987), the Court held that whether an employee's speech addresses a matter of public concern is determined by the content, form, and context of the speech, as revealed by the entire record.*

A. Protected Speech

◆ *When an employee speaks on a matter of public concern, and is then disciplined, courts use a balancing test to determine whether the employee's right to speak outweighs the employer's right to promote workplace efficiency.*

An Illinois school district fired a high school teacher for sending a letter to the editor of a local newspaper criticizing the board and district superintendent for their handling of school funding methods. The letter particularly criticized the board's handling of a bond issue and allocation of funding between school educational and athletic programs. The teacher also charged the superintendent with attempting to stifle opposing views on the subject. The board held a hearing at which it charged the teacher with publishing a defamatory letter. It then fired the teacher for making false statements. An Illinois court affirmed the board's action, as did the Illinois Supreme Court, which held the teacher's speech was unprotected by the First Amendment because his teaching position required him to refrain from statements about school operations.

The U.S. Supreme Court disagreed that public employment subjected the teacher to deprivation of his constitutional rights. **The state interest in regulating employee speech must be balanced with individual rights. The Court outlined a general analysis for evaluating public employee speech, ruling that employees are entitled to constitutional protection to comment on matters of public concern.** The public interest in free speech and debate on matters of public concern was so great that it barred public officials from recovering damages for defamatory statements unless they were made with reckless disregard for their truth. Because there was no evidence presented that the letter damaged any board member's professional reputation, **the teacher's comments were not detrimental to the school system, but only constituted a difference of opinion**. Since there was no proof of reckless disregard for the truth by the teacher and the matter concerned the public interest, the board could not constitutionally terminate his employment. The Court reversed and remanded the case. *Pickering v. Board of Educ.,* 391 U.S. 563, 88 S.Ct. 1731, 20 L.Ed.2d 811 (1968). [IL]

◆ *Where employees can be disciplined or discharged for legitimate reasons, the First Amendment will not protect them from the adverse action unless the action was taken in response to protected speech.*

An untenured teacher was not rehired after a number of incidents that led the school board to conclude he lacked tactfulness in handling professional matters. After the board decided not to reemploy the teacher, he asked for and received a list of the board's reasons. The board gave general reasons for its failure to rehire him and noted that he had made an obscene gesture and had given an on-air opinion about school dress codes at a local radio station. The teacher sued for reinstatement on the grounds that his discussion with the radio station was protected by the First Amendment and that to refuse reemployment was a violation of his free speech rights. An Ohio federal court and a court of appeals agreed, and ordered reinstatement with back pay. The school board appealed to the U.S. Supreme Court.

The Court first rejected the school board's argument that the Eleventh Amendment barred private lawsuits against local political subdivisions such as a school district. City and county governments were not "states" within the meaning of the Eleventh Amendment. However, the Court overturned the lower court decisions, holding that apart from the actions for which the teacher might claim First Amendment protection, the board could have chosen not to rehire him on the basis of several other incidents. The radio station incident, while clearly implicating a protected right, was not the substantial reason for nonrenewal. The board could have reached the same decision had the teacher not engaged in constitutionally protected conduct. **A marginal employee should not be able to prevent dismissal by engaging in constitutionally protected activity and then hiding under a constitutional shield as protection from all other actions that were not constitutionally protected.** The lower courts were instructed to determine whether the board's decision could have been reached absent the constitutionally protected activity of phoning the radio station, and, if such a decision could have been reached, whether remedial action to correct the violation would be necessary. *Mt. Healthy City School Dist. v. Doyle*, 429 U.S. 274, 97 S.Ct. 568, 50 L.Ed.2d 471 (1977). [OH]

◆ *The Tenth Circuit upheld a jury verdict which found an Oklahoma administrator had participated in the wrongful termination of a professor.*

An Oklahoma university assistant professor was appointed to a tenure-track position. He complained to an administrator about overcrowding in his classroom and other safety concerns, and e-mailed university officials and the state fire marshal about these issues. Department faculty and an interim department chair approved the professor's tenure application, but the university vice-president of academic affairs recommended against renewing his one-year contract. The professor sued university officials in a federal district court after his contract was not renewed, alleging retaliation for exercising his speech and association rights. A jury returned a verdict in his favor, finding the board of regents liable for $34,959 and the vice president liable for $53,063. The court denied the vice president's motion to vacate the judgment and he appealed.

The Tenth Circuit held a court will grant a motion for judgment to set aside a verdict only if the evidence leads to one conclusion that is not susceptible to reasonable inferences supporting the verdict. **The vice president failed to present sufficient evidence from the trial transcript that he was not personally involved in undermining the professor's tenure application. He could be held liable for wrongful termination if he set in motion a series of** events that he knew or reasonably should have known would cause others to deprive the professor of his constitutional rights. The court affirmed the judgment for the professor. *Garrett v. Hibler*, No. 02-6300, 80 Fed.Appx. 82, 2003 WL 22457045 (10th Cir. 2003). [OK]

◆ *The U.S. Court of Appeals, Second Circuit held a 42 U.S.C. § 1983 action could not be brought against a Connecticut university board of trustees because the board was not a "person" within the meaning of § 1983.*

A technical college denied emeritus status to a retired professor. He sued the college board of trustees in a federal district court for retaliation in violation of his First Amendment and equal protection rights. The court granted the trustees' motion for summary judgment, and the professor appealed to the Second Circuit. The court noted the constitutional claims had been pleaded under 42 U.S.C. § 1983, a federal law that creates no rights itself, but provides a cause of action for rights secured by the U.S. Constitution and laws. **A § 1983 action can be brought only against a "person." The court held a university board of trustees is an entity, not a "person" under § 1983.** The order for summary judgment in the board's favor was correct. *Gaby v. Board of Trustees of Community Technical Colleges*, 348 F.3d 62 (2nd Cir. 2003). [CT]

◆ *The Court of Appeals of California held a professor did not show a university deprived him of his First Amendment and due process rights.*

The professor agreed to teach a course abroad, and arranged for substitutes to teach his classes without informing his department. The university claimed this was unprofessional conduct and demoted him. An arbitrator reversed the decision, and the professor sued the university for civil rights violations and breach of contract. A court awarded the university summary judgment. Two years later, the professor sued the university again, alleging it retaliated against him for filing a grievance and filing the previous lawsuit. A court again held for the university. The professor filed a third action against the university for First Amendment violations and defamation. The court awarded summary judgment to the university, and he appealed to the Court of Appeal of California.

The court stated that to succeed on a First Amendment retaliation claim, the professor had to establish his prior lawsuits involved the public concern. Evaluation of the constitutional protection due an employee's speech requires examining its content, form, and context. The court characterized the grievance and lawsuits as "speech involving individual personnel disputes," which would not be relevant to the public's evaluation of the university. The professor did not inform the public about his demotion, nor did he use it as an example of how the university was interfering with its obligations to students or taxpayers. There was no evidence that the professor personally heard any of the statements forming the basis for his defamation claim, and the court affirmed the judgment in all respects. *Aviel v. California State Univ., Hayward*, No. A102092, 2003 WL 22810321 (Cal. App. 1st Dist. 2003). [CA]

◆ *An Illinois college avoided liability in a speech rights action by a discharged employee. However, the court denied summary judgment to the college and supervisory employees for a related retaliation claim.*

The employee worked as an account manager and sold more contracts than any other person in her department. However, she failed to complete required time sheets and was the subject of complaints about her sarcasm and criticism of others. The employee refused to contribute to a "team fund" for gift certificates, meetings and catered lunches. She complained that the fund was not approved by the college and was unethical. The employee then received a warning to "stop the abusive behavior" and reduce her absenteeism. After another warning several months later, the college fired her.

The employee sued the college and two supervisors in a federal district court for speech rights violations and retaliation. The college and supervisors argued her decision to opt out of the team fund was for purely personal reasons and did not involve the public concern. The court denied the supervisors' motion concerning the speech rights claim. **The misuse of public funds is a matter of public concern and the employee presented sufficient evidence to go forward with this claim against the supervisors. The court agreed with the college that it could not be held vicariously liable for the supervisors' conduct, since they had no policymaking authority.** Although the college was entitled to judgment for this claim, the court denied the remainder of its motion. *Carpanzano v. College of Dupage*, No. 03 C 4358, 2004 WL 442606 (N.D. Ill. 2003). [IL]

◆ *An employee's complaints about the lenient disciplining of a co-worker were not protected free speech.*

An Ohio university employee sought a promotion to a better position and had to compete for the job against a co-worker. The co-worker stated that she was going to bring a gun in and kill the employee, and fellow employees reported the threats to a university official. After the co-worker admitted making the remarks, the official determined that she was not dangerous. However, he placed her on administrative leave and required her to undergo counseling. The employee then received the promotion. When she later approached the HR department to discuss her concerns about the discipline meted out, and filed numerous grievances, retaliatory actions were allegedly taken against her. She sued under 42 U.S.C. § 1983, asserting First Amendment violations. An Ohio federal court ruled against her, noting first that **she had not been speaking out on a matter of public concern, but had rather addressed internal employee matters.** Second, even if her speech had been of a public nature, it undermined the university's daily operations (because it was disruptive) and therefore was not protected under the balance-of-interests tests established by *Pickering*, above. *Serrato v. Bowling Green State Univ.*, 252 F.Supp.2d 550 (N.D. Ohio 2003). [OH]

◆ *A professor could not show that his speech was on a matter of public concern so as to be protected under the First Amendment.*

A professor at a state university in Florida filed several complaints against various colleagues alleging, among other things, misrepresentations in tenure applications. The Florida Ethics Commission dismissed his complaints. He asked for a transfer to another campus and, while there, filed ethics complaints against two other professors. After those complaints also were dismissed, he was transferred again. He sued the university and various co-workers under 42

U.S.C. § 1983, alleging that he was retaliated against for exercising his First Amendment rights. The university and co-workers sought to dismiss the case. A state court refused to do so, but the Florida District Court of Appeal held that the lawsuit should have been dismissed. Not only was the university entitled to sovereign immunity as an arm of the state, but **the professor failed to demonstrate that he had spoken out on a matter of public concern**. His complaints concerned personal matters and not public interests. As a result, under *Pickering*, above, he was not entitled to constitutional protection. *Board of Regents of the State of Florida v. Snyder*, 826 So.2d 382 (Fla. App. 2002). [FL]

◆ *A dean's refusal to terminate certain courses amounted to protected speech under the First Amendment.*

The dean of a community college was directed to terminate the engineering and machine tool technology programs, but refused to do so. He asserted that terminating the programs would violate Illinois law because of the large number of students currently enrolled in them. When the college fired him for refusing to follow the directive, he sued it under the First and Fourteenth Amendments and for wrongful discharge. The college sought to dismiss his claims. A federal court ruled for the college on the Fourteenth Amendment claim because the dean had no constitutionally protected property right in continued employment. However, it refused to dismiss the First Amendment claim because **the dean had established a *prima facie* case of retaliation. He was fired for refusing to terminate the courses**—a matter of public concern. The court also refused to dismiss the wrongful discharge claim. *Butts v. Triton College*, 2001 WL 1298723 (N.D. Ill. 10/23/01). [IL]

◆ *A directive issued to limit contact with prospective student-athletes violated the First Amendment as an unconstitutional prior restraint.*

The mascot of the University of Illinois is "Chief Illiniwek," a figure some believe is insulting to American Indians. After certain members of the university community contacted prospective student-athletes to discuss whether they wanted to participate in an athletic program that promoted stereotypes and biases, the chancellor of the university sent out an e-mail requiring all communication with potential student-athletes to be authorized by the athletic director. The university maintained that the directive was issued to ensure compliance with NCAA rules on the amount of contact schools can have with prospective student-athletes. A coalition of students and faculty who objected to the use of the mascot sued the chancellor for violating their First Amendment rights, and a federal court judge ruled that the directive was unconstitutional. He issued a temporary restraining order against the directive. The judge then held that **the directive was an unconstitutional prior restraint that was not narrowly tailored to achieve a legitimate purpose**. It prohibited more speech than was necessary to comply with the NCAA's rules. As a result, the university violated the First Amendment by issuing the directive. The issue of damages was to be resolved at a later trial. *Crue v. Aiken*, 204 F.Supp.2d 1130 (C.D. Ill. 2002). [IL]

◆   *A university could prevent an employee from using a vulgar phrase as part of her e-mail signature.*

A part-time university student also worked at one of the university's graduate schools. She altered her e-mail messages so that the phrase, "The truth shall set you free, but first it will piss you off! Gloria Steinem," would automatically appear as part of her e-mail signature. When her supervisor instructed her to remove the quote from work-related e-mails because the word "piss" was vulgar and inappropriate, she did so, then challenged the directive internally. After she lost her internal challenge, she sued the university and her supervisor for violating her speech rights under the First Amendment. A Wisconsin federal court ruled in favor of the defendants, and the Seventh Circuit Court of Appeals affirmed. It rejected the employee's argument that the university had created a limited public forum with its e-mail system such that it could not engage in viewpoint discrimination against her. The court also found that her speech was not on a matter of public concern. Further, **even if her speech had been of a public nature, the university's interest in regulating inappropriate language outweighed her interest in speaking**. The university had appropriately directed her to cease using the e-mail signature. *Pichelmann v. Madsen*, 31 Fed.Appx. 322 (7th Cir. 2002). [WI]

◆   *A professor's controversial remarks in an underground newspaper were protected by the First Amendment.*

A professor at a California community college wrote and published an underground newspaper, in which he made a number of controversial statements of a vaguely threatening nature against the president and the board of trustees. The chancellor of the community college district reprimanded the professor for violating the district's policies on workplace violence, discrimination and harassment. He ordered the professor to cease all verbal threats and attend an anger management program. The professor sued under the First and Fourteenth Amendments. A federal court ruled for the professor on the First Amendment claim, but dismissed the Fourteenth Amendment equal protection claim. On further appeal, the Ninth Circuit Court of Appeals affirmed in part, ruling that a portion of the district's workplace violence policy was unconstitutional. **Where the policy prohibited the making of "violent behavior overtones," it was unconstitutionally vague.** Also, the professor's speech was on a matter of public concern and outweighed the administrative interest in suppressing that speech. Thus, the district violated the professor's First Amendment rights by reprimanding him for his newspaper writings. *Bauer v. Sampson*, 261 F.3d 775 (9th Cir. 2001). [CA]

◆   *A university may have violated a professor's First Amendment rights by denying him a promotion after he publicly denounced the large amount of feminist literature in the curriculum.*

A tenured professor who taught American literature courses at Portland State University spoke out publicly against feminist criticism of male writers in American literature and against the increase of feminist-oriented courses in the English department. He alleged that two colleagues opposed and delayed his promotion to full professor and that they and other members of the department recommended that he not receive merit pay increases and salary raises proportionate to his qualifications. He also alleged that the defendants succeeded in reducing the courses he taught and that they ridiculed, harassed and humiliated him.

In his 42 U.S.C. § 1983 lawsuit against his colleagues, a federal court granted summary judgment to the defendants. The Ninth Circuit reversed, noting that a college professor cannot be arbitrarily disciplined for speaking freely. **Any member of a college faculty would know that denying a staff member a promotion because of his speech on educational policy would violate his constitutional rights.** However, the allegations that the defendants limited his course offerings and denied him a position on a search committee were not covered by § 1983. Professors do not have property rights to the units assigned their courses, the length of courses or their place on a college search committee. *Hollister v. Tuttle*, 210 F.3d 1033 (9th Cir. 2000). [OR]

◆   *A Virginia law that prohibits state employees from accessing sexually explicit material on state-owned computers did not violate the constitutional rights of a group of professors.*

A Virginia law required state employees to obtain written approval from an agency head before using an agency-owned or leased computer to access, download, print or store information with sexually explicit content. Six professors from various public universities in Virginia sued state officials in federal court, asserting that the law violated their First Amendment rights of free speech and academic freedom. The court granted pretrial judgment to the professors, finding that the law infringed on their constitutional rights.

The state officials appealed to the U.S. Court of Appeals for the Fourth Circuit, which reversed. The court noted that the law did not prohibit all access to explicit material by state employees, since they still could view such material on computers not owned or leased by the state. Access to materials through the use of state-owned or leased computers involved a professor's role as an employee, not as a private citizen. **Since the law did not regulate state employee speech that was of public concern, it did not violate the professors' First Amendment speech rights.** The court also rejected the professors' alternative argument that the law violated their particular right to academic freedom. Any right of academic freedom belonged to the university and was not an individual right. *Urofsky v. Gilmore*, 216 F.3d 401 (4th Cir. 2000). [VA]

◆   *University professors could not be barred from testifying against the state in various lawsuits.*

A Texas state university policy and a state law prohibited university professors and state employees from taking employment as consultants or expert witnesses in litigation against the state, or when doing so would create a conflict with the state's interests. A number of professors sued to have the policy and the law struck down as unconstitutional. They asserted that their free speech and equal protection rights were being violated. A federal court granted the professors a preliminary injunction, and the state appealed. The Fifth Circuit Court of Appeals affirmed, finding that the policy and the law were impermissibly overbroad under the First Amendment. **The professors' rights to testify (whether for a fee or not) on a matter of public concern outweighed the state's right to prevent its employees from creating a conflict by testifying against it.** Although the court acknowledged that there could be times when the state's interest would outweigh the interests of the professors, the policy and the law at issue here prohibited all speech, even that which would not adversely affect the state's interest in the efficient delivery of public services. The court further noted that although some of the professors were being paid as expert witnesses or consultants, their speech did not qualify as commercial speech, for which less protection would be available. The policy and the law were struck down. *Hoover v. Morales,* 164 F.3d 221 (5th Cir. 1998). [TX]

◆   *Where a university allowed the history department to use a display case, it could not regulate the type of expression employed.*

The history department of a Minnesota university maintained a display case in a university building hallway. Two student members of the university history club proposed that professors pose in photographs depicting their areas of historical interest for a display in the case. Eleven professors posed in period costumes and their pictures were displayed with their written comments. **The university's affirmative action officer observed that two of the photographs showed professors posed with weapons and declared them insensitive and inappropriate.** The university chancellor agreed to remove the pictures, and the students and professors filed a federal district court action against the chancellor and university, asserting constitutional violations. The court granted the university's summary judgment motion. However, the court denied summary judgment to the chancellor on the issue of qualified immunity, finding that his actions violated the clearly established First Amendment rights of the professors and students.

The chancellor appealed to the U.S. Court of Appeals, Eighth Circuit, which reversed the district court decision, but later granted a petition to review the matter. On review, **the court found that the history display was an appropriate use of the display case and that once the university recognized the use of the case by the history department, it could not discriminate against different types of speech being expressed there**. The chancellor's decision to discriminate against the viewpoint expressed by the professors and students violated clearly established First Amendment rights. Because there was no valid reason for curtailing this expression, the district court had correctly denied the chancellor's summary judgment motion for qualified immunity. *Burnham v. Ianni,* 119 F.3d 668 (8th Cir. 1997). [MN]

◆   *In* Waters v. Churchill, *511 U.S. 661 (1994), the U.S. Supreme Court held a reasonable belief of workplace disruption can be enough to outweigh a speaker's rights under the First Amendment.*

The chairman of the Black Studies department at City College of New York gave a speech proclaiming bias in the state public school curriculum. His remarks included derogatory statements against Jews. The college board of trustees then voted to limit his term as department chair to one year instead of the usual three. The professor sued the college, its board of trustees and individual trustees in a New York federal court for violating his First Amendment rights. The court conducted a jury trial and determined that **the professor had been demoted because of his speech, even though the speech did not disrupt department operations.** The jury also determined that the trustees had been motivated by a reasonable expectation that the speech would cause disruption and that some of the trustees had acted with malicious intent to violate his constitutional rights. The court ordered reinstatement and awarded punitive damages to the professor. The U.S. Court of Appeals, Second Circuit, affirmed the decision in part and remanded the case for correction of some inconsistencies in the damage award. However, the U.S. Supreme Court vacated and remanded the case for reconsideration.

On remand, the court of appeals reviewed the case in light of *Waters v. Churchill*, 511 U.S. 661, 114 S.Ct. 1878, 128 L.Ed.2d 686 (1994), a Supreme Court decision that reduced the burden on a government employer to demonstrate the actual disruptiveness of an employee's speech. *Waters* held that employment termination was permitted where only a likelihood of disruption existed. It was unnecessary to demonstrate an actual disruption if termination was based on the employer's reasonable belief that a disruption could occur. Because the jury had found that **the professor's speech had a reasonable potential for interfering with college operations**, the demotion had not been improperly motivated. The trustees had not violated the professor's First Amendment rights, and the district court's judgment was reversed and remanded. *Jeffries v. Harleston*, 52 F.3d 9 (2d Cir. 1995). [NY]

B. Religion and Free Speech

The First Amendment, in addition to providing free speech rights, contains the Establishment Clause, which prohibits Congress from making any law respecting the establishment of religion. The Free Exercise Clause of the First Amendment bars Congress from making any law that prohibits the free exercise of religion. Like the speech provisions of the First Amendment, the religion clauses apply only to governmental action.

◆ *A Kansas university's display of a controversial statue did not violate the Establishment Clause, because the display had a secular purpose and its primary effect was not hostility toward the Roman Catholic Church.*

Washburn University selected five statues to be placed on its campus as part of an annual sculpture exhibit. One of the statues was titled "Holier than Thou." It depicted a Roman Catholic bishop wearing a miter and a stole, with a "grotesque" negative expression. A tenured professor of biology and a student president of a Catholic campus center sued the university and its officials in a federal district court, asserting the statue had an anti-Catholic message that violated the Establishment Clause. The university moved for dismissal.

The court utilized the test from *Lemon v. Kurtzman*, 403 U.S. 602 (1971) to determine if the university violated the Establishment Clause. **It rejected arguments by the student and professor that the statue promoted bigotry and hatred toward Catholics and their faith. There was no evidence the**

statue was selected because of its religious message, or that the university had a policy of antagonism towards Catholicism. A reasonable person would not find the statue conveyed an anti-Catholic message. The court held the display of the statue had a secular purpose that did not foster hostility toward the Catholic Church. The university did not violate the Establishment Clause, and the court entered judgment in its favor. *O'Connor v. Washburn Univ.*, 305 F.Supp.2d 1217 (D. Kan. 2004). [KS]

◆   *If a public college or university creates a public forum for speech, it cannot prohibit religious speech. However, where no public forum is created, reasonable restrictions can be imposed.*

A physiology professor at the University of Alabama occasionally mentioned his religious beliefs during classes. He also scheduled an after-class discussion group entitled "Evidence of God in Human Physiology," which several of his students attended. Although he stated that his remarks were his own personal bias, a group of his students complained to the head of the physiology department. **The department head, after meeting with the dean and the school's attorney, drafted a memo directing the professor to stop interjecting his personal religious beliefs in class and not to hold the optional classes.** The professor petitioned the president of the university for a rescission of the order, but the president affirmed the restrictions. The professor filed suit in federal court under 42 U.S.C. § 1983 seeking an injunction lifting the restrictions placed on his speech. The professor moved for summary judgment. **The trial court determined that the university had created a public forum for the exchange of ideas, and that the university's interests were not sufficient to justify restricting the professor's freedom of speech.** The court granted summary judgment in favor of the professor. The university appealed to the U.S. Court of Appeals, Eleventh Circuit.

The appeals court rejected the district court's determination that a classroom constituted a public forum. It relied on the U.S. Supreme Court's decision in *Hazelwood School Dist. v. Kuhlmeier*, 484 U.S. 261, 108 S.Ct. 562, 98 L.Ed.2d 592 (1988), in which the Court stated that "school facilities may be deemed to be public forums only if school authorities have ... opened those facilities for indiscriminate use by the general public." If the facilities, as in this case, have been reserved for other intended purposes, no public forum has been created. **Where no public forum exists, school officials may impose reasonable restrictions on the speech rights of students and teachers. Accordingly, the appeals court held that the professor's classroom was not a public forum and the university could reasonably regulate his speech.** In addition, the university could prohibit the professor from promoting and scheduling optional classes. The court reversed the district court's judgment. *Bishop v. Aronov*, 926 F.2d 1066 (11th Cir. 1991). [AL]

◆   *The Supreme Court held the act of certifying a union by the National Labor Relations Board (NLRB) infringed on a Catholic school's rights.*

The right of employees of a Catholic school system to join together and be recognized as a bargaining unit was successfully challenged in a case decided by the U.S. Supreme Court. In this case, the unions were certified by the NLRB as bargaining units, but the diocese refused to bargain. The court said that the religion clauses of the U.S. Constitution, which require religious organizations to finance their educational systems without governmental aid, also free the religious organizations of the obviously inhibiting effect and impact of unionization of their teachers. The court agreed with the employer's contention that **the very threshold act of certification of the union by the NLRB would necessarily alter and infringe upon the religious character of parochial schools**, since this would mean that the bishop would no longer be the sole repository of authority as required by church law. Instead, he would have to share some decision making with the union. This, said the Court, violated the religion clauses of the U.S. Constitution. *NLRB v. Catholic Bishop of Chicago*, 440 U.S. 490, 99 S.Ct. 1313, 59 L.Ed.2d 533 (1979). [IL]

◆ *Two nuns hired to perform secular services for a New Jersey university could bring a breach of contract action after being discharged.*

A Catholic university hired the nuns for computer science department positions. Their probationary contracts had no religious conditions and were used for both lay and clerical faculty. The university later decided the nuns were a "disruptive influence" and should be dismissed. Instead of following university procedures, university officials consulted a Marist brother who was an administrator for the university. He conferred with the nuns' Ursuline superiors who refused the nuns permission to renew their contracts. The university dismissed the nuns under Roman Catholic canon law, which prohibited "accepting duties outside the institute without permission of the legitimate superior." The nuns sued the university in a state court, which upheld their breach of contract claim. A state appeals court reversed the decision.

The nuns appealed to the New Jersey Supreme Court, which considered **whether matters of religion precluded a civil court action under the Free Exercise Clause**. It distinguished between religious school employees who "spread the faith" and those with "secular obligations." The court held the "ministerial function test" prohibited court intervention only when the employment activity involved direct participation in religious activities. The nuns had not counseled students as to spiritual affairs or moral matters and had performed primarily secular tasks. The court found **the nuns had not performed any "ministerial functions." They had been hired for their computer skills, not for their clerical value.** There was no indication that the contracts were to be governed by canon law. The court held that state courts had jurisdiction over their claims and reversed the holding of the court of appeals. *Welter v. Seton Hall Univ.*, 608 A.2d 206 (N.J. 1992). [NJ]

C. Loyalty Oaths

◆ *A loyalty oath could not be administered to two applicants who objected to it on religious grounds.*

Two Jehovah's Witnesses applied for positions with the California Community College District. As part of state-mandated preemployment procedures, the district required the applicants to sign an oath swearing "true faith and allegiance" and to "support and defend" the United States and

California Constitutions. The applicants refused to take the oath due to their religious beliefs, and the district rejected their applications.

The applicants sued the district under the Religious Freedom Restoration Act of 1993 (RFRA), challenging the validity of the loyalty oath as a condition precedent for employment. A California federal court held that **requiring the applicants to take an oath that violated their religious tenets placed an undue burden on their right to free exercise of religion**. The district failed to assert that the loyalty oath furthered a compelling government interest or was the least restrictive means of achieving that interest. Although employee loyalty was a compelling interest, the evidence failed to establish that a loyalty oath effectively achieved this goal. An alternative oath directed to an applicant's actions rather than his or her beliefs would be equally effective and less restrictive. Because the loyalty oath could not be justified under the compelling interest test articulated in the RFRA, the court enjoined the district from administering the loyalty oath to the applicants. *Bessard v. California Community Colleges*, 867 F.Supp. 1454 (E.D. Cal. 1994). [CA]

[*Editor's Note*: The U.S. Supreme Court held that the RFRA was unconstitutional as applied to state actions in *City of Boerne, Texas v. Flores*, 521 U.S. 507, 117 S.Ct. 2157, 138 L.Ed.2d 624 (1997).]

◆ *In 1955, as McCarthyism waned, the Supreme Court invalidated a New York City charter provision that purported to deprive Communist Party members of their Fifth Amendment right against self-incrimination.*

Section 903 of New York City's charter provided that any city employee who used the Fifth Amendment's self-incrimination privilege to avoid answering a question relating to official conduct would lose tenure and be ineligible for future city employment. An associate professor of German at Brooklyn College was called before the U.S. Senate Judiciary Committee's Internal Security Subcommittee to testify about subversive influences within the nation's educational system. The professor testified that he was not a member of the Communist party and was completely willing to answer questions about his political affiliation from 1941 to the present date. However, he refused to answer questions about his political beliefs during 1940 and 1941 on the grounds that his answers might incriminate him. After the professor testified, the college suspended him even though he had taught there 27 years and was entitled to tenure under New York state law. Three days later, his position was vacated in accordance with § 903. If not for § 903, because he was tenured, the professor would have been entitled to notice, a hearing and the opportunity to appeal an unfavorable decision, with discharge for just cause being the only appropriate result.

The professor sued, challenging the constitutionality of § 903. He argued that the section violated the Privileges and Immunities Clause of the Fourteenth Amendment since it effectively imposed a penalty on the exercise of a federally guaranteed right in a federal proceeding. He also argued that it violated his due process rights under the Fifth and Fourteenth Amendment because the statute did not provide a reasonable basis for his termination. The case reached the U.S. Supreme Court, which held that **the statute violated the Due Process Clause** and therefore did not rule on the Privileges and Immunities Clause claim. The Court also held that taking the self-incrimination privilege could not automatically be interpreted to mean that the teacher had been a Communist Party member. The Court held that such an arbitrary dismissal violated due process. *Slochower v. Board of Educ.*, 350 U.S. 551, 76 S.Ct. 637, 100 L.Ed. 692 (1955). [NY]

◆ *A state could not require teachers to file annual affidavits listing every organization they belonged to in the past five years.*

The Arkansas legislature established **a statute that required every teacher employed by a state-supported school or college to file an annual affidavit listing every organization to which he or she had belonged in the past five years**. A teacher who had worked for an Arkansas school system for 25 years and who was a member of the NAACP was told he would have to file such an affidavit before the start of the next school year. After he failed to do so, his contract for the next year was not renewed. He filed a class action lawsuit against the school district in a federal district court.

The court found that the teacher was not a member of the Communist Party, nor of any organization advocating the violent overthrow of the government. It upheld the statute, finding that the information requested by the school district was relevant. The Supreme Court of Arkansas had previously upheld the statute's constitutionality in a case brought by other teachers. The U.S. Supreme Court agreed to hear both cases and consolidated them for a hearing. The Court noted that the state certainly had a right to investigate teachers, since education of youth was a vital public interest. It stated that the requirement of the affidavit was reasonably related to the state's interest. However, the Court held that **requiring teachers to name all their associations was an interference of teacher free speech and association rights**. The Court ruled that because fundamental rights were involved, governmental screening of teachers was required to be narrowly tailored to the state's ends. Because the statute went beyond what was necessary to meet the state's inquiry into the fitness of its teachers, the Court ruled it unconstitutional. *Shelton v. Tucker,* 364 U.S. 479, 81 S.Ct. 247, 5 L.Ed.2d 231 (1960). [AR]

◆ *The Supreme Court struck down a Florida loyalty oath statute as unconstitutionally vague.*

A Florida law required all state employees to submit a written oath, certifying that they had never lent counsel, advised, aided or supported the Communist party. Failure to submit such an oath resulted in the employee's immediate termination. A teacher who had taught in the same Florida school district for nine years was dismissed when he refused to sign the oath. The teacher sought a declaration that the statute was unconstitutional and an injunction to prevent its enforcement. A Florida trial court refused to grant an injunction, and the Florida Supreme Court affirmed this decision. After determining that the case was based on federal law and was properly a matter in which it had jurisdiction, the U.S. Supreme Court struck the statute down as a violation of the Fourteenth Amendment's Due Process Clause. **The statute was too vague to pass constitutional standards.** It compelled state employees to take the oath or face immediate dismissal. Because the statute lacked objective standards, no employee could truthfully take the oath. Statutes that made persons of average intelligence guess at their possible meanings and applications violated the Due Process Clause because they did not constitute true rules or standards. The Court reversed the Florida court decision, ruling for the teacher. *Cramp v. Board of Public Instruction of Orange County,* 368 U.S. 278, 82 S.Ct. 275, 7 L.Ed.2d 285 (1961). [FL]

◆ *Likewise, a Washington statute aimed at prohibiting subversives from becoming teachers was too vague to be constitutional.*

Faculty members at the University of Washington brought a class action suit to declare two state statutes unconstitutional. One statute required all state employees to take loyalty oaths, and the other required all teachers to take an oath as a condition of employment. Both oaths dealt with employee loyalty to the U.S. Constitution and to the government. The public employee statute applied to all public employees and defined a "subversive person" as one who conspired to overthrow the government. The Communist Party also was named as a subversive organization. Persons designated as subversives or Communist Party members were ineligible for public employment. The U.S. Supreme Court held that the statutes were vague and overbroad, and violated the Fourteenth Amendment's Due Process Clause. The statutes were too unspecific to provide sufficient notice of what conduct was prohibited. This constituted a denial of the teachers' due process rights. **The university could not require its teachers to take an oath that applied to some vague behavior in the future**, especially since there were First Amendment freedom of speech and association claims at stake. *Baggett v. Bullitt,* 377 U.S. 360, 84 S.Ct. 1316, 12 L.Ed.2d 377 (1963). [WA]

◆ *An Arizona statute that prohibited even associating with the Communist Party was struck down. The statute should have prohibited only those employees with a "specific intent" to do something illegal.*

An Arizona teacher who was a Quaker refused to take an oath required of all public employees under Arizona law. The oath swore that the employees would support both the Arizona and the U.S. Constitutions as well as state laws. The legislation also stated that anyone who took the oath and supported the Communist party or the violent overthrow of government would be discharged from employment and charged with perjury. The teacher sued for declaratory relief in the Arizona courts, having decided she could not take the oath in good conscience because she did not know what it meant.

The case eventually reached the U.S. Supreme Court, which held that political groups may have both legal and illegal aims and that there should not be a blanket prohibition on all groups that might have both legal and illegal goals. Such a prohibition would threaten legitimate political expression and association. The Court held that mere association with a group cannot be prohibited without a showing of "specific intent" to carry out the group's illegal purpose. It went on to say that **the Arizona statute was constitutionally deficient because it was not confined to those employees with a "specific intent" to do something illegal**. The statute infringed employee rights to free association by not punishing specific behavior that yielded a clear and present danger to government. The statute was struck down as unconstitutional. *Elfbrandt v. Russell,* 384 U.S. 11, 86 S.Ct. 1238, 16 L.Ed.2d 321 (1965). [AZ]

◆ *In 1967, the Supreme Court held that New York statutory prohibitions on treasonable and seditious speech by public employees were unconstitutionally vague. The statute might have allowed dismissal of employees who believed in such a doctrine, without actually advocating it.*

A group of faculty members at the privately owned University of Buffalo in New York continued their employment when the university merged into a state-operated university. They had to comply with a state plan that disqualified subversive persons from public employment. Four professors refused to sign a certificate that they were not Communists and that if they ever had been, they had notified the state university's president. One instructor was dismissed immediately. Two more continued to teach until their contracts ran out. Another was dismissed after refusing to answer under oath whether he had ever been a Communist party member. They sued. The U.S. Supreme Court examined the statute (which allowed the removal of public school teachers for "treasonable or seditious" utterances or acts) and held that **such words were too vague to allow teachers to know the difference between seditious and nonseditious utterances or acts**. In addition, another section of the statute allowed dismissal of any person who "by word of mouth or writing willfully and deliberately advocates, advises or teaches the doctrine" of the violent overthrow of government. The Court struck it down as too vague and sweeping, stating that it might allow dismissal of an employee who merely believes in such a doctrine, without actually advocating it. *Keyishian v. Board of Regents,* 385 U.S. 589, 87 S.Ct. 675, 17 L.Ed.2d 629 (1967). [NY]

◆ *The Supreme Court held that the line between permissible and impermissible conduct must be clearly drawn in loyalty oaths.*

A teacher was offered a position with the University of Maryland. However, he refused to take a loyalty oath required by the university for its employees. The oath required the employee to swear that he was not engaged in any attempt to overthrow the government by force or violence. The teacher brought suit challenging the oath's constitutionality. The U.S. Supreme Court decided that the oath's constitutionality had to be considered in conjunction with the state statute allowing the university board of regents to establish the oath. In addition, free speech rights were implicated because the First Amendment protects controversial as well as conventional speech. The Court held that **the authorizing statute was unconstitutionally vague and overbroad. It falsely assumed that someone belonging to a subversive group also supported the violent overthrow of the government.** The statute also put continuous surveillance on teachers by imposing a perjury threat. Such a concept was hostile to academic freedom, limiting the free flow of ideas in places of learning. The Court ruled that the line between permissible and impermissible conduct must be clearly drawn. **Because the statute failed to clearly define prohibited behavior, it was unconstitutional.** *Whitehill v. Elkins,* 389 U.S. 54, 88 S.Ct. 184, 19 L.Ed.2d 228 (1967). [MD]

D. Academic Freedom

In Sweezy v. New Hampshire, *354 U.S. 234, 77 S.Ct. 1203, 1 L.Ed.2d 1311 (1957), the Supreme Court stated "the essentiality of freedom in the community of American universities is almost self-evident.... Scholarship cannot flourish in an atmosphere of suspicion and distrust. Teachers and students must always remain free to inquire, to study and evaluate, to gain new maturity and understanding; otherwise our civilization will stagnate and die." However, academic freedom is not an absolute principle. The teacher's right to speak on a given matter must be balanced against the college or university's right to forward legitimate pedagogical interests.*

◆ *An Indiana university did not violate a professor's academic freedom by terminating his employment for poor job performance.*

Indiana State University hired an African history professor under a contract specifying a seven-year probationary period. A personnel committee recommended against reappointing him after two years, based on its finding that his performance was mediocre. The professor claimed a department chairperson advised him not to associate with other African professors and to become more involved with African-American activities. After exhausting his university appeals, the professor sued the university in a state court for due process and First Amendment violations. The university removed the case to a federal district court, which held his constitutional claims were meritless.

The professor appealed to the U.S. Court of Appeals, Seventh Circuit. It held that to succeed on a due process claim, the professor had to show the existence of a mutually explicit understanding of continued employment. A review of the contract showed the university had broad discretion to decide whether to reappoint him. As the professor did not establish a property interest in continued employment, his due process claim failed. His liberty interest claim failed because he could not show the university publicly communicated its denial of his re-appointment and that the communication damaged his good name. **The professor's academic freedom claim was meritless. The statements by the department chairperson resembled employment advice. They were not connected with the performance of employment duties,** and did not suppress the professor's First Amendment rights. Moreover, he was never sanctioned for having spoken about any issue. Accordingly, the court affirmed the judgment. *Omosegbon v. Wells*, 335 F.3d 668 (7th Cir. 2003). [IN]

◆ *If a professor's "philosophical counseling activities" were on a matter of public concern, a university might have violated his First Amendment rights by ordering him to cease those activities.*

A professor at the City College of New York, who was involved in "philosophical counseling activities" on campus, was instructed by college officials to cease those activities. He sued under 42 U.S.C. § 1983, alleging First Amendment and due process violations. A federal court granted the college's motion to dismiss the lawsuit, but the Second Circuit vacated that decision. Here, **the lower court should have determined what was involved in the professor's "philosophical counseling activities"** to ascertain whether the speech was on a matter of public concern so as to be protected under the First Amendment. The court remanded the case. *Marinoff v. City College of New York*, 63 Fed.Appx. 530, 2003 WL 1228032 (2d Cir. 2003). [NY]

◆ *A college was held to have inappropriately fired a professor for conduct and comments he made during class.*

A former professor at a Colorado junior college sued the college for terminating his employment on the basis of allegedly inappropriate classroom conduct and speech. The case arose when **a number of students complained he used an inappropriate teaching style and made offensive comments in class.** He allegedly discussed the presence of tampons in a sewer plant while lecturing about animal parasites, referred to human oral and anal sex and male orgasms during a lecture about the transmission of parasites, used euphemisms to describe feces, and implied that students were "dumb." He inappropriately referred to comments student evaluations and discussed matters unrelated to course content during class. A jury awarded the professor over $550,000.

The Tenth Circuit Court of Appeals affirmed the ruling for the professor. It noted that teachers enjoy some First Amendment protection in their classroom speech and cited to *Keyishian v. Bd. of Regents*, 385 U.S. 589 (*see* Section I.C., above), and *Tinker v. Des Moines Indep. Community School Dist.*, 393 U.S. 503 (1969). Although not every word uttered in class is protected by academic freedom, the jury found the termination was not reasonably related to legitimate pedagogical interests. As the college had failed to object to having the jury decide that question, the verdict could not be set aside. *Vanderhurst v. Colorado Mountain College Dist.*, 208 F.3d 908 (10th Cir. 2000). [CO]

◆ *A professor fired for teaching pornography was able to survive a motion to dismiss his claim for violating his academic freedom rights.*

An adjunct assistant professor of Humanities at a New York college also was hired to be an English instructor. **He conducted a lesson aimed at reducing the use of repetitive words and ideas in essay writing and allowed the students to choose the topic. They chose sex. He modified it to relationships/sex and warned the students against using sexually explicit terms**, as doing so would alienate readers. He wrote down ideas suggested by the students on the blackboard, but used initials to represent sexually explicit terms. Subsequently, he was fired for violating the college's sexual harassment policy and for teaching pornography. He sued under a number of theories, one of which was that the college had violated his academic freedom rights under the First Amendment. The court refused to dismiss the action, finding that the university had failed to properly move for dismissal on the claim. However, it indicated that he was unlikely to win on his claim. *Vega v. State Univ. of New York Bd. of Trustees*, 67 F.Supp.2d 324 (S.D.N.Y. 1999). [NY]

◆ *A public university professor did not have a right to determine what would be taught in his classroom.*

A professor at a Pennsylvania university taught a course entitled "Introduction to Educational Media." One of his students complained that he used the class to advance religious ideas. For example, his syllabus for at least one class included an emphasis on bias, censorship, religion and humanism, and listed numerous publications discussing those issues as required or recommended reading. The vice president for academic affairs wrote the professor, directing him to cease and desist from using "doctrinaire materials" of a religious nature. When **the new chair of the education department became concerned that the professor was still advancing religious issues,** he and the department faculty voted to reinstate an earlier syllabus, and he cancelled certain book orders. Eventually, the professor was suspended with pay, although he returned the next semester to teach several courses.

The professor sued the university for violating his free speech rights, and the case reached the U.S. Court of Appeals, Third Circuit. The court of appeals held that **a public university professor does not have a First Amendment right to determine what will be taught in the classroom.** Outside the classroom, the professor had a right to advocate for the use of certain curriculum materials. However, inside the classroom, he did not have a right to use those materials without permission. The university was allowed to make content-based decisions when shaping its curriculum. *Edwards v. California Univ. of Pennsylvania*, 156 F.3d 488 (3d Cir. 1998). [PA]

II. DEFAMATION

Defamation consists of an oral (slander) or written (libel) communication that injures a person's reputation. The defamatory material must have been disclosed to third parties who understand that the material refers to the plaintiff. Also, the plaintiff's reputation must have suffered in the minds of the third parties, and there must be a tangible (usually economic) injury. Several absolute defenses exist to a defamation lawsuit including truth, consent and opinion. The defense of privilege is common in employment cases.

◆ *The Court of Appeal of California held newly-discovered evidence found in an e-mail could undermine a university's defense in a defamation case.*

A state university vice president received an external review report which stated that an assistant health education professor was not meeting standards for a tenured university professor, "resulting in a weak program." The report was distributed to seven other administrators. The professor sued Northridge and several others for defamation and invasion of privacy in a state trial court. The court granted their motion for summary judgment, and the professor appealed to the court of appeal. While his appeal was pending, new evidence was found on a computer hard drive, and he requested a special writ.

The court granted the writ and reversed entry of summary judgment. **To establish his defamation claim, the professor had to show there was an intentional publication of a factual statement that was false, unprivileged, and had a natural tendency to injure him or cause special damages.** The trial court had found the allegedly defamatory statements were protected by a common interest privilege. It held there was no triable issue concerning malice by the university officials, which would defeat the privilege. Newly found evidence on a computer hard drive revealed an e-mail including the report and an allegedly defamatory statement. As the e-mail raised a triable issue of fact on the issue of malice, the court granted the writ, and reversed the entry of summary judgment. *Fischbach v. Trustees of California State Univ.*, Nos. B159589, B165926, 2004 WL 179471 (Cal.App. 2d Dist. 2004). [CA]

◆ *A university was not liable for refusing to rehire a manager who couldn't get along with his superiors.*

A construction manager for Miami University of Ohio had a deteriorating relationship with is supervisor and eventually resigned. Before the resignation became effective, he applied for another position, but was not selected when the university's director of architecture recommended against it because of his poor people skills. He also was not selected for a field representative position. He sued for defamation and tortious interference with a business relationship, but the Ohio Court of Claims ruled against him. There was no defamation because **the architecture director's stated objections to hiring the manager were not false, but rather protected opinions**. And even if the statements were of a factual nature, they were privileged because they were made in a reasonable manner, for a proper purpose and in good faith. Also, since the director had an interest in selecting people who could work well together, he was justified in opposing the manager for the open positions. Thus, there was no tortious interference with a business relationship. *Reece v. Miami Univ.*, 2003 WL 21061398 (Ohio Ct. Cl. 5/3/03). [OH]

◆ *A professor did not defame an administrator by accusing him of covering up mismanagement where the administrator did not show a false statement.*

A Louisiana university professor created a Web site where he accused the university's vice president of external affairs of covering up mismanagement at the university and called him the "vice president of *excremental affairs*, [who] has been shoveling so long that he is cracking under the strain." The vice president sued the professor for defamation, and a state trial court refused to dismiss the case. The Louisiana Court of Appeal reversed, ordering the lawsuit dismissed. Here, the vice president failed to show that the professor's objectionable statements were false. Clearly, the professor's speech was on a matter of public concern — the management of a public university — and the statements were not made with reckless disregard for the truth. In fact, **the professor maintained that they were true, and the vice president failed to show they were false**. Moreover, the hyperbole used was not actionable as defamation. *Baxter v. Scott*, 847 So.2d 225 (La. App. 2003). [LA]

◆ *A professor's accusations against a college's CFO could be construed as defamatory.*

A CPA served as the chief financial officer of a Texas college. A mathematics professor publicly accused him of commingling college funds with money from a foundation, falsifying financial records, and skimming interest from college investments. After an audit report cleared the CFO of any wrongdoing, the professor continued to repeat the accusations. The CFO sued for defamation, and a state court granted pretrial judgment to the professor on the ground that his letter to the Texas Board of Public Accountancy was protected by judicial privilege. The Texas Court of Appeals reversed, finding an issue of fact as to whether the CFO was defamed. Here, even if the initial report to the board was protected, **after the report cleared the CFO, the professor continued to accuse him of skimming funds from college investments**. The case required a jury trial. *Alaniz v. Hoyt*, 105 S.W.3d 330 (Tex. App. 2003). [TX]

◆ *A professor was awarded $3 million in a defamation action against a former student.*

A University of North Dakota student stalked and harassed her physics professor, sending him harassing and sexually explicit e-mails, and making false statements about him. She claimed the communications were either consensual or privileged. The student relations committee suspended her indefinitely, and the professor sued her for defamation and intentional interference with a business relationship. She then posted statements about him on her Web site, and he amended his complaint to include those statements in his defamation action. A jury awarded the professor $3 million in damages, and the North Dakota Supreme Court upheld the award. **The Internet postings plus the defamatory statements she made while attending UND justified the large damages award.** *Wagner v. Miskin*, 660 N.W.2d 593 (N.D. 2003). [ND]

◆ *A professor who resigned could sue a university for defamation and due process violations.*

A tenured associate professor of accounting at the University of Delaware received satisfactory performance evaluations until he had a dispute with the chair of the accounting department. The department chair then gave him unsatisfactory ratings, removed him from a departmental committee chairmanship, assigned him freshman courses, and discussed his teaching methods with colleagues. Later, the Association to Advance Collegiate Schools of Business changed the professor's listing from academically qualified to academically unqualified. The professor retired, then sued the university and various employees, alleging violations of due process and defamation, among other claims. The university sought to dismiss the lawsuit. Denying the motion in part, **the court found evidence that the professor was constructively discharged**. Here, a workplace environment was created that was so unpleasant as to force the professor to resign. And though he availed himself of the grievance process, the university did not properly follow the procedures. Also, the report listing the professor as academically unqualified was defamatory, and the university would have to defend itself by asserting a qualified privilege. *Stiner v. University of Delaware*, 243 F.Supp.2d 106 (D. Del. 2003). [DE]

◆ *A professor and a university could not be sued for defamation in Texas over an article displayed on a Web site in New York*

After a Harvard University professor wrote an article criticizing senior members of the Reagan administration for allowing the Lockerbie terrorist bombing despite clear advance warnings, the Columbia University School of Journalism posted the article on its Web site. One of the members of the administration, who resided in Texas, sued the university and the professor in a

Texas federal court. The court dismissed the case based on lack of personal jurisdiction, and the Tenth Circuit Court of Appeals affirmed. Here, **the "passive" Web site maintained by the university in New York did not support personal jurisdiction in Texas** because there were not sufficient contacts to justify requiring the university to defend itself in Texas. *Revell v. Lidov*, 317 F.3d 467 (5th Cir. 2002). [TX]

◆ *A scientific article that criticized a medical procedure for ineffectiveness could not be construed as defamatory.*

A biochemist co-authored an article about the benefits of an assay (a medical science research test) in determining whether silicone gel could be detected from leaking silicone breast implants. Three years later, three medical researchers at a Texas university published an article based on their research into the immunogenicity of silicone, in which they opined that the use of assays was questionable. They did not use the biochemist's assay in their study, but they named him in a footnote and implied that his assay also was of questionable value. After their article was published, the biochemist complained to the university, which conducted an independent inquiry into the researchers' work and writing, and concluded that the article was sloppy, contained careless mistakes, and did not support their conclusion that the biochemist's assay was ineffective. The article was retracted, and the researchers apologized in writing to the biochemist.

The biochemist then brought a libel action against the researchers, who defended by asserting that the article constituted their opinion and as such could not be construed as libel. They also asserted that they were immune to suit as state employees, and that there were no false statements in their article. A state court ruled in favor of the researchers, and the Texas Court of Appeals affirmed. Here, **the article (written as a medical science research article) was incapable of a defamatory meaning**. It did not attack the biochemist personally, but rather questioned the effectiveness of his assay. Moreover, two other articles had been published the same year that also questioned the effectiveness of his assay. Finally, the biochemist produced no evidence that the article contained false statements, an essential element of his claim. Under these circumstances, the court refused to hold that the article amounted to libel. *Ezrailson v. Rohrich*, 65 S.W.3d 373 (Tex. App. 2001). [TX]

◆ *A professor deemed to be a public figure could not succeed on his defamation lawsuit against a student reporter.*

When a student reporter wrote that a professor obtained tenure only after successfully suing the college for race discrimination, and added that the lawsuit was a possible explanation for the professor's outspoken racial views and the administration's reluctance to openly censure the professor, the professor sued the reporter for defamation. A state court ruled that **the professor was a public figure based on his participation in public lectures and writings that attracted national media attention**. The court then made several evidentiary rulings and held that no defamation occurred. The Massachusetts Court of Appeals affirmed. The trial court properly allowed an editorial from the *Washington Post* to be admitted (calling for the professor's removal because of his use of a book published by the Nation of Islam) because it showed that the professor's reputation could have been damaged by articles other than the one written by the student. *Martin v. Roy*, 767 N.E.2d 603 (Mass. App. 2002). [MA]

◆ *A university official slandered a student by accusing him of sexual misconduct.*

Two university students went drinking at an off-campus bar to celebrate the female student's birthday. When they returned to campus, they engaged in sexual conduct on two occasions during the night at the male student's dorm room. Under questioning by campus security, the female student stated that she did not remember the events of the previous night. The male student was then charged with sexual assault in violation of the school's code of conduct. After a hearing, he was expelled. Criminal charges also were filed against him, though the trial resulted in a hung jury, and the charges were then dropped. Subsequently, in a newspaper article, his parents accused the university of granting preferential treatment to the female student. A university assistant director responded, through the newspaper, that the male student "definitely committed sexual battery, from the information that was gathered." The male student then sued the university and the assistant director for defamation. A trial court ruled for the defendants, but the Ohio Court of Appeals reversed. Here, **the assistant director's statement was not mere opinion; rather, it implied that factual evidence supported the assertion of sexual battery**. Further, the assistant director did not have a qualified privilege to make the statement because her remarks went beyond the scope of the university's interest. *Mallory v. Ohio Univ.*, 2001 WL 1631329 (Ohio App. 12/20/01). [OH]

◆ *A newspaper could not repeat a defamatory statement without determining the truth of the statement.*

In a newspaper commentary written by a nonemployee, a professor was identified as having been reprimanded for numerous complaints of sexual harassment. The commentary also stated that, as revealed in recently unsealed court papers, the professor had been accused of masturbating during a faculty meeting, but that no sanctions were imposed for that offense. The professor sued the newspaper and the writer for defamation, conceding that he had been accused of masturbating but denying that the accusation was true. The newspaper defended the action by claiming the privilege of fair reporting of judicial proceedings and by asserting that the accusation was true. A trial court granted summary judgment to the defendants.

The Superior Court of New Jersey, Appellate Division, reversed. It noted that **the privilege was not available because the report was not full, fair and accurate**. First, the report implied that the masturbation incident came after the reprimand for sexual harassment, when in fact the accusation had come some 10 years earlier. Second, the report implied that the professor had been charged in the court action, which was not true. And third, by stating that the professor had not been sanctioned, the report implied that he had been found guilty or liable. The court also found that, **in order to assert the defense of truth, the newspaper had to show more than that the accusation had been made. It**

had to show that the accusation was true as well. Otherwise, it could escape liability by merely repeating what someone else (perhaps an unreliable gossip) had said first. The defamation action could continue. *Fortenbaugh v. New Jersey Press,* 722 A.2d 568 (N.J. Super. A.D. 1999). [NJ]

◆ *A university employee could not show defamation where he admitted the facts upon which the statement was based.*

The University of Kentucky hired a manager for its College of Engineering's machine shop. The dean of the college informed the manager that he could do private consulting work the equivalent of one day per week. The dean's understanding was that the machinist would not use shop machinists in his private consulting work. However, the manager believed that he could use shop facilities, materials and machinists. He contracted for outside work and used university machinists and materials for the jobs, but never reimbursed the university for the use of the machines, materials or the machinists' work. Subsequently, an audit was conducted. The report stated that it appeared that the manager had violated university policy as well as criminal law regarding theft and misapplication of property. The university fired the manager, who sued for wrongful discharge and defamation, among other claims.

A state court dismissed his claims and he appealed. The Court of Appeals of Kentucky affirmed, noting that **the manager could not show defamation because he had conceded that he used university machinists for his personal work.** Because truth is a defense to a defamation action, the manager could not show that the statement about him violating university policy was defamatory. Further, a statement in the form of an opinion (like this one was) could be defamatory only if it implied the existence of undisclosed defamatory facts. **Here, the audit report stated the facts upon which the opinion was based and therefore did not imply the existence of undisclosed defamatory facts.** *Buchholtz v. Dugan,* 977 S.W.2d 24 (Ky. App. 1998). [KY]

◆ *A supervisor's statements that an employee did not follow up on assignments and did not get along well with her co-workers was not defamatory.*

An Illinois woman worked as the director of corporate relations for a private university for nine years. She was then approached by an organization about a comparable position. She was interviewed by a number of people at the organization and was told that the interviews had gone well. She believed that she was the leading candidate for the position and after another interview, she was told that she was going to be recommended for the job. Before her final interviews, the organization's director spoke to her supervisor at the university who stated that she "did not follow up on assignments" and did not get along well with her co-workers. Her final interviews were then canceled. She sued the university for defamation and intentional interference with prospective economic advantage. The trial court dismissed the case. The appellate court reversed, and the university appealed to the Illinois Supreme Court.

The court held that to state a claim of intentional interference with prospective economic advantage, **the employee had to show that she had a reasonable expectancy of getting a position with the organization. Here, the employee had not completed all of the interviews and her beliefs that**

she was the leading candidate and that all of the interviews went well were completely subjective. She did not attribute these assessments to anyone at the organization and did not support them with adequate evidence. Finding that the employee was nothing more than a candidate for the position with further interviews pending, the court held that she had no reasonable expectation of employment. The court also noted that the supervisor's statements could have been innocently construed to mean that the employee did not fit in with the university and did not perform well in that particular position. Since they were not necessarily comments on her lack of ability in her profession, they did not qualify as defamation *per se.* The court reversed the appellate court's decision. *Anderson v. Vanden Dorpel,* 667 N.E.2d 1296 (Ill. 1996). [IL]

◆ *A professor who labeled an engineer a "crank" was found not liable for defamation.*

A mathematics professor employed by an Indiana private university wrote a book entitled *Mathematical Cranks* in which he addressed a publication written by a Wisconsin engineer. The professor noted that the engineer's article read as if written by someone "whose mind will not be changed by anything" and labeled the engineer a "crank." The professor explained that the spectrum of mathematical cranks ran from the "slightly eccentric" to "people who are convinced that they have the truth, that it is revolutionary, and that mathematicians are engaged in a vast conspiracy to suppress it." The engineer filed a defamation lawsuit against the professor in a U.S. district court, alleging that the professor had acted with actual malice in writing the article. The district court granted the professor's motion to dismiss on the ground that the word "crank" was mere "rhetorical hyperbole," a well-recognized category of privileged defamation. The engineer appealed to the Seventh Circuit.

The court of appeals affirmed, holding that where one scholar calls another a "crank" for having taken a position that the first scholar considers patently wrong, the second does not have a remedy in defamation. **To call a person a "crank" is basically a colorful and insulting way of expressing disagreement with the owner's idea**, and it therefore belongs to the language of controversy rather than the language of defamation. This was especially clear where, as in the present case, the word was used in a work of scholarship. Scholars have their own remedies for unfair criticisms of their work. If the professor's criticisms of the engineer were unsound, the engineer could publish a rebuttal in the same journal in which he published the article that the professor attacked. *Dilworth v. Dudley,* 75 F.3d 307 (7th Cir. 1996). [IN]

◆ *A university was privileged to make otherwise defamatory statements in the following case.*

A New Jersey private university accepted the resignations of three department managers in the wake of their alleged diversion of university property for private gain. The university published a statement to members of the faculty and the administration that certain equipment had been used off campus on personal projects, that the estimated losses totaled approximately $10,000, and that three staff members had submitted their resignations. Reports in two university publications (for both students and alumni) expressly connected these three individuals with the alleged improprieties. The university declined to elaborate on any of the employees' cases or resignations and described them as "mutually arrived at decisions." One manager sued the university and certain officials, alleging that statements in the university publications were defamatory.

The Superior Court of New Jersey, Appellate Division, noted that **private corporations, including private universities, have a qualified privilege to communicate with contributors, employees and other persons involved in their activities regarding alleged employee wrongdoing.** It also noted that dissemination of information to the media may be the only method for such communication under some circumstances. Here, the university administration had an interest in informing the university community about the investigation rather than allowing it to remain the subject of vague and exaggerated rumors that could have damaged the university's reputation. *Gallo v. Princeton Univ.,* 656 A.2d 1267 (N.J. Super. A.D. 1995). [NJ]

III. STUDENTS

A. Religion and Free Speech

◆   *The Establishment Clause does not prevent private citizens from using public facilities for religious purposes. In fact, if a facility is made available to the public, religious groups cannot be excluded from using it.*

The University of Missouri at Kansas City, a state university, made its facilities available for the general use of registered student groups. **A registered student religious group that had previously received permission to conduct its meetings in university facilities was informed that it could no longer do so because of a university regulation that prohibited use of its facilities for the purposes of religious worship or teaching.** Members of the group sued in federal court, alleging that the regulation violated their First Amendment rights to free exercise of religion and freedom of speech. The court upheld the school's regulation, but the U.S. Court of Appeals, Eighth Circuit, reversed, stating that the regulation was discriminatory against religious speech and that the Establishment Clause does not bar a policy of equal access in which facilities are open to groups and speakers of all kinds.

The Supreme Court agreed with the court of appeals' assessment, stating **that the university policy violated the fundamental principle that state regulation of speech must be content-neutral**. It is obligatory upon the state to show that the regulation is necessary to serve a compelling state interest and that it is narrowly drawn to achieve that end. The state was unable to do that here. The state's interest in achieving greater separation of church and state than is already ensured under the Establishment Clause was not sufficiently "compelling" to justify content-based discrimination against religious speech of the student group in question. *Widmar v. Vincent,* 454 U.S. 263, 102 S.Ct. 269, 70 L.Ed.2d 400 (1981). [MO]

◆   *The U.S. Supreme Court held that the University of Virginia could not withhold authorization for payments to a printer on behalf of a Christian student organization.*

The University of Virginia collected a mandatory $14 student activity fee from full-time students each semester. The fees supported extracurricular activities that were related to the educational purposes of the university. University-recognized student groups could apply for funding by the activities fund, although not all groups requested funds. University guidelines excluded religious groups from student funding as well as activities that could jeopardize the university's tax-exempt status. A university-recognized student group published a Christian newspaper for which it sought $5,862 from the activities fund for printing costs. The student council denied funding because the group's activities were deemed religious under university guidelines. After exhausting appeals within the university, group members filed a lawsuit in the U.S. District Court for the Western District of Virginia, claiming constitutional rights violations. The court granted summary judgment to the university, and its decision was affirmed by the U.S. Court of Appeals, Fourth Circuit.

The students appealed to the U.S. Supreme Court. The Court observed that **government entities must abstain from regulating speech on the basis of the speaker's opinion.** Upon establishing a limited public forum, state entities must respect the forum by refraining from the exclusion of speech based upon content. **Because the university had opened a limited public forum by paying other third-party contractors on behalf of student groups, it could not deny the religious group's claim for funds on the basis of its viewpoint.** Allowing the payment of the group's printing costs amounted to a policy of government neutrality for different viewpoints. The Court distinguished the student fee from a general tax and placed emphasis on the indirect nature of the benefit. The Court reversed the lower court decisions, ruling that access to public school facilities on a neutral basis does not violate the Establishment Clause of the First Amendment. *Rosenberger v. Rector and Visitors of Univ. of Virginia,* 515 U.S. 819, 115 S.Ct. 2510, 132 L.Ed.2d 700 (1995). [VA]

◆   *Virginia Military Institute's daily "supper prayer" violated the Establishment Clause by coercing cadets to participate in a religious ritual.*

Virginia Military Institute (VMI) is a state-operated college that closely regulated the personal behavior of cadets. Each night, cadets marched in formation and were called to attention in the mess hall for a prayer read by a chaplain. Cadets had to remain standing and silent while the prayer was read, but were not obligated to recite the prayer, close their eyes, or bow their heads. VMI denied a request by some cadets to ignore the supper prayer, and they commenced a federal lawsuit, asserting it violated the Establishment Clause. The court granted summary judgment to the cadets, and issued an order prohibiting VMI from continuing the prayers. It held VMI's superintendent was entitled to qualified immunity in the action. The parties appealed.

The Fourth Circuit Court of Appeals applied the "coercion test" of *Lee v. Weisman,* 505 U.S. 577 (1992) and *Santa Fe Indep. School Dist. v. Doe,* 530 U.S. 290 (2000). Under *Lee* and *Santa Fe,* **"school officials may not, consistent with the Establishment Clause, compel students to participate**

in a religious activity." The record showed VMI's educational philosophy was based on coercion. Because of VMI's coercive atmosphere, the Establishment Clause precluded school officials from sponsoring an official prayer, even for mature adults. However, VMI's superintendent was entitled to qualified immunity, as the cadets' rights to be free from prayer at a public military college were not clearly established at the time. *Mellen v. Bunting*, 341 F.3d 312 (4th Cir. 2003). [VA]

◆ *A federal district court held a Pennsylvania university's code of conduct was overbroad and thus violated the First Amendment.*

Shippensburg University's catalogue contained a code of conduct establishing student rights and responsibilities and regulating student behavior. The code prohibited "acts of intolerance directed toward other community members." The term "acts of intolerance" was not defined. The university's racism and cultural diversity statement prohibited racial and ethnic intimidation and harassment. Two students sued the university in a federal district court, asserting the code and diversity statement violated their First Amendment rights to speech, association and free exercise of religion.

The university sought dismissal, asserting the provisions were not subject to First Amendment scrutiny because they were "merely aspirational and precatory." **The court held five of the provisions disputed by the students were overbroad because they restricted speech and conduct that was protected by the First Amendment.** Among the provisions held unconstitutional were the statements that "acts of intolerance directed toward other community members will not be tolerated" and "the expression of one's beliefs should be communicated in a manner that does not provoke, harass, intimidate, or harm another." **The court held unconstitutional the code provisions stating a student's actions should mirror the university's racial and diversity ideals and the university's definition of racism.** The university did not show it had a history of campus disruption that would allow these provisions. The court granted the students' motion for a preliminary injunction concerning the five unconstitutional provisions, and denied the university's motion to dismiss the case. *Bair v. Shippensburg Univ.*, 280 F.Supp.2d 357 (M.D. Pa. 2003). [PA]

◆ *A federal district court dismissed claims that an assignment to read a religious-related book violated student free exercise rights.*

An orientation program held by the University of North Carolina, Chapel Hill (UNC) required incoming freshman to read a book that explored Islam. UNC stated it was highly relevant in light of the then-recent terrorist attacks. Although the program had an exception for students with religious objections, several incoming students sued UNC in a federal district court for Free Exercise Clause violations. **The court considered UNC's motion for dismissal, and noted the book was not a religious reading.** It found the orientation program was an academic exercise. The court stated UNC had attempted to engage students in a scholarly debate about a religious subject, and encourage them to express their opinions. Students who objected to reading the book could refrain from doing so. **UNC did not compel the affirmation of**

any particular religious belief, favor any religious dogma, or punish the expression of any particular religion. As UNC did not ask students to compromise or give up their religious beliefs, the court granted its motion to dismiss the action. While the court dismissed the claims against the university, it permitted the students to file a second amended complaint to add new factual allegations. *Yacovelli v. Moeser*, No. 1:02CV596, 2004 WL 1541594 (M.D.N.C. 2004). [NC]

◆   *A federal district court dismissed an Illinois student's claim that a college conduct code violated his First Amendment speech rights.*

The student got into an argument with a college employee. The employee signed a complaint, saying the student scared her when he used profane language and yelled at her in a public place. The campus police arrested him. The college later expelled the student for violation of a college code of conduct prohibition on the use of abusive language towards members of the college community. The student sued the college in an Illinois federal district court, claiming the code of conduct violated his First Amendment speech rights. **The court held the conduct code did not prohibit legally protected speech. The college had to be allowed to impose discipline for a wide variety of unanticipated conduct that could disrupt the educational process.** The court granted the college's motion to dismiss the case. *Cady v. Suburban College*, 310 F. Supp.2d 997 (N.D. Ill. 2004). [IL]

◆   *A student had no First Amendment right to have his master's thesis kept by the university library where he failed to comply with professional guidelines.*

A graduate student at a California university wrote his master's thesis and obtained approval of the version he submitted for review. He later attempted to file his thesis in the university library with two new pages in which he criticized administrators with profanity. The thesis committee and a dean refused to allow the thesis to be filed because the extra pages did not meet professional standards for publication. Even though the university never filed a copy of the thesis, the student received a master's degree. He then sued the university, asserting he should have been allowed to file the revised thesis, and asserting due process violations because he did not receive a formal hearing.

A federal court ruled against the student, and the Ninth Circuit affirmed. Here, **the thesis was a curriculum assignment with pedagogical objectives that required him to comply with professional guidelines. Because he failed to do so, he could not claim a First Amendment right** to have his thesis filed. He also failed on his due process claim because the defendants' decision to defer granting his degree was an academic one that was careful and deliberate. *Brown v. Li*, 308 F.3d 939 (9th Cir. 2002). [CA]

◆   *Where a Washington college allowed secular demonstrations, it could not place restrictions on a demonstration based on religion.*

The dean of a community college allowed an anti-abortion demonstration on campus. His office received a number of complaints, leading him to ask campus security to remove the demonstrators. When they refused to leave, police were called, and a demonstrator was arrested. He later sued the dean and the head of campus security under 42 U.S.C. § 1983 for violating his First Amendment rights. A federal court granted pretrial judgment to the defendants, but the Ninth Circuit Court of Appeals reversed. It stated that **a "no religious instruction or worship" condition imposed by the dean violated the First Amendment as a content-based restriction on speech**. Only if that restriction was necessary to achieve a compelling state interest, and was narrowly designed to accomplish that interest, would it be constitutional. The court also held that the dean was not entitled to immunity under § 1983 because he should have known that placing the "no religion" restriction on the demonstration violated the First Amendment. There also was a question of fact, requiring a trial, as to whether the security head was entitled to immunity. *Orin v. Barclay*, 272 F.3d 1207 (9th Cir. 2001). [WA]

♦ *A Mormon student's lawsuit failed because requiring her to perform scripts containing language she found religiously offensive did not violate her First Amendment rights.*

When a student who belonged to the Church of Jesus Christ of Latter-day Saints auditioned for the university's Actor Training Program, the instructors asked her if there was anything she would be uncomfortable doing as an actor. She replied that she would not take her clothes off, take the name of God or Christ in vain, or use the word "fuck." The student was accepted into the program, and her professors encouraged her to overcome her objection to certain language. Nevertheless, she omitted words and phrases she found objectionable from one of her performances without approval. At the end of her first semester, she was informed by her instructors that she would no longer be allowed to censor language she found objectionable. The student then left the program and sued in federal court, claiming the requirement to use religiously objectionable language violated her constitutional rights to free exercise of religion and free speech. She sought damages under 42 U.S.C. § 1983.

The court found that the student's constitutional rights were not violated. Here, the instructors' stance on the use of offensive language was derived from an aesthetic principle encouraging all actors to challenge themselves and not to specifically deprive the student of her free exercise rights. As such, the court rejected the student's free exercise claim. The court also rejected the student's free speech claim. Citing *West Virginia State Board of Education v. Barnette*, 319 U.S. 624 (1943), the court recognized that a state entity cannot force a student to advocate a particular ideological point of view. Here, **the instructors were not forcing the student to adopt or promote an ideological view**: they merely asked her to read some lines which she found offensive. The court dismissed the case. *Axson-Flynn v. Johnson*, 151 F.Supp.2d 1326 (D. Utah 2001). [UT]

♦ *Temporarily suspending the showing of a religious film did not result in liability.*

The Board of Regents of Oklahoma State University (OSU) temporarily suspended the showing by the university Student Union Activities Board (SUAB) of *The Last Temptation of Christ*, a film depicting Jesus descending from the cross to marry, father children and return to the cross. An association of students and faculty members advocating free speech rights filed a lawsuit in the U.S. District Court for the Northern District of Oklahoma, seeking declaratory relief. The regents lifted the suspension, and the film was shown. The court held that school officials could not be held liable for damages under 42 U.S.C. § 1983, and the association appealed.

The U.S. Court of Appeals, Tenth Circuit, **rejected the association's argument that the regents had violated the constitutional rights of its members by imposing content-based censorship**. The regents had merely imposed a temporary suspension while obtaining a legal opinion concerning OSU's potential liability if it chose to allow the showing of the film. **The regents could not be held liable for violating any clearly established constitutional rights,** and the regents' action did not violate constitutional restraints on censorship. Because the SUAB and OSU were closely related in funding and staffing, the regents had merely displayed caution in their decision-making process. *Cummins v. Campbell*, 44 F.3d 847 (10th Cir. 1994). [OK]

◆ *Graduation prayers were allowed at Indiana University.*

In a case involving graduation prayers at Indiana University, the U.S. Court of Appeals, Seventh Circuit, distinguished the ceremonies from public school ceremonies involving younger students. **There was no element of coercion requiring students to participate in the large, impersonal university commencement exercises**, and many students and family members remained in their seats during the prayer. Adult students were unlikely to succumb to peer pressure and could choose not to attend the ceremony without suffering any severe consequences. The court agreed with the university that the prayers solemnized the ceremony, did not endorse any particular religion and allowed the university to continue a 155-year-old tradition. *Tanford v. Brand*, 104 F.3d 982 (7th Cir. 1997). [IN]

B. Retaliation

◆ *The Third Circuit upheld the dismissal of a case filed by a student claiming he was arrested in retaliation for accusing an instructor of discrimination.*

A white Jewish student argued with an African-American computer lab instructor over his use of computer lab facilities. A college policy permitted computer use by students enrolled in active, on-going classes, but prohibited access for personal use. At the time, the student was not enrolled in an active, ongoing class and was using computers for his own use. He wrote a letter to the college president complaining about the denial of lab use. The dispute continued for eight months, and resulted in the student's forcible removal from the computer lab by Pittsburgh police officers. He was arrested for trespass, but charges were later withdrawn. The student sued the college and officials including the instructor in a federal district court for speech rights violations and breach of contract. He claimed violation of his First Amendment rights based on the letter he wrote to the college president.

A federal district court awarded summary judgment to the college and officials, and the student appealed. The U.S. Court of Appeals, Third Circuit, said that **to prevail in a speech rights retaliation claim, the student had to** show he engaged in protected speech and the college retaliated against him for making the speech. **The court found his letter was not a matter of public concern and was thus not protected activity.** The student's contract claim failed because no contract ever existed between the college and student. The college was not required to provide him with written notice of every regulation governing the use of its facilities to enforce its regulations. The court affirmed the judgment for the college and officials. *Feldman v. Community College of Allegheny*, No. 00-3355, 85 Fed.Appx. 821, 2004 WL 50784 (3d Cir. 2004). [PA]

◆ *An expelled student could proceed with his First Amendment retaliation claim against Connecticut university officials.*

A Connecticut university student criticized the university administration and filed an ethics complaint against the university president. After the interim vice president and dean of student affairs accused him and two other students of making unauthorized changes to over 30 grades in violation of the university handbook, a hearing was conducted and the student was expelled. The university upheld the student's expulsion, but dropped proceedings against the two others. The student sued the university in a federal district court, alleging violations of his speech and due process rights.

The university sought to dismiss the lawsuit on Eleventh Amendment immunity grounds, and a federal court granted the motion in part. As an arm of the state, the university could not be liable for negligence. Also, the student received appropriate due process in the hearing and expulsion procedures used by the university. However, **there was a fact issue as to whether he had been expelled in retaliation for his speech against the administration**. The court refused to dismiss that claim and ordered a trial. *Brown v. Western Connecticut State Univ.*, 204 F.Supp.2d 355 (D. Conn. 2002). [CT]

C. Newspapers and Yearbooks

◆ *A dean who tried to exercise prior restraint over a college newspaper's content was not entitled to qualified immunity.*

Students at an Illinois state university held positions on the student newspaper and also were appointed to the Student Communications Media Board. According to board policy, only students determined newspaper content; no censorship or prior approval by university officials was allowed. When the dean of student affairs notified the newspaper's printing company that a university official had to review and approve the paper's content before each issue was printed, the students brought a lawsuit under the First Amendment against a number of university officials.

An Illinois federal court dismissed all the defendants except the dean, and the Seventh Circuit Court of Appeals affirmed. It noted that she was not entitled to qualified immunity because **the prohibition against censorship within the university setting was clearly established** at the time she took the challenged actions. Although the Supreme Court had held in *Hazelwood School Dist. v. Kuhlmeier*, 484 U.S. 260 (1988), that high school officials have broad powers to censor school-sponsored newspapers if their actions are supported by valid educational purposes, the greater maturity level of college students made censorship of college newspapers untenable. *Hosty v. Carter*, 325 F.3d 945 (7th Cir. 2003). [IL]

◆ *A university violated the First and Fourteenth Amendment rights of the yearbook editor when it confiscated yearbooks for being "inappropriate."*

The editor of Kentucky State University's yearbook during the 1993–1994 school year decided to be innovative and, for the first time, gave the yearbook a theme: "Destination Unknown." The theme reflected the students' uncertainty about life after college and the pending question of whether the university was to become a community college. The yearbook included pictures from KSU events as well as current national and world events. KSU's vice president for student affairs objected to the final product. She opposed the yearbook's cover, theme, the lack of captions under many photos and the inclusion of current events unrelated to KSU. **The vice president and other university officials prohibited the yearbooks from being distributed and confiscated them.** The editor and another student sued the school on behalf of all KSU students in federal court, claiming their First and Fourteenth Amendment rights were violated. The court dismissed the suit, finding that the yearbook was a nonpublic forum because it was not intended to be a journal of expression, but rather a record of the events at KSU for its students. The students appealed

Although it is well established that a high school yearbook is not a public forum and is therefore subject to strict control by school officials, the Sixth Circuit determined that **a college yearbook was a limited public forum**. KSU's written policy toward the yearbook gave the student editors control over the publication because it did not allow a faculty/staff advisor to change the yearbook in order to alter the content. In addition, **the language of the university's student publication policy indicated that such publications were intended to be limited public forums**. The policy begins by saying, "The Board of Regents respects the integrity of student publications and the press, and the rights to exist in an atmosphere of free and responsible discussion and of intellectual exploration." The Sixth Circuit remanded the matter to the district court for further proceedings. *Kincaid v. Gibson*, 236 F.3d 342 (6th Cir. 2000). [KY]

◆ *Insulting statements that cannot be reasonably interpreted as stating facts cannot form the basis of a defamation action.*

A student newspaper at a Virginia university published an article describing the success of a student placement program. The article quoted a university official who facilitated student participation in the program and referred to her as "Director of Butt Licking." **The official filed a Virginia circuit court action against the student newspaper for defamation and use of insulting words** in violation of state law. The court held that the newspaper reference was void of any literal meaning and not reasonably susceptible to interpretation as containing factual information. The official appealed to the Supreme Court of Virginia, which observed that **statements that cannot reasonably be interpreted as stating facts about a person cannot form the basis of a defamation action**. The court rejected the official's claim that she was entitled to present her case to a jury on grounds that literal interpretation of the offensive phrase imputed to her a criminal violation of the state sodomy statute and was defamatory. It also rejected her assertion that the statement injured her reputation and held her up to ridicule by implying that she lacked integrity. The court affirmed the judgment for the newspaper. *Yeagle v. Collegiate Times*, 497 S.E.2d 136 (Va. 1998). [VA]

◆   *Where student editors refused to publish an advertisement they believed was defamatory, they could not be held liable under the First Amendment.*

An attorney wrote two articles that were highly critical of his law school, which were published in the law school's newspaper. He also sought to have a classified advertisement placed in the paper, soliciting material that would discredit certain faculty and administrators at the school for the purpose of assisting him in a federal civil rights action against the school. He also sought in the ad to urge students who had been discriminated against by the school's criminal defense clinic to join his Office of Civil Rights complaint against the clinic. When the paper's three student editors refused to publish the ad, fearing that it was defamatory and would expose them and the paper to litigation, the attorney sued the students and the school under the First Amendment. The U.S. District Court for the Eastern District of New York noted that **the student editors were not state actors (a requirement for a claim brought under the First Amendment) and** that **the school did not exercise control over the newspaper**. As a result, the attorney's claim could not succeed. The court dismissed the lawsuit. *Leeds v. Meltz*, 898 F.Supp. 146 (E.D.N.Y. 1995). [NY]

◆   *Student journalists were entitled to receive campus arrest reports in the following case.*

A group of student journalists and an organization that promoted the rights of the student press brought a lawsuit against the U.S. Department of Education and the Secretary of Education. **They sought to enjoin the government from enforcing a provision of the Family Educational Rights and Privacy Act (FERPA), which allows the complete withdrawal of federal funding from any university that discloses personally identifiable student records.** The journalists alleged that this prohibition, as applied to campus security arrest reports, violated their First Amendment right to receive information. The journalists moved for an injunction in a federal district court to immediately halt enforcement of FERPA's prohibition.

After resolving numerous procedural matters, the court examined the burdens imposed by FERPA and balanced them against the corresponding governmental interest. The journalists argued that the general arrest reports, which are provided by local law enforcement officials, do not distinguish which arrestees are students. Further, any attempt at matching those lists to student records is difficult and makes the effort to report campus crime ineffectual. The government maintained that the burden was trivial. **The court held that the government's position was "untenable," and that its interests were outweighed by the rights of the journalists.** A temporary injunction was issued that prevented the withdrawal of federal funding from any campus that disclosed its arrest reports. *Student Press Law Center v. Alexander*, 778 F.Supp. 1227 (D.D.C. 1991). [DC]

◆   *A Texas university could not forbid some newspapers while allowing others to be distributed.*

Southwest Texas State University had a policy forbidding the distribution of newspapers that contained advertisements. The university did not regulate the distribution of newspapers or literature without advertisements. The regulation also did not apply to the student-run university newspaper, which contained many advertisements. Aside from these restrictions, the university fostered an environment of free expression. A group of students and a small, politically oriented, local newspaper that had attempted free distribution on campus sued the university, claiming that its "no solicitation" policy violated the First Amendment.

A federal district court held for the university, and the students appealed to the U.S. Court of Appeals, Fifth Circuit, which stated that **the university was a limited public forum. As such, its ability to regulate expressive conduct was limited**. There was no evidence that handing out free newspapers would affect the university's academic mission or crime rate. The regulation was not narrowly tailored to meet the privacy, litter, or congestion interests of the university. Moreover, the fact that the university did not regulate publications without advertisements illustrated the tenuous nature of those arguments. The regulation was declared unconstitutional. *Hays County Guardian v. Supple*, 969 F.2d 111 (5th Cir. 1992). [TX]

◆   *Following its ruling in* Healy v. James, *408 U.S. 169 (1972), the Supreme Court held that, at the collegiate level, the conduct of students and the dissemination of ideas–no matter how offensive, could not be curtailed based solely on the "conventions of decency."*

A graduate student at the University of Missouri was expelled for distributing on campus a newspaper that violated university bylaws since it contained forms of "indecent speech." The newspaper was found objectionable for two reasons. First, on the front cover was a political cartoon of policemen raping the Statue of Liberty and the Goddess of Justice with a caption that read "… with Liberty and Justice for All." Secondly, the issue contained an article entitled "Mother Fucker Acquitted," which discussed the trial and acquittal on an assault charge of a New York youth. The student sued the university in a federal district court, for First Amendment violations.

The court denied relief, and the Eighth Circuit affirmed. On further appeal, the U.S. Supreme Court held the student should be reinstated. It stated that **while a university has an undoubted prerogative to enforce reasonable rules governing student conduct, it is not immune from the sweep of the First Amendment**. The Court noted that *Healy v. James* (Section D, below) makes it clear that the mere dissemination of ideas–no matter how offensive to good taste–may not be shut off in the name of "conventions of decency" alone. *Papish v. University of Missouri*, 410 U.S. 667, 93 S.Ct. 1197, 35 L.Ed.2d 618 (1973). [MO]

D. Gay Rights

◆   *A university violated the speech rights of two organizations by prohibiting them from using facilities they had reserved.*

A female graduate student at the University of Massachusetts sought to secure a classroom for two organizational meetings on two different nights. The meetings were sponsored by the Reproductive Rights Network and the Coalition for Lesbian and Gay Civil Rights, among other organizations. The student asked her professor for assistance in scheduling the space and was authorized to call and reserve the room in the professor's name. A staff meeting was held on the morning of the first scheduled meeting, at which concerns were expressed about the effect of having the organizations meet on campus. **Officials were concerned that the university would be perceived as a sponsor, thus detrimentally affecting public and private fundraising.** However, the university allowed the first meeting to take place. None of the anticipated problems from allowing the meeting to occur came to pass. Nevertheless, the university closed the building where the second meeting was to take place, and 17 police officers prevented people from entering.

A trial court found that the university had violated the organizations' free speech rights, and entered an injunction to prevent the university from interfering with the organizations' rights to use university facilities for political speech. However, the court found that the university had not violated the Massachusetts Civil Rights Act. The Appeals Court of Massachusetts upheld the injunction, but also found that the university had violated the MCRA. **The university's failure to publish an explicit, content-neutral policy, containing objective standards on the use of university facilities allowed it unbridled discretion to deny use of its facilities to groups on the basis of the content of their speech.** Further, the use of numerous police officers to secure the building amounted to "threats, intimidation or coercion" under the MCRA, even though no physical confrontation occurred. The court remanded the case for a determination of reasonable attorney's fees and costs. *Reproductive Rights Network v. President of the Univ. of Massachusetts*, 699 N.E.2d 829 (Mass. App. 1998). [MA]

◆   *The military could be prohibited from recruiting on a school's campus because of its discriminatory policies toward homosexuals.*

An unincorporated student organization representing gay and lesbian law students attending the University of Connecticut School of Law opposed the appearance of military recruiters at the school because of military policies that discriminated on the basis of sexual orientation. **It filed a lawsuit against university trustees in a state trial court, seeking a temporary order and declaration that the state Gay Rights Law prohibited on-campus military recruiting efforts.** The court issued a temporary order prohibiting law school officials from permitting any organization that discriminated on the basis of sexual orientation, including the military, from using on-campus employment recruiting facilities. The law school and trustees appealed.

The Supreme Court of Connecticut observed that the state Gay Rights Law protected members of the organization against discrimination. The school and trustees argued that another statute, which required institutions to treat all employment recruiters alike, required that they allow access to the military. The supreme court disagreed, stating that the school had to provide equal access to the military, not preferential treatment. **Because no civilian employer with discriminatory practices would be allowed to recruit on campus, the military was prohibited from on-campus appearances.** The court affirmed the trial court judgment for the student organization. *Gay and Lesbian Law Students Ass'n v. Board of Trustees, Univ. of Connecticut*, 236 Conn. 453, 673 A.2d 484 (1996). [CT]

◆ *A state university could not refuse to recognize gays, lesbians and bisexuals when it recognized other student groups.*

An Alabama statute prohibits any college or university from spending public funds or using facilities to sanction, recognize or support any group promoting lifestyles or actions prohibited by state sodomy and sexual misconduct laws. It also prohibits any group from permitting or encouraging persons to engage in homosexual lifestyle and activity. **A university-recognized organization representing gay, lesbian and bisexual students attending the University of South Alabama was denied access to funding.** It filed a lawsuit against the state of Alabama claiming that the statute violated its members' rights under the First Amendment to the U.S. Constitution. The organization sought a declaration that the act was unconstitutional and an order that would forbid the university from denying it access to university facilities.

The court commented that the First Amendment prohibits viewpoint discrimination and requires government entities to abstain from regulating speech based on the desire to restrict a speaker's opinion. **A state university making its facilities and funding available to different student organizations may not withhold access to persons holding a particular viewpoint without violating the First Amendment.** The statute clearly violated the First Amendment by targeting the gay student organization's speech and access to university funds. States cannot exclude particular viewpoints with respect to an idea even where a compelling state interest in the idea exists. The court issued the declaration sought by the organization but denied its application for an injunction as unnecessary. *Gay Lesbian Bisexual Alliance v. Sessions*, 917 F.Supp. 1548 (M.D. Ala. 1996).

The attorney general then moved for a partial stay pending appeal to the U.S. Court of Appeals, Eleventh Circuit. The court denied the motion, observing the state's failure to adequately show a possibility of prevailing on the merits of the case. The court also denied the organization's motion for an injunction to enforce the declaratory judgment as unnecessary. *Gay Lesbian Bisexual Alliance v. Sessions*, 917 F.Supp. 1558 (M.D. Ala. 1996). [AL]

E. Student Activity Fees

◆ *The U.S. Supreme Court held that the University of Wisconsin could assess a mandatory activity fee to fund student extracurricular programs.*

The University of Wisconsin required all students to pay the university a non-refundable activity fee to support registered student groups. Students who objected to the collection and use of their student fees to support objectionable political and ideological expression sued university regents in a federal district court, asserting that the program violated their speech rights. The court held that the fee program compelled students to support political and ideological activity with which they disagreed in violation of the First Amendment. It prohibited the university from using student fees to fund registered student organizations engaged in such activity. The U.S. Court of Appeals, Seventh Circuit, affirmed in part, finding that the student activity fee program was not germane to the university's mission and burdened student speech.

The U.S. Supreme Court found that the university assessed the fee to facilitate the free and open exchange of ideas among students. Objecting students could insist upon certain safeguards regarding the compelled support of expressive activities. To insist upon germaneness to the university's mission would contravene the purpose of the program, which was to encourage a wide range of speech. The Court found it inevitable that the fees would subsidize some speech that students would find objectionable, and it declined to impose a constitutional requirement upon the university compelling it to refund fees to students. Viewpoint neutrality was the proper standard for the protection of the First Amendment rights of the objecting students. **The university could require students to support extracurricular speech of other students in a viewpoint neutral manner**, and the parties had stipulated in this case that the program was viewpoint neutral. The university had wide latitude to adjust its extracurricular speech programs to accommodate students. The Court reversed and remanded the case for further proceedings on the issue of whether a referendum by students undermined constitutional protection for viewpoint neutrality. *Board of Regents of Univ. of Wisconsin System v. Southworth*, 529 U.S. 217, 120 S.Ct. 1346, 146 L.Ed.2d 193 (2000). [WI]

On remand to the district court, the court determined the university's updated fee system, which set forth various criteria groups had to meet before obtaining funding and required the student government to determine which groups received funding, was unconstitutional because it was not viewpoint neutral. Under the new system, the university's student government made funding decisions with little on no oversight. The court further determined the criteria used to determine whether a group received funding was too subjective. The university was ordered to establish a funding system for student groups that was viewpoint neutral. *Fry v. Board of Regents of Univ. of Wisconsin System*, 132 F.Supp.2d 744 (W.D. Wis. 2000). [WI]

◆ *Oregon students could be required to pay fees that supported a nonpolitical public interest research group.*

The University of Oregon required students, as a condition of matriculation, to pay incidental fees that contributed to the support of the Oregon Student Public Interest Research Group (OSPIRG) Education Fund. A number of students sued to have the fees declared unconstitutional. The Ninth Circuit Court of Appeals first held that the university and the state board of higher education were immune from liability under the Eleventh Amendment. However, the officials responsible for the administration of the fees could be sued. The court then held that the fees were not unconstitutional. **This was not** a case of compelled membership in an objectionable organization. Students were not required to join the OSPIRG Education Fund. Nor did the fees go to an organization that did political lobbying because the OSPIRG Education Fund was separate from the OSPIRG (the political arm of the group). Here, the fees were allocated among scores of campus organizations representing many diverse viewpoints. Further, the OSPIRG Education Fund provided college students with hands-on experience in recognizing, researching and solving the problems of society. This furthered the university's educational mission. *Rounds v. Oregon State Bd. of Higher Educ.*, 166 F.3d 1032 (9th Cir. 1999). [OR]

◆ *A California university could require students to pay student fees that funded political activities.*

The Associated Students of the University of California (ASUC) administers student government and extracurricular activities at the University of California, Berkeley. The ASUC senate conducts student government through 30 elected student representatives. During the school year, the senate meets weekly and sometimes debates controversial public issues including gay and lesbian rights, gun control, and marijuana legalization. A group of students and student organizations challenged the mandatory collection of student fees of which a part funded ASUC senate political activities. They filed a lawsuit against university regents in a California superior court. The court held for the regents, and the Court of Appeal of California affirmed the judgment. However, the Supreme Court of California remanded the case for a determination of whether senate activities violated the speech and association rights of dissenting students by using their fees to support certain ideological and political views.

The superior court again held for the regents, and the dissenting students appealed to the court of appeal. The court reviewed trial court findings that the financial burden on the dissenting students was minimal and that senate activities accounted for only 4 percent of total ASUC expenditures. The senate's primary function was to administer and govern ASUC activities, and the senate was not dedicated to achieving a particular political or ideological outlook. **The expenditure of mandatory fees did not violate the test described by the supreme court since the educational benefits provided by the ASUC senate outweighed the advancement of political and ideological interests** and was not merely incidental to those interests. The court affirmed the judgment for the regents. *Smith v. Regents of the Univ. of California*, 65 Cal.Rptr.2d 813 (Cal. App. 1st Dist. 1997). [CA]

◆ *In the following case, the Supreme Court held that rights to association may not be disregarded or limited.*

A group of students desired to form a local chapter of Students for a Democratic Society (SDS) at a state-supported college. They were, however, denied recognition as a campus organization. The students sued for declaratory and injunctive relief. A federal district court held the college's refusal to recognize the group, in light of the disruptive and violent nature of the national organization, was justifiable. The U.S. Court of Appeals for the

Second Circuit affirmed, stating that the students had failed to avail themselves of the due process of law accorded to them and had failed to meet their burden of complying with the prevailing standards for recognition.

The U.S. Supreme Court held that **the lower courts erred in disregarding the First Amendment interest in freedom of association that the students had in furthering their personal beliefs**. It also held that putting the burden on the students (to show entitlement to recognition) rather than on the president (to justify nonrecognition) was also in error. The Court stated that insofar as the denial of recognition was based on the group's affiliation with the national SDS, or as a result of disagreement with the group's philosophy, the president's decision violated the students' First Amendment rights. A proper basis for nonrecognition might have been that the group refused to comply with a rule requiring them to abide by reasonable campus regulations. Since it was not clear that the college had such a rule, and whether the students intended to observe it, the case was remanded to the district court for resolution. *Healy v. James*, 408 U.S. 169, 92 S.Ct. 2338, 33 L.Ed.2d 266 (1972). [CT]

F. Commercial Speech

◆   *The Supreme Court has held that restrictions on commercial free speech need not be subjected to as rigorous an analysis to determine the restrictions' reasonableness. As long as the restriction is reasonable, it will be upheld.*

The State University of New York (SUNY) prohibited private commercial enterprises from operating in SUNY facilities. Campus police prevented a housewares manufacturer from demonstrating and selling its products at a party hosted in a student dormitory. The manufacturer and a group of students sued SUNY in a federal district court, stating that the policy violated the First Amendment. The court held for SUNY, stating that the student dormitories did not constitute a public forum for purposes of commercial activity, and the restrictions were reasonable in light of the dormitories' purpose. The Second Circuit Court of Appeals reversed, stating that it was unclear whether the policy directly advanced SUNY's interest and whether it was the least restrictive means of achieving that interest. The U.S. Supreme Court granted review and stated that the court of appeals erred in requiring the district court to apply a least restrictive means test. The Court stated that **regulations on commercial speech require only a reasonable "fit" between the government's ends and the means chosen to accomplish those ends**. The Court reversed and remanded the case. *Board of Trustees of the State Univ. of New York v. Fox*, 492 U.S. 469, 109 S.Ct. 3028, 106 L.Ed.2d 388 (1989). [NY]

◆   *A student newspaper lost its First Amendment challenge to a Pennsylvania statute sanctioning businesses that advertise alcohol in any school publication.*

The Pitt News filed suit seeking to prevent the enforcement of "Act 199," a 1996 amendment to the state's liquor code, that sanctioned advertisers of alcohol products in school newspapers. The U.S. Court of Appeals, Third Circuit, ruled that the newspaper could not sued because it could not demonstrate that its constitutional rights were being violated, and it could not sue on behalf of third parties. **The paper's loss of advertising revenue and**

subsequent decrease in the length of the publication did not demonstrate that its First Amendment rights were violated. *The Pitt News v. Fisher*, 215 F.3d 354 (3d Cir. 2000), *cert. denied*, 121 S.Ct. 857 (2001). [PA]

◆ *A university's radio station did not have to allow the KKK to underwrite a program.*

A not-for-profit public broadcast radio station operated by the University of Missouri (and a member of National Public Radio) received a request from the state coordinator for the Ku Klux Klan to underwrite a number of 15-second spots on the station's "All Things Considered" program. This would require the station to acknowledge the gift by reading a message from the Klan stating that it was a white Christian organization standing up for the rights and values of white Christians and leaving contact information. Although this did not violate any of the station's enhanced underwriting guidelines, the station's general manager asked the university's chancellor what to do. The chancellor decided that allowing the underwriting would result in a loss of revenue to the station of at least $5 million from donor support and lost tuition, and she rejected the offer. The state coordinator and the Klan sued the station manager, asserting that the station could not reject the offer because it was a public forum, and could not discriminate on the basis of viewpoint.

The U.S. District Court for the Eastern District of Missouri held that **the station did not have to accept the Klan's offer to underwrite "All Things Considered." The station's employees had the discretion to choose which underwriting offers to accept, and the underwriting program could not be deemed a public forum.** Further, the decision to reject the offer was not based on viewpoint but on business considerations. The court granted pretrial judgment to the station manager. The Eighth Circuit Court of Appeals affirmed. It noted that the underwriting spots constituted governmental speech and that the government could exercise discretion over what it chose to say. Since the station had the right to reject the proposed spots, the Klan's lawsuit could not succeed. *KKK v. Bennett*, 203 F.3d 1085 (8th Cir. 2000). [MO]

◆ *A college dean could not restrict a student editor from accepting an advertisement from a strip club and bar.*

A Michigan student held the position of editor-in-chief of her community college newspaper. She printed an advertisement of a Canadian bar where the drinking age was only 19 and the dancers were nude. When the school's dean prohibited her from printing any more of the bar's advertisements, the student sued the school in a federal court, alleging violations of her free speech rights and intentional infliction of emotional distress. The court noted that if the editor had the authority to run the newspaper, the school would have to have a compelling interest in restricting her speech in it.

Where commercial speech is lawful and not misleading, and where the governmental interest in restricting that speech is substantial, then the government may restrict the speech if the means it employs are narrowly tailored to meet its objective. The newspaper was independent of the school because the editor-in-chief had the full authority to decide its content, policies and personnel. The dean's policy of exerting final control over what could be published in the newspaper was not narrowly tailored to achieve the government's interests. It burdened substantially more speech than was necessary and violated the student's free speech rights. *Lueth v. St. Clair County Comm. College*, 732 F.Supp. 1410 (E.D. Mich. 1990). [MI]

G. Student Elections

◆   *A college president's cancellation of a student election may have violated the First Amendment.*

The student newspaper at the College of Staten Island endorsed student union candidates, some of whom were also part of the newspaper's staff, for elected student government positions. After a complaint was filed, the Student Election Review Committee postponed the election. The college president then reviewed the disputed issue of the newspaper and agreed that it improperly endorsed the student union candidates, compromising the electoral process. She declared the results of the election void and ordered a new election. The student union candidates swept both elections. When a lawsuit was filed against the president and the university, asserting that the president violated the First Amendment by canceling the election, a court held that there were **issues of fact as to whether the president's decision was a constitutionally permissible content-based determination** or impermissible viewpoint discrimination. As a result, it refused to award pretrial judgment to the student plaintiffs. *Husain v. Springer*, 193 F.Supp.2d 664 (E.D.N.Y. 2002). [NY]

◆   *A university could not put spending limitations on student council candidates without violating the First Amendment.*

A California university student ran unopposed for a seat on the student-run legislative council. After he was elected, the elections commission discovered that he spent $233.40 on his campaign despite student association regulations limiting campaign spending to $100. He was disqualified from holding the position and sued under the First Amendment. He sought a preliminary injunction reinstating him to the position during the litigation, and a federal court ruled in his favor. It stated that the Eleventh Amendment did not preclude awarding injunctive relief. Further, the student met the requirements for obtaining such relief. He was likely to succeed on the merits of his claim because campaign spending restrictions directly affect freedom of speech; he would suffer irreparable injury if the injunction was not granted; and **allowing him to represent the students who elected him was in the public interest**. The student was reinstated to his seat on the legislative council. *Welker v. Cicerone*, 174 F.Supp.2d 1055 (C.D. Cal. 2001). [CA]

CHAPTER FIVE

Employment

I. WRONGFUL TERMINATION AND BREACH OF CONTRACT

A. Breach of Contract

Breach of contract claims arise from written contracts; academic custom and usage, including faculty handbooks; First Amendment issues based on the use of religious criteria in employment decisions; application of the American Association of University Professors (AAUP) guidelines; and reliance on oral statements implying or modifying an employment contract.

1. Written Contracts

◆ *A Colorado state college followed appropriate procedures in terminating an employee's position when it became unable to fund it.*

A certified employee held a classified position under the state personnel system. His position did not receive regular state funding, and when special funding and interim funds were exhausted, the college eliminated it and dismissed him. An administrative law judge held the decision was not arbitrary or an abuse of discretion, and the state personnel board agreed. The employee appealed to the Court of Appeals of Colorado, which stated reorganizations and layoffs involve practical and financial concerns. There are no credibility determinations to be made in terminating an employee based on a lack of funds. In contrast, disciplinary terminations do require credibility determinations and require the employer to act on the basis of "merit and fairness."

The court held the employee lacked a property interest in his abolished position. Although a public employee has a continued interest in employment, there can be no reasonable expectation that a position will never be abolished. The human resources manager who processed the layoff complied with a statutory layoff matrix based on classification structure, employment history, performance evaluations, and veteran status. As there was no error in the board's order, the court affirmed it. *Velasquez v. Department of Higher Educ.*, 93 P.3d 540 (Colo. App. 2003). [CO]

◆ *A professor who served as a dean under a four-year appointment was properly terminated when the appointment expired.*

A Tennessee state university entered into a contract with a professor for a four-year appointment as Dean of the College of Education. At the end of four years, the professor was terminated and demoted to the rank of tenured professor with a corresponding reduction in pay. He brought an action before the Tennessee Claims Commission, asserting breach of contract and wrongful discharge. The commission ruled that the university had to pay the professor the difference between his salary as a dean and his salary as a professor. However, the Court of Appeals of Tennessee reversed. It found **no evidence that the professor was entitled to continue receiving a dean's salary after his appointment expired**. The contract only provided that he would be entitled to a tenured position. *Emans v. Board of Regents of State of Tennessee*, 2002 WL 31443206 (Tenn. App. 11/1/02). [TN]

◆ *A doctor who signed a non-compete agreement could violate it where he was not harming the university's legitimate business interests.*

A Florida university hospital employed a doctor who signed a non-compete agreement stating that he would not engage in a "community-based clinical practice within a radius of 50 miles" of the university hospital for a two-year period following his employment. After leaving the university, the doctor began working in a community-based clinical practice within 50 miles of the university hospital. The university sued, seeking to enforce the non-compete agreement. The doctor argued that he was not causing irreparable injury to the university hospital's "legitimate business interests" because no former patients of the university hospital followed him to his current practice. A trial court found that the doctor violated the terms of the non-compete agreement but that his new practice did not interfere with the university hospital's legitimate business interests. The Florida District Court of Appeal affirmed. Since **none of the doctor's former patients were now receiving treatment from him**, and since his current practice was not attempting to recruit prospective university patients, the court refused to enforce the non-compete agreement. *University of Florida, Bd. of Trustees v. Sanal*, 837 So.2d 512 (Fla. App. 2003). [FL]

◆ *Despite some procedural irregularities, a board of trustees could vote not to renew a college president's contract.*

A Texas college hired a president under a three-year contract, which contained an option for a three-year extension. Toward the end of the initial term, the board of trustees met by teleconference and voted not to renew the president's contract. He was given notice of the nonrenewal in compliance with the terms of his contract. He then sued the college for breach of contract, asserting that the termination notice was invalid because the vote against renewing his contract occurred at a meeting that was not called in compliance with the college's bylaws. A state court granted pretrial judgment to the college, and the Texas Court of Appeals affirmed. Even though the teleconference was called in an irregular manner, that was insufficient to void the board's decision not to renew the president's contract. **Although the board's actions at that meeting were voidable, they could be ratified (and were) at a later meeting.** Further, the president lacked standing to challenge the procedural violations. The president was not able to regain his job. *Swain v. Wiley College*, 74 S.W.3d 143 (Tex. App. 2002). [TX]

◆ *In the absence of approval by University of Louisiana trustees, a coach who sought a promotion to athletic director had no claim against the system.*

The men's basketball coach for Northwestern State University also sought the athletic director position when the AD announced his retirement. The coach was informed of a plan to name him athletic director/head basketball coach. The university president sent a letter to the coach outlining the plan, but noting that it would not be official until approved by the Board of Trustees for the University of Louisiana System. The Board never approved the appointment of the coach to the AD position. When the president retired and an acting president was appointed, the acting president initiated a nationwide search for a new AD and invited the coach to apply. The coach instead sued the board for breach of contract and detrimental reliance. A Louisiana trial court ruled in favor of the board, finding that there was no contract to be breached.

The court determined that since the board of trustees never approved the change in positions, no contract was ever formed. It also rejected the coach's contention that he turned down a job offer to be athletic director at the University of South Alabama because he had been promised the same position at NSU. The only evidence offered in support of this position was a letter from Southern Alabama's AD stating what the contract terms would be if the coach were offered a position. This letter was not a job offer. **Because the coach could not establish a contract or that he relied on a promise made by NSU to his detriment, he failed to establish a case** under state law, and the university was entitled to a judgment in its favor. The trial court decision was affirmed. *Barnett v. Board of Trustees*, 809 So.2d 184 (La. App. 2001). [LA]

◆ *A college did not breach a professor's employment contract when it reopened her position after the EEOC investigated whether the school had discriminated against other applicants for the position.*

The professor was hired as a full-time, permanent history instructor for Southeast College. An applicant for the position then sent a letter to the college's human resources department claiming the professor received preferential treatment. The applicant also filed a formal complaint with the EEOC, claiming he had been discriminated against on the basis of age, religion, sex and national origin. After an investigation, the EEOC did not find evidence of discrimination, but it noted errors in the college's screening of applicants. As a result, the college decided to re-post the position and moved the professor into an adjunct position with a month-to-month contract.

The professor then sued for breach of her employment contract. She also claimed that the applicant had defamed her in his various formal complaints. The court granted pretrial judgment to the college on the breach of contract claim and to the applicant on the defamation claim. The Texas Court of Appeals affirmed the ruling in favor of the college on the professor's breach of contract claim. It noted that **the professor's employment contract stated that she was subject to a probationary period during her first year as a full-time professor, which allowed the college to reassign her during her first year.** The appellate court reversed the ruling for the applicant on the defamation issue. The applicant's comments alleging the professor misrepresented her qualifications and was unduly favored by the college administrators could possibly have been defamatory. This issue was remanded for a trial. *Thorpe v. Alsaeed*, 2000 WL 567617 (Tex. App. 5/11/00). [TX]

◆ *A New Mexico public university was not immune to suit in an action brought under a written contract.*

A tenured professor in pediatric medicine at the University of New Mexico began serving as the director of the division of developmental disabilities under a written contract that provided $5,000 for his administrative duties. After the professor helped the university obtain a grant to establish a center for training and research in developmental disabilities, he became the director of the center and his administrative salary increased to $10,000. A few years later, after a review of the center, the dean of the medical school informed the professor that his directorship would be on probation for the rest of the year. The following year, he was removed as director of the center, and the year after that, his administrative salary returned to $5,000. The professor sued the university for breach of contract, and a state trial court denied the university's claim of governmental immunity. The Supreme Court of New Mexico affirmed that decision, noting that the professor's action against the university was based on a written contract. Since a state statute provided that governmental entities were immune from actions based on unwritten contracts, **the implication was that the government could be sued under valid written contracts.** *Handmaker v. Henney*, 992 P.2d 879 (N.M. 1999). [NM]

◆ *A liquidated damages clause in a coach's contract was valid and enforceable where the amount of harm caused by the coach's early departure was difficult to ascertain, and where the amount was reasonable.*

After a Vanderbilt University football coach joined another school, a Tennessee federal court awarded Vanderbilt $281,886.43 under the employment contract. The sum included a liquidated damages amount for the two-year time period covered by a contract extension the coach had earlier signed. The coach appealed, alleging that the liquidated damages provision was unenforceable as a penalty and that the contract extension was not binding upon him. The U.S. Court of Appeals, Sixth Circuit, reversed and remanded, **holding that the liquidated damages clause was not a penalty and that it was enforceable. By leaving early, the coach would harm Vanderbilt more than by just the cost of replacing him.** However, a question of fact existed as to whether the two-year contract extension was enforceable. Although the coach had signed the contract, he had told the athletic director that the extension would not be "final" until his attorney-brother looked at it. The court remanded the case for a determination as to whether the brother had to approve the contract extension before the coach could be held bound by its terms for damages and, if so, whether the brother's failure to object to the contract's language constituted *de facto* approval. *Vanderbilt Univ. v. DiNardo*, 174 F.3d 751 (6th Cir. 1999). [TN]

◆ *A coach had no cause of action under a contract where he was paid through the term of the contract despite having his duties taken away.*

The head football coach at a private Pennsylvania college was sent a letter each year offering him employment for the following year. To accept, he would sign and return a copy of the letter to the president of the college. After an unsuccessful football season, a number of football players wrote to college officials, expressing their dissatisfaction with the coach. The officials laid out new terms and conditions for his employment the following year. When he did not respond, he was informed that his employment would not be continued. **He was paid for the rest of the year pursuant to his contract but was relieved of all duties.** The coach sued the college and three of his players for breach of contract and intentional interference with employment relations. The Superior Court of Pennsylvania rejected the coach's argument that his employment was governed by the college's personnel manual, which contained "just cause" and conflict resolution provisions. The court found no evidence that the manual was intended to contradict the terms of his annual contract and held that **a reasonable person would not have interpreted the provisions as converting his contracts into permanent employment.** The court also found that the players did not intentionally interfere with the coach's employment contract. The coach's case was dismissed. *Small v. Juniata College*, 682 A.2d 350 (Pa. Super. 1996). [PA]

◆   *Transferring a professor to a non-teaching staff position was not a breach of contract where there was no reduction in pay and where the contract called for the professor to teach and/or serve the college.*

A professor employed by a Georgia private art college developed personality conflicts with several colleagues in the video department. His colleagues complained and requested that the college transfer the professor out of the department. The college complied with the request, reassigning the professor to a non-teaching "staff" position in an ancillary video production unit with no reduction in salary. The new position was consistent with his training and experience. The professor wanted to teach, but refused to accept the college's offer to place him as a visiting teacher in a county public school system. He filed a lawsuit in a Georgia trial court, alleging breach of contract and seeking damages. The trial court granted pretrial judgment to the professor. The college appealed to the Court of Appeals of Georgia. The court of appeals held that the professor's contract, which required him to devote his time "to teaching and/or service to the college," recognized the flexibility necessary in the effective administration of a college. The trial court's reliance on the professor's transfer from "faculty" to "staff" as the basis for its ruling was misplaced. **Considering the nature of the new position, as opposed to its classification, the court held that the transfer was not a breach of contract.** *Johnson v. Savannah College of Art*, 460 S.E.2d 308 (Ga. App. 1995). [GA]

◆   *Professors who were contractually entitled to the rank of professor for life were not entitled to lifetime employment where they signed annual employment contracts.*

Two faculty members at a Pennsylvania private university were promoted to professor in 1965. The contracts provided that "the distinctive rank of professor is an appointment for life." However, the contract also provided that they would receive a salary for the following academic year only. Between 1965 and 1990 both professors entered into similar annual contracts with the university, except that the appointment for life clause was deleted. In 1982, the university modified its retirement policy to make retirement mandatory for tenured faculty members who reached the age of 70. Pursuant to this policy, both professors were retired from active faculty status. The professors challenged the mandatory retirements in court, and the case eventually reached the Superior Court of Pennsylvania.

The university contended that **while the rank of professor was a lifetime rank, employment as a member of the faculty was year by year.** The superior court agreed, noting that employment relationships are generally terminable at will. In holding for the university, the superior court noted its reluctance to interpret employment contracts as guaranteeing employment for life. Rather, it gave effect to the intent of the parties as reasonably manifested by the language of their written agreement. Here, the language of the contract clearly entitled the professors to retain their rank for the remainder of their life. However, the faculty members were not guaranteed employment for life. The duration of each employment contract was for a period of one academic year only. *Halpin v. LaSalle Univ.*, 639 A.2d 37 (Pa. Super. 1994). [PA]

◆ *A written contract that did not specify an exact term of employment did not alter the at-will employment relationship.*

A Texas Baptist college hired an administrator in 1969 pursuant to a written contract that did not specify an exact term of employment. Throughout the early years of the administrator's 23-year term of employment, the college's president allegedly assured him that his job was secure as long as his work was satisfactory. However, in 1992, the administrator resigned in lieu of termination. He then filed a constructive discharge lawsuit, alleging breach of contract and that the college's new president had tortiously interfered with his employment contract. A Texas trial court granted pretrial judgment to the college and the president, and the administrator appealed.

The Court of Appeals of Texas held that **a contract without a specified term of employment did not alter the administrator's at-will status.** Moreover, even assuming that oral promises of lifetime employment were made and that the president had authority to make them, the administrator's breach of contract action based on this oral representation was barred by the statute of frauds. Finally, because the president was an agent of the college and an agent could not be personally liable for tortious interference with its principal's contracts, this claim had also been properly dismissed. The trial court ruling was affirmed. *Massey v. Houston Baptist Univ.* 902 S.W.2d 81 (Tex. App.–Houston 1995). [TX]

2. Handbooks

◆ *A college that failed to provide a professor with written evaluations as required by the faculty handbook did not have to renew his contract.*

A private college in New York employed a nontenured probationary assistant professor in its accounting department under a series of one-year contracts. The faculty handbook called for written evaluations to be provided each teacher, but the college failed to provide them. After the professor organized and participated in a student protest aimed at the accounting department's curriculum, the college sent him a letter along with his proposed contract notifying him that upon expiration of the contract, it would not be renewed. The letter indicated that **the basis for nonrenewal was the impaired collegiality and confidence between the professor and the accounting department.** He signed the one-year, nonrenewable contract that accompanied the letter and became unemployed at the end of the year.

The professor sued the college for breach of contract in a state trial court where pretrial judgment was granted to the college. The New York Supreme Court, Appellate Division, affirmed the lower court decision in favor of the college. It noted that the nonrenewal of the professor's contract was solely related to his failure to get along with his colleagues and was not related to his teaching skills, which the college conceded were excellent. Also, even though the college failed to provide written evaluations as called for in the faculty handbook, **there was no duty to automatically renew the professor's contract if he was found to be an excellent teacher.** The college's decision not to renew the professor's contract did not amount to breach of contract. *DeSimone v. Siena College*, 663 N.Y.S.2d 701 (A.D. 3d Dept. 1997). [NY]

◆   *Where a professor failed to follow the procedures outlined for challenging his discharge, his lawsuit for breach of contract failed.*

Several allegations of plagiarism were leveled against a private college professor regarding a book he published in 1983. The college proposed to reduce the professor in rank and pay, but he filed a grievance against it and was reinstated to a full professorship. However, at the same time, he was notified that he would be fired at the end of the year. A grievance committee and the president of the college upheld the termination and dismissed the professor's grievance. The professor failed to commence an article 78 proceeding to review the president's determination. Instead, he brought suit in a New York trial court for breach of contract. The court dismissed the breach of contract action, stating that the professor should have brought an article 78 proceeding to challenge the validity of the grievance decision. On appeal to the New York Supreme Court, Appellate Division, the court noted that **the college had followed the procedures provided in the handbook governing employment termination.** The professor's sole remedy if he was dissatisfied with his discharge was to commence an article 78 proceeding. Accordingly, the trial court had properly dismissed the breach of contract claim. *Klinge v. Ithaca College*, 663 N.Y.S.2d 735 (A.D. 3d Dept. 1997). [NY]

◆   *Where a professor maintained that a handbook created a contract, and that the university breached that contract, her claim failed because the university followed the procedures outlined in it.*

A private Iowa university hired a part-time lecturer into a faculty position under a one year contract and told that she would be evaluated annually. She received excellent reviews and eventually became a tenure track professor. Before becoming eligible for tenure, the professor began to have difficulties with the art department's new chairperson concerning the submission of her work for review as part of her annual evaluation. The professor objected to the lack of stated criteria and noted that her graphic design work, often created in a commercial setting, did not easily fit into the category "scholarly and artistic development." The chairperson found her work insufficient in this area. After three more annual appointments she was fired. She challenged this decision before an academic committee, stating she was denied her procedural rights, but the committee disagreed. The professor sued the university for breach of contract, and the case reached the Supreme Court of Iowa.

The court found that although the professor was employed under a series of one-year contracts, she was more than an at-will employee. In order for the professor to prove that her faculty handbook was an enforceable employment contract, she had to show that it was sufficiently definite in its terms to create an offer, that it was communicated and accepted by her so as to create acceptance and that she continued working, so as to provide consideration. The court found that here, **the handbook created an enforceable contract but also found that the university did not breach that contract.** The handbook did not state that any particular criteria should be used to evaluate the professor's work and it did not allow her to demand that the university use more or different criteria than what was currently used. Furthermore, **all the grievance procedures described in the handbook were given to the professor.** She was given adequate warning, told she could remedy the situation by providing sufficient documentation of her commercial work and given full access to the appeals process. *Taggart v. Drake Univ.*, 549 N.W.2d 796 (Iowa 1996). [IA]

◆   *Where a handbook's language clearly indicated an intent not to create a contract, none was formed.*

A carpenter foreman at a Pennsylvania private college was discharged, allegedly for abuse of college time and materials and for submitting false time sheets. However, the foreman alleged that the college had a longstanding policy and practice of allowing its employees to use scrap materials and allowing them to perform personal projects during "nonbusy" work time. The employee handbook outlined the four disciplinary steps, ranging from an oral warning to discharge, but stated that the steps were merely intended as a guide to both supervisors and employees. The handbook also contained an introductory letter from the college president that stated that the handbook was "intended to serve as an introduction and guide to expectations at the college."

The foreman filed suit in a Pennsylvania federal court, alleging breach of contract and detrimental reliance. He contended that the employee handbook and the college policies constituted a binding contract which entitled him to continued employment. The court disagreed, ruling that the foreman was an at-will employee subject to discharge with or without cause. Here the foreman failed to overcome the at-will presumption. **The president's disclaimer in his introductory statement and the precatory language in the handbook clearly indicated an intent not to create an employment contract.** The court dismissed the breach of contract and detrimental reliance claims. *Raines v. Haverford College*, 849 F.Supp. 1009 (E.D. Pa. 1994), *Anderson v. Haverford College*, 851 F.Supp. 179 (E.D. Pa. 1994). [PA]

◆   *Where a handbook provided that it was subject to modification at any time, it did not provide contractual rights over and above those existing in the at-will relationship.*

A Massachusetts resident was hired as an associate director of admissions at a Rhode Island private university. He later became a member of the university president's advisory council. A new president took office and "philosophical differences" developed between the two men. The university informed the associate director that he would be replaced, but that he would be appointed to a new position through the summer of the following year. The university's personnel policy manual provided that employees with over 10 years of service would be given severance pay and that all employees would receive a written warning prior to termination. However, **the manual was subject to modification at any time.**

After his termination, the associate director sued the university in federal court, alleging breach of contract, breach of an implied covenant of good faith, and wrongful termination. The associate director first contended that the university breached the contract created by the employment manual (providing that he receive severance pay and adequate notice prior to his termination). The court disagreed, noting that **employment manuals which can be modified at any time do not provide additional contractual rights to at-will employees.** Absent a violation of an express statutory standard, an employer of an at-will employee is not subject to an implied covenant of good faith. Similarly, wrongful termination claims by at-will employees fail unless the employer violates a statute. The claims were dismissed. *Dunfey v. Roger Williams Univ.*, 824 F.Supp. 18 (D. Mass. 1993). [MA]

◆ *Where a college failed to follow procedures in a handbook on achieving tenure, it was required to conduct another tenure review.*

A New York private college hired an art history professor for a newly created tenure track position. According to the faculty manual, once a professor was hired, consideration for tenure was governed by procedures set forth in the manual. The evaluation subcommittee and the advisory committee recommended that tenure be granted. However, the dean gave a negative recommendation based on declining enrollment in art history courses. During the tenure review, the president's participation was limited to his consultation with the dean in contravention of express provisions in the faculty manual. The board of trustees voted to deny tenure to the professor. A New York trial court vacated the denial and directed the college to conduct another tenure review.

The college appealed. The New York Supreme Court, Appellate Division, held the college had failed to follow its own procedures in conducting the professor's tenure review. **The college did not adhere to the process set forth in the faculty manual** insofar as that process contemplated an active role for the president of the college. The court also held that the college had failed to apply its own substantive criteria in evaluating the professor for tenure. Student involvement, the crucial factor in the dean's negative recommendation, was not among the enumerated criteria in the faculty manual. While enrollment could be an appropriate consideration in the decision whether to create or continue a tenure-track position, it was not an appropriate consideration in the tenure review of a particular faculty member. The appellate division court affirmed the order requiring the college to conduct another tenure review. *Bennett v. Wells College*, 641 N.Y.S.2d 929 (A.D. 4th Dept. 1996). [NY]

3. AAUP Guidelines

◆ *A professor could not use the AAUP guidelines, which had been incorporated into his contract, to modify the intent of the contract.*

A professor and a New Jersey private university entered into five separate employment contracts, each of which incorporated the terms of the university's collective bargaining agreement with the American Association of University Professors (AAUP) guidelines. However, the professor's applications for tenure were denied due to his lack of a doctorate degree and his failure to publish. His contract for a sixth academic year stated that his associate professor position was a "non-tenured position." In the following year, he was appointed as an associate dean but continued to teach three credits per semester without additional compensation. He was fired several years later because his overall performance was found to be "significantly below expectations." The professor filed a lawsuit in a New Jersey superior court, alleging that he had acquired *de facto* tenure under the provisions of the AAUP contract. The AAUP contract required that faculty members who had taught for 14 continuous academic semesters be granted tenure. The superior court held for the university, and the professor appealed to a state appellate division court.

The appellate division court noted that **the provision requiring tenure for faculty members teaching 14 continuous semesters was a subsidiary provision that should not be interpreted so as to conflict with the principal purpose of the contract.** The court rejected the professor's disproportionate emphasis on the provision to support his tenure claim. The interpretation of the probationary appointments provision urged by the professor unlawfully conflicted with the principal purpose of the university's formal tenure policy, which placed substantive and procedural prerequisites on the acquisition of tenure. The superior court ruling was affirmed. *Healy v. Fairleigh Dickinson Univ.*, 671 A.2d 182 (N.J. Super. A.D. 1996). [NJ]

◆   *A seminary breached a professor's employment contract by refusing to follow its own regulations.*

The executive committee of a seminary's board of trustees ordered the president of the seminary to reduce the budget by at least $50,000. As a result, a 62-year-old tenured faculty member, who had taught there for 31 years, was fired. The faculty member sued for breach of contract. The seminary agreed that the contract was subject to the AAUP Recommended Institutional Regulations on Academic Freedom and Tenure. This document, along with the faculty promotion and tenure policy of the seminary, contained provisions governing the firing of a tenured faculty member.

The seminary claimed that the document did not require it to allow the fired teacher to participate in "any way at any stage" of the proceedings. The court observed, however, that **the regulations required any faculty member facing termination to be allowed to participate in the dismissal proceedings before a faculty group and the governing board.** It noted that without an opportunity to be heard, the faculty member had no opportunity to have pertinent issues reviewed and discussed in a meaningful way. The court therefore ruled that the seminary failed to follow its own regulations since the language of the document clearly expressed that an aggrieved faculty member had a "contractual right to request a review of his termination." In this case, the discharged faculty member was denied that opportunity, which meant that the seminary had breached his contract. *Linn v. Andover-Newton Theological School*, 638 F.Supp. 1114 (D. Mass. 1986). [MA]

◆ *Where a part of the AAUP guidelines was excluded from an employment contract, the university did not have to follow the procedures listed in that part.*

A private Louisiana university dismissed a tenured professor for alleged professional incompetence. She sued the university for reinstatement of tenure and employment. She argued that the university, after agreeing to modify her existing employment contract, failed to apply Paragraph Seven of the AAUP guidelines, which provide procedures for the termination of a tenured professor. The trial court held that the college had no obligation to comply with Paragraph Seven, and the professor appealed to the state court of appeal.

On appeal, the professor argued Paragraph Seven of the AAUP guidelines was an implied provision in her employment contract. Her contract incorporated the provisions listed in the university's faculty handbook, which provided procedures for the termination of faculty appointments. The appellate court held that **the faculty handbook and the contract clearly excluded Paragraph Seven of the AAUP guidelines. As a result, the paragraph did not apply to any procedures established by the university for the termination of tenured professors.** The court further stated that there was no merit to the professor's argument that the college agreed to modify her original employment contract. The court affirmed the trial court's decision. *Olivier v. Xavier Univ.*, 553 So.2d 1004 (La. App. 4th Cir. 1989). [LA]

◆ *The AAUP guidelines were held not to apply in a case where teachers' contracts were not terminated but rather not renewed.*

Three teachers were employed at Talladega College under employment contracts with a term of one year from August 1984 to August 1985. In May 1985, each received a letter from the college president notifying them that their employment with the college would end in August 1985. The teachers sued the college in an Alabama circuit court for breach of contract. The court ruled for the college, and the teachers appealed to the Alabama Supreme Court. They claimed that the *Procedural Standards in Faculty Dismissal Proceedings* published by the American Association of University Professors (AAUP) were incorporated within their employment contracts. The teachers filed a breach of contract and wrongful termination lawsuit, alleging that the AAUP standards favored them because the standards applied to any nontenured teacher "whose term appointment has not expired."

The state supreme court stated that although the AAUP standards were neither expressly nor impliedly a part of the teachers' contracts, it would apply the standards for purposes of the appeal. The court concluded that the title of the publication and the publication's provisions indicated that the standards applied only to dismissals of college faculty members. **The standards did not apply here since the teachers' contracts were not cancelled prior to their completion.** The teachers completed their performance through August 1985, and were paid for the entire term. They had no valid claims since they were not dismissed but rather were simply not reemployed for the next year. One of the teachers claimed that he had achieved *de facto* tenure status since he had been employed for over seven years. The court disagreed, noting that the faculty handbook required that permanent tenure be extended only to persons specifically elected by the board of trustees and that the "acquisition of tenure

... is not automatic after seven years of teaching..." The decision in favor of the college was affirmed. *Hill v. Talladega Col.*, 502 So.2d 735 (Ala. 1987). [AL]

4. Implied Contracts

◆   *The Supreme Court of New Hampshire upheld a jury verdict which found that reappointment letters created an employment contract.*

A New Hampshire college audio-visual director worked for 11 years under annual reappointment letters describing terms such as his salary, employment period and duties. The college discharged the director prior to the end of the term of a reappointment letter. He sued the college for breach of contract in the state court system, alleging termination without good cause. The case went to trial, which resulted in a verdict for the director. The court denied the college's motion for a directed verdict. The college appealed to the state supreme court. It reviewed the terms of the reappointment letters, and held a reasonable jury could find they constituted an employment contract. The fact that they stated 12-month terms was persuasive evidence that the director was not an "at-will" employee. The reappointment rights section of the College Handbook stated employees could be disciplined for just cause. The court held a reasonable jury could find the college was obligated to follow this provision. Since there was sufficient evidence for a jury to find an employment contract existed, the denial of a directed verdict was not an abuse of discretion, and the jury verdict was upheld. *Dillman v. New Hampshire College*, 838 A.2d 1274 (N.H. 2003). [NH]

◆   *The Second Circuit affirmed a decision for Yale University on contract and tort claims by a professor who was terminated from Yale Medical School.*

The professor completed two three-year employment terms at the school, and was promoted to a five-year term as an associate professor. A year later, Yale notified him that his employment would not be renewed at the end of the term. The professor was excluded from a private organization created by the school. He completed his employment term, then sued Yale in a federal district court, alleging contract and tort claims. The court held for Yale, and the professor appealed to the U.S. Court of Appeals, Second Circuit.

Although the professor contended Yale breached his employment contract by excluding him from membership in the organization, his employment contract included no such terms. The contract described only the duration of his employment term and his benefits–no other details were included. The court rejected the professor's argument that inclusion within the organization was an implied-in-fact agreement, and denied his constructive discharge claim. Yale's decision to exclude him from the organization did not intentionally inflict emotional distress. Accordingly, Yale was entitled to summary judgment. *Franco v. Yale Univ.*, No. 03-7060, 80 Fed.Appx. 707, 2003 WL 22716754 (2d Cir. 2003). [CT]

◆   *An employee suing for breach of contract could not assert a bad faith claim against a private research institute.*

A medical researcher at Baylor Research Institute claimed that Baylor and various officials breached his employment contract by "unilaterally imposing oppressive and unreasonable requirements on his research activities." He sued for breach of contract and bad faith, among other claims, and a Texas federal court dismissed the bad faith claim. The court noted that under Texas law, there is no implication of a general duty of good faith and fair dealing in contracts. A duty of good faith is only imposed in special relationships. As a result, the bad faith claim could not proceed. *Curiel v. Baylor Research Institute*, 2003 WL 21283200 (N.D. Tex. 5/28/03). [TX]

◆ *A compensatory damage award to a coach who relied on an athletic director's invalid commitment of a two-year position was upheld by the Alabama Supreme Court.*

When the Savannah State University head basketball coach expressed reservations about taking a one-year position with Alabama State University, the ASU AD advised him by letter that if he was not appointed head coach for a second season, he could be assured a position as first assistant coach for the second season. The coach then quit his job and moved his family to Alabama. The AD had made the commitment without securing approval from ASU's president, who had sole authority to bind the university in employment matters. The president rejected the assurance and told the AD to inform the coach that he only had a one-year contract. The AD waited until after the 1995–96 season to reveal to the coach his true status. The coach was not hired permanently. He sued ASU and various officials in a state trial court. Citing statutory immunity, the court dismissed all the claims, except those brought against the AD.

After a jury sided with the coach and awarded him compensatory and punitive damages, the AD appealed to the Alabama Supreme Court. The AD argued that the coach had failed to prove the elements of promissory fraud. He also questioned whether the coach had proven that the AD had intentionally deceived him. The court noted that **the jury had evidence from which it could find that the AD, knowing his lack of authority and knowing the coach's insistence upon a term of more than one year, made an offer that exceeded his authority.** Further, the AD was not entitled to state-agent immunity because his misrepresentations were willful, malicious, fraudulent or in bad faith. The court upheld the compensatory damage award, noting the coach's lost income, mental anguish and mounting debts, all arising from the fact that he left his Georgia position to take the ASU job, and once terminated, was unable to find suitable work in Alabama. The court, however, reversed the award of punitive damages. The coach was ordered to give back the punitive damage portion of the award; if he refused, the court would reverse the entire award and order a new trial. *Williams v. Williams*, 786 So.2d 477 (Ala. 2000). [AL]

◆ *Where written and oral evidence was too vague to support an implied contract, the employment remained at will.*

An Oklahoma junior college was dissatisfied with its new president's job performance and offered suggestions for improvement. After he failed to make the requisite improvements, his employment with the college was terminated. He filed breach of contract, wrongful discharge and intentional infliction of emotional distress (IIED) claims against the college in an Oklahoma trial court. At trial, the president introduced a standard rejection letter from the college, a college manual highlighting suggested termination procedures, and evidence of oral assurances of "lengthy employment." However, both parties acknowledged that either could have terminated the employment relationship at any time. The trial court entered pretrial judgment in favor of the college, and the president appealed to the Court of Appeals of Oklahoma.

The court noted that **factors indicating an implied contract of job security include evidence of additional consideration, longevity of employment, employee handbooks, detrimental reliance on oral assurances, and promotions or commendations.** Here, the written and oral evidence was too vague to support an implied contract. Further, because the employee was never asked to perform illegal acts and was never prohibited from discussing employment matters, his wrongful discharge claim was dismissed. Finally, the dismissal of his breach of contract and wrongful discharge lawsuits precluded the IIED claim. The district court's ruling was affirmed. *Beck v. Phillips Colleges*, 883 P.2d 1283 (Okl. App. 1994). [OK]

◆   *Negotiations and documentation were sufficient to constitute a two-year contract in the following case.*

A private university conducted a federally-funded research project in collaboration with the government of Ecuador. The research project involved the appointment of a field sociologist who was to live in Ecuador for two years. **The university selected a sociologist but the parties never signed a contract.** The sociologist accepted a temporary appointment and commenced working even before he was placed on the university's payroll. He traveled to Ecuador with some of his staff for three months to do preliminary research and obtain housing for his family. When the sociologist returned to the U.S. to arrange his move to Ecuador, a dispute arose between him and the staff over research methodology. **The university staff decided not to appoint the sociologist** and gave him a written notice that he would not be hired.

When the university claimed that no employment contract existed, the sociologist sued, seeking general damages of over $111,000 and punitive damages of over $335,000. The trial court held that the university had hired the sociologist for a period of two years for a salary of $30,000 per year but that no contractual breach had occurred. The court awarded damages of $22,379 to the sociologist. The reduced damages reflected mitigation for his acceptance of employment at another institution. A New York appellate division court affirmed the trial court decision, finding that the negotiations and the documentation constituted a two-year employment contract. *Merschrod v. Cornell Univ.*, 527 N.Y.S.2d 109 (A.D. 3d Dept. 1988). [NY]

◆   *By proposing a new contract, an Iowa teacher was offering to rescind the original contract, and he could not complain when he was asked to resign.*

After four months, an Iowa teacher met with his college's president to discuss his duties and salary because he was disappointed with his original employment contract. At this meeting, the teacher proposed a new employment contract on a form the college had used for his prior contract. The unsigned contract provided for an increase in his annual salary for the remaining eight months on his original contract. The following day the parties met again and the college president asked the teacher to resign. The teacher refused, relying on his original employment contract. Subsequently, the teacher received a letter from the president indicating that his position was to be declared open.

The teacher left his job and sued the college in an Iowa trial court for breach of contract. The trial court held that the teacher's proposed employment contract, prepared on the college's form, showed an intent to terminate the parties' original contract. The court entered judgment for the college, and the Court of Appeals of Iowa affirmed. It held that **when the teacher presented the new employment contract, it was an offer to rescind the original contract. The president accepted this rescission** in the letter the teacher received declaring that his position was open. As a result, neither party had any obligation under the rescinded contract. *Wiysel v. William Penn College*, 448 N.W.2d 712 (Iowa App. 1989). [IA]

B. Employee Misconduct

Employee misconduct includes a variety of actions such as inappropriate, unethical, or criminal behavior. In addressing such actions, educational institutions may be bound by faculty handbooks or requirements for hearings.

◆ *A Kansas court held a campus police officer's conduct was improper, but did not constitute gross misconduct or conduct unbecoming an officer.*

A Kansas university police officer stopped a student for speeding. Most of the stop was recorded by an in-car video camera. The student became greatly upset when the officer ran a license check and said her license was suspended. The officer then turned off the camera. His written report stated he informed the student her license was suspended, issued her a citation, noted her car was legally parked, and suggested that a friend drive her car away. The police department investigated to determine what happened after he turned off the camera. The student claimed the officer said she could park her car in front of her apartment herself. After the investigation, the university dismissed the officer for falsifying his incident report and violating the in-car video policy. An administrative tribunal upheld the action, finding his actions were "gross misconduct or conduct unbecoming a state officer or employee."

A Kansas state court upheld the discharge, and the officer appealed. The Court of Appeals of Kansas stated that to prove "intentional" conduct, there had to be evidence he willfully concealed wrongdoing. Under the state employment securities law, **"gross misconduct" was "conduct evincing extreme willful or wanton misconduct." In order for misconduct to be "gross," "it must be aggravated, extreme, or wanton in nature, evincing a knowing and reckless disregard for the rules, policies, or other standards of appropriate behavior."** The court held that while the officer's report was inaccurate, the evidence was insufficient to support a finding of intentional falsification of a police report. His deactivation of the camera was a technical violation that did not constitute gross misconduct. The court reversed the judgment and ordered the officer to be reinstated with back pay and benefits. *Jones v. Kansas State Univ.*, 81 P.3d 1243 (Kan. App. 2004). [KS]

◆ *A North Dakota instructor failed to counter a college's evidence that there was adequate cause to fire her for neglect of duties and incompetence.*

Bismarck State College (BSC) notified a tenured commercial art instructor it intended to dismiss her for disclosing a student's confidential information to a classroom of students. BSC alleged the disclosure violated state higher education board policy and federal law and demanded she apologize to the student. BSC later found the instructor's apology inappropriate and told her it considered her behavior to be a neglect of duty. She challenged the sufficiency of this notice. BSC amended the notice to include charges of neglecting teaching responsibilities by ending a class a month early and failing to clean up her classrooms. It also alleged incompetent teaching, an inappropriate pattern of behavior and incompetence. BSC then fired the instructor for cause. An administrative law judge (ALJ) upheld the dismissal and a state district court affirmed the decision, granting BSC's motion for summary judgment.

The Supreme Court of North Dakota found the trial court had properly ordered summary judgment on the instructor's breach of employment contract claim. She failed to present any facts to show why a jury would not have found adequate cause to fire her. The instructor presented no facts to support her wrongful termination and conspiracy charges, and the order for summary judgment was affirmed. *Peterson v. North Dakota Univ. System*, 678 N.W. 2d (N.D. 2004). [ND]

◆ *An Idaho State University accountant was properly fired for misconduct that amounted to insubordination.*

The accountant received satisfactory performance reviews until she got a new boss, who became more critical. After an argument with her supervisor, she was given a written reprimand for refusing to accept a reasonable assignment (insubordination and conduct unbecoming a state employee). While on a medical leave, she made a threatening phone call to a university medical clinic, and was issued a second written reprimand. She later raised a commotion in the financial services office, and exhibited contumacious behavior at a grievance meeting, which led her supervisor to recommend termination. She challenged the dismissal, and the case made its way to the Idaho Supreme Court, which upheld it. Here, **the record established four incidents of misconduct that supported the decision to let her go**. Also, the misconduct that occurred while she was on medical leave was sufficiently related to her employment to constitute a ground for dismissal. *Horne v. Idaho State Univ.*, 69 P.3d 120 (Idaho 2003). [ID]

◆ *A professor was fired for assaulting his department chair and not for complaining about the university's smoking policy.*

A Texas state university hired an associate professor who soon complained about the university's lack of a no-smoking policy. Over the next two years, he continued to complain about the smoking policy even though the university agreed to designate certain areas as smoke-free zones. The university continued to renew his contract, but refused to do so in the third year after he pushed his department chairman and engaged in other misconduct. He sued the university for violating the Texas Whistleblower Protection Act, but a state court ruled against him. The Texas Court of Appeals affirmed, noting that **there was insufficient evidence that the professor was fired for his complaints about the smoking policy**. It was not until after he assaulted the department chair that he was fired. *Ginn v. Stephen F. Austin State Univ.*, 2003 WL 1882264 (Tex. App. 4/17/03). [TX]

◆ *A team's poor performance and the coach's questionable behavior were the reasons why the coach was fired.*

An Ohio university hired a men's lacrosse coach, but within a few years, the new athletic director began to have concerns about the team's performance. Also, one person complained that the coach used vulgar language in front of the team, and another person alleged that the coach grabbed a player by the facemask and jerked the player's head back and forth. The athletic director decided not to renew the coach's contract, and the coach sued. He asserted age discrimination (he was 58 and was replaced by a 29-year-old), disability discrimination (he had high blood pressure and an irregular heartbeat) and breach of contract (claiming the university had a duty to find him another job in the athletic department). A trial court ruled for the university, and the Ohio Court of Appeals affirmed. Here, the few age-related comments made by the athletic director did not amount to age discrimination. Also, his heart-related problems did not amount to a handicap under state law. Finally, **nothing in the operating manual required the university to find the coach another job in the athletic department after firing him**. *Caldwell v. Ohio State Univ.*, 2002 WL 992379 (Ohio App. 5/16/02). [OH]

◆ *A professor's good-faith refusal to turn over student grades to her supervisor was not insubordination.*

A tenured associate professor refused to comply with her supervisor's request to turn over student grades to evaluate the professor's program. She asserted the student handbook's privacy policy only permitted the registrar to release grades and that no other department could release them without written student consent. The supervisor then issued the professor a written reprimand which was placed in the professor's personnel file. An administrative law judge upheld the reprimand, finding her refusal to comply with the request amounted to insubordination because compliance would not threaten her health or safety.

A state court affirmed the ALJ's decision. The West Virginia Supreme Court of Appeals held **the professor was not insubordinate because the privacy policy was ambiguous, and he reasonably believed the request was invalid**. As a result, she had a good-faith belief that she should not comply. The court ordered the reprimand to be expunged from her personnel file. *Butts v. Higher Education Interim Governing Bd./Shepard College*, 2002 WL 1334483 (W.Va. 6/17/02). [WV]

◆ *Where an employee refused to discuss matters relating to a grievance she had filed, she could not be discharged for insubordination.*

An administrative employee and her supervisor at the University of Alaska did not get along. The supervisor delivered a memorandum to the employee requiring her to meet regarding problems in the office. The employee attended the meeting. The supervisor then delivered a second memorandum which gave the employee three months to improve her performance and which required a written response. The employee notified her supervisor that the information contained in the second memorandum was inaccurate and that she was going to file a grievance. She then refused to discuss any matters relating to the grievance. The next day, the supervisor delivered a third memorandum, which placed the employee on unpaid leave and scheduled a pre-termination hearing. After the hearing, the employee was discharged. She sought a review of the decision, and the case reached the Supreme Court of Alaska.

The supreme court found insufficient evidence that the employee had been insubordinate so as to justify her discharge. She had provided a written response to the second memorandum in the form of a grievance letter, and **her refusal to talk with her supervisor about matters relating to the grievance was not insubordination.** Further, even if, as the university contended, the employee refused to communicate at all with her supervisor, that refusal resulted from an ambiguous and unclear order. **Because the employee reasonably believed that the supervisor was asking her to discuss grievance-related matters, she was entitled to refuse to do so.** The court found the termination unjustified. *Nyberg v. University of Alaska*, 954 P.2d 1376 (Alaska 1998). [AK]

◆ *Where a handbook provided that dismissal was the only form of discipline for misconduct, a college should not have imposed a lesser punishment.*

A New York college faculty handbook provided that dismissal was the only expressly authorized punishment for misconduct and that tenured professors remained subject to annual renewal. Each professor's offer of renewal was delivered on a single sheet of paper containing a footnote that incorporated the college faculty handbook by reference. An associate professor received a promotion after he published a book in 1985. Upon review, the dean and the provost concluded that the professor was guilty of plagiarism and demoted him from full professor to associate professor, reduced his salary, and restricted his academic duties in the 1993-1994 school year. His offer of renewal did not contain the footnote, but the cover letter stated that the appointment was subject to the terms of the handbook. The professor reluctantly accepted the demotion and sued the college in a New York court for breach of contract and intentional infliction of emotional distress (IIED).

The court held that, given the unequivocal assurance found in the cover letter, the contract continued to incorporate the handbook provisions on tenure renewal and faculty discipline for the 1993-1994 school year. Here, **a jury could find that the college properly imposed a punishment, in the form of demotion, for the misconduct of the professor without following the rule mandated in the handbook.** The provost arguably imposed a limited punishment, in the form of a punitive renewal contract that was not clearly contemplated by the handbook, rather than the sanction of termination expressly authorized. The court then dismissed the IIED claim, holding that the college's actions were not sufficiently outrageous to state such a claim. However, the professor stated an emotional injury claim against two of the professors who may have needlessly and indiscriminately disclosed the plagiarism charges to members of the campus community in violation of college rules. *Klinge v. Ithaca College*, 634 N.Y.S.2d 1000 (Sup. 1995). [NY]

◆ *An instructor who made no voluntary attempt to repay a student loan was properly terminated.*

An instructor at a North Carolina technical institute was notified by her employer that it believed she was in violation of North Carolina law regarding repayment of her state-funded student loans. At a hearing, she testified that there was a clerical error on the part of the lender. Shortly thereafter her employer determined that there was no clerical error, nor any voluntary attempt to pay the state. She was fired. The instructor alleged wrongful termination and brought suit against the college in a state court. After two adverse rulings, the instructor appealed to the Court of Appeals of North Carolina. North Carolina law provides that "employees of the state who owe money to the state must make full restitution of the full amount as a condition for continued employment." **Without deciding whether the repeated garnishment of income tax amounted to "repayment," the court agreed that the lack of a voluntary attempt at repayment justified the termination.** *Battle v. Nash Technical College*, 404 S.E.2d 703 (N.C. App. 1991). [NC]

C. Tenure and Promotion Denials

State tenure laws create property rights in public employment that vest school employees with certain procedural rights. These rights vary from state to state according to the type of personnel action. Tenured employees are generally entitled to notice and an opportunity to respond to the charges, a hearing with the right to confront and cross-examine witnesses, and the right to be represented by counsel. These and related procedural protections are referred to as due process rights. Absent a state statute specifically governing tenure at private educational institutions or a claim of discrimination, tenure disputes at private schools rest on principles of contract law.

1. Supreme Court Decisions

◆ *Two U.S. Supreme Court decisions,* Board of Regents v. Roth, *408 U.S. 564, 92 S.Ct. 2701, 33 L.Ed.2d 548 (1972) and* Perry v. Sindermann, *408 U.S. 593, 92 S.Ct. 2694, 33 L.Ed.2d 570 (1972), help define employee due process rights.*

The *Roth* case explained that **in order for a teacher to be entitled to due process, the teacher must have a "liberty" or "property" interest at stake.** The teacher in *Roth* was hired at a Wisconsin university for a fixed contract term of one year. At the end of the year, he was informed that he would not be rehired. No hearing was provided and no reason was given for the decision not to rehire. In dismissing the teacher's due process claims, the Supreme Court stated that no liberty interest was implicated because in declining to rehire the teacher, the university had not made any charge against him such as incompetence or immorality. Such a charge would have made it difficult for the teacher to gain employment elsewhere and thus would have deprived him of liberty. As no reason was given for the nonrenewal of his contract, the teacher's liberty interest in future employment was not impaired and he was not entitled to a hearing on these grounds.

The Court declared that because the teacher had not acquired tenure he possessed no property interest in continued employment at the university. To be sure, the teacher had a property interest in employment during the term of his one-year contract, but upon its expiration the teacher's property interest ceased to exist. The Court stated: **"To have a property interest in a benefit, a person clearly must have more than an abstract need or desire for it. He must have more than a unilateral expectation of it. He must, instead, have a legitimate claim of entitlement to it."**

The *Sindermann* case involved a teacher employed at a Texas university for four years under a series of one-year contracts. When he was not rehired for a fifth year, he brought suit contending that due process required a dismissal hearing. The Supreme Court held that "a person's interest in a benefit is a 'property' interest for due process purposes if there are such rules and mutually explicit understandings that support his claim of entitlement to the benefit that he may invoke at a hearing." Because the teacher had been employed at the university for four years, the Court felt that he may have acquired a protectible property interest in continued employment. The case was remanded to the trial court to determine whether there was an unwritten "common law" of tenure at the university. If so, the teacher would be entitled to a dismissal hearing.

Roth and *Sindermann* emphasize, first, that there must be an independent source for a liberty or property interest to exist. Such interests are not created by the Constitution, but arise by employment contract or by operation of state tenure laws. Second, if a liberty or property interest is not established, no requirement of due process exists under the Fourteenth Amendment. Third, **if a teacher possesses a liberty or property interest in employment, then due process is required and the teacher may not be dismissed without a hearing.** A tenured teacher, or an untenured teacher during the term of his or her contract, possesses a property interest in continued employment. An untenured teacher who is not rehired after expiration of his or her contract is entitled to a due process hearing if the decision not to rehire is accompanied by a finding of incompetence or immorality, because the teacher's liberty of employment would be impaired by such a finding. However, probationary employees or at-will employees generally do not enjoy the due process protections.

2. Claims of Discrimination

◆   *An Ohio university did not breach its employment contract when it fired a medical department professor who was a native of India.*

The professor worked in the department of psychiatry under a one-year, non-tenured contract. The university renewed his contract for a second year, when it also hired a new department chair. The professor alleged the chair disliked him because he was Indian. At the end of the year, the chair notified him his contract would not be renewed. A university grievance committee found the non-renewal decision was not motivated by discrimination or personal animosity. The professor sued the university in a state court for breach of contract and intentional infliction of emotional distress. He added claims against the department chair for intentional infliction of emotional distress.

The court granted summary judgment to the university and chair, and the professor appealed. **The Court of Appeals of Ohio held that all employment in the state is "at-will" so that either party may sever the employment relationship at any time and for any reason. The renewal of an untenured professor is discretionary.** Since the professor had not published or applied for funding for the past two years, he failed to fulfill his contract performance requirements. The university had a legitimate reason not to renew his contract. The court affirmed the judgment, rejecting the professor's claims for intentional infliction of emotional distress against the university and chair as they did not engage in outrageous conduct. *Adityanjee v. Case Western Reserve Univ.*, 806 N.E.2d 583 (Ohio App. 3rd 2004). [OH]

◆ *Where a female professor failed to meet a university's publishing requirements for a tenure candidate, she could not succeed on her sex discrimination claim.*

An Indiana university hired an assistant professor for the anatomy department at its medical school. Her tenure track required her to demonstrate proficiency in three areas: research, teaching and service. In order to meet the research standards, she had to publish one-to-two peer-reviewed research papers per year and be listed as either the first or a senior author. After three years, the promotion and tenure committee admonished her for her low publishing rate. When she submitted her candidacy for tenure, she had published only five peer-reviewed papers—only once as a senior author and never as the first author. The anatomy department denied tenure, and she sued for gender discrimination. A federal court ruled for the university, and the Seventh Circuit affirmed. Here, **the professor was unable to show that less qualified male candidates had been awarded tenure** because the males with similar publishing rates had received tenure under less stringent standards. Their departments did not have the same publishing standards. *Lim v. Trustees of Indiana Univ.*, 297 F.3d 575 (7th Cir. 2002). [IN]

◆ *A professor from the University of Redlands lost her discrimination case because she failed to prove she was denied tenure because she is Jewish.*

A professor in the university's art department applied for tenure in 1995. The chair of the department recommended her for tenure, but with some reservations. At the same time, another art professor was up for tenure. The professor supported her colleague for tenure, but observed that he often told her she didn't listen to him. She claimed he had an "inability to recognize genuine differences of opinion" and had "difficulty with clear verbal communication." After she submitted her review, the department chair withdrew her support for the professor, believing the review proved the professor could not interact effectively with her colleagues or accept criticism. The Faculty Review Committee subsequently denied her tenure. An appeals committee recommended tenure, but the university president ultimately decided not to grant tenure, advising her to apply the next year. Once again, she was denied tenure. The appeals committee concluded her review was not fair because the dean may have been prejudiced against her. It recommended she be allowed to reapply in three years. The president upheld the denial and rejected the committee's recommendation to allow the professor to reapply, finding no prejudice by the dean. As a result, the professor sued the university for breach of implied contract, breach of implied covenant of good faith and fair dealing, fraud, and religious discrimination. A trial court ruled for the university.

The professor appealed, contending that the university's proffered reasons for the denial were merely pretextual. The California Court of Appeal concluded that the denial of tenure was not related to the fact that the professor was Jewish, it was due to academic politics at the university. **The court conceded she may have been treated unfairly, but it did not find any of the university's decisions about denying her tenure were related to her religion.** A reasonable juror would conclude that any perceived prejudice was based on the incident with her colleague and not the fact that she was Jewish. Even if various faculty members made comments about her not teaching classes on certain Jewish holidays, this did not demonstrate discrimination since she suffered no adverse consequences for not teaching on those days. The court affirmed the trial court's decision. *Slatkin v. University of Redlands*, 88 Cal.App.4th 1147, 106 Cal.Rptr.2d 480 (Cal. App. 2001). [CA]

◆ *A fully tenured professor was unable to show a New York university discriminated against him on the basis of his national origin and/or age as a result of its reorganization plan because he suffered no adverse employment action due to the plan.*

An East Indian was hired by the University of Rochester in 1963 as a professor of statistics and assigned to the program in statistics, which was part of the math department. In 1967, the professor received tenure. That same year, the university established a department of statistics. Five years later, he was promoted to the rank of full professor of statistics and biostatistics. In 1997, the university conducted a reorganization, which included the professor's department. As a result, the professor retained his full-tenure status, with a primary appointment in the program of statistics and a secondary appointment in the biostatistics department. The professor sued the university for discrimination on the basis of race, national origin, religion and age. The district court held for the school, and the professor appealed.

The Second Circuit affirmed, finding the professor failed to establish a *prima facie* case of discrimination. While he was a member of a protected class and qualified for his position, **he failed to show that he suffered an adverse employment action.** Inconvenience or alteration in job responsibilities was not enough to constitute an adverse employment action. **The professor retained full-tenure status, remained on faculty committees and received the same pay and benefits.** Except for a subjective perception that his current position was less prestigious, the professor made no showing of materiality and offered no evidence that the reorganization had a discriminatory purpose. *Mudholkar v. University of Rochester*, 229 F.3d 1136 (2d Cir. 2000). [NY]

◆ *Where a professor obtained tenure through an internal grievance process, she was not subjected to discrimination in violation of Title VII.*

Despite a departmental recommendation to grant tenure to a professor of philosophy employed by Vanderbilt University, the acting dean of the relevant college informed the professor that her employment with the university would end the following year. The professor filed a grievance with the professional ethics committee, which concluded that irregularities had occurred and forwarded the matter to the promotion and tenure committee. Meanwhile, the professor sued the college in a Tennessee federal court for national origin and gender discrimination in violation of Title VII. However, before the court considered the case, the tenure committee awarded the professor tenure, and granted her an award of back pay. The professor claimed the back pay award was insufficient to compensate her for the emotional distress and damage to her reputation, but the district court granted pretrial judgment to the university. The U.S. Court of Appeals, Sixth Circuit, affirmed, holding that **because the professor successfully obtained tenure through the university's internal grievance process, no adverse employment action ever occurred.** Accordingly, no violation of Title VII was committed. *Dobbs-Weinstein v. Vanderbilt Univ.,* 185 F.3d 542 (6th Cir. 1999). [TN]

◆ *Where legitimate reasons existed for denying tenure to an instructor, her age discrimination claim failed.*

A 58-year-old instructor at a private Illinois university applied for tenure. Two tenure committees recommended against granting tenure, and the university denied her application. The instructor filed charges of age discrimination with the EEOC and an internal grievance with a faculty appeals committee. Due to procedural problems, the appeals committee recommended that the university give the instructor another year to apply for tenure. The next year, the tenure committees unanimously rejected her application. The instructor again filed an internal grievance, and the appeals committee found procedural errors. However, the university upheld the decision to deny her tenure. After the university rejected her appeal, she sued. A federal court granted the university pretrial judgment, and the instructor appealed.

The Seventh Circuit held the university had a legitimate, nondiscriminatory reason for its decision to deny tenure. Its decision was based on the unanimous view of the two tenure committees that **the instructor failed to demonstrate the "high level of performance expected of a tenure applicant"** which included: 1) a significant level of involvement in curriculum innovation, instructional research and programmatic design that would be expected of a tenure candidate, 2) significant service to the institution, and 3) an exhibited commitment to the university in terms of significant leadership or contribution in areas of institutional importance. One of the committees also noted a lack of reference letters from her colleagues and little evidence of significant scholarly presentations. Although the instructor presented some evidence of decisions disfavoring older employees, she failed to supplement the information by engaging in a detailed comparison of her own qualifications (or those of the other older candidates denied tenure) to those of younger candidates who were granted tenure. The judgment of the lower court was affirmed. *Vanasco v. National-Louis Univ.,* 137 F.3d 962 (7th Cir. 1998). [IL]

3. Collegiality and Animosity

◆ *A federal district court dismissed an Illinois professor's constitutional rights violation claims.*

The professor was disciplined after having confrontations with other faculty members. After a no-confidence vote by the faculty, he lost his position as a member and chair of a college personnel committee. He was also removed from the University Council Personnel Committee position. The professor sued university officials in a federal district court for denial of due process and equal protection rights. The court dismissed the claims against the board and officials on Eleventh Amendment grounds, finding they were not subject to constitutional claims for damages. The claims of deprivation of property and liberty without due process lacked merit. Although the professor had a property interest in his employment as a tenured faculty member, he did not have any interest in membership on committees. As he did not show damage to his good name, reputation, honor or integrity, the court dismissed his claim based on deprivation of a liberty interest. Since the university did not take adverse employment action against the professor, such as termination, demotion, or a loss of pay and benefits, he failed to allege any significant legally cognizable injury, and the case was dismissed. *Ganesan v. NIU Bd. of Trustees*, No. 02 C 50498, 2003 WL 22872139 (N.D. Ill. 2003). [IL]

◆ *Even though collegiality was not listed as a specific factor for tenure or promotion review, a university could consider it when evaluating a teacher.*

A teacher at a Maryland university sought an early review for tenure and a promotion. When both were denied, she sued the university for breach of contract, asserting that it had improperly considered collegiality (defined by the court as "the capacity to relate well and constructively to the comparatively small bank of scholars on whom the ultimate fate of the university rests" and as "the relationship of colleagues") in its decision-making process. She claimed that the university could only evaluate teaching, research and service. The university claimed that although nothing in the contract mentioned collegiality, it was inherently a part of the contract and therefore a proper consideration in both tenure and promotion decisions.

The Court of Special Appeals of Maryland ruled in favor of the university, finding that **collegiality was a proper factor for review.** It noted that the American Association of University Professors had even contemplated as much in its Statement on Professional Ethics. **Collegiality plays an important role in both teaching and service.** Finding insufficient evidence that the university breached either the contract or its implied covenant of good faith and fair dealing, the court ruled that the teacher's claim could not succeed. *University of Baltimore v. Iz*, 716 A.2d 1107 (Md. App. 1998). [MD]

◆ *While a university professor may have been denied tenure because of personal animosity, the law could offer him no remedy.*

An English and drama professor sued Wesley College for wrongfully denying him tenure. The professor claimed that the president of the college held such personal animosity towards him that he intentionally undermined his tenure application by providing misleading materials to the Board of Trustees. The Trustees, after assessing negative financial figures for the college and a lack of students interested in the degree program for drama, denied the professor tenure. Without tenure, the college would only renew the professor's employment contract for one additional year. The Court of Chancery of Delaware ruled in favor of the Trustees. Because the college faced a $300,000 operating deficit and was in danger of facing financial insolvency, the Trustees could properly adopt plans to eliminate the budget deficit, including personnel cutbacks. Even though the professor presented evidence of personal animosity toward him, he did not present evidence that the president lied to the trustees. Finally, the court held that **personal animosity, in and of itself, could not constitute the foundation of a lawsuit.** *Hudson v. Wesley College,* 1998 WL 939712, No. 1211 (Del. Ch. 12/23/98). [DE]

◆ *A university could deny tenure to a professor based on lack of collegiality.*

A professor employed part-time by a Louisiana private university was promoted to full-time probationary faculty status in 1987. He was again promoted to associate professor in 1991 and entered into a series of one-year contracts with the university. Each contract constituted a new appointment with the university for that respective year. The faculty handbook provided that "each non-tenured member of the ordinary faculty is considered to be on probation" but that "tenured faculty contracts may not be terminated except for cause." Although the faculty exercised the primary right of determination in matters of faculty status, the university conciliation committee could request reconsideration of tenure decisions. The faculty ultimately denied the professor's application for tenure based on his alleged lack of "collegiality" and refused the conciliation committee's request for reconsideration. The professor filed suit in a Louisiana trial court, alleging breach of contract. The trial court held for the university, and the professor appealed. The Court of Appeal of Louisiana held that **any ambiguity with regard to the employment relationship should be construed in favor of employment-at-will.** The professor was a non-tenured employee who could be terminated at the expiration of his annual contract without cause. Consequently, he was permissibly denied tenure based on lack of collegiality. A contrary ruling would improperly destroy the distinction between probationary and tenured faculty. The holding of the trial court was affirmed. *Schalow v. Loyola Univ. of New Orleans,* 646 So.2d 502 (La. App. 4th Cir. 1994). [LA]

4. Handbooks and Procedures

◆ *A Mississippi court dismissed a professor's lawsuit because she failed to exhaust the university's grievance process.*

Mississippi Valley State University discharged an assistant professor who also served as director of the Department of Field Experience. The professor did not appeal the decision through the university's three-step appeal process. Nearly two years after being discharged, she sued the university and university officials in a state court for tortious discharge and interference with her employment contract. The court dismissed the case as untimely under a one-year statute of limitations. The Court of Appeals of Mississippi agreed with the university that the triggering event for the statute of limitations was the date of the termination letter, not the professor's last day of work. Therefore, an action brought two years after the date of the letter was untimely. Regardless of the timeliness of the claims, the professor failed to exhaust her administrative remedies by not first proceeding through the university's appeal process. Therefore, the court did not have jurisdiction. *Black v. Ansah*, No. 2001-CA-01909-COA, 2003 WL 21267089 (Miss. App. 2003). [MS]

◆ *When Harvard followed its handbook in denying tenure, a professor's breach of contract action against it was dismissed.*

After an associate professor of government at Harvard was denied tenure, he grieved the matter, claiming that Harvard's provost was biased against him and influenced the ad hoc committee that had recommended against tenure. The reviewing committee ruled that the grievance was without merit, and the professor sued for breach of contract. A state court refused to dismiss the lawsuit, but the Appeals Court of Massachusetts reversed, holding that the lawsuit should have been dismissed. Nothing in the university's handbook prevented the provost from submitting an opinion regarding the professor's abilities. Also, there was no requirement that the ad hoc committee be composed of specialists in the professor's field. Since **Harvard did not violate the tenure evaluation procedures outlined in its handbook**, the breach of contract lawsuit should have been dismissed. *Berkowitz v. President & Fellows of Harvard College*, 789 N.E.2d 575 (Mass. App. 2003). [MA]

◆ *A professor lost her challenge to tenure denial by failing to follow procedural court rules.*

An assistant professor of health, physical education, recreation and coaching was evaluated for tenure after five years. She was rated above average in teaching and service, but below average in scholarly activity, and was denied tenure. She sued the university under Title VII and the Fourteenth Amendment, asserting equal protection violations. After pretrial judgment was granted to the university, the professor appealed to the Seventh Circuit, which affirmed. Here, the professor committed procedural errors by failing to comply with local court rules. Also, she was unable to show an equal protection violation. She was not treated differently than other similarly situated tenure candidates, and **she had no liberty interest claim because the university did not make any stigmatizing remarks in connection with the denial of tenure**. *Hedrich v. Board of Regents of Univ. of Wisconsin System*, 274 F.3d 1174 (7th Cir. 2001). [WI]

◆ *Where procedural errors by a tenure committee did not prejudice a professor, his breach of contract claim failed.*

An Ohio university professor sought tenure consideration and was notified by a superior that the Retention, Promotion and Tenure Committee wanted to discuss his monitoring of two former graduate students, whose masters theses he rejected. Although tenure track procedures called for a two-week notice, he was only given one day's notice prior to the committee meeting. After the meeting, the committee denied him tenure based on his conduct toward the two graduate students. He received the minutes from the tenure meeting later than he should have. When he sued for breach of contract, the Ohio Court of Appeals ruled against him, finding that the two procedural errors did not substantially prejudice his rights. **There was no indication that the professor had been unable to prepare an adequate response as a result of the improper notice or the delay in receiving the minutes.** *Galiatsatos v. University of Akron,* 2001 WL 1045513 (Ohio App. 9/13/01). [OH]

◆ *A university did not have to grant tenure to an assistant professor merely because a handbook described tenure procedures.*

A Louisiana private university assistant professor was classified as a probationary regular appointment, with the prospect of tenure. The faculty handbook explained that appointments during the probationary period were made for one year, with written notification of reappointment made annually. Tenure-track professors were eligible for tenure if they met the university's expectations for tenured faculty. During the professor's third-year review, he was informed that he had a low number of publications. During his sixth-year review, the provost rejected all recommendations that he be given tenure. A committee determined that the provost had not acted improperly. Thereafter, the professor sued the university for breach of contract in a state court, which granted the university's motion for pretrial judgment. The professor appealed to the Court of Appeal of Louisiana, Fourth Circuit.

On appeal, the professor argued the university had breached his contract by denying him promotion and tenure. The university argued that there was no factual support for his claim that a contract existed that promised him tenure. The professor asserted that a contract was formed by the parties mutually agreeing to be bound by certain terms and conditions described in the faculty handbook. However, a handbook is a unilateral expression of company policy, and the publishing of that policy does not evidence a meeting of the minds. **Here, the professor did not claim that he was promised tenure; he claimed that he understood that the faculty handbook constituted such a promise** because each party mutually agreed to be bound by the terms and conditions set forth therein. Because there was no proof of a contract promising tenure, the trial court correctly ruled for the university. *Schwarz v. Administrators of the Tulane Educ. Fund,* 699 So.2d 895 (La. App. 4th Cir. 1997). [LA]

◆ *A handbook designed as a guide for the faculty did not create a property right to tenure.*

An assistant German professor at a Texas university was notified his contract would not be renewed for financial reasons. The professor asked that he be allowed to undergo the tenure approval process so he could tell potential employers he was being considered for tenure. According to the faculty handbook, he was eligible for tenure consideration. He was not, however, granted tenure. He sued the university in a federal district court, claiming he was denied due process of law in being refused tenure and in being fired. A jury agreed, but the judge overturned the jury's decision. The professor appealed to the U.S. Court of Appeals, Fifth Circuit. The court stated **the handbook was a guide for the faculty and not a self-contained policy document. It did not** create a constitutionally protected property right in continued employment or an assurance of tenure. The handbook was not a contract. The only process due to the professor was the exercise of professional judgment in a non-arbitrary fashion. Since there was evidence to support the termination, it was not arbitrary. *Spuler v. Pickar*, 958 F.2d 103 (5th Cir. 1992). [TX]

◆ *A probationary professor did not have a property interest in being granted tenure.*

A probationary professor at the University of Oklahoma was denied tenure despite the unanimous recommendation of the members of her department. The tenure committee had denied tenure because it felt her research was deficient. Claiming that the tenure committee breached university procedures by performing an independent evaluation of her scholarship, the professor sued the university in a state court, arguing that she had a property interest in being granted tenure. The Court of Appeals of Oklahoma disagreed. The court stated that **there was no evidence to suggest that tenure was meant to be granted routinely or that it could be withheld only "for cause." Once tenure was granted, a property interest would arise, but not until then.** In addition, it was within the power of the committee to perform an independent evaluation of the teacher's scholarship. *Stern v. University of Oklahoma Bd. of Regents*, 841 P.2d 1168 (Okla. App. 1992). [OK]

◆ *Even though a university offered one-year contracts to a teacher for more than seven years, she was not entitled to tenure by default.*

A nontenured assistant professor at a Georgia university was given a series of one-year contracts for each academic year. Although university policy stated that no regular eighth-year contract should be given unless an award of tenure had already been made, the university offered the professor an eighth one-year contract without offering her tenure. It then offered her a final contract for her ninth year. She sued, asserting that since she had taught at the university for eight years, she was either entitled to tenure or had already acquired tenure by default (tenure *de facto*). A federal court granted pretrial judgment to the university, and the Eleventh Circuit Court of Appeals affirmed. **The university's policy of allowing contracts for nontenured professors for only seven years did not create an entitlement to tenure** where the university offered a teacher an eighth year of employment. The professor could not show that she had been tenured *de facto* where she failed to show that a past practice of the university allowed for automatic tenure. She presented no evidence that tenure *de facto* had ever occurred at the university. She was not entitled to tenure. *Gray v. Board of Regents of the Univ. System of Georgia*, 150 F.3d 1347 (11th Cir. 1998). [GA]

◆ *A Georgia appellate court held that the decision to deny tenure did not have to be unanimous in order for the denial to be effective.*

A university employed a professor under a series of annual contracts. Each contract incorporated portions of the university's faculty handbook but made no explicit references to the faculty handbook tenure section. University policy was to discharge tenure track faculty members if they remained untenured upon completing their seventh annual contract. The university denied the professor tenure in his fifth, sixth and seventh years of employment. He claimed that the university deviated from its faculty handbook procedures. He also claimed that tenure decisions required a joint determination by the dean and appropriate chairpersons, and a specific recommendation to the university with supporting data. In his final unsuccessful attempt at gaining tenure, **the dean and division chairperson had disagreed on whether to grant tenure. The professor claimed that the handbook required a unanimous decision by the dean and chairperson in order to effectively deny tenure.**

The professor sued the university, and a trial court ruled in the university's favor. The Georgia Court of Appeals affirmed. It agreed that the faculty handbook tenure provisions formed a part of the professor's employment contract. However, it found no merit to his claim that tenure recommendations from the dean and division chairperson must be unanimous. While supporting data should have been provided, failure to do so did not injure the professor. Nothing in the employment contract or faculty handbook indicated the right to a board of trustees review. The professor had already received three opportunities to obtain tenure and no further consideration was due. *Moffie v. Oglethorpe Univ.*, 367 S.E.2d 112 (Ga. App. 1988). [GA]

5. Other Tenure and Promotion Cases

◆ *Kentucky university trustees were entitled to official immunity for their discretionary acts in denying a professor's application for tenure.*

A University of Louisville assistant professor applied for tenure after 11 years with the university. The university board of trustees denied the application and discharged him. The professor sued the university and trustees in a state court, which dismissed his claims for tortious interference with contractual relationships and breach of contract. The professor appealed to the Court of Appeals of Kentucky, where the trustees claimed official immunity. **The court held qualified official immunity applies to the negligent performance by an officer or employee of discretionary acts or functions performed in good faith within the scope of the employee's authority. The court found the trustees' evaluations were based on personal deliberations and were discretionary.** Because the professor offered no evidence of bad faith on the part of the board members, the court correctly dismissed the tortious interference claim. His contract expired at the end of its present term, and the court affirmed the judgment. *Haeberle v. University of Louisville*, 2004 WL 595257 (Ky. App. 2004). [KY]

◆ *A California court held a temporary community college instructor was not a regular employee under the college system's academic classification system.*

The instructor taught less than 60 percent of the hours required for a full-time assignment and was deemed a temporary employee. He submitted three grant requests and worked on them during the intercession so as to not exceed the 60 percent rule. The college later rescinded one of the grant awards because it believed his work during the intercession might count toward the 60 percent rule.

The college denied a request by the instructor's union for reclassification as a permanent employee and he petitioned a state court for relief. The court held his projects constituted "teaching" and that he exceeded the 60 percent rule. It ordered the college to reclassify the instructor as a permanent employee, and the university appealed to the Court of Appeal of California.

The court noted the California Code established three classifications for community college instructors including probationary contract employees, tenured regular employees, and temporary employees, who could be terminated at the discretion of the governing board. **Pursuant to the code, a temporary employee who teaches full time for a complete school year and is re-hired for the next school year will automatically be reclassified as a contract employee.** The court held an instructor teaching adult or community college classes less than 60 percent of a full-time assignment must be classified as a temporary employee. It distinguished statutory teaching requirements from the research and grant projects, which it characterized as "faculty work." Since these projects could not be considered "teaching" under the statute, the instructor did not exceed the 60 percent rule and should not be reclassified. The trial court's judgment was reversed. *Kamler v. Marin Community College Dist.*, No A098114, 2003 WL 21493662 (Cal. App. 2003). [CA]

◆ *Athens State College did not violate the Alabama Fair Dismissal Act when the director of a volunteer program lost her job.*

During the 1970s, the college began sponsoring the Retired Senior Volunteer Program. The college provided operating space and equipment for the program; it also managed RSVP funds through a separate account. In 1989, the Alabama Department of Examiners of Public Accounts (DEPA) determined that state law prohibited the college's sponsorship of RSVP. A subsequent attorney general opinion declared sponsorship by the college permissible, as long as it complied with three conditions. In 1995, DEPA found that providing operating space and equipment constituted monetary support in violation of the attorney general's conditions. Subsequently, the college discontinued the RSVP program and discharged the director. Although the director kept her job when the United Way began sponsoring the program, she appealed the college's decision to discontinue the program. An employee panel decided that the college should have reinstated the director to a non-teaching position.

A state court upheld the panel's decision, and an appeals court affirmed, finding that the state Fair Dismissal Act had the same general purpose as the state Teacher Tenure Act. The court directed the college to place the director in a non-teaching position. The Alabama Supreme Court reversed. The court carefully reviewed the language of both statutes and determined that each law had a separate purpose. The court drew a distinction between teachers, who are certified to teach in a specific field, and non-teachers, who may not be "presumptively qualified" to perform in another non-teaching position. The intent of the Fair Dismissal Act is to provide non-teacher employees with procedural protections in connection with their terminations. In applying the Act to the director's claim, **the high court found no evidence to suggest that she was qualified to perform other non-teaching positions at the college**. When the college withdrew its sponsorship of the program, the director's position was eliminated. Consequently, she lost her job due to a "justifiable decrease in jobs in the system." Moreover, **the college complied with the procedures set forth in the Fair Dismissal Act**. *Ex parte Athens State College*, 795 So.2d 709 (Ala. 2000). [AL]

◆ *A tenured professor's challenge to an amended appraisal policy, which permitted consideration of previous evaluations, passed constitutional muster because it was not applied retrospectively.*

In 1997, the Colorado State Board of Agriculture, which oversees Colorado State University, amended its performance appraisal policy and adopted a new policy for review of tenured faculty. A professor who was granted tenure in 1981 received unsatisfactory performance reviews for 1997 and 1998, based in part on previously issued evaluations. He sued, alleging the amended policy was improper because it was applied retrospectively. The court held for the university, and the professor appealed.

The Colorado Court of Appeals evaluated the policy, first to determine if the drafters intended a retroactive effect and second to determine if the policy, as applied, was retrospective. The court found that the new policy did not alter disciplinary provisions, but provided for a new two-step review of tenured faculty. The court also noted that the policy was "retroactive," though not necessarily unconstitutional. Therefore, the critical issue became whether the policy affected any of the professor's vested rights. In making this determination, the court determined that the amended policy "[did] not take away or impair vested rights, [did not] create a new obligation, [did not] impose a new duty, or attach a new disability." Instead, **the professor had previously been subjected to disciplinary provisions and was still subjected to those provisions, regardless of the amended policy. The new policy merely created a new procedural framework**. As the university's new policy was not retrospective, the court affirmed the judgment. *Johnson v. Colorado State Bd. of Agriculture*, 15 P.3d 309 (Colo. App. 2000). [CO]

◆ *The spouse of a member of a board of trustees was not eligible for promotion due to the potential conflict of interest that would occur.*

An accountant employed by the Long Beach Community College District for over 25 years applied for a new accounting position. At the time she applied, her husband had been a member of the college's Board of Trustees for over two years. The accountant was deemed ineligible for the position by the college's director of human resources because of her husband's position, the California conflict of interest statute, and several state Attorney General Opinions interpreting the conflict of interest statute. The college hired the top ranked external candidate. The accountant then filed a petition with a state trial court seeking the job. The trial court denied her request, finding that Section 1091.5 of the California conflict of interest statute allowed her to keep her present position once her husband was elected to the Board of Trustees, but that the same section barred her promotion to a different position.

The appeals court agreed with the college that the conflict of interest statute barred the accountant from being promoted to the disputed supervisory position. The accountant's assertion that she was entitled to the position based on one of the exceptions contained in the conflict of interest statute was rejected by the court, as the disputed exception only allowed the spouse of a board of trustees member to retain any position held for at least one year as of the time the spouse was elected to the board. Since the accountant had held her position for approximately five years before her husband's election, she was statutorily allowed to keep that position, but was barred from being promoted to the new position. The trial court decision was affirmed. *Thorpe v. Long Beach Community College Dist.*, 83 Cal.App.4th 655, 99 Cal.Rptr.2d 897 (Cal. App. 2000). [CA]

◆ *A professor's position as associate dean was not a protected property interest preserved by her tenured faculty position.*

The University of North Dakota hired a professor in the School of Communication. She was also given administrative duties as the director of the School of Communication and as the associate dean of the College of Fine Arts and Communication. In 1995, she was told by her senior administrators to improve her administrative performance. Eventually, she was dismissed from her administrative duties, but remained a faculty member. She sued in federal court, alleging that her discharge from the administrative positions violated her protected property interests under tenure. The court dismissed her claim that she had a protected property interest in her administrative positions. Citing the North Dakota State Board of Higher Education Policy Manual, which was included in her employment contract, the district court noted that tenure does not extend to administrative positions.

The Eighth Circuit Court of Appeals agreed, noting that the professor's administrative position was at will, which does not evoke a protected property interest. In fact, the letter of understanding supplementing her employment contract stated, "Associate Deans have no specific term, but rather serve at the pleasure of the Dean." The circuit court found that the professor's position as director of the School of Communication included a three-year contract, but **her protected property interest had been satisfied because the university had fully compensated her for the salary associated with the position even though she did not serve out the full term.** *Rakow v. State of North Dakota*, 208 F.3d 218 (8th Cir. 2000). [ND]

◆ *A university could deny tenure to a professor with electronic publications on the ground that her work was not published in refereed journals.*

An associate professor at a New York university went before a tenure review committee and received a 3 to 2 vote in her favor. Nevertheless, the dean of the school of education recommended to the university president that she be denied tenure because of her lack of publications in peer-reviewed, scholarly (refereed) journals. The professor specialized in computer applications in occupational therapy and had developed a number of computer applications. **Her work had been published electronically or in non-print media.** After tenure was denied, she claimed that the review process had been flawed and that she had not been allowed to demonstrate her computer materials to the committee. The case reached the New York Supreme Court, Appellate Division, which held that there was no record of the review being arbitrary, capricious or tainted by bad faith. Here, the dean had recommended against tenure because she believed that the professor needed to theoretically justify and validate through research the computer applications she had developed. However, **the university had conducted the review process in substantial compliance with its procedures.** As a result, the court refused to overturn the university's decision to deny tenure. *Loebl v. New York Univ.*, 680 N.Y.S.2d 495 (A.D. 1st Dept. 1998). [NY]

◆   *Where a university conducted a fair review of a professor's record before denying tenure, the professor could not succeed in his lawsuit against it.*

Washington State University hired a professor with eight years' teaching experience and promised to review him for tenure after three years instead of six. However, at the review, his research record revealed that he had been a co-author on all his publications, and they were not in top-tier journals. He had also received poor teaching scores. After he was denied tenure, he sued the university for breach of contract, discrimination and misrepresentation. The case reached the Supreme Court of Washington, which ruled in favor of the university. **The court found that the university had considered the professor's full teaching and publication record, and that the procedure used had been fair.** None of the professor's claims could survive. *Trimble v. Washington State Univ.*, 993 P.2d 259 (Wash. 2000). [WA]

◆   *A university was liable for breach of contract where it failed to deliver on a promised raise.*

A professor and his wife, both employed at a Florida university, were offered jobs at a Texas university. The professor met with his supervisors and discussed the offer, at which time the dean of the college of social sciences promised him that he would match the offer within three years. The professor and his wife decided to stay in Florida. When the university failed to raise the professor's salary to the agreed-upon level, the professor sued the university for fraud and breach of contract. A jury awarded him $65,000 for breach of contract and $86,450 for the fraudulent misrepresentations made by university officials. The trial court overturned the jury's verdict, finding that sovereign immunity barred both the fraud and breach of contract claims. The Court of Appeal of Florida agreed that the fraud claim was barred by sovereign immunity. However, it held that **the breach of contract claim survived. Because the dean was acting within the scope of his employment when he entered into the contract with the professor, the court reinstated the jury's verdict on the breach of contract claim.** *Parker v. State of Florida Bd. of Regents*, 724 So.2d 163 (Fla. App. 1st Dist. 1998). [FL]

◆   *An associate professor could not sue a university for denying him a promotion where he was found to have withdrawn his request for the promotion.*

An assistant professor of anesthesiology at the University of West Virginia's School of Medicine attained tenure and a promotion to associate under guidelines that called for him to demonstrate "excellence" in teaching and service, and a level of "satisfactory" in the area of research. The university modified the guidelines to require "excellence" in research. When the associate professor applied for the position of professor, he was informed that he would be evaluated under the new guidelines and that he did not qualify for promotion under them. **He then wrote two letters, informing the university that he declined to be evaluated under the new guidelines,** and filed an administrative grievance, requesting that the old guidelines be used in evaluating him for promotion. He also asserted that the university was retaliating against him for two earlier grievances he had filed in which he had obtained substantial dollar amounts. An administrative law judge (ALJ) determined that the associate professor had withdrawn his request for promotion, and the case reached the state Supreme Court of Appeals.

The court agreed with the ALJ that the associate professor had withdrawn his request for promotion. Even though his letters stated that he declined to be evaluated under the new guidelines, and there was some question as to whether this meant that he was withdrawing his promotion request, the ALJ had concluded that the letters were a withdrawal. Since this determination was not clearly wrong, it could not be reversed The associate professor's claim had to be dismissed. *Graf v. University of West Virginia Bd. of Trustees*, 504 S.E.2d 654 (W.Va. 1998). [WV]

◆ *A university did not have a duty to avoid making negligent misrepresentations to a teacher.*

A professor at an Oregon community college took a leave of absence to work as a visiting professor at a nearby university and, at the end of the year, applied for a permanent tenure-track position there. He was offered the position but before accepting, he received his student evaluations. They were well below those of the average teacher at the university and the professor asked a dean whether the poor evaluations would affect his chances of obtaining tenure. The dean told him that the evaluations would not be a problem. The professor resigned his position at the community college and accepted the job at the university. Over the next year, **his student evaluations did not improve, and the following year he was offered a nonrenewable one-year contract.**

The professor sued the university, alleging the dean negligently misrepresented the affect of his poor evaluations on tenure. A jury found for the professor, and the university appealed. The Supreme Court of Oregon found that the university did not owe the professor a duty to avoid making negligent misrepresentations. The parties were in a contractual relationship and both were acting on their own behalf. **The university employee handbook did not require the university to provide employees information regarding their job security,** and created no duty to avoid negligent misrepresentations. Finally, the court held that the employer-employee relationship does not create a special duty of care. The court affirmed the decision for the university. *Conway v. Pacific Univ.*, 924 P.2d 818 (Or. 1996). [OR]

◆ *Even though two physicians had an understanding that tenure would be a formality, a university was not required to grant it.*

A private, Maryland university recruited two physicians to join its pediatric cardiology department. Both were tenured professors at different universities and dealt primarily with the department director in their negotiations. After interviews with other university officials, the physicians were offered professor positions. The physicians began to have difficulties in the department. Other doctors and staff complained that they were difficult to get along with, had poor management skills and failed to adequately monitor research projects. Because the physicians had not yet been approved for tenure, the university terminated their employment. They sued the university for breach of contract, alleging that the director had orally assured them that the approval process was a formality and that they would receive tenure. The jury found that the physicians had accepted contracts for tenured professorships and that the university did not have just cause to fire them. The university appealed.

The Court of Special Appeals of Maryland held that the jury could have properly found that the approval process was a formality and that the physicians' tenured positions were assured. However, **the director did not have the authority to bind the university to a guarantee of tenure since the university never told him that the physicians could bypass the approval process.** Although the director may have believed that the physicians would have little difficulty obtaining tenure, there was no indication that the tenure committees shared this belief. Accordingly, the court reversed the trial court's decision. *Johns Hopkins Univ. v. Ritter*, 689 A.2d 91 (Md. App. 1996). [MD]

◆ *A college could not dismiss tenured professors for financial reasons where the board of trustees did not declare a state of financial exigency.*

An Illinois college entered into contracts with tenured faculty members, which provided that they could be discharged if the board of directors declared that the college was in a state of financial exigency. The college encountered severe financial difficulty, and signed an agreement to become part of an Illinois university, but the board never declared a state of financial exigency. The parties signed an indemnification agreement and the university promised to give tenured appointments to at least 26 members of the college's tenured faculty. It then offered eleven five-year contracts, and dismissed three professors with two years' salary. Two of the three dismissed professors sued the university for breach of their tenure contracts. The trial court granted pretrial judgment to the university, and the professors appealed.

The Appellate Court of Illinois held **the financial distress of the college leading to the affiliation with the university did not extinguish the college's obligations under the faculty manual.** Because the board of trustees had improperly failed to declare a state of financial exigency and no other contractual provision justified their dismissal, the professors' tenure rights had not expired. Neither the college nor its contractual obligations were extinguished when it became part of the university. Although the American Association of University Professors' guidelines caution against portable or transferable tenure, the court held that whether the parties intended that tenure be extinguished if the college affiliated with another university was a question of fact to be determined at trial. The trial court ruling was reversed and the case was remanded for further proceedings. *Gray v. Loyola Univ. of Chicago*, 652 N.E.2d 1306 (Ill. App. 1st Dist. 1995). [IL]

D. Letters of Intent

A letter or statement of intent regarding future employment is generally not enforceable against an employer unless the letter evinces a bilateral understanding that employment will be forthcoming. A unilateral, subjective expectation on the part of an employee (or future employee) is insufficient to subject an employer to liability.

◆ *A department chair was immune from personal liability in a lawsuit arising out of a rescinded job offer.*

An assistant professor at a New York university decided to pursue other positions and interviewed with the department chair at a Wisconsin public university. She received an offer from a school in Buffalo but contacted the department chair to find out if he had made a decision before deciding whether to accept the Buffalo job. When he offered her a job, she turned down the Buffalo job and resigned from her current position. However, after a committee refused to extend the tenure track for her from three to five years, she was notified that the Wisconsin university did not intend to offer her a position. She sued the chair and the board of regents. After granting her partial relief against the board, a trial court held that the chair was entitled to immunity. The Wisconsin Court of Appeals affirmed. **The department chair's actions were neither ministerial nor "malicious, willful and intentional."** His discretionary acts were within the scope of his employment and he was entitled to immunity. *Bicknese v. Sutula*, 635 N.W.2d 905 (Wis. App. 2001). [WI]

◆ *Where an employee received a letter that only confirmed his compensation, and not the duration of the employment, he could be discharged during the school year.*

A manager employed by a Missouri university received letters each year confirming his reappointment and compensation for the following school year. Ten years after his initial hiring, he received a letter that confirmed only his proposed compensation. The school discharged him in November of that same year. The manager filed a wrongful discharge lawsuit against the university in a Missouri trial court. The trial court dismissed the claim, and the manager appealed to the Missouri Court of Appeals. The court of appeals held that the compensation letter sent to the manager was insufficient to establish a contract. The court noted that **a statement of duration was an essential element of an employment contract.** An indefinite hiring at a set amount per year was a hiring at will and could be terminated by either party at any time. Moreover, even if the letters received from the university in prior years formed a series of one-year contracts, the university purposely excluded the language "reappointing" the manager for another year. Any previous contract the manager had with the university had expired by the time he was discharged, and the university was not under any obligation to rehire him. *Clark v. Washington Univ.*, 906 S.W.2d 789 (Mo. App. E.D. 1995). [MO]

◆ *A letter addressing the use of laboratory facilities at a university did not amount to a contract requiring the university to provide such facilities.*

A Northwestern University medical school professor sued the university claiming that it had harassed him into resigning from his tenured position. He alleged that the university had failed to assign him new patients for research and removed him from the patient rotation hospital calendars. He filed a lawsuit against the university in an Illinois court, which held in his favor. The court issued a temporary restraining order preventing the university from changing the professor's research practices. A state appellate court reversed the decision and remanded the case for additional proceedings.

On remand, the circuit court enjoined the university from evicting the professor from his laboratory facilities. It based its decision on a partially written agreement allegedly requiring the university to provide the professor with adequate facilities to continue and expand his research. The university sought a reversal of the circuit court's injunction. The university's request was denied and it again appealed to an Illinois appellate court. The appellate court reversed the circuit court decision. **Although the agreement mentioned the laboratory facilities, it did not clearly reflect an agreement between the university and the professor for his continued use of the facilities.** The professor was not entitled to the injunction allowing him continued use of the laboratory facilities. *Williams v. Northwestern Univ.*, 523 N.E.2d 1045 (Ill. App. 1st Dist. 1988). [IL]

E. Investigations, Hearings and Procedural Disputes

Several substantive and procedural rights surround employment decisions, particularly when an employee has a property interest in employment. The rights afforded to the employee may include administrative remedies, collective bargaining grievance procedures and state or federal court actions.

1. Investigations

When administrative agencies attempt to investigate discrimination charges, they frequently issue subpoenas for school employment records and may seek testimony from school officials regarding employment decisions. Schools are often reluctant to provide such information because of two factors: 1) the First Amendment's assurance that the government will not entangle itself in religious affairs (applicable only to religious schools), and 2) the perceived need to protect the integrity of the peer review process (applicable regardless of religious affiliation). While the lower courts are split on whether to allow broad inquiries by federal authorities into private school employment records, the U.S. Supreme Court has ruled that investigations by state agencies should be allowed to proceed unhampered by the federal courts.

◆ *A private college had to disclose certain records to the EEOC in the following case.*

A professor, who had been employed at a Pennsylvania private college for three years, was denied tenure after he was reviewed by the school's Professional Standards Committee. The committee, composed of the dean and five faculty members, recommended that tenure not be granted to the professor. The committee's recommendation was also reaffirmed by the college's grievance committee. The professor then filed a complaint with the EEOC alleging discrimination based on his French national origin. The EEOC issued a subpoena for the committee's records. Although the EEOC offered to accept the records with names deleted, the school refused to disclose them. The EEOC then filed suit in federal district court to compel the college to comply with the subpoena. The district court ordered disclosure of the records and the college appealed. The court of appeals affirmed, holding that **although the disclosure might burden the tenure process or invade the privacy of other professors, the records had to be disclosed because they were "relevant" to the EEOC's case.** The college appealed to the U.S. Supreme Court, but its petition for review was denied. *Franklin & Marshall College v. EEOC*, 476 U.S. 1163, 106 S.Ct. 2288, 90 L.Ed.2d 729 (1986). [PA]

◆   *The U.S. Supreme Court required a university to comply with an EEOC subpoena seeking peer review information.*

After the University of Pennsylvania, a private institution, denied tenure to an associate professor, she filed a charge with the EEOC alleging discrimination based on race, sex and national origin in violation of Title VII. During its investigation, the EEOC issued a subpoena seeking disclosure of the professor's tenure-review file and the tenure files of five male faculty members identified as having received more favorable treatment. The university refused to produce a number of the tenure-file documents and asked the EEOC to modify the subpoena to exclude "confidential peer review information." The EEOC refused and successfully sought enforcement of its subpoena through a federal district court. The U.S. Court of Appeals, Third Circuit, affirmed and rejected the university's claim that policy considerations and First Amendment principles of academic freedom required recognition of a qualified privilege or the adoption of a balancing approach that would require the EEOC to demonstrate a showing of need to obtain peer review materials. The U.S. Supreme Court then held that **a university does not enjoy a special privilege requiring a judicial finding of necessity prior to access of peer review materials.** The Court was reluctant to add such a privilege to protect "academic autonomy" when Congress had failed to do so in Title VII. The Court also stated that "academic freedom" could not be used as the basis for such a privilege. The Court affirmed the lower court decisions. *University of Pa. v. EEOC*, 493 U.S. 182, 110 S.Ct. 577, 107 L.Ed.2d 571 (1990). [PA]

2. Hearings and Procedural Disputes

◆   *When a property right to employment exists, due process requires that the employee receive notice and an opportunity to be heard before being dismissed.*

In two consolidated cases, the U.S. Supreme Court considered what pretermination process must be afforded a public employee who can be discharged only for cause. In the first case, a security guard hired by a school board stated on his job application that he had never been convicted of a felony. Upon discovering that he had in fact been convicted of grand larceny, the school board summarily dismissed him for dishonesty in filling out the job application. He was not afforded an opportunity to respond to the dishonesty charge or to challenge the dismissal until nine months later. In the second case, a school bus mechanic was fired because he had failed an eye examination. The mechanic appealed his dismissal after the fact because he had not been afforded a pretermination hearing. The Supreme Court held that **because the employees possessed a property right in their employment, they were entitled to a pretermination opportunity to at least respond to the charges against them.** The pretermination hearing need not fully resolve the propriety of the discharge, but should be a check against mistaken decisions. The Court held that in this case the employees were entitled to a pretermination opportunity to respond, coupled with a full-blown administrative hearing at a later time. *Cleveland Bd. of Educ. v. Loudermill*, 470 U.S. 532, 105 S.Ct. 1487, 84 L.Ed.2d 494 (1985). [OH]

◆ *When the disciplinary action is something less than termination, the protections afforded by due process are not the same as required in* Loudermill.

A police officer employed by a Pennsylvania state university was arrested in a drug raid and charged with several felony counts related to marijuana possession and distribution. State police notified the university of the arrest and charges, and the university's human resources director immediately suspended the officer without pay pursuant to a state executive order requiring such action where a state employee is formally charged with a felony. Although the criminal charges were dismissed, university officials demoted the officer because of the felony charges. The university did not inform the officer that it had obtained his confession from police records and he was thus unable to fully respond to damaging statements in the police reports. He filed a federal district court action against university officials for failing to provide him with notice and an opportunity to be heard before his suspension without pay. The court granted pretrial judgment to the officials, but the U.S. Court of Appeals, Third Circuit, reversed and remanded the case.

The U.S. Supreme Court agreed to review the case, and stated that the court of appeals had improperly held that a suspended public employee must always receive a paid suspension under *Cleveland Bd. of Educ. v. Loudermill*, above. The Court held that **the university did not violate due process by refusing to pay a suspended employee charged with a felony pending a hearing.** It accepted the officials' argument that the Pennsylvania executive order made any presuspension hearing useless, since the filing of charges established an independent basis for believing that the officer had committed a felony. The Court noted that **the officer here faced only a temporary suspension without pay, and not employment termination as in *Loudermill*.** The Court reversed and remanded the case for consideration of the officer's arguments concerning a postsuspension hearing. *Gilbert v. Homar*, 520 U.S. 924, 117 S.Ct. 1807, 138 L.Ed.2d 120 (1997). [PA]

◆ *A university followed the proper procedures when it fired a professor for sexual harassment.*

A tenured anthropology professor at Baylor University took several students on a university-sponsored academic field trip to Guatemala. While there, he engaged in inappropriate sexual contact with female students and made crude sexual remarks to them. A student reported his conduct to university officials upon returning, and an investigation found the student's accusations to be true. When the professor refused to accept a demotion and mandated counseling, a hearing was conducted, after which the tenure committee recommended the professor's termination. The president fired the professor, who sued for breach of contract and defamation.

A jury held that the university breached its contract with the professor, but the Texas Court of Appeals reversed. The inclusion of an American Association of University Professors statement in the employment manual did not mean that the manual incorporated the AAUP's termination procedures. **The university had clearly set forth its termination procedures and followed them in this case.** The professor received written notice of the charges against him and had an opportunity to challenge the evidence and confront witnesses at the hearing. The termination was upheld. *Fox v. Parker*, 2003 WL 132424 (Tex. App. 1/15/03). [TX]

◆   *The Court of Appeals of North Carolina held state law precluded administrative review of layoff actions involving state university employees.*

Permanent state funding reductions forced the University of North Carolina at Chapel Hill to eliminate staff positions in various departments. Three employees who were included in the reduction of force pursued grievances that were upheld under university procedures. All three employees filed petitions with the state office of administrative hearings (OAH), alleging they were improperly laid off. A state trial court denied the university's dismissal motions and held the OAH had jurisdiction to determine if just cause supported the layoffs. **The state court of appeals held the OAH only had jurisdiction to hear state employee cases involving demotion, retaliation for opposition to discrimination and disputes relating to veterans preferences.** The state legislature enacted a law that intentionally excluded reductions in force based on procedural violations from OAH jurisdiction. The court directed the trial court to grant the university's dismissal motions. *University of North Carolina v. Feinstein*, No. COA03-225, 2003 WL 22948517 (N.C. App. 2003). [NC]

◆   *A university was not liable for firing a professor for harassment prior to a hearing.*

A professor at a New York university was rumored to have sexually harassed a female student. Although no grievance or complaint was filed under the university's grievance procedures, the university took the student's information, gathered other information, and decided to fire the professor. When the student failed to appear at the arbitration hearings mandated by the collective bargaining agreement, the termination was rescinded and the charges against the professor were dismissed. He nevertheless sued the university for failing to follow its own rules when disciplining him. A jury awarded him $25,000 in damages, but the Second Circuit Court of Appeals reversed. Here, **the professor failed to show that the university was required to follow the grievance procedures exclusively when making a finding that an employee had engaged in illegal discrimination.** Because the university's grievance procedures gave it the flexibility to discipline the professor without formal hearings, there was no breach of duty by the university. *Garcia v. State Univ. of New York at Albany*, 320 F.3d 148 (2d Cir. 2003). [NY]

◆   *Even if a university violated an employee's procedural due process rights, he did not suffer any harm so as to be entitled to judicial relief.*

A paraprofessional library assistant at a South Carolina university was accused of sexual harassment. Although no formal charges were filed, he was issued several reprimands, which were withdrawn from his file after he challenged them. Several years later, his new assistant accused him of gender discrimination and of making sexual advances toward males in a specific library. The director of the Equal Opportunity Programs office notified him of the allegations but failed to provide him with witness names or details. After yet another complaint, the university temporarily reassigned the employee, then issued him a reprimand and permanently reassigned him, still without providing him with witness names or details of its investigation.

The employee sued the university for violating his due process rights, and a federal court ruled against him. The Fourth Circuit affirmed, noting that even though the EOP office may have violated the employee's procedural due process rights, he could not show that he was deprived of a property interest in employment. **He only had a right to continued employment with the university, not to continued employment in a particular position. Also, he did not suffer a reduction in pay** upon his reassignment. *Parkman v. University of South Carolina*, 44 Fed.Appx. 606 (4th Cir. 2002). [SC]

◆   *By seeking arbitration, a fired employee limited his judicial review rights.*

A physician at the University of Minnesota was accused of sexual harassment and was fired. He grieved the decision through three stages and, at Phase III, the termination was upheld. At that point, he requested Phase IV binding arbitration, which also resulted in an adverse decision. When the physician then challenged that decision before the Minnesota Court of Appeals, the court ruled that he could not do so. He either had to seek judicial review after Phase III or pursue his remedies under the federal Uniform Arbitration Act before a district court, both of which he failed to do. *University of Minnesota v. Woolley*, 659 N.W.2d 300 (Minn. App. 2003). [MN]

◆   *College officials were not entitled to immunity in a lawsuit brought by a teacher accused of misconduct and barred from campus.*

A music instructor at a Nebraska public college taught for 29 years before retiring. He directed a performance group called "Chorale" in addition to teaching, and continued to work in a part-time capacity after he retired until the college eliminated his position. At that time, the college informed him it was banning him from campus, pending an investigation into alleged embezzlement. The college's letter also accused him of permitting Chorale to have inappropriate sexual overtones in their performances. He sued the college and its officials under 42 U.S.C. § 1983, alleging violations of his substantive and procedural due process rights as well as his free speech and freedom of association rights under the First Amendment. **The college and officials**

asserted qualified immunity and sought a dismissal. A federal court dismissed the substantive due process claims, but refused to dismiss the others.

The Eighth Circuit Court of Appeals affirmed. The instructor was entitled to a name-clearing hearing because the accusations of dishonesty and immorality were stigmatizing and were known by faculty members at several campuses. He had a liberty interest in his name and reputation, and the college officials were not entitled to qualified immunity after refusing to provide the hearing. Finally, since the college was a public forum, its officials should have determined whether banning the instructor from campus was the least restrictive way to serve a compelling interest. They were not entitled to qualified immunity on the First Amendment claims either. *Putnam v. Keller*, 332 F.3d 541 (8th Cir. 2003). [NE]

◆ *A police officer whose contract was not renewed could not sue for due process violations.*

A Kentucky university hired a police officer under an annual contract. It later suspended him with pay for his involvement in the dubious arrest of several students. He did not challenge the suspension. When the university refused to renew his contract the following year, he sued it under 42 U.S.C. § 1983, asserting due process and equal protection violations. A federal court ruled in favor of the university, and the Sixth Circuit affirmed. It noted that he could not succeed because **he could not show that he had a legitimate expectation of continued employment with the university**. The university's personnel manual did not create a property interest in employment, nor did it require the university to reappoint him. *Baker v. Kentucky State Univ.*, 45 Fed.Appx. 328 (6th Cir. 2002). [KY]

◆ *An at large professor might have been qualified for another position so as to avoid a reduction in force.*

A university hired a dean for its college of business and management, but because of a faculty restructuring, gave him an "at large" executive appointment. Later, the college merged with the college of professional studies and he was retained as a tenured professor. Finally, a financial crisis caused a reduction in force, in which he lost his job. He sued the university, claiming that he should have been exempt from the RIF because of his status as an at large professor. The court ruled for the university, and the DC Court of Appeals affirmed in part. Here, **the university had the authority to conduct a RIF and release faculty members**. However, the university never made an initial finding as to whether the professor might have qualified for placement in another department because of his at large status. Thus, that issue had to be remanded to the university. *Hahn v. University of Dist. of Columbia*, 789 A.2d 1252 (D.C. 2002). [DC]

◆ *A North Dakota professor was properly fired where he was able to confront witnesses and challenge evidence in two hearings before his termination.*

A university professor served as chairman of the physics department until his relationships with other faculty members deteriorated and he was removed as chairman. He criticized the department in a number of letters that he sent to university officials and local newspapers. Subsequently, the university received numerous complaints from students about his poor teaching performance. More than 90 percent of his introductory students transferred out of his class in one semester. The university then sent him a letter of termination that listed six grounds for his firing, including his libelous conduct, his disciplinary record, and his lack of cooperation with faculty members. He obtained a hearing before a special review committee, which ruled in his favor, but the president of the university rejected the committee's findings.

The committee on faculty rights then upheld the dismissal. The professor sued the university in a federal district court under 42 U.S.C. § 1983 for violating his First and Fourteenth Amendment rights. The court ruled for the university and the professor appealed to the Eighth Circuit. It noted that while two of the professor's letters addressed matters of public concern, most of them did not. The professor could not claim First Amendment protection for all the letters, and the allegedly libelous material in the unprotected letters could be used as a reason for termination. Also, **the professor received due process in that he was given notice of the charges against him and an opportunity to respond**. Thus, his Fourteenth Amendment claim could not succeed. *de Llano v. Berglund*, 282 F.3d 1031 (8th Cir. 2002). [ND]

◆   *A Wisconsin professor had six months to petition for review after tenure was denied.*

The health, physical education, recreation and coaching department at a Wisconsin university evaluated an assistant professor it was considering recommending for tenure. Her teaching and service were above average, but her research was below average because none of the four articles she had submitted for publication had yet been published. The department decided not to recommend tenure. A grievance panel determined that the department should have considered her manuscripts. However, when the executive committee met, she had to submit revised drafts because she failed to keep copies of the originals. The committee refused to consider the revised drafts and voted to deny tenure. When she later sought judicial review, the university sought to dismiss her petition because it was not filed within the statutory 30-day deadline for contested tenure cases. A trial court dismissed the petition, but the Wisconsin Court of Appeals reversed. **Cases involving denial of tenure were not contested cases, but rather uncontested**. As such, she had six months to petition for review, and her petition was timely filed. The court remanded the case for further proceedings. *Hedrich v. Board of Regents of Univ. of Wisconsin System*, 635 N.W.2d 650 (Wis. App. 2001). [WI]

◆   *A ruling granting a grievance hearing to six non-tenured employees of the Tennessee state university and community college system was upheld by a state appellate court.*

The six plaintiffs were non-tenured support staff from different schools in the university system, holding such positions as roofer, security officer, custodian and library assistant. They were terminated for poor performance, but were denied grievance hearings. Each filed a separate suit against the university system, and the trial courts ruled that the university system acted arbitrarily by denying them grievance hearings in violation of Tenn. Code Ann. § 47-8-117.

On appeal, the cases were consolidated. The university system argued that the plaintiffs were "at-will-employees" and could therefore be terminated at any time with or without good cause. The Tennessee statute addressing at-will employees requires educational institutions to establish a grievance procedure for their support staff for complaints relating to adverse employment actions such as "termination for cause." Termination for cause involves any termination in which the employee was fired for a job-related reason: for example, failure to follow a supervisor's directions, poor job performance or failure to execute assigned duties. However, an employee who has been terminated as part of a reduction in the work force has not been terminated for cause because the termination was not related to job performance. Here, **the plaintiffs were all fired for reasons related to their job performance, which entitled them to grievance hearings** under the statute. The decisions of the trial courts were upheld. *Lawrence v. Rawlins*, 2001 WL 76266 (Tenn. App. 1/30/01). [TN]

◆   *Where a state university violated a professor's procedural due process rights, but no proof of actual injury was shown, the professor was only entitled to $1.00 in nominal damages.*

A tenured professor at a West Virginia university was issued a letter of reprimand by a dean, who cited a number of deficiencies, including that the professor's second job with Dupont was interfering with his duties. The professor replied that the letter lacked specifics and was without a basis in fact. Subsequently, the university discharged him by letter. He appealed through the university's appeal system. After a hearing, it was determined that the discharge had been for just cause, but that the failure to hold a per-termination hearing required the university to pay the professor back pay. The university appealed. The Supreme Court of Appeals of West Virginia held that **the university had improperly terminated the professor without providing him an opportunity to respond. This was a violation of his due process rights.** However, the court then found that the termination was proper and that no proof of actual injury had been shown from the denial of procedural due process. As a result, the award of back pay was reversed, and the university only had to pay nominal damages of $1.00. *Barazi v. West Virginia State College*, 498 S.E.2d 720 (W.Va. 1997). [WV]

◆   *A college could not violate a professor's due process rights where the state was not involved and the college was entirely private.*

A tenured professor at a New York private college was fired. He filed suit against the college in state court, alleging that his discharge violated due process. After the court dismissed the case, he appealed to the New York Supreme Court, Appellate Division. The appellate court noted that students and **instructors at private colleges have no right to due process in the colleges' proceedings unless they can show that the state was involved in the challenged activity.** The professor argued that all private colleges and universities in New York are included in the University of the State of New York and are subject to regulation and inspection by the Board of Regents. The court, however, found that **mere regulation is not enough to show state**

involvement. Rather, there must be a sufficiently close relationship between the state and the action of the entity so that the action can be regarded as an activity of the state itself. Because that was not the case here, the court found that the professor had no due process rights and it affirmed the trial court's decision. *Moghimzadeh v. College of Saint Rose*, 653 N.Y.S.2d 198 (A.D. 3d Dept. 1997). [NY]

◆ *A professor who was fired following a sexual harassment complaint failed to show a due process violation.*

A Vermont private college ended its "presumptive tenure" plan pursuant to measures undertaken to downsize the school. Professors with presumptive tenure were entitled to five-year contract extensions absent misconduct or exigent circumstances. A male student at the college filed a complaint with the sexual harassment committee under an interim policy, alleging that a professor forced him to have sexual relations with him. The interim policy was more comprehensive than the older policy with respect to the informal and formal procedures in cases alleging sexual harassment. The professor received notice of the complaint and a hearing, but was told that only witnesses with potential direct knowledge of the incident would be permitted to testify. After extensive deliberations, the committee unanimously recommended termination of the professor's employment. The president dismissed his appeal, and the professor sued for breach of contract and for violating his due process rights. A jury awarded him damages, and the college appealed to the Second Circuit.

The court noted that the jury had reasonably interpreted the handbook as constituting a contract of employment between the professor and the college. However, there was insufficient evidence in the record for a reasonable jury to find that the college adopted the interim policy in violation of handbook procedures. The professor failed to present any evidence establishing that he was discharged without cause; he had merely asserted his innocence in a conclusory manner. There was also insufficient evidence to find for the professor on his claim that the college had breached its duty of good faith and fair dealing. **The committee's conduct did not deprive the professor of any substantive or procedural rights he had under his employment contract.** *Logan v. Bennington College Corp.*, 72 F.3d 1017 (2d Cir. 1995). [VT]

◆ *A professor was not entitled to an injunction allowing him to remain in his position.*

A California private university established an accredited department of emergency medicine. The university appointed a professor of surgery with limited experience in emergency medicine as the chairman of the department. However, the university removed the professor from his position after the Accreditation Council announced its intention to withdraw accreditation of the program based on his lack of experience. The professor sought a preliminary injunction in a state trial court, alleging violations of his due process rights and civil service rules. The trial court granted the professor a preliminary injunction, and the university appealed to the California Court of Appeal.

The professor contended that his removal from the position required application of predisciplinary protections mandated by county civil service rules. The court of appeal disagreed, holding that the university bylaws vested such decisions in the president. Because the professor was not likely to prevail on the merits of the claim, and because the university was more likely to be harmed by the injunction than the professor, the court reversed the order granting the injunction. Finally, the court of appeal held that **the alleged improprieties surrounding the professor's dismissal did not allege state action necessary to implicate due process protections.** The university was a private institution and the professor's position was not governmental. *Shoemaker v. County of Los Angeles*, 43 Cal.Rptr.2d 774 (Cal. App. 2d Dist. 1995). [CA]

◆ *A federal appeals court could remand a case to state court after dismissing the federal cause of action. It did not have to dismiss the case–thereby defeating the plaintiff's claims because of the statute of limitations.*

An employee of Carnegie-Mellon University (CMU) filed a lawsuit in a Pennsylvania state court charging that CMU violated the federal Age Discrimination in Employment Act (ADEA). He also alleged violations of state laws. CMU was allowed to remove the case from state court to a U.S. district court because the alleged violation of the ADEA gave federal court jurisdiction over the entire lawsuit. The employee subsequently discovered that the federal claim could not be successful because he had failed to file a timely age discrimination charge with a federal or state agency. He requested that the federal claim be deleted and that the case be remanded to state court. The federal court granted this request. CMU then requested that the U.S. Court of Appeals, Third Circuit, order the lower court not to remand the case to the state court. The court of appeals denied that request and CMU appealed.

The U.S. Supreme Court noted that when a case is removed from state to federal court because it contains a federal claim, the federal court can exercise jurisdiction over the entire case, including claims arising under state law. However, the federal and state law claims must arise from the same "operative fact," in this case the employee's dismissal. In cases where the federal claim is dropped from the lawsuit after removal, a federal court has discretion to dismiss the case and let the plaintiff start over again in state court. The question in this case, however, was **whether the federal court has discretion to remand the case to the state court, thereby preserving state law claims that would otherwise be lost if state statutes of limitation have run before the plaintiff can start again in state court.** The Supreme Court asserted that federal courts have such discretion and ruled that the employee's case could be remanded to the Pennsylvania court in which it was filed, thus preserving his state law claims. *Carnegie-Mellon Univ. v. Cohill*, 484 U.S. 343, 108 S.Ct. 614, 98 L.Ed.2d 720 (1988). [PA]

◆ *An employee could not invoke the grievance procedures of a staff handbook because he was a high-level managerial employee.*

A Louisiana man worked for Tulane University for more than 30 years as the director of the university's physical plant department. He was eventually discharged for poor job performance and because he and his immediate supervisor were unable to resolve their differences. Upon his discharge, the director sought to invoke the grievance procedures outlined in the university's staff handbook. The university responded that the grievance procedures were unavailable to high-level managerial employees. He then sued the university. After a federal court determined that he was an at-will employee and had no contractual right to a grievance proceeding, the director appealed to the U.S. Court of Appeals, Fifth Circuit. The court first noted that **because the handbook was not an employment contract, and because the university had not entered into an oral contract with the director concerning the handbook's grievance proceedings, the director had no right to invoke its protections.** The court also held that the director could not show that he had justifiably relied on the availability of the grievance procedures. The court affirmed the decision in favor of the university. *Gilbert v. Tulane Univ.*, 909 F.2d 124 (5th Cir. 1990). [LA]

F. Wrongful Termination

An at-will employee may be discharged at any time without cause unless an agreement exists which limits the employer's right to terminate employment. Public policy also restricts an employer's right to discharge an employee.

◆ *An Illinois court denied a professor's claims against a university for defamation, breach of contract and invasion of privacy.*

A divinity school was considering an associate professor for tenure when the administration received complaints about the way he ran his classes. A tenure committee conducted an investigation and learned that students considered him rude and abrasive. They reported he deviated from class topics and was unprofessional. School administrators spoke with the professor several times about these concerns and warned him that failure to change his conduct would result in termination. The professor denied the charges and the school suspended him. He claimed the charges harmed his professional reputation and that communications to students and faculty about termination constituted defamation. He sued the school for defamation and breach of contract. The court dismissed the defamation claim and characterized the termination of his contract as a "buy-out," since it paid the professor in full.

The professor appealed to the Appellate Court of Illinois, which rejected contract claims relating to the university handbook, which allowed the interviewing of students about classroom decorum. **The university did not breach his contract by failing to renew it after extending the tenure review process.** Under the faculty constitution, notice of termination was to be given by March 1 of the year, except in cases of moral turpitude. Since the professor did not receive notice by this deadline, he argued colleagues and students would infer he was fired on grounds of moral turpitude. The court rejected his claim and affirmed the judgment. The invasion of privacy claim failed because the professor did not show the university put him in a false light. *Green v. Trinity Int'l Univ.*, No. 801 N.E.2d 1208 (Ill. App. 2d Dist. 2003). [IL]

◆ *A Florida District Court of Appeal held a whistleblower complaint was properly dismissed by the state human relations commission.*

After being discharged, a community college provost filed a complaint with the Florida Commission on Human Relations, accusing college trustees of violating the state whistleblower act. The commission dismissed her complaint because the college was not a "state agency" under state law. The provost appealed to a state district court of appeal. The court found the list of statutory terms for the definition of "state agency" included any official, officer, commission, board or department of the executive branch of state government. For the provost to establish the commission's jurisdiction to investigate her claim, she would have to show the board of trustees was part of the executive branch. However, state law described community colleges as state political subdivisions, and emphasized the difference between political subdivisions and state agencies. As the board of trustees was not a board of the executive branch of state government, the commission lacked jurisdiction to investigate the complaint. *Caldwell v. Board of Trustees Broward Community College,* 858 So.2d 1199 (Fla. App. 4th Dist. 2003). [FL]

◆ *The Supreme Court of Iowa held that opposition to a co-worker's discharge was not "protected activity."*

Drake University investigated a security officer for an arrest he made during the annual Drake Relays. The officer was placed on desk duty for three months, then discharged. A university shift sergeant defended the officer's actions and offered to testify on his behalf. The university asked the sergeant to stop discussing the incident with the press, but he continued to talk openly about it. The university then demoted him one rank, resulting in a pay cut. The sergeant resigned and sued the university in an Iowa court, asserting he was constructively discharged for engaging in protected activity. The court awarded the university summary judgment. The state appeals court affirmed.

The state supreme court held that **to succeed in a wrongful discharge claim, the sergeant had to establish his advocacy established a clearly defined public policy that would be undermined by his termination**. He would also have to show his termination resulted from his participation in a protected activity and for no other reason. **The court found that opposing a co-worker's wrongful termination was not a "protected activity" under state law.** While public policy protected employees offering truthful testimony at legal proceedings, there was no indication the discharged officer had intended to sue the university. The court affirmed the judgment for the university. *Shoop v. Drake Univ.,* 672 N.W.2d 335 (Iowa 2003). [IA]

◆ *A university was entitled to immunity in a wrongful refusal to hire case.*

A New York mathematical physicist sought employment at the Lawrence Livermore National Laboratory, which is operated by the University of California pursuant to a contract with the federal government. He sued university regents in a federal district court, claiming breach of contract because the university agreed to employ him but then wrongfully refused to hire him when he could not obtain a required security clearance from the U.S. Department of Energy (DOE). The court held that the Eleventh Amendment, which provides for state immunity from lawsuits, barred his breach of contract action. The U.S. Court of Appeals, Ninth Circuit, reversed the decision and the U.S. Supreme Court agreed to review the case.

On appeal, the physicist contended that the Eleventh Amendment was inapplicable in this case because any award of damages would be paid by the DOE and not the state of California. The Supreme Court rejected this argument, finding that **an entity's potential legal liability, not its ability to discharge the liability or to require a third party to reimburse it, was the relevant inquiry when determining the immunity issue. The Eleventh Amendment protects a state from the risk of adverse judgments even though the state may be indemnified by a third party.** The Court reversed the court of appeals' judgment. *Regents of Univ. of California v. Doe,* 519 U.S. 425, 117 S.Ct. 900, 137 L.Ed.2d 55 (1997). [CA]

◆ *A university employee could not show that he was fired because of complaints he made about co-workers stealing.*

A receiving clerk in the maintenance department at a Florida university complained to university security officers that his supervisor and co-workers were stealing university property. He was then allegedly subjected to certain retaliatory actions, including a glued office lock, a smoke-filled office, and interference with his radio transmissions. He later asked to take a leave, but his request was rejected when the university determined that he had already exhausted his leave time. He took the time off anyway and was fired. **He sued the university for retaliation under the state whistleblower act**, and a state court ruled against him. The Florida District Court of Appeal affirmed. Here, even if the employee's complaint about stealing was protected speech, he failed to show a causal connection between his complaint and his firing. For being absent without leave, he would have been fired regardless of the complaint. Also, as for the retaliatory actions, he was unable to prove that management was either implicated in the attacks or that it condoned them. *Amador v. Florida Bd. of Regents,* 830 So.2d 120 (Fla. App. 2002). [FL]

◆ *A professor could sue an agency that supervised his grant work under the state's whistleblower act when it removed him from the project before he could release his results.*

A professor at the University of Louisville received a $500,000 grant to evaluate the effect of welfare reform on Kentucky families. The university then entered into a contract with the Cabinet for Families and Children regarding the monitoring of the professor's research. As part of the contract, the CFC paid one-third of the professor's salary and benefits while he worked on the project. The university also reduced the professor's workload by one-third during the two years he was involved in the project. The results of the study indicated that welfare reform had a negative effect on black and Appalachian families, and the professor informed the CFC that he would release his report during a public hearing. Before that could happen, the CFC got the university to remove the professor from the project and return him to full-time teaching. The professor sued the CFC under the state whistleblower act, and the Kentucky Court of Appeals found that he could do so. It rejected the CFC's argument that it was not the professor's employer, noting that **the CFC supervised the professor's work and paid part of his salary. Thus, it was an employer subject to the whistleblower act.** *Cummings v. Cabinet for Families and Children,* 2002 WL 1943758 (Ky. App. 8/23/02). [KY]

◆ *A fired university employee had to pursue administrative relief before she could sue for wrongful discharge.*

After a Texas university employee was fired, she sued the university for wrongful termination under the telephone hotline anti-retaliation provision of the Texas Workers' Compensation Act. Alternatively, she asserted violations of the state whistleblower act. The Texas Court of Appeals ruled against her, noting that **university employees were not entitled to judicial relief for employer retaliation under the workers' compensation act.** Also, her failure to comply with the administrative requirements of the whistleblower act meant that she could not sue under that statute either. *University of Texas Medical Branch at Galveston v. Savoy,* 86 S.W.3d 782 (Tex. App. 2002). [TX]

◆ *Although a coach should not have been fired for retaliating against a player, the university could still fire her for lying.*

A black basketball player at the University of Southern Florida filed a complaint with the university's Equal Opportunity Affairs office, accusing her coach of race discrimination. She played basketball the following year, then was dismissed from the team after composing and singing a song implying that the coach was going to be removed from her job. She then filed a second EOA complaint, claiming she had been dismissed from the team in retaliation for the first complaint. During an investigation, the coach maintained that she did not know the student was involved in the first complaint against her. The university fired her for retaliating against the player and for dishonesty in her sworn statement that she did not know of the student's involvement. The Florida District Court of Appeal ruled that the university should not have fired the coach for retaliating against the player. **Since a year had passed between the first complaint and the player's dismissal from the team, there was no retaliation.** However, on remand, the university would be allowed to fire the coach for dishonesty if it so chose. *Winters v. Florida Bd. of Regents,* 834 So.2d 243 (Fla. App. 2002). [FL]

◆ *Project documents did not prevent a university from eliminating an employee's position.*

A university assigned an employee to work on a project updating the university's financial software system for Y2K compatibility. Several months later, the employee's position was eliminated as part of a reorganization and, after he unsuccessfully applied for a number of other jobs, he was fired. He sued the university for breach of contract, asserting that the project work plans amounted to a contract. The university asserted that the work plans did not constitute an employment contract and that, even if they did, it had not breached the contract. A court found in favor of the university, and the California Court of Appeal affirmed. **The work plans did not prohibit the university from conducting the reorganization or from firing the employee**

when it had no work for him. *Jenkins v. California Institute of Technology*, 2002 WL 31529092 (Cal. App. 11/15/02). [CA]

◆ *A mold-sensitive employee could not prove that she was disabled under Michigan law.*

A Michigan university employee developed a pulmonary condition as a result of high concentrations of mold in her office. She was granted a medical leave, but her position was eliminated while she was on leave, and she was terminated. She sued the university for damages. The case reached the Michigan Court of Appeals, which ruled that the university was not liable for an intentional tort because she failed to show that it knew she was unusually sensitive to mold and that she was certain to become ill because of that sensitivity. Also, she could not show that she was disabled under state law because **her breathing was usually impaired only when she was exposed to high concentrations of mold**. This was not a substantial limitation of a major life activity. However, she was entitled, as an at-will employee, to nominal damages for breach of contract. *Leonard v. Board of Governors of Wayne State Univ.*, 2003 WL 1919530 (Mich. App. 4/22/03). [MI]

◆ *An adjunct music instructor was denied renewal of his employment contract based on his unprofessional conduct, not his organizational activities.*

Three adjunct music instructors at a Minnesota college distributed a survey to other adjuncts concerning salary and benefit issues. They presented the survey results to the department chairmen and informed them that they intended to hold elections for a formal committee. The adjuncts were elected to the Adjunct Faculty Committee (TAFC), and obtained recognition for it from the Faculty Affairs Committee. In light of the actions taken by the three organizers, one of the department chairmen recommended disciplinary action. The dean of the college declined, but decided to discuss professional expectations with each of the three instructors before offering them new one-year contracts. One instructor was not rehired, based on his conduct during his meeting with the dean. He filed a complaint with the National Labor Relations Board, alleging the non-renewal was due to his organizing activities, in violation of federal law. An administrative law judge held the failure to extend a contract to him constituted an unfair labor practice. The NLRB adopted the ALJ's findings and ordered the college to reinstate the instructor.

The Eighth Circuit Court of Appeals rejected the NLRB's characterization of the instructors' meetings with the dean as a means of forcing them into abandoning their TAFC activities. Evidence from the dean's meeting with one of the retained instructors indicated they simply disagreed about the instructor's involvement with TAFC. In contrast, **the non-retained instructor used vulgarities and called the music department a "laughingstock" during his meeting with the dean**. The court found that the instructor's behavior during the meeting demonstrated unprofessional conduct and disrespect for the music department. Moreover, the court did not believe that the instructor's conduct was provoked. Because it was the instructor's conduct during the meeting that led to his termination, and not his organizing activities, the university met its burden of establishing that the termination decision would have been made regardless of the instructor's protected activities. The Eighth Circuit refused to enforce the NLRB's reinstatement order. *Carleton College v. NLRB*, 230 F.3d 1075 (8th Cir. 2000). [MN]

◆ *The Mississippi Court of Appeals held that neither coercion nor misrepresentation existed in the execution of a settlement agreement between a college and its provost.*

The provost of William Carey College was employed pursuant to an annual employment contract. After he disagreed with the board of trustees over the college's application for a federal education grant, the board determined that his actions undermined his relations with the college, and decided not to renew his contract. Eventually, the provost and the college entered into a settlement agreement, under which the provost agreed not to file a civil action against the college or any of its officials. About two years later, the college entered into a settlement agreement with the U.S. Department of Justice following an investigation into alleged violations of the False Claims Act. Upon learning of this agreement, the provost sued the college and its officials in a Mississippi court. The court granted pretrial judgment for the college, upon finding that the provost was unable to show that coercion or misrepresentation existed that would set aside his settlement agreement. The court of appeals upheld the ruling for the college. **A contractual employment relationship existed between the provost and the college, which was not the sort of relationship under which the school owed the provost fiduciary duties**. Even if the provost could have established a fiduciary relationship, he was unable to show that he was coerced into signing the agreement. In fact, the record revealed that in his capacity as a licensed attorney, the provost had "aggressively negotiated" the terms of the settlement agreement before signing it. *Braidfoot v. William Carey College*, 793 So.2d 642 (Miss. App. 2000). [MS]

◆ *An employee alleging retaliatory discharge was entitled to a trial.*

While conducting a study on the interaction between passive smoking and contact with radioactive materials for the University of Chicago, **an employee noticed that human test subjects had been exposed to dangerously high levels of radiation. After insisting that the matter be reported to the federal government, the employee was fired.** The employee filed suit, claiming that his termination was retaliatory, but a trial court dismissed the case because the employee did not allege that a criminal statute, state law or actual violation was involved. The Illinois Appellate Court reversed and remanded the case. It held that the employee merely had to allege that he had a good-faith belief that a violation of public policy occurred in order for the case to go to trial. *Stebbings v. University of Chicago*, 726 N.E.2d 1136 (Ill. App. 2000). [IL]

◆ *When a junior college attempted to discharge a teacher for writing anonymous letters critical of the college district's president, she brought a variety of claims against it.*

When anonymous letters critical of the president of a junior college district were distributed, the president took action to determine who had written them. He authorized the search of personnel files and data from employees' computers. The governing board later concluded that a teacher had written the letters and issued her a notice that it intended to dismiss her. She sued, denying that she had written the letters, and obtained a temporary restraining order that put her on paid administrative leave. Subsequently, the governing board withdrew the charges against her, but reserved the right to reinstate them.

A California federal court found that the Eleventh Amendment prevented her lawsuit for money damages against the junior college district and its governing board. It then held that the teacher did not have a reasonable expectation of privacy in the material on her computer or in her personnel file such that the search could be ruled unconstitutional under the Fourth Amendment. However, **she stated a valid claim under the First Amendment even though she claimed not to have written the letters. If the attempted discharge was due to the belief that she had written the letters, then it did not matter if she did not write them**. She would still have a claim under the First Amendment. The court dismissed most of her claims, but held that she could re-file in state court. *Wasson v. Sonoma County Junior College Dist.*, 4 F.Supp.2d 893 (N.D. Cal. 1998). [CA]

◆ *An employee's wrongful discharge claim failed where she could not show that her firing had been related to her reports of theft in the office.*

A Massachusetts private college employee reported the apparent theft of funds from the office in which she worked. She was employed at will, and after her reports of theft, she was discharged. She brought suit against the college and her former supervisor in the superior court, claiming wrongful discharge and intentional interference with her employment contract. The court granted pretrial judgment in favor of the college and her former supervisor. She appealed unsuccessfully to the Appeals Court, then appealed to the Supreme Judicial Court of Massachusetts.

The lower court had held that as an at-will employee, she could not obtain redress from her former employer when it discharged her for reporting the theft of funds. In certain circumstances, however, an at-will employee may maintain an action against her former employer for wrongful discharge. Public policy is violated when an employer discharges an employee for reporting criminal activity even if the reports were made only within the employing units. Here, there was no dispute that the woman was an at-will employee. She therefore had an obligation to support her claim that she was discharged for reporting criminal conduct to her superiors. However, **she had no facts to support her claim, and the record contained nothing showing that the college discharged her for a reason contrary to a well-established public policy.** Further, she failed to show that her supervisor intentionally interfered with her employment contract because she was unable to prove that he knowingly induced the college to break the contract, that his interference, in addition to being intentional, was improper in motive or means, and that she was harmed by his actions. Rather, the record stated several examples of problems she was having on the job. Therefore, the court affirmed the grant of pretrial judgment for the college and the supervisor. *Shea v. Emmanuel College*, 682 N.E.2d 1348 (Mass. 1997). [MA]

◆ *An employee was allowed to proceed in his lawsuit against a college for retaliation.*

A security officer employed by a Vermont private college sought workers' compensation benefits after he was injured on the job. The college denied his claim but the state Department of Labor and Industry reversed and granted him benefits. The officer alleged the college then discriminated against him by badgering him to come back to work, changing his employment duties and responsibilities, requiring him to work night shifts in breach of a previous agreement, changing his work hours, giving him unfairly low job evaluations, and challenging his right to receive workers' compensation. He was also demoted and placed on probation for six months based on a student's complaint. The security officer did not return to work following his demotion, alleging stress-induced depression prevented him from working.

The college fired the officer after his short-term disability benefits ran out, and he sued it for retaliatory discrimination and intentional infliction of emotional distress. A state court granted pretrial judgment to the college, and the officer appealed. The Supreme Court of Vermont held that **employees have a private right of action under the workers' compensation act when an employer allegedly discharges them or discriminates against them for filing a workers' compensation claim.** Although the college articulated a legitimate, nondiscriminatory reason for the officer's discipline, the court found factual issues remained concerning whether he was discriminated against for filing a workers' compensation claim, and whether the severity of the disciplinary action resulting from the student's complaint was the result of discriminatory treatment. Finally, the court dismissed the officer's intentional infliction of emotional distress claim. *Murray v. St. Michael's College*, 667 A.2d 294 (Vt. 1995). [VT]

◆ *A wrongful discharge claim failed where the employee was paid through the end of his contract.*

A licensed veterinarian contracted with a Missouri private university to work for its animal facilities department from July 1989 through June 1990. The interim director ultimately notified him that his services would not be needed in 1990 but that he would remain on the payroll until the expiration of his current contract. The veterinarian filed a wrongful discharge lawsuit in a Missouri trial court, alleging that he had been discharged in retaliation for reporting infractions of the federal Animal Welfare Act. The trial court granted pretrial judgment to the university, and the court of appeals transferred the case to the Supreme Court of Missouri.

The supreme court held that only discharged at-will employees may state a wrongful discharge cause of action. Here, **because the veterinarian had not been discharged (his contract had expired), his claim had been properly dismissed.** Given the significant differences between employees at will and contractual employees, the court rejected the veterinarian's contention that the failure to renew an employment contract should be treated the same as the discharge of an employee at will. The court declined to consider whether a separate (as yet unrecognized) tort or theory of damages should have been alleged in place of the wrongful discharge claim. Whether liability exists for wrongful failures to renew contracts or what type of damages may be recovered for a breach of contract in "whistleblower" situations were still open questions. *Luethans v. Washington Univ.*, 894 S.W.2d 169 (Mo. 1995). [MO]

II. EMPLOYEE BENEFITS

Like their counterparts in the public sector, many private schools offer a broad range of employment benefits to employees. These benefit programs are subject to federal civil rights laws such as Title VII and the Equal Pay Act as well as income tax laws. Employer-employee disputes concerning benefits will generally be resolved according to contract law rules (see Section I).

A. Retirement Benefits

◆ *A university could require a semi-retired professor to teach during the spring semester.*

A professional pianist worked for an Ohio university as a music professor and "artist in residence." After over 30 years with the university, the professor signed a three-year "limited-service agreement for retired faculty," under which he was allowed to participate in the university's "supplemental retirement program" in exchange for teaching eight or nine semester hours each fiscal year. He taught during the summer semesters that year at his request, but was assigned to teach in the spring semester the following year. He objected to that assignment, and the university eventually determined that he had effectively withdrawn from his retirement program obligations by refusing to accept the assignment. The professor sued for breach of contract, and a magistrate judge ruled for the university. The Ohio Court of Claims affirmed. Under the terms of the retirement program, **the university had the sole discretion to assign the hours and responsibilities of the professor**. *Rose v. Bowling Green State Univ.*, 784 N.E.2d 213 (Ohio Ct. Cl. 2003). [OH]

◆ *A professor could not enroll in an early retirement program where he waited too long to submit his application.*

An Ohio state university instituted an early retirement incentive program, which Ohio law authorized as long as enrollment did not exceed 5 percent of eligible employees. A professor/associate dean applied for the program but then withdrew his application. He later attempted to resubmit his application, but the university denied his request. After resigning, the professor sued, seeking an order that he be enrolled in the early retirement program. A state court ruled in his favor, but the Court of Appeals of Ohio reversed. Here, the university had improperly expanded the program to allow more than 5 percent of eligible employees to participate. As a result, **even though the professor's initial application would have placed him in the eligible 5 percent, his resubmitted application came after the 5 percent threshold had already been met**. He was ineligible for the program. *Bee v. University of Akron*, 2002 WL 31387127 (Ohio App. 10/23/02). [OH]

◆   *A discharged professor could proceed with his lawsuit for unpaid pension benefits.*

After 10 years teaching, a tenured assistant professor was notified that he would be reassigned to an administrative position. While trying to agree on a position, the professor performed no services for the university, which then stopped paying his salary and began dismissal proceedings against him. The university did not complete the proceedings because it determined that he had abandoned his job. When he sued for reinstatement and backpay, a New York court dismissed the case on the grounds that he should have filed an Article 78 proceeding against the university. An appellate court reversed, but the lawsuit was dismissed when he failed to appear. He later sued for unpaid salary and pension contributions, asserting that the university had never formally fired him. A federal court dismissed the case, but the Second Circuit reversed in part, finding that **if his employment status claim was valid, he might be able to succeed on his pension claim**. However, his claim for unpaid salary had been properly dismissed. *Yoon v. Fordham Univ. Faculty and Administrative Retirement Plan*, 263 F.3d 196 (2d Cir. 2001). [NY]

◆   *Where a university reasonably modified a retirement plan, it was not liable for violating ERISA.*

A professor employed by a New York private university retired in 1977 and began receiving benefits under the school's contributory retirement plan. The board of trustees amended the plan periodically to provide cost of living adjustments (COLAs) to plan members or their beneficiaries. Subsequently, the retirement committee amended the COLA and the board of trustees amended the plan again to provide that "the retirement committee shall have exclusive authority and discretion to construe any disputed term." After the retirement committee denied the professor's claim for additional benefits, he filed suit against the retirement plan and the university under the Employee Retirement Income Security Act (ERISA) in a state trial court. The case was ultimately transferred to a U.S. Magistrate Judge. The magistrate judge granted the university's motion for pretrial judgment, and the professor appealed to the U.S. Court of Appeals, Second Circuit.

The retirement committee contended that it had properly modified the earlier increases by calculating what each retiree's monthly benefit would have been under the amended COLA, subtracting the value of increases actually given, and adding the difference to each retiree's monthly benefits. The professor contended that the base figure to which the above formula would be applied should include all prior COLAs. The court ruled that **the retirement committee had discretion to construe any uncertain or disputed term.** Consequently, the court applied the arbitrary and capricious standard of review. Because the retirement committee's interpretation of the statute was reasonable, the court affirmed the magistrate judge's ruling in favor of the university. *Jordan v. Retirement Committee of Rensselaer Poly. Inst.*, 46 F.3d 1264 (2d Cir. 1995). [NY]

◆ *A professor was entitled to sue after a college improperly fired him and terminated his retirement benefits.*

A Wisconsin professor was promoted to president of a private college. He signed an employment agreement for a three-year term with the understanding that the agreement could be terminated by either party with one year's notice. **The professor also entered into a retirement agreement with the school that provided him with four payments of $30,000 over the three-year term, as long as he did not retire or terminate his employment.** The college terminated his employment, without the required one-year notice, after two retirement payments had been made. The professor sued the college for the payments and for the wages he would have earned from the time of termination to the time the contract was to have expired. The trial court ruled in favor of the college, stating that the statute of limitations had tolled and there was no consideration for the retirement payments. The professor appealed to the Wisconsin Court of Appeals.

The professor argued that the statute of limitations had not run because he was suing for wages unearned. The court of appeals agreed, stating that the statute of limitations is shorter when suing for wages earned than when suing for wages unearned. Further, it stated that there was consideration for the retirement payments. Continuation of employment may consist of a detriment to the promissee or a benefit to the promissor. For the professor to receive retirement benefits, he was required to remain at the college and not retire or accept other employment. Thus, he gave up exercising a legal right, which is valid consideration. The court of appeals reversed the trial court's decision. *Lovett v. Mt. Senario College,* 454 N.W.2d 356 (Wis. App. 1990). [WI]

B. Welfare Benefits

◆ *A police instructor was not entitled to disability benefits because his injuries predated his membership in the state retirement system.*

The instructor was involved in two automobile accidents during his employment by a state university. He had been involved in an accident prior to his employment by the university that caused severe injuries to his spine, for which he underwent spinal fusion surgery and received psychiatric treatment for post-traumatic stress disorder. After going to work for the university, the instructor was involved in another motor vehicle crash and was diagnosed as having a sprain. His third accident occurred when he was going to work. After this accident, the instructor underwent a second cervical fusion operation. He applied for disability benefits based on his cervical injury and mental illness. A medical board denied his request, and a hearing officer upheld the denial. The hearing officer found the instructor's disability predated his university employment and his membership in the state retirement system.

The state retirement system adopted the hearing officer's findings, and the instructor appealed to the Court of Appeals of Kentucky. The court found medical testimony supported the hearing officer's finding that the instructor's physical and mental disabilities resulted from the first automobile accident and predated his university employment. The court rejected his argument that his injuries from the third accident occurred during the course of his employment because he changed his route to obtain water for use in his police training class.

The record showed the instructor traveled just a mile out of his way and was not on campus when the accident occurred. **The university did not file an accident report or a workers' compensation claim, which would have indicated the accident was in the course of his employment.** The court affirmed the denial of benefits. *Morris v. Kentucky Retirement Systems*, No. 2002-CA-001570-MR, 2003 WL 21834980 (Ky. App. 2003). [KY]

◆   *The Court of Appeals of North Carolina upheld a decision to deny permanent and total disability benefits to a library assistant.*

A 55-year-old library assistant worked at North Carolina State University for 22 years before injuring herself when she slipped on a wet floor. The university workers' compensation disability benefits coordinator authorized health care, and a specialist diagnosed the assistant with a small wrist fracture. Another doctor diagnosed her with fibromyalgia and degenerative disc disease. Physicians explained that while these injuries were probably aggravated by the fall, the fall did not cause them. The university denied that the assistant's back injuries were related to her fall and the state industrial commission denied her claim for permanent total disability compensation.

The state appeals court noted only one physician had initially testified the assistant was permanently and totally disabled. However, after being asked if she met the statutory definition of "permanently and totally disabled," he retracted his statement. **Most of the medical testimony placed the assistant's disability at five to ten percent permanent partial disability, indicating she could perform light duty work with some restrictions**. The commission did not abuse its discretion by denying the assistant an opportunity to show a change in her condition. Since the commission's findings were supported by competent evidence, its decision was affirmed. *Hunt v. North Carolina State Univ.*, 582 S.E.2d 380 (N.C. App. 2003). [NC]

◆   *Community college teachers who did not work during the summer were not entitled to state-paid health care benefits.*

Two teachers at community colleges in Washington worked under contract for each quarter they taught at more than 50 percent of a full-time schedule. They did not teach during the summer. When they sued to get state-paid health benefits for the summer months, a trial court ruled that because they were not employees during the summer, they were not entitled to state-paid health benefits. The Washington Court of Appeals affirmed the ruling against them. **Even though they worked a nine-month period, they did so by virtue of quarterly contracts and thus did not qualify as career seasonal/instructional employees**. Also, despite the fact that they did not qualify for unemployment in the summer (because they received reasonable assurances of employment for the following quarter), they were not technically employed during that time. *Mader v. Health Care Authority*, 37 P.3d 1244 (Wash. App. 2002). [WA]

◆   *A New Hampshire college could provide less insurance benefits for mental illnesses than for physical illnesses.*

A college professor was treated for depression through medication and outpatient medical care. The college funded its own health care plan, which contained an annual limit of $3,000 for outpatient mental health benefits and a lifetime cap of $10,000. After the professor reached the lifetime cap, he filed a grievance, arguing that the cap violated a state statute and the collective bargaining agreement by providing less benefits for mental illnesses than physical illnesses. An arbitrator ruled that neither the state statute nor the bargaining agreement had been violated, and the Supreme Court of New Hampshire upheld that decision. **Because the college was not an insurer, it was not subject to the statute requiring equal health insurance coverage for mental and physical illnesses.** *Marshall v. Keene State College,* 785 A.2d 418 (N.H. 2001). [NH]

♦ *A New Jersey college was forced to reinstate health insurance for an employee who failed to pay her premium after becoming mentally incompetent.*

The college offered a health plan that was governed by the Employee Retirement Income Security Act (ERISA) and the Consolidated Omnibus Budget Reconciliation Act (COBRA). An employee suffered from cerebral atrophy and became hospitalized and mentally incompetent. She failed to pay a premium, and her insurance was canceled. A representative notified her employer of her incompetency. Following the representative's judicial empowerment as legal guardian, he paid the premiums which would have come due. However, her employer contended that it could not be forced to reinstate coverage. The guardian sought reinstatement in a federal court. Although ERISA and COBRA speak to the nonpayment of premiums, neither directly speak to nonpayment of premiums due to incompetency.

The court considered the policies underscoring the statutes, which included "the continued well being and security of employees." Common law provides that the actions of an incompetent are disregarded. It followed that an incompetent's inaction should also be disregarded. Further, an earlier case ruled that an insured is not bound to give notice of a disability when made unable to do so by the disability insured against. **The employee was rendered unable to appreciate the fact that her premium was due. The court held that the school could be required to accept the premium and reinstate coverage.** The motion for dismissal was denied and the case was allowed to proceed to trial. *Sirkin v. Phillips Colleges,* 779 F.Supp. 751 (D.N.J. 1991). [NJ]

C. Discrimination

♦ *A California institute could not discontinue disability benefits to an employee who turned 65 because he was not receiving pension benefits.*

A research scientist at a California research and education institute was diagnosed with Parkinson's disease and took a medical leave of absence. He eventually became eligible to receive long-term disability benefits through the institute's insurance plan but he retained his employee status and his right to return to work if his health improved. While still receiving his disability benefits, he turned 65 years old and became eligible for retirement. Had the scientist chosen to retire, his pension benefits would have been slightly more than his disability benefits. **Although he did not retire (and thus did not receive pension benefits), the institute offset his disability benefits with the**

amount of pension benefits he would have received by retiring, thereby reducing his income to zero. The scientist filed suit against the institute in state court, alleging violations of the Age Discrimination in Employment Act (ADEA) and a state statute. The institute cross-claimed for the amount of disability benefits it had inadvertently paid him after he turned 65, removed the case to federal court and filed a motion to dismiss. The motion was granted and the employee appealed to the U.S. Court of Appeals, Ninth Circuit.

The court noted that this was not a case of double dipping, which the ADEA was designed to prevent. In order to preclude employees from receiving both long-term disability benefits and pension benefits for which the employee is eligible, the ADEA allows employers to offset the amount of disability benefits with the amount of pension benefits. The institute argued that since the employee was eligible to retire, he was eligible to receive the pension benefits, and therefore it could offset them. The court disagreed. **Because the employee had not retired, he was not receiving any pension benefits.** The court also noted that the ADEA expressly prohibits any employee benefit plan from requiring or permitting involuntary retirement. The primary effect of the institute's policy was to leave an employee without an income unless he or she retired, and the court held that a reasonable person in the employee's position would feel that he had no choice but to retire. Finding that **the offsetting of long-term disability benefits is only allowed when pension benefits are being paid concurrently,** the court found that the institute's disability plan violated the ADEA. The district court's decision was reversed. *Kalvinskas v. California Institute of Technology*, 96 F.3d 1305 (9th Cir. 1996). [CA]

D. Income Tax Laws

◆ *An employee welfare benefit plan established by an association of Christian schools was not entitled to tax exempt status.*

The American Association of Christian Schools, a tax exempt association of Christian schools located in all 50 states, established a "welfare plan" providing health, disability, and life insurance as well as other benefits to employees of member schools. The welfare plan, which was a separate legal entity, sued the IRS for a refund, contending that it was exempt from paying federal income taxes under §§ 501(c)(3), (4) and (9) of the Internal Revenue Code. The court observed that under § 501(c)(3), groups organized and operated exclusively for religious purposes were exempt from paying federal income taxes. The welfare plan did not meet the operational test of the provision because **it could not show that it was operated exclusively for a tax-exempt religious purpose.** Here, the welfare plan essentially sold insurance coverage. Because the welfare plan had a significant nonexempt purpose, the welfare plan was not exempt under § 501(c)(3). The presence of a significant non-exempt purpose also prevented the welfare plan from being eligible for § 501(c)(4)'s "social welfare" exemption.

The welfare plan also argued that it was exempt from federal taxation because it was a voluntary employees' beneficiary association (VEBA) under § 501(c)(9). The court observed that one of the requirements for being a VEBA is that the organization be controlled by either its membership, an independent trustee or a board of trustees, at least some of whom were designated by, or on behalf of, the employees themselves. Here, because the AACS welfare plan board was self-perpetuating, it failed to meet any one of these criteria. Even though school employees had some say in selecting the pastors of the churches, the court noted that when an employee selected a pastor who served on the board of trustees of the welfare plan, he or she was acting as a church member and not as an employee of the school. The welfare plan was not tax exempt and its request for a refund was denied. On appeal, the decision was affirmed. *American Ass'n of Christian Schs. Voluntary Employees Beneficiary Ass'n Welfare Plan Trust v. U.S.*, 850 F.2d 1510 (11th Cir. 1988). [AL]

◆ *A Wisconsin religious school was not entitled to a refund of federal income taxes paid on behalf of employees who received fringe benefits in lieu of a higher salaries.*

Marquette University, a tax-exempt educational institution, provided certain fringe benefits to its employees from 1973 to 1978 with commensurate salary reductions, but did not withhold federal income tax on the amounts by which the salaries of participating employees were reduced. The university paid taxes on those amounts after they were assessed by the IRS and then sued the government seeking a refund. The Internal Revenue Code defines gross income as "all income from whatever source... including... compensation for services...." The court observed that this included income obtained in any form, whether services or property, and that the university would be obligated to locate a specific statutory section which allowed it to exclude the questionable amounts from "gross income." **The three benefits at issue were parking spaces, recreation center memberships and tuition payments by the university for certain employees' children at area high schools.**

The university claimed that the tuition payments remitted to the area high schools were scholarships and therefore were exempt from taxation. The district court ruled, however, that the tuition payments were not scholarships since the payments had been deducted from the salaries of the employees and remitted to the high schools by the university and were therefore to be considered part of the employees' taxable gross income. The university also contended that waived parking fees and recreation center memberships were not taxable income. The district court observed that "entertainment, medical services, or so called 'courtesy' discounts furnished by an employer to his employee generally are not considered as wages subject to withholding if such facilities or privileges are of relatively small value and are offered by the employer merely as a means of promoting the health, goodwill, contentment, or efficiency of its employees." However, the court concluded that the benefits here did not meet the criteria since they were considered significant enough to be deducted from the employee's wages and were only available to employees who agreed to the salary reduction in return for the benefits. **The university's attempt to recover the taxes paid was rejected by the court.** *Marquette Univ. v. U.S.*, 645 F.Supp. 1007 (E.D. Wis. 1986). [WI]

◆ *Although wage cuts used to purchase annuity contracts were not taxable as income, they were subject to social security taxation.*

John Carroll University is a not-for-profit institution exempt from federal income taxes under §§ 501(a) and 501(c)(3) of the Internal Revenue Code. The university established a retirement annuity plan for employees in which participating employees agreed to take salary cuts in exchange for contributions by the university on their behalf toward the purchase of annuity contracts. The university's contributions were excludable from the employees' gross income for federal income tax purposes. When the university filed claims for refunds of FICA taxes paid for certain years, the IRS denied the university's claim for one year and failed to rule on the claims for two other years. The university sued the IRS in U.S. district court seeking a refund of FICA taxes for the years in question totaling $79,147 plus interest.

At issue was whether taxpayers acting pursuant to salary reduction agreements are exempt from FICA taxes paid on amounts contributed prior to January 1, 1984, toward the purchase of retirement annuities. The court observed that in 1965, the IRS decided that amounts withheld because of a salary cut agreement are to be included in the employee's taxable wage base for FICA tax purposes, even though the amounts withheld are excluded from gross income for federal income tax purposes. The court reasoned that if retirement annuity contributions were not included in the FICA wage base, individuals could control which part of their wage was to be included in the FICA wage base. In denying the university's claim, the court also referred to a 1981 U.S. Supreme Court decision in which the court held that **"the term 'wages' must be interpreted consistently for purposes of both income tax withholding and FICA."** The district court held a 1984 Act which applied FICA taxation to remuneration paid on or before March 4, 1983 made retroactive taxation possible. **The contributions of the university to the annuity plans were therefore subject to FICA taxes** and the university's claim was dismissed. *John Carroll Univ. v. U.S.*, 643 F.Supp. 675 (N.D. Ohio 1986). [OH]

III. UNEMPLOYMENT AND WORKERS' COMPENSATION

A. Unemployment Benefits

The Federal Unemployment Tax Act (FUTA), 26 U.S.C. § 3301 et seq., establishes a federal program to compensate people temporarily unemployed. Although the federal Department of Labor oversees the program, states meeting specific criteria administer the program. A major exemption from coverage, in § 3309(b)(1) of the Act, states: "This section shall not apply to service performed ... in the employ of (A) a church or convention or association of churches, or (B) an organization which is operated primarily for religious purposes and which is operated, supervised, controlled, or principally supported by a church or convention or association of churches."

◆   *The Supreme Court of Hawaii held that a student, who was also a university employee, was not entitled to receive unemployment benefits.*

The student attended the University of Hawaii for five consecutive academic years. He was hired as a university peer counselor full-time during a summer when he did not attend school. The student resumed his studies at the university that fall. The next year, he filed an unemployment insurance claim. The state Department of Labor and Industrial Relations determined the wages from his summer job could be considered for the purpose of unemployment benefits, since he was not enrolled or regularly attending classes during the summer session. The university appealed that decision.

An appeals officer found the student's services could be considered for benefits. A state trial court noted Hawaii law made students ineligible for unemployment benefits if they were enrolled or regularly attended classes while working for a university. The court applied a "primary relationship test" which focused on the student's primary relationship to the university. It held the student's services were excluded from the unemployment statute's definition of "services." The Supreme Court of Hawaii held that **because the student attended classes full-time for five consecutive academic years, his primary relationship was that of a student**. He would have been ineligible for summer work with the school without his status as a student. Since the summer job was excluded from the code's term "employment," the court affirmed the judgment. *University of Hawaii v. Befitel*, No. 24270, 2004 WL 1345017 (Haw. 2004). [HI]

◆ *A professor not on tenure track and whose contract was not renewed was entitled to unemployment benefits.*

An Ohio university hired a visiting assistant professor under a one-year contract, which stated that it was not a tenure-track position and that it would not lead to a tenure-track position. At the end of the year, the university did not renew her contract, and she applied for unemployment compensation benefits. An administrative official determined that **she was entitled to benefits because the university's decision not to renew her contract resulted from lack of work**. A review commission and a state court upheld that decision, and the Ohio Court of Appeals affirmed. Despite the university's assertion that the professor should be ineligible for benefits because she voluntarily entered into a one-year contract, the court credited testimony by the university's director of employment relations that the university did not have any work available for the professor at the end of her contract. The professor was entitled to benefits. *Case Western Reserve Univ. v. Ohio Unemployment Compensation Review Comm'n*, 2003 WL 1924645 (Ohio App. 4/24/03). [OH]

◆ *Maryland's labor and employment statute does not require a finding of intent in cases of termination for misconduct to deny unemployment benefits.*

A senior lab technician employed by Johns Hopkins University came to work one day armed with a hockey stick and began smashing desks, filing cabinets and other objects. Campus security and the Baltimore police were called. The technician was apprehended and taken to the emergency room. He was involuntarily admitted to JHU's affective disorder unit for observation and released nine days later. He was diagnosed with bipolar disorder. Based on this violent incident and other performance deficiencies, he was fired. He filed a claim for unemployment benefits and a claims examiner denied them. On appeal, a hearing examiner reversed that decision, finding competent evidence indicating that his bipolar disorder caused his actions, and that they could not be characterized as intentional misconduct. A state court upheld this decision and JHU appealed.

The Maryland Court of Special Appeals reversed. It reviewed the three grounds for disqualification—misconduct, gross misconduct and aggravated misconduct—and determined that the statutory language does not require intentional misconduct in order to be disqualified from receiving benefits. Moreover, the court distinguished civil cases from criminal cases, noting that criminal conduct involves an analysis of intent. However, **in civil cases, an individual is held accountable for his or her conduct regardless of whether that "conduct is a product of a mental deficiency."** Thus, the lower court erred in finding that the technician was entitled to unemployment benefits because his misconduct was not intentional. The appeals court concluded that the technician should have been temporarily disqualified from receiving unemployment benefits for a period of between five and 10 weeks. The judgment was reversed and the matter remanded for further proceedings. *Johns Hopkins Univ. v. Board of Labor, Licensing and Regulations*, 134 Md.App. 653, 761 A.2d 350 (Md. App. 2000). [MD]

◆ *A student worker who lost his job was not entitled to unemployment benefits because the job was deemed incidental to his studies.*

A university graduate student in cinema-television obtained a job in the School of Business Administration at the University of Southern California. His job category was student worker even though it was described as "faculty assistant" by the business school. It was a "nonbenefits position" available only to students. This meant that the university did not provide a funding pool for unemployment benefits for the position. The student ultimately lost his job and was denied unemployment benefits under California Unemployment Insurance Code § 642. This section provides that "employment" (for unemployment insurance purposes) does not include services performed for a school by an enrolled student who is regularly attending classes. However, regulations promulgated pursuant to this statute provide that, "if the course of study is incidental to the employment, the exemption shall not apply."

The case reached the California Court of Appeal, Second District, where the student contended that his studies were incidental to his employment. Specifically, **he alleged that his job in the business school was not exempt from unemployment compensation benefits because it did not directly further his course of study. The court of appeal disagreed,** noting that the student was employed in a position available only to students regularly enrolled at the university. Consequently, even though the position was in a different department, it was incidental to his studies. *Davenport v. California Unemp. Ins. Appeals,* 30 Cal.Rptr.2d 214 (Cal. App. 2d Dist. 1994). [CA]

B. Workers' Compensation

◆ *Legislation that waived sovereign immunity for some state employees but not for university employees did not violate the Equal Protection Clause.*

A maintenance employee at Texas A & M University (TAMU) suffered on-the-job back injuries and filed a claim for workers' compensation benefits. The university discharged him and he sued it in a state court, alleging he was terminated in retaliation for filing the claim. The court dismissed the case, finding the state had immunity for lawsuits filed by university employees. The employee appealed to the state court of appeals. The Texas Workers' Compensation Act generally offers coverage for all state employees, but not for TAMU employees. The employee argued this distinction violated the Equal Protection clause by discriminating against those employees. **The court held government employees are not a protected class for equal protection analysis. The state did not waive its sovereign immunity for lawsuits brought by TAMU employees**, and the judgment was affirmed. *Richards v. Texas A&M Univ.*, 131 S.W.3d 550 (Tex. App. 2003). [TX]

◆ *A university employee was allowed to file a review petition because he alleged a new medical condition resulted from a work-related injury.*

A Villanova University employee received workers' compensation benefits for a sprained shoulder. Soon after returning to work, he experienced kidney problems. He then filed a review petition claiming he developed nephrotic syndrome as a result of taking medication to treat his work-related shoulder injury. Villanova disputed the claim, but a workers' compensation judge (WCJ) granted the employee's petition, finding he suffered a work-related neck injury. The case reached the Commonwealth Court of Pennsylvania, which held the review petition was properly filed. The court upheld the WCJ's credibility determinations, but agreed with Villanova as to the work-related injury issue. The notice of compensation payable listed only a shoulder injury, and the record indicated Villanova never acknowledged a neck injury. The WCJ erred in stating the employee suffered a neck injury. *Villanova Univ. v. WCAB*, 840 A.2d 1074 (Pa. Cmwlth. 2003). [PA]

◆ *A hearing officer's decision to deny workers' compensation benefits was reversed to determine whether the injury was covered.*

A fellow at Georgetown University Hospital had ankle pain from wearing tight shoes at a banquet. Her supervisor administered a nerve block to prevent her from limping. The fellow received another nerve block injection with low doses of steroids, and her ankle became ulcerated, requiring surgery. She sued the university for personal injury. A hearing officer found the injury did not occur in the course of her employment. As a result, it was not compensable under the Workers' Compensation Act and the fellow could pursue her personal injury claims. Georgetown appealed to the District of Columbia Court of Appeals, which noted there was sufficient evidence to support a presumption of compensability based on a work-related event. The hearing officer had considered evidence that the injury was caused by tight shoes, but failed to address the significance of injections performed at the workplace. The record established the fellow was limping at work and received the nerve block to relieve her pain so that she could make her hospital rounds. Since the hearing officer's decision was not supported by substantial evidence, the case was reversed and remanded. *Georgetown Univ. v. District of Columbia Dep't of Employment Serv.*, 830 A.2d 865 (D.C. 2003). [DC]

◆ *A deputy workers' compensation commissioner improperly allowed a claimant to introduce a cumulative injury theory at an administrative hearing.*

A University of Iowa custodian sought workers' compensation benefits for back injuries he suffered while dumping heavy trash at work. Based on his statements, the university prepared a defense to a specific injury theory. During a hearing, the custodian claimed he had previous back trouble and disputed the actual date of the injury. A deputy commissioner determined the custodian suffered a cumulative traumatic injury on the last day he worked. An Iowa trial court reversed the decision, finding the university was prejudiced by the new and unexpected theory. The Court of Appeals of Iowa affirmed. It stated **due process requires that a party receive notice of the issues to prevent surprise and to provide an opportunity to prepare.** The cumulative injury theory was raised for the first time at the workers' compensation hearing. As a result, the university was denied the opportunity to investigate and was unable to present expert witnesses to defend against the new theory. The trial court properly reversed the commissioner's decision. *University of Iowa Hospitals and Clinics, v. Waters*, 670 N.W.2d 432 (Iowa App. 2003). [IA]

◆ *The South Carolina Workers' Compensation Commission wrongly held the statute of limitations had run on a claim for repetitive trauma injury.*

An operating room technician's job duties entailed heavy lifting, such as removing trash bins from operating rooms, moving equipment, and lifting and transporting patients. He complained to his supervisor of bad circulation in his legs. While the technician received medical attention, no work restrictions were imposed. He complained to his family physician about back pain on two later occasions but did not seek treatment for lower back pain for three years. After tests revealed the technician had a disc herniation, he applied for workers' compensation benefits. The state workers' compensation commissioner denied his claim as barred by a two-year state statute of limitations.

A state trial court reversed the decision. The university appealed to the Court of Appeals of South Carolina. **The court noted the technician suffered from a repetitive traumatic injury. These injuries generally have a gradual onset, making it difficult to determine the actual date of injury.** Even assuming the technician knew his back pain was work-related when he first noticed it, the statute of limitations did not begin to run until his last day of work. The court affirmed findings that the claim was timely filed, and his injury arose out of and in the course of his employment. *White v. Medical Univ. of South Carolina*, 586 S.E.2d 157 (S.C. App. 2003). [SC]

◆ *A New York court held the state workers' compensation commission did not abuse its discretion in denying a claimant's request for a full board review.*

Yitka Kozak was employed by the State University of New York at Old Westbury. In March 1998, Kozak left her position and filed a claim for workers' compensation benefits. She alleged that she suffered mental anxiety and depression as a result of a personnel decision that was made by the university. A Workers' Compensation Law Judge (WCLJ) denied Kozak benefits, finding that her alleged mental injuries were not compensable under New York's Workers' Compensation Law because they resulted from lawful employment decisions. The Workers' Compensation Board upheld that determination, and Kozak's application for full board review was denied. The Appellate Division noted that Kozak was not challenging the merits of the WCLJ's decision, but was merely making a procedural request. Kozak failed to offer any new evidence to support her request, arguing only that the WCLJ's determination was not supported by substantial evidence. The court found no abuse of discretion and affirmed the decision. *Kozak v. SUNY at Old Westbury*, 768 N.Y.S.2d 421 (N.Y. App. 3d Dept. 2003). [NY]

◆ *A New York university had to pay the medical expenses of a secretary who was hospitalized on an emergency basis due to a work-related illness.*

The secretary left her position due to respiratory aliments caused by pollutants in her workplace. A specialist in environmental and occupational medicine diagnosed her with multiple chemical sensitivities and recommended her admission into the environmental care unit at a Texas hospital. The secretary remained there for five weeks, incurring over $69,400 in medical costs. The university refused to pay her expenses because her hospitalization was not pre-authorized. A state workers' compensation judge ordered the university to pay the costs, finding them causally related to the secretary's medical condition. The university appealed to a state appellate division court, arguing there was no evidence her admission was an emergency. **The court found that the compensation judge had credited the specialist's testimony that the hospitalization was made on an emergency basis.** Accordingly, the decision was affirmed. *Langenmayr v. Syracuse Univ.*, 765 N.Y.S.2d 914 (N.Y. App. Div. 2003). [NY]

◆ *A Delaware court reversed an award of benefits to a security guard that was made without considering her pre-existing conditions.*

The University of Delaware hired a security service officer who soon suffered a ruptured disc in her lower lumbar spine. Following surgery, she returned to her position without restriction. Two years later, the officer needed additional surgery and several years after that, she injured her back at home. Following another surgery, the officer returned to work without restriction. She was then injured while trying to break up a fight on campus. She continued to work, but a few weeks later, her back stiffened and she underwent three additional surgeries to correct the problem. The officer became unable to perform her job duties, and applied for workers' compensation benefits.

The state industrial accident board heard testimony from a university expert, who stated only half of the officer's prior injuries and surgeries were work-related. The Board rejected this allocation and decided to award the officer the entire amount of permanent impairment she claimed. A state superior court held the officer's back problems were not the result of a natural degenerative condition. Therefore, an appointment provision applied, and she should have been awarded only half of the permanent partial impairment she claimed for work-related injuries. The board's decision was reversed, and the case was remanded for further proceedings. *State of Delaware v. Neff*, No. Civ.A. 02A-12-006SCD, 2003 WL 22064099 (Del. Super. 2003). [DE]

◆   *A federal district court determined that more discovery was necessary to determine if an injured federal work-study student was an employee of Tulane University limited to workers' compensation.*

While attending Tulane, a work-study student worked as a lab assistant between 1992 and 1994 on a university-run project run in conjunction with Coastal Catalyst Oil Co. The student claimed that while working on this project, she was improperly exposed to a wide variety of toxic chemicals, but did not learn of the exposure until the fall of 1999, after being diagnosed with heavy metal poisoning. In October 2000 the student sued Tulane and Coastal Catalyst.

A Louisiana federal court examined whether the student's exclusive remedy against her work-study "employer" was workers' compensation. Courts throughout the country have reached different conclusions about whether particular work-study students were "employees" for workers' compensation purposes. In *Dustin v. DHCI Home Health Services*, 673 So.2d 356 (La. App. 1st Cir. 1996), a Louisiana appeals court held that a student at a medical support personnel training school was not an employee of the hospital. But *Walters v. United States*, 458 F.2d 20 (8th Cir. 1972), held that a work-study student assigned to a federal facility was a federal employee entitled to compensation under the Federal Employees' Compensation Act. It noted that **a work-study student's status as an "employee" depends on the particular facts of the case interpreted in light of the specific workers' compensation statute.** Here, more discovery was needed regarding the student's work placement to determine if she was an employee of Tulane. In addition, a detailed analysis of the federal work-study program and the Louisiana workers' compensation act was required. *Grant v. Tulane Univ.*, 2001 WL 245785 (E.D. La. 3/9/01). [MD]

◆   *A union representative was not entitled to workers' compensation benefits when she slipped and fell on her way back to work from a union meeting.*

A Connecticut university employee was a local union representative. While returning to work after a union meeting during her lunch break, she fell on a sidewalk not under the control of the university and injured her arm. The meeting had been a weekly meeting and not a grievance or negotiating session. Her employer was not allowed to attend the meeting and her attendance was voluntary. She filed for workers' compensation benefits and after a hearing, the workers' compensation commissioner found her injury compensable because the coming and going to the meeting was part of her employment or incidental to it. He noted that the meeting had been for the mutual benefit of the employee and the university. The university appealed to a workers' compensation review board, which reversed the commissioner's decision.

The Supreme Court of Connecticut noted that when employees leave work for lunch or for other functions not related to work, they are outside the scope of their employment if they are injured. However, if the activity is work related, the employee can fall within the workers' compensation act's coverage if he or she can show that the activity benefited the employer. **Traditionally, attendance at union meetings has been held not to benefit employers, but more recent decisions have looked at the particular nature of the union activity.** For example, grievance hearings and negotiation settlements have been held to benefit employers. Because the employee here was only attending a weekly meeting, the court found that she was not acting within the scope of her employment or performing an activity that benefited her employer. The court affirmed the board's decision. *Spatafore v. Yale Univ.*, 684 A.2d 1155 (Conn. 1996). [CT]

IV. LABOR RELATIONS

The National Labor Relations Act (NLRA), as amended by the Labor Management Relations Act (LMRA), 29 U.S.C. § 141 et seq., governs unionization and collective bargaining matters in the private sector, including private education. States are also subject to the dictates of the act. The NLRA was passed to protect the rights of employees to organize, or to choose not to organize, and to ensure that commerce is not interrupted by labor disputes. Managerial employees are unprotected by the NLRA.

A. Appropriate Bargaining Units

◆ *In certain circumstances, faculty members at private educational institutions can be considered managerial employees.*

Yeshiva University's faculty association had petitioned the National Labor Relations Board (NLRB) for certification as bargaining agent for all faculty members. The NLRB granted certification but the university refused to bargain. After the U.S. Court of Appeals declined to enforce the NLRB's order that the university bargain with the union, the NLRB appealed to the U.S. Supreme Court, which upheld the appeals court. The Supreme Court's ruling was based on its conclusion that Yeshiva's faculty were managerial employees. It stated:

> The controlling consideration in this case is that the faculty of Yeshiva University exercise authority which in any other context unquestionably would be managerial. **Their authority in academic matters is absolute.** They decide what courses will be offered, when they will be scheduled, and to whom they will be taught. They debate and determine teaching methods, grading policies, and matriculation standards. They effectively decide which students will be admitted, retained, and graduated. On occasion their views have determined the size of the student body, the tuition to be charged, and the location of a school. When one considers the function of a university, it is difficult to imagine decisions more managerial than these. To the extent the industrial analogy applies, the faculty determines within each school the product to be produced, the terms upon which it will be offered, and the customers who will be served.

The Court noted that its decision applied only to schools that were "like Yeshiva" and not to schools where the faculty exercised less control. **Schools where faculty do not exercise binding managerial discretion do not fall within the scope of the managerial employee exclusion.** *NLRB v. Yeshiva Univ.*, 444 U.S. 672, 100 S.Ct. 856, 63 L.Ed.2d 115 (1980). [NY]

◆   *A District of Columbia court remanded an NLRB decision recognizing a bargaining unit for college faculty members.*

Approximately 60 full-time faculty members at LeMoyne-Owen College attempted to form a collective bargaining unit. The college denied the request because it considered them managerial employees who were exempt from NLRA coverage. The faculty petitioned the NLRB for recognition as a bargaining unit. The college opposed the petition, citing the Supreme Court's decision in *NLRB v. Yeshiva Univ.*, above, as controlling precedent. The NLRB regional director found the college's faculty were not managerial employees and certified the bargaining unit. The college sought review, arguing the regional director deviated from *Yeshiva* and other precedents.

The NLRB found the college guilty of an unfair labor practice when it refused to bargain with the new bargaining unit. The college petitioned for review of the NLRB's order. The District of Columbia Circuit Court remanded the case. While deference is generally afforded to the NLRB's authority to certify bargaining units, the decision in this case departed from precedent without explanation. The NLRB had an obligation to explain itself. The college made a reasoned argument based on the *Yeshiva* case. The regional director did not explain why the college's argument should be rejected. The court remanded the case to the NLRB for further proceedings. *LeMoyne-Owen College v. NLRB*, 357 F.3d 55 (D.C. Cir. 2004). [DC]

◆   *A Michigan court upheld a determination by the State Employment Relations Commission to deny a petition to merge two bargaining units.*

Kendall College of Art and Design is a sub-unit within Ferris State University. Kendall retains its own academic governance and operates autonomously. Although the university has the authority to make changes to Kendall, it has not exercised that power. The Ferris Faculty Association, which represented full-time faculty members at the university, petitioned to add the Kendall bargaining unit to its bargaining unit. The Kendall unit was composed of both full-time and part-time faculty members.

The Michigan Employment Relations Commission denied the petition, and the association appealed. The Court of Appeals of Michigan explained a commission's determination of appropriate bargaining units was factual, and could not be disturbed unless there was a lack of competent, material, and substantial evidence. In reaching its decision, the commission focused on Kendall's academic autonomy from the university and the differences between the two educational institutions. The court rejected the association's argument that the commission erred in considering the bargaining history of the Kendall union. **Bargaining history is a relevant factor in considering whether a bargaining unit is appropriate.** The commission acknowledged the need "to avoid fractionalization or multiplicity of bargaining units." As the Kendall bargaining unit served its members well, it was an appropriate bargaining unit. The commission's decision was affirmed. *Ferris Faculty Ass'n v. Ferris State Univ.*, No. 243885, 2004 WL 144671 (Mich. App. 2004). [MI]

◆ *A state labor relations board used incorrect tests to determine whether two employees were "confidential employees" who were ineligible for the union.*

A union sought to represent all classified and specialist employees at an Illinois college. In the representation election, the union won by a single vote. The college challenged the result, asserting that two of the employees should not have been allowed to vote because they were "confidential employees" under the state labor relations act. One was a secretary; the other was a research associate—both reported to an assistant vice president for administrative affairs. An administrative law judge determined that the employees were confidential employees, and the state labor relations board upheld that decision. The Appellate Court of Illinois reversed and remanded the case, finding that the board used the wrong tests to determine whether the employees were "confidential." Here, **although the college asserted that the employees were going to be performing duties related to the collective bargaining process, they had not yet done so**. Thus, the board should have determined whether there was a reasonable expectation that future job duties would satisfy the definition of a confidential position. *One Equal Voice v. Illinois Educ. Labor Relations Bd.*, 777 N.E.2d 648 (Ill. App. 2002). [IL]

◆ *There must be a broad measure of control for faculty to be considered management.*

The faculty of Florida Memorial College, a private, nonprofit four-year liberal arts college, established a union pursuant to a NLRB directive. The college filed a petition with the NLRB claiming that under the U.S. Supreme Court's decision in *NLRB v. Yeshiva University*, above, the faculty should be prevented from forming a union due to its managerial/supervisory status. After the National Labor Relations Board (NLRB) dismissed the college's petition, the college continued in its refusal to bargain with the union. The NLRB asked the U.S. Court of Appeals, Eleventh Circuit, to enforce the NLRB order.

The court of appeals observed that the college faculty here was not managerial or supervisory. Unlike *Yeshiva's* faculty, **the faculty in this case asserted insufficient control in almost every one of the areas examined by the Supreme Court in *Yeshiva*.** Among other things, the Florida Memorial College faculty lacked a comprehensive governing organization which provided meaningful input as to administrative and academic matters. Although faculty members sat on various administrative committees at the college, their influence was diluted since they were appointed by college administrators and because the committees included a number of administrators and students. Further, the faculty had no effective control over curriculum, student policies, faculty hiring, tenure or termination. Also, the fact that there was an absence of tenure at the college indicated that the faculty was nonmanagerial. The court of appeals ordered the college to comply with the NLRB's collective bargaining order. *NLRB v. Florida Memorial College*, 820 F.2d 1182 (11th Cir. 1987). [FL]

◆ *Where faculty had little control over management decisions, they could not be deemed managerial employees.*

The Cooper Union for the Advancement of Science and Art, a private institution of higher education located in Manhattan, had an enrollment of 900 to 1,000 students and employed 55 to 60 full-time faculty members. In 1974, the Cooper Union Federation of College Teachers was certified to represent a bargaining unit of full-time faculty members and librarians. In 1980, however, after the U.S. Supreme Court's decision in *NLRB v.Yeshiva University*, the school withdrew its recognition of the bargaining unit and refused to bargain with it. The U.S. Court of Appeals, Second Circuit, noted several distinctions between Cooper Union and Yeshiva. Cooper Union's **faculty had no "effective recommendation or control" of management decisions,** and lacked the authority possessed by the Yeshiva faculty. Also, the Cooper Union faculty had little or no authority over financial concerns and other nonacademic matters and merely had restricted access to ordinary office supplies. In addition, the authority of Cooper Union's faculty over academic matters was relatively weak. In light of these differences, the court ruled that the holding of the *Yeshiva* case could not be applied to Cooper Union. Therefore, the Cooper Union faculty was held to be nonmanagerial and was entitled to the protection of the NLRA. The court affirmed the decision of the NLRB and ordered Cooper Union to bargain with the faculty bargaining unit. *NLRB v. Cooper Union for the Advancement of Science & Art*, 783 F.2d 29 (2d Cir. 1986). [NY]

◆ *The Second Circuit refused to enforce a National Labor Relations Board (NLRB) order requiring a New York college to bargain with a union because supervisors belonged to the union.*

The Security Department Membership (SDM) is the organization certified by the NLRB to represent Quinnipiac College's security personnel in collective bargaining. Quinnipiac refused to bargain with SDM, maintaining the organization was improperly certified because it included supervisors, who are excluded from collective bargaining under the NLRA. SDM was certified to include six dispatchers, four traffic-control officers, two shift supervisors and 18 assistant supervisors, four of whom act as shift supervisors at certain times. Quinnipiac objected to the inclusion of the two shift supervisors and the assistant supervisors who acted as shift supervisors. The NLRB conducted a hearing in response to the college's objection, but concluded the shift supervisors were not "supervisors" under the act. The board ordered Quinnipiac to bargain with SDM, but the college refused. The NLRB petitioned the U.S. Court of Appeals, Second Circuit to enforce the order.

The NLRA defines "supervisor" as an employee who has the authority to hire, transfer, suspend, lay off, recall, promote, discharge, assign, reward, discipline or responsibly direct other employees, or address grievances. According to the Second Circuit, Quinnipiac's shift supervisors made assignment decisions based on their own expertise and experience, despite the existence of college procedures. Shift supervisors also disciplined employees. Although security directors had to review any disciplinary procedures taken by the shift supervisors, they still amounted to a supervisor's duty. Lastly, the shift supervisors responsibly directed other security employees. In declining to enforce the NLRB's order, the Second Circuit remanded the matter, with the suggestion that the board review the membership of SDM and consider eliminating the shift supervisors from the bargaining unit. *NLRB v. Quinnipiac College*, 256 F.3d 68 (2d Cir. 2001). [NY]

◆ *An exclusive bargaining representative which is duly elected by school employees should have the sole voice in discussing employment-related matters with the employer.*

In a U.S. Supreme Court case, Minnesota community college faculty members brought suit against the State Board for Community Colleges. **The faculty alleged that a state statute requiring public employers to engage in official exchanges of views only with their professional employees' exclusive representatives on certain policy questions violated their First Amendment rights.** Under the statute, public employers were required to bargain only with the employees' exclusive bargaining representative. The statute gave professional employees, such as college faculty members, the right to "meet and confer" with the employer on matters outside the scope of the collective bargaining agreement. The faculty members objected to the "meet and confer" provision, saying that rights of professional employees within the bargaining unit who were not members of the exclusive representative were violated. The Supreme Court held that the "meet and confer" provision did not violate the faculty members' constitutional rights. **There was no constitutional right to force public employers to listen to the members' views.** The fact that an academic setting was involved did not give them any special constitutional right to a voice in the employer's policymaking decisions. Further, the state had a legitimate interest in ensuring that its public employer heard one voice presenting the majority view of its professional employees on employment related policy questions. *Minnesota Comm. College Ass'n v. Knight*, 465 U.S. 271, 104 S.Ct. 1058, 79 L.Ed.2d 299 (1984). [MN]

◆ *In 1999, the Supreme Court held that public university regents could set standards for faculty instructional workloads for the purpose of emphasizing undergraduate instruction, and that such standards could be removed from the collective bargaining table.*

The Ohio legislature passed a statute requiring state universities to adopt faculty workload policies and made them an inappropriate subject for collective bargaining. The law was enacted to address the decline in the amount of time faculty spent teaching, as opposed to time spent on research. Any university policy prevailed over the contrary provisions of collective bargaining agreements. One university adopted a workload policy pursuant to the law and notified the collective bargaining agent that it would not bargain over the policy. As a result, **the professors' union filed a state court action, seeking an order that the statute violated public employee equal protection rights.** The Supreme Court of Ohio struck down the statute, finding the collective bargaining exemption was not rationally related to the state's interest of encouraging public university professors to spend less time researching at the expense of undergraduate teaching.

The U.S. Supreme Court accepted the university's appeal, and held that the state supreme court had not applied the correct standard of review under the Equal Protection Clause. In equal protection clause cases that do not involve fundamental rights or suspect classifications, there need only be a rational relationship between disparity of treatment and some legitimate government purpose. In this case, the disputed statute met the rational relationship standard.

Ohio could reasonably conclude that the policy would be undercut if it were subjected to collective bargaining. **The state legislature could properly determine that collective bargaining would interfere with the legitimate goal of achieving uniformity in faculty workloads.** The Ohio Supreme Court decision was reversed and remanded. *Central State Univ. v. American Ass'n of Univ. Professors, Central State Univ. Chapter,* 526 U.S. 124, 119 S.Ct. 1162, 143 L.Ed.2d 227 (1999). [OH]

B. Agency Fees

◆ *Compelled agency fees cannot be used to support political viewpoints.*

In 1977, the U.S. Supreme Court held that the First Amendment prohibited states from compelling teachers to pay union dues or agency fees where their labor unions used the fees for purposes that were unrelated to collective bargaining. Compelled support of collective bargaining representatives implicated free speech, freedom of association, and freedom of religion concerns. However, some constitutional infringement on those rights was justified in the interest of peaceful labor relations. Thus, as long as the union acted to promote the cause of its membership, individual members were not free to withdraw their financial support. However, **compelled agency fees could not be used to support political views and ideological causes that were unrelated to collective bargaining issues.** *Abood v. Detroit Bd. of Educ.,* 431 U.S. 209, 97 S.Ct. 1782, 52 L.Ed.2d 261 (1977). [MI]

◆ *In order to justify agency fees, the activities for which the fees are collected must be germane to collective bargaining activity, be justified by the government's interest in labor peace (and the avoidance of free riders), and present only an insignificant burden on employee speech.*

The exclusive bargaining representative of the faculty at a state college in Michigan entered into an agency-shop arrangement with the college requiring nonunion bargaining unit employees to pay a service or agency fee equivalent to a union member's dues. Employees who objected to particular uses by the unions of their service fee brought suit under 42 U.S.C. § 1983, claiming that using the fees for purposes other than negotiating and administering the collective bargaining agreement violated their First and Fourteenth Amendment rights. A federal district court held that certain collective bargaining expenses were chargeable to the dissenting employees, the U.S. Court of Appeals affirmed and the U.S. Supreme Court granted certiorari. The Court first noted that chargeable activities must be "germane" to collective bargaining activity and be justified by the policy interest of avoiding "free riders" who benefit from union efforts without paying for union services. It then stated that **the local union could charge the objecting employees for their *pro rata* share of costs associated with chargeable activities of its state and national affiliates, even if those activities did not directly benefit the local bargaining unit**. The local could even charge the dissenters for expenses incident to preparation for a strike, which would be illegal under Michigan law. However, lobbying activities and public relations efforts were not chargeable to the objecting employees. The Court affirmed in part and reversed in part the lower courts' decisions and remanded the case. *Lehnert v. Ferris Faculty Ass'n*, 500 U.S. 507, 111 S.Ct. 1950, 114 L.Ed.2d 572 (1991). [MI]

◆ *A union's objection procedures for challenging non-members' dues were constitutional.*

Two University of Alaska professors challenged their union's procedures for calculating non-members' dues. Under the collective bargaining agreement, if they declined union membership, they had a choice of either objecting to the use of their dues for unrelated union activities (and paying a reduced agency fee) or requesting that an arbitrator determine if the non-member fee was accurate. Under the second option, the arbitrator had the option of raising the amount. A federal court ruled that the union's procedure was constitutional, and the Ninth Circuit Court of Appeals affirmed. Here, the procedures complied with the requirements set forth by the U.S. Supreme Court in *Chicago Teachers Union v. Hudson*, 475 U.S. 292 (1986). **The professors received an adequate explanation of the basis for calculating the agency fee, and they were provided with a reasonably prompt opportunity to challenge the amount of the fee before an impartial decisionmaker**. *Carlson v. United Academics-AAUP/AFT/APEA AFL-CIO*, 265 F.3d 778 (9th Cir. 2001). [AK]

◆ *An Illinois local failed to provide adequate procedural protections to nonbargaining unit members who objected to its nonrepresentational activities.*

In federal court, a group of nonbargaining unit members, employed by a university as clerical employees, filed a class action suit against the union. The nonmembers asserted that the union's fair share fee collection procedure failed to provide sufficient safeguards, thereby violating the First and Fourteenth Amendments. The union moved to dismiss the complaint. The court interpreted the union's response as a pretrial judgment motion and ruled in favor of the union. The employees appealed.

The Seventh Circuit reversed. Pursuant to the Illinois Educational Labor Relations Act (IELRA), the amount of fair share fees "can neither exceed union dues nor include any costs related to supporting candidates for political office." In *Hudson v. Chicago Teachers Union, Local No. 1*, 475 U.S. 292 (1986), the U.S. Supreme Court required a union to satisfy the following three prongs in collecting these fees: (1) the union must provide "an adequate explanation of the basis for the fee"; (2) provide the non-member with a reasonable opportunity to protest the fee amount; and (3) establish "an escrow account for the amounts in dispute." Here, the union had the university collect 100 percent of union dues from both members and nonmembers, even though the fair share fee calculated for two of the disputed years amounted to about 85 percent of full dues. When an objection was filed, the non-member fees were then held in an escrow account, which could not be accessed by the union. **The collection of fees, based on an advance reduction approach, was not as problematic as the dispute resolution procedure**. Under the IELRA, objectors were deprived of 15 percent of their funds for a year, a portion of which was not even being disputed. In addition, the fee objections had to be renewed annually. These burdens violated the *Hudson* test. *Tavernor v. Illinois Federation of Teachers*, 226 F.3d 842 (7th Cir. 2000). [IL]

◆ *In response to challenges by non-union public school and state university teachers against the union for assessing them certain agency fees, a court of appeals held that union officials' salaries were chargeable, but expenses related to a two-day strike by university faculty were not.*

Public school teachers and state university instructors sued the Massachusetts Teachers Association for charging them agency fees for activities the teachers claimed were not part of doing business as a bargaining representative. The Massachusetts Labor Relations Commission examined the MTA's expenditures for 1990–1991 to determine which expenses were chargeable to non-union members and which were not. The commission concluded that the MTA had demanded $26.77 in excess service fees from each of the non-union members.

The Massachusetts Court of Appeals largely upheld the commission's ruling, finding that unions are not required to submit evidence showing that each expense incurred for a conference or meeting is exclusively incurred in furtherance of a chargeable activity. The MTA's accounting expenses were chargeable, according to the court, except for the 14 hours the accounting staff devoted to non-chargeable activities. **The union president and vice-president's salaries were overhead and therefore chargeable in proportion to the union's overall chargeable activities**. Discussions the union had about a statewide strike to publicize the condition of public education funding were not chargeable. Expenses related to two days in 1991 when faculty at the University of Massachusetts at Amherst withheld services to protest the lack of funding for their collective bargaining agreement were also not chargeable, even though the university administration approved of and participated in the protest. Because the faculty had withheld services, the two-day action was a strike, and the expenses incidental to it were not chargeable. Nor were the costs of flyers distributed during 1991 commencement exercises at the University of Massachusetts at Boston chargeable to non-union members. Distribution of the flyers was a public relations activity not germane to the union's collective bargaining functions. However, expenses related to an article that appeared in a union magazine providing pointers on how to communicate during a strike or some other unusual event were chargeable. *Belhumeur v. Labor Relations Commission*, 432 Mass. 458, 735 N.E.2d 860 (Mass. App. 2000). [MA]

C. Collective Bargaining Agreements

◆ *A California court rejected a nurse's claim that her dismissal from a student clinic violated her due process and collective bargaining rights.*

A nurse practitioner who worked at a university clinic examined a student and determined she was 24 weeks pregnant. The student wanted to abort the pregnancy, but the nurse recommended against it, saying the pregnancy was too advanced. The nurse later urged the student to put the baby up for adoption and told her that a colleague at the clinic was interested in adopting it. A supervisor learned of the plan and admonished the nurse for unethical conduct. The student later had the baby, and the colleague took it home from the hospital. The university discharged the nurse and her grievance was denied. She then requested a hearing that was later cancelled by a union representative based on insufficient notice of witnesses and the university's refusal to allow her to issue subpoenas. A hearing was held in the nurse's absence, and the hearing officer upheld the dismissal. The nurse appealed to a state trial court, which dismissed the case. The nurse appealed.

The Court of Appeal of California found the nurse had no right to invoke arbitration. It also rejected her claims that the hearing officer was biased, and the proceedings were inherently unfair. The university's failure to provide her with a witness list seven days before the hearing did not prejudice her case. By then, the nurse had already gone through the grievance procedure and knew the identity of the witnesses. Her inability to subpoena witnesses did not render the process unfair. **Since the nurse voluntarily failed to appear for her hearing, she could not now complain it was unfair to hold it in her absence**, and the judgment was affirmed. *Nelson v. Regents of the Univ. of California*, No. D040623, 2004 WL 339340 (Cal. App. 4th Dist. 2004). [CA]

◆ *Hawaii could not enact a law eliminating state university employee rights to collectively bargain.*

A Hawaii law prohibited the state university system from negotiating over "cost items" during the 1999-2001 biennium. Because wages, hours, pensions, and other terms and conditions of employment were "cost items," public employee unions sued, seeking a declaration that the law was unconstitutional. The Hawaii Supreme Court struck down the law. Even though the state constitution gave the legislature the ultimate authority over collective bargaining "as provided by law," that authority was granted within the framework of existing **federal law that granted employees the right to bargain collectively**. Since the law would deny public employees the right to bargain collectively, it could not stand. *United Public Workers, AFSCME, Local 646, AFL-CIO v. Yogi*, 62 P.3d 189 (Haw. 2002). [HI]

◆ *A union could use a university's e-mail system to contact members where the collective bargaining agreement did not prohibit it.*

The union representing Oregon University System employees negotiated a collective bargaining agreement that allowed union officers and stewards to "have access to electronic bulletin boards under specified conditions." The union then began using e-mail to transmit information to its members' work computers. The university objected to this practice, claiming that the bargaining agreement did not allow the union to use e-mail in that way. After two arbitrators determined that the university could prohibit union officials from using the e-mail system, the Oregon Court of Appeals determined that the union's use of e-mail neither violated the terms of the bargaining agreement nor breached its duty of good faith and fair dealing. **The bargaining agreement was silent with respect to the union's use of e-mail**. Thus, there was no breach of contract and no bad faith. *Oregon Univ. System v. Oregon Public Employees Union, Local 503*, 60 P.3d 567 (Or. App. 2002). [OR]

◆ *Adjunct faculty members were allowed to join a union in New Hampshire.*

A labor association seeking to represent 147 adjunct faculty members at a New Hampshire state college petitioned for certification by the Public Employees Labor Relations Board. The university system opposed the petition, arguing that adjunct faculty are temporary employees who are excluded from bargaining because of their temporary status. A hearing officer granted the petition, allowing instructors who were currently teaching, and those who had taught two of the last three semesters, to join the union. The PELRB upheld that decision, and the adjunct faculty voted in favor of the union.

The case reached the Supreme Court of New Hampshire, which found that there is some expectation that adjunct faculty members will return annually— they are compensated for longevity. The court affirmed the PELRB's decision that **adjunct faculty members are not temporary employees**. Even though the contracts they signed did not include an expectation of continued employment, that fact did not necessarily diminish the adjunct faculty members' **reasonable expectation of continued employment**. The fact that adjunct instructors taught one-third of the college's courses indicated that they were not just "last-minute" hires. The court remanded the case to consider who was eligible for union membership. The PELRB did not provide an explanation for why only adjuncts who were currently teaching or who had taught two of the last three semesters were eligible. *In re Univ. System of New Hampshire*, 795 A.2d 840 (N.H. 2002). [NH]

◆ *The DC Circuit adopted a test for determining whether a religious institution can exempt itself from NLRB jurisdiction for purposes of collective bargaining.*

The University of Great Falls, which is operated by the Sisters of Providence (a Roman Catholic religious order) refused to recognize or bargain with the Montana Federation of Teachers. The university maintained that the NLRB lacked jurisdiction because the school was a religiously run institution, and also asserted that the Religious Freedom Restoration Act barred the NLRB from ordering it to engage in collective bargaining. The union petitioned the NLRB for relief, and the regional director examined the university's mission, courses and operation before ruling that the NLRB had jurisdiction. The NLRB upheld that determination, and the university appealed to the U.S. Court of Appeals, DC Circuit. The appellate court vacated the NLRB's decision and order. It stated that the NLRB had improperly engaged in an examination of the university's religious character.

The court adopted **a three-part test for determining whether an institution can avail itself of the exemption in *NLRB v. Catholic Bishop of Chicago*,** 440 U.S. 490 (1979) [see Chapter Four, § I.B]—where the Supreme Court held that the NLRB did not have jurisdiction over religious institutions. Under this test, an institution must: 1) provide a religious educational environment and hold itself out as such, 2) be organized by a nonprofit, and 3) be "affiliated with, or owned, operated or controlled directly or indirectly, by either a recognized religious organization or with an entity, membership of which is determined, at least in part, with reference to religion." Here, the university easily passed that test. As a result, the NLRB did not have jurisdiction, and the university did not have to bargain with the union. *University of Great Falls v. NLRB*, 278 F.3d 1335 (D.C. Cir. 2002). [MT]

◆   *Where a no-smoking policy was not included in a collective bargaining agreement, a university did not have to bargain over the policy.*

The University of Alaska's Board of Regents adopted a policy that excluded smoking from university facilities that were open to the public. It later amended the policy to prohibit smoking in motor vehicles. Prior to the adoption of the policy, the union representing certain university employees formally requested bargaining. One union member learned of the revised smoking policy but continued to smoke in the vehicle assigned to him. He was censured for smoking in the vehicle and circulated a petition signed by 30 union members asking the union to negotiate the non-smoking policy. The union presented the proposal to the university, which refused to bargain, asserting that the policy was a permissive subject for which it had no obligation to bargain. **The parties reached a collective bargaining agreement that was ratified by the union membership containing no express reference to the non-smoking policy.** The agreement contained a reservation of rights clause stating that bargaining unit members agreed to follow all university policies not specified in the agreement and reserving the right to change university policies.

The union filed an unfair labor practice against the university, asserting that the non-smoking policy was a mandatory subject of bargaining. The state labor relations agency determined that the policy was a mandatory subject of bargaining, but that the union had contractually waived it by executing the collective bargaining agreement. On appeal, the Supreme Court of Alaska observed that **because the collective bargaining agreement contained no specific reference to the non-smoking policy, the union had contractually waived its right to bargain on that issue** by agreeing to the contract. The union could also be deemed to have waived its right to bargain under the reservation of rights section of the agreement. The court affirmed the agency ruling that the union had waived bargaining on the policy by entering into the agreement. *University of Alaska v. University of Alaska Classified Employees Ass'n,* 952 P.2d 1182 (Alaska 1998). [AK]

◆   *A law requiring Massachusetts employees to take days off or to work for deferred pay violated the Contract Clause of the Constitution by substantially impairing the state's obligations under the collective bargaining agreements. Such impairment was neither reasonable nor necessary.*

In the face of a perceived fiscal crisis, **Massachusetts implemented a mandatory furlough program for almost all state employees.** Under the program, employees could take unpaid days off, work without pay and receive bonus paid vacation days after the beginning of the next fiscal year, or work without pay and receive a lump sum payment upon terminating employment with the state. The amount of mandated days off increased with the amount of compensation an employee earned. After faculty and various professional staff at several of the state's community colleges, and unions representing employees in the state college system challenged the program, the case reached the Supreme Judicial Court of Massachusetts.

The court found that **the program violated the Contract Clause of the U.S. Constitution by substantially impairing the state's obligation to pay compensation to affected employees under their collective bargaining agreements.** Further, the state was unable to show that the impairment was both reasonable and necessary to serve an important state purpose. Because the increasing fiscal deficit problems were reasonably foreseeable at the time the state entered into the collective bargaining agreements with the employees, the substantial impairment of the employees' rights under those contracts (after the contracts were signed) could not be reasonable. The court struck down the mandatory furlough program. *Massachusetts Community College Council v. Commonwealth*, 649 N.E.2d 708 (Mass. 1995). [MA]

◆ *A law allowing Hawaii to postpone employees' pay by a few days was unconstitutional.*

To remedy a budget crisis, Hawaii passed a law authorizing the state to postpone by a few days, at six different times, the dates on which state employees were to be paid. It also declared that the postponements were "not subject to negotiation" by the state employees' unions. University of Hawaii faculty members and their union sued in federal district court to stop the state from implementing the act, and the district court granted the injunction. The case then reached the Ninth Circuit Court of Appeals, which affirmed. It held that **the law violated the U.S. Constitution's Contract Clause by substantially impairing the state's obligation to honor its collective bargaining agreements with the unions**. The law not only changed the employees' pay dates, but also removed "the whole subject from the bargaining table." It could not be justified as reasonable and necessary because there were less drastic ways to reduce the state's financial obligations. *University of Hawaii Professional Assembly v. Cayetano*, 183 F.3d 1096 (9th Cir. 1999). [HI]

◆ *Florida could not renege on a contract that promised pay raises to public employees.*

During the collective bargaining process, unions representing public employees in Florida reached an impasse with the state. The legislature resolved the impasse by authorizing a 3 percent pay raise, which the unions ratified. Subsequently, state officials projected a shortfall in public revenues, causing the legislature to convene a special session and postpone the pay raises. Several months later, the legislature responded to continuing revenue shortfalls by eliminating the pay raises altogether. When the unions sued, a state trial court ruled in their favor, and the state appealed. The Supreme Court of Florida affirmed the ruling against the state. **Here, the state had a fully enforceable agreement with the unions that it could not break unless there existed no other reasonable alternative means of preserving the contract, in whole or in part.** The state could not nullify the pay raises simply because that was the most expedient solution. By appropriating public money to fund the pay raises, the state and all its branches became bound by the agreement. The court ordered the state to take the necessary steps to implement the pay raises. *Chiles v. United Faculty of Florida*, 615 So.2d 671 (Fla. 1993). [FL]

D. Arbitration

◆ *The Commonwealth Court of Pennsylvania held the right to make curriculum decisions was solely the managerial right of a university.*

A state university resolved a dispute with an employee association over its curriculum approval process in 1974. The parties' settlement agreement established a four-step course approval process, allowing the input of departments and faculty members for course proposals. While a curriculum committee had input in the process, final course approval rested with the university president. In 2000, the president included a chemical biotechnology program in the curriculum without the committee's approval. The association filed a grievance, alleging the university violated the collective bargaining agreement. After the grievance was denied, the union invoked arbitration. The arbitrator issued an award for the association, finding the 1974 agreement was a grievance settlement that became part of the collective bargaining agreement. The arbitrator held for the association, and the university appealed.

The commonwealth court explained **an arbitration award will be vacated only if it is without foundation or concerns a matter outside the collective bargaining agreement. The court held that curriculum decisions are inherently managerial matters that are not subject to collective bargaining.** The state Public Employee Relations Act (PERA) did not require public employers to collectively bargain over matters of inherent managerial policy. Under the PERA, curriculum decisions were not subject to collective bargaining. While the 1974 agreement established a procedure for making curriculum changes, it did not deprive the university president of the power to make final decisions. The court rejected the union's characterization of committee approval as a "past practice." The university established that the authority to approve curriculum changes was never included in the collective bargaining agreement. As the arbitrator erred in finding the committee had authority to approve curriculum changes, the court vacated the award. *State System of Higher Educ. v. Association of Pennsylvania State College and Univ. Facilities*, 834 A.2d 1235 (Pa. Cmwlth. 2003). [PA]

◆ *A Massachusetts employee association's decision not to invoke arbitration did not breach its duty of fair representation.*

The Massachusetts Maritime Academy employed an instructor under two one-year temporary appointment letters. He filed a grievance to protest the academy's decision denying him tenure. The Massachusetts State College Association represented academy employees and presented the case before a grievance committee. After the committee denied the grievance, the association decided not to invoke arbitration. The instructor filed a charge against the association with the state labor relations commission for unfair representation in refusing to proceed with his grievance to arbitration. The commission dismissed the charge, finding the association did not act arbitrarily.

The state appeals court affirmed the commission's decision. In reviewing the record, the court found the commission carefully reviewed the association's actions. **The association complied with its representational obligation under the terms of the collective bargaining agreement by filing the**

grievance, explaining the procedure to the instructor, and representing him before the grievance committee. The decision not to invoke arbitration was a reasonable determination based on the evidence. The temporary appointment letters undermined the instructor's claim that he was promised tenure. The commission's decision was affirmed. *Gable v. Labor Relations Comm'n*, 59 Mass. App. 1101, 793 N.E.2d 1286 (Mass. App. 2003). [MA]

◆ *An Alaska university could raise non-union salaries to redress past inequities in pay.*

The University of Alaska suspended a 3 percent salary increase for all employees due to a perceived financial crisis. A teachers' union filed a grievance, and union employees received the salary increase. Non-union employees did not get the raise. Two years later, the university commissioned a study to identify underpaid employees, and decided to award certain non-union employees a 2.6 percent salary increase. The union and six female faculty members filed another grievance, asserting that they were entitled to the 2.6 percent raise. Before that grievance was resolved, a third grievance was filed and settled, in which 26 faculty members received pay increases. The second grievance then went to arbitration, and the arbitrator found that the pay raise to non-union employees was not motivated by illegal discrimination. However, he ordered the university to perform a new compensation study and apply a 2.6 percent pay increase to correct any identified inequalities.

The case reached the Supreme Court of Alaska, which refused to uphold the arbitrator's award. **The arbitrator committed "gross error" in finding that the university violated the collective bargaining agreement where there was no illegal discrimination**. The raise was an attempt to redress past salary inequities in a fair and equitable manner; not an attempt to discriminate against women or union members. *University of Alaska v. Alaska Community Colleges' Federation of Teachers*, 64 P.3d 823 (Alaska 2003). [AK]

◆ *The arbitration provision of a union-negotiated collective bargaining agreement—under which employees supposedly waived their right to a federal forum with respect to federal discrimination claims—was not enforceable in the following case.*

A clerical employee for New York University filed a discrimination suit against the school after she was fired for not returning to work when her leave under the Family Medical Leave Act expired. She claimed that the collective bargaining agreement, which governed the terms of her employment, explicitly prohibited discrimination by her employer. The university filed a motion to stay the action because the collective bargaining agreement stipulated that all disputes under the agreement would be arbitrated. The trial court denied the university's motion to stay pending arbitration and the university appealed.

The Second Circuit affirmed. Under *Alexander v. Gardner-Denver Co.*, 415 U.S. 36 (1974), an employee who is subject to a collective bargaining arbitration clause is not precluded from bringing suit in federal court. In addition, the Supreme Court's decision in *Wright v. Universal Maritime Service Corp.*, 525 U.S. 70 (1998), stated that **employees only waive their rights under a federal statute if a collective bargaining agreement**

explicitly states that is the case. Here, the applicable agreement did not specifically state that employees waived their statutory right to bring discrimination claims in federal court. The Second Circuit ruled the arbitration clause was not "clear and unmistakable," as required by *Wright*. The fact that the agreement stated that discrimination laws were relevant—but did not explicitly state that discrimination claims must be arbitrated—demonstrated that the arbitration clause did not, under *Wright*, force the employee to waive her right to sue. *Rogers v. New York Univ.*, 220 F.3d 73 (2d Cir. 2000). [NY]

◆ *An arbitrator's decision was entitled to deference in a dispute over discovery of information.*

When a professor complained to her union that she was denied a merit compensation award based on her involvement with the union, the union filed a grievance on her behalf and requested from the university documentation regarding all merit applications and merit recommendations. The university denied the request. The grievance proceeded to arbitration, and the union filed an unfair labor practice charge against the university. During the arbitration, the union was supplied with the requested information. Ultimately, the arbitrator denied the professor's claim. The Delaware Public Employee Relations Board held the university committed an unfair labor practice by denying the request for discovery information. The Delaware Supreme Court held **the board should have deferred to the arbitrator's decision**. The collective bargaining agreement provided specific timelines under which the university had to comply with the arbitrator's requests for information, and the discovery and merit award issues were fully resolved by the arbitrator's ruling. *Delaware State Univ. Chapter of American Ass'n of Univ. Professors v. Delaware State Univ.*, 813 A.2d 1133 (Del. 2003). [DE]

V. PRIVACY RIGHTS

◆ *A North Carolina court held Congress clearly intended to abrogate sovereign immunity for federal wiretapping violations in actions against people or entities other than the U.S. government.*

A North Carolina university employee worked as a personal assistant for a department director. She learned the director had audio tape recorders and was taping the personal phone conversations of a coworker. When the employee advised the director she knew about the recordings, he stated her conversations were not being taped. The director created a standard operating procedure for downloading recordings of phone calls that permitted access to a support technician and telecommunications supervisor. He later installed computer software that allowed him to eavesdrop on all department employee telephone conversations. The employee sued the director, other university officials and the university in a state court for violating federal wiretapping laws.

The court denied motions for pretrial judgment by the university and officials, and they appealed to the Court of Appeals of North Carolina. **The court held a state university and its officials are entitled to sovereign immunity in state court actions for federal law violations if Congress does**

not clearly expresses the intent to disallow immunity. Congress had clearly stated the intent to abrogate sovereign immunity for federal wiretapping law violations in 18 U.S.C. § 2520(a). **The Electronic Communications Privacy Act of 1986 and the USA Patriot Act of 2001 broadened the wiretapping law to allow recovery against a person or entity other than the U.S. government**. The trial court had properly denied the director and university's claims to immunity, and the appeals court affirmed the judgment. *Huber v. North Carolina State Univ.*, 594 S.E.2d 402 (N.C. App. 2004). [NC]

◆ *The private consideration of applicants for a university president violated the Minnesota Open Meetings Law and Government Data Practices Act.*

The University of Minnesota Board of Regents searched for a new president for the university. Some applicants requested anonymity, and the board voted to screen them privately. The board denied information requests by media organizations about unsuccessful candidates. The organizations sued the board in the state court system for an order forcing disclosure of the information, and enjoining the university from holding closed meetings. The court entered summary judgment for the media, and the board appealed.

The state court of appeals noted that **the government data privacy act made public all personnel data on current and former applicants for employment by a statewide agency**. The names of applicants were considered "private data," except for finalists. Since the university was a statewide agency, and because the candidates were deemed "finalists," the court held the data practices act applied to procedures for selecting a university president. The only exception to the open meetings law applied to disciplinary proceedings, and did not apply in this case. Accordingly, the court affirmed the decision to grant the media organizations' motion. *Star Tribune Co. v. University of Minnesota*, 667 N.W.2d 447 (Minn. App. 2003). [MN]

◆ *Statutory colleges operated by a private university had to comply with freedom of information requests.*

A New York citizen filed Freedom of Information Law requests on two statutory colleges that were technically part of the State University of New York system, but that were operated by Cornell University, a private institution. The colleges refused to disclose the information sought (on a possible agricultural technology park, and research on genetically modified organisms), and an article 78 proceeding ensued, where the colleges were ordered to comply with the FOIL request. The New York Supreme Court, Appellate Division, affirmed. Even though the statutory colleges were operated by a private university, the legislature had authorized the dissemination of such information by Cornell, and **the requested information concerned a public interest**. Accordingly, the colleges had to release the requested information. *Alderson v. New York State College of Agriculture*, 749 N.Y.S.2d 581 (A.D. 3d Dept. 2002). [NY]

◆ *While an Indiana university had no privacy rights, its administrators did.*

A professor at the University of Evansville was fired. He then created a Web site and e-mail addresses incorporating the letters "UE," a common abbreviation for the school's name, as well as portions of the names of the university president, vice president for academic affairs and dean of the college of arts and sciences. He sent e-mail messages that appeared to originate from those individuals, nominating them for positions at other schools, and placed articles on his Web site alleging wrongdoing by the president and other university employees. The university and the three administrators sued him for invasion of privacy, and a trial court granted a permanent injunction preventing the former professor from continuing that activity. The Supreme Court of Indiana held that **the university, as a corporate entity, had no right of privacy under state law**. However, the administrators did have such rights, and the court largely upheld the injunction with respect to them. He could continue to send in nominations under his own name; he just could not do so where he was creating the appearance that they originated elsewhere. *Felsher v. University of Evansville*, 755 N.E.2d 589 (Ind. 2001). [IN]

◆ *A teacher and a professor were held not to have violated the Electronic Communications Privacy Act in the following case.*

A private Delaware college employed a computer programmer who alleged the college president often mistakenly printed out e-mail messages in the office where the programmer worked, and that he would either return them to the president's assistant, or place them in a folder beside the printer. After the programmer was discharged, he told a paralegal teacher that the college was foolish to fire him, as he had "seen things" on the computer screens. He mentioned he had seen an e-mail relating to an English professor's breach of contract lawsuit against the college. The teacher then called the English professor and recounted the conversation she had with the programmer. Neither the paralegal teacher nor the professor saw any e-mail until a lawsuit was filed against them and the programmer by the college. The college sued the teacher and professor for violations of the federal Electronic Communications Privacy Act (ECPA) and state law. They moved for dismissal.

The court held the ECPA prohibits people from attempting, intentionally intercepting, or procuring another to intercept any electronic communication. **A reasonable jury could not conclude that the teacher or professor took affirmative steps to intercept or access the president's e-mail**, because there was no evidence that they possessed the capability to take those steps or join forces with someone who did. Title I also prohibits any person from using or disclosing to any other person the contents of any electronic communication while knowing or having reason to know that the information was obtained through the illegal interception of an electronic communication. The court held that there was insufficient evidence to conclude that the teacher and professor should have known that the programmer intercepted the e-mail in violation of the ECPA. Also, the college had not shown that the programmer had acquired the e-mails while they were being transmitted. He could have merely seen them on the screen. This would not violate the ECPA. Fact issues precluded pretrial judgment with respect to the programmer. However, the court granted the teacher's and professor's motions for pretrial judgment. *Wesley College v. Pitts*, 974 F.Supp. 375 (D. Del. 1997). [DE]

◆ *A coach was not liable to a former player for defamation or contract interference where there was no showing of damages.*

The head basketball coach and women's athletic director at the University of Wisconsin-Madison accused a standout women's player of forming an inappropriate relationship with an assistant coach. The head coach called a team meeting to announce the suspension of the assistant coach, and when the player interrupted the meeting, the head coach stated that she was a "disgrace" to the team and university. The player resigned from the team. She later agreed to share an apartment with another player for the following year. **The head coach discouraged the player from living with the former teammate, and the former player filed a lawsuit against the head coach** in a Wisconsin trial court for defamation, invasion of privacy, tortious interference with the apartment sharing agreement, and intentional infliction of emotional distress. The court granted the coach's pretrial judgment motion for the defamation and contract interference claim. Following a jury trial, the court entered judgment for the coach on the remaining claims. The former player appealed dismissal of the defamation and contract interference claims to the Court of Appeals of Wisconsin. **The court agreed with the trial court's decision, finding no evidence of special damages that might justify the defamation claim. There also was no showing of an inability to locate another roommate.** Because there was no showing of extreme emotional distress, the trial court had properly dismissed the claims against the coach. *Bauer v. Murphy*, 530 N.W.2d 1 (Wis. App. 1995). [WI]

VI. OVERTIME AND WAGE DISPUTES

The payment of wages is generally covered by either the Fair Labor Standards Act or a comparable state law.

◆ *A California trade school qualified as an institution of higher learning, and its instructors were professionals who did not qualify for overtime pay.*

The school received state accreditation and became a degree-granting institution in 2002. Its instructors held certificates of authorization for service under the Education Code. The state division of labor standards enforcement notified the school its instructors were not exempt from overtime pay under an administrative wage order. The school sought a declaration that its instructors were exempt from overtime pay as professional employees. A state trial court agreed, and held the instructors were exempt from the overtime wage order. The state court of appeal held the school qualified as a "college." It complied with statutory requirements to obtain accreditation. **The "teaching exception" was not limited to institutions granting bachelor's or higher degrees.** The division relied on outdated records and evidence in arguing trade schools were not exempt as not meeting the definition of "higher learning." Instead, the boundaries of California's education system had expanded to include a much broader category of institutions. **Since the professional exemption was not limited to instructors at institutions granting baccalaureate degrees or higher, the school's instructors were entitled to the professional exception,** and the court affirmed the judgment. *California School of Culinary Arts v. Lujan*, 112 Cal.App.4th 16, 4 Cal.Rptr.3d 785 (Cal. App. 2d Dist. 2003). [CA]

◆ *A New York court held that a fee required by medical schools from physicians as a condition of employment violated state Education Law.*

Ophthalmologists who worked as full-time assistant professors at Columbia University wanted to continue practicing ophthalmology and remain on the faculty. In exchange for allowing them to change their appointments to part-time, Columbia requested that they pay a 10 percent "Dean's Tax" on all their practice income. When they refused, their appointments were terminated. The doctors sued Columbia in a state trial court, which held in their favor. A state appellate division court held that the **payment of the "Dean's Tax" as a condition of employment constituted illegal fee-splitting**. Because the doctors were no longer employees, and because Columbia was no longer providing them with benefits, facilities or malpractice insurance, the request was a violation of law. The court directed Columbia to review the applications for part-time appointments and affirmed the judgment. *Odrich v. Trustees of Columbia Univ.*, 764 N.Y.S.2d 448 (A.D. 1st Dept. 2003). [NY]

◆ *Washington community college instructors were not entitled to overtime wages.*

Part-time instructors from five community colleges in Washington brought a lawsuit alleging that the colleges violated the state's Minimum Wage Act by failing to compensate them for overtime work. Their wages were determined by multiplying their classroom hours by a negotiated hourly rate that included payment for time spent on course preparation, grading and office hours. However, they asserted that they were not exempt professional employees paid on a salary basis because the colleges docked their pay for time missed after all their accrued sick and annual leave was exhausted. The case reached the Washington Supreme Court, which ruled against them. It noted that as long as **their predetermined wages were not subject to reduction because of variations in the quality or quantity of work performed**, they still could be considered salary basis employees. Under U.S. Department of Labor regulations adopted by the court, deductions for missed time after accrued sick and annual leave expire do not alter an employee's professional status. *Clawson v. Grays Harbor College Dist. No. 2*, 61 P.3d 1130 (Wash. 2003). [WA]

◆ *A teacher who also worked for the university as a nurse was entitled to an accounting over discrepancies in her pay.*

As part of her contract, a teacher at a Mississippi nursing school was required to work at a school-operated clinic. Although she would earn more income by doing so, she also had to contribute half of any earnings over $10,000 to the clinic. In practice, the clinic held her earnings until the end of the year, then paid her her share. The agreement between the parties specified that all disputes were to be arbitrated. When the teacher noticed that she received only $767 one year, while the clinic kept $6,000, she requested an explanation and an accounting. The dean refused the request and then fired the teacher when she refused to continue working at the clinic. She filed a petition for an accounting with the Mississippi Chancery Court, and the university sought to compel arbitration. The court held that **the teacher was entitled to an accounting** and that the university waived its right to demand arbitration. On appeal, the Mississippi Supreme Court ruled that the university did not waive its right to demand arbitration by delaying its demand. However, the teacher was entitled to an accounting, which was not subject to arbitration. *University Nursing Associates PLLC v. Phillips*, 842 So.2d 1270 (Miss. 2003). [MS]

◆ *A coach obtained over $135,000 for fraud and FLSA violations after the athletic director who hired him refused to pay him.*

The athletic director at an Illinois community college hired a basketball coach in March 1999 and promised him a teaching position in physical education for the following fall. The coach began his duties right away, but was not paid. In August, he filled out paperwork for the teaching position. He also made informal complaints to the athletic director, then filed a formal complaint regarding the payment of wages. After the athletic director told him he would not be paid for the work he had done the previous seven months, he sued under the Fair Labor Standards Act. A jury awarded him $10,562 on that claim, as well as $52,526 in compensatory damages for the athletic director's fraud, and $75,000 in punitive damages. The district court judge reversed the fraud claim, but the Seventh Circuit Court of Appeals reversed the district court judge. It found sufficient evidence to support the jury's determination that **the coach had justifiably relied on the athletic director's misrepresentations to his detriment**. The award in favor of the coach was reinstated. *Hefferman v. Board of Trustees of Illinois Community College Dist. 508*, 310 F.3d 522 (7th Cir. 2002). [IL]

◆ *A former university employee could sue two officials in their individual capacities for retaliating against her under the FLSA.*

A Colorado university employee retired after almost 30 years, requesting payment for 224 hours of overtime. The university paid her $5,673 but later determined that she was an exempt employee under the FLSA and that it had overpaid her by $5,120. It ordered her to return the money, but her former department chairman instead suggested that she be allowed to work off the amount through a temporary position. However, when she could not find a position, she learned that a dean and assistant dean had allegedly told employees not to hire her because she was dishonest and had broken the law. She sued the dean and assistant dean for retaliating against her for the exercise of her FLSA rights. The case reached the Supreme Court of Colorado, which held that **the dean and assistant dean were not entitled to sovereign immunity because they were being sued in their individual capacities**. So even if the state might indemnify them for defending themselves in the lawsuit against them, they were not entitled to immunity. Next, the court addressed the notice requirements of the Colorado Governmental Immunity Act, which the employee admittedly failed to meet. The court stated that the FLSA preempted the notice requirements of the CGIA such that the employee could continue her lawsuit. *Middleton v. Hartman*, 45 P.3d 721 (Colo. 2002). [CO]

◆ *Probationary campus police officers were not entitled to overtime for attending EMT classes.*

A Massachusetts university hired four campus police officers as probationary employees. As a condition of employment, the officers were required to obtain and retain certification as emergency medical technicians within one year of their hire date. The four officers took the EMT course at the university and completed the course. Although they were not paid for attending EMT classes after work, they were compensated when EMT classes occurred during their regular working hours. They sued the university under the FLSA, seeking overtime pay for time spent working toward their EMT certification. A federal court ruled in their favor, but the First Circuit reversed. It noted that the Portal-to-Portal Act of 1947 precluded liability. **The Portal-to-Portal Act permits an employer to avoid paying an employee for activities that are "preliminary or postliminary" to the principal activities the employee is engaged to perform.** Here, that condition was satisfied because the officers were attending the EMT classes during their probationary period, and they did not perform any EMT-related work until after obtaining certification. Thus, they could be characterized as students during their probationary period for purposes of avoiding overtime compensation. *Bienkowski v. Northeastern Univ.*, 285 F.3d 138 (1st Cir. 2002). [MA]

VII. LEAVES OF ABSENCE

The Family and Medical Leave Act of 1993 (FMLA), 29 U.S.C. §§ 2601–2654, makes available to eligible employees up to 12 weeks of unpaid leave per year: 1) because of the birth of a son or daughter of the employee and in order to care for such son or daughter; 2) because of the placement of a son or daughter with the employee for adoption or foster care; 3) in order to care for the spouse, or a son, daughter, or parent, of the employee, if such spouse, son, daughter or parent has a serious health condition; or 4) because of a serious health condition that makes the employee unable to perform the functions of the position of such employee. 29 U.S.C. § 2612.

The FMLA exempts small businesses and limits coverage of private employers to those engaged in commerce or in activities affecting commerce and who employ 50 or more employees for each working day during each of 20 or more calendar workweeks in the current or preceding calendar year. 29 U.S.C. § 2611. To be eligible for leave, an employee must have been employed by the covered employer for at least 12 months, and must have worked at least 1,250 hours during the 12 month period preceding the commencement of the leave. 29 U.S.C. § 2611.

If the employer provides paid leave for which the employee is eligible, the employee may elect, or the employer may require the employee, to substitute the paid leave for any part of the 12 weeks of leave to which the employee is entitled under the act. 29 U.S.C. § 2612. When the need for leave is foreseeable, the employee must provide reasonable prior notice (generally, at least 30 days for birth or placement of a child, and at least 30 days for planned medical treatment, unless the employee does not have 30 days in which to provide notice). 29 U.S.C. § 2612. The employee also must make efforts to schedule the leave so as not to unduly disrupt the employer's operations. Further, where spouses are employed by the same employer, they can be limited to a total of 12 weeks of leave for the birth or adoption of a child or for the care of a sick parent. 29 U.S.C. § 2612.

An employer may require medical certification to support a claim for leave for an employee's own serious health condition or to care for a seriously ill child, spouse or parent. If the certification is for the employee's health condition, it must contain a statement that the employee is unable to perform the functions of his or her position. 29 U.S.C. § 2613. If the certification is for a child, spouse or parent, it must include an estimate of the amount of time the employee is needed to care for the family member.

Further, an employer may require, at its own expense, a second opinion. 29 U.S.C. § 2613. An employer also may require an employee on leave to report periodically to the employer on his or her leave status and intention to return to work. 29 U.S.C. § 2614. The regulations implementing the FMLA [29 CFR Part 825] define "serious health condition" to include treatment two or more times by a health care provider, and a period of absence to receive multiple treatments "for a condition that would likely result in a period of incapacity of more than three consecutive calendar days in the absence of medical intervention or treatment." 29 CFR § 825.114.

An employee needing leave for a serious health condition may, if medically necessary, take leave intermittently or on a reduced leave schedule that reduces the employee's usual number of hours per workweek or per workday. However, if an employee requests leave on such a basis, the employer may require the employee to transfer temporarily to an alternative position that better accommodates the intermittent or reduced leave, provided that the position has equivalent pay and benefits. 29 U.S.C. § 2613.

During leave, any pre-existing health benefits provided to the employee by the employer must be maintained. However, **the employer is under no obligation to allow the employee to accrue seniority or other employment benefits during the leave period**. 29 U.S.C. § 2614. Upon return from leave, the employee must be restored to the same or an equivalent position. 29 U.S.C. § 2614. However, the statute contains an exemption for certain highly compensated employees, allowing an employer to deny restoration if: 1) such denial is necessary to prevent substantial and grievous economic injury to the operations of the employer, 2) the employer notifies the employee of its intent to deny restoration on such basis at the time the employer determines that such injury would occur; and 3) in any case in which the leave has commenced, the employee elects not to return to employment after receiving such notice. 29 U.S.C. § 2614.

It is unlawful for an employer to interfere with, restrain, or deny the exercise of or the attempt to exercise, any right provided under the FMLA. 29 U.S.C. § 2615. It is also unlawful for an employer to discharge or in any other matter discriminate against any individual for opposing a practice made unlawful under the act, or for participating in any inquiry or proceeding relating to rights established under the act. 29 U.S.C. § 2615.

Rights established under the FMLA are enforceable through civil actions. An employer who violates § 2615 will be liable for money damages resulting from the violation, and an additional amount equal to the actual damages as liquidated damages. The employer also may be required to provide equitable relief, including employment, reinstatement or promotion. 29 U.S.C. § 2617. Where an employer can prove to the satisfaction of the court that it acted in good faith and had reasonable grounds to believe that its acts or omissions were not a violation, the court may, in its discretion, limit the employer's damages liability to the actual damages and refuse to award liquidated damages. 29 U.S.C. § 2617. The prevailing plaintiff in an action under the FMLA also is entitled to reasonable attorney's fees, expert witness fees, and other costs of the action.

Actions brought under the FMLA must be brought not later than two years after the date of the last event constituting the alleged violation for which the action is brought, or within the last three years of the last event if the violation is wilful. 29 U.S.C. § 2617. An employee's right to bring a civil action terminates if the Secretary of Labor files an action seeking relief with respect to that employee. 29 U.S.C. § 2617.

The FMLA sets forth special rules for employees of local educational agencies who are employed principally in an instructional capacity. These rules apply to the scheduling of intermittent leave based on planned medical treatment, and leave beginning or ending during the five-week period prior to the end of an academic term. 29 U.S.C. § 2618.

The FMLA further provides that it does not modify or affect any federal or state law prohibiting discrimination on the basis of race, religion, color, national origin, sex, age or disability. 29 U.S.C. § 2651. It also states that nothing in the act shall be construed to supersede any provision of any state or local law that provides greater family or medical leave rights than the rights established under the FMLA or any amendment to it. 29 U.S.C. § 2651. Further, **nothing in the FMLA is to be construed to diminish the obligation of an employer to comply with any collective bargaining agreement or any employment benefit plan or program that provides greater family or medical leave rights to employees than the rights established under the FMLA**. 29 U.S.C. § 2652. Nor shall rights established for employees under the FMLA be diminished by any collective bargaining agreement or by any employment benefit plan or program. 29 U.S.C. § 2652.

◆ *A federal court held a New York university did not violate an employee's FMLA rights by terminating her position while she was on FMLA leave.*

A research nurse was placed on medical leave for being intoxicated at work. The university did not inform her it considered her leave to be under the FMLA. It sent the nurse a letter, stating the conditions of her leave and its concern with her performance. The university agreed to take no adverse action if she confirmed her admittance into a treatment program. The letter stated the university would consider the time she spent receiving treatment to be medical leave, and it continued to pay her for 12 weeks. The nurse applied for a professional assistance program, but the treatment center later reported she had relapsed. Doctors did not recommend she return to work, and the university discharged the nurse for failing to submit the reports required by the letter.

The nurse sued the university in a federal district court, alleging it interfered with her FMLA rights by firing her while she was on medical leave. She said the university violated the FMLA by not informing her she was being placed on FMLA leave, requiring the progress reports, and discharging her. The court held the nurse did not prove she was denied any FMLA benefits. The university granted her 12 weeks of paid leave, and **was not obligated to offer her a position after she took leave. The nurse was incapable of performing the job's essential functions. The university could discharge her while she was on leave, as long as it did not do so because she took FMLA leave**. The court dismissed the case. *Geromano v. Columbia Univ.*, 322 F.Supp.2d 420 (S.D.N.Y. 2004). [NY]

◆ *New York University (NYU) Law School did not terminate a security guard in violation of the FMLA.*

The guard's attendance was inconsistent, and while he received warnings for tardiness and absenteeism, no disciplinary action was taken. After an accident, the guard was placed on leave and received workers' compensation benefits for a back injury. His supervisor requested additional medical documentation to support the need for extended leave. The guard eventually returned to work, but later claimed he re-injured his back. He stopped reporting to work and received workers' compensation benefits. When his workers' compensation benefits were cut off, he applied for leave under the FMLA. The guard submitted an incomplete FMLA form request. NYU rejected the medical information supplied by his chiropractor and scheduled another physical examination. After the examination, the guard did not return to work.

NYU officials terminated the guard's employment, and an arbitrator refused to overturn the action. He sued NYU and his supervisor in a federal district court for wrongful termination in violation of the FMLA. The court stated **the FMLA has a two-year statute of limitations that may be extended to three years for a "willful" violation of the statute.** There was no evidence that NYU or its officials interfered with the guard's FMLA application. NYU provided him an FMLA kit and other assistance. Since he did not establish a "willful" violation by NYU, the three-year statute of limitations did not apply. **NYU's failure to return the guard to his former position was not an FMLA violation in any event, because he was not on FMLA leave at the time and was returned to his original position**. The court awarded NYU summary judgment. *Porter v. New York Univ. School of Law*, No. 99 Civ. 4693 (TPG), 2003 WL 22004841 (S.D.N.Y. 2003). [NY]

◆ *An employee failed to show that she was discriminated against for requesting maternity leave.*

A university employee held a position classified as half-faculty/half-staff. When she requested maternity leave, she claimed that the university began to retaliate against her by requiring her to teach summer school and by reducing her accrued maternity leave. When she sued for discrimination under state law, the case reached the Minnesota Court of Appeals. The court held that even though the employee had presented a *prima facie* case, **the university had set forth a legitimate, nondiscriminatory reason for its adverse actions**. First, the employee had wrongly accrued maternity leave at the full-staff rate. Second, she was given the summer school assignment based on her past summer teaching experience. Because she could not show that the university's reasons for its actions were actually a pretext for discrimination, she could not succeed on her claim against it. *Cierzan v. Hamline Univ.*, 2002 WL 31553931 (Minn. App. 11/19/01). [MN]

◆ *A college employee could be fired for failing to return to work after her FMLA leave expired.*

A Morehouse College administrative assistant sustained injuries in a car accident and took leave under the FMLA and the college's similar family and medical leave policy. After returning to work, she notified the college that she was pregnant. A few months later, the college placed her on administrative leave while it investigated the office where she worked. It continued to pay her salary as well as full benefits. When the investigation ended, the office's director was fired for failing to follow directions and for running another business out of the office. However, because the assistant was due to give birth in a few weeks, the college kept her on administrative leave. After the birth of her child, the assistant failed to comply with the college's FMLA notification requirements. When she still had not returned to work five months after the birth of her child, she was fired for job abandonment. She sued the college under the FMLA for failing to give her timely notice of when her FMLA leave started and for refusing to allow her to select the starting date of her FMLA leave. She wanted the leave to start two months after the child was born so that the leave still would be under way at the time she was fired. A Georgia federal court ruled in favor of the college, finding that the FMLA leave started on the birth of her child even though she was not officially notified that the administrative leave had ended until after that time. Also, **the college could run her paid leave concurrently with her FMLA leave and require her to return to work after 12 weeks**. *Johnson v. Morehouse College*, 199 F.Supp.2d 1345 (N.D. Ga. 2002). [GA]

◆ *A professor on paid approved leave did not have to return monies paid for doing a seminar on the university's behalf.*

An Ohio university professor took an approved and paid faculty improvement leave, during which he participated in three seminars on the university's behalf. He was paid $4,230 for doing the seminars, but the university asked him to return the money on the grounds that state law prohibited him from receiving additional money while on paid faculty improvement leave. When the professor refused to pay the money to the university, a lawsuit ensued. A trial court ruled in favor the professor, and the Ohio Court of Appeals affirmed. Here, **the statute at issue did not require the professor to repay the seminar money because that money was not part of his salary**. The statute only provided that he could not be paid more than he would have been paid for performing his regular duties during the leave. Further, the professor had received payment for his involvement in the seminars throughout his 20-year tenure at the university and that money was not designated as salary. *University of Akron v. Sellers*, 2002 WL 219568 (Ohio App. 2/13/02). [OH]

CHAPTER SIX

Employment Discrimination

I. RACE AND NATIONAL ORIGIN DISCRIMINATION

Title VII of the Civil Rights Act of 1964, later amended in 1991, 42 U.S.C. § 2000e et seq., prohibits discrimination in employment based upon race, color, sex, religion or national origin. It applies to any institution, affecting commerce, which has 15 or more employees. Title VII exempts employment decisions based on religion, sex or national origin where these characteristics are "bona fide occupational qualifications reasonably necessary to the operations of that particular business or enterprise." The First Amendment also may preclude consideration of such claims against religious schools. However, no such exemptions exist for race-based discrimination. Other federal statutes cover discrimination based upon age and disability.

The prohibition against race and national origin discrimination in employment extends to all "terms or conditions of employment," including hiring and firing decisions, promotions, salary, seniority, benefits, and work assignments. Title VII applies to both public and private institutions.

A. Race Discrimination

◆ *The Sixth Circuit held an Ohio university's stated reasons for not renewing the contract of an African-American professor may have been pretextual.*

An African-American professor's contract was not renewed at the end of an academic year. She contacted the university's vice provost, who promised to investigate the matter. He allegedly remarked that the college dean "was trying to get rid of the black professors," and that "I don't know what's going on, they're a bunch of racists over there." The professor sued the university in a federal district court, claiming it discharged her based on her race in violation of Title VII and state law. The university moved for summary judgment, arguing she failed to present either direct or circumstantial evidence of race discrimination. The district court agreed and granted the motion.

The Sixth Circuit focused on the vice provost's comments, which suggested that the university's action was not actually motivated by the reasons given. The district court had improperly discounted them as "too isolated" to show pretext. The vice provost oversaw the affirmative action process at the university and was required to ensure that deans complied with affirmative action requirements. Although he was not directly involved in the decision-making process, his role was not "too isolated" to justify summary judgment. The professor was entitled to a further opportunity to show the university did not renew her contract for the reasons it stated. The entry of summary judgment for the university was reversed, and the case was remanded for additional proceedings on the issue of pretext. *Carter v. University of Toledo*, 349 F.3d 269 (6th Cir. 2003). [OH]

◆ *An African-American assistant chancellor identified sufficient evidence of discrimination to avoid pretrial dismissal of her lawsuit.*

The assistant chancellor received merit increases and a contract extension during her first years with a Wisconsin university. She later criticized a university newsletter as offensive for its depiction of minorities, and advocated for a female basketball coach who was attempting to negotiate scheduling accommodations due to difficulties with her pregnancy. When the university's athletic director resisted making the accommodations, the assistant chancellor reminded him he had accommodated a male coach. She also informed the chancellor that the female coach might file a Title IX complaint. The assistant chancellor's contract was not renewed, allegedly because of staff complaints accusing her of micro-managing her office. She sued the university and officials in a federal district court for race and gender discrimination and for retaliating against her because she exercised her First Amendment rights.

The court found there were no substantial negative performance issues leading up to the decision not to renew the assistant chancellor's contract. There was sufficient evidence she was meeting expectations and the reasons for not renewing her contract were suspect to avoid pretrial dismissal of her race and sex discrimination claims. The remarks about the campus newsletter and coach's pregnancy accommodations constituted protected speech. **The court held that speech about compliance with the law is a matter of public concern. As there was evidence the university had retaliated against the assistant chancellor and stated false reasons for not renewing her contract, the court denied summary judgment** to the university and officials. *Walker v. Board of Regents of Univ. of Wisconsin*, 300 F.Supp.2d 836 (W.D. Wis. 2004). [WI]

◆ *The Eleventh Circuit held a student's poor performance during a residency program, and not his race, led to his dismissal from the program.*

The student was a native of the Netherland Antilles, and he was in a five-year surgical residency program at the University of South Florida. The department chair notified him he would have to repeat his fourth year due to his poor score on the national ABSITE examination. Eventually, the university allowed him to contract as a fourth-year resident while performing fifth-year work. It would review his performance after six months and promote him if his work was acceptable. However, the university dismissed the student for not attending conferences, low ABSITE scores and performance problems.

The student sued the university in a federal district court for breach of contract and race discrimination in violation of Title VII. The court held for the university. He appealed to the Eleventh Circuit. The court held the university was entitled to Eleventh Amendment immunity for the contract claim, as it did not clearly consent to being sued in federal court. **The student failed to show employment discrimination under Title VII, because he did not show similarly-situated surgical residents were treated more favorably. He had significant performance problems including poor patient care and low ABSITE scores.** Accordingly, the court affirmed the judgment. *Maynard v. Board of Regents of Div. of Univ., Florida Dep't of Educ.*, 342 F.3d 1281 (11th Cir. 2003). [FL]

◆ *No discrimination occurred where a black security guard received a 75 percent tuition break while a white employee received a 100 percent deduction.*

A black security guard at the Twin Cities campus of a private university in Minnesota enrolled in classes at the campus and received a 75 percent tuition discount even though tuition remission was not normally offered to employees at that campus, and despite the fact that the university determined it would not benefit from his degree. He also was allowed to attend class while on duty and was compensated for his time in class. Later, the guard learned that a white administrative assistant at the campus was granted 100 percent tuition remission for classes taken outside her work hours because the university determined that her receipt of a bachelor's degree would benefit the university.

After the guard complained, his duties and hours were briefly changed, and he was subjected to derogatory comments by several co-workers. He sued the university under Title VII for race discrimination and retaliation, but a federal court ruled against him. The Eighth Circuit affirmed, noting that **the guard failed to show he was treated less favorably than similarly situated white employees**. Also, the brief change to his hours and duties did not amount to an adverse employment action, and the stray comments were made by non-decision-makers. *Saulsberry v. St. Mary's Univ. of Minnesota*, 318 F.3d 862 (8th Cir. 2003). [MN]

◆ *A white police officer could sue a college for race discrimination when it promoted three black candidates over him.*

An Ohio community college hired a white male for a part-time police officer position. He applied for three full-time officer positions and, though qualified and recommended by the Selection Advisory Committee, was passed over in each case for an African-American candidate. He sued the college for reverse discrimination. A federal court granted pretrial judgment to the college, finding that he failed to show background circumstances supporting a suspicion that the college discriminated against him. The Sixth Circuit Court of Appeals reversed, finding issues of fact over whether the head of security, who was black, discriminated against him. **He had presented evidence that he was substantially more qualified than the candidates who were ultimately promoted**, and a jury would have to decide whether he was entitled to relief. *Zambetti v. Cuyahoga Community College*, 314 F.3d 249 (6th Cir. 2002). [OH]

◆ *A black applicant could not show that discrimination was the real reason a university refused to hire him for a coaching position.*

A university placed an ad for a football coach, including among the requirements that the applicant have successful college coaching experience. A black semi-professional football coach applied for the job but was not interviewed because he had no prior college coaching experience. He sued the university under Titles VI and VII of the Civil Rights Act, and under 42 U.S.C. § 1981. A Connecticut federal court ruled against him, accepting the university's argument that **prior successful college coaching was a legitimate nondiscriminatory requirement for the job**. It was essential to ensure the adequate administration of the football team, as well as compliance with applicable NCAA rules and the recruiting process. Not only was there no direct evidence of discrimination, there also was insufficient statistical evidence that the university's requirement had a disparate impact on black coaches. *Jackson v. University of New Haven*, 228 F.Supp.2d 156 (D. Conn. 2002). [CT]

◆ *A state university could be sued under Title VII because of states' history of discrimination against women and minorities.*

An Illinois state university fired an assistant microbiology professor, who challenged her termination administratively and lost. She then sued the university under Title VII for race, gender and national origin discrimination, and also asserted a 42 U.S.C. § 1983 claim for equal protection violations. The university sought to dismiss the lawsuit, claiming Eleventh Amendment immunity under Title VII and that the persons sued under § 1983 were not "persons" under the statute. A federal court rejected the university's claims, and the Seventh Circuit affirmed. Acknowledging Supreme Court rulings that states have immunity to some age and disability discrimination lawsuits, the court noted that **states had a history of discrimination on the basis of race, gender and national origin, justifying the sweeping nature of Title VII.** Thus, Title VII passed the "congruence and proportionality" test and validly eliminated states' sovereign immunity. The court also allowed the § 1983 claim to proceed for injunctive relief only. *Nanda v. Board of Trustees of Univ. of Illinois*, 303 F.3d 817 (7th Cir. 2002). [IL]

◆ *A university president may have violated Title VII by adjusting salaries for female and minority faculty on the basis of flawed statistical evidence.*

An Arizona university, after conducting an investigation, determined that hiring and salary disparities existed with respect to female and minority faculty. The university's president increased salaries for female and minority faculty members whose salaries fell below the predicted salaries of similarly situated white males. Subsequently, an outside study concluded that the methodology employed in the investigation was flawed and that the statistical disparity was not significant enough to show gender or minority bias. A number of white male professors then sued the president under Title VII and 42 U.S.C. §§ 1981 and 1983 for violating their equal protection rights.

A federal court ruled for the president, but the Ninth Circuit reversed in part. It upheld the grant of qualified immunity on the §§ 1981 and 1983 claims, finding that even though **the president violated equal protection rights by adjusting salaries on the basis of race and gender without a compelling reason for doing so,** he did not understand that he was violating those rights at the time. However, with respect to the Title VII claims, the court found an issue of fact as to whether the salary increases had been necessary to eliminate a "manifest imbalance." This issue had to be litigated. *Rudebusch v. Hughes*, 313 F.3d 506 (9th Cir. 2002). [AZ]

◆ *An employee failed to prove that the denial of a promotion was discriminatory.*

The director of minority student affairs at an Ohio university had a Ph.D. in counseling psychology and also was a licensed psychologist. When the university embarked on a cost-saving program to reduce its deficit, it eliminated and restructured a number of positions. It also created two new jobs, which it filled without following established hiring procedures. The director complained about the appointments as being violative of the university's affirmative action plan, and the university rescinded the appointments, reopening the hiring process. Nevertheless, the director did not get the job she sought. She sued the university under Title VII for race discrimination, but a federal court ruled against her. Even though she was a member of a protected class, was qualified for the position, and was subjected to an adverse action by being denied the promotion, **she could not prove that a less-qualified candidate was selected in her stead**. The university clearly spelled out its reasons for choosing the white candidate, indicating that it had selected the best-qualified applicant. *Ogletree v. Ohio Wesleyan Univ.*, 2002 WL 31409367 (S.D. Ohio 10/18/02). [OH]

◆ *Transfers of two employees to lateral positions could not be deemed race discrimination.*

Triton College employed a black woman as an associate vice president of affirmative action and human resources until she complained of stress. The college then reorganized the department she worked for and created a new position for her. She perceived the new position to be a demotion and, after a two-month leave for medical reasons, resigned without responding to the college's offer of the job. The college also employed a black computer systems specialist in its information systems department until a reorganization forced the employee's transfer to an audio-visual equipment assistant position with no reduction in pay or benefits. He also took a medical leave for six months, then resigned without responding to the college's offer.

The employees filed race discrimination charges with the EEOC, then sued the college under Title VII in an Illinois federal court. The court held for the college, and the Seventh Circuit affirmed. **Neither employee suffered an adverse employment action.** The first employee was transferred to a lateral position based on her complaints about stress, and the second employee did not suffer an adverse employment action because he did not lose any compensation or benefits. Also, neither employee could show that other similarly situated employees were treated more favorably. *Adams v. Triton College*, 35 Fed.Appx. 256 (7th Cir. 2002). [IL]

◆ *An Ohio community college was not bound by its affirmative-action policy to promote an African-American female over a more qualified applicant.*

An African-American employee applied for the new position of assistant vice president of academic and student affairs. Out of 40 candidates, the employee was one of three who made it past the initial review process. However, her supervisor ultimately hired a white male, who had the professional experience needed for the position. Immediately after learning she had not been selected for the position, the employee resigned and sued the college for race and gender discrimination along with constructive discharge.

The Ohio Court of Appeals noted that **the college's affirmative-action plan did not require it to pass over a more qualified candidate to hire a less qualified one**. Although the employee was a minority female who arguably could have been considered for the position, the supervisor asserted that the other candidate was the most qualified applicant. The employee failed to prove that the supervisor's reasons for not hiring her were based on her gender or race. The court also rejected the employee's claim that the college committed race discrimination by paying her less than two white employees in similar positions. An independently conducted study found legitimate and non-discriminatory reasons for the employee's lower salary. *Minter v. Cuyahoga Community College*, 2000 Ohio App. LEXIS 598 (Ohio App. 2/17/00). [OH]

◆ *An affirmative action plan did not violate Title VII where it was not based strictly on racial quotas.*

The University of Nevada hired minority faculty members under an unwritten affirmative action policy to rectify an imbalance in the faculty's racial composition. A white female applicant was hired for $5,000 less than an African-American male applicant in a similar position. The pay gap widened due to merit increases, and she filed a complaint against the state university system for violation of the Equal Pay Act and Title VII. A jury ruled that the applicant was entitled to $40,000, and the university system appealed.

The Supreme Court of Nevada reversed, holding that the university's affirmative action plan did not violate Title VII because it was not strictly based on race but **allowed the university to make employment decisions on criteria including educational background, publishing history, teaching experience and areas of specialization**. The plan did not violate the Equal Pay Act because the university demonstrated a legitimate business reason for the wage disparity between the two employees–obtaining a culturally diverse faculty. *University and Community College System of Nevada v. Farmer*, 930 P.2d 730 (Nev. 1997). [NV]

B. National Origin Discrimination

◆ *Where the reason for denying tenure may have been a pretext for discrimination, a university was not entitled to pretrial dismissal.*

An Ohio university employed an Iranian-born Muslim as a tenure track assistant professor. He was promoted to an associate professor and given his third year pre-tenure peer review. Although his review was largely positive, it also contained suggestions for improvement. Typically, faculty members on a pre-tenure track received a sixth-year review in addition to the third-year review. However, the professor did not receive his sixth-year review because the chairman of the department failed to notify the department that the review was due. A university grievance panel found that the professor should receive a proper review, but the university continued to deny him tenure on three different occasions. When the professor sued the university for **national origin and religious discrimination**, the university moved for pretrial judgment.

The court noted that although the professor was a member of a protected class and suffered an adverse employment action, genuine issues of material fact existed as to whether he was qualified to receive tenure. The evidence showed that the professor's research, publications, collaborative work, and service were adequate for tenure in the opinion of outside reviewers. Additionally, **some evidence existed that nonprotected employees were treated differently**. Moreover, a material issue existed as to whether the university's proffered reasons for the denial of tenure were pretextual. The professor alleged that he met all university expectations prior to the chairman's membership in the faculty, and he provided evidence that the chairman gave preference to American-born or Jewish employees. Thus, the court denied pretrial judgment to the university. *Amini v. Case Western Reserve Univ.*, 5 F.Supp.2d 563 (N.D. Ohio 1998). [OH]

◆ *A tenure review committee did not demonstrate a discriminatory bias against a professor when it denied her tenure.*

A Pakistani Muslim was hired as an associate professor at a New York university. Upon review of her publications and reference letters for tenure, the history department personnel committee almost unanimously recommended her for tenure. However, the nondepartmental *ad hoc* committee unanimously denied tenure. The professor sued the university in federal court, asserting **national origin and religious bias** on the part of certain members such as the chairperson. The professor conceded that no discussion of her national origin or religion occurred during the committee's deliberations, but inferred that the chairperson was able to affect the outcome of the committee vote by means of her negative, but facially nondiscriminatory comments.

The court found that **the professor failed to show discriminatory animus by the chairperson, who had not influenced the committee's decision** because of the mere fact that she participated in deliberations. Each member of the committee had grave reservations about the quality of the professor's work before the *ad hoc* committee meeting, and those conclusions were reached without any substantive input from the chairperson. Furthermore, the chairperson did not contribute at all to the hostile questioning of the professor's witnesses. As a result, the court granted the university pretrial judgment. *Jalal v. Columbia Univ.*, 4 F.Supp.2d 224 (S.D.N.Y. 1998). [NY]

◆ *It was permissible for a university to promote more qualified white employees over a lesser-qualified black employee even though all the employees were technically qualified for the job.*

A private university in New York passed over for promotion a clerical employee of African-American descent. The reason given was her failure to obtain a college degree. It instead hired a white male employee with a management and accounting degree. However, the clerical employee met all of the minimum requirements necessary to fill the position. The university passed over the clerical employee twice more under similar circumstances. When her performance evaluations began to decline, she filed a federal district court action against the university, alleging race and gender discrimination in violation of Title VII and Title IX. The university moved for dismissal.

The court held that the employee had stated a *prima facie* case for adverse employment action since she was a member of a protected class, had applied for the promotional positions and was passed over in favor of a white male despite her qualification for the positions. However, the university successfully rebutted the inference of discrimination created by the employee since **it had legitimate, nondiscriminatory reasons for hiring the white males, who were more experienced in the relevant areas and had managerial experience**. The court rejected the employee's claim that the decline in her evaluations was the result of race discrimination, as it appeared to be the result of personal animosity between the employee and manager. Because the employee failed to demonstrate that the employer created a hostile work environment, the claims under Title VII and Title IX were dismissed. *Carter v. Cornell Univ.*, 976 F.Supp. 224 (S.D.N.Y. 1997). [NY]

◆ *A university may have committed national origin discrimination against a white professor by hiring a Hispanic professor as the director of its Spanish language program.*

A white male professor at a private university in New York served as the acting director of the university's Spanish language program. When the university decided that a full-time director should be hired, despite his strong credentials and recommendations, the professor was passed over in favor of a Hispanic male. He sued the university for national origin discrimination in violation of Title VII, and a federal court granted pretrial judgment to the university. It stated that although the professor had presented sufficient evidence to establish a *prima facie* case, it would not second-guess the nondiscriminatory reason proffered by the university for the selection of the chosen candidate—that he was a better classroom teacher.

On appeal to the U.S. Court of Appeals, Second Circuit, the professor reiterated that his qualifications were superior to those of the selected candidate, that the university had deviated from its own prescribed practices in seeking to fill the position, and that university officials had indicated that he would not be seriously considered for the position because of their desire to find a minority candidate. **The evidence he presented was sufficient to support a finding that the university's reason for rejecting him was pretextual**, and the case required a trial. *Stern v. Trustees of Columbia Univ.*, 131 F.3d 305 (2d Cir. 1997). [NY]

◆ *A college was allowed to deny a sabbatical to a qualified Filipino priest while granting it to an unqualified nursing instructor.*

The priest worked for a South Dakota Catholic college that denied him a paid sabbatical leave. However, the college granted a nursing instructor's requested leave for a two-year period to complete her Ph.D. even though she lacked the requisite seniority. As the reason for its decision, the college noted that it was seeking accreditation for a four-year bachelor's degree nursing program that required faculty members to upgrade their credentials by obtaining Ph.D. degrees. The college also noted that the priest's application was not sufficiently focused and did not fit the needs of the college. The priest resigned and sued the college for race, national origin, gender, and age discrimination in violation of Title VII and the ADEA. The court held that although the priest established a *prima facie* case, **the college had articulated legitimate, nondiscriminatory reasons for the denial of his sabbatical application**. Consequently, the court ruled for the college. The court also dismissed the priest's constructive discharge claim, ruling that he failed to produce any evidence that he quit as a reasonably foreseeable consequence of the college's allegedly harassing actions. The Eighth Circuit affirmed. *Roxas v. Presentation College*, 90 F.3d 310 (8th Cir. 1996). [SD]

◆ *A university's different treatment with respect to tenure applicants created a presumption of unfair treatment in the following case.*

A female math professor of Indian descent was denied tenure by a District of Columbia private university based in part on her allegedly serious mathematical errors in several papers published by Indian math journals. The university handbook provided that an applicant for tenure be judged in four areas: research and scholarly publications, teaching, service to the university, and community and professional development. The professor alleged that male, non-Indian professors were treated more favorably in the tenure application process. She sued for Title VII sex and national origin discrimination, and breach of contract. The university moved for pretrial judgment.

The court rejected the university's motion, ruling that issues of fact existed regarding the professor's qualifications. Several outside evaluators had recommended that the professor be awarded tenure. Moreover, the alleged errors in her published papers and the accuracy of the chairman's highly critical reports were questions of fact for a jury. Because a male, non-Indian professor was ultimately promoted to tenure during the same period of time, the court held that the professor stated a *prima facie* case of sex and national origin discrimination. The court also held that **the university's different treatment with respect to the tenure applicants allegedly proved the university's nondiscriminatory reasons to be pretextual**. Finally, as issues of fact precluded pretrial judgment with respect to the breach of contract claim, the court held the case had to go to trial. *Nayar v. Howard Univ.*, 881 F.Supp. 15 (D.D.C. 1995). [DC]

C. Individual Liability

◆ *University officials could be sued for race discrimination under 42 U.S.C. §§ 1981 and 1983.*

An East Indian math professor was denied several promotions and appointments. He sued the university and various officials under Title VII and 42 U.S.C. §§ 1981 and 1983, asserting race and national origin discrimination. A New York federal court dismissed his claims against the university, but held that he could proceed with his § 1981 and § 1983 claims against the officials. The court stated that **the Eleventh Amendment does not protect university officials who may have acted in violation of federal law because their actions would not be considered actions by the state**. *Kulkarni v. City Univ. of New York*, 2001 WL 1415200 (S.D.N.Y. 11/13/01). [NY]

◆ *In the following case, a federal court explained the reasoning behind why, in most jurisdictions, individuals cannot be held liable under Title VII.*

A white, Jewish, New Jersey woman worked as an assistant professor in the theater department of a private university. She alleged that the chairman of the department, a black, male professor, conspired with the dean and the president to deny her tenure. She further alleged that the chairman discriminated against her in numerous other ways. She filed a complaint with the EEOC, which issued her a right-to-sue letter. She then sued the university, the chairman and the two officials for racial, gender and religious discrimination in violation of Title VII, among other claims. The defendants filed a motion to dismiss, arguing the chairman of the department and the two officials could not be held individually liable under Title VII.

Title VII defines an employer as "a person engaged in an industry affecting commerce that has 15 or more employees and any agent of such a person." The court noted that courts disagree over whether this provision allows individual liability, but it followed those courts that have held that the language imputes liability only on the employer and not on the employer's agents. It stated that **the statute does not cover businesses with less than 15 employees** in an attempt to protect small entities from the costly burdens of discrimination claims. Therefore, it would be logical to assume that the statute also would protect individuals from these burdens. Further, in the Civil Rights Act of 1991, **damage awards are calibrated with regard to how many employees an employer has**. Because similar damages are not calibrated with regard to individuals, the court held that Congress had no intention of imposing individual liability. The court dismissed the claims against the chairman and the two university officials. *Schanzer v. Rutgers Univ.*, 934 F.Supp. 669 (D.N.J. 1996). [NJ]

◆   *A temporary employee who was denied a permanent position failed in her claim of discrimination in the following case.*

A private college in New Hampshire hired a black woman as a temporary employee in its dining service program. When she applied for a permanent position, her application was rejected, ostensibly because she had accrued too many absences during her temporary employment. During that temporary employment, one of her supervisors made several comments that were derogatory and of a racial nature. The employee filed a charge of race discrimination with the EEOC, then brought suit against the college and certain supervisors in the U.S. District Court for the District of New Hampshire alleging both sex and race discrimination in violation of Title VII and Title IX, among other claims.

The college and the supervisors moved for judgment on the pleadings, arguing that the Title VII claim should be dismissed to the extent that it alleged sex discrimination because the employee failed to make a specific allegation of discrimination on the basis of sex to the EEOC. The court granted this motion because **the employee failed to exhaust her administrative remedies** by claiming only race discrimination in the charge to the EEOC. Accordingly, only the Title VII race discrimination claim could proceed. The court also granted the supervisors' motion to dismiss because **there was no individual liability under Title VII in New Hampshire**. The court then dismissed the Title IX claim because the dining service program was not an education program or activity within the meaning of Title IX even though the dining service employed some students who were enrolled in federal work-study programs. **The employee did not allege that she was a student; thus, her Title IX claim failed.** The court dismissed in part the claims against the college and the supervisors. *Preyer v. Dartmouth College*, 968 F.Supp. 20 (D.N.H. 1997). [NH]

D. 42 U.S.C. § 1981

Section 1981 of the Civil Rights Act (42 U.S.C. § 1981) makes it unlawful for any person or entity to discriminate on the basis of race in the making and enforcement of contracts, therefore providing an alternative basis for race discrimination claims. Section 1981 applies not only at the initiation of contracts, but also at any time during the life of the contract.

◆ *The U.S. Supreme Court has held that persons of Arab descent are protected from racial discrimination under 42 U.S.C. § 1981.*

The case involved an Arab-American Muslim professor who sued St. Francis College in a U.S. district court after St. Francis denied his tenure request. The Pennsylvania district court ruled that § 1981, which forbids racial discrimination in the making and enforcement of any contract, does not reach claims of discrimination based on Arab ancestry. It held that Arabs were Caucasians, and that since § 1981 was not enacted to protect whites, the Arab professor could not rely upon that statute. The professor appealed. The U.S. Court of Appeals, Third Circuit, reversed in favor of the professor, and St. Francis appealed to the U.S. Supreme Court.

Section 1981 states that "[a]ll persons shall have the same right to make and enforce contracts ... as is enjoyed by white citizens...." In affirming the court of appeals' decision, the Supreme Court noted that although § 1981 does not use the word "race," the Court has construed the statute to forbid all racial discrimination in the making of private as well as public contracts. It observed that all who might be thought of as Caucasian today were not thought to be of the same race at the time § 1981 became law. The Court cited several sources to support its decision that **for the purposes of § 1981, Arabs, Englishmen, Germans and certain other ethnic groups are not to be considered a single race**. If the professor could prove that he was subjected to intentional discrimination because he was an Arab, rather than solely because of his place of origin or his religion, he would be entitled to relief under § 1981. The court of appeals' decision in favor of the professor was affirmed, and the case was remanded for trial. *St. Francis College v. Al-Khazraji*, 481 U.S. 604, 107 S.Ct. 2022, 97 L.Ed.2d 749 (1987). [PA]

◆ *A professor's federal lawsuit against a university failed.*

A professor at the University of Toledo was disciplined after the National Science Foundation accused him of plagiarism. The professor sued the university and various officials under 42 U.S.C. §§ 1981, 1983 and 1985(3). He also sued under state law. An Ohio federal court granted pretrial judgment to the university, and the Sixth Circuit affirmed. **The professor could not succeed on his § 1981 and § 1985(3) claims because he was not a member of a protected class.** Nor could he define himself as a class of one—this is allowed only under egregious circumstances, which were not present here. The court also held that his § 1983 claim against the school could not succeed because universities are not "persons" under that statute, and the Eleventh Amendment bars suits against state entities in federal court. The § 1983 claim against the various officials also failed because the professor did not specify that he was suing them in their individual capacities. The court refused to extend jurisdiction over the state law claims and dismissed the lawsuit. *Underfer v. University of Toledo*, 36 Fed.Appx. 831 (6th Cir. 2002). [OH]

◆ *Where an employee failed to prove that the discrimination against her was intentional, her lawsuit under § 1981 could not succeed. However, she stated a possible claim for retaliation.*

An African-American woman was employed by a private university in the District of Columbia for 13 years. After being appointed the acting dean of students and serving in that capacity for over two years, she applied for the permanent position of dean of students. The university considered her application but eventually selected a white male for the job. The employee then returned to her previous position as director of student services and held that position until the university laid her off as part of a budget reduction. She sued the university in federal court, asserting discrimination under 42 U.S.C. § 1981.

The court noted that **to make out a claim under § 1981, the employee had to show that the university had intentionally or purposefully discriminated against her.** Here, although the employee had made out a *prima facie* case by demonstrating that she was a member of a protected class, that she was qualified for the position, that she was not hired, and that someone outside the protected class received the job, the university had proffered legitimate, nondiscriminatory reasons for hiring someone else. After it ruled for the university, the employee appealed to the District of Columbia Circuit Court of Appeals. That court affirmed in part, finding that the employee had presented insufficient evidence that discrimination motivated either adverse decision. However, there was an issue of fact as to whether the university had retaliated against her. *Carney v. American Univ.*, 151 F.3d 1090 (D.C. Cir. 1998). [DC]

II. SEX DISCRIMINATION

Sex discrimination is prohibited by Title VII, the Equal Pay Act, and by state statutes. These laws apply to public and private institutions of higher education. Colleges and universities may not engage in sexually discriminatory employment practices unless the employee's gender is a bona fide occupational qualification. The First Amendment may preclude sex discrimination claims against religious schools where the position involved is a religious one.

A. Different Treatment

◆ *The Third Circuit affirmed a jury verdict for a male who was passed over for a coaching position in favor of a female applicant.*

A men's crew team assistant coach at the University of Pennsylvania applied to coach the woman's rowing team. A female university associate athletic director conducted the search. The men's team head coach highly recommended the assistant coach, describing him as the "superior" candidate. However, the associate director refused to interview him, or any of the 33 other male applicants. She granted interviews to four of the 20 females who applied for the job. The university athletic director eventually selected a female candidate. The assistant coach sued the university in a federal district court for gender discrimination in violation of Title VII. After a trial, a jury returned a verdict of over $115,000 for the assistant coach. The university appealed.

The university claimed the female candidate was selected because of her knowledge of NCAA and Ivy League rules, her fundraising skills and administrative abilities. The court noted the job posting emphasized coaching duties, such as training, selection of racing lineups, and instruction in rowing techniques. **The inconsistency between these skills and the female candidate's abilities were especially suspect in light of evidence that the assistant coach was a superior technical coach. A jury could reasonably have found the university altered its coaching priorities to hire the female candidate.** Accordingly, the judgment was affirmed. *Medcalf v. Trustees of Univ. of Pennsylvania*, No. 02-2861, 2003 WL 21843021 (3d Cir. 2003). [PA]

◆ *A basketball coach could sue a college for sex discrimination under Title VII but not under Title IX.*

The women's basketball coach at a New York college complained about the disparate treatment of the women's team and filed a complaint with the U.S. Department of Education's Office for Civil Rights. Subsequently, the college let her contract expire. She then sued under Title VII and Title IX, as well as under a number of state common law causes of action. A federal court examined the college's motion to dismiss the lawsuit and decided to grant the motion only in part. Here, **the coach could not sue for employment discrimination under Title IX**; however, she could bring a cause of action for disparate treatment of the women's team under that statute. Also, she could sue for employment discrimination under Title VII. The court dismissed the common law claims against the college, however. *Brusseau v. Iona College*, 2002 WL 1933733 (S.D.N.Y. 8/21/02). [NY]

1. Defenses to Different Treatment

◆ *A lesbian professor was denied tenure because of her poor teaching performance, not because of discriminatory motives.*

The professor was denied tenure by a New York college, allegedly because of numerous negative comments made by students on their evaluation forms. She sued the college in a federal district court, asserting sex discrimination and retaliation in violation of Title VII. The college moved for summary judgment, asserting that its reasons were not a pretext for unlawful discrimination. It said the denial of tenure was based on the professor's mediocre job performance. To support its decision, the college noted student evaluations describing her as "overly critical," "condescending," "insulting," "intimidating," and "rude."

The court found the student evaluations were gender-neutral, not biased against women and lesbians, as the professor claimed. She was regarded as a "modest scholar with an adequate service record" and many colleagues rated her as a below-average professor. These were legitimate, non-discriminatory reasons for denying her tenure. The professor's advocacy for "greater sexual and racial diversity in the workplace" was not protected activity. **An employer's failure to follow an affirmative action policy is not an unlawful practice.** As the professor did not oppose any unlawful employment practice, there was no retaliation by the university. The university was entitled to summary judgment. *Byerly v. Ithaca College*, 290 F.Supp.2d 301 (N.D.N.Y. 2003). [NY]

◆ *There was no discrimination where poor job performance provided a legitimate reason for an adverse employment action.*

Louisiana State University opened the position of admissions counselor for applications. A female university employee with a poor job performance history decided not to apply because she was led to believe that the position required frequent travel when in fact it did not. Approximately six months later, the employee was notified that she would be fired in 90 days because of poor job performance unless her work skills improved. After a dispute with her supervisor, the employee met with an Equal Opportunity Compliance officer and complained of alleged misrepresentations regarding the admissions counselor position as well as maternity leave harassment. A few days later, she received notice that she would be fired, and she resigned. The employee sued the university for gender discrimination and retaliatory discharge under Title VII. The university moved for pretrial judgment.

Although the employee was a member of a protected class and was not hired for the admissions counselor job, she failed to establish that she was qualified for the position because of her previous performance problems. Even if she had established a *prima facie* case of gender discrimination, the university offered a legitimate nondiscriminatory reason for why she wasn't hired—poor job performance. The employee did not offer any evidence that the university's proffered reason was pretextual. The court also rejected the employee's claim of retaliatory discharge. Even though her meeting with the Equal Opportunity Compliance officer was a protected activity, she failed to establish a causal connection between the meeting and the adverse employment decision. The court granted the university's motion for pretrial judgment. *Keenan v. State of Louisiana*, 985 F.Supp. 658 (M.D. La. 1997). [LA]

◆ *Where a fair process was used to hire an athletic director, a claim of sex discrimination failed. The applicant who was not hired could not state a claim under Title IX.*

A female assistant athletic director for a private Rhode Island university served as the acting athletic director while a search committee conducted a nationwide search for a qualified athletic director. The assistant applied for the position, but a male applicant from outside the university was hired. The assistant then returned to her original duties. She began to have increasing difficulty working with the new athletic director, and received reprimands. Eventually, she was fired. The dean of students investigated her allegations of sex discrimination, but concluded that no factual basis existed to support them. The assistant then sued the university under Title IX.

The court determined that a private cause of action existed under Title IX for employment discrimination against a federally funded education program. However, the assistant failed to produce sufficient evidence to support her claim. **The search committee had conducted a nationwide search, ranked applicants on a point system, and then held interviews.** Once the committee had narrowed the number of applicants, it submitted the top three applicants for review. The applicant ultimately hired had been ranked first, while the assistant had been ranked fourth. The conduct and composition of the search committee also reasonably suggested a gender-neutral approach toward the hiring of the new athletic director. There was an effort to include women on the search committee, and sufficient evidence demonstrated that **the assistant's application had been fully reviewed**. The court held for the university. *Bedard v. Roger Williams Univ.*, 989 F.Supp. 94 (D.R.I. 1997). [RI]

◆ *Denial of tenure because of insufficient merit to the quality of scholarship was held not to be a pretext for discrimination.*

A female associate professor at a private Illinois university twice applied for tenure and was twice denied. In each instance, a male professor was granted tenure. Under the university's tenure process, an *ad hoc* committee recommended that tenure be denied or granted based on materials created by the candidate and letters from scholars in the candidate's field. A faculty review committee then either accepted or rejected the *ad hoc* committee's recommendations, and the dean would deny or recommend tenure to the provost. In both of her applications for tenure, the *ad hoc* committee recommended a denial of tenure. After the second denial, the professor appealed to a university appeals panel, alleging sex discrimination. While the appeal was pending, the professor filed a charge with the EEOC. Her appeal was denied, and she sued the university for sex discrimination and retaliation.

The professor presented a *prima facie* case of discrimination by showing that she was a member of a protected class, she was qualified for tenure, and individuals not in the protected class were granted tenure. **The university then offered a legitimate and nondiscriminatory reason for denying tenure by stating that the quality of her scholarship was not of sufficient merit.** The professor had to show that this reason was a pretext for discrimination. After considering all the evidence, the court found no indications that the university's reason was pretextual. The court also failed to find a causal link between the provost's denial of her appeal and her charge with the EEOC. The court found for the university on both the sex discrimination and retaliation claims. *Schneider v. Northwestern Univ.*, 925 F.Supp. 1347 (N.D. Ill. 1996). [IL]

◆ *A private university in Rhode Island did not discriminate when it reopened a position, rather than offering it to a female candidate, after two male candidates turned it down.*

A Rhode Island university opened a search for a position and narrowed the field to two male candidates and one female candidate. The position was offered to the first two choices, both men. After they turned down the job, the university did not offer the female applicant the job, but instead reopened the search. The applicant sued the university in a federal district court alleging sex discrimination. The court held for the university, ruling that there had never been unanimous support for the applicant's nomination and that **the applicant did not meet the unique requirements of the position in terms of**

accomplishments and peer recognition. The U.S. Court of Appeals, First Circuit, held that the university had not discriminated against the applicant. Rather it had stated legitimate, nondiscriminatory reasons for reopening the search. The university had proven by clear and convincing evidence that its reasons were valid. Because **the applicant was significantly less qualified than the two men**, the university properly decided it should reopen the search rather than appoint the applicant. The court of appeals affirmed the district court's decision. *Lamphere v. Brown Univ.*, 875 F.2d 916 (1st Cir. 1989). [RI]

◆ *Discriminating on the basis of sex is allowed where gender is a bona fide occupational qualification, as shown by the following case where a male janitor was not allowed to work in a women's dormitory.*

A male custodian at a Minnesota private university worked in a women's dormitory on campus. He had held this position for nearly six years. The university reorganized its custodial operations and, pursuant to recommendations from a consulting firm, adopted a new gender policy for custodians. In effect, the new policy prohibited custodians from working in dormitories where students of the opposite sex resided. During the reassignment process, the custodian bid for his old position in the women's dormitory. The university refused and assigned him to another position where the "same sex policy" was not in effect. The custodian sued the university in a federal district court, alleging that sex was not a bona fide occupational qualification (BFOQ) for custodial work in a women's dormitory.

The court stated that **sex could be a BFOQ if an essential part of the custodian's job intruded upon the students' legitimate privacy interests**. Here, the male custodian had to schedule his work in the women's dormitory within certain admissible hours. Time was lost both at the beginning and end of the day for this reason. Also, female residents frequently interrupted the custodian while he was working in the dormitory bathrooms. Finally, "peeping incidents" on campus and the embarrassment and inconvenience to female residents due to the bathroom closings brought up legitimate privacy concerns. Thus, the policy change was justified. *Hernandez v. University of St. Thomas*, 793 F.Supp. 214 (D.Minn. 1992). [MN]

2. Religious Entanglement

◆ *A Wisconsin civil rights act provided no protection to a female teacher whose contract with a seminary was not renewed. Because the position involved was a religious one, the statute did not apply.*

A part-time female teacher employed by a Wisconsin Roman Catholic theological seminary was selected to organize, develop, and lead the newly implemented department of field education. The purpose of the department was to increase seminary students' pastoral development outside the classroom. The Catholic Church promulgated an administrative policy requiring that directors of field education be experienced priests. Based on these policy guidelines, the seminary declined to renew the director's contract. The director challenged the seminary's action with the Labor Industry Review Commission, alleging sex discrimination in violation of the Wisconsin Fair Employment Act (WFEA). At a hearing, an administrative law judge determined that the seminary was wholly sectarian in purpose and ruled that the Equal Rights Division lacked jurisdiction over religious institutions such as the seminary. A Wisconsin trial court affirmed, and the director appealed.

The Court of Appeals of Wisconsin held the Equal Rights Division could investigate employment discrimination complaints but **could not enforce employment discrimination laws against religious associations when the employment position served a "ministerial" or "ecclesiastical" function**. As a general rule, if the employee's primary duties consist of teaching, spreading the faith, church governance, supervision of a religious order, or supervision or participation in religious ritual and worship, he or she should be considered ministerial or ecclesiastical. Because the director performed several of these duties, the Equal Rights Division was constitutionally precluded from enforcing the WFEA against the seminary. *Jocz v. Labor and Industry Review Comm'n*, 538 N.W.2d 588 (Wis. App. 1995). [WI]

◆ *An EEOC investigation and lawsuit was impermissibly entangled with religion, as they interfered with the selection and training of clergy.*

A Catholic university hired a nun as an associate professor. Her tenure application was denied, and she appealed to a school committee, alleging differential treatment. The university responded that her scholarship, measured primarily by her publications, was not up to its standards. She filed a complaint with the EEOC, which filed suit on her behalf in a federal district court against the university, alleging sex discrimination and retaliatory conduct. The trial judge dismissed the case, finding that the application of Title VII to the case would violate the Free Exercise and Establishment Clauses. The professor appealed to the U.S. Court of Appeals, District of Columbia Circuit.

The professor argued that the district court improperly used **the ministerial exception, which exempts the selection of clergy from Title VII**, and similar statutes. The court of appeals found that the exception did apply since the professor's duties included spreading the faith and participation in religious worship. The court held that the EEOC's investigation and lawsuit violated the First Amendment since they resulted in an impermissible entanglement with religious decision-making and interfered with a procedure of critical importance to the Catholic Church, its ability to select and train its clergy. The university's interest in employing faculty of its choice outweighed the government's interest in eliminating discrimination and, therefore, the professor's claims were barred by the Free Exercise and Establishment Clauses. The district court's decision was affirmed. *EEOC v. Catholic Univ. of America*, 83 F.3d 455 (D.C. Cir. 1996). [DC]

◆ *A female professor's liberal views on abortion could legitimately be considered in a hiring decision by a religious university.*

A female professor at Marquette University was repeatedly denied a position as associate professor of theology. The professor sued Marquette under Title VII of the Civil Rights Act of 1964, alleging that it had refused to hire her because she was a woman. She also claimed that Marquette had discriminated against her on the basis of her religious views, *i.e.*, her liberal views on abortion. The district court ruled against the professor, holding that the First Amendment prohibited any court from considering her claim since Marquette's interest in the integrity of its theology department was an overriding factor. The court of appeals concluded that the professor's Title VII claim failed as a matter of law because **the record clearly indicated that she would not have been granted the associate position even if she were a man**. It agreed with the district court's observation that Marquette was exempt from Title VII under the provision that permits a university to hire and employ employees of a particular religion if it is owned by that religion. The professor's liberal abortion views could legitimately be considered in whether the professor ought to be hired as an associate professor. The district court's decision was upheld. *Maguire v. Marquette Univ.*, 814 F.2d 1213 (7th Cir. 1987). [WI]

3. Procedural Issues

◆   *The U.S. Supreme Court held that a Title VII "charge" did not have to be verified by oath or affirmation at the time it was filed with the EEOC. As long as the charge was filed within the 300-day deadline, the oath or affirmation could come later.*

Five months after a Virginia college denied tenure to a professor, he faxed a letter to an EEOC field office claiming he had been subjected to gender, national origin and religious discrimination. He then filed charges with the state and, 313 days after the denial of tenure, he filed a verified "Form 5 Charge of Discrimination." When he sued the college under Title VII, the college sought to dismiss the case on the grounds that he had failed to comply with the 300-day statute of limitations. A federal court found that the faxed letter was not a "charge" of discrimination within the meaning of Title VII, and that the verification could not relate back to the letter. The Fourth Circuit agreed, but the U.S. Supreme Court reversed, noting that **the faxed letter to the EEOC could qualify as a "charge" under Title VII**, and that the verification could relate back to the letter. Nothing in Title VII required the charge to be verified at the time it was made. The Court remanded the case for further proceedings. *Edelman v. Lynchburg College*, 535 U.S. 106, 122 S.Ct. 1145, 152 L.Ed.2d 188 (2002). [VA]

◆   *In a 1980 employment case brought under Title VII, the Supreme Court concluded that the statute of limitations began to run on the date the teacher was denied tenure, rather than on his final employment date.*

A black Liberian teacher taught at a state-supported Delaware college that was attended predominantly by blacks. The faculty committee on tenure recommended that he not be given tenure, and the college faculty senate and board of trustees adhered to this recommendation. The teacher then filed a grievance with the board's grievance committee, which took the case under advisement. The college offered him a one-year "terminal contract" in accordance with state policy. After the teacher had signed the terminal contract without objection, the grievance committee denied his grievance. The teacher then attempted to file a complaint with the EEOC. However, he was notified that he would first have to exhaust state administrative remedies if he wanted to file a claim under Title VII. After the appropriate state agency waived its jurisdiction, the EEOC issued a right-to-sue letter.

The teacher then sued the college for discriminating against him on the basis of his national origin in violation of Title VII and 42 U.S.C. § 1981. The district court dismissed the teacher's claims as untimely because the Title VII complaint had not been filed with the EEOC within 180 days and the § 1981 claim had not been filed in federal court within three years. The U.S. Court of Appeals, Third Circuit, reversed, holding that the limitations on Title VII and § 1981 did not begin to run until the teacher's terminal contract expired.

The U.S. Supreme Court reversed the court of appeals' decision, finding that **both the Title VII and § 1981 claims were untimely**. The teacher's complaint did not state that the college discriminated against him on the basis of national origin; it simply concentrated on the college's denial of tenure. The teacher had failed to make out a *prima facie* case of employment discrimination under Title VII, because he had stated no continuing violation of his civil rights. In fact, the teacher had received essentially the same treatment accorded to other teachers who were denied tenure. The statute of limitations began to run when the teacher was denied tenure, specifically, on the date when the college had offered him a terminal contract. *Delaware State College v. Ricks*, 449 U.S. 250, 101 S.Ct. 498, 66 L.Ed.2d 431 (1980). [DE]

◆   *The Supreme Court compelled a private college to disclose employment records in an administrative proceeding before the EEOC.*

In *EEOC v. Franklin & Marshall College*, 775 F.2d 110 (3d Cir. 1985), a professor, who had been employed at a private school in Pennsylvania for three years, was denied tenure. The school's professional standards committee, composed of the dean and five faculty members, recommended that tenure not be granted to the professor. The committee's recommendation was reaffirmed by the college's grievance committee. The professor then filed a complaint with the EEOC, alleging discrimination based on his French national origin. The EEOC issued a subpoena for the committee's records. Although the EEOC offered to accept the records with names deleted, the school refused to disclose them. The EEOC then sued to compel the college to comply with the subpoena. The court ordered disclosure of the records. Before the court of appeals, the college argued that "the quality of a college and ... academic freedom, which has a constitutional dimension, is inextricably intertwined with a confidential peer review process." The court of appeals held that **although the disclosure might burden the tenure process or invade the privacy of other professors, the records had to be disclosed because they were "relevant" to the EEOC's case**. The records were ordered disclosed to the EEOC. The college appealed to the U.S. Supreme Court, but its petition for review was denied. *Franklin & Marshall College v. EEOC*, 476 U.S. 1163, 106 S.Ct. 2288, 90 L.Ed.2d 729 (1986). [PA]

◆   *The Supreme Court ruled that a state administrative proceeding on a Title VII discrimination claim filed in state court could be appealed to the federal court system when the state administrative proceeding remained unreviewed by state courts.*

The University of Tennessee Agricultural Extension Service discharged a black employee, allegedly for inadequate work and misconduct on the job. The employee requested a hearing under the state Uniform Administrative Procedures Act to contest his termination. Before his administrative hearing took place the employee also filed a claim in a U.S. district court under federal civil rights laws, alleging that his dismissal had been racially motivated. The district court entered a temporary restraining order halting the state administrative hearing, but it later allowed the hearing to go forward. The hearing officer determined that the dismissal had not been racially motivated. The university moved to dismiss the employee's federal court lawsuit because it already had been resolved in the administrative hearing. The district court agreed and dismissed the case. The Sixth Circuit reversed, allowing the case to remain in federal court. The university appealed the decision to the U.S. Supreme Court, which held that the case should be heard by the district court. It ruled that **a state administrative proceeding on a Title VII claim not reviewed by a higher state board could be heard in federal court**. Since the decision made at the employee's administrative hearing was not reviewed by the state courts, it had no preclusive effect. The employee had the right to introduce his claim anew. *University of Tennessee v. Elliot*, 478 U.S. 788, 106 S.Ct. 3220, 92 L.Ed.2d 635 (1986). [TN]

◆ *In an employment discrimination lawsuit filed under Title VII, the aggrieved party bears the burden of proving that the employer's refusal to hire is a pretext for unlawful discrimination.*

In an employment discrimination case against a state college, a federal district court ruled that the college had discriminated against a professor on the basis of sex. The U.S. Court of Appeals, First Circuit, affirmed the decision, ruling that Title VII of the 1964 Civil Rights Act, 42 U.S.C. § 2000e *et seq.*, required the college to prove absence of discriminatory motive. In a per curiam opinion, the U.S. Supreme Court held that this burden was too great. It ruled that **in an employment discrimination case, the employer need only "articulate some legitimate, nondiscriminatory reason for the employee's rejection."** In other words, the employee has the burden of proving that the reason for the employee's rejection was a mere pretext. The Court vacated the court of appeals' decision and remanded the case for reconsideration under the lesser standard. *Trustees of Keene State College v. Sweeney*, 439 U.S. 24, 99 S.Ct. 295, 58 L.Ed.2d 216 (1978). [NH]

◆ *A $50,000 damage award and an order to apologize were struck down where a federal court failed to make the proper analysis of whether discrimination had occurred.*

A Canadian citizen began a post-doctoral fellowship at a Tennessee university doing work on the cloning of specific gene sequences, where part of her salary was paid by a grant. She later sought and obtained a salary commensurate with that paid to two male post-doctoral fellows and was moved into a "research associate" position that provided greater benefits. When her relationship with the doctor in charge of the research deteriorated, she accused him of scientific misconduct and sexual harassment. He sought to have her grant money terminated. She filed a sex discrimination and retaliation complaint with the EEOC. After the Immigration and Naturalization Service informed the university that she had been denied permanent residency status, it fired her. She sued the doctor and the university under Title VII and 42 U.S.C. § 1983. A federal court ruled in her favor, but the Sixth Circuit vacated and remanded the case. Here, the lower court failed to determine **whether the employee was treated differently than her male co-workers**. Also, the court noted that the employee could pursue her sex discrimination claim under both Title VII and § 1983. However, she would be limited to one recovery. *Woodruff v. Ohman*, 29 Fed.Appx. 337 (6th Cir. 2002). [TN]

◆   *Claims of sexual harassment and discrimination were allowed to proceed where there were issues of fact as to what really happened.*

The assistant director of Afro-American studies at the University of Pennsylvania brought suit for race discrimination after she was fired. She also claimed that after she complained of sexual harassment, she was retaliated against by university officials. The university moved for pretrial judgment, but the court denied the motion, finding that **she had raised an issue of fact as to whether she had been subjected to a hostile work environment by virtue of 20 alleged incidents of harassing conduct**. Because the university failed to show that the work environment was not hostile, a trial would have to be held on that issued. There also were issues of fact as to whether the university retaliated against the assistant director, and whether it treated her harassment claims differently than claims brought by white employees. *Roberts v. University of Pennsylvania*, 2001 WL 1580304 (E.D. Pa. 12/11/01). [PA]

◆   *Where a tenure denial was discriminatory, the First Circuit held that a federal court could order tenure to be granted.*

A Boston University professor became eligible for tenure review. She was evaluated in three areas: scholarship, teaching and service to the university. Excellence had to be demonstrated in two of the three areas. She had published one book and three essays, and had received a grant to write another book. She also had advised 15 to 20 undergraduate students in scheduling their classes, had conducted a "women's literature discussion group," and had served on various university committees. Her department, the tenure committee and the dean all recommended that she be tenured. However, the assistant provost, the provost and the president recommended against tenure to the trustees, who denied tenure. She then sued the university for sex discrimination.

A jury found that the professor had been denied tenure because of her sex, and the court granted the professor tenure. The university appealed to the First Circuit Court of Appeals, which noted that the evidence introduced by the professor as to her qualifications had been properly admitted. Thus, it had been reasonable for a jury to determine that tenure denial was discriminatory. **Although a court order to grant tenure was a rarity, the court held that such an order was appropriate where it was simply attempting to make the professor "whole."** The ruling granting the professor tenure was affirmed. *Brown v. Trustees of Boston Univ.*, 891 F.2d 337 (1st Cir. 1989). [MA]

B. Harassment

Sexual harassment is a form of sex discrimination prohibited by Title VII of the Civil Rights Act of 1964 and by Title IX of the Education Amendments of 1972. However, to be actionable under Title VII, the harassment must be severe or pervasive, and it must be based on gender.

In 1998, the U.S. Supreme Court held that in Title VII sexual harassment suits employers may have a defense available where no tangible adverse action is taken against the employee. In such cases, the employer can avoid liability by showing that it exercised reasonable care to prevent and promptly correct any harassing behavior, and that the employee unreasonably failed to use those procedures or otherwise avoid harm.

1. Title VII

◆ *Alabama college officials were entitled to qualified immunity in a suit alleging same-sex sexual harassment.*

Four security officers employed by an Alabama community college claimed their supervisor subjected them to sexual harassment over a 15-year period. They accused him of touching them and other male employees inappropriately and of constantly making sexual remarks and gestures. The officers sued the college and its officials in a federal district court, alleging the harassment violated their equal protection rights, and college officials violated their constitutional rights by failing to stop the misconduct. The court held the officials were entitled to qualified immunity.

The officers appealed to the Eleventh Circuit Court of Appeals, which held the officials were entitled to immunity unless they violated the officers' clearly established statutory or constitutional rights. **For a constitutional right to be clearly established, a governmental official must be aware an action is obviously wrong in the light of preexisting law.** Although a 1998 U.S. Supreme Court decision found a same-sex harassment claim actionable under Title VII against a private employer, the decision did not place governmental officials on notice that this conduct violated the officers' constitutional rights. **Since same-sex discrimination was not clearly a violation of the Equal Protection Clause at the time of the harassment, the officials were entitled to qualified immunity.** *Snider v. Jefferson State Community College*, 344 F.3d 1325 (11th Cir. 2003). [AL]

◆ *A professor did not suffer any adverse action under Title VII because she retained her position and benefits.*

A Georgia university assistant professor received excellent performance evaluations and was chosen for a candidate selection committee to fill a vacant position. She was upset by the majority's recommendation to hire a male for the position and allegedly shook her fist at other committee members. The faculty voted not to renew the professor's contract on the grounds that she was insulting and hostile to colleagues. School deans rejected the faculty's recommendation based on her previous positive performance evaluations. The faculty voted not to renew her contract the next year and the deans did not interfere with the decision. Although the faculty senate eventually voted to retain the professor, she sued the university and officials in a federal district court for First Amendment and Title VII violations.

The court granted summary judgment to the university, and the professor appealed. The Eleventh Circuit Court of Appeals found she suffered no serious or tangible effects from the university's actions. Moreover, any emotional distress was too insubstantial to be considered adverse employment action. **Since the professor did not suffer any adverse action under Title VII, there was no basis for a First Amendment retaliation claim. The court explained that "an important condition of employment" must be involved in a First Amendment retaliation claim.** She did not suffer a reprimand, demotion, or discharge, so the court affirmed the judgment. *Stavropoulos v. Firestone*, 361 F.3d 610 (11th Cir. 2004). [GA]

◆ *"A tangible employment action" occurs when a supervisor threatens an employee with discharge unless the employee acquiesces to sexual demands.*

A secretary for a California university began a sexual relationship with her supervisor. She later stated her belief that he would discharge her if she did not comply with his advances. After their relationship ended, she requested a transfer. The university denied the request and established a committee to investigate her sexual harassment allegations. The committee found insufficient evidence of sexual harassment, but it offered the secretary a position working for a female professor in a different department. She rejected the offer and sued the university and supervisor for sexual harassment. A federal district court awarded summary judgment to the university, finding the secretary did not suffer a "tangible employment action."

The secretary appealed to the Ninth Circuit, which held an employee can establish a "tangible employment action" by showing she complied with a supervisor's sexual demands to avoid termination. If there is a tangible employment action under Title VII, the employer can be held vicariously liable for the supervisor's unlawful conduct. The court found the secretary did not show her continued employment was conditioned upon consenting to sexual relations with the supervisor. **Although he created an uncomfortable environment, there was no evidence establishing a connection between continuing employment and his request for sex.** The court noted the university investigated the allegations as soon as it learned of them. Even though it did not think there was sufficient evidence of sexual harassment, it offered to transfer the secretary and asked the supervisor to resign. As the university took reasonable corrective measures, the court affirmed the judgment. *Holly D. v. California Institute of Technology*, 339 F.3d 1158 (9th Cir. 2003). [CA]

◆ *A three-year lapse between reported sexual harassment and the discharge of a Wisconsin professor doomed her retaliation claim.*

A research scientist with the U.S. Department of Veteran Affairs (VA) worked part time as an associate professor of neurology at a Wisconsin medical college. When she charged another professor with sexual harassment, her supervisor at the college warned her filing a sexual harassment charge could be a "career limiting move." However, the supervisor investigated her complaint. Three years later, the professor lost her VA research position. The college then discharged her because her VA research responsibilities were the basis of her faculty appointment. The professor sued the college in a federal district court for retaliation in violation of Title VII. The court granted the college's motion for summary judgment and the professor appealed.

The U.S. Court of Appeals, Seventh Circuit stated that **a Title VII claim based on retaliation required evidence of statutorily protected activity that results in adverse employment action. The professor's retaliation claim failed because of the time lapse between her sexual harassment complaint and her discharge three years later**. The delay was too great to imply a causal connection between protected activity and adverse employment action. The supervisor's comment that a complaint could be a "career limiting move" was not direct evidence of retaliation. As the professor did not show she was treated less favorably than similarly situated employees, the court affirmed the decision. *Myklebust v. Medical College of Wisconsin*, No. 03-2882, 97 Fed.Appx. 652, 2004 WL 957935 (7th Cir. 2004). [WI]

◆ *A North Carolina university police officer alleged sufficient facts to support Title VII claims that she was sexually harassed by a supervisor.*

The officer claimed the supervisor made lewd remarks, touched her inappropriately and accosted her in a parking lot. She complained to other supervisors, who offered her no assistance. The officer claimed the harassment caused her mental distress and depression. She received psychiatric treatment and eventually lost her job at the university. The officer sued the university in a federal district court under Title VII for hostile work environment, adding a Title IX claim for sexual harassment and a claim for constitutional rights violations by the university and its officials. The university moved for dismissal of the Title VII and constitutional claims.

The court relied on *Shaw v. First Union Nat'l Bank*, 202 F.3d 234 (4th Cir. 2000) to test the Title VII hostile work environment claim. It held **the officer demonstrated harassment that was sufficiently pervasive or severe to create an abusive work environment. The supervisors who did not assist her had actual knowledge of harassing behavior which created an unreasonable risk of harm.** While the supervisors were potentially liable for failing to act, punitive damages were unavailable against university officials. The university's motion to dismiss the case was denied. *Alston v. North Carolina A&T State Univ.*, 304 F.Supp.2d 774 (M.D.N.C. 2004). [NC]

◆ *A jury would have to decide whether a professor was fired in retaliation for his wife's sexual harassment complaint against the department chair.*

Husband and wife biochemists took jobs with the University of Massachusetts Medical Center. For the next nine years, the husband received good performance reviews and salary increases. Shortly after funding problems led the university to recommend merging the lab the husband directed with another lab, the wife accused the department chairman of sexual harassment. The husband was then relieved of most of his teaching duties and given his first negative evaluation. The following year, the acting chairman of the department accused the husband of scientific misconduct, banned the wife from the lab where she had worked, informed her that her contract would not be renewed, and gave the husband a second negative evaluation.

The husband filed a complaint alleging retaliation for his wife's complaint of sexual harassment. Several years later, the husband was accused of being deliberately unproductive, and he and his wife were both fired. The husband sued under Title VII, state law and 42 U.S.C. § 1983 for violation of an asserted First Amendment right to intimate association. A state court refused to let the case go to a jury and ruled in favor of the university. The Appeals Court of Massachusetts reversed, finding that a jury should have been allowed to examine whether the university's adverse action against the husband was taken because of the wife's sexual harassment complaint. Although **the university had presented evidence of the husband's lack of productivity and the independent nature of the decision to fire him**, a jury had to decide if the real motivator was retaliation. Also, the § 1983 claim was allowed to proceed. *Mole v. University of Massachusetts*, 787 N.E.2d 1098 (Mass. App. 2003). [MA]

◆   *An Alabama state university employee could sue for same-sex harassment under Title VII.*

A campus police officer at the University of Alabama claimed that his immediate supervisor, a male, subjected him to such severe sexual harassment that a hostile work environment was created. He sued the university under Title VII. The university sought to dismiss the case, arguing that it was immune from liability under the Eleventh Amendment. The court denied the motion for immunity, and the Eleventh Circuit Court of Appeals affirmed. Since **Title VII did not create new constitutional rights apart from those granted by the Equal Protection Clause**, Congress did not exceed its power when it enacted Title VII. As a result, the university was not entitled to immunity. Also, the court stated that the university could be liable for same-sex harassment under Title VII even though the discriminatory conduct did not have a sexual overtone. Where a supervisor displays hostility to members of the same sex in the workplace, a hostile work environment claim can be brought under Title VII according to the Supreme Court's decision in *Oncale v. Sundowner Offshore Services, Inc.*, 523 U.S. 75 (1998). The court remanded the case for further proceedings. *Downing v. Board of Trustees of Univ. of Alabama*, 321 F.3d 1017 (11th Cir. 2003). [AL]

◆   *A university was liable for its agent's harassing behavior, but its good faith efforts to end the harassment prevented an award of punitive damages.*

A Louisiana woman worked as an office manager for a doctor at Tulane University and later began a consensual sexual relationship with him. After the relationship ended, she claimed that he began to harass her—breaking into her desk, searching her belongings and stripping some of her job duties. Her mental health suffered, and she eventually left Tulane. When she sued the doctor and the university under Title VII, a federal court dismissed the claims against the doctor, but allowed the claims against the university to go to a jury.

The jury awarded her $300,000 in compensatory damages as well as back pay and front pay of more than $128,000. The court dismissed her claim for punitive damages. On appeal, the Fifth Circuit affirmed, noting that there was sufficient evidence that the doctor harassed the manager because of her gender and not just because of the failed relationship. Since he was acting as an agent of the university by doing so, the jury verdict against the university was proper. Also, punitive damages had appropriately been denied because despite the doctor's behavior, **the university acted in good faith to end the harassment by putting her on paid administrative leave and seeking another position for her within the university system.** *Green v. Administrators of Tulane Educ. Fund,* 284 F.3d 642 (5th Cir. 2002). [LA]

◆ *Conduct that was only "bothersome and uncomfortable" did not amount to harassment.*

An economics professor at Florida Atlantic University told university officials that she was having problems with the chair of the search committee that hired her. **Her complaints included the way he "looked her up and down," late-evening calls to her home, inappropriate touching and questions, and compliments on her clothing and jewelry.** She characterized the behavior as sexual harassment and filed an internal complaint. An attempt to informally resolve the complaint was unsuccessful. The professor filed a charge with the EEOC, then sued the chair of the search committee and the university's board of regents. She alleged violations of 42 U.S.C. § 1983 and Title VII, based on both hostile environment and *quid pro quo* sexual harassment. A jury returned a verdict in favor of the chair on the § 1983 claims, but found the board of regents liable under Title VII for sexual harassment and retaliation, and awarded damages of $95,000 on the two claims.

The U.S. Court of Appeals, Eleventh Circuit, reversed. It noted that a plaintiff must establish that the offensive behavior is severe and pervasive enough to alter the conditions of her employment, and not only that she perceived her work environment to be hostile and abusive, but also that a reasonable person would perceive the environment to be hostile and abusive. Here, it was obvious the professor subjectively perceived the alleged harassment to be severe and pervasive. However, even the most serious conduct alleged—that the chair placed his hand on the professor's knee and touched the hem of her dress—were only two incidents over a period of six or seven months. **Because each incident was momentary and did not interfere with the professor's job performance, the alleged harassment could not be considered severe and/or pervasive.** Accordingly, the incidents did not rise to the level necessary to be considered harassment. *Gupta v. Florida Bd. of Regents,* 212 F.3d 571 (11th Cir. 2000). [FL]

◆ *An instructor's Title VII claim failed where the complained of behavior was not directed at him because of his sex, nor was it severe and pervasive enough to be considered harassing.*

A full-time male instructor employed by Shawnee State University was given the title Coordinator of Sports Studies. He alleged that the female dean of education then began sexually harassing him, including **touching and rubbing his shoulder, grabbing his butt and making a related offensive comment.** Shortly after one of the allegedly harassing incidents, the instructor was stripped of his position by the dean. She also recommended him for termination. Several days later, a university provost rescinded the termination recommendation. Later that year, the instructor was placed on permanent disability retirement. Almost two years after the termination incident, the instructor sued under Title VII. His complaint was dismissed, and he appealed to the Sixth Circuit.

The court of appeals agreed with the lower court that no adverse employment action had been taken because the coordinator position was not an actual position at the university, but merely a title. The court also noted that the university promptly reinstated him. Further, **many of the perceived slights and abuses were not directed at the instructor because of his gender, which is a requirement for a Title VII violation**. Although several of the incidents were directed at the instructor because he was male and involved sexual suggestions, these incidents were not severe or pervasive enough to be considered sexual harassment. Accordingly, the decision dismissing the instructor's complaint was upheld. *Bowman v. Shawnee State Univ.*, 220 F.3d 456 (6th Cir. 2000). [OH]

◆ *A supervisor who was brusque with both men and women and who made only one gender-specific comment about women did not engage in sexual harassment.*

The director of the campus bookstore at a State University of New York was accused of failing to respond to complaints of sexual harassment by a male employee. The complaints spanned a period of approximately 17 months. Once the director's supervisor was informed of the harassment, he fired the alleged harasser. The supervisor also fired the director over her lack of response to the matter. The director sued under Title VII and Section 296 of the New York Executive Law, claiming that the supervisor created a hostile work environment and that her termination was retaliatory. A federal court ruled for the defendants, and the Second Circuit Court of Appeals affirmed.

First, the director admitted that **her supervisor never used inappropriate gender-based language, never made inappropriate gender-based comments, never used profanity and never physically touched her or threatened her**. The supervisor's remark about a woman not being "right for the job" when a position became available was too isolated and/or occasional to constitute a hostile environment within the meaning of Title VII. At most, the incidents of which the director complained demonstrated that her supervisor was a rude person. In examining the retaliation claim, the court determined that the defendants articulated legitimate, nondiscriminatory reasons for discharging her — mishandling the sexual harassment problem between the two bookstore employees, and acting unprofessionally after being told she was being discharged. This was sufficient to support both the initial termination decision and the subsequent decision to move up the termination date. *Rizzo-Puccio v. College Auxiliary Services Inc.*, 216 F.3d 1073 (2d Cir. 2000). [NY]

◆ *An Indiana federal court held that a single instance of harassing conduct could create a hostile work environment if the conduct was severe enough.*

An Indiana university employee alleged a supervisor grabbed her, kissed her, and reached inside her blouse and groped her. She managed to get away from him and immediately went to the restroom where she vomited. However, she did not report the incident until three months later. At that time, a university official said, "Oh no, not again." The university conducted an investigation that resulted in the supervisor's resignation. When the employee sued for sexual harassment under Title VII, the university sought to dismiss the action, maintaining that one instance of harassment was not enough to create a hostile work environment, that it had acted promptly in its investigation, and that the employee had waited too long to report the incident.

The court refused to dismiss the case. It noted that **the alleged incident was severe enough to create a hostile work environment**. Further, although the university acted promptly once it learned of the incident, it arguably had knowledge of previous instances of misconduct by the supervisor. Thus, there was an issue of fact as to whether the university should have taken action to prevent the attack. Finally, the court could not say that a three month delay in reporting the assault was unreasonable. The case would have to proceed to trial. *Fall v. Indiana Univ. Bd. of Trustees*, 12 F.Supp.2d 870 (N.D. Ind. 1998). [IN]

2. Title IX

◆   *The former women's basketball coach for Delaware State University lost her Title VII gender discrimination suit against the university because she should have filed a Title IX claim.*

Although DSU claimed the coach was fired for poor job performance, the coach maintained her termination was in response to her frequent complaints that the women's athletic program did not receive the same benefits as the men's program. The coach's lawsuit alleged gender discrimination and retaliation under Title VII of the Civil Rights Act of 1964. The U.S. District Court for the District of Delaware ruled that she failed to establish a *prima facie* case. The coach "confused discrimination based on her sex with discrimination based on her association with women's athletics." **She did not demonstrate that she was discriminated against for being a woman**, as opposed to being fired for her complaints about the women's athletic program. Additionally, the fact that she was replaced by a woman did not help her case. Her retaliation claim also failed because it addressed an activity protected under Title IX of the Educational Amendments of 1972, rather than Title VII. Despite the coach's claim that she suffered retaliation for complaining about a potential Title IX violation, **she did not show she suffered retaliation for complaining about discrimination based on her sex**, as required by Title VII. The court granted pretrial judgment to DSU. *Lamb-Bowman v. Delaware State University*, 152 F.Supp.2d 553 (D. Del. 2001). [DE]

◆   *A professor's claim that Title IX was violated when a college fired him for sexual harassment failed.*

A Minnesota man working as a professor at a private college was accused of violating the college's sexual harassment policy because of his sexual contact with a student. He was later fired, and the student sued the professor and college. She later settled these claims, but the professor counterclaimed against the college and its president, alleging a violation of Title IX, breach of contract, defamation and tortious interference with contract. Both sides filed for pretrial judgment. The court noted that although courts have recognized a cause of action under Title IX on behalf of students who are discriminated against by educational programs, few courts have found that employees of educational institutions have a cause of action for damages under Title IX. **Because Title VII provides a comprehensive system for redressing employment discrimination, courts have refused to infer one in Title IX.** The court dismissed that claim. However, it noted that the college did not follow the sexual harassment procedures contained in the faculty manual and therefore issues of fact existed on the breach of contract claim. The professor's motion was denied. The college's motion was granted in part and denied in part. *Cooper v. Gustavus Adolphus College*, 957 F.Supp. 191 (D.Minn. 1997). [MN]

◆   *A lawsuit against a university for harassment by a supervisor could not be dismissed where fact issues were in doubt as to what the university knew.*

A male supervisor at a Maryland private university allegedly sexually harassed two female employees. When they reported the incidents, they alleged that no action was taken and that one of them was assigned to a less desirable position. They also maintained that the university failed to distribute to them its policy manual prohibiting sexual harassment. They filed Title IX hostile work environment claims against the university in a Maryland federal court, which examined the university's motion for pretrial judgment and determined that claims brought under Title IX for abusive work environments should be analyzed under Title VII standards. It then found that the alleged conduct was severe and pervasive enough to warrant a trial on the facts. Here, **the university arguably had actual or constructive notice of the harassment**, and a jury would have to decide whether liability should be imputed to the university. *Ward v. Johns Hopkins Univ.*, 861 F.Supp. 367 (D. Md. 1994). [MD]

C. Equal Pay Issues

The Equal Pay Act (EPA) requires that employers pay males and females the same wages for equal work. Employees are protected by the EPA as long as the employer is engaged in an enterprise affecting interstate commerce. The EPA has been interpreted by the courts to require only that the jobs under comparison be "substantially" equal. Strict equality of the jobs under comparison is not required. The EPA requires equal pay for jobs involving "equal skill, effort, and responsibility, and which are performed under similar working conditions, except where such payment is made pursuant to (i) a seniority system; (ii) a merit system; (iii) a system which measures earnings by quantity or quality of production; or (iv) a differential based on any other factor other than sex." Many cases alleging disparate pay rates based on sex include claims under Title VII and analogous state laws.

◆   *A Louisiana professor failed to show an EPA violation because she did not show her job was "substantially equal" to a male professor's.*

The professor worked as an adjunct for nine years before becoming a tenured associate. The university turned her down twice for a full professorship before doing so after 11 years. She claimed the university violated the EPA by paying her less than a male professor doing the same work she did and that she was more experienced than anyone else in her department. The professor sued the university in a state court for EPA violations. The case went before a jury, which rejected the university's evidence that the pay disparity reflected the different starting dates and annual performance reports of the two professors. The university appealed to the Court of Appeal of Louisiana, which held the **professor did not show her job was substantially equal to that of the male professor or involved the same skills**. Because of this, she failed to show an EPA violation, and the court reversed the judgment. *Ramelow v. Board of Trustees of Univ. of Louisiana*, 870 So.2d 415 (La. App. 3d Cir. 2004). [LA]

◆   *A Minnesota assistant women's hockey coach lost his EPA and Title VII action because he did not prove he suffered any adverse employment action.*

The assistant coach learned the university paid him $13,000 per year less than a female assistant coach. He complained to the director of women's athletics, and then asserted the head coach retaliated against him and gave him a poor performance evaluation. The male assistant coach resigned and sued the university in a federal district court for EPA and Title VII violations. **The court noted the female assistant coach performed many job duties that the male assistant coach did not perform, such as recruiting and public relations. Their positions were not "substantially equal" under the EPA**.

The male assistant coach appealed to the Eighth Circuit, which upheld the EPA ruling. **It also rejected his Title VII retaliation claim because the performance evaluation was not an "adverse employment action."** The assistant's discomfort with the situation was not enough to create an adverse employment action under Title VII. As his working conditions were not so intolerable as to force his resignation, the court affirmed the judgment for the university. *Horn v. University of Minnesota*, 362 F.3d 1042 (8th Cir. 2004). [MN]

◆   *University officials were not entitled to immunity in an action regarding salary increases for female faculty members.*

The University of Minnesota entered into a consent decree to settle a sex discrimination class action lawsuit that began in the 1970s. The decree provided for the distribution of $3 million in salary increases to female faculty members. A male professor sued, asserting the regression analysis used by the university to provide the salary increases amounted to unlawful sex discrimination by failing to take into account rank and market value. A federal court granted judgment to the university, but the Eighth Circuit remanded the case for a trial. **There was a genuine issue of material fact as to whether there was a salary imbalance based on gender that justified the salary increases.** *Maitland v. University of Minnesota*, 155 F.3d 1013 (8th Cir. 1998).

On remand, the board of regents requested legislative immunity, and the university defendants requested Eleventh Amendment immunity. The court denied both requests. The Eighth Circuit affirmed. **The board members were not entitled to legislative immunity.** Although the regents are given the power to enact laws for the state government, they are considered administrators, not legislators. The court also held that Congress did not exceed its Fourteenth Amendment authority when it enacted Title VII, so the university was not entitled to Eleventh Amendment immunity. The court affirmed the judgment. *Maitland v. University of Minnesota*, 260 F.3d 959 (8th Cir. 2001). [MN]

◆ *Six female professors could not sue for wage discrimination where they waited over three years to file the lawsuit.*

In 1997, an Iowa university appointed its graduate school director the acting vice president of academic affairs. He conducted a statistical analysis of faculty salaries and discovered some discrepancies. He then hired a consulting firm to conduct an in-depth review of salaries and, two years later, the firm found that gender was not a statistically significant predictor of faculty salaries. The university nevertheless increased salaries for a number of male and female faculty members. Six female professors sued the university in November 2000 under Title VII and the Equal Pay Act, but a federal court dismissed their lawsuit on the grounds that **it was not timely filed**. Here, the last payment disparities allegedly occurred in 1997 and, since they were discrete discriminatory acts, the professors could not use the continuing violation doctrine to extend the statute of limitations. The professors' pay after that time was a lingering effect that was not actionable. *Inglis v. Buena Vista Univ.*, 235 F.Supp.2d 1009 (N.D. Iowa 2002). [IA]

◆ *An employee's discrimination claims failed where the college presented legitimate reasons for its decisions.*

A clerk at an Oklahoma community college complained over a number of years that she had the same responsibilities as a male assistant but that she was paid less. In 1997, she was promoted to assistant but was not given a raise because she already made more than an entry-level assistant. In 1998, she stated that she was going to hire a lawyer to help her obtain equal pay. Two days later, the employee and the rest of her department learned that overtime pay would no longer be available. She told a supervisor that she would not be able to complete all her work as a result. During that meeting, the two got into a heated confrontation, and the supervisor recommended to an executive vice president that the employee be fired. The college fired the employee. She sued under the Equal Pay Act, Title VII and 42 U.S.C. § 1983, and a federal court dismissed her claims.

The Tenth Circuit affirmed. Here, the Equal Pay Act claim failed because the male assistant had greater responsibilities until she was promoted, and had greater seniority after her promotion. **The Title VII retaliation claim failed because the college offered a legitimate reason for her termination—** insubordination. And the § 1983 claim failed because she was an at-will employee with no constitutionally protected property interest in continued employment with the college. *Lewis v. Board of Regents for Tulsa Community College*, 2002 WL 1316810 (10th Cir. 6/18/02). [OK]

◆ *An Equal Pay Act claim failed where the two professors being compared were not in substantially similar positions.*

A female professor at an Illinois university believed that she was being paid less than a similarly situated male professor. She sued the university under the Equal Pay Act. A federal court ruled for the university, noting that the university had presented legitimate reasons for paying the male professor more. First, he was recruited while he was a full professor at another university; she did not become a full professor until 13 years after her hiring. Second, the male professor received an appointment to a chair position and served on a department publication and committee. Thus, the two professors were not similarly situated. **She did not perform work requiring equal skill, effort and responsibility under similar working conditions.** *Pinkston v. University of Chicago*, 2001 WL 1609395 (C.D. Ill. 12/12/01). [IL]

◆ *A university violated Title VII and the Equal Pay Act by paying a female doctor less than a male.*

A female doctor at a Texas university had full-tenure status and was paid $64,000 per year. Another female doctor in the department informed the department chair that her husband (also a doctor) was dissatisfied with his job and that she might leave the department if he got another job. The department chair hired her husband for $83,000 a year to keep her from leaving the department. When the female doctor sued the university under Title VII and the Equal Pay Act, **a federal jury awarded her $91,000 in back pay, $20,000 in compensatory damages and an annual salary equal to the male doctor's.**

On appeal, the Fifth Circuit upheld the award. First, the university could not claim that his grant-obtaining abilities were better than hers because the department did not have a policy of factoring that in when making salary determinations. Also, this was not a case where market forces allowed for paying him more; the university hired him to keep his wife from leaving. Finally, the university was not entitled to Eleventh Amendment immunity. *Siler-Khodr v. University of Texas Health Science Center San Antonio*, 261 F.3d 542 (5th Cir. 2001). [TX]

◆ *The Second Circuit affirmed a jury verdict of $117,929.98 to a female professor who sued Marist College under the Equal Pay Act and Title VII.*

After the jury rendered its verdict for the professor, both sides appealed different aspects of the decision. The college argued that the verdict should be overturned because the professor did not make specific comparisons with her male counterparts, but rather the group as a whole. Thus, the university argued that the professor failed to state a *prima facie* case.

The professor claimed that a special jury verdict form erroneously instructed the jury to ignore her claim under Title VII if it found that any violation of the Equal Pay Act by the college was not willful. The appeals panel rejected the college's argument, finding that the five variables the professor's expert used to isolate comparable positions were effective. The variables were rank, years of service, division, tenure status and degrees earned. Turning to the professor's argument on appeal, the circuit court pointed out that while the Equal Pay Act and Title VII must be construed in harmony, particularly where claims made under the two statutes arise out of the same discriminatory pay policies, another consideration comes into play. One of the major differences between the Equal Pay Act and Title VII is the requirement regarding intent. **Under Title VII, a plaintiff alleging disparate treatment must demonstrate discriminatory intent, while an Equal Pay Act plaintiff does not have to make this showing.** Accordingly, the jury verdict form was appropriate. The district court decision was upheld. *Lavin-McEleney v. Marist College*, 239 F.3d 476 (2d Cir. 2001). [NY]

◆   *Illinois State University was not entitled to immunity under the EPA.*

An EPA suit was filed by a group of tenured and tenure-track female instructors. They claimed that they received less compensation than male instructors. The case reached the Seventh Circuit, which held that Congress had clearly intended to abrogate the States' Eleventh Amendment immunity in crafting the Equal Pay Act and that the abrogation was a valid exercise of Congressional authority. The university argued that gender discrimination claims are evaluated based on intermediate scrutiny and that the Equal Pay Act unconstitutionally raised its burden by subjecting it to the strict scrutiny test. However, **the court found that the Act's language allowed the university to avoid liability by showing that the wage disparity was based on a factor other than gender**. Accordingly, the Act did not subject the university to liability that it would not otherwise be subjected to under the federal Constitution. Further, Congress enacted this legislation based on a history of gender discrimination. Thus, the university was not entitled to Eleventh Amendment immunity from the instructors' Equal Pay Act claims. *Varner v. Illinois State Univ.*, 226 F.3d 927 (7th Cir. 2000). [IL]

◆   *In a later case, the Seventh Circuit restated its position on immunity.*

An English professor at a Wisconsin university resigned after 22 years and then sued under Title IX and the Equal Pay Act, alleging that she had been compensated at a lower rate than male professors with similar experience and education. The university sought to dismiss her claims, asserting that the **Eleventh Amendment** barred her claims against it. The court denied the motion to dismiss, and the Seventh Circuit Court of Appeals affirmed. *Cherry v. University of Wisconsin System Bd. of Regents*, 265 F.3d 541 (7th Cir. 2001). [WI]

◆   *Female faculty members could not bring a class action lawsuit against the University of Washington for discrimination in their compensation.*

The plaintiffs sued the University of Washington for gender discrimination and equal pay violations under state law. The complaint listed five class representatives who were professors or former professors at the university's medical and dental schools. The lead plaintiff was a full professor in the department of oral and maxillofacial surgery pathology who allegedly was consistently compensated less than her male counterparts.

The plaintiffs sought a declaratory judgment finding the school systematically discriminated against class members. They also sought an order prohibiting the university from engaging in future discrimination, forcing the school to continue assessing unequal treatment among male and female faculty members, and compelling the university to take active steps to eliminate future discrimination through training, adjustments in hiring and other measures. A state court agreed to certify the proposed class, but the Washington Court of Appeals reversed. It found that **the professors failed to establish a common course of conduct that would support a class action lawsuit**. *Oda v. State*, 44 P.3d 8 (Wash. App. Div. 1 2002). [WA]

D. Pregnancy Discrimination

Pregnancy discrimination is prohibited by Title VII of the Civil Rights Act of 1964. However, a religious school can discipline employees for failing to comply with religious teachings. Thus, where sex outside of wedlock is prohibited, for example, a teacher can be discharged for such activity. The school must merely ensure that it treats men and women alike.

◆ *A pregnancy discrimination case could not be dismissed where the employee presented evidence she was discharged because of her pregnancy.*

A community college hired an Illinois woman as a secretary. A few months later, her supervisors informed her that her work was not satisfactory and that she would have to improve if she wanted to keep her job. Over the next two months her work improved. She then learned that she was pregnant and informed her supervisors of that fact. Ten days later, they informed her that they were recommending that she be fired. Rather than appeal that recommendation internally, she hired an attorney and, after her employment was terminated, sued the college and various college officials for pregnancy discrimination. The defendants sought to dismiss the lawsuit. The court noted that where an indirect method of proving discrimination is employed, the employee must prove that she was doing her job well enough to meet her employer's legitimate expectations. However, **where, as here, the direct method of proof is used, even an employee who cannot prove that she was satisfying her employer's legitimate expectations is protected by Title VII**, though evidence about the employee's job performance may play an important role in the court's assessment of the direct case. Because there was a question of fact as to whether the discharge was because of pregnancy, the court refused to dismiss the case. *Suarez v. Illinois Valley Community College*, 688 F.Supp. 376 (N.D. Ill. 1988). [IL]

E. Sexual Orientation

◆ *The denial of health care benefits to same sex partners of employees was held to violate the Alaska Human Rights Act.*

The University of Alaska denied health insurance benefits to the domestic partners of two employees because the domestic partners were neither spouses nor dependents. The employees sued the university for violating the state Human Rights Act, and the case reached the Supreme Court of Alaska. The university conceded that it had discriminated against the employees on the basis of their marital status, but asserted that providing lower health care benefits to single employees did not violate the Human Rights Act because the legislature did not intend to prohibit the kind of discrimination it was practicing. **Noting that the Human Rights Act prohibits discrimination on the basis of marital status, the supreme court held that the university had violated the Act.** *University of Alaska v. Tumeo*, 933 P.2d 1147 (Alaska 1997). [AK]

◆ *Denying health care benefits to domestic partners of gay and lesbian state university employees violated Oregon's Constitution.*

The Oregon Court of Appeals determined that a public health sciences university violated the state constitution's privileges and immunities clause by maintaining **a practice of denying health insurance coverage to the domestic partners of its homosexual employees.** The case arose after three university nurses applied for insurance coverage for their domestic partners. The benefits manager refused to process the application because the university provided health insurance to spouses, not unmarried partners. After the state employee benefits board upheld the denial of benefits, the nurses sued. The state court of appeals held that Oregon's employment discrimination statute protected the nurses on the basis of their sexual orientation. However, the university did not violate that statute. Rather, the university violated the state constitution's privileges and immunities clause (which requires governmental entities to make benefits available on equal terms to all Oregon citizens). **Because homosexuals cannot marry under Oregon law, the university's health insurance benefits were made available on terms that, for gay and lesbian couples, were a legal impossibility.** *Tanner v. Oregon Health Sciences Univ.*, 971 P.2d 435 (Or. App. 1998). [OR]

III. RELIGIOUS DISCRIMINATION

Title VII generally prohibits religious discrimination. However, religious hiring preferences are permitted if the institution is substantially "owned, supported, controlled, or managed" by a religious organization or if the curriculum "is directed toward the propagation of a particular religion."

◆ *A Texas professor was unable to establish that a university improperly fired him based on his religious beliefs.*

The professor asserted that as the only Jewish professor in a predominantly Arab or Muslim department, he was subjected to a hostile work environment. He contended the university required him to teach a course on his Sabbath, while accommodating Muslim colleagues during Ramadan. A colleague observed the professor's class and found that he was not teaching or applying the required subjects. His supervisor rated his performance "unsatisfactory" and "unacceptable," and the university discharged him. The professor sued the university in a state court for age and religious discrimination. The court awarded the university summary judgment, and the professor appealed.

The Court of Appeals of Texas held that to prevail in his religious discrimination claim, the professor had to show the university knew of his good faith religious beliefs, that they conflicted with a job requirement, and that he suffered an adverse employment action for failing to comply

with the requirement. In view of the substantial evidence indicating the professor's performance was poor, the court concluded the university had legitimate, non-discriminatory reasons for discharging him. Accordingly, summary judgment for the university was affirmed. *Brauer v. Texas A&M Univ.*, No. 13-01-868-CV, 2003 WL 22415369 (Tex. App. 2003). [TX]

◆ *A federal district court dismissed an Illinois employee's charges of discrimination and retaliation against a college.*

The college assigned the employee to advise students in a center operated by the Chicago Public Schools (CPS). He claimed the center mistreated him because he wore dreadlocks and a kofi to observe his religion. The employee filed an administrative complaint alleging race discrimination against CPS. He later claimed the college discharged him in retaliation for filing the claim. The employee then sued CPS in a federal district court for Title VII violations. The case was dismissed because CPS had never been his employer.

The employee filed a new action against the college for race and religious discrimination and retaliation. The complaint alleged the college retaliated against him after it learned of his discrimination claim against CPS. The court noted the discrimination charges referred to only retaliation and said nothing about the college engaging in discriminatory practices. It therefore dismissed the race discrimination claim. **The court said that in a Title VII retaliation claim, the retaliatory actions must be those of the employer or an agent of the employer. Since the college and CPS were separate and independent from one another, charges against one could not be imputed to the other.** For that reason, the court dismissed the retaliation claim. *Flowers v. Columbia College Chicago*, No. 03 C 9247, 2004 WL 1459346 (N.D. Ill. 2004). [IL]

◆ *A Massachusetts professor failed to show religious discrimination and also failed to timely file his claim.*

A tenured professor at a Massachusetts university was interrupted at home while observing the Jewish holy day of Yom Kippur. He complained to a dean and from then on was not disturbed while observing religious days at home. However, he claimed that the incident caused a hostile work environment to develop and resulted in retaliation against him. He filed a religious discrimination complaint against the university. The Superior Court of Massachusetts dismissed his claim because he had waited more than six months to file his claim. **There was no evidence that the professor experienced continuing harassment** that would allow him to pursue his case under the continuing violation doctrine. Moreover, he suffered no disciplinary action and was still employed by the university. *Berger v. Brandeis Univ.*, 2002 WL 31433433 (Mass. Super. 10/31/02). [MA]

◆ *An employee who quit under adverse conditions could proceed with her lawsuit for religious discrimination under Title VII.*

A recruiter for the University of Chicago Hospitals was an Evangelical Christian Baptist who recruited people at churches and church job fairs. She got a new boss who directed her to remove all religious items from her desk. She also was told that she could no longer recruit at churches and church job fairs.

Although she had previously received good reviews, under the new boss, she was warned that she would be fired if her performance did not improve. Shortly before her vacation, another recruiter was hired to perform essentially the same duties. During a phone call while she was on vacation, she was asked about some missing applicant test scores, and was told that was the "last straw" and to "be prepared" when her leave was over. When she returned from vacation, she found her desk packed up and her office being used for storage. She resigned and filed a complaint with the EEOC, which sued on her behalf for constructive discharge on the basis of religion. An Illinois federal court granted pretrial judgment to the university hospitals, holding that she was not subjected to conditions that would make a reasonable person quit. The Seventh Circuit reversed, holding that **Title VII also protects employees who have been told that termination is coming and who decide to quit rather than wait to be fired**. *EEOC v. University of Chicago Hospitals*, 276 F.3d 326 (7th Cir. 2002). [IL]

◆   *An Orthodox Jewish professor's claims of religious discrimination, hostile work environment and retaliation were allowed to go to trial.*

At the start of an Orthodox Jewish professor's first year as an associate professor in the School of Education at William Paterson College of New Jersey, her department chair allowed her to arrange her schedule around religious holidays and did not count as sick days the days she missed for religious holidays. During her third year of employment, she was charged sick days for religious holidays. She also was charged a sick day for a Jewish holiday that fell on a day she was not scheduled to teach. The professor was continually asked why she could not attend meetings on Friday nights and Saturdays, even though she had explained her wish to observe the Sabbath. After her termination, she sued under Title VII and the New Jersey Law Against Discrimination for religious discrimination, hostile work environment and retaliation. The district court granted pretrial judgment to the university, finding no intentional discrimination on the basis of religion.

The Third Circuit Court of Appeals reversed, noting that the district court applied the wrong standard when evaluating the professor's hostile environment claim. Rather than require a showing of discriminatory animus, the court should have asked **whether a reasonable fact finder could view the evidence as showing that the professor's treatment was attributable to her religion**. Although the college provided legitimate nondiscriminatory reasons for its decision not to retain the professor, she was able to cast doubt on the legitimacy of those reasons such that the lawsuit could proceed. *Abramson v. William Paterson College of New Jersey*, 260 F.3d 265 (3d Cir. 2001). [NJ]

◆   *A Tennessee religious college could fire a lesbian employee who worked closely with students.*

A Baptist college in Tennessee offered baccalaureate degrees in nursing and health sciences. It did not offer any religion degrees and required only one three-hour course in religion for its degree programs. It also did not require its faculty, staff members or students to be Baptists. The college hired a student services specialist to work with students in planning activities of various campus student organizations. The college learned that the employee was a lesbian, who also was a minister at a Christian church that advertised itself as being open to gays and lesbians. Because the college's Baptist constituency believed homosexuality to be sinful, the college asked for the employee's resignation. When she refused to provide it, she was fired. She sued the college and its parent corporation for religious discrimination under Title VII, claiming that she was fired because of her different religious beliefs.

The U.S. District Court for the Western District of Tennessee granted pretrial judgment to the defendants. It noted that **religious organizations may discriminate on the basis of religion in certain circumstances** (for example, where an educational institution employs individuals of a particular religion to perform work connected with the carrying on by such institution of its activities). Here, the court found that the college qualified as a religious educational institution even though it did not offer any degrees in religion or theology. Further, even if it were not exempted from Title VII, it did not discriminate against the employee. **Its reason for firing her—that she had assumed a leadership role in an organization espousing beliefs diametrically opposed to its own—was not a pretext for discrimination.** The employee's claim could not succeed. *Hall v. Baptist Memorial Health Care Corp.*, 27 F.Supp.2d 1029 (W.D. Tenn. 1998). [TN]

◆ *A Missouri Christian college could fire a Catholic teacher without violating Title VII.*

A Catholic faculty member at a Presbyterian college conducted a survey of fellow faculty members. Subsequently, the dean instructed him to stop the survey. He alleged that he then failed to receive raises or received less than average raises for seven years, after which he was fired. He sued the college for discrimination on the basis of religion and for retaliation. A Missouri federal court dismissed his lawsuit. It stated that the college (as a Christian college) was exempt from Title VII's prohibition against religious discrimination. Further, **even though the employee—as a Catholic—was a Christian, the college still could disagree with his religious views. Therefore, if the college in fact discharged him because of his religious views, it could lawfully do so under Title VII.** With respect to the retaliation claim, the court noted that the employee had not been engaged in protected activity under Title VII. As a result, he could not prove that the college had retaliated against him in violation of that statute even if it took adverse action against him because of the survey. *Wirth v. College of the Ozarks*, 26 F.Supp.2d 1185 (W.D. Mo. 1998). [MO]

◆ *A private university that had established a divinity school qualified as a religious educational institution under Title VII.*

An Alabama private university received a bequest to establish a divinity school and entered into a contract with a professor to teach in both the divinity school and the undergraduate departments of religion and English at the university. Because the professor and the dean of the divinity school did not share the same theological views, the university eventually removed the professor from the divinity school teaching schedule. He filed a Title VII claim of religious discrimination against the university in the U.S. District Court for the Northern District of Alabama. The university sought pretrial judgment on the grounds that it qualified for a religious exemption under the statute. The district court granted the motion, and the professor appealed.

The U.S. Court of Appeals, Eleventh Circuit, held the university qualified for the religious educational institution exemption under § 702(a) of Title VII. The university received approximately seven percent of its annual budget (over $4 million) from the Alabama Baptist Convention. Further, both the Internal Revenue Service and the U.S. Department of Education recognized the university as a religious educational institution and granted it exemptions on that basis. The court then examined § 703(e)(2) of **Title VII, which grants an exemption to schools, colleges, universities and other educational institutions that are owned, supported, controlled or managed in whole or substantial part by a religious association**. Here, the university's receipt of seven percent of its budget from the convention amounted to substantial support. Accordingly, as an alternative to the court's § 702 holding, the university qualified as an educational institution supported in substantial part by a religious association and thus protected by the exemptions in Title VII. The court affirmed the district court's decision. *Killinger v. Samford Univ.*, 113 F.3d 196 (11th Cir. 1997). [AL]

IV. AGE DISCRIMINATION

The Age Discrimination in Employment Act (ADEA), 29 U.S.C. § 621 et seq., prohibits age discrimination against individuals at least 40 years of age. As part of the Fair Labor Standards Act, it applies to institutions with 20 or more employees and which affect interstate commerce. Although state employees can no longer sue under the ADEA (see Kimel v. Florida Bd. of Regents, *below), state statutes and the Equal Protection Clause can provide relief. With respect to private employers, the ADEA remains in force.*

A. ADEA

◆ *Recently, the Supreme Court held that state employees could not sue their employers under the ADEA.*

Two associate professors at the University of Montevallo sued the university in an Alabama federal court under the ADEA. They alleged that the university had discriminated against them on the basis of their age, that it had retaliated against them for filing charges with the EEOC, and that its College of Business, where they were employed, used an evaluation system that had a disparate impact on older faculty members. The university sought to dismiss the action on the grounds of Eleventh Amendment immunity, and the district court agreed, finding that the ADEA did not eliminate the state's immunity.

A group of current and former faculty and librarians of Florida State University and Florida International University filed suit against the Florida Board of Regents under the ADEA, alleging that the board refused to require the two state universities to allocate funds to provide previously agreed-upon market adjustments to the salaries of eligible university employees. They maintained that this failure had a disparate impact on the base pay of employees with a longer record of service, most of who were older. The board sought to dismiss the action under the Eleventh Amendment, but the court refused to do so.

On appeal to the Eleventh Circuit, the court of appeals consolidated the cases and held that the ADEA did not abrogate (do away with) the states' Eleventh Amendment immunity. The U.S. Supreme Court then agreed to review the case and affirmed the court of appeals' decision. It noted that **although the ADEA contains a clear statement of Congress' intent to eliminate the states' immunity under the Eleventh Amendment, such action exceeded Congress' authority under § 5 of the Fourteenth Amendment** (which grants Congress the power to enact laws under the Equal Protection Clause). The Court observed that although state employees cannot sue their employers for discrimination under the ADEA, they are not without remedies. Every state has age discrimination statutes, and almost all of them allow the recovery of money damages from state employers. *Kimel v. Florida Bd. of Regents*, 528 U.S. 62, 120 S.Ct. 631, 145 L.Ed.2d 522 (2000). [AL]

◆   *The U.S. Supreme Court issued a ruling affecting the right of a former private university employee to have his case returned to state court rather than dismissed at the federal court level.*

A private university employee sued the university in a Pennsylvania trial court, claiming that the school had violated the ADEA. He also brought state law claims for wrongful discharge, breach of contract and other violations. The employee was allowed to remove the case from state court to federal court because the alleged violation of the ADEA gave federal court jurisdiction over the entire lawsuit. The employee then discovered that he had failed to file a timely age discrimination charge with a federal or state agency. He requested that the federal claim be deleted and that the case be remanded to the state court in which it was filed. The federal court granted his request, and the U.S. Court of Appeals, Third Circuit, upheld that request. The U.S. Supreme Court concluded that **federal courts can remand a case back to state court if such action would best accommodate the values of economy, convenience, fairness and comity**. The employee's case could be remanded to the Pennsylvania trial court in which it was filed. *Carnegie-Mellon Univ. v. Cohill*, 484 U.S. 343, 108 S.Ct. 614, 98 L.Ed.2d 720 (1988). [PA]

1. Applicability to Religious Schools

◆   *The ADEA did not to apply in the following case involving a seminary.*

A Missouri seminary allegedly dismissed an employee because of his age. He sued the seminary in a federal district court under the ADEA. The seminary brought a motion for pretrial judgment, stating that the ADEA was inapplicable because the institution was pervasively religious. The court agreed. It considered the U.S. Supreme Court's decision in *NLRB v. Catholic Bishop of Chicago*, 440 U.S. 490, 99 S.Ct. 1313, 59 L.Ed.2d 533 (1979), in which the Court held the National Labor Relations Act inapplicable to church-operated schools. The court ruled that although the ADEA was a remedial statute rather than a regulatory statute such as the NLRA, the ruling in *Catholic Bishop* applied here. Because application of the ADEA could implicate enforcement by the EEOC, government regulatory powers were involved. Thus, **since the**

potential existed for impinging the seminary's religious freedoms, the
court ruled that the ADEA was inapplicable. It granted the seminary's
motion for pretrial judgment. *Cochran v. St. Louis Preparatory Seminary*, 717
F.Supp. 1413 (E.D. Mo. 1989). [MO]

◆   *However, an Ohio federal court held that the ADEA could be applied to a*
religious institution.

An employee at Xavier University, an institution operated by the Order of
Jesuits, sued the university under the ADEA in an Ohio federal court. The
university asserted that the court had no authority to rule on the case because
the university, as a religious institution, was exempt from the ADEA's
provisions. The court observed that because the ADEA gave no indication that
religious institutions were exempt from its provisions, the issue became
whether application of the ADEA to the university would violate the Free
Exercise and Establishment Clauses of the First Amendment. It then held for
the employee, noting that the Fourth Circuit held in *Ritter v. Mount St. Mary's*
College, 814 F.2d 986 (4th Cir. 1987), that **application of the ADEA to a**
religious institution did not present a significant risk of infringement on
the institution's First Amendment rights. Here, the facts gave no indication
that enforcement of the ADEA would violate the religion clauses of the First
Amendment. Accordingly, the university was not entitled to have the case
dismissed. *Soriano v. Xavier Univ.*, 687 F.Supp. 1188 (S.D. Ohio 1988). [OH]

2. Releases and Settlements

◆   *A fired security officer could not use the OWBPA to avoid signing a*
settlement agreement.

When the director of protective services at a New York university was fired
at the age of 67 (after 16 years on the job), he sued under the ADEA for age
discrimination. The university maintained that the real reasons for the firing
were his poor communication skills and his inability to work with other
employees and supervisors. During a settlement conference, no agreement was
reached. But a second conference was held several months later, at which the
employee agreed to accept $199,000 in exchange for a release of his claims
prior to the settlement date. However, he later refused to sign the agreement on
the grounds that he did not have enough time to consider it under the Older
Workers Benefit Protection Act. The court ordered him to sign the agreement
because **the waiver was knowing and voluntary under the OWBPA**. He had
had several months to consider the agreement between conferences, and had
been represented by an attorney throughout the settlement process. *Manning v.*
New York Univ., 2001 WL 963982 (S.D.N.Y. 8/22/01). [NY]

◆   *A private university could require a former employee to withdraw her*
EEOC claim in order to obtain a settlement award.

A Tennessee woman who worked for a private university received a letter
of reprimand and filed two grievances against her supervisors as a result.
Subsequently, the head of the department and another supervisor asked her to
sign a voluntary resignation letter and when she refused, she was discharged.

Eight days later, she filed an age discrimination charge with the EEOC. The university conducted a grievance hearing before the associate dean of students who found no evidence of age discrimination or harassment. However, she recommended that the employee be placed on paid administrative leave for six months with a reasonable letter of recommendation to help her find another position within the university system. The university informed the employee that it would accept the recommendation of the hearing officer subject to the employee's agreement to withdraw her EEOC charge. When the employee refused to do so, the university declined to implement the recommended resolution. The employee then sued the university for retaliation in violation of the ADEA. The court found that the university had not taken an adverse employment action against the employee. **Requiring an employee to withdraw an EEOC claim in order to have a recommended settlement award implemented is not an adverse employment action.** The court ruled for the university. *Hansen v. Vanderbilt Univ.*, 961 F.Supp. 1149 (M.D. Tenn. 1997). [TN]

3. Defenses

◆ *The Supreme Court held that two employees could not pursue their age discrimination claims in state court because they waited too long to sue.*

Two employees of the University of Minnesota claimed that the university tried to force them to accept early retirement at the age of 52 and, when they refused to retire, reclassified their jobs to lower their salaries. They sued the university in federal court under the ADEA and also alleged age discrimination under the Minnesota Human Rights Act as a supplemental claim. The university asserted that it was immune to suit under the Eleventh Amendment and, after the U.S. Supreme Court ruled in *Kimel v. Florida Bd. of Regents*, 528 U.S. 62 (2000), that states are immune to lawsuits brought by individuals under the ADEA, a federal court dismissed their lawsuit. They then sought to sue the university in state court under state law, alleging that the statute of limitations was tolled during the time they were pursuing their federal court action. The case reached the U.S. Supreme Court, which ruled against them. The Court held that the federal law at issue here (which tolls the statute of limitations on certain state law actions while a plaintiff pursues a related claim in federal court) did not apply to claims that are dismissed under the Eleventh Amendment. **Since the state had immunity in the federal action, there was no tolling of the state action up until the time the federal action was dismissed.** *Raygor v. Regents of Univ. of Minnesota*, 534 U.S. 533, 122 S.Ct. 999, 152 L.Ed.2d 27 (2002). [MN]

◆ *There was no discrimination where a university reorganized a department and let a professor go.*

Loyola University employed an "over 40" doctor in its medical school's pathology department under a non-tenured contract. Due to financial considerations, the department's chair was directed to reorganize the department. He restructured a laboratory, taking away one of the doctor's duties and giving it to two younger, male doctors who had advanced knowledge and ability. Later, he recommended that the doctor's contract not be renewed. She appealed her termination through the university's administrative process, but when that was unsuccessful, she sued for age and sex discrimination. An Illinois federal court ruled for Loyola, and the Seventh Circuit Court of Appeals affirmed. **Loyola had asserted a legitimate, nondiscriminatory reason for terminating her employment**–budgetary issues–and had let both male and female employees go. There was no discrimination. *Kowal-Vern v. Loyola Univ. of Chicago*, 66 Fed.Appx. 649 (7th Cir. 2003). [IL]

◆ *Even though a university could not be sued by ex-employees under the ADEA, it could be sued by the EEOC.*

The University of Wisconsin Press, a nonprofit publishing company affiliated with the university's graduate school, laid off four workers between the ages of 46 and 54. All were replaced by younger workers. When the four workers complained to the Equal Employment Opportunity Commission, the EEOC agreed to prosecute the case. A federal jury concluded that the university willfully violated the ADEA, and the Seventh Circuit affirmed. The court of appeals first noted that even though the university was immune to lawsuits under the ADEA brought by the individual workers, it was not immune to a lawsuit brought by the EEOC. Next, the court noted that there was ample evidence to support the jury's verdict. The decision to lay off the employees was made without any consideration of their respective job skills, without input from their supervisors, and without any discussion with the employees. Further, **the jury's finding that the violation was willful was upheld because university officials were not educated on their obligations under the ADEA**. The award against the university was upheld. *EEOC v. Board of Regents of Univ. of Wisconsin System*, 288 F.3d 296 (7th Cir. 2002). [WI]

◆ *An employee's age discrimination lawsuit failed where the university that fired him offered a legitimate nondiscriminatory reason for so doing.*

A 43-year-old man was employed as a carpenter at a private Illinois university. He began writing letters to the office manager, who was six months pregnant. He continued to write personal letters to her and began bringing gifts for her and the baby. After complaining to another manager about the letters and gifts, the office manager spoke to the carpenter and asked him to stop writing her. However, the carpenter continued to write and send her gifts. After the manager returned from maternity leave, she again complained about the carpenter's continued behavior. That same day, the carpenter was summoned to a meeting with his supervisors, who told him about the manager's complaints. After he refused to resign, he was fired for sexual harassment. Shortly thereafter, he was replaced by a 32-year-old man.

The carpenter sued the university in an Illinois federal court, alleging that his discharge violated the ADEA. The court ruled for the university, and the U.S. Court of Appeals, Seventh Circuit, affirmed. The university had articulated a legitimate, nondiscriminatory reason for the discharge—sexual harassment. Therefore, the only remaining issue was whether the reason given by the university was pretextual. Here, **the carpenter produced no evidence to support his claim of age discrimination.** *O'Connor v. DePaul Univ.*, 123 F.3d 665 (7th Cir. 1997). [IL]

◆ *A professor was not entitled to a promotion simply because he received*
satisfactory evaluations as an assistant professor.

An assistant professor employed by an Indiana private university retired
after having been denied a promotion to associate professor. The promotion and
tenure committee stated as reasons for the rejection that his work as a teacher
was not superior, his service to the university community was limited, and that
he had not achieved distinction in performance. The professor countered that he
was viewed as a satisfactory member of the faculty, and that he would have
been promoted to associate professor on several earlier occasions but for his
lack of a Ph.D. and budgetary shortfalls. The professor also observed that a
younger person was promoted to associate professor in 1991-92. The professor
filed an age discrimination lawsuit against the university. The Seventh Circuit
held that **the professor's argument failed to distinguish between competent
and superior achievement. Satisfactory performance as an assistant
professor did not entitle him to the promotion.** The court ruled in favor of
the university. *Kuhn v. Ball State Univ.*, 78 F.3d 330 (7th Cir. 1996). [IN]

4. Evidence of Discrimination

◆ *A 61-year-old Illinois university administrator's ADEA claim failed*
because she did not show she was treated less favorably than younger persons.

The administrator was promoted into a new position at the age of 61.
Shortly after starting, she learned she had to work a significant amount of
overtime to timely complete required financial reports. The administrator was
unwillingly to put in these hours. A supervisor claimed she made mistakes
because of her poor computer skills. Although he rated her performance
"acceptable," he identified areas in which she could improve and noted she
would have to work additional hours to meet her goals. After another similar
evaluation, the administrator stormed out of a meeting with the supervisor, and
he placed her on a 60-day performance improvement plan.

The administrator showed no signs of improvement after 60 days, and the
university discharged her. She sued the university in a federal district court for
age discrimination under the ADEA. The university argued she could not prove
younger employees were treated more favorably than she was treated. The
**court held that while discrimination may be implied by the hiring of a
younger person for a position, the administrator made no such showing.**
The university was entitled to summary judgment as the evidence did not
support the complaint. *Vera v. University of Chicago*, No. 02 C 9124, 2004 WL
1123817 (N.D. Ill. 2004). [IL]

◆ *An age discrimination claim failed where a 55-year-old applicant made it*
to the stage of finalist.

A Wisconsin technical college advertised for an instructor of psychology,
listing the minimum criteria as a masters' degree in psychology with a
sociology minor preferred. The college received 29 applications, of which the
top 10 were numerically rated. Only the three highest-rated candidates received
interviews. The fifth-rated applicant was a 55-year-old male with a doctorate
degree in teaching with a psychology minor and relatively little teaching

experience. He claimed that the college's hiring practices were biased in favor of young women, observing that the three top-ranked candidates were all women and that only one was over 40. He sued the college in a federal district court for age discrimination. The court entered pretrial judgment for the college, and the applicant appealed.

The U.S. Court of Appeals, Seventh Circuit, agreed with the applicant that it was only necessary for him to show some evidence that the college's reasons for rejecting his application were pretextual. However, **his presence among the job finalists undermined his age discrimination theory, and although there were irregularities in the college's hiring policies, there was no evidence of discrimination**. The court affirmed the judgment for the college. *Senner v. Northcentral Technical College*, 113 F.3d 750 (7th Cir. 1997). [WI]

◆ *No discrimination was found in the following case, even though the department head had referred to a teacher as "too old."*

A 61-year-old professor at a North Carolina technical college had trouble adapting to a new curriculum. The department chair repeatedly admonished the professor to discontinue teaching the outmoded curriculum. After one confrontation within earshot of students, the professor challenged the department chair to a fistfight. The department chair subsequently stated that the college needed "new blood," because the professor was "outdated, too old, behind the times and unable to teach at the pace required." The college declined to extend the professor's contract beyond the following summer. A younger applicant was hired in his place. The college also denied the request for a hearing, although the personnel policy provided for review of all contractual decisions. The professor sued the college under the ADEA.

The district court first held that the department chair's statements did not constitute direct evidence of discrimination. Here, the only arguably discriminatory statement was the department chair's reference to the professor as "too old." The other comments merely reflected the college's desire that older employees remain current in their job knowledge. Further, such allegedly discriminatory comments were unlawful only if acted upon. Although the college replaced the professor with a younger employee, **there was a lack of direct evidence establishing discriminatory intent**. The professor also failed to establish that the college's nondiscriminatory reasons (his teaching of outmoded material and his confrontation with the department chair) were pretextual. *Fisher v. Asheville-Buncombe Technical Community College*, 857 F.Supp. 465 (W.D.N.C. 1993). [NC]

◆ *An insurer had to reimburse a school that violated the ADEA because the school did not act with the specific intent of violating the ADEA.*

A private school terminated an older tenured professor in order to meet budgetary requirements. The professor sought and obtained damages for the school's violation of the ADEA. The school then filed suit against its insurer for reimbursement. A Massachusetts federal court granted pretrial judgment to the insurer, and the appeals court reversed. On remand, the insurer was required to prove that the school knowingly violated the ADEA in order to avoid payment of the reimbursement costs under a policy exclusion. The district court found for the school. Both parties appealed to the First Circuit.

The main issue on appeal was **whether an actor of an intentionally committed wrongful act also must have had a "specific intent" to do something against the law in order to invoke the policy exclusion and thus preclude insurance coverage** for damages arising from a violation of the ADEA. Here, the court held that "specific intent" was absent, and the insurer was obliged to reimburse the school for its loss. Since the dean of the school was not familiar with the ADEA, he could not possibly have acted with the requisite "specific intent." Thus, the holding of the district court was not clearly erroneous and was affirmed. *Andover Newton Theological School v. Continental Cas. Co.*, 964 F.2d 1237 (1st Cir. 1992). [MA]

B. Mandatory Retirement

◆ *A professor who was subjected to mandatory retirement was not entitled to an injunction prohibiting her retirement.*

A world-renowned professor at a New York private university turned 70 years of age in 1993. As a full-time tenured professor, she had a student assistant, full use of the library and computer facilities, and was responsible for advising graduate students. The university informed her that she would be retired from her tenured position when she reached the age of 70 pursuant to its mandatory retirement policy. The professor rejected a part-time position as an adjunct professor after she retired and then filed suit in the U.S. District Court for the Southern District of New York, alleging age and sex discrimination and seeking an injunction prohibiting her retirement from her tenured position.

Although the mandatory retirement age was permissible under an exemption in the ADEA, the professor contended that it did not apply because the college's tenure policies did not strictly comply with the 1940 Principles on Academic Freedom and Tenure. The district court disagreed, ruling that the college's substantial compliance with the 1940 principles was sufficient to fall within the ADEA § 12(d) exemption. Consequently, **the college's mandatory retirement of the professor was permissible**. The court then held that the professor stated a valid Title VII sex discrimination claim. However, the court noted that the professor failed to establish the requisite "irreparable harm" necessary to justify a preliminary injunction prohibiting her removal from the tenured position (until resolution of the Title VII claim). The professor was not being placed in severe financial difficulty nor was she being "isolated" or "academically deprived." Rather, she merely faced reductions and limitations. Thus, the mandatory retirement did not violate the ADEA, and the professor was not entitled to a preliminary injunction. *Pollis v. New School for Social Research*, 829 F.Supp. 584 (S.D.N.Y. 1993). [NY]

◆ *Where a retired security guard did not sue for age discrimination until 10 years after the mandatory retirement policy was changed, he could not succeed.*

A man was hired in 1966 by Columbia University as a resident hall security guard and worked in that position for 22 years until retiring at the age of 65. The guard believed that he was required to retire because of his age. Ten years later, he learned that the mandatory retirement age was being changed at the time of his retirement. He claimed that this change should have applied to him. He sued the university and his former union.

The university moved for pretrial judgment, and the union moved for dismissal. The question in this case was whether the guard's actions were barred by the applicable statute of limitations. The normal time limit for these claims is six months from when the claimant could successfully have brought the claims. In some cases, this is interpreted as meaning either **when the claimant knew, or should have known, about the action**. The guard argued that the claims against the union should include a failure to notify him of the change in retirement age. However, the court held that his action against both the school and the union had accrued upon the execution of the change of mandatory retirement age, and that **the guard should have known about the claim at that time**. The facts that persuaded the court included ongoing negotiations at the time the guard retired, the union holding monthly meetings that the guard failed to attend, and the negotiations being well publicized. The court dismissed the claims as being time-barred. *Walker v. Columbia Univ. in City of New York*, 756 F.Supp. 149 (S.D.N.Y. 1991). [NY]

C. State Statutes

◆ *A graduate student could not sue for discrimination under Kentucky's employment laws because she was not an employee of the university.*

A 44-year-old graduate student studying psychology received a Regent's Fellowship that provided her with full tuition and a yearly stipend. She lost her fellowship after her third year of study due to her failure to have her thesis proposal approved by a department committee. She remained in the graduate program for another year, but was subsequently dismissed. The student filed an unsuccessful grievance, then sued for sex and age discrimination in violation of Kentucky law and the university handbook.

A state court granted the university's motion for pretrial judgment, finding the student had no cause of action under the state discrimination statutes because she was not an employee of the university. The Kentucky Court of Appeals affirmed. **It rejected the student's assertion that her duties as a psychologist during her studies resembled employee duties, not academic work.** Although the student may have developed a therapist-patient relationship with one clinic patient, it was clear that nearly all of her duties and activities were in connection with her academic work rather than providing a service to the university, and therefore, an employer-employee relationship did not exist. *Stewart v. University of Louisville*, 65 S.W.3d 536 (Ky. App. 2001). [KY]

◆ *Where an employee was not qualified for a position, she could not successfully sue for discrimination.*

An Ohio private college hired a female applicant to implement and develop a new degree completion program in organizational management. She signed a one-year contract for the period September 1992 to August 1993. Her supervisor notified her five months later that her contract would not be renewed because she had allegedly failed to work closely with the faculty, failed to recruit program faculty, and failed to develop the organizational, communication and management skills that were necessary to perform the position. The college hired another female in her place. The employee sued for sex, age, and religious discrimination. She testified that her supervisor deliberately excluded her from committee meetings, acted differently toward women of her age, and appeared to be "more comfortable" in a male environment. The trial court ruled for the college, and the employee appealed.

The Court of Appeals of Ohio held that because the employee had been replaced by another woman, she failed to establish an essential element of her sex discrimination claim. Moreover, with respect to her age and religious discrimination claims, even assuming that the employee could state a *prima facie* case as to each claim, there was insufficient evidence from which a rational trier of fact could conclude that the college's articulated reasons for the nonrenewal were pretextual. In fact, **not only did the employee lack the necessary skills, she acknowledged that communication problems existed between her and her supervisor**. Accordingly, the trial court had properly ruled in favor of the university. *Doerter v. Bluffton College*, 647 N.E.2d 876 (Ohio. App. 3d Dist. 1994). [OH]

◆ *State human rights laws mirror Title VII. They generally prohibit religious discrimination except by religious organizations.*

A Jewish vice-president at a New York Catholic university was discharged, allegedly because of poor job performance. He filed suit in a New York trial court, alleging that he was subjected to increased scrutiny and then discharged because of his Jewish faith in violation of the Human Rights Law. The trial court granted pretrial judgment to the university, and the vice-president appealed to the New York Supreme Court, Appellate Division. The appellate division affirmed, ruling that the university was exempt from the prohibition against religiously motivated discharges. The vice-president appealed to the Court of Appeals of New York.

The court of appeals noted that the New York Human Rights Law permits religious organizations to "giv[e] preference to persons of the same religion" or "to promote the religious principles for which it is established or maintained." **However, the court held that the university could not "discriminate against the vice-president for reasons having nothing to do with the free exercise of religion and then invoke the religious exemption as a shield against its unlawful conduct."** Here, disputed issues of fact as to whether the university engaged in unlawful discrimination precluded pretrial judgment in its favor. The holding of the appellate division was reversed. *Scheiber v. St. John's Univ.*, 84 N.Y.2d 120, 615 N.Y.S.2d 332 (N.Y. 1994). [NY]

◆ *Five years after settling a discrimination claim against a college, a professor was allowed to sue the college despite a release she had signed.*

An economics professor at a New York college initiated several state and federal lawsuits against the college alleging discrimination. She claimed the college was liable for age and sex discrimination because it reduced her employment status from full-time to three-fourths status after she turned 65. Subsequently, the professor executed a settlement agreement with the college. In return, the college agreed to continue her employment as an adjunct professor teaching six courses per year until she turned 70. The agreement also stated that the professor released the college from: "any manner ... of [lawsuits] which now exist or may hereinafter arise..." College officials allegedly informed her that due to college policy, she would not be employed beyond her 70th birthday. She then sued the college. A trial court held for the college, and the professor appealed. The issue before the appellate division court was **whether the settlement agreement precluded the professor from suing the college for age discrimination after she reached age 70**. The court observed that the settlement agreement released the college from the professor's original age discrimination lawsuit in exchange for its promise to employ her until she turned 70. It held that the new lawsuit was not barred by the settlement agreement. This was due to the fact that the college officials allegedly stated that the college had a policy of not hiring professors over 70 years of age. This presented **a fresh discrimination claim upon which the professor could sue**. The lower court decision was reversed. *Jochnowitz v. Russell Sage College*, 523 N.Y.S.2d 656 (A.D. 3d Dept. 1988). [NY]

V. DISABILITY DISCRIMINATION

Section 504 of the Rehabilitation Act of 1973, 29 U.S.C. § 794, prohibits discrimination against qualified individuals with disabilities in programs or activities receiving federal financial assistance. The Americans with Disabilities Act of 1990 (ADA), 42 U.S.C. § 12101 et seq., extends protection to both private and public employees. It also prohibits discrimination against employees who are associated with disabled individuals (for example, an employee with a disabled son or daughter).

A. Liability

◆ *The U.S. Supreme Court concluded that Congress exceeded its authority by allowing monetary damage awards against states in ADA cases.*

Two Alabama state employees alleged that they were discriminated against by their employers in violation of the ADA. One was a state university nursing director who was demoted upon her return from a medical leave to undergo treatment for breast cancer. The other was a youth services department security officer with chronic asthma and sleep apnea who alleged that the department refused to provide him with reasonable accommodations to mitigate the effects of his disabilities. They sued the state in federal court for monetary damages under the ADA. The court consolidated the cases and granted judgment to the state. The U.S. Court of Appeals, Eleventh Circuit, reversed the judgment.

The U.S. Supreme Court reversed, holding that the ADA did not validly abrogate Eleventh Amendment immunity in lawsuits seeking monetary relief. The Eleventh Amendment ensures that no state may be sued in a federal court without first consenting to be sued. However, Congress may abrogate this immunity where it does so unequivocally and under a valid grant of constitutional authority. The Supreme Court noted that legislation enacted under § 5 of the Fourteenth Amendment must demonstrate "congruence and proportionality between the injury to be prevented or remedied and the means adopted to that end." Here, there was no such congruence and proportionality.

Congress identified negative attitudes and biases against individuals with disabilities as reasons for enacting the ADA, but did not identify a pattern of irrational discrimination by the states. **This limited evidence fell far short of showing a pattern of unconstitutional discrimination.** Congress thus exceeded its authority by authorizing suits for money damages under the ADA against the states. *Board of Trustees of Univ. of Alabama v. Garrett*, 531 U.S. 356, 121 S.Ct. 955, 148 L.Ed.2d 866 (2001). [AL]

◆ *A Texas university medical center was entitled to Eleventh Amendment immunity in an ADA case.*

The center hired a police officer who refused to be sprayed with pepper spray during training because of his chronic rhinosinusitis, nasal polyposis, and allergic rhinitis. He claimed the center failed to reasonably accommodate his disabilities and relied on job criteria that precluded individuals with disabilities from obtaining employment. The officer sued the center in a state court for ADA violations. The center removed the case to a federal district court and moved for dismissal. **The court recognized the center was a state entity. It held the officer's claim for monetary damages was barred under *Board of Trustees of Univ. of Alabama v. Garrett*, above.** The center did not waive its Eleventh Amendment immunity by removing the case from state to federal court. Since the monetary claims were barred by Eleventh Amendment immunity, and since the center never waived its immunity, the ADA claims were dismissed. *Keithly v. University of Texas Southwestern Medical Center*, No. Civ. A. 303CV0452L, 2003 WL 22862798 (N.D. Tex. 2003). [TX]

◆ *A New York university employee raised material issues of fact concerning the university's ability to accommodate her disability.*

The employee had Systemic Lupus Erythematosus. Due to pain and fatigue, she was allowed to work only seven hours per day. During the next eight years, the employee took several leaves of absence for her disability and child care needs. The university warned her about excessive absences and tardiness, but promoted her to a departmental administrative position. The employee received a positive employment evaluation in her first year in the position, but her absences then increased dramatically. A university official said her absences were disruptive and ordered her to return to work by a specific date. The employee instead presented the university with a physician's note and requested an indefinite leave of absence. Her initial application for long-term disability benefits was denied, and the university discharged her.

Although the employee was later awarded long-term disability benefits and was reinstated on long-term disability leave, she sued the university in a federal district court for ADA violations. **The court focused on her ability to perform the essential functions of her position.** While the university contended the employee had to work for eight hours each day, she presented evidence she rarely needed to work overtime and that she had performed her essential job functions during a seven-hour shift for several years. The court accepted the employee's explanation that she was forced to apply for long-term disability benefits because the university did not offer her reasonable accommodations. Based on her employment history and inconsistencies in the parties' versions of events, the court denied the university's summary judgment motion. *James v. Trustees of Columbia Univ.*, No. 01 Civ. 8873(LBS), 2003 WL 23018797 (S.D.N.Y. 2003). [NY]

◆ *A Massachusetts university librarian with rheumatoid arthritis was entitled to further opportunities to prove her claim of disability discrimination.*

The librarian's arthritis caused pain and exhaustion, and made it difficult for her to carry, lift and shelve materials. She asked the university to create an accommodation for her by assigning others her role of carrying materials, climbing stairs, and shelving articles and books. The university declined, even after a doctor sent a letter confirming the librarian had rheumatoid arthritis and should not lift over 10 pounds. The university insisted the librarian shelve books on a daily basis and never offered her an accommodation. Instead, it recommended she take a short-term disability leave.

The librarian sued the university in a state court for discrimination under the Massachusetts Civil Rights Act (CRA) and Massachusetts Equal Rights Act (MERA). The court dismissed the case and she appealed. **The Court of Appeals of Massachusetts considered whether shelving, paging and retrieval tasks were essential functions for the job, and whether the librarian could have performed these functions with a reasonable accommodation.** As the evidence about the job's essential functions was conflicting, and the trial court did not address the issue of reasonable accommodation, the order for summary judgment was inappropriate. The court vacated the judgment on the CRA claim, but affirmed the dismissal of the MERA claim, as this law created no independent right to sue. *Cargill v. Harvard Univ.*, 804 N.E.2d 377 (Mass. App. 2004). [MA]

◆ *The Fifth Circuit decided that a teacher at a community college in Texas raised sufficient factual issues to bring his ADA case to a jury.*

The instructor had slurred speech as the result of an accident, but never requested any accommodations. The president of the college transferred him from the college banking program, stating the program was not running well and that the instructor's handicap could have contributed to the problem. The next year, the instructor was informed that his contract was not going to be renewed, based on an allegation that he had been intoxicated while teaching, and that the banking program had improved since he had been removed.

An investigation revealed **the claim of intoxication had been based on the instructor's slurred speech and unsteady gait, both of which were due to his accident**. The instructor sued the college, alleging it discriminated against him on the basis of a perceived disability. A federal magistrate judge disagreed and entered judgment for the college. The Fifth Circuit, however, determined there were enough facts in dispute to entitle the instructor to bring his case to a jury. **There was evidence that the college perceived him to be disabled and transferred him to a full-time teaching position because of his limited speaking ability.** The case had to be presented to a jury. *McInnis v. Alamo Community College Dist.*, 207 F.3d 276 (5th Cir. 2000). [TX]

◆ *After-acquired evidence of misconduct could not justify a discharge based on disability.*

A wheelchair-bound teacher at a North Carolina community college taught classes at a county jail preparing inmates to take their high school equivalency exams. After she broke her back and then her leg, she was told she would not be offered another contract at the jail because of the college's concerns about her safety and the school's liability if she were to suffer another accident at the jail. Less than 10 days later, the college received anonymous phone calls alleging misconduct by the teacher (including drug use, sex with inmates, providing prisoners with drugs and bullets, and carrying a loaded weapon).

The college notified the teacher that she was fired 10 days after she was notified her contract would not be renewed. She sued the college for disability discrimination under state and federal law, and the case eventually reached the North Carolina Court of Appeals. It noted that because the trial court had found that the teacher's disability was the reason for the termination, **it should not have used the after-acquired evidence of misconduct to dismiss the teacher's lawsuit**. However, the after-acquired evidence could be used to limit the relief available (like limiting backpay and barring reinstatement). *Johnson v. Board of Trustees of Durham Technical Community College*, 577 S.E.2d 670 (N.C.App. 2003). [NC]

◆ *A university failed to make a reasonable accommodation where it refused to consider reassigning a disabled employee.*

A clerical employee of the University of Arizona had carpal tunnel syndrome and myofascial pain syndrome, which prevented her from performing her heavy word-processing duties. She became unable to perform her work despite accommodations provided by the university and requested reassignment to a position with less word-processing work. The university considered the transfer request under its general personnel policy by requiring her to go through a competitive hiring process.

The employee was not reassigned, and the university fired her. She sued the university under the ADA, § 504 and Arizona law. The court rejected the university's claim that the ADA does not mandate affirmative action efforts by employers. It noted the ADA and § 504 are comprehensive antidiscrimination laws designed to prohibit discrimination on the basis of disability through the requirement of reasonable accommodation. Reasonable accommodation, contrary to the university's claim, requires employers to evaluate possible ways to structure work for individuals with disabilities. **The university had failed to demonstrate that it had conducted any analysis to determine whether reassignment was reasonable or whether it presented an undue hardship.** *Ransom v. State of Arizona Bd. of Regents*, 983 F.Supp. 895 (D. Ariz. 1997). [AZ]

◆ *After a jury found that a private New Hampshire college had discriminated against a professor with morbid obesity, the college was ordered to reinstate her and pay part of her claimed damages.*

A religious studies professor employed by a New Hampshire private college was morbidly obese. She had difficulty walking more than 500 yards and performing some of her daily activities. At a faculty meeting, the president of the college referred to the need to educate both the mind and the body, and stated that the faculty needed to be an example to the students in this respect. The professor was later told that her contract would not be renewed for the following year. She sued the college for violating the ADA.

The court denied the professor's motion for a preliminary injunction, finding that she was unlikely to succeed on the merits of her ADA claim and that her morbid obesity did not substantially impair her ability to walk or work. The college then filed a motion to dismiss, which was denied. The jury returned a verdict on the ADA claim of $68,974, and $137,500 on the breach of contract claim, and the court directed the parties to address the issue of reinstatement. The court noted that a victim of discrimination is entitled to be made whole through the use of equitable remedies. Accordingly, the first choice is reinstatement. Because the professor succeeded on her ADA claim, **the court directed the college to reinstate her as a full-time faculty member.** The court also found that the jury awards were duplicative and limited her recovery to the larger award of $137,500. *Nedder v. Rivier College*, 972 F.Supp. 81 (D.N.H. 1997). [NH]

B. Defenses

◆ *Generally, a seniority system takes precedence over ADA accommodation.*

In a case involving an airline employee with a bad back, who was seeking a mailroom position, **the U.S. Supreme Court held that as a general rule, an accommodation under the ADA is not reasonable if it conflicts with an employer's seniority rules.** However, employees may present evidence of special circumstances that make a "seniority rule exception" reasonable in a particular case. *US Airways, Inc. v. Barnett*, 535 U.S. 391, 122 S.Ct. 1516, 152 L.Ed.2d 589 (2002). [CA]

◆ *An alcoholic employee could be fired for failing to comply with a return to work agreement.*

An administrative employee at Columbia University took several unauthorized leaves of absence and eventually told his supervisors that he was an alcoholic and that he needed to enter a treatment program. He continued to have problems, missing meetings and failing to return messages. He was finally offered a "return to work" agreement detailing conditions he had to satisfy in order to retain his job. Under the agreement, he had to supply documentation that he had successfully completed a treatment program and also provide weekly progress reports after his in-patient treatment ended. He provided the documentation regarding the treatment program, but failed to supply the weekly progress reports, and the university fired him. When he sued under the ADA and the Rehabilitation Act, a federal court dismissed the lawsuit. Here, **the university had provided a legitimate nondiscriminatory reason for the termination** — his failure to comply with the return to work agreement. *Mayo v. Columbia Univ.*, 2003 WL 1824628 (S.D.N.Y. 4/7/03). [NY]

◆ *A university could fire a dyslexic security officer for unsatisfactory performance.*

A New York state university hired a security officer as a probationary public safety officer. Under the civil service laws, he could be fired at any time after two months of employment and before completion of his 52-week probationary period. His two-month review was satisfactory, but his next review was not. During a discussion of the second review, the officer admitted for the first time that he was dyslexic. University officials offered him training opportunities and increased his responsibilities. Although his third evaluation showed some improvement in his recordkeeping, university officials became concerned about his judgment and ethics after two incidents involving campus parking violations. The university fired the officer, who sued under the ADA and the Rehabilitation Act. A federal court dismissed the lawsuit, noting that **the officer was neither disabled nor regarded as disabled**. Here, the termination was because of unsatisfactory performance, not because of the learning disability. *Smith v. State Univ. of New York*, 2003 WL 1937208 (N.D.N.Y. 4/23/03). [NY]

◆ *An employee suing for disability discrimination under state law should have filed a charge with the state agency rather than the EEOC.*

A groundskeeper at a Texas university medical center was responsible for maintaining an area of ground near a large bird sanctuary. After contracting histoplasmosis — a disease caused by inhaling spores from an organism that thrives in areas enriched by bird droppings — she complained about the environmental risks caused by the birds. She claimed that she was then offered the choice of resigning or being fired. She quit, then filed a charge with the EEOC. Later, she sued in federal court under state law and had her lawsuit dismissed. When she sued again in state court for disability discrimination, **her lawsuit was again dismissed because she failed to exhaust her administrative remedies**. Reporting her disability discrimination claim to the EEOC was not the same as reporting it to the Texas Commission on Human Rights. *Smith v. University of Texas Southwestern Medical Center*, 101 S.W.3d 185 (Tex. App. 2003). [TX]

◆ *A custodian with tennis elbow was not disabled under the ADA.*

A custodian at Villanova University injured his elbow while lifting trash bags at work. After being diagnosed with tennis elbow, he was put on light-duty assignments for a time, then had all his work restrictions lifted except for a weight-lifting limitation. He later reinjured the elbow. When the university ordered him to undergo a work-hardening program to evaluate his physical capacities, he refused and was fired for insubordination. He filed a grievance and was offered reinstatement, but never responded to the offer. Instead, he sued the university under the ADA. A Pennsylvania federal court ruled in favor of the university, finding that the custodian did not qualify for protection under the ADA because **his tennis elbow did not substantially limit him in a major life activity**. Here, his injury was of short duration, and he was able to perform tasks of central importance to most people's daily lives (personal hygiene, household chores). *Cella v. Villanova Univ.*, 2003 WL 329147 (E.D.Pa. 2/12/03). [PA]

◆   *A professor fired for unprofessional conduct failed in his ADA lawsuit against the university.*

An Arizona university hired an adjunct professor and later promoted him to chair of the College of Arts and Sciences. The professor insisted on employing a veteran with a service-related knee injury, gout, hepatitis C and other ailments to a computer assistant position. He then began accumulating reprimands for unprofessional conduct and was demoted before eventually being fired. He sued the university under the ADA, asserting that he had been retaliated against for advocating on behalf of a disabled student. An Arizona federal court ruled in favor of the university. It noted that although none of the student's conditions necessarily supported a finding of disability under the ADA, his conditions were sufficient for the professor to have a reasonable belief that he was advocating on behalf of a disabled person. However, **the university set forth a legitimate, nondiscriminatory reason for its actions — the professor's unprofessional conduct**. Here, in contravention of university policy, he had allowed a dog to ride in a university van, allowed students to take their own vehicles on a field trip, and allegedly drank with students at a bar. *Garber v. Embry-Riddle Aeronautical Univ.*, 259 F.Supp.2d 979 (D. Ariz. 2003). [AZ]

◆   *An employee with lifting restrictions could be fired for threatening a supervisor.*

A custodian at an Iowa university was diagnosed with a pulmonary embolism and was issued medical work restrictions limiting his lifting to 25 pounds and prohibiting him from snow shoveling. The lifting restrictions were later changed to 30, then 50 pounds. Some time after that, the custodian threatened the life of his supervisor. At that point, the university decided to fire him. He sued, asserting that the real reason for the termination was disability discrimination. A federal court dismissed the case, finding that **the custodian failed to prove he was disabled under the ADA**. Here, even though his ability to breathe was substantially limited when he engaged in activities that required heavy lifting, he could participate in normal activities without any limitation on his ability to breathe. Thus, he was not disabled. Further, even if he could show a disability under the ADA, the university had offered a legitimate nondiscriminatory reason for the discharge—the threat of violence toward the supervisor. *Dose v. Buena Vista Univ.*, 229 F.Supp.2d 910 (N.D. Iowa 2002). [IA]

◆   *A narcoleptic hospital resident could be fired where he couldn't perform his duties due to his impairment.*

An anesthesiology resident at a New York university hospital failed to respond to his emergency beeper on three occasions and was fired. He was later diagnosed with narcolepsy. He then sued the hospital and various physicians for disability discrimination, and the defendants sought to have the case dismissed. After a trial court dismissed the doctors from the suit, the New York Supreme Court, Appellate Division, dismissed the hospital. Although the resident suffered from a disability, which caused the behavior that got him fired, **the hospital had asserted a legitimate reason for firing him**–his narcolepsy prevented him from performing the essential functions of the job.

Timashpolsky v. SUNY Health Science Center at Brooklyn, 761 N.Y.S.2d 94 (A.D. 2003). [NY]

◆ *The failure of an employee of the University of Oregon to contact the university's employment manager about alternative positions doomed her state law accommodation claim.*

Co-workers of an employee with depression who worked a modified schedule became concerned about her behavior and reported it. Two supervisors sent the employee a memo stating that she would need a release from her counselor and doctors saying that she could return to work full time, with the ability to perform all job functions. The employee produced a letter from a doctor allowing her to work full-time hours, but stipulating that she be transferred to a less stressful department. However, by that time, the university had eliminated her position. It recommended that she contact the university employment manager to find out if there were any positions available within her salary range and for which she was qualified; if not, she would be removed from the payroll. The employee sued the university instead. The court dismissed the suit. The Oregon Court of Appeals affirmed. Here, the employee never contacted the personnel office. State law mandates that the disabled employee cooperate with the employer's efforts for accommodation. **Since the employee never looked into alternative job placements, there was no way of knowing whether the university could have properly accommodated her and it therefore had no further obligation to her.** *Flug v. University of Oregon*, 170 Or.App. 660, 13 P.3d 544 (Or. App. 2000). [OR]

◆ *Where a professor suffered from a mental impairment that prohibited him from being able to teach, he was not entitled to the protections of the ADA.*

A man was hired by a Massachusetts university under a special appointment with teaching as his primary function. Several female students complained that the professor pressured them to attend a party at his house. The professor later took an underage student out to dinner, bought her a glass of wine and allegedly made suggestive remarks. He was given a formal reprimand and after another complaint by a female faculty member, he was notified that any further occurrences would result in his dismissal. Nonetheless, he later took another underage student off campus and purchased alcohol for her.

The university began termination proceedings. The professor then asserted that he suffered from a depressive disorder that reduced his inhibitions. He requested that he be allowed to continue in his position with extra monitoring as a reasonable accommodation. The university fired him, and he filed suit, alleging violations of the ADA and § 504. The court noted that to be a qualified individual under the ADA, an individual must be able to perform the essential functions of his or her position. The professor admitted that in his present condition, he was not qualified to teach students because of his inability to conform his conduct to appropriate boundaries. However, **because teaching was an essential function of his position, he was not a qualified individual under the ADA.** The court dismissed the case. *Motzkin v. Trustees of Boston Univ.*, 938 F.Supp. 983 (D. Mass. 1996). [MA]

◆   *An employee with an impairment was not covered under the ADA where the restrictions on his ability to walk were not significant.*

A Pennsylvania man who worked for a private university suffered an injury to his hip that caused him to limp. He was unable to walk more than a mile or so at a time and had to climb stairs at a slower pace while holding the rail. Six years later, when the employee was 68 years old, the university discharged him as part of its university-wide reduction in force. He sued the university for age discrimination in violation of the ADEA and disability discrimination in violation of the ADA. The court first determined that a supervisor's question to the employee concerning when he planned to retire, made approximately one year before the layoff, was merely a casual remark that resulted from the employee's child's graduation from college.

The court next determined that **the employee's trouble in climbing stairs and his ability to walk only one mile without pain did not substantially limit his ability to walk under the ADA.** Further, the university had asserted a legitimate, nondiscriminatory reason for its employment decision — the RIF. The court granted the university's motion for pretrial judgment. The Third Circuit affirmed, noting that in order for his condition to qualify as a disability, it would have to significantly restrict his ability to walk as compared with an average person in the population. However, he was able to walk and did not need a cane or crutches to aid him. Although his ability to walk was moderately restricted, he was not disabled. *Kelly v. Drexel Univ.*, 94 F.3d 102 (3d Cir. 1996). [PA]

◆   *An instructor was not protected under the ADA where she was not able to meet the attendance requirements of the job.*

A part-time medical assistance instructor at a Virginia private college suffered from an autoimmune system disorder. She frequently missed work because of her condition and also missed work to take care of her son, who suffered from gastro-esophageal reflux disease. The college permitted the instructor to take sick leave and to take breaks whenever she felt ill. It granted her requests for accommodation and permitted her to keep flexible hours. The instructor was also permitted to take a leave of absence to be with her son while he was undergoing surgery. However, her request for additional time off to take care of his postoperative problems was denied. The instructor resigned, and signed a report prepared by the college stating that her separation was "mutual." She then sued the college under the ADA in a federal district court.

The court held for the college, and the instructor appealed to the Fourth Circuit Court of Appeals. It held **an employee who cannot meet the attendance requirements of a job is not protected by the ADA. The instructor's absences had rendered her unable to function effectively as a teacher.** Consequently, she was not a "qualified individual with a disability" under the ADA. The court also rejected her claim that the discharge constituted discrimination based on her association with her disabled son. *Tyndall v. National Education Centers*, 31 F.3d 209 (4th Cir. 1994). [VA]

◆ *An alumni association may not be a private club and thus may have to comply with the ADA.*

A New York man was hired by the alumni association of the United States Military Academy to solicit contributions from alumni. His wife suffered from Lyme disease, chronic fatigue syndrome and depression, and consequently was unable to accompany her husband to various association social events. Allegedly because of this and other problems caused by his wife's illness, the employee was treated in a discriminatory manner by his superiors and was eventually fired. He and his wife sued the association under the ADA and state law. The court dismissed the ADA claim asserted by the employee's wife, finding that she had no standing to sue the association for discrimination. **The association then argued that it was a bona fide private membership club exempt from ADA coverage.**

The court noted that to qualify for this exemption, the association had to show that it existed for recreational or social purposes, was legitimate and private, and required meaningful conditions for membership. Here, the association's primary function was to raise money and not to involve itself with fraternal activities. Although a tax-exempt status is evidence of the private nature of a club, the court found that here it was granted because the association was so closely integrated with the academy. Finding that **a genuine issue of fact existed as to whether the association qualified as a private club**, the court refused to dismiss the employee's ADA claim. *Willson v. Ass'n of Graduates of U.S. Military Academy*, 946 F.Supp. 294 (S.D.N.Y. 1996). [NY]

C. Contagious Diseases

In 1998, the U.S. Supreme Court held that a person with HIV was protected by the Americans with Disabilities Act despite the fact that she was not yet exhibiting any symptoms of the disease. Since the HIV infection substantially impaired her ability to reproduce, she could not be discriminated against unless her condition presented a direct threat to the health and safety of others. Bragdon v. Abbott, *524 U.S. 624, 118 S.Ct. 2196, 141 L.Ed.2d 540.*

◆ *The Supreme Court held that a person with a contagious disease was entitled to the protections of the Rehabilitation Act.*

A Florida elementary school teacher was discharged because of her continued recurrence of tuberculosis. She sued the school board under § 504 of the Rehabilitation Act, which prohibits entities that receive federal funding from discriminating against individuals with disabilities. A federal court dismissed her suit, but the Eleventh Circuit reversed, holding that persons with contagious diseases fall within § 504's coverage. The case then reached the U.S. Supreme Court, which held that **tuberculosis was a disability under § 504**. The disease attacked the teacher's respiratory system and affected her ability to work. It would be unfair to allow an employer to distinguish between a disease's potential effect on others and its effect on the afflicted employee in order to justify discriminatory treatment. Accordingly, she was entitled to reinstatement or front pay if she could show that despite her disability, she was otherwise qualified for her job with or without a reasonable accommodation.

School Bd. of Nassau County v. Arline, 480 U.S. 273, 107 S.Ct. 1123, 94 L.Ed.2d 307 (1987). [FL]

◆   *The transfer of an HIV-positive employee was not discriminatory where the employee had committed infractions that resulted in risks to others.*

A New York medical college employed a phlebotomist who was HIV positive. The college had a policy in place requiring employees to wear gloves on both hands when drawing blood. After the employee violated that policy on at least three occasions, the college reassigned her to the billing department. The employee brought suit against the college in a state trial court, alleging that it had discriminated against her based on her HIV-positive disability. The case was transferred to the New York Supreme Court, Appellate Division, which held that **the college did not discriminate against the employee by reassigning her**. The court noted that the employer was unaware of any similar infractions by any other employees. Thus, it had provided a legitimate, nondiscriminatory reason for the transfer that was supported by substantial evidence. *Friedel v. New York State Div. of Human Rights*, 632 N.Y.S.2d 520 (A.D. 1st Dept. 1995). [NY]

VI. RETALIATION

Title VII prohibits an employer from taking action against an employee because the employee has filed or has participated in the investigation of a discrimination complaint. In Robinson v. Shell Oil Co., *519 U.S. 337 (1997),* **the U.S. Supreme Court held a former employee of a corporation could bring a retaliatory discrimination lawsuit against his former employer after he was given a negative employment reference following his filing of an EEOC complaint. Title VII protects not only current employees but also former employees from retaliatory actions.**

◆   *A business professor claimed Kentucky State University (KSU) retaliated against her for filing a federal wage and sex discrimination lawsuit.*

The professor taught business courses at KSU for 15 years. For most of that time, she was the only female professor in her division. Her salary was 31 percent less than her male counterparts and 13 percent less than males in lower-ranking positions. KSU justified the professor's lower salary as the result of her very low incoming salary. The professor claimed KSU retaliated against her after she sued the university in a federal district court for unequal pay. She contended the dean of the business school threatened to discharge her after she filed the complaint. The professor filed a second action against the university in a federal district court for gender-based discrimination and retaliation. The court granted the university's request for summary judgment, and the professor appealed to the U.S. Court of Appeals, Sixth Circuit.

The court found significant evidence from which a court could decide that intentional gender discrimination was a substantial factor in the pay disparity at KSU. The professor presented enough conflicting evidence to support inferences that the dean's actions were retaliatory. The conflicting evidence called for a trial, not summary judgment. The court reversed the summary judgment and remanded the case for a trial. *Smith v. Kentucky State Univ.*, No. 02-5652, 97 Fed.Appx. 22, 2004 WL 785280 (6th Cir. 2004). [KY]

◆ *The U.S. Court of Appeals, Tenth Circuit, held in favor of a university that faced charges of retaliation by an adjunct professor.*

A University of Kansas assistant professor was denied tenure, then discharged. She sued the university in a federal district court for discrimination under Title VII. She was then appointed to an adjunct lecturer position, but was denied principal investigator (PI) status, which would have allowed her to act as a director of grant applications. Meanwhile, a jury ruled for the university in her discrimination lawsuit. The next month, the professor applied for an administrative position with the university, but was not interviewed for it. Claiming the university denied her the administrative position and PI status in retaliation for filing her Title VII lawsuit, she brought a second action against the university in a federal district court for retaliation. The court granted summary judgment to the university, and the professor appealed.

The U.S. Court of Appeals, Tenth Circuit, held that to establish adverse employment action under Title VII, the professor had to show the university acted in a way that meant a significant change in her employment status. The court found the decisions to confer the adjunct lecturer title on the professor and deny her PI status were not significant changes in employment. The university's decision not to hire the professor as an administrator was not retaliation. **The university presented legitimate, non-discriminatory reasons for declining to hire her for that position. Because the professor offered no evidence to show the school's non-discriminatory reasons were a pretext for discrimination or retaliation, the court affirmed the judgment.** *Annett v. University of Kansas*, 371 F.3d 1233 (10th Cir. 2004). [KS]

A. Former Employees

◆ *A university was held to have retaliated against a professor for reporting same-sex harassment by another professor.*

A male professor at a dental school in Texas was allegedly subjected to sexual harassment by another male professor at the school. When he complained about the harassment, the school conducted an investigation but was unable to determine whether it had occurred. However, after the investigation, the professor alleged that the school retaliated against him, discontinuing a stipend he had been receiving, denying his request for paid leave, and eventually terminating him because of his failure to return from unpaid leave (he had requested an extension of leave, which the school denied). He sued the school in federal court under Title VII and obtained an award of over $380,000. On the school's appeal, the Fifth Circuit affirmed in part. Here, **there was sufficient evidence to suggest that a hostile work environment had been created by the harassment. Also, the school had retaliated against the professor**, and the school's president had sent an e-mail to all 8,000 employees stating that the professor had failed to return from leave and painting him in a negative light. This justified the award of front pay against the school. *Mota v. University of Texas Houston Health Science Center*, 261 F.3d 512 (5th Cir. 2001). [TX]

◆ *A college's actions were held not to be retaliatory because the conduct occurred after the employment relationship had ended, and did not impact on the employee's future employment.*

An African-American part-time gospel choir director employed by a New Jersey private college was discharged after the position was eliminated for budgetary reasons. After student protests, the college decided to fund the choir, but as an elective course with academic credit. Because all faculty members were required to have a college degree, the college rejected the director's application for the new position in favor of a female African-American candidate with a Master of Arts degree in music performance. The director filed a race discrimination charge with the EEOC, which was settled. Pursuant to the agreement, she entered into a temporary contract with the college as a director of the extracurricular gospel choir. In spite of written admonitions that the college preapprove any campus visits after the temporary contract expired, she attended a campus protest and returned to lead a "Gospel Sing Fest."

After the EEOC dismissed a second discrimination complaint, the director sued for unlawful retaliation under Title VII. The district court granted the college's motion for pretrial judgment, and the director appealed to the U.S. Court of Appeals, Third Circuit. The director contended that actionable retaliation includes all conduct that "arises out of the employment relation." The court of appeals disagreed, ruling that **an employer's significant wrongful post-employment conduct must "touch an employment relationship."** The university's requirement that the director obtain its approval before entering its campus was not an "employment practice" because the director was not the college's employee when the requirement was imposed. The requirement did not affect her actual or proposed employment anywhere else. Consequently, the college's actions did not give rise to a retaliation claim. The court affirmed the district court's decision. *Nelson v. Upsala College*, 51 F.3d 383 (3d Cir. 1995). [NJ]

◆ *Two former employees who brought retaliation claims against a college were allowed to proceed with their lawsuit.*

A Hispanic woman worked in the human resources department of a private Texas college. She misplaced a file room key but did not tell anyone because she was afraid that the director of the department would yell at her. She had previously complained that the director treated her in a racially discriminatory manner. The employee contacted a secretary in another department to ask for assistance in obtaining a duplicate key. The secretary also had had problems with her supervisor and had previously complained that her supervisor treated her in a sexually discriminatory manner. She obtained a duplicate key and gave it to the employee. When their supervisors discovered that they did not follow the proper key replacement procedure, both employees were fired. They sued, alleging Title VII claims for national origin and gender discrimination, based on theories of unlawful retaliation and hostile work environment. The court dismissed the lawsuit, and the employees appealed.

The U.S. Court of Appeals, Fifth Circuit, noted that to show claims of unlawful retaliation, **the employees needed to show that they were engaged in activities protected by Title VII, that an adverse employment action occurred and that a causal link existed between the protected activities and the adverse employment action.** Here, each employee presented evidence that she was treated differently because of either her national origin or her gender in violation of Title VII. Also, both employees were subjected to an adverse employment action. Finally, the court noted that there was an issue of fact as to whether there was a causal link between the protected activities and their dismissal. Finding that the college's reason could be a pretext for unlawful retaliation, the dismissal of the retaliation claim was reversed. *Long v. Eastfield College*, 88 F.3d 300 (5th Cir. 1996). [TX]

B. Defenses

◆ *A Texas state court agreed with a private religious university that it could not consider an employment case that was previously brought in federal court.*

A former university department chair sued the university in federal court for Title VII violations based on his removal from office and retaliation for an earlier lawsuit he filed against the university. Before the federal court ruled on the case, the employee filed a breach of contract and fraud action against the university in the state court system. The federal court awarded the university summary judgment, declaring that religious education institutions are exempt from Title VII. The Court of Appeals of Texas then held the state court action was barred by the equitable doctrine of *res judicata*, which precludes actions that have already been litigated between the same parties and involve the same factual basis. *Bishop v. Baylor Univ.*, No. 10-01-080-CV, 2003 WL 22996902 (Tex. App. 2003). [TX]

◆ *A math teacher assigned to remedial and introductory courses failed to show that the assignments were retaliatory.*

A mathematics instructor of Burmese origin worked for a community college in Washington and did some things that angered his fellow instructors, like changing the grade of a student who was not in his class. He received a written reprimand for that action. However, he later obtained tenure despite a "no" vote from the tenure review committee when he appealed to the board of trustees. Afterward, he received teaching assignments for remedial courses as well as a few introductory college-level and post-calculus courses. He sued the college for discrimination and retaliation (for challenging the tenure denial).

A state court let the discrimination claim proceed, but granted pretrial judgment to the college on the retaliation claim. He appealed. The Court of Appeals of Washington affirmed. Here, the instructor did not engage in protected activity when he challenged the tenure decision. And even if he did, his class assignments were not adverse employment action. **The college had a legitimate reason for making the assignments.** His teaching style differed from the "Harvard reform calculus method" recently adopted by the math department. *Tan v. State of Washington*, 2003 WL 1849185 (Wash. App. 4/9/03). [WA]

◆ *A retaliation claim failed where the professor could not show that it had occurred because of opposition to an unlawful employment practice.*

A professor employed by a private, Alabama university often supported his students when they complained of discrimination by the university. A female student informed him that because of her gender she was being discriminated against. He directed her to the appropriate school officials and then personally notified a university dean and the provost. He was told by the officials to keep the matter private, but in the next month, he informed a university trustee of his concerns about the situation. After this, his relationship with the university deteriorated significantly and he was given repeated warnings to forget the situation. He was then told that the university was not going to renew his contract because he had informed the trustee of the discrimination complaint. He sued the university and its officials for violations of Title VII and Title IX.

An Alabama federal court dismissed the claims. In considering the professor's retaliation claim under Title VII, the court noted that he had to show that he was discriminated against because he opposed an unlawful employment practice. **Here, the student did not claim that she was discriminated against in employment and therefore, the professor's Title VII claim for retaliation failed. With regard to Title IX, the court found no express remedy for retaliation in the statute** and refused to imply one. Even if it could imply such a remedy, the court nonetheless found that because the professor himself was not alleging gender discrimination, his claim was too far removed from the coverage of Title IX. *Holt v. Lewis*, 955 F.Supp. 1385 (N.D. Ala. 1995), *affirmed*, 109 F.3d 771 (11th Cir. 1997). [AL]

◆ *A retaliation claim failed because the university had proffered a legitimate nondiscriminatory reason for its nonrenewal of the professor's contract.*

A female assistant professor was denied tenure by a New York private university, allegedly because she lacked a Ph.D. and a sufficient record of scholarly research. The professor rejected several offers for part-time adjunct positions and filed a complaint against the university with the New York Human Rights Commission, alleging that she had been denied tenure on the basis of her sex. She was permitted to teach in adjunct status without a contract for an additional two years, despite the university's policy of not allowing persons to teach without signed contracts. During settlement negotiations, the university offered her a five-year adjunct contract with a 60 percent pay increase in exchange for her withdrawal of the sex discrimination complaint. The professor declined the offer, and the university unconditionally refused to consider her for additional available adjunct positions.

The professor filed a second complaint with the commission, alleging that the university had retaliated against her for not withdrawing her sex discrimination complaint. The commission held that the university had retaliated against the professor but dismissed the discrimination claim. The case reached the Court of Appeals of New York. It held **the record was devoid of evidence that the university had a subjective retaliatory motive for the nonrenewal**. The professor's failure to agree to any of the university's adjunct offers over the course of two years belied her assertion that the nonrenewal was in retaliation for her failure to withdraw the discrimination claim. Rather, her adjunct status was not renewed because of her protracted tactical decisions not to execute a series of adjunct contracts, in favor of her relying completely on her achieving full tenure in the pending discrimination proceeding. Moreover, the university's enforcement of its policy prohibiting adjuncts from teaching without a signed contract was a legitimate nondiscriminatory reason for the nonrenewal. *Pace Univ. v. N.Y. City Comm'n on Human Rights*, 85 N.Y.2d 125, 647 N.E.2d 1273 (N.Y. 1995). [NY]

◆ *An employee who asserted she was discharged for complaining about her supervisor's homosexuality could not prove retaliation.*

An associate director of nursing employed by a Washington, D.C. private university hospital frequently complained that the director showed partiality to two subordinate employees by granting them extensive overtime pay, choice working assignments, and lenient disciplinary action. She alleged that the director's behavior undermined her authority, contradicted hospital policy, and adversely affected department morale. She also believed the favoritism stemmed from the subordinates' homosexual relationships with the director. After the university fired the associate director, she sued it for retaliatory discharge. A awarded damages to the associate director and the university appealed to the District of Columbia Court of Appeals.

The court held **the associate director did not establish she was engaged in protected activity or that she opposed unlawful practices. Allegations of cronyism or favoritism generally are insufficient to state a claim for retaliatory discharge.** The court rejected the associate director's assertion that based on the work environment, university officials should have known a complaint of unlawful discrimination was being made. Because the associate director failed to state a *prima facie* retaliation claim, her action was dismissed and the trial court's ruling was reversed. *Howard Univ. v. Green*, 652 A.2d 41 (D.C. App. 1994). [DC]

C. Causal Connection

◆ *A former assistant director of development at the Art Institute of Chicago alleged sufficient facts to survive a motion to dismiss her retaliatory discharge action.*

The assistant director worked for the Gene Siskel Film Center at the Art Institute of Chicago. She agreed to post names of the Siskel family on a donor wall as a condition for accepting a donation by the family. A vice president of the center admonished her for listing more than one name in violation of the Institute's "one gift, one name" policy, even though the president and four other officials had approved the action. Two days before a public dedication, the director of the center instructed the assistant director to "steer…Gene Siskel's widow…away from the donor wall during the press preview." She refused to comply with the directive and was discharged for insubordination.

The assistant director sued the institute in a federal district court for retaliatory discharge. **The court held the critical factor in this case was whether the assistant director reasonably believed her supervisors were involved in an illegal or unlawful act.** The institute had accepted the donation on the condition that the entire Siskel family would be listed on the donor wall. Supervisors instructed her to remove their names just two days before the dedication and without discussing the change with the family. The sudden change in plans was sufficient for the assistant director to reasonably believe the institute was engaging in fraudulent activity. She presented sufficient evidence to survive the institute's motion to dismiss the case. *Tanzer v. Art Institute of Chicago*, No. 02 C 8115, 2003 WL 21788850 (N.D. Ill. 2003). [IL]

◆   *A three-year span between a sexual harassment complaint and an adverse employment decision was too great to permit an inference of retaliation.*

A teacher at a Kansas university accused the vice president of academic affairs of improper sexual advances. The university resolved the complaint through a settlement in which she dropped the charges in exchange for a three-year lecturer position. In that position, she received positive reviews, and the university decided to make the position a tenure position. However, she was not selected for it because she lacked the requisite background in educational technology. She sued the university for retaliation, but a federal court ruled against her. The Tenth Circuit affirmed, noting that she relied too much on inference to try to prove retaliation. Even though the five-member search panel had been chaired by a good friend of the vice president, **her mere speculation about the vice president's influence was not sufficient to prove retaliation**. Also, three years had passed since she had made the complaint. Finally, the candidate selected was qualified for the position. *Adams v. Washburn Univ. of Topeka*, 66 Fed.Appx. 819 (10th Cir. 2003). [KS]

◆   *An employee failed to show a link between her helping other workers file sexual harassment complaints and her termination.*

A supervisor/curator in the Ocean Drilling Program at Texas A&M University helped five female co-workers file sexual harassment complaints against staffers in the program over several years. She alleged that as a result, she received no raises for three years. When the program was later reorganized to cut costs and make it more efficient, her position was consolidated with that of her superior. A university official created the requirements for the new position and decided that the new curator would have to hold a Ph.D. The supervisor/curator had only a bachelor's degree and was fired after the consolidation. She sued for retaliation under Title VII, and a jury found in her favor, awarding her $466,000. The Fifth Circuit reversed the award, finding **no causal link between her protected activity and her termination**. Here, over a year had elapsed since the last harassment complaint had been filed. Also, she failed to show that the university official in charge of setting the new position's requirements even knew she had assisted co-workers with sexual harassment complaints. *Mato v. Baldauf*, 267 F.3d 444 (5th Cir. 2001). [TX]

◆   *Because there was no connection between an employee's firing and his complaints to the Michigan Department of Civil Rights, he could not succeed on his retaliation claim.*

The male coordinator of cultural events for Kirtland Community College was supervised by the dean of student services. When the dean asked a female employee out, he learned that she was romantically involved with the coordinator. The coordinator claimed his relationship with the dean then deteriorated. He alleged that the dean's continuing adverse treatment caused him physical and psychological problems so severe that he had to take a personal and FMLA leave from his job. The coordinator was fired when he returned to work, ostensibly for insubordination and job abandonment. He sued for retaliation under the state Civil Rights Act, violation of the FMLA, and other claims. The jury found no violation of the FMLA, but found in favor of the coordinator on his retaliation claim and awarded him $100,000 in damages. The trial court awarded the coordinator attorneys' fees and costs in connection with the retaliation claim.

The Michigan Court of Appeals concluded the trial court should have overruled the jury's verdict on the retaliation claim. **The coordinator did not engage in any protected activity under the Civil Rights Act that could be said to have led to an adverse employment action.** Although he was fired shortly after he complained to the Michigan Department of Civil Rights, he failed to show a causal link between his complaints and the decision to fire him. The college also produced a memo written a week before the coordinator's first complaint, stating that the coordinator's "poor attitude" justified not renewing his contract. Therefore, the coordinator's complaints could not be considered a "significant factor" in the decision to fire him. *Barrett v. Kirtland Community College*, 628 N.W.2d 63 (Mich. App. 2001). [MI]

◆ *To succeed on a claim of retaliation under Title VII, an employee (or former employee) must show a causal connection between the protected activity and the adverse employment action.*

A Texas business school discharged an African-American admissions representative. The representative applied for another position with the U.S. Internal Revenue Service (IRS), which requested a reference from the school. The school responded that the representative was below average in the categories of quality of work, judgment, dependability and flexibility. It also noted that he was discharged due to his tardiness and insubordination. The school contended that the evaluation was based on observations of the representative during his employment. The representative filed a Title VII lawsuit against the school, alleging race discrimination and retaliation with respect to his discharge, the school's failure to promote him, and its allegedly false references to the IRS. The school moved for pretrial judgment.

The court held that the representative's failure to obtain a right-to-sue letter precluded his discrimination claim with respect to his discharge and denial of promotion. Next, the court noted that Title VII prohibits retaliation for an employee's past discrimination charges. However, although the representative could premise a Title VII retaliation claim on the school's post-employment retaliatory conduct, his self-serving, generalized testimony stating his subjective belief that discrimination had occurred was insufficient to show a causal connection between the protected activity and the adverse employment action. Further, **there was nothing in the record that could support a finding that the appraisal was motivated by malice or retaliatory intent** or that the school's explanation of the appraisal was pretextual. The court granted the school's motion for pretrial judgment. *Fields v. Phillips School of Business & Technology*, 870 F.Supp. 149 (W.D. Tex. 1994). [TX]

◆ *Multiple discrimination and retaliation claims failed in the following case involving a private college counselor.*

An African-American female was hired as a talent search counselor for a Mississippi private college to plan services and activities designed to encourage the retention of first-generation college students. A year later, she applied for the position of educational talent search coordinator. However, an African-American male was hired to fill this position. The counselor filed a written grievance in accordance with college procedure stating that the vacancy had not been properly posted and that she had been mistreated by her supervisor. The position became available again in 1992, but the college revised the job qualifications to require administrative supervisory experience. The counselor was again rejected, this time in favor of an African-American female who met the revised job qualifications. The counselor filed suit in a U.S. district court, alleging that the college retaliated against her for filing a sex discrimination grievance in violation of Title VII, 42 U.S.C. § 1981 and the Fourteenth Amendment. The college moved for pretrial judgment.

The court held that the counselor failed to state a *prima facie* case under Title VII. Although she asserted an adverse employment action (failure to promote her), she failed to establish that she had engaged in statutorily protected expression or that any causal connection existed between the allegedly protected expression and the adverse employment action. Specifically, her grievance had merely asserted that the job vacancy was not properly noticed and that she had been treated unfairly by her supervisor. She had not complained of sex discrimination. Further, since the change in job qualifications occurred almost 16 months after she filed her grievance, **there was no causal connection between her grievance and the college's failure to promote her**. Next, because § 1981 does not apply to sex discrimination claims, the court dismissed this claim. Finally, an action taken by a private college (even funded by federal grants) failed to allege state action necessary to assert a Fourteenth Amendment claim. The court granted pretrial judgment to the college and dismissed all the claims against it. *Aldridge v. Tougaloo College*, 847 F.Supp. 480 (S.D. Miss. 1994). [MS]

CHAPTER SEVEN

Intellectual Property

I. INTRODUCTION

In determining who owns the patent rights to an invention, courts look at the nature of the relationship between the inventor and the employer. Where the inventor is hired to invent something, the employer retains all patent rights; and where the inventor is hired under a general contract of employment, the inventor will retain ownership rights. However, most cases fall somewhere in between these two: for example, where a university hires a professor or a graduate student to teach and do research. The ambiguity this creates has led colleges and universities to enter into pre-employment assignments of intellectual property rights that specifically lay out the rights of both parties. Sometimes this is done by written agreement–other times, by use of a faculty handbook.

Generally, copyright rights are treated more laxly than patent rights. Perhaps this is because of tradition but, whatever the reason, a professor who writes a book is likely to retain all ownership rights to the work. In contrast, the professor who invents a new printing press that will produce a better book likely will not own the rights to that work. However, copyright policies are becoming more common, due largely to the fact that computer programs, which are potentially very lucrative, are copyrightable.

With respect to patent rights, professors usually are required to assign creations and patent rights to the colleges and universities that employ them in exchange for a percentage of the royalties. The issue becomes trickier when dealing with graduate students. Some universities require graduate students to assign patent rights, while others do not.

A number of states have enacted statutes to limit the extent to which employers can claim an interest in employee inventions. However, those statutes generally provide that if the employer provides resources, or if the invention relates to the employer's business, the employer can require assignment of intellectual property rights. It is only where the employer has no involvement at all that the employee can claim full rights to an invention. This chapter focuses on copyright and patent cases in higher education.

II. COPYRIGHTS

Article I, Section 8 of the U.S. Constitution provides that Congress can secure for limited times to authors and inventors the exclusive right to their respective writings and discoveries. From this provision came the Copyright Act and the patent system.

Section 107 of the Copyright Act states:

17 U.S.C. § 107

The fair use of a copyrighted work, including such use by reproduction in copies ... for purposes such as criticism, comment, news reporting, teaching (including multiple copies for classroom use), scholarship, or research, is not an infringement of **copyright**. In determining whether the use made of a work in any particular case is a fair use the factors to be considered shall include—

(1) the purpose and character of the use, including whether such use is of a commercial nature or is for nonprofit educational purposes;
(2) the nature of the copyrighted work;
(3) the amount and substantiality of the portion used in relation to the copyrighted work as a whole; and
(4) the effect of the use upon the potential market for or value of the copyrighted work.

◆ *Publishing companies must obtain permission from free-lance writers before reusing their works in electronic databases.*

In 2001, the U.S. Supreme Court determined that permission was required for inclusion of free-lancers' works in electronic databases. Copyright law allows publishers to reuse free-lancers' contributions when a collective work, such as a magazine issue or an encyclopedia, is revised, but the Court said that massive databases such as NEXIS do not fit within that provision of the law because they are not revisions of previously published collective works. The decision was the result of a lawsuit that was filed against New York Times Co., Newsday Inc., Time Incorporated Magazine Co., LEXIS/NEXIS and University Microfilms International in U.S. District Court for the Southern District of New York, alleging violation of free-lance writers' copyrights in articles they wrote that were included in complete issues of the publishers' products. *New York Times Co., Inc. v. Tasini*, 533 U.S. 483, 121 S.Ct. 2381, 150 L.Ed.2d 500 (2001). [NY]

◆ *The U.S. Court of Appeals for the First Circuit rejected a Tufts University visiting lecturer's claims based on the terms of a publishing contract involving a publisher and a professor at another college.*

The lecturer had co-authored the second and third editions of an undergraduate textbook with a professor and director of the graduate nutrition program at another college. The third edition agreement assigned all present and future copyrights of the third and future editions to the book's publisher. The lecturer and professor contracted with the same publisher for a fourth edition that increased the lecturer's share of royalties from 25 to 40 percent. The professor failed to meet deadlines set by the agreement, and the publisher suggested she assign more work to the lecturer. The professor refused, and the lecturer notified the publisher she was withdrawing from the project. She also stated her revisions could not be used without her permission. The publisher sent the lecturer an acknowledgement that she would receive 12.5 percent of the fourth edition royalties–half her compensation under the third edition agreement. She signed the acknowledgement, but later discovered her revisions were included in the fourth edition and that the professor was listed as its sole author.

The lecturer copyrighted her revisions and brought a multi-count federal district court complaint against the publisher and professor for copyright infringement and breach of contract. The court held the lecturer had assigned her copyright interest to the publisher under the fourth edition revisions. The publisher was not obligated to terminate its contract with the professor when she failed to meet her deadlines. The First Circuit affirmed the decision, holding the lecturer could not claim a copyright interest in her fourth edition revisions. Based on the terms of the third and fourth edition agreements, she had "assigned ... all present and future copyrights" of the third and future editions to the publisher. **The publisher was the sole copyright owner of the third edition, and consequently the fourth "revised edition." There was no breach of contract by the publisher, because it had the option to extend the deadlines and did so for legitimate financial reasons.** *Zyla v. Wadsworth*, 360 F.3d 243 (1st Cir. 2004). [MA]

◆   *Brown University retained its copyrights to photographs taken by a member of its staff under the "works for hire" doctrine.*

Brown University hired a full-time professional photographer to capture images of academic life and natural campus settings for its publications. He was also allowed to shoot pictures on his own initiative. The university purchased photographic equipment for him, arranged for student assistants, and provided him with access to the university's darkroom. Brown's copyright policy contained a provision regarding the ownership of copyrightable materials. After 24 years, Brown severed its relationship with the photographer as part of a reduction in force. He sued Brown in a federal district court, claiming ownership of 97 photographs in his possession.

The court focused on several sections of the Copyright Act of 1976. **Under § 201(b), titled "Works Made for Hire," the court explained that ownership rights of works by an employee typically vest with the employer.** It determined the photographs were "works for hire" owned by Brown. **The court distinguished between the photographs and the "faculty exception" from the works for hire rule.** Equitable considerations often mandate that a scholar retain the copyright to works, notwithstanding the work made for hire doctrine. **The faculty exception did not apply in this case because Brown officials often directed what images should be photographed.** There was no document indicating a conveyance of ownership rights by Brown to the photographer. The language of the policy was too imprecise to use as evidence to support the photographer's claim of such a transfer. By his own admission, he did not think about copyright ownership in the photos until after his relationship with Brown was severed. As Brown owned the photographs and did not transfer ownership rights to the photographer, the court granted summary judgment to Brown. *Foraste v. Brown Univ.*, 290 F.Supp.2d 234 (D.R.I. 2003). [RI]

◆   *Where two state university officials may have had some involvement in violating copyright law, they were not entitled to immunity.*

A New York university hired a filmmaker to produce a documentary on Italian-American theater. A lawsuit eventually arose when the filmmaker asserted that the university interfered with her right to market the documentary and failed to account to her for monies received from the sale and/or distribution of the documentary. In addition to the university, she sued the chancellor and an institute director. She alleged that part of the documentary was made up of some previously copyrighted material. She also alleged that the defendants improperly removed another documentary from her workplace. She sought an injunction to prevent the chancellor and institute director from continuing to violate copyright law. The chancellor and director sought to dismiss the claims against them, but a federal court refused to do so. **Even though the university was entitled to Eleventh Amendment immunity, the two individuals were not.** The case would have to proceed to trial. *Salerno v. City Univ. of New York*, 2001 WL 1267158 (S.D.N.Y. 10/23/01). [NY]

◆   *By refusing to pay permission fees to copyright holders, a copy shop violated the Copyright Act.*

A commercial copy shop reproduced substantial segments of copyrighted works and bound them into "coursepacks," which were sold to students so that they could fulfill reading assignments given by professors at the University of Michigan. The copy shop acted without the permission of the copyright holders, claiming that the fair use doctrine eliminated the need for it to obtain permission. The fair use doctrine states that the fair use of a copyrighted work for teaching, scholarship or research, among other uses, is not an infringement of copyright. In this case, a number of copyright holders sued the copy shop claiming that its reproduction of material was not fair use. A federal court agreed and awarded damages against the copy shop. It also found that the infringement was willful.

On appeal, the U.S. Court of Appeals, Sixth Circuit, noted that by reproducing copies for students without paying the copyright holders the permission fees that other copy shops paid, **the copy shop was reducing the potential market for or the value of the copyrighted works**. Since one of the potential uses of a copyright is to grant a license to reproduce part of the work for use in a classroom, and since the copyright holders were willing to grant those licenses, by refusing to pay the permission fees, the copy shop violated the Copyright Act. The court also noted that the purpose and character of the use was of a commercial nature, that the material being reproduced was creative in nature, and that the amount and substantiality of the reproduced segments in relation to the works as a whole were quite large (between 5 and 30 percent). The court affirmed the finding that the copy shop had infringed the copyright holders' rights. However, **it refused to find that the infringement had been willful**. It remanded the case for reconsideration of the damages. *Princeton Univ. Press v. Michigan Document Services*, 99 F.3d 1381 (6th Cir. 1996). [MI]

◆   *A copy shop violated the Copyright Act by copying excerpts from books and putting them in course packets. This was not "fair use" under the act.*

Several New York publishers sued Kinko's for copyright infringement as a result of the store's **policy of copying excerpts from books, compiling them into course "packets," and selling them to college students**. Kinko's admitted that it copied the works, but asserted that doing so was a fair use under the Copyright Act, and that since it had been doing this type of copying for 20 years, the publishers could not now claim copyright infringement.

A federal district court held that Kinko's had infringed the copyrights. First, the usage was commercial in nature, rather than for nonprofit educational use. Second, the amount and substantiality of the copied works weighed against Kinko's because the portions copied were critical parts of the copyrighted works. Third, and most importantly, **the effect of the use on the value of and market for the works weighed against Kinko's**. Thus, the copying did not amount to fair use under the Copyright Act. Further, the court accepted the publishers' assertion that although they had known Kinko's was copying their works for 20 years, they did not know that Kinko's had been infringing on their copyrights all that time. It ordered Kinko's to obtain permission in the future, to pay any licensing fees required, and to pay $510,000 in statutory damages for past infringement. *Basic Books, Inc. v. Kinko's Graphics Corp.*, 758 F.Supp. 1522 (S.D.N.Y. 1991). [NY]

◆   *New York's Standardized Testing Act requires testing agencies to file reports on standardized tests with the Commissioner of Education and also requires the filing of copyrightable test questions.*

The American Association of Medical Colleges (AAMC), a nonprofit educational association, sponsors a medical school testing program, the central feature of which is the MCAT exam. The AAMC holds copyrights in the MCAT test forms, test questions, answer sheets, and reports. When the state of New York enacted the Standardized Testing Act, requiring disclosure of this copyrighted information, the AAMC sued to enjoin the application of the Act. It claimed that the Act was preempted by the federal Copyright Act and moved for pretrial judgment, which the court granted. The court found that the purpose and character of the use was noncommercial and educational, and that disclosure of the test questions would prevent their reuse.

The Second Circuit Court of Appeals reversed, finding that there were issues of fact that precluded a grant of pretrial judgment. If the disclosure of material were considered "fair use," then there would be no Copyright Act violation. However, if the state Act facilitated infringement, then the Copyright Act would preempt it. **Here, the state's goal of encouraging valid and objective tests was laudable, and there was a question of fact as to whether the test questions could be used again after being disclosed.** As a result, the fourth and most important fair use factor–the effect of the use upon the potential market for or value of the copyrighted work–did not necessarily weigh in favor of the AAMC. The court remanded the case for further proceedings. *Association of American Medical Colleges v. Cuomo*, 928 F.2d 519 (2d Cir. 1991). [NY]

◆   *A federal district court agreed with four educational testing agencies, including the College Entrance Examination Board, that the required disclosure of test questions under a New York law violated federal copyright law.*

New York education law requires college testing services to file copies of their test questions and statistical reports with the state education commissioner. A number of testing agencies claimed that the statute violated federal copyright law, and filed a lawsuit against the governor and other state officials. In view of the result in a similar case filed by the Association of American Medical Colleges, the parties entered into a stipulation under which the testing agencies disclosed questions for only some of the tests administered in the state and were allowed to administer a fixed number of undisclosed tests. The court then considered a motion by the agencies for temporary relief. The agencies argued that the compelled disclosure of the test questions violated federal copyright law and did not meet the fair use exception to federal copyright law. The state argued that **the public had an interest in ensuring the fairness and objectivity of standardized admission tests** and had a strong need to evaluate the scoring process. It also claimed that disclosure did not violate copyright laws because of the lack of any commercial purpose.

The court agreed with the testing agencies that the disclosure of test questions violated federal copyright law and issued a preliminary injunction. The court also found that the agencies were entitled to the presumption of irreparable injury that normally accompanies the showing of copyright infringement. However, because of the many factual issues existing in the case, the court issued an order preserving the status quo, under which only some tests administered in the state would be subject to the disclosure law pending further proceedings. *College Entrance Examination Bd. v. Pataki*, 889 F.Supp. 554 (N.D.N.Y. 1995). [NY]

Three of the testing agencies sought an order completely barring enforcement of the state law or alternative relief. A fourth agency submitted a statement indicating that it would comply with the order by disclosing three testing forms administered in New York during the test year and an additional form traditionally administered in the state in low-volume administrations.

The testing agencies asserted that the wording of the preliminary order would prevent the Graduate Record Examination (GRE) program from offering at least one administration in the state, and that the status quo provision of the order did not account for changing circumstances in testing from year to year. They further asserted that the preliminary order contravened **the principle in copyright infringement cases that the status quo sought to be preserved is the state of non-infringement.**

The court held that the preliminary order struck the correct balance between competing interests, including that of the students who would take the examinations. There was no need to strictly comply with the rule that the status quo to be preserved is a state of non-infringement, since the parties had agreed by stipulation to provide for limited disclosure of test forms. The court modified the preliminary order to accommodate the GRE program's phase-out of paper and pencil administrations. *College Entrance Examination Bd. v. Pataki*, 893 F.Supp. 152 (N.D.N.Y. 1995). [NY]

◆   *A public university in Texas was entitled to immunity in a lawsuit filed by an author who asserted copyright violations.*

The author asserted that the University of Houston violated federal copyright law by publishing her book without consent and violated the Lanham Act by naming her as the selector of plays in another book without her permission. She sued the university in a federal court, which refused to dismiss the case on the basis of immunity. The Fifth Circuit held that the university had impliedly waived Eleventh Amendment immunity by contracting with the author, because Congress had imposed statutory waivers of immunity in both the Copyright and Lanham Acts.

The U.S. Supreme Court remanded the case for reconsideration under *Seminole Tribe of Florida v. Florida*, 517 U.S. 44 (1996), which held that abrogation of a state's Eleventh Amendment immunity requires an expression of Congressional intent and a constitutionally valid exercise of power. On remand to the Fifth Circuit, the author asserted that the university impliedly waived state sovereign immunity and that Congress retained the power to abrogate state immunity in both federal acts under Article I of the Constitution.

The court held that the *Seminole Tribe* case had rejected the implied waiver theory relied upon by the author. Under *Seminole Tribe*, a state's waiver of immunity cannot be implied simply because the state conducts business in an area subject to federal regulation. **The express provisions of the Copyright and Lanham Acts purporting to require this consent were outside the power of Congress under Article I.** The court also rejected the author's alternative argument that she had been deprived of property without due process of law by the university's purported violations of federal law.

The author's statutorily created right to protect her name from misappropriation under the Lanham Act was not a property right protected by the Due Process Clause of the Fourteenth Amendment. **Congress had no power to subject states to federal court lawsuits for Lanham Act violations.** The copyright claim was one for breach of contract, which could not be treated as a procedural due process violation in federal court. The author's theory of recovery amount to a direct end-run around *Seminole Tribe*, and her claims against the university had to be dismissed. *Chavez v. Arte Publico Press*, 157 F.3d 282 (5th Cir. 1999). [TX]

Subsequently, the Supreme Court decided *Florida Prepaid Postsecondary Educ. Expense Bd. v. College Savings Bank*, 527 U.S. 627, 119 S.Ct. 2199, 144 L.Ed.2d 575 (1999) and *College Savings Bank v. Florida Prepaid Postsecondary Educ. Expense Bd.*, 527 U.S. 666, 119 S.Ct. 2219, 144 L.Ed.2d 605 (1999). The Fifth Circuit again considered the case and held that the

Copyright Remedy Clarification Act was not a valid exercise of legislative authority as applied to the states. As a result, the university was entitled to be dismissed from the suit under the Eleventh Amendment. *Chavez v. Arte Publico Press*, 204 F.3d 601 (5th Cir. 2000). [TX]

III. PATENTS

A patent is a legally protected property interest that gives the owner the right to exclude others from making, using, selling, offering for sale, or importing the invention covered by the patent. Patents generally run for a period of 20 years from the effective filing date of the patent application. To be patentable, an invention must be useful, new or novel, and non-obvious.

◆ *The Eleventh Amendment bars federal court lawsuits by private parties against states under the Patent Remedy Act and the Lanham Act.*

In 1999, the Supreme Court decided two cases involving the same parties and the same dispute. In *Florida Prepaid Postsecondary Educ. Expense Bd. v. College Savings Bank*, 527 U.S. 627, 119 S.Ct. 2199, 144 L.Ed.2d 575, **the Court held that Congress' abrogation, under the Patent Remedy Act, of states' sovereign immunity from patent infringement suits was not constitutional**. Building on its earlier decision in *Seminole Tribe of Florida v. Florida*, 517 U.S. 44, 116 S.Ct. 1114, 134 L.Ed.2d 252 (1996), where it held that Congress does not have the power to abrogate a state's sovereign immunity under Article I of the Constitution, the Court found that Congress had overstepped its bounds. Although patents can be considered property within the meaning of the Due Process Clause, there was no indication here that the Patent Remedy Act had been enacted under the authority of the Fourteenth Amendment. Rather, the legislation was authorized by Article I and thus improperly removed states' sovereign immunity.

The case arose after College Savings Bank, which owned and marketed a patented investment methodology designed to finance the costs of college education, discovered that the state of Florida was selling a similar product. The bank brought separate actions against the state for patent infringement and false advertising under the Lanham Act. In the patent infringement action, the Court determined that Florida could not be sued without its consent where it had merely engaged in interstate commerce.

In the false advertising action, the Court held that **the Trademark Remedy Clarification Act also did not validly abrogate states' Eleventh Amendment immunity from a suit brought under the Lanham Act**. Although Congress may remove a state's sovereign immunity under § 5 of the Fourteenth Amendment, there must be a property interest involved for it to do so. However, there was no property interest at stake in a false advertising suit under the Lanham Act. Further, the state of Florida had not constructively waived its immunity by engaging in interstate commerce. *College Savings Bank v. Florida Prepaid Postsecondary Educ. Expense Bd.*, 527 U.S. 666, 119 S.Ct. 2219, 144 L.Ed.2d 605 (1999). [FL]

◆   *A pharmaceutical company had to pay $54 million in damages for*
fraudulently obtaining a patent based on work by university researchers.

Two University of Colorado researchers worked under an agreement with
a pharmaceutical company. They discovered certain multivitamins were not
supplying proper amounts of iron to pregnant women and published an article
suggesting a reformulation to increase iron absorption. The researchers sent an
advance copy to the doctor they had been working with at the company. The
company then obtained a patent on the reformulation of the multivitamin
without notifying the university. It copied and plagiarized portions of the article
in the patent application. The university foundation sued the company in a
federal district court for wrongfully obtaining the patent. The court found the
company liable for fraudulent nondisclosure. It noted the company would have
had to pay the university for the rights to the reformulation, and calculated the
royalty rates at approximately $22 million. The court held the university could
recover equitable damages for unjust enrichment and determined the company
had been unjustly enriched in the amount of $23 million. It also ordered
exemplary damages in the amount of $500,000 for each inventor, based on the
company's "clandestine and deceptive conduct," and "fraud, malice, and willful
and wanton misconduct." The court ordered the company to pay a total award
of $54 million. *University of Colorado Foundation v. American Cyanamid Co.*,
216 F.Supp.2d 1188 (D. Colo. 2002). [CO]

The U.S. Court of Appeals, Federal Circuit, rejected the company's
argument that the damage award for unjust enrichment created a state-based
patent law that was inconsistent with the federal statutory scheme. The court
held this was not the issue in this case. The unjust enrichment claim was based
on the wrongful use of research and did not interfere with the federal patent
scheme. The researchers satisfied state law requirements for unjust enrichment,
as it would be unjust to allow the company to retain profits acquired through
misconduct. **The district court had properly awarded damages based on
incremental profits that were directly attributable to the misconduct. The
court upheld the district court's findings establishing inventorship.** Clear
and convincing evidence indicated the researchers were the sole inventors of
the patent. Substantial evidence supported the damage award, including the
award of exemplary damages, and the court affirmed the judgment for the
researchers and university. *University of Colorado Foundation v. American
Cyanamid Co.*, 342 F.3d 1298 (Fed. Cir. 2003). [CO]

◆   *A patent claimed by a New York university was invalid because it did not*
comply with the written description requirement of federal patent law.

Researchers at the University of Rochester developed a method for
identifying a prostaglandin synthesis inhibitor. The university received two
U.S. patents, one of which was based on a method that inhibited PGHS-2
prostaglandins. After four pharmaceutical manufacturers began using the
method, the university filed a federal district court action against them for
patent infringement. The court held the patent did not meet statutory written
description requirements and merely described a theory, not an invention. The
patent did not satisfy statutory enablement grounds, as it did not allow those
skilled in the art to make and use the invention without undue experimentation.

The university appealed to the Federal Circuit. It held **the patent failed the written description requirement, as its description was "vague." It did not disclose the structure or physical properties of any compounds.** While it was not necessary for the university to describe the exact chemical compound of an inhibitor, its description of a non-steroidal compound that inhibits the activity of the PGHS-2 gene product was insufficient for statutory purposes. **It would not provide a researcher, skilled in this area, with sufficient information to understand what it claimed to accomplish and how to perform the method.** The court affirmed the judgment for the manufacturers. *University of Rochester v. G.D. Searle & Co.*, 358 F.3d 916 (Fed. Cir. 2004). [NY]

◆   *A West Virginia university could not compel a student to assign second-generation patents to it under the university's patent policy.*

The student created a "half-wave bifilar contrawound toroidal helical antenna." He asked the university to submit patent applications for the antenna, and it did so. The student changed his mind and received a patent for the same invention. He then filed another application to provoke an interference with the university's application for second-generation patents. The university sued the student in a federal district court for breaching his duty to assign the patent as required by a university policy, and the student counterclaimed for breach of an implied contract. The district court issued an order for the university.

On appeal, the Federal Circuit held the student in breach of his obligation to assign the applications. He refused to sign the university's assignment forms and drafted new ones that only conveyed the rights to patent applications listed in the district court order. The court granted the university's motion to enforce the order and denied the student's motion for relief. The case reached the Federal Circuit again. The university argued the student's assignments failed to include three second-generation patents. **The court held the original assignment covered only the exact invention, its "immediate lineal descendants" and similar categories. The second-generation patents were excluded from these categories**, and the professor was not obligated to assign them to the university. **The university could not use its patent policy to compel assignment of the second-generation patents.** As the ownership of these patents had not been decided yet, the case was reversed and remanded. *University of West Virginia v. VanVoorhies,* 342 F.3d 1290 (Fed. Cir. 2003). [WV]

◆   *The corporate sponsor of genetic research at a state university was the rightful owner of a patentable invention.*

A molecular biologist assigned all intellectual property rights arising out of his research at Washington State University (WSU) to WSU by agreeing to the terms of WSU's faculty manual. WSU had in turn assigned its intellectual property rights to a corporate sponsor under a research collaboration agreement. The biologist began research on a plant fat metabolism project, for which he also used a laboratory at Ohio State University (OSU). He discovered the FAD2 gene, one of several genes that encoded the fatty acid desaturase enzyme. The sponsor and biologist entered into an agreement recognizing him and another scientist as the inventors of the FAD2 gene and assigning his entire right, title and interest in the gene to the sponsor. The biologist further agreed to cooperate with the sponsor's patent application. He later refused to cooperate until he received a reasonable royalty. The sponsor sued the biologist in a federal district court for a declaratory judgment that it exclusively owned the FAD2 gene, and to enforce his contract duties. The biologist counterclaimed for a declaration that he was the sole owner and inventor of the FAD2 gene and requesting rescission of his assignment. The court held for the sponsor.

On appeal, the Sixth Circuit held that while the Federal Circuit has exclusive jurisdiction over federal patent law, this was a contract dispute. It held **inventorship is an issue of patent law, but ownership of a patent is not a federal patent law question. The WSU faculty manual established a legally binding contract between the biologist and WSU.** Faculty members assigned their ownership of intellectual property to WSU, which in turn assigned ownership to the sponsor under the research collaboration agreement. The consequence of these two agreements was that all rights to the FAD2 patent were transferred to WSU, and then to the sponsor. OSU had waived any rights to the FAD2 patent. Even if it did not, **the faculty manual obligated the transfer of the biologist's intellectual property rights to WSU.** Summary judgment for the sponsor was affirmed. *E.I. Du Pont de Nemours & Co. v. Okuley*, 344 F.3d 578 (6th Cir. 2003). [OH]

◆ *Inventions by a pharmaceutical concern and a university were separately patentable as their molecules had different chemical structures.*

Eli Lilly and Co. filed a reissue application surrendering a patent covering deoxyribonucleic acid (cDNA), a sequence code for human protein C. At the same time, Lilly filed a patent interference claim against the University of Washington concerning a university-held patent that also related to the sequence of human protein C. The university denied any interference, asserting the cDNA molecules had different chemical sequences. The Board of Patent Appeals and Interferences agreed, finding Lilly's invention was not the same as the university's. Lilly was dissatisfied with the board's ruling and moved to define the interfering subject matter by proposing two alternative constructions of the cDNA: a narrow construction and a broad construction. The board applied a two-part test and rejected Lilly's contentions. Regardless of whether the claim was construed as a genus or a species, Lilly's reissue application and the university's claim did not define the "same patentable invention." There was no interference-in-fact, and the matter was dismissed.

Lilly appealed to the Federal Circuit, which explained that under 37 C.F.R. § 1.601(n), the "'same patentable invention' means that the one invention of one party anticipates or renders obvious the other party's invention." Since the claimed interference involved genus/species inventions, it was unclear whether the genus claim or the species claim was invented first. **The court found it possible that both a genus claim and a species claim could be separate, patentable inventions. The director resolved the issue by presuming that both Lilly's invention and the university's invention were "prior art."** This meant that the university's invention was assumed to be prior art of Lilly's invention and vice versa. Although the court acknowledged Lilly's assertion that a one-way test should be applied, it was within the director's discretion not to accept it. The court upheld the use of the two-way test and affirmed the board's decision. *Eli Lilly & Co. v. Board of Regents of Univ. of Washington*, 334 F.3d 1264 (Fed. Cir. 2003). [WA]

◆   *A university could not employ the "experimental use" defense in a patent infringement action filed against it by a former professor.*

Duke University hired a research professor from Stanford who had obtained two patents for devices/technology used in his lab: a "microwave electron gun" and a "free-electron laser oscillator." The professor worked as the director of Duke's laser research lab and, along with the university, contracted with another school to build a "microwave gun test stand" under a government contract awarded to the other school. After a disagreement over management of the lab and use of lab equipment, the professor was removed as director and eventually resigned from the university. He then sued Duke for patent infringement resulting from the continued use of equipment that incorporated his patented technology. A federal district court dismissed the case, finding Duke was entitled to the "experimental use" defense. The Federal Circuit reversed in part, noting that the lower court had improperly drawn a distinction between a research grant and a government contract for services. The court noted that **the experimental use defense should be applied in limited circumstances where use was "for amusement, to satisfy idle curiosity, or for strictly philosophical inquiry."** It did not matter that Duke was a nonprofit entity. The court remanded the case for an evaluation of the grant and a determination of which uses of the electron gun fell within the scope of the grant. *Madey v. Duke Univ.*, 307 F.3d 1351 (Fed. Cir. 2002). [NC]

◆   *A university and its licensee could not patent a discovery about the best time to harvest and eat certain vegetables.*

Johns Hopkins University owned three patents based in part on the discovery of the beneficial effects of harvesting and eating broccoli and cauliflower at the two-leaf stage, when they contain the highest levels of glucosinates and Phase 2 enzymes, which reduce the risk of developing cancer. The patents also contained a method for preparing the sprouts in order to increase their protective properties. The university licensed the patents to a company, then joined the company in a lawsuit against competitors for violating the patents. The defendants asserted that the portions of the patents that referred to the eating and growing of sprouts should be invalidated by prior art. A Maryland federal court ruled in favor of the defendants, and the Federal Circuit Court of Appeals affirmed. It noted that under 35 U.S.C. § 101, a patent can be obtained for inventing or discovering any new composition of matter or any new improvement thereof. However, **the university and its licensee did not create a new kind of sprout or develop a new growing method**. They merely discovered that the vegetables contained glucosinates and Phase 2 enzymes (anti-cancer agents). Those elements were inherent in the sprouts. Since prior art unquestionably included growing, harvesting and eating the sprouts, the patents were invalidated to the extent they tried to protect that activity. *Brassica Protection Products, LLC v. Sunrise Farms*, 301 F.3d 1343 (Fed. Cir. 2002). [MD]

◆ *A university's patent policy validly required two researchers to assign all rights to their inventions to the university.*

The University of New Mexico's patent policy stated that all inventions developed during the course of research funded by the university or employment at the university belonged to the university. The policy also required the inventors to cooperate with the university in the patent process. Two researchers of chemical compounds completed work that led the university to submit 11 different patent applications regarding two compounds. The researchers assigned their rights in the patents to the university. However, two years later, the university submitted five continuation-in-part patent applications, and the researchers did not assign their rights under these applications to the university. When the university entered into a licensing agreement with a company regarding the two compounds, a dispute arose over the ownership of the patents. A New Mexico federal court assigned a special master, who concluded that the researchers had to assign their rights to one of the compounds to the university. With respect to the second compound, the court conducted a trial and determined that the university owned those patents as well. On appeal, the Federal Circuit largely affirmed. The researchers were to be listed as inventors, but **the university's patent policy, which was incorporated into the researchers' employment contracts, clearly made the university the owner of the patents**. *Regents of the Univ. of New Mexico v. Scallen*, 321 F.3d 1111 (Fed. Cir. 2003). [NM]

◆ *Two researchers lost their right to continuing royalties when the patent on minoxidil expired.*

Two Colorado university researchers discovered that minoxidil stimulates hair growth. At approximately the same time, a drug company discovered the same thing. Because of competing patent claims, the Patent & Trademark Office held an interference proceeding, which resulted in the parties entering into an "interference settlement agreement." The agreement granted the researchers a minimum of $100,000 a year for the first six years after minoxidil was available commercially. After six years, with the researchers having received more than $26 million in royalties, the drug company's patent expired, and the royalty payments ceased. The researchers sued, asserting that they were entitled to three more years of royalty payments, but a federal court ruled against them. The Tenth Circuit Court of Appeals affirmed. **Even if the settlement agreement was ambiguous, the royalty payments terminated with the expiration of the patent.** The federal Hatch-Waxman Act did not extend the term of the patent for three more years. It merely permitted the Food and Drug Administration "to grant a drug manufacturer an extended 'exclusivity' period." Since the Act was enacted four months after the parties signed their agreement, the parties could not have intended for its provisions to apply. *Grant v. Pharmacia & Upjohn Co.*, 314 F.3d 488 (10th Cir. 2002). [CO]

◆ *A university showed that a company infringed its patent by surreptitiously disassembling a prototype device and stealing the design.*

Kent State University, through two subsidiaries, developed a "polymer-free liquid crystal display device" commonly used in digital watches and notebook computer screens. The university later learned that a company was using a similar polymer-free liquid crystal display device and sued to enforce its patent. The company responded by seeking a declaratory judgment that the university's patent was invalid. After a company engineer testified that he and others surreptitiously disassembled a prototype, photographed its component parts and then reassembled the device, a jury found that the company had infringed on the university's valid patent and awarded the university $1.5 million in damages.

A federal court upheld jury findings that **the company had infringed the university's patent**, noting that the patent was not "invalid for indefiniteness." The terms used in the patent application were not indefinite when construed in the context of the entire patent document. Also, even though the jury found that the company had committed both **literal infringement** (misappropriation of all essential elements in the patent) and **infringement under the doctrine of equivalents** (infringement that involves a device performing the same function as the patented device in substantially the same way to achieve the same result), the court found no inconsistency and simply reformed the verdict to show a finding of literal infringement. The court did, however, lower the damage award to $175,000 based on a reasonable royalty determination at the time the infringement occurred. *Advanced Display Systems, Inc. v. Kent State Univ.*, 2002 WL 1489555 (N.D. Tex. 7/10/2002). [TX]

◆ *A claim for co-inventor status failed where the claimant could not document his contributions.*

Researchers at an Illinois university obtained a patent on an invention based on the concept that virus-like particles (VLPs) could be produced after the expression of truncated L1 proteins in *E. coli*. The patent application listed four co-inventors. Subsequently, the president of a company sued the university, claiming that he was a co-inventor because he contributed the concept that VLPs could be produced after expression of truncated L1 in *E. coli*. The university asserted that he was not a co-inventor, and a federal court ruled in its favor. The president presented testimony of one of the four co-inventors that he contributed the concept, but the court rejected that testimony because the co-inventor had a substantial financial interest in the company in the form of stock options. **The president presented no lab notes, contemporaneous documentation or scientific articles regarding his alleged contribution to the project.** Based on the lack of clear and convincing evidence, the court found that the president was not a co-inventor. *MediGene AG v. Loyola Univ. of Chicago*, 2001 WL 1636425 (N.D. Ill. 12/19/01). [IL]

◆ *A university could not continue to receive royalty payments on expired patents.*

In the early 1970s, a Tulane University research team created a modified LH-RH molecule, which the university patented. Under a patent license agreement reached in 1982, the university gave an exclusive license to a Swiss company in exchange for a 6 percent royalty rate on net sales in countries where a licensed patent was in force for the life of the patent. In countries where no patent was in force, a 3 percent royalty was to be paid for 10 years. Four years after the agreement was signed, the company developed a new product based on the patented molecule. A dispute erupted over royalty payments for the new product, and a new agreement was signed in 1988 wherein the university accepted a reduced royalty rate for 10 years. In 1994, the patents licensed to the company expired, and it ceased paying royalties to the university. The university sued.

A Louisiana federal district court held for the company with respect to the 1982 agreement, noting that the university was prohibited from receiving royalties in countries where its patent had expired. **The university could only be paid royalties on existing patents.** However, the court then stated that parts of the 1988 agreement were ambiguous. The university claimed that the agreement required the company to pay it a 3 percent royalty for 10 years regardless of the existence of a patent. The court held that this issue had to be litigated. *Administrators of the Tulane Educ. Fund v. Debio Holdings, S.A.*, 177 F.Supp.2d 545 (E.D. La. 2001). [LA]

◆ *An employee's lawsuit against a company could not succeed, but her claims regarding inventorship of certain patents were allowed to go forward.*

An employee of the University of Chicago held a Ph.D. in molecular genetics and cell biology. She conducted research there in the alteration of DNA under the supervision of her advisor, who held an endowed chair, a distinguished service professorship in virology at the university. After 14 years, she was allegedly barred from future work in the laboratory and was told that she would be fired if she did not resign. She learned that **the university had patented three inventions involving altered Herpes Simplex Viruses, listing either itself or a subsidiary corporation as the owner of the patents.** She sued the university, the subsidiary, the advisor and a private company co-founded by the advisor that was licensed to use the patents, alleging a number of claims, including that she should have been listed as the sole inventor of one of the inventions and as a joint inventor on the other two. The advisor and the private company sought to be dismissed from the lawsuit.

The U.S. District Court for the Northern District of Illinois noted that the advisor was not a proper party to the cause of action regarding patent ownership because he was not an owner of the patents. Further, the employee had consented to work for the university under its rules of employment, one of which was that all inventions would be owned by the university. The court also found that the advisor had no fiduciary duty to the employee regarding the patenting of laboratory discoveries. However, it refused to dismiss the cause of action for conversion against the advisor. There was an issue of fact as to whether the advisor had taken her diagrams, drawings, writings and documentation. Finally, the court dismissed the action against the private company, as it had not authorized any of the acts alleged by the employee. In fact, it did not come into existence until after much of the alleged activity had occurred. Only the conversion claim remained against the advisor. *Chou v. University of Chicago*, 2000 U.S. Dist. LEXIS 2002 (N.D. Ill. 2/18/2000).

On appeal to the U.S. Court of Appeals for the Federal Circuit, a significant number of the employee's claims were reinstated. The claims relating to the inventorship of the disputed patent, and most of the claims arising from the inventorship dispute, should not have been dismissed, as the employee had standing to challenge the inventorship of the disputed material, and the advisor and university were proper parties to this aspect of the dispute. **Even though the employee would have been required to assign her invention to the university once the patent was issued, she was eligible for certain financial incentives if she was listed as the inventor or co-inventor of the disputed patent. Therefore, she had standing to bring the ownership claim.** The employee's state law claims for fraudulent concealment, breach of fiduciary duty, unjust enrichment, and breach of contract implied in law against the advisor were erroneously dismissed by the district court. The employee was entitled to a trial on these claims, along with her claims against the university for fraudulent concealment, breach of fiduciary duty, and breach of express contract. The circuit court upheld the dismissal of all of the employee's claims against the private company, with the exception of the inventorship claims. The case was remanded for trial. *Chou v. University of Chicago*, 254 F.3d 1347 (D.D.C. 2001). [IL]

◆   *Where conflicting evidence was presented to a jury, its award for breach of a licensing agreement was upheld.*

A professor of obstetrics and gynecology at the Medical College of Wisconsin invented a cervical cancer screening procedure and assigned the patent to the college. The college licensed exclusive worldwide rights to market the procedure to a company. Subsequently, the company sued the college and the professor for breaching the licensing agreement, and a jury ruled in its favor, awarding the company $10 million to compensate it for its losses. **The college and professor appealed the amount of the damage award, asserting that the company was a start-up business that had never been profitable and that the award of $10 million was speculative. Thus, the award did not meet the standard of reasonable certainty.** The Court of Appeals of Wisconsin affirmed the award. It noted that the company was not a new and untried business venture because there was credible evidence in the record of its history, progress and experience since its inception to justify the award. Since there was sufficient evidence to support the jury's award, the court could not overturn it. *NTL Processing, Inc. v. Medical College of Wisconsin*, 616 N.W.2d 114 (Wis. App. 2000). [WI]

◆   *A university could not modify a patent policy unilaterally to decrease the amount it owed a professor.*

The University of California hired an associate professor to teach and do research in the department of pomology. The professor concentrated his research on the genetics of strawberries. At the time of his hire, the professor signed a patent agreement, which provided that employees were required to assign inventions and patents to the university and that they would be assigned royalties pursuant to the university's patent policy. **The patent policy stated that employees would get 50 percent of the net royalties and fees received from their inventions. Subsequently, the university announced its intention to revise the patent policy**, reducing the percentage of royalties it would pay to inventors. When the professor invented six new strawberry cultivars, he informed the university, which notified him that the inventions would be governed by the revised patent policy. The professor sued the university for a declaration that the original patent agreement was in effect and that he was entitled to 50 percent of the net royalties. The trial court granted him pretrial judgment, and the university appealed.

The California Court of Appeal affirmed the decision for the professor. Because the written patent agreement signed by the professor was a valid contract, the university could not unilaterally modify it. **Even though the patent agreement did not state that the professor would get 50 percent royalties, it did state that the patent policy would be followed.** Further, the patent policy in place at the time of signing declared that employees would receive 50 percent of net royalties. As a result, the patent policy was incorporated into the patent agreement and could not be modified by the university without the professor's consent. The policy was not a mere personnel policy that the university could unilaterally modify. *Shaw v. Regents of the Univ. of California*, 58 Cal.App.4th 44, 67 Cal.Rptr.2d 850 (Cal. App. 3d 1997). [CA]

◆ *A state university could not obtain a dismissal of the lawsuit brought against it to determine the validity of a patent because the act of acquiring a patent requires a waiver of Eleventh Amendment immunity.*

Two companies attempted to negotiate the sale of a limited-use license in a Dynamic Cooling Device technology that would be used in conjunction with a laser skin treatment process they marketed. The University of California, which owned the patent on the technology, granted an exclusive license to another corporation. The two companies sued the university, seeking a legal judgment that the patent was invalid, and the university sought to dismiss the lawsuit on the grounds that it was immune from suit under the Eleventh Amendment. A federal court noted that this was not a case like *College Savings Bank* and *Florida Prepaid*, above, where a state was merely engaging in "otherwise lawful activity." Rather, this was a case asserting the invalidity of a patent–an integral part of the patent scheme as a whole. The court stated that **the Patent Remedy Act clearly and unmistakably requires a waiver of Eleventh Amendment immunity upon the acquisition of a patent (with respect to a declaratory suit over the validity of a patent).** Congress could require such a waiver because a patent constitutes a gift or gratuity bestowed by the federal government. Accordingly, the court denied the university's motion to dismiss the suit. *New Star Lasers, Inc. v. Regents of the Univ. of California*, 63 F.Supp.2d 1240 (E.D. Cal. 1999). [CA]

◆ *A university was entitled to damages for a company's willful infringement of its patents, but it was not entitled to a repatriation order compelling the return of material exported from the country.*

A doctor working with Johns Hopkins University discovered an antigen that appears on the surface of immature stem cells but not on the surface of mature cells. This allowed for the relatively pure suspension of stem cells that could be used for transplantation after radiation therapy. The university applied for and received two patents with respect to this discovery. Four years later, **a scientist at a research center developed a method of physically separating** stem cells from mature cells that was similar to the method disclosed in the university's patents. The scientist formed a company that began to use the method and also developed machines that it sold to be used in conjunction with the antibody to perform the scientist's separation method. The company knew of the university's patents. However, obtained an opinion letter, which stated that the claims in the patents were invalid and unenforceable.

In the infringement lawsuit that arose, the U.S. District Court for the District of Delaware held that **the company had infringed on the patents**. A jury then assessed over $2.3 million in damages against the company for willful infringement, and the court ordered the company to repatriate all clones or subclones it had exported from the country. The company appealed to the U.S. Court of Appeals, Federal Circuit, which agreed that the company had infringed the patents, that **the infringement had been willful, and** that **the damages award was proper**. However, it found that the repatriation order was improper and also found that there was an issue of fact yet to be tried as to whether the claims in one of the patents were anticipated or obvious based on evidence the district court refused to admit. The court affirmed in large part the holding of the district court in favor of the university. *Johns Hopkins Univ. v. CellPro, Inc.*, 152 F.3d 1342 (Fed. Cir. 1998). [DE]

IV. TRADEMARKS

A trademark, defined at 15 U.S.C. § 1127, is any word, name, symbol or device, or any combination thereof used to identify and distinguish goods, including a unique product, from those manufactured or sold by others, and to indicate the source of the goods, even if the source is unknown. Service marks are identical to trademarks in all respects except that they are intended to indicate the origin of services, rather than goods. Trade dress is defined as the total image of a product, and includes features such as size, shape, color, color combinations, texture, graphics or sales techniques. Although trademark issues arise in higher education, they occur much less frequently than copyright and patent issues.

Section 43(a) of the Lanham Act, 15 U.S.C. § 1125(a), creates a federal cause of action for unfair competition in interstate commercial activities. It forbids unfair trade practices involving infringement of trade dress, service marks or trademarks, even in the absence of federal trademark registration. See, for instance, Two Pesos, Inc. v. Taco Cabana, Inc., *505 U.S. 763 (1992). Under § 43(a), civil liability exists in cases where a person "on or in connection with any goods or services, ... uses in commerce any word, term, name, symbol, or device, or any combination thereof, or any false designation of origin, false or misleading description of fact, or false or misleading representation of fact, which—*

> *(A) is likely to cause confusion, or to cause mistake, or to deceive as to the affiliation, connection, or association of such person with another person, or as to the origin, sponsorship, or approval of his or her goods, services, or commercial activities by another person, or*

(B) in commercial advertising or promotion, misrepresents the nature, characteristics, qualities, or geographic origin of his or her or another person's goods, services, or commercial activities..."

According to one court, the "touchstone test" for a violation of § 43(a) is the likelihood of confusion resulting from the defendant's adoption of a trade dress similar to the plaintiff's. See Original Appalachian Artworks, Inc. v. Toy Loft, Inc., *684 F.2d 821 (11th Cir. 1982).*

♦   *The Nebraska Supreme Court denied an apparel store owner's claim for damages and injunctive relief against the University of Nebraska for wrongful use of a registered trade name.*

In late 1995, the Nebraska Athletic Department created an Authentic Shop, which would sell to the public apparel and equipment identical to that used by its teams and staff. The university began this process by test-marketing the idea to gather purchasing statistics for a new store. That same year, the university's board of regents filed an application with the Nebraska secretary of state to register the trade name "Husker Authentics" for the purpose of selling licensed goods. However, because the university did not file the requisite proof of publication of the name with the secretary and the county clerk as required by law, the registration was canceled without notice to the university. Taking all this in was Brent White, who owned and operated two businesses, Nebraska Spirit and Team Spirit Industries. White was well aware of the university's plans to open a store in 1997, which would, he believed, be a direct competitor with his stores. The day White learned that the university's registration of the trade name had been canceled because of improper publication, he filed his own application for registration of the trade name Husker Authentics. The Collegiate Licensing Company (CLC), the university's exclusive licensing agent, then got involved in the dispute. White had the CLC's approval to produce and manufacture the university's indicia from 1995 to 1998. The CLC sent White a letter claiming he was in violation of his license agreement and that failure to transfer his registration to the university within 15 days would result in immediate termination of his licensing agreement. White then canceled his agreement with CLC. Ignoring White's preemptive strike, the university opened a store called Husker Authentic on Aug. 27, 1997. Seven days later, White filed a petition requesting that the school be enjoined from using the disputed trade name. Later that month, White added a damages claim.

The university argued, among other things, that there had been a violation of common-law and statutory trade name and trademark rights. A state district court considered the arguments and found for the university, concluding that White's registration had been improperly granted because he had not actually used the trade name prior to registration. White appealed. The Nebraska Supreme Court found the district court's decision to be correct, but on different grounds, citing the work the university had done in test-marketing the concept. It further concluded that this afforded the school the common-law right to the trademark and any subsequent registration was therefore invalid. **Because the university owned the common-law right to "Husker Authentics," White could not properly register the disputed trademark.** The lower court's cancellation of White's registration was upheld. *White v. Board of Regents of the Univ. of Nebraska*, 260 Neb. 26, 614 N.W.2d 330 (Neb. 2000). [NE]

◆   *Villanova University was granted a preliminary injunction against its athletic booster club barring the organization from using various trademarks associated with its sports teams, "The Wildcats."*

In 1995, the Blue White Club (previously the Wildcat Club) and Villanova executed an agreement that formally affiliated the two entities, detailed their specific roles and outlined the organization's use of Villanova's sports trademarks. The agreement expired in 1996. After failing to reach a new agreement, the club's members voted to become an independent entity, and the university officially terminated the affiliation agreement. It told the organization that it was no longer authorized to solicit funds for the university, its athletic programs or athletic scholarships. On May 23, 2000, **the university notified the club's legal counsel that the club must cease and desist all use of the University's names and marks.** Since the termination of the parties' affiliation, the club changed its mission to raising funds for non-athletic scholarships. It continued to solicit funds and to use the designations "Wildcat Club," "Villanova Alumni Educational Foundation," "Villanova Alumni," "Villanova," and "Villanova Wildcats," as well as the image of a wildcat.

Villanova then sued the Blue White Club, alleging that since the university had disassociated itself from the club, the club engaged in "service mark infringement, service mark dilution, tortious interference with prospective contractual relations and breach of contract." The school also filed a motion for a preliminary injunction, requesting that the booster club cease use of the trademark words or any other name or mark "confusingly similar thereto." The Blue White Club maintained that it was free to use the designations. The club contended that the suit was merely an attempt to divert its significant credit card royalty income to the university. Villanova claimed that it sued only because the club ignored its repeated requests to stop using its trademarks.

The club filed a countersuit against Villanova, seeking a court order giving the club the right to use the Wildcat designations without university approval. In addition, it sought more than $1.2 million in endowment funds that it claimed to have raised for the university. The Blue White Club alleged that after its repeated refusals to submit itself to the university's jurisdiction, Villanova's president, the former university athletic director, and the former vice president for development conspired to tortiously interfere with the club's fund-raising activities to cause it to go out of business. **The court granted a preliminary injunction to Villanova, barring the club from using the "Villanova" and "Wildcat" designations.** The university and club were competing with each other in their fund-raising efforts, and the club's use of university designations could easily confuse outside parties. *Villanova Univ. v. Villanova Alumni Educ. Foundation, Inc.*, 123 F.Supp.2d 293 (E.D. Pa. 2000). [PA]

◆   *The practice of registering a domain name that is a common misspelling of someone else's domain name was found to violate the Anticybersquatting Consumer Protection Act in the following case.*

The Third Circuit concluded "Typosquatting"–the registration of Internet domain names that are misspellings of trademarks or service marks belonging to others–violates the Anticybersquatting Consumer Protection Act (ACPA). Joseph C. Shields operates the Web site www.joecartoon.com, which receives more than 700,000 hits per month. Additionally, products bearing Shields' work have been sold nationally in gift shops and online. On an issue of first impression, the Third Circuit ruled that John Zuccarini violated the ACPA by registering several variations on Shields' domain name, including joescartoon.com, joecarton.com, joescartons.com, joescartoons.com and cartoonjoe.com. "A reasonable interpretation of conduct covered by the phrase 'confusingly similar' is the intentional registration of domain names that are misspellings of distinctive or famous names, causing an Internet user who makes a slight spelling or typing error to reach an unintended site," the appeals court wrote. The circuit court characterized Zuccarini's conduct as an example of conduct the ACPA was developed to address. *Shields v. Zuccarini*, 254 F.3d 476 (3d Cir. 2001). [PA]

◆   *In the following case, the University of Florida was unable to demonstrate a violation of § 43(a) of the Lanham Act by the producer of a commercial study guide because it was unable to prove two of the three elements of a § 43(a) violation. There was no proof that the university had information that was inherently distinctive or that had acquired a secondary meaning, and the information was not primarily nonfunctional.*

A publishing company hired students to take lecture notes from various courses offered by the University of Florida to produce commercial study guides for sale to other students at the university. The university claimed that this arrangement violated federal copyright law, and it sued the publisher in a federal district court for copyright infringement, false representation of origin and deceptive advertising. The court entered judgment for the publisher, and the university appealed to the U.S. Court of Appeals, Eleventh Circuit. It argued that the district court had improperly denied its motions for judgment on the statutory and common law copyright infringement claims, and that the court erred in directing verdicts for the publisher on the false representation of origin and deceptive advertising claims.

The court held that the university was not entitled to judgment on the copyright infringement claims, since this would require the court to review the propriety of the district court's pretrial rulings, which did not evaluate evidence that was later presented at trial. The university also failed to demonstrate liability for false representation of origin under § 43(a) of the Lanham Act (15 U.S.C. § 1125(a)). It failed to satisfy the three elements for § 43(a) liability, namely that **(1) the mark sought to be protected is inherently distinctive or has acquired a secondary meaning, (2) the mark is primarily nonfunctional and (3) the defendant's mark is confusingly similar**.

The university had conceded that the information it sought to protect was functional and nondistinctive, and there was no merit to its argument that it was entitled to Lanham Act protection by satisfying the third element alone. Because there was no substantial evidence that the university's information was both distinctive and nonfunctional, the court affirmed the directed verdicts on the false representation of origin and deceptive advertising claims. *University of Florida v. KPB, Inc.*, 89 F.3d 773 (11th Cir. 1996). [FL]

◆ *Where an invention was created on university time, with university materials, by employees who were paid to do the work that led to the invention, the employees had no ownership rights to the invention.*

In one of the few cases addressing the issue of ownership rights to an invention, the Supreme Court of North Carolina held that **professors and researchers employed at North Carolina State University did not acquire any interest in a secret process for the use of Lactobacillus acidophilus they discovered using resources provided them by the university**. The employees here were hired, among other things, to do exactly what they did. Their invention was created on university time, with university materials, and they were paid to do the work. When they notified the university of their discovery, it was determined that the process was not patentable. A trademark was then obtained, and a nonprofit dairy foundation was selected to develop and market the process. Subsequently, the employees sued the university and the foundation to impose a constructive trust on the royalties received. The state supreme court ruled against them. It found that because the university owned the process immediately upon its discovery, the employees never possessed an interest in the process that would allow them to share in the royalties. Further, the university's patent policy did not apply because the process was not patentable. Finally, the university did not owe the employees a fiduciary duty to pay a percentage of the royalties. *Speck v. North Carolina Dairy Foundation*, 319 S.E.2d 139 (N.C. 1984). [NC]

CHAPTER EIGHT

School Liability

I. NEGLIGENCE

Negligence refers to acts or omissions demonstrating a failure to use reasonable or ordinary care. Negligence may refer to inadvertence, carelessness, or the failure to foresee potential harm. Some overlap exists between negligence and intentional misconduct cases. A pattern of negligence by schools and colleges that shows a conscious disregard for safety may be deemed "willful misconduct," a form of intentional conduct discussed in Section II of this chapter.

◆ *An injured student at the University of Colorado could file a claim with either the Board of Regents or the Attorney General's office.*

The student was struck by a dry erase board that was not properly secured to the wall. It fell and hit her in the head while she was sitting at her desk. Pursuant to the state's Governmental Immunity Act (GIA), she filed a notice of claim with the university's Board of Regents. The next day, her claim was transmitted to the Office of University Counsel. The university sought to dismiss for lack of jurisdiction, arguing that she was required to file her complaint with the Attorney General's (AG) office. The Supreme Court of

Colorado found that the student could file her claim with either the university's Board of Regents or the AG's office. The GIA allowed the student the option of filing with either the Board of Regents or with the AG's office. *University of Colorado v. Booth*, 78 P.3d 1098 (Colo. 2003). [CO]

◆   *A University of Oregon employee could not sue under the state Tort Claims Act because she waited too long to notify the university of her intent to sue.*

The employee suffered from depression and was placed on administrative leave when her supervisors became alarmed by her comments relating to postal workers and her shooting prowess. They told her she could return to work after gaining a medical release indicating she could perform all of her job functions. Over the next year, through her attorney, she exchanged correspondence with the university's counsel. She then sued the university, asserting a violation of the Tort Claims Act based on intentional infliction of emotional distress. The trial court granted the university summary judgment. The Supreme Court of Oregon affirmed, ruling that the employee's letters to her university supervisors failed to indicate an intent to sue. Therefore, the letters did not establish actual notice for purposes of the 180-day deadline in the Tort Claims Act. Although a plaintiff only had to inform the other party in general terms of an intent to bring a claim, the employee was unable to satisfy that standard. Her letters revealed no indication that she intended to sue the university. *Flug v. University of Oregon*, 73 P.3d 917 (Or. 2003). [OR]

A. Duty of Care

Most personal injury lawsuits brought against colleges and universities assert negligence, which has three general components: 1) a duty on the part of the school or school officials to protect others from unreasonable risk of harm, 2) the school's failure to exercise the duty of care appropriate to the risk involved, and 3) an injury or loss caused by such failure.

◆   *A university was liable for a pedestrian's injuries where it did not maintain a walkway properly, even though a safer route was available.*

A pedestrian was walking through a New York university's campus courtyard when she slipped and fell on ice. She sued the university for negligence in maintaining its courtyards and pathways. A jury found that the university could not be held liable because it had a direct and safer alternative path on campus and the pedestrian chose to take the more dangerous one. The Supreme Court, Appellate Division disagreed. It held that the university had to act reasonably in maintaining the campus property and ensuring it is kept in a safe condition. Just because there was a safer alternative route on campus did not mean the university did not have to maintain the pathway where the pedestrian fell. The university was liable for the pedestrian's injuries. *Witherspoon v. Columbia Univ.*, 777 N.Y.S.2d 507 (N.Y. A.D. 2d Dep't 2004). [NY]

◆   *A student did not have to show the existence of a special relationship with a university to prove it owed him a duty of care.*

A student enrolled in an earth science course at the University of Utah went on a required off-campus field trip to examine the fault lines in the Salt Lake City area. While on the outing, a classmate lost her footing, grabbed onto him and caused him to slip and fall. The student sustained injuries when he fell and sued the university, claiming it was negligent in allowing students to cross a "dangerous area" on a school-sponsored field trip. The university moved to dismiss, arguing there was no special relationship between the student and the university that gave rise to a duty. The trial court granted the university's motion, and the student appealed. The Court of Appeals of Utah reversed and remanded the case, finding the student was not required to show a special relationship existed between him and the university in order to maintain his suit. Because the student was on **a school-sponsored field trip**, and was directed by university officials to cross the icy sidewalk where the accident occurred, the university was required to exercise ordinary and reasonable care. *Webb v. University of Utah*, 88 P.3d 364 (Utah App. 2004). [UT]

◆ *A New York university was not liable for a student's gunshot injuries because even if it was negligent, it did not cause the harm.*

A student at the University of Rochester attended several fraternity and sorority parties on campus in an area named fraternity quad. Due to a rash of robberies in the prior week, the university had placed 19 security guards on patrol. Eight security guards patrolled the quad area. The student was shot by a non-student while the security guard assigned to that part of the campus was in an office doing paperwork. The student sued the university for negligence. The New York Supreme Court, Appellate Division, ruled that the university was not liable for the gunshot injuries. The student **failed to show that any negligence on the part of the university was a proximate cause of his injuries**. Even if the university owed him a duty to protect him from criminal activity, and even if the university breached its duty to provide adequate security, this breach was not the proximate cause of his injuries. *Colarossi v. University of Rochester*, 770 N.Y.S.2d 237 (N.Y. A.D. 2003). [NY]

◆ *A college was not liable for a student's injuries sustained during an off-campus assignment.*

A student at a California community college was thrown from a pickup truck while on a homework assignment for a course designed to train guides for horse-packing trips. The assignment required her to camp and map out a route for a three-day "pack trip." She became a paraplegic and sued the college and instructor, alleging negligence in planning and supervising the assignment. A trial court found that the defendants had no duty to ensure the student had a safe means of transportation. Also, the defendants were immune. The California Court of Appeal affirmed, determining that the college had no duty to protect the student during the off-campus assignment. As a general rule, colleges and their employees are not liable for off-campus student injuries. Here, neither the instructor nor any other school employee supervised the assignment. Courts impose greater responsibility upon adults than they place on elementary-and secondary-aged students to make transportation decisions. *Stockinger v. Feather River Community College*, 4 Cal. Rptr. 3d 385 (Cal. App. 2003). [CA]

◆ *A student was unable to show that a university's annual barbecue led him to suffer an injury as a result of a fight in a dormitory room.*

On the day Fordham University held its annual barbecue, a nonalcoholic event, some students drank alcohol at the event and in the dorm rooms. In one dormitory, two groups of students began to argue, and a student was hit in the eye. He sued the university, alleging that inadequate security at the barbecue caused his eye injury. The New York Supreme Court, Appellate Division, found **no evidence that the aggressor attended the barbecue. Moreover, the student was injured not at the event but at a dorm room.** Further, there were no previous incidents of fights during the annual barbecue that would have placed the university on notice that it needed to have a heightened security presence during the event. *Peterson v. Fordham Univ.*, 761 N.Y.S.2d 33 (N.Y. A.D. 2003). [NY]

◆ *A university had no duty to protect a student who slipped and fell on ice.*

A student at the University of Akron was walking from the campus parking lot, carrying her video camera, when she slipped and fell on an icy sidewalk. She was treated for injuries to her right wrist and shoulder. She sued the university, alleging negligence and seeking to recover $1,500 for her personal injuries. The university denied liability, asserting that it had no duty to protect her from the obvious hazard that resulted from the natural occurrence of snow and ice. The Court of Claims of Ohio agreed with the university. **The hazard was obvious** and the student was deemed to have knowledge of the condition. There was no negligence. *Lee v. University of Akron*, No. 2003-03132-AD, 2003 WL 21694740 (Ohio Ct. Cl. 2003). [OH]

◆ *A college was not liable for negligence when a resident assistant did not get medical assistance for a student's guest, who had passed out.*

An Iowa college student's guest drank at least 12 shots of vodka and passed out. The student informed the resident assistant (RA), of the guest's condition and was instructed to watch her. At some point, the student engaged the guest in sexual intercourse, which he claimed was consensual. The guest claimed it was sexual assault. The student also allegedly permitted two friends to fondle the guest's breasts. She brought a damages action against Simpson College for negligence under the theory of respondeat superior, based on the failure of the RA to obtain medical attention for her. A federal court granted the college summary judgment. The Eighth Circuit affirmed. It refused to find that the RA assumed a legal duty to come to the guest's aid. Since the RA did not specifically act to take control of the guest, he had no legal duty to obtain medical aid for her. *Freeman v. Busch*, 349 F.3d 582 (8th Cir. 2003). [IA]

◆ *A university did not have a greater duty to protect a 15-year-old student than it had to its other students.*

A 15-year-old matriculated at the University of Alabama and performed well her first semester. However, she then began drinking, doing drugs, and was rumored to be engaged in sexual activity with football and basketball players. On two occasions, university officials confronted her about the rumored sexual activity, which she denied. Later, she stopped attending classes and failed out of school. She then sued the university under Title IX, alleging that the university had a duty to prevent her from engaging in sexual activity that interfered with her classroom performance, which it breached. She asserted that the college stood *in loco parentis* (in the place of her parents) because of her age. An Alabama federal court disagreed. **Even though high schools stand in** *loco parentis*, **and even though she was of high school age, the university did not have increased obligations toward her.** Further, she had denied engaging in any sexual activity when confronted by university officials. Thus, the court dismissed the case. *Benefield v. Board of Trustees of Univ. of Alabama at Birmingham*, 214 F.Supp.2d 1212 (N.D. Ala. 2002). [AL]

◆   *A student who was shot could proceed with his lawsuit against a college and a fraternity for negligence.*

A Missouri student enrolled in a private college for the summer semester and moved into a fraternity house. After a confrontational phone call, the student attempted to lock the front door, but the latch malfunctioned and popped open. Ten minutes later, two men entered the house and shot him. He sued the college and the fraternity for negligence, asserting that they breached a duty to maintain the premises in good repair. The college and fraternity maintained that they had no duty to prevent a third person from performing an intentional criminal act, and that even if they had a duty to maintain and repair the house, the student could not show that a breach of that duty caused his injuries under the law. A state court granted pretrial judgment to the defendants, but the Missouri Supreme Court reversed. It found issues of fact as to **whether the student was in a landlord-tenant relationship with either of the defendants so as to impose a duty of care**. There also was a jury question as to whether the breach of that duty was the proximate cause of the student's injuries. *Letsinger v. Drury College*, 68 S.W.3d 408 (Mo. 2002). [MO]

◆   *The University of Maine may have been negligent in failing to prevent a sexual assault that occurred in one of its dorms because, under state law, it has a duty as a business to protect its "invitees."*

A student participated in a pre-season summer soccer program at the University of Maine. The university allowed participating students to live on campus during the program. The student stayed in a dorm and attended a fraternity party, after which a young man offered to escort her back to her dorm. When she reached her room, the man followed her in and sexually assaulted her. The student and her parents sued the university for negligence and breach of an implied contract. The court granted pretrial judgment to the university. She appealed. The Supreme Judicial Court of Maine reversed the dismissal of the negligence claim. It found that the university owed a duty of care to the student. Under Maine law, **a business (such as the university) has a duty to protect its "invitees" from reasonably foreseeable danger. A sexual assault in a college dormitory is foreseeable** and is one of the reasons the university went through the trouble of establishing safety measures in the dorms. Here, the student had never seen or met with the resident assistant on her floor; there were no group meetings offering instruction on rules and regulations regarding safety within the dorms; and there were no signs posted in the dorms informing residents who should or should not be allowed in. The negligence claim was allowed to proceed, but the court affirmed dismissal of the contract claim. *Stanton v. University of Maine System*, 773 A.2d 1045 (Me. 2001). [ME]

◆ *A university did not have a special duty of care to a student who was successful in his second suicide attempt, even though university officials were aware of his first attempt and did not notify his parents.*

University of Iowa resident assistants (RAs) were called to an off-campus dormitory to defuse a situation between an 18-year-old freshman and his girlfriend regarding the student's alleged attempt to commit suicide. The RAs suggested the student go to a counselor, which he agreed to do. The next day, another university official suggested to the student that he arrange for counseling from the university's counseling service. He again agreed. The student refused to allow his parents to be contacted. About three weeks later, the student committed suicide in his dorm room. His parents filed a wrongful death lawsuit against the university, claiming that it negligently failed to notify them of the student's previous suicide attempt. A trial court ruled for the university, and the Iowa Supreme Court affirmed. The university did not have a "special duty of care" toward the student as a result of its knowledge of his previous suicide attempt. Here, the university tried to help the student by referring him to counseling, offering encouragement and seeking permission to inform his parents of the situation. **The university neither increased the risk that the student would commit suicide nor led him to abandon other avenues of relief.** *Jain v. State of Iowa*, 617 N.W.2d 293 (Iowa 2000). [IA]

◆ *Negligence claims by a Montana State University researcher, who contended he was deported because he followed erroneous advice from the university's legal services office, were dismissed.*

In 1996, a citizen of China was granted American resident status and hired by the university as an HIV researcher. In 1997, he and his wife were involved in a domestic dispute, and he was arrested and charged with assault. The couple went to the university's legal services office for advice. An employee there advised the researcher to plead guilty to "Family Member Assault." She had been told by an attorney that the Immigration and Naturalization Service would not deport the researcher until he was convicted of two misdemeanors; however, in 1996, Congress amended immigration law to allow the deportation of immigrants who were convicted of domestic violence. The researcher pled guilty to family member assault, and the INS notified him that he was subject to deportation. The researcher hired a new attorney, withdrew his guilty plea, and then pled guilty to violating the state's assault statute. Based on the new conviction, a federal judge ordered him deported. The researcher then sued the employee and the university's legal services office for professional negligence. A trial court dismissed his lawsuit.

The Supreme Court of Montana affirmed. The researcher had argued that his second guilty plea was not a violation of the state's domestic violence statute and therefore could not warrant deportation. The court disagreed, noting that the federal judge who ordered deportation concluded the second offense was just as much a violent crime against his wife as the initial offense.

Although the employee had misinformed the researcher, her advice did not lead to his current predicament, which was based on his second plea, made on the advice of his new attorney. Thus, the researcher could not prove that he would have avoided deportation if it had not been for the employee's advice, and his professional negligence claim was not viable. *Fang v. Bock*, 28 P.3d 456 (Mont. 2001). [MT]

◆ *Rowan College was not liable for damages when one of its students was killed by a violence-prone ex-boyfriend on campus. The school did not have a duty to protect the student despite its previous efforts to help her leave the relationship.*

The student's boyfriend often displayed violent behavior. Local police were summoned to his home twice. The student volunteered at Rowan's radio station and told the manager about her boyfriend's violent tendencies. The manager recommended that she get out of the relationship, but she did not do so right away. When she moved out of his home, the dean of liberal arts and sciences agreed to grant her emergency campus housing free of charge. On Aug. 12, 1996, the student told the radio station manager that she was meeting the boyfriend in the radio station parking lot. The boyfriend killed the student, then himself. The student's family sued the college and school officials, seeking money damages under 42 U.S.C. § 1983. The lawsuit claimed the university knew of the boyfriend's propensity for violence toward the student and therefore had a duty to use reasonable care to protect her.

A federal court granted the university pretrial judgment because, as a state school, it was immune from suits seeking money damages unless it created or exacerbated the danger presented to the student. Here, Rowan did not create or exacerbate the situation. The student was an adult who voluntarily engaged in contact with the boyfriend. **The school's assistance in offering free housing and counseling did not create a duty to protect the student, nor did it create or exacerbate the situation.** The college officials involved in the situation did not act with deliberate indifference towards the student. *Nannay v. Rowan College*, 101 F.Supp.2d 272 (D.N.J. 2000). [NJ]

◆ *A university owed a student a duty to use reasonable care in assigning her to a practicum location.*

A graduate student in psychology at a private Florida university was assigned to an internship (practicum) at a family services agency that was about 15 minutes away from the university's campus. One evening, while leaving the agency, the student was abducted at gunpoint, robbed and sexually assaulted. She sued the university, alleging that it had been aware of a number of criminal incidents that had occurred at or near the agency's parking lot and that it had breached its duty of care to her by assigning her to an unreasonably dangerous internship site. The university sought to dismiss the case, arguing that it did not owe the student a duty of care because it did not own, operate or control the parking lot where the abduction had taken place. A trial court agreed. The court of appeal reversed, and the Florida Supreme Court affirmed. It noted that **because the university required the student to take the internship, and because it assigned her to a specific location, it also assumed the duty of**

acting reasonably in making that assignment. Since the university had knowledge that the internship location was unreasonably dangerous, a jury would now have to decide whether the university acted reasonably in placing the student there. The jury also would have to consider the student's knowledge that the internship site was unreasonably dangerous, and assess fault accordingly. *Nova Southeastern Univ. v. Gross*, 758 So.2d 86 (Fla. 2000). [FL]

◆ *Where a resident assistant received a serious injury off campus from a student who had been expelled, she was not entitled to recover from the university for her injuries.*

A student at Marquette worked for the university as a resident assistant (RA). One of her duties was to supervise the dormitory room check-out procedure whenever a student left the dorm. When a summer participant in a nationwide program for disadvantaged pre-college students was expelled from the university for inappropriate behavior, the RA was told to supervise the participant when she checked out of her room. The participant was aggressive and uncooperative during the check-out procedure, and eventually the campus police were called. However, by the time they arrived, the participant had gone. The next night, the RA went to a downtown club where she saw the participant. Although she was uncomfortable, she did not leave. Around midnight, as she was leaving, she noticed that the participant also was leaving. The participant taunted her and then hit her in the face with a broken bottle, causing serious injuries.

The RA sued the university for negligence, and a jury ruled that the university was 80 percent responsible for her injuries. The Court of Appeals of Wisconsin reversed, noting that **even if the university was negligent, the injury was too far removed from the negligence to warrant imposing liability on it.** Further, it was highly unforeseeable that the university's negligence would bring about the kind of harm that resulted. Also, allowing a recovery here could lead to lawsuits based on incidents even more remote in time and place. The RA was not entitled to recover anything from the university. *Conroy v. Marquette Univ.*, 582 N.W.2d 126 (Wis. App. 1998). [WI]

◆ *A university psychology professor could be liable for negligence where he failed to refer a student to someone qualified in suicide prevention.*

A university student with a history of psychological problems sought the guidance of a professor of psychology, who also was a psychologist. The professor discovered that the student suffered from depression and had experienced suicidal fantasies almost since elementary school. He only saw the student three times, pursuant to the university's policy of providing only short-term care, and then gave him a list of four people that he could contact for further treatment. None of them were psychiatrists or specialists in suicide prevention. The student selected a specialist in eating disorders, whom he met with for over two years. However, he then terminated his treatment and committed suicide. His mother sued the professor for negligent referral and the university on the basis of *respondeat superior* as the professor's employer. The court refused to let the case go to the jury, and the mother appealed to the Supreme Court of Rhode Island. The supreme court remanded the case for further proceedings on whether the professor negligently referred the student. **A jury could have reasonably concluded that the professor was negligent in failing to refer the student to someone qualified in suicide prevention** or to someone who could prescribe medication that would reduce his suicidal inclinations. *Klein v. Solomon*, 713 A.2d 764 (R.I. 1998). [RI]

◆ *Where a university knew of a dangerous condition and failed to fix it, it was liable for injuries resulting from that condition.*

A student at Louisiana Tech University and her roommate notified the residence assistant on several occasions that the air conditioner in her dorm room was leaking water onto the floor. Although the university twice attempted to fix the problem, leaks reoccurred within 48 hours of each repair. When the student's mother visited her, she slipped on the wet floor, fell, and hurt her knee. After undergoing surgery, she and her husband sued the university and their daughter for negligence. A trial court found the university 100 percent liable for the woman's injuries. It awarded her over $550,000 and awarded her husband $25,000. The university appealed to the Court of Appeal of Louisiana, which amended and affirmed the lower court's ruling. First, it found that the student was 25 percent at fault for her failure to warn her mother of the wet floor. Because she had knowledge of the dangerous condition, she had a duty to warn. However, **the university also had knowledge of the problem and had attempted to fix it twice before. It had the greater responsibility and thus was 75 percent responsible for the woman's injuries.** The court adjusted the damage award to reflect the percentage of fault, awarding the woman $413,000 and her husband $18,000 to be paid by the university. *Varnell v. Louisiana Tech Univ.*, 709 So.2d 890 (La. App. 2d Cir. 1998). [LA]

◆ *A private university was not liable for negligently hiring or failing to supervise a debate coach who murdered one of his students.*

A student at an Alabama university was a member of the debate team. After the university hired a new debate coach, the team became nationally competitive. During his junior year, the student participated in a practice debate. His team lost. Later that evening, the coach murdered the student. The coach was sentenced to life imprisonment. The student's parents sued the university and coach, alleging that the coach had been acting within the scope of his employment when he killed their son and that the university negligently hired and failed to supervise him. The university was dismissed from the lawsuit, and the parents were awarded $12 million against the coach. They appealed the decision to dismiss the university to the Supreme Court of Alabama.

The court noted that to be acting within the scope of employment, an employee must be pursuing an act that is incident to his employment or that the employer set in motion. It does not arise simply because the act occurred while the person was in the employment of another but rather, it must be shown that the act was at most only a slight, rather than a radical deviation from the employer's business. Here, **the murder of the student was a radical deviation from the university's business and therefore was not within the scope of the coach's employment**. It was not foreseeable that the coach would commit a murder while working for the university. Therefore, the university was not liable for negligently hiring or failing to supervise him. The court affirmed the trial court's decision. *Copeland v. Samford Univ.*, 686 So.2d 190 (Ala. 1996). [AL]

◆   *A private college employee's failure to warn others or call the police upon encountering a man carrying a gun and smelling like alcohol on campus did not result in school liability for negligence.*

A man entered the chapel of a Montana private college, where he encountered a priest who was preparing for mass. The man became loud and boisterous. The priest smelled alcohol on his breath and noticed that he had a handgun stuck in the front of his pants. He escorted the man out of the chapel and then returned to conduct mass. The man then entered the college's cafeteria and shot a food service employee and another worker. The other worker died, and the food service employee sued the college for negligence. She alleged that the college, through the priest and others who observed the man prior to the shooting, was negligent for failing to warn others or call the police. A jury found for the college, and the Supreme Court of Montana affirmed. The employee had presented evidence that the college breached its duty to provide reasonable security and a reasonably safe place to work. However, the college had presented evidence that it had never before had a problem with transients on campus, had never had a serious crime occur on campus and that the man did not threaten anyone and did not resist when the priest ushered him out of the chapel. The jury's decision was not clearly erroneous. *Peschke v. Carroll College*, 929 P.2d 874 (Mont. 1996). [MT]

◆   *A student advisor may have a duty to control his student and his failure to exercise reasonable care to protect minors potentially at risk from the student's behavior may lead to liability.*

A psychiatric post-graduate student at a New York medical school was accepted into its division of psychoanalytic training in 1986. He told his advisor-instructor that he was a pedophiliac and that he intended to enter into child psychiatry as a profession. Deeming the information confidential, the advisor never attempted to prevent the student from treating children. When the student allegedly sexually assaulted and threatened a mentally retarded 10-year-old minor whom he had been treating for possible suicidal ideation, the minor suffered severe personal injuries. Several years later, the minor sued the school and the advisor in a Connecticut federal court, alleging that the advisor had negligently failed to control the student or to warn his parents of the student's foreseeable conduct. The defendants moved to dismiss the minor's claims.

First, the district court held that the extended statute of limitations for actions involving the sexual abuse of a minor was not limited to the actual perpetrators of the abuse and therefore applied with respect to the advisor. Second, the court held that the advisor at least arguably had a duty to control the student. **The advisor had official authority over the student and had reason to know that he posed a specific threat to minor patients.** Further, he had reasonable mechanisms to control the student's behavior without compromising the confidentiality of his disclosures. For example, steps could have been taken to "redirect the student's professional development." Finally, the court noted that "a psychiatrist who knows or should know that a patient poses a threat to a victim or class of victims has a duty to warn such victims of such danger." **The advisor should have known that a self-confessed pedophiliac who intended to pursue child psychiatry posed a foreseeable threat of harm to minor patients.** Because both the advisor and the college had failed to exercise reasonable care to protect the minor, the court denied the motions to dismiss. *Almonte v. New York Medical College*, 851 F.Supp. 34 (D. Conn. 1994). [CT]

B. Premises Liability

◆ *An Ohio university did not have to protect an invitee from an open and obvious danger.*

The Court of Claims of Ohio ruled in favor of Miami (Ohio) University, which faced charges of negligence when a student's mother injured her foot while attending her daughter's campus volleyball game. The mother was directed to sit in the balcony area of the university's gymnasium. As she proceeded up the steps towards the balcony area, she tripped over a concrete step and broke her foot. The mother sued the school for negligence by failing to maintain the balcony area in a reasonably safe condition. The university contended the area where the mother tripped was adequately lit. The court found that **the university did not have a duty to protect the mother from hazards that are so obvious and apparent that she would be reasonably expected to discover and protect against them on her own.** The court held that the mother failed to produce sufficient evidence to establish that the step was dangerous by being hidden or indiscernible. *Schetter v. Miami Univ.*, 2004 WL 1399138 (Ohio Ct. Cl. 2004). [OH]

◆ *A university and its contractor weren't vicariously liable for the negligent acts of a subcontractor.*

A deliveryman sued a university and its contractor for injuries he received when a door fell on him while he was making a delivery on school grounds. The door had not yet been installed and was leaning against a wall. The university had hired a contractor to install the door, and the contractor had subcontracted the installation. The trial court granted summary judgment for the school and its contractor, and the New York Supreme Court, Appellate Division, affirmed. When a property owner hires an independent contractor for a job, it is not liable if that contractor is negligent unless there is a duty or the owner knows about an inherent danger. The university and contractor offered evidence to show that none of their employees supervised or were involved in the door's installation. Since the deliveryman failed to submit evidence to the contrary, there was no liability. *Laecca v. New York Univ.*, 777 N.Y.S.2d 433 (N.Y. A.D. 1st Dep't 2004). [NY]

◆ *A college that leased premises to a professor did not breach its duty to inspect or repair the property.*

A professor moved into faculty housing, which she leased from her employer, Marymount College. When she called the management service to complain about a leaking toilet and a non-working dishwasher, the service fixed the toilet but not the dishwasher. After the second visit to repair the dishwasher, she found her kitchen flooded. As she crossed the kitchen floor to turn the water valve off, she slipped on the wet linoleum floor and injured herself. She sued Marymount and the service for negligence and premises liability, claiming they failed to properly inspect the premises and remove dangerous plumbing materials. A trial court ruled for the defendants, and the Court of Appeal of California affirmed. Marymount's obligation to inspect was limited to only those defects or dangerous conditions that could be discovered by a reasonable inspection. Even if the service had not inspected her unit, **she failed to show the leak could have been detected via a reasonable inspection**. *Henowick v. Marymount College*, No. B158103, 2004 WL 604138 (Cal. App. 2004). [CA]

◆   *A negligence claim filed by an injured food service worker was rejected because the university did not control the area where the fall took place.*

An employee of a company that provided food services at Fordham University fell down an interior staircase that connected the kitchen of the cafeteria to the basement of the student center. She claimed the steps were slippery because that is where they took down the garbage. She also said the metal strip at the edge of the step was worn away. She suffered injuries and sued the university and the Jesuits of Fordham. The New York Supreme Court, Appellate Division, noted that control of the stairway was the critical issue in assessing liability. The evidence was unrefuted that **the Jesuits did not own, manage, or control the student center where the employee fell**. Only company employees handled the kitchen trash, and no member of the Fordham maintenance staff handled kitchen trash or used the stairway. Moreover, there was no evidence that the university had either actual or constructive notice of the stairway's alleged defective condition. *Garcia v. Jesuits of Fordham, Inc.*, 774 N.Y.S.2d 503 (N.Y. A.D. 2004). [NY]

◆   *A Texas university was not liable for a diver's injuries under the Recreational Use Statute.*

A member of the public, who paid a nominal fee to use the East Texas Baptist University outdoor pool, injured her back while attempting to dive. She claimed the diving board "double bounced". She sued the university for premises liability, negligence, and gross negligence, arguing the diving board's lever support was improperly positioned. The trial court granted the university's motion for summary judgment. The Court of Appeals of Texas affirmed, finding that it did not breach its duty of care to the diver under the Recreational Use Statute. The university was only "liable for injuries incurred through its willful, wanton, or grossly negligent conduct." Although the university acknowledged that the lever would shift after extensive use, the shifting did not cause problems suggesting that divers were at risk. A university lifeguard testified that in her 10 years of lifeguarding she never received any complaint that the diving board was functioning improperly, and never observed any defects or problems with the diving board, either before or after the injury. *Howard v. East Texas Baptist Univ.*, 122 S.W.3d 407 (Tex. App. 2003). [TX]

◆ *A student failed to show that snow and ice on a sidewalk constituted a nuisance* per se.

A student at Eastern Michigan University slipped on a snow-covered sidewalk and hit his head. He sued the university, alleging that snow, ice and debris that accumulated on the sidewalk constituted a nuisance *per se*. The university moved for summary judgment. The trial court determined the sidewalk did not constitute a nuisance *per se*. The Court of Appeals of Michigan affirmed. By definition, a nuisance *per se* is "an activity or condition, which constitutes a nuisance at all times and under all circumstances, without regard to care." Based on this definition, the snowy, icy sidewalk did not constitute a nuisance *per se*. *Hajek v. Eastern Michigan Univ. Bd. of Trustees*, No. 245574, 2004 WL 136746 (Mich. App. 2004). [MI]

◆ *A university avoided a premises liability suit under the landowner immunity provisions of the California Civil Code.*

A non-student went to a California university to walk on its track for exercise. As she walked toward the infield, she crossed a lane line and failed to see a steeplechase pit. She fell into the pit and sustained injuries. She sued the university for premises liability. The trial court granted the university's motion for summary judgment based on immunity provisions provided for private landowners under section 846 of the Civil Code. The Court of Appeal of California affirmed. Even though section 846 does not specifically include the term "walking" within the list of activities that are examples of activities undertaken for a "recreational purpose," the court found that this was not a limiting list. Walking is an activity serving a recreational purpose under section 846. *Brown-Alkire v. University of LaVerne*, No. B162191, 2003 WL 22054277 (Cal. App. 2003). [CA]

◆ *A university might be liable for injuries sustained by a student who mistakenly walked into a glass panel.*

A student at the University of Southern California mistakenly walked into a large glass panel that flanked the exit doors. The glass shattered, and falling glass shards injured her. She sued the university for negligence, claiming that the glass panels that were too thin to resist the impact of walking into them. A trial court found that the student was unable to establish causation because the breach did not result in her injuries. The California Court of Appeal reversed in part. It found that the trial court erred in its analysis of the causation issue. Causation required a showing that the university's act or omission was a "substantial factor" in causing the injury. Here, the width of the glass panels did not meet Building Code standards in 1968, which indicated that the glass panels should have been 5/16 inch thick rather than 1/4 inch thick. The university's negligence contributed to the injury enough to be a "substantial factor." Although the student admitted that she was not watching where she was going, this admission did not negate the causation element. Instead, it merely raised an issue of comparative negligence. A trial was required. *Chin v. University of Southern California*, No. B161246 2003 WL 21696282 (Cal. App. 2003). [CA]

◆ *A university-owned housing complex was not liable for a student's injuries suffered in an unforeseeable assault.*

A student served as a resident advisor at a student apartment complex owned and operated by Ohio State University. He and his friends attended a party in Hallway 2 of the complex. When an argument broke out between some high school students and a college student, he attempted to intervene. He was assaulted by the high school students and sustained injuries. He sued the complex for negligence in providing security. A trial court ruled in favor of the complex, and the Ohio Court of Appeals affirmed. Here, **he failed to show that the complex breached a duty to protect him** or that the complex could have reasonably foreseen his injuries. This was the first time an assault had occurred at a party at the complex. Further, the student's lease agreement stated that any security measures taken by the complex could not be treated by the student as a guarantee against or reduction in crime. It also stated that the complex would not be liable to the student for any injuries or damage. *Reichman v. Campus View Village*, 2002 WL 31831398 (Ohio App. 12/16/02). [OH]

◆ *A rape victim could proceed with her lawsuit against a university where the expert who testified that the dorm was safe was not properly qualified to do so.*

An Ohio university student was raped while taking a shower in the women's bathroom on the 12th floor of her co-ed dorm. Her assailant was never apprehended. She sued the university for negligence, asserting that it failed to provide a security system that worked properly. **She claimed it breached its duty of reasonable care by failing to install locks on either the bathroom doors or the shower doors.** At trial, an expert hired by the university testified regarding the safety of the dorm, and the court ruled in favor of the school. The Ohio Court of Appeals reversed, finding that the lower court improperly admitted the expert's testimony without a proper foundation. Here, the expert based his opinion on conversations with the head of the residence halls and the campus chief of police. However, he never visited the dorm, and neither the chief nor the residence hall head testified or gave deposition testimony. The court remanded the case for further proceedings. *Shivers v. University of Cincinnati*, 2002 WL 31722466 (Ohio App. 12/5/02). [OH]

◆ *A university was liable for negligence where it knew a floor was not suitable for a dance performance but used it anyway, causing injury to a dancer.*

An Indiana state university dance theatre was scheduled to perform at a high school, but did not conduct an on-site inspection of the auditorium floor. Instead, the director of dance contacted a teacher, who told her that it was a basic wooden stage. The teacher's daughter, who also happened to be a member of the dance theatre, informed an assistant professor that the floor was slippery and not completely smooth. She asked that a portable floor be brought in for the performance. The university chose not to do so. During the performance, one of the dancers was stuck in the knee by a 14-inch sliver of wood. She required two surgeries and sued the university for negligence. A court granted the university governmental inspection immunity, but also found that **the university had knowledge of the dangerous floor, creating a duty to protect**

apart from its duty to inspect. A jury awarded the student $150,000 in damages, and the Indiana Court of Appeals upheld the award. Here, the university had knowledge of an unreasonable risk and failed to protect its dancers from that risk. *Board of Trustees of Ball State Univ. v. Strain*, 771 N.E.2d 78 (Ind. App. 2002). [IN]

◆ *A student failed to prove that silk-screening chemicals caused her respiratory problems.*

A student at a state college in Nebraska experienced shortness of breath while working on a silk-screen project and had to go to the emergency room. When she returned with a doctor's note stating that she should not enter the classroom, her instructor told her she had to complete the project or fail the class. He opened all the windows and doors, and the student was able to complete the project. She was later diagnosed with reactive airways disorder syndrome and **sued the college for negligently exposing her to toxic chemicals**. A trial court ruled for the college, and the Nebraska Court of Appeals affirmed. Here, the student failed to prove that her limited exposure to the silk-screening chemicals caused her injuries. *Roth v. Board of Trustees of Nebraska State Colleges*, 2001 WL 1402075 (Neb. App. 11/13/01). [NE]

◆ *A university was not liable for the death of a student who fell off the roof of its natatorium.*

A Louisiana university constructed a roof over its swimming pool. The roof's apex stood 56 feet tall, with both sides sloping down to just a few feet off the ground. After campus police reported that a number of students had climbed the roof while intoxicated, and that several of them had fallen and sustained injuries, university officials discussed whether anything should be done about the roof. However, they decided to take no action because the students who had climbed the roof had all appeared to be intoxicated. Subsequently, a 23-year-old senior who had been drinking (and who had a blood alcohol level of .073) decided to climb the roof on his way back to his fraternity house. After reaching the roof's peak, he slipped and fell, suffering head injuries that resulted in his death less than a week later. His parents filed a wrongful death lawsuit against the university and various state entities.

After a trial court dismissed the case, the Court of Appeal of Louisiana affirmed. It noted that **the danger of falling off a roof is open and obvious to everybody. As a result, the roof was not unreasonably dangerous, and the defendants owed no duty to prevent the student from climbing it.** Because there was no hidden defect or disrepair associated with the roof—that is, it was functioning exactly as a roof is supposed to—it was not an unreasonable condition of the roof that caused the injury, but the student's reckless act of climbing it. The university was not negligent and therefore not liable for the student's death. *Robertson v. State of Louisiana*, 747 So.2d 1276 (La. App. 1999). [LA]

◆ *A Texas university was not liable under the state's tort claims act for sexual misconduct that occurred in a dorm room.*

The parents of two minor children sued a state university under the Texas

Tort Claims Act after they discovered that a student had taken numerous pictures and videos of their children in sexually explicit poses. Some of the incidents took place in the student's dormitory room, leading the parents to allege premises liability as well as vicarious liability (on the grounds that the university knew the student was a pedophile and yet continued to rent him a room). The university sought to dismiss the lawsuit, asserting sovereign immunity. A state court denied the motion. The Court of Appeals of Texas noted that **the state could be liable for premises liability where a condition or use of tangible real property resulted in personal injury**. However, the use of the dorm room here did not cause the injuries to the minor children. It was merely the site at which the student committed his illegal actions. Accordingly, there was no premises liability for the student's sexual misconduct. Further, even if university employees knew of the student's proclivity towards pedophilia, which the university denied, there could be no liability under the tort claims act because the misuse of that knowledge was not a use of real property as would allow for a waiver of sovereign immunity. The court vacated the lower court's decision and dismissed the case. *Lamar Univ. v. Doe*, 971 S.W.2d 191 (Tex. App. 1998). [TX]

◆ *In a similar case the following year, a similar result was achieved: no liability for a counselor's sexual assault of two youths.*

A counselor in a summer youth program held at a Texas university raped a participant while they were on a field trip at a hotel. Later that night, the counselor returned to the university and attempted to rape another participant who had not gone on the field trip. This assault occurred in a dorm room. Both participants sued the university to recover for their injuries. The university claimed immunity, while the participants claimed that the use of state money to rent a hotel room or a dormitory room was a use of real or personal tangible property that waived immunity under the Texas Tort Claims Act. The Texas Court of Appeals ruled in favor of the university, noting that **the money used to rent the rooms (and the rooms themselves) did not cause the injuries to the participants. The rooms were no more than the settings in which the attacks occurred.** *Scott v. Prairie View A&M Univ.*, 7 S.W.3d 717 (Tex. App.–Houston. 1999). [TX]

◆ *A private university could be held liable for negligence even though it did not own the property where a student's accident occurred.*

A private university in New York conducted some classes on the campus of another private college. While attending a university class on the college campus, a student was injured when she slipped and fell on a walkway. She sued both the university and the college in a New York trial court, asserting that both institutions were responsible for maintenance of the premises and that they had breached a duty of care to her. The university moved to dismiss the complaint on the ground that it neither owned nor maintained the premises and therefore owed no duty to the student. The trial court denied the motion, and the university appealed. The New York Supreme Court, Appellate Division, affirmed because **the university failed to present documentary evidence conclusively establishing that it had no control over or responsibility for**

maintenance of the common areas of the college campus. Even though the university did not own the property where the accident occurred, it still might be liable for negligence. *Smuckler v. Mercy College*, 663 N.Y.S.2d 869 (A.D. 2d Dept. 1997). [NY]

◆   *Although landowners owe persons lawfully on their property a duty of reasonable care, they are not required to be guarantors of safe passage.*

A commuter left her job in Virginia amid freezing rain that had begun only an hour earlier. She traveled by subway to a metro station that led to a plaza owned by a Washington, D.C. private university. When she reached the top of the escalator, freezing rain was coating the concrete, fences and surrounding cars. The commuter began sliding immediately after she left the escalator and ultimately fractured her ankle when she fell on the icy pavement. She received medical treatment for her injuries and filed a negligence lawsuit against the university in the U.S. District Court for the District of Columbia. The university filed a motion for pretrial judgment. The court held that the university had neither a statutory nor a common law duty to clear freezing rain while the storm was in progress. Although landowners owe persons lawfully on their property a duty of reasonable care, they are not required to be guarantors of safe passage. **Landowners are not responsible for damages caused by their failure to remove snow and ice until a reasonable time has elapsed after cessation of the storm.** Because the university did not have such an opportunity and the storm persisted at the time of the accident, the negligence lawsuit had to be dismissed. Further, because the plaza could not be considered a sidewalk, the university was not liable under the District of Columbia Snow Removal Statute. The court granted the university's motion for pretrial judgment. *Battle v. George Washington Univ.*, 871 F.Supp. 1459 (D.D.C. 1994). [DC]

◆   *A private vocational school had a general duty to exercise reasonable care and not to expose its students to unreasonable risks of injury or harm.*

A student at a Louisiana private vocational school proceeded to a small bathroom to collect a urine specimen for the laboratory instruction portion of one of her classes. Upon entering the bathroom, she tripped and fell over a toilet plunger and landed on her back. Because she was focused on her classroom duties, she failed to observe the plunger, which was occasionally used to prop open the bathroom door. An MRI examination and a CAT scan indicated that she suffered from a herniated disk. The student sued the vocational school, seeking compensation for her injuries. The trial court awarded $12,500 in general damages and $3,835 in past medical expenses, finding that her back injuries were more likely due to the fall than to degeneration. The vocational school appealed to the Court of Appeal of Louisiana, which noted that the student had to prove: **1) that the school's conduct was the cause-in-fact of the injury, 2) that the school owed a duty of care to the student, and 3) that this duty was breached**. The school had a general duty to exercise reasonable care and not to expose its students to unreasonable risks of injury or harm. Here, given the small confines of the bathroom and the fact that the plunger had been improperly used as a doorstop on other occasions, the finding of liability was not clearly erroneous. Also, the student was not negligent under comparative fault principles. The holding of the trial court was affirmed. *Butler v. Eastern College of Health Vocations, Inc.*, 631 So.2d 1254 (La. App. 5th Cir. 1994). [LA]

C. Defenses

Several defenses exist that either protect institutions from liability or reduce institutional liability. Public institutions, of course, generally are protected by sovereign immunity.

Under certain circumstances, private institutions also may seek immunity under state charitable immunity statutes. However, the institutions must meet the requirements of the statutes to qualify as charitable organizations.

More commonly, institutions defend against liability by demonstrating a student's assumption of the risk or contributory negligence. Statutes of limitations provide an additional defense in lawsuits that have been filed after the specific time period designated in such statutes for filing claims.

◆ *A student could not hold a university liable when she fell off a ladder while climbing down from a bed.*
A university student painted her dorm room. Another student (whose roommate would be away for the weekend) let her stay in her room while the paint dried so that she could avoid the fumes. She slept in a loft-style bed that was constructed by the fathers of the students who lived in the room, and injured herself when she fell off a ladder while descending to the floor. She sued the university, the students who invited her to stay with them, and their fathers. A trial court ruled in favor of the defendants, and the Michigan Court of Appeals affirmed. Here, **the ladder presented an "open and obvious danger,"** and it also **was not unreasonably dangerous**. Nothing was wrong with the ladder. The student simply lost her balance and fell to the floor. *VanNieuwenhuyzen v. Madonna Univ.*, 2002 WL 1747963 (Mich. App. 7/26/02). [MI]

◆ *A professor who left personal property in his old office for four years could not recover when the property vanished.*
After a biology professor was accused of sexual harassment on several occasions, he was relieved of his teaching duties and reassigned to another office. He was informed that he should remove his personal property from the office and laboratory space he had been using. He failed to do so. Two years later, the Tennessee Board of Regents determined that the professor was guilty of "capricious disregard of accepted standards of professional conduct" and fired him. He hired movers to pack up and remove his belongings, but did not take all his personal property with him. Two years after that, he returned to retrieve his property and found it missing. He filed a complaint with the Tennessee Claims Commission seeking return of his property or monetary compensation. The commission denied his claim. The Tennessee Court of Appeals upheld that decision. Here, **the university was not negligent. Rather,**

the professor abandoned his property. If there was wrongdoing here, it was committed by the professor, who continued to occupy space after he had been ordered to leave. *Wells v. State of Tennessee*, 2001 WL 1545501 (Tenn. App. 12/5/01). [TN]

1. Immunity

◆ *The design immunity provision of California's government code barred recovery to a concert-goer injured in a fall.*

The concert-goer fell down a few stairs at UCLA and sued for premises liability, claiming that the steps were a dangerous and hazardous condition and were in violation of the safety codes. UCLA moved for summary judgment, arguing that the design immunity provision of the government code barred the plaintiff's recovery. The trial court granted UCLA's motion. The California Court of Appeal affirmed. The stairs met building code and safety requirements, and the lack of guardrails and barriers was part of the design. The campus fire marshal approved the plans for the stairway and testified that a guardrail or barrier was not necessary for a riser less than 30 inches tall. The stairway plans were based on a reasonable design. **The design immunity provision does not require that the building be perfectly designed.** *Ying v. Regents of the Univ. of California*, No. 2d Civil No. B162112, 2003 WL 21983727 (Cal. App. 2003). [CA]

◆ *A dormitory at a public university did not satisfy the "public-building" exception to governmental immunity.*

A student at the University of Michigan lived in a dormitory, that was locked 24 hours a day. In order to gain entrance, students used a courtesy telephone at the top of a short stairway outside the residence. After using the telephone, the student lost her balance and fell down the stairs, injuring herself. She sued the university, claiming that the telephone was placed too close to a narrow step and that its location created a defective and dangerous condition. Because the university was protected by sovereign immunity, she asserted that the dormitory was a public building under the public building exception to sovereign immunity. The Supreme Court of Michigan held that **the public building exception did not apply to a residence hall at a public university**. Mere public ownership was insufficient to meet the public building exception. The critical issue was whether the university intended to limit the public's access to the dormitory. Here, public access was limited by the courtesy telephone and that entry was granted only by a resident. The university was entitled to sovereign immunity. *Maskery v. Board of Regents of Univ. of Michigan*, 664 N.W.2d 165 (Mich. 2003). [MI]

◆ *A university was not entitled to sovereign immunity for injuries caused by a sprinkler.*

A Texas woman and her husband were cycling along a trail adjacent to the shot put field on the campus of Stephen F. Austin University. Unexpectedly, she was struck by a stream of water shooting out of a sprinkler head located on the shot put field. The water hit the right side of her head with such force that she was knocked off her bicycle. As a result of the fall, she sustained injuries. She sued the university under the state's tort claims act. The university moved to dismiss, asserting that sovereign immunity barred the action. A trial court denied the motion, finding the placement and operation of the sprinkler system constitutes policy implementation under the tort claims act. Such activity was not protected by sovereign immunity. The Court of Appeals of Texas affirmed. Although the decision to water the campus was discretionary, making the university immune on that issue, **the decision as to how and when to water the campus was not discretionary**. Instead, it was a maintenance activity conducted at the operational level. *Stephen F. Austin State Univ. v. Flynn*, No. 12-03-00240-CV, 2004 WL 100395 (Tex. Ct. App. 2004). [TX]

◆   *A state university could not be held liable for an resident advisor's murder at the hands of a student.*

A graduate student at Purdue University worked as a resident advisor (RA) and reported to campus police that a student had marijuana in his dorm room. He later discovered that the student's roommate had cocaine on him and reported that to the police as well, despite a death threat from the roommate. Later, the roommate shot the RA, then killed himself. The RA's estate sued the university, the campus police and various officials for wrongful death, asserting violations of 42 U.S.C. § 1983. A trial court dismissed the action, but the Indiana Court of Appeals reversed in part. Although **the university and the campus police were "arms of the state" under § 1983 and thus immune from liability under the Eleventh Amendment**, the university officials and individual police officers were "persons" under § 1983 and could be sued. The court also noted that the state never assumed a duty to protect the RA, and it did not have a "special relationship" with him such that a duty to protect could be inferred. The court remanded the case for further proceedings against the individual defendants. *Severson v. Board of Trustees of Purdue Univ.*, 777 N.E.2d 1181 (Ind. App. 2002). [IN]

◆   *A state university was entitled to charitable immunity in a lawsuit brought by a student.*

A student at Montclair State University fell down an amphitheater staircase on campus, fracturing his ribs and elbow. He spent several days in the hospital and sued the university for damages. The university asserted that it was immune under the New Jersey Charitable Immunity Act, and a trial court agreed. Because the student was a "beneficiary" under the Act, the university was entitled to charitable immunity. The appellate division court reversed that decision, but the New Jersey Supreme Court reinstated the trial court's ruling. Here, the university was formed for a nonprofit purpose; it was organized for educational purposes; and it was promoting those goals at the time the student (beneficiary) was injured. **Nothing in the Act required that an entity be a private nonprofit institution in order to qualify for charitable immunity.** As a result, the public university was entitled to have the lawsuit against it dismissed. *O'Connell v. State of New Jersey*, 795 A.2d 857 (N.J. 2002). [NJ]

◆   *The associate housing director at Murray State University was not entitled to immunity in a lawsuit brought by the mother of a student who died in a dormitory fire.*

A fire started in the dorm where the student lived. His mother contacted the associate director of the university's housing office, who allegedly described the incident as "minor" and assured her that the fire was "nothing to worry about." Five days later, another fire was set in the same location. This time, the student was unable to escape and died of smoke inhalation. His mother later learned that the suspected cause of both fires was arson. As a result, she sued the associate director for negligent misrepresentation, claiming that if he had told her the school suspected arson was the cause of the fires, she would have removed her son from the dorm after the first fire. The suit also claimed that the director of public safety at the university breached his duty to ensure the safety of the students by not having an adequate security system in place. The defendants moved to dismiss the suit, claiming immunity because they did not knowingly commit a wrongful act. The defendants argued that since the mother's complaint alleged "negligent misrepresentation," they were immune. The district court agreed and dismissed the suit.

On appeal, the U.S. Court of Appeals, Sixth Circuit, upheld the district court's dismissal of the claims against the director of public safety, but found the associate director of the housing office was not entitled to immunity. Despite the fact that the mother was suing for negligent misrepresentation, the court interpreted her allegation as claiming that the associate director intentionally misrepresented the cause of the first fire. **Since the facts alleged by the mother were sufficient to support a claim for intentional misrepresentation, the associate director was not entitled to immunity.** *Minger v. Green*, 239 F.3d 793 (6th Cir. 2001). [KY]

◆   *A Texas athletic director was entitled to immunity in a former baseball coach's lawsuit against him.*

When the Athletic Director (AD) of the University of Texas learned the baseball coach was paying his son, allegedly a volunteer coach, for the son's participation in summer youth baseball camps, the athletic director took his concerns to a university vice president. An investigation was conducted, and an audit concluded that a separate account set up by the coach to pay his son and others violated university rules. The AD recommended that the coach be fired. However, the coach resigned, then sued. The AD asserted that he had immunity. A Texas trial court ruled for the AD, and the coach appealed. The Texas Court of Appeals held that the AD was entitled to immunity. The AD's recommendation to remove the coach from his position was a discretionary act based on the investigation, audit and the AD's experience. Thus, the AD acted in good faith and within the scope of his authority. *Gustafson v. Dodds*, 2001 WL 359685 (Tex. App.– Austin, 8/23/01). [TX]

◆   *A university was entitled to qualified immunity where the students suing it could not show that they had been deprived of a property interest in their education.*

Two student-athletes at an Illinois state university were accused of raping another student. They maintained that the sex had been consensual, and that the accusation of rape had followed from the refusal by one of them to continue a relationship with the student. One of the student athletes was acquitted of all criminal charges, and the other was never charged. Both were, however, required to appear before a hearing board, where one was expelled and the other was suspended indefinitely. The student athletes sued the university and various officials, alleging that they were deprived of a property interest in their education without due process of law. An Illinois federal court dismissed the case, finding that the university was entitled to qualified immunity because the student athletes failed to show that the university violated a clearly established constitutional right, and also that the Eleventh Amendment barred their suit. They appealed to the Seventh Circuit Court of Appeals, which affirmed. **Even if children have a property interest in attending elementary and secondary public schools, the student-athletes had not shown that Illinois state law provided them with a property interest in higher education.** The court also noted that the university, as an arm of the state, was immune from suit under the Eleventh Amendment. *Lee v. Board of Trustees of Western Illinois Univ.*, 202 F.3d 274 (7th Cir. 2000). [IL]

◆ *Two students who were injured while traveling to another college to play a soccer game could not sue their college because of a state law granting the college immunity.*

Two members of a community college soccer team were injured when the van they were riding in was involved in a highway accident. While traveling to another college for a soccer match in a van owned by the community college and driven by an assistant coach, the van blew a tire. The coach lost control of the vehicle, causing it to travel across two lanes of oncoming traffic and to flip several times. The players sued the college and the coach to recover for their injuries. The college claimed it could not be sued, citing a California statute that granted immunity to colleges for field trips or excursions in connection with school-related social, educational, cultural, athletic or college band activities to and from places. The statute provided that **persons taking such field trips or excursions are deemed to have waived all claims against the college or the state for any injuries that might result**. The California Court of Appeal affirmed the trial court's grant of pretrial judgment in favor of the college. Since extracurricular sports programs are "school-related athletic activities," the trip to the other college was covered by the immunity statute, and the students' lawsuit could not succeed. *Barnhart v. Cabrillo Community College*, 90 Cal.Rptr.2d 709 (Ct. App. 6th Dist. 1999). [CA]

◆ *A graduate student's lawsuit against a public university was barred by the Eleventh Amendment.*

A doctoral candidate at the City University of New York (CUNY) decided to switch his major after completing the required classes and written exams, but before completing his dissertation and oral exam. The history department approved the change, and the student found another professor to advise him. Over a year later, the director of the department notified the student that he would have to take more classes and re-take his major written exam. The student contacted the dean of students, who allegedly stated that he believed the student had been wronged by the history department and its director. However, he never convened a hearing. The student then took a two-year leave of absence and transferred to another program at another university. He sued CUNY, the dean of students and the history department director (in their official capacities) for money damages, including lost income and tuition, alleging that the director was a political leftist who was sympathetic to the PLO, and that the director had taken wrongful action against him because he was a committed and active Zionist. The defendants sought to dismiss the case under Eleventh Amendment immunity, and a federal court granted their request. **Because the state (and not the City of New York) would ultimately be responsible for indemnifying CUNY, the Eleventh Amendment applied to bar the lawsuit against all the defendants.** *Weiss v. City Univ. of New York*, 1999 WL 203354 (S.D.N.Y. 4/12/99). [NY]

◆ *A university student who was raped after getting into the front seat of a taxi in Mexico could not sue the university that sponsored her trip.*

While participating in a university-sponsored cultural immersion program in Mexico, a student was raped at knifepoint by a taxi driver. The student sued the university for her injuries. It sought to dismiss the case, asserting that it was immune from liability. The Court of Appeals of Minnesota ruled in favor of the university. It noted that the university was immune from liability for its discretionary decisions. First, the decision to use host families to provide housing was a discretionary decision. So too was the decision not to provide transportation for students in the program. The court also found that the university had warned the student about getting into the front seat of a taxi. It was not required to do more. **Because the university was not the guarantor of the student's safety, and because its decision to design and construct a program allowing students to be immersed in another country's culture was discretionary, the university was entitled to statutory immunity.** *Bloss v. University of Minnesota Bd. of Regents*, 590 N.W.2d 661 (Minn. App. 1999). [MN]

◆ *Aside from the Eleventh Amendment, state constitutions also provide immunity.*

A graduate student at an Arkansas university failed to obtain his doctorate in Marketing within the seven-year period allowed by the university. He asserted that the professor under whom he was working caused his failure by acting in bad faith and by giving him an unworkable dissertation topic, and then by giving him inaccurate, arbitrary and false information. He sued the board of trustees of the university, as well as several officials and employees for fraud, among other claims. A state court dismissed his suit on the basis of sovereign immunity under the Arkansas Constitution, and the state supreme court affirmed. **Although a person can sue state officials or agencies to stop bad faith and arbitrary and capricious actions, the student's complaint failed to show that any act of the university was in bad faith or arbitrary.** He acknowledged that the university had the discretion to grant an extension to the seven-year period, and that it did not grant extensions in every case. The court also found that the individual defendants were entitled to immunity. *Grine v. Board of Trustees, Univ. of Arkansas*, 2 S.W.3d 54 (Ark. 1999). [AR]

◆   *A Virginia college and professor were not entitled to charitable immunity where the professor was not acting on behalf of a charitable institution at the time he injured a beneficiary.*

A professor at a Virginia college established a program with the Boys and Girls Club of Hampton Roads, under which students in the professor's recreation programming class were required to spend six hours observing the children and volunteering at the club. The students were required to return to the classroom, design programs for the children, then implement the programs at the club. The professor went to the club to observe his students and help them out when needed. While he was there observing one day, a student asked him to watch a door leading to the weight room. She was giving a talk on wellness and body conditioning to 13- to 18-year-olds and wanted to keep younger students not involved in the program out of the room. The professor closed the door, amputating the right thumb of a minor who had his hand on the doorframe. The minor sued the professor and the college, who sought to dismiss the action on the basis of charitable immunity. The Supreme Court of Virginia noted that the club was a charity and that the minor was a beneficiary of the club. However, **it refused to award the defendants charitable immunity because, at the time of the injury, the professor was not engaged in the work of the charity. Rather, he was carrying out his duties as a professor**, observing a student and acting as a "doorkeeper." The court remanded the case for further proceedings. *Mooring v. Virginia Weslayan College*, 514 S.E.2d 619 (Va. 1999). [VA]

◆   *The New Jersey charitable immunity statute provided protection to a religious university in a negligence lawsuit arising from the university's operation of a pub on campus.*

A Catholic university in New Jersey operated a pub on campus solely for students and their guests. The pub was not operated for profit, it was subsidized by the student government association, and its employees were students. A 21-year-old senior at the university went with several friends to the pub and slipped in a puddle that was apparently left when a serving cart was moved. He sued the university in a state trial court seeking to recover for his injuries. The court denied the university's motion for a directed verdict, and a jury returned a verdict in favor of the student. The university appealed to the Superior Court of New Jersey, Appellate Division.

On appeal, the court noted that the university had deemed the pub to be part of a student's socialization process and a factor in the development of a well-rounded person. The question was whether the state's charitable immunity statute applied to the university while it was running the pub for students and their guests. **Under the statute, nonprofit corporations, societies or associations organized exclusively for religious, charitable, or educational purposes could not be held liable for negligence where the person injured as a result of the negligence was a beneficiary, to whatever degree, of the works of the nonprofit corporation, society or association.** Because the student was a beneficiary of the university to some degree while patronizing the pub, the university was entitled to charitable immunity under the statute. The court noted that the fact that the pub had since been replaced by a campus coffee house was not critical to the immunity analysis. Since the university had reasonably concluded that a campus experience ought to include opportunities to mature in an environment enriched not only by study and classes, but by diverse forms of social interchange within the university setting, the student was a beneficiary at the time of his injury, and the university was entitled to immunity. *Bloom v. Seton Hall Univ.*, 704 A.2d 1334 (N.J. Super. A.D. 1998). [NJ]

2. Assumption of Risk

◆ *A student's personal injury action was barred because she signed the university's release.*

A student registered for a seven-week basic rock-climbing course at Cornell University. As part of the registration process, she watched a safety video and signed a release, which precluded her from holding the university liable for any injuries caused by use of the climbing wall and for injuries that resulted from her own negligence. She also signed a contract promising not to climb above a yellow "bouldering" line without required safety equipment. On the day of her fall, she was climbing above the yellow "bouldering" line without safety equipment. She lost her footing and fell, then sued the university for her injuries. The university moved to dismiss the matter based on the release. The trial court granted the university's motion, and the New York Supreme Court, Appellate Division, affirmed. **The release language was unambiguous. It pointed out the dangers of rock climbing, and it clearly stated that the university could not be held responsible.** *Lemoine v. Cornell Univ.*, 769 N.Y.S.2d 313 (N.Y. A.D. 2003). [NY]

◆ *One who participates in sports can impliedly assume the risks that are inherent in that sport, including negligent instruction and supervision. Moreover, signing a release may absolve a school and its employees from liability.*

A student at a private west coast university enrolled in an introductory scuba diving course. At the beginning of the course he signed a "Liability Release." This document released the outside diving firm teaching the course and the Professional Association of Diving Instructors (PADI) from liability. The student completed the course, became certified, and then enrolled in an advanced scuba class taught by an adjunct professor. The student once again executed a liability release, this time naming PADI and the university. While with the instructor and two other students, he died of an air embolism as a result of ascending too rapidly from a deep dive. The mother of the student brought a wrongful death action. She alleged that the instructor negligently caused her son's death and that the university was vicariously liable for the negligence of its agent. The instructor and the school countered with the affirmative defenses of release liability and assumption of risk. They were granted pretrial judgment, and the mother appealed to the Court of Appeals of Washington.

In affirming the trial court's decision, the appellate court determined that though the fall liability release did not name the fall instructor, he was nonetheless included as an employee of the university. The general rule is that a pre-injury release of the employer from liability also releases the employee. **The instructor owed no greater duty of care than the school, which was released by contract from liability.** Next, in addressing the assumption of risk issue, the court noted that one who participates in sports impliedly assumes the risks, that are inherent in that sport. The student had the option of not taking the class, and he was aware of the dangers. Moreover, **by signing the release he expressly assumed the risks of the sport.** Negligent instruction and supervision clearly were risks associated with being a student in a scuba course and were encompassed in the broad language of the release contract. *Boyce v. West*, 862 P.2d 592 (Wash. App. Div. 1993). [WA]

◆   *A university could be liable for a student's injuries from attempting to dunk a basketball if he did not assume the risk of injury.*

A student at Cornell University, while playing in a pick-up basketball game, attempted to dunk the ball. He hit his hands on the rigid rim of the basket and fell to the floor, landing on his wrists and sustaining injuries. He and his parents sued the university for negligence, claiming that rigid rims unreasonably increase the risk to a player who is attempting to dunk a basketball. They asserted that the university should have used break-away rims, which give way on contact. The university moved for pretrial judgment, asserting that the student assumed the risk of injury when he attempted to dunk the ball over the rigid rim. **The student asserted that although he knew that he risked falling after attempting the dunk, he did not know of the increased risk that resulted from a rigid rim.** Because he had never been able to jump high enough to dunk the ball before, he did not know how unsafe it could be on a rigid rim. The U.S. District Court for the Northern District of New York held that the risk of hanging up on a rigid rim was not necessarily one that would be perceived by every adult. As a result, it refused to grant pretrial judgment to the university. *Traub v. Cornell Univ.*, 1998 U.S. Dist. LEXIS 5530 (N.D.N.Y. 4/15/98). [NY]

◆   *Because football is an inherently dangerous sport, a student could not sue after sustaining injuries in a football class.*

A California college student enrolled in an "advanced football" class, which taught appreciation of football and football strategy. Part of the class was devoted to offensive and defensive drills. These were non-contact drills, where the offensive players would try to complete a play, and the defensive players would try to stop that play. Once a pass was caught and the offensive player was touched, for example, the play would stop. While attempting to catch a pass, the student was inadvertently hit in the face by a defensive player's elbow. The student sustained injuries and sued the college. After the trial court found that the student had assumed the risk of injury, it dismissed the case. The student appealed. The California Court of Appeal affirmed the lower court's ruling. It noted that there are two kinds of assumption of risk: primary and secondary. Primary assumption of risk occurs when a person participates in an activity that carries an inherent risk of injury, and is a complete bar to recovery. Secondary assumption of risk occurs when a defendant breaches a duty of care to a person, but the person nevertheless knowingly encounters the risk created by the breach. This does not create a complete bar to recovery. Rather, comparative negligence principles are used to allocate fault between the parties. **Here, because the risk of injury was inherent in the sport of football, primary assumption of risk barred any recovery by the student.** *Fortier v. Los Rios Community College Dist.*, 45 Cal.App.4th 430, 52 Cal.Rptr.2d 812 (Cal. App. 3d Dist. 1996). [CA]

◆ *Where a student signed waivers assuming the risk of injury, she could not sue a university after sustaining an injury.*

After signing two waivers of liability and an authorization of medical treatment, an Indiana university student participated in a motorcycle training course for beginners. She drove a motorcycle provided by the university into a tree, breaking her arm. She then sued the university for negligence, including failure to provide appropriate equipment and failure to provide appropriate instruction. A state court granted pretrial judgment to the university, and the student appealed. The Court of Appeals of Indiana held that the waivers were not void as against public policy. Here, **the student had agreed that she assumed the risk of injury by participating in the class.** Further, the university did not owe her a statutory duty that voided the waivers she signed. Because the waivers were valid, the university was not liable for the student's injury. *Terry v. Indiana State Univ.*, 666 N.E.2d 87 (Ind. App. 1996). [IN]

◆ *A university was not liable for injuries a student sustained while sledding into a parking lot.*

When a rare winter snowstorm hit northern Louisiana, a university student went sledding with some fellow students. While riding on a plastic garbage can lid, the student (on his eighth trip down the hill) collided with the concrete base of a light pole in the football stadium parking lot. He sustained head and back injuries resulting in permanent paralysis from the mid-chest down. He and his parents sued the university and the state for negligence, asserting that the university had encouraged dangerous sledding activities and had failed to put cushions on the light poles. A state court granted pretrial judgment to the defendants, finding that the danger of striking a fixed object while sledding was apparent and obvious. The court of appeal reversed. The Supreme Court of Louisiana noted that a number of people had testified that the light poles were visible, and that they had tried to warn the student that he was approaching the pole. **Because the conditions of the property were not unreasonably dangerous, and because the dangers of the light poles were apparent and obvious, the university did not have a duty to protect the student.** Further, the university encouraged sledding only in proper areas and with the use of good judgment. Finally, there was no special relationship between the university and the school that created a duty to protect. The supreme court reversed the lower court decision and ruled in favor of the university. *Pitre v. Louisiana Tech Univ.*, 673 So.2d 585 (La. 1996). [LA]

◆ *A university did not negligently fail to warn when its representatives were unaware of the harm that could result from experiments it was conducting.*

The U.S. Court of Appeals, Fourth Circuit, upheld a lower court's ruling against a diver who allegedly suffered organic brain damage while participating in a simulated deep diving experiment conducted by a Duke University laboratory. The diver was experienced and held a degree in oceanographic technology. He signed an "informed consent" form that detailed the many risks associated with the experiments. After setting the world record for a simulated deep dive of 2,250 feet, the diver suffered organic brain damage. He sued the university in federal court under various legal theories, including fraud and negligent failure to warn him of the program's risks. The district court ruled against him. The court of appeals agreed with the lower court that because the participant was a highly educated, sophisticated diver who knew that brain damage could result from the experiments, his fraud claim against the university could not succeed. **Even if the university's representatives had concealed the risks of the experiment from the participant, he could not have been harmed since he already knew of those risks** but participated in the experiments anyway. The court then determined that there was no evidence that the university's representatives were aware that organic brain damage could result from the experiments. The university could not have been guilty of negligent failure to warn him of the risks. *Whitlock v. Duke Univ.*, 829 F.2d 1340 (4th Cir. 1987). [NC]

D. Damages

The nature and extent of damage awards generally depends upon the nature of the injury and the conduct of the parties. Compensatory damages serve to compensate an injured party for his or her injuries such as medical expenses or pain and suffering.

Punitive damages, on the other hand, are not designed to compensate for loss. Instead, they serve to punish the offending party because of the party's willful and wanton conduct.

◆ *Patients who never faced a medically verified substantial risk of contracting HIV did not suffer recognizable damages.*

Six patients received various treatments from several students at an Illinois private university's dental clinic during 1990 and 1991. In July of 1991, the university sent a letter to the patients informing them that a dental student who provided care to the patients was infected with HIV. While the university stated that it was unlikely that they were infected with HIV, it strongly recommended that the patients be tested for the virus. The patients sued the university and the dental student in a state court, which dismissed their claim. The patients appealed to the Appellate Court of Illinois, First District, which held that **in the absence of a particularly substantial risk of HIV infection, their reasonable fears were not severe enough to warrant compensation**. Because the patients never faced a medically verified substantial risk of contracting HIV, they did not suffer recognizable damages. Therefore, the court affirmed the judgment dismissing the complaint. *Doe v. Northwestern Univ.*, 682 N.E.2d 145 (Ill. App. 1st Dist. 1997). [IL]

◆   *A community college was liable for injuries sustained when a friend of the basketball coach, driving at the coach's direction, got in an automobile accident.*

The head basketball coach of a Kansas community college recruited an Ohio high school senior to play on his team and invited him for a visit. He asked a friend to pick the student up at the airport. The friend lacked a driver's license and liability insurance, and his car was not registered. He was supposed to drive the student to a hotel in El Dorado, but initially traveled to Hutchinson, where the coach already had taken several other recruits to watch a tournament. When the friend arrived in Hutchinson, he called the coach, who told him to drive the student to El Dorado. On the way there, the friend ran a stop sign and collided with a tractor-trailer rig. The friend died, and the student and the semi driver sustained injuries. They sued the college and the coach in federal court, asserting *respondeat superior* liability (that the friend was the servant or employee of the defendants and that he was acting within the scope of his authority at the time of the accident). The court agreed, and **a jury then found the defendants 90 percent liable, assessing 10 percent liability to the semi driver. The student was awarded over $2 million in damages, and the semi driver received over $270,000.** The defendants then moved for a new trial. While that motion was before the court, they settled their case with the student. With respect to the semi driver, the court denied the motion for a new trial. The award of damages was not excessive. *Foster v. Board of Trustees of Butler County Community College*, 771 F.Supp. 1122 (D. Kan. 1991). [KS]

◆   *An injured student under 21 years of age and unemancipated could not recover damages for medical expenses paid by his parents, although his parents were entitled to bring a recovery suit.*

After a student at an east coast private college fell out the window of his dormitory room and was injured, he brought a negligence action against the college in a New York trial court. The jury found him 50 percent at fault and awarded him $2.378 million, of which he was entitled to one-half. The incident occurred when he fell five stories to the ground through the sliding sash of his dormitory room window while attempting to open the window. On appeal to the Supreme Court, Appellate Division, the court reversed the findings of the trial court and ordered a new trial. The appellate court found that **the question of negligence was impermissibly taken away from the jury** and that the trial court erred in permitting the student to recover for past medical expenses paid by his parents. The court noted that the parents had the absolute duty to pay the medical expenses of the student since he was under 21 years of age and unemancipated. Although the parents could have brought an action to recover the expenses so incurred, they did not do so. **The student could not maintain an action on his own behalf to recover expenses incurred by his parents.** Since this issue should not have been part of the damages calculation and because of the error on the negligence question a new trial was ordered. *Radcliffe v. Hofstra Univ.*, 606 N.Y.S.2d 333 (A.D. 2d Dept. 1994). [NY]

◆   *Where a private college did not act willfully or wantonly toward the safety of its students, an injured student was not entitled to punitive damages.*

Two intoxicated students threw a smoke bomb under the door of another student's room, causing a fire. The fire resulted in death to one student and injuries to another. The fire alarm failed to warn the students. A lawsuit charged the school and students with wrongful death and other claims. The suit demanded compensatory relief as well as punitive damages. The school moved for pretrial judgment on the demand for punitive damages. **Punitive damages are available only when the wrongdoer has acted willfully or wantonly.** The court first examined the dormitory supervision system. The plan included having floor and hall monitors, and occasional meetings with residents on safety and other issues. It was not shown that this system was lacking or that the school acted willfully or wantonly in the supervision of its students. Also, the lack of a policy forbidding the use of alcohol by anyone less than 21 years of age did not encourage the drinking that led to the fire. The school relied on Delaware law in this area. Finally, the fire alarm system was appropriate for the conditions at the school. Therefore, the school was found not to have acted willfully or wantonly toward the safety of the students. Pretrial judgment was granted for the school on the punitive damages issue. *Sterner v. Wesley College, Inc.*, 747 F.Supp. 263 (D. Del. 1990). [DE]

II. INTENTIONAL CONDUCT

Schools may be found liable for the intentional acts or omissions of school personnel. Additionally, courts have found schools liable for intentional acts of third parties on or near school grounds. In those cases, courts may hold that the school should have foreseen the potential for misconduct.

A. Teacher Misconduct

Common lawsuits against teachers include those claiming intentional infliction of emotional distress, defamation, or sexual misconduct. Often, accusations of inappropriate sexual behavior may result in civil as well as criminal action against the teacher.

♦ *A university student could sue for sexual harassment by an instructor under both Title IX and 42 U.S.C. § 1983.*
   An Arkansas university student reported sexual harassment by one of her instructors. After the university fired the instructor, the student remained dissatisfied with the university's complaint resolution process and sued the university, instructor and certain university officials under 42 U.S.C. § 1983 and Title IX. The student sought injunctive relief and monetary damages under § 1983 and raised several claims under Title IX including strict liability for the instructor's action under the theories of *respondeat superior*, failure to train and failure to ensure that the university's sexual harassment policy was known to employees. The court dismissed several claims on the basis of Eleventh Amendment immunity and qualified immunity, but refused to dismiss the § 1983 claims for injunctive relief against the university and for injunctive relief and monetary damages against the instructor and university assistant president. The Title IX claims against the university, instructor and officials also were retained.

The university and officials appealed to the U.S. Court of Appeals, Eighth Circuit, which rejected the university's claim that Title IX was an unconstitutional exercise of congressional authority. The act came within Congress' powers under the Fourteenth Amendment. There was also no merit to the claim that § 1983 was preempted by the Title IX claim, because the U.S. Supreme Court has held that Title IX enforcement mechanisms are not exclusive. The student's claim for strict liability under the theory of *respondeat superior* was dismissed. However, **she was entitled to pursue her remaining § 1983 and Title IX claims against the university since she had a clearly established right not to be harassed.** The court remanded these claims to the district court. *Crawford v. Davis*, 109 F.3d 1281 (8th Cir. 1997). [AR]

◆ *If a professor's spanking of a student was sexual in nature, then the university could be liable to the student under Title IX.*

While enrolled in a biology class at a Virginia university, a female student took a make-up examination, which her professor immediately evaluated. After reviewing the exam, the professor told her that her performance was unsatisfactory and invited her to his office to review the test. The professor, after reviewing the test with the student, placed her over his knees and spanked her repeatedly with his hand. He then told her that she could re-take the test the next day, but that she should bring a hairbrush with her because he was going to spank her again, even harder, if she did not achieve a certain score. The student left the professor's office and sought medical treatment for sore buttocks. She initiated criminal and administrative proceedings against the professor, which resulted in the professor's conviction for misdemeanor assault and placement on probation by the university. Subsequently, she sued the university under Title IX, asserting *quid pro quo* sexual harassment (that she was required to submit to the harassment as a condition of receiving an educational benefit). The university sought pretrial judgment. The U.S. District Court for the Eastern District of Virginia held that **there were questions of fact as to whether the professor's actions in spanking and threatening to spank the student were sexual in nature. However, there was no question that the university was liable for the professor's actions.** Thus, if the spanking and threatened spanking amounted to *quid pro quo* sexual harassment, the university would be liable. The court refused to grant pretrial judgment to the university. *Kadiki v. Virginia Commonwealth Univ.*, 892 F.Supp. 746 (E.D. Va. 1995). [VA]

◆ *When a student settled a slander claim against a college, he could not pursue the claim against the professor who committed the act.*

A sociology professor allegedly ordered a student to leave his classroom, then slandered him in a 30-minute tirade to the remaining students. Subsequently, the student entered into a settlement agreement with the college, which released the college, its officers, agents and employees from any liability for any alleged slander committed by the professor. The release did not prevent the student from suing the professor for actions outside the scope of his authority as an employee. When the student sued the professor for slander, a state trial court granted pretrial judgment to the professor. The Supreme Court of Montana affirmed, finding that **the student was statutorily barred in his suit against the professor by reason of his settlement with the college. A state law provided that recovery against a governmental entity barred recovery against the employee whose wrongful act caused the harm.** *Stansbury v. Lin*, 848 P.2d 509 (Mont. 1993). [MT]

◆ *A Louisiana appellate court held a professor liable for defamation and intentional infliction of emotional distress for comments he made to other students about an incident with the defamed student.*

A first-year professor at a private Louisiana law school recounted an embarrassing experience during which a female law student fell off her chair in a local nightclub. Upset at the comment, the female law student asked, "why didn't you help me up?" The professor replied, "I ain't picking no slut up off the floor." When confronted by the chancellor, the professor denied calling her a slut. During a subsequent class, the professor threatened to give bad grades to any student who testified against him. Eventually, the professor publicly apologized, and the law student was allowed to transfer to another class. She suffered emotional injuries and sued the professor for defamation and intentional infliction of emotional distress (IIED). The trial court held that although defamation had occurred, the law student had failed to prove IIED or loss of reputation and granted her only $1,500 plus interest and costs. The professor appealed to the Court of Appeal of Louisiana. The court of appeal determined that **the professor's statements amounted to defamation** *per se* (on its face). Consequently, the court presumed that **the statements were both false and malicious.** The professor was liable for damages as well as for IIED. Thus, the defamatory comments, coupled with the emotional distress, justified an increase in damages to $5,000. *Smith v. Atkins*, 622 So.2d 795 (La. App. 4th Cir. 1993). [LA]

◆ *A university could not be held liable for a professor's "battery" against a woman.*

While at a woman's house as a social guest, a university professor walked up behind the woman and touched her back with both of his hands, mimicking the movement of pressing and releasing the keys of a piano keyboard. He did this to demonstrate the sensation of the movement by a pianist, not to cause any harm. However, the woman sustained injuries as a result of the touching and sued the university under the Idaho Tort Claims Act. The university asserted that it was immune from liability because the touching amounted to a "battery" under the law. The university, as a governmental entity, was immune from liability for any injuries arising out of a battery committed by an employee. The case reached the Supreme Court of Idaho, which held that for a civil battery to be committed, there need not be any intent to cause harm; there need only be an act that causes an intended contact with another person that is unpermitted and that is harmful or offensive. **Here, the professor's touching of the woman was without her permission, intentional and, despite intent to the contrary, harmful. As a result, it was battery.** The university could not be held liable for battery under the state tort claims act. *White v. University of Idaho*, 797 P.2d 108 (Idaho 1990). [ID]

B. Employee Misconduct

Other school employees, such as principals, counselors, or custodians, also may be subject to lawsuits based on intentional infliction of emotional distress, criminal behavior, or other misconduct.

◆   *A university instructor's physical assault of a student did not result in school liability because the assault was not in furtherance of the school's business and therefore fell outside the scope of employment.*
    A student at a New York university enrolled in a non-credit karate course offered during the summer session. The class was held in the school's physical education building. According to the student, he was told by the instructor to do a reverse push-up. After he refused, believing that it was unsafe, the instructor struck him several times. He was taken to the hospital and later sued the school in the Court of Claims for his injuries. The school asserted that it should not be held vicariously liable for the student's injuries because the instructor was not an employee but an independent contractor.
    The court noted that although there was an issue as to whether students could reasonably believe that the instructors of the non-credit courses were employees of the school, it did not need to resolve this issue since the karate instructor's conduct was outside the scope of his employment. **The school did not authorize the use of violence and such actions were not within any discretionary authority given to the instructor.** The assault was not in furtherance of the school's business and therefore fell outside the scope of employment. The school could not be held vicariously liable for such actions. *Forester v. State*, 645 N.Y.S.2d 971 (Ct. Cl. 1996). [NY]

◆   *A private college did not become liable for a priest's sexual assault of a boy because it was not reasonably foreseeable.*
    A priest employed as a campus minister by a private college and as a chaplain at a hospital was accused of sexually assaulting a boy. The priest knew the boy and his family through the boy's school and parish. The alleged assaults took place in the evening at the priest's residence, where the boy was staying because of his family's friendship with the priest. The boy was neither a patient at the hospital nor a student at the college. After the assault, the boy's parents sued the college and the hospital, alleging *respondeat superior* liability and negligent supervision. The college and the hospital filed motions to dismiss, which the trial court granted. The parents appealed to the Court of Appeals of Ohio, which noted that **for an employer to be liable under the theory of** *respondeat superior***, the employee's act must be committed within the scope of employment.** This means that it must be calculated to facilitate or promote the business for which the person was employed. Here, the court held that sexual assault diverted from the straight and narrow performance of the priest's job, as it was not reasonably foreseeable to the college or hospital that the priest would commit such an act against someone who was neither a student at the college nor a patient at the hospital. His relationship with the boy was in no way related to his roles as campus minister or hospital chaplain. The court also found no liability as to the negligent supervision claim. The trial court's

decision was affirmed. *Gebhart v. College of Mt. St. Joseph*, 665 N.E.2d 223 (Ohio App. 1st Dist. 1995). [OH]

◆ *An employee's lawsuit against co-workers for "aiding and abetting" in a sexual assault by another co-worker failed because the co-workers' actions were not a direct or deliberate cause of the assault.*

A New York woman employed by a private university as an animal attendant was repeatedly subjected to "rude and vulgar" behavior from the stable attendant. Her co-workers at the university knew of the stable attendant's "demeaning and malevolent attitude toward women" and his history of "hostile physical aggression toward women." After the stable attendant assaulted the animal attendant, she sued the university and two co-workers, alleging that they "aided and abetted" the assault and that they were liable for intentional infliction of emotional distress (IIED). The defendants moved for pretrial judgment, which the court denied. The Supreme Court, Appellate Division, noted that "merely harboring a dangerous person or giving tacit approval" did not constitute aiding or abetting the assault. Rather, in order to prevail on this claim, the defendants had to "overtly encourage the offensive behavior." Here, **the co-workers' contribution to a hostile work environment could not be interpreted as a "direct or deliberate" cause of the assault**. Therefore, the aiding and abetting charge was dismissed. Further, the IIED claim could not survive because the stable attendant's crude and inappropriate comments were not sufficiently "atrocious and intolerable" to establish such a cause of action. The holding of the lower court was reversed. *Shea v. Cornell Univ.*, 596 N.Y.S.2d 502 (A.D. 3d Dept. 1993). [NY]

C. Third-Party Misconduct

Liability for third-party misconduct can arise when someone connected with the school is injured by a third party while outside school property, or when an individual not affiliated with the school enters school property and injures someone connected with the school. Often, third-party misconduct involves some type of criminal behavior, such as physical or sexual assault. Claims against schools arise when students seek to hold the school liable for negligence, alleging that the school failed to provide a safe and secure environment.

◆ *Lawsuits filed against Texas A&M after a tragic bonfire accident were allowed to continue by a federal appeals court.*

In 1999, a bonfire stack collapsed on the campus of Texas A&M University, killing 12 students and injuring 27 others. A university special commission report exonerated university officials, finding that their actions did not rise to the level of deliberate indifference. However, numerous lawsuits arose, alleging violations of 42 U.S.C. § 1983 under a state-created danger theory. A federal district court dismissed the lawsuits, but the Fifth Circuit reversed and remanded. The court of appeals noted that the record supported a finding of deliberate indifference. The plaintiffs presented evidence that university officials allowed the bonfire stack to increase over the years to a pile of burning trash weighing more than 3 million pounds. A university official had described the stack as the "most serious risk management activity at the university." Nevertheless, university officials did not use their authority to control the stack's building or destruction. The plaintiffs even asserted that the university encouraged students to add to the stack as a "marketing tool to lure prospective students" and to gain alumni donations. Based on all this evidence, the Fifth Circuit found that the plaintiffs established their § 1983 claim. The district court's decision was reversed, and the case was remanded. *Scanlon v. Texas A&M Univ.*, 343 F.3d 533 (5th Cir. 2003). [TX]

◆ *A college could declare an alumnus "persona non grata" and bar him from campus.*

Over the course of his nine years at a college, a student exhibited disruptive behavior on campus and began receiving psychiatric treatment. His mother allegedly warned a nurse that he might act violently at his graduation ceremony, and security guards questioned him shortly before the ceremony began. However, the ceremony took place without any trouble. A month later, the student was declared "persona non grata" by the college and was barred from the campus. He eventually sued the college and the nurse. A state court ruled for the defendants, and the New York Supreme Court, Appellate Division, affirmed. Here, **since he had graduated, he was no longer a student and was not entitled to due process as a result of the college barring him from campus.** Further, his claims against the nurse could not succeed because he could not show that she breached a duty to keep information confidential. *Godinez v. Siena College*, 733 N.Y.S.2d 262 (N.Y. A.D. 2001). [NY]

◆ *A college student, who was sexually assaulted by two men after consuming alcoholic beverages at an off-campus bar, could not maintain a suit against the college.*

A 17-year-old college freshman at a four-year private school gained entrance to an off-campus tavern through the use of her student ID card. The bar was named after the college's mascot and displayed college memorabilia. After consuming alcoholic beverages, the student left the bar with two men and was sexually assaulted. A parent of the student sued the college on her behalf, claiming that the college had breached its duty of care toward the student in several respects. The first claim asserted that the school breached a duty to provide a campus environment free from foreseeable harm. The college stressed that the tavern was not on campus grounds, the student's activities were unrelated to her curriculum, and that the college had no knowledge of the potential for assault. The court refused to impose liability under these circumstances. The second claim asserted that the school failed to advise the student concerning state law and the dangers associated with drinking. However, the student admitted she knew of these matters. Further, the court stated that no such duty should be imposed upon a college. The final claim concerned duties associated with **an *in loco parentis* relationship**. This relationship **would place a duty on the college to act toward a student as would a parent**. Although courts have almost universally rejected such a notion, the girl's parent argued that the *in loco parentis* relationship should be required because the girl was only 17 years old. The court noted that such a relationship is not within the expectations of either the college or students. It refused to impose the duty, and all claims were dismissed. *Hartman v. Bethany College*, 778 F.Supp. 286 (N.D. W.Va. 1991). [WV]

◆ *Although a woman was injured while on a university campus, the university's alleged lack of security was not the legal cause of her injuries.*

A woman was grabbed from behind, stabbed, beaten and raped while on a university campus. Nearly an hour later, two motorists heard her screams, but the assailant fled before they arrived. The woman sued the university for negligence. At trial, her independent security expert found many faults with the security provided by the school. The university's expert testified that the security was adequate. The jury returned a verdict for the woman, and she accepted a reduced judgment of $1,288,888. The university appealed, contending that there was no causal connection between its negligence and the woman's injury. The court of appeal agreed. It assumed, without deciding, that the university breached a duty by failing to provide adequate security to prevent the injury. However, that abstract negligence could not be the legal cause of the woman's injury. Noting that absolute safety was not an achievable goal and that increased security meant increased costs, the court was not willing to make landowners guarantors of their patrons' personal safety. **The court concluded that the causation element "imposed rational limits on liability" and avoided turning a third party (the university) into a vicarious criminal.** Thus, the university's alleged lack of security was not the legal cause of the injury. *Nola M. v. University of Southern California*, 20 Cal.Rptr.2d 97 (Cal. App. 2d Dist. 1993). [CA]

◆ *Although a church-operated college owned a parking lot adjoining a state university childcare center, a patron of the center had no special relationship with the college that required imposing liability on the college.*

A church-operated Illinois college owned a parking lot adjoining a state university childcare center. Persons dropping off their children at the center customarily used the parking lot, and the practice was acknowledged by a college official. The college employed off-duty police officers to patrol its campus area, including the parking lot. No serious incidents had been reported in the parking lot, and the most serious incident on the campus had involved harassment and bottle-throwing by local high school students. However, a patron of the daycare center was abducted from the parking lot at gunpoint after dropping off her child. She was then sexually assaulted and slashed with a knife. She sued the college in federal court for her injuries, claiming that the college had voluntarily undertaken police protection for the parking lot. Her husband also sued for loss of consortium. The court granted the college's motion for pretrial judgment, and the patron and her husband appealed to the U.S. Court of Appeals, Seventh Circuit.

According to the court, Illinois law imposed no duty upon parties to protect third parties from criminal attack. Exceptions existed when there was a special relationship between the parties or when a criminal attack was reasonably foreseeable. Here, the patron had no special relationship with the college, as she was not on college property by invitation or for the benefit of the college. **Although the college had undertaken a duty to protect persons who were lawfully on its campus, it was not liable for injuries resulting from crimes that were not reasonably foreseeable.** Because there was no evidence that any attack resembling the one suffered by the patron had ever occurred near college property, the abduction was unforeseeable. The court affirmed the lower court's decision. *Figueroa v. Evangelical Covenant Church*, 879 F.2d 1427 (7th Cir. 1989). [IL]

◆   *Without a specified statutory duty, there was no legal requirement for a school to prevent student injuries on adjacent property.*

A California law school opened its library until midnight for use by its students. Criminal activity had occurred in the immediate area, but the school provided no security. The school provided no student parking or lighting. An unknown assailant attacked and stabbed a student about 10:00 p.m. one night. The assault occurred on city-owned property that was adjacent to the school. The student sued the school, arguing that a special relationship existed between the school and its students. He asserted that the school should have taken reasonable, inexpensive measures such as providing additional security or lighting to protect him from foreseeable criminal activities. The student argued that the school had "control" of the sidewalk area and had a duty to assume the responsibility of protecting the area. The trial court held for the school, and the California Court of Appeal upheld that decision. Without a specified statutory duty, there was no legal requirement for the school to prevent student injuries on adjacent property. **Mature students were considered "business invitees" whose legal status was not analogous to the relationship between minor school students and their schools.** Hence, there was no special relationship between the school and its students. The school had not created the risk and did not control the area where the assault occurred. *Donnell v. California Western School of Law*, 246 Cal.Rptr. 199 (Cal. App. 4th Dist. 1988). [CA]

◆   *A stockbroker who occasionally used the library at Oregon State University (OSU) was appropriately excluded from campus after OSU officials issued exclusion notices for stalking two students.*

The stockbroker was an OSU alumnus who used the library and attended public events on campus. An OSU student obtained a temporary protective stalking order against him in 1993, prohibiting any contact with her and excluding him from named OSU premises, including the fifth and sixth floor of the library. However, the order did not ban him from campus. In 1995, OSU security services published a policy providing for written trespass warnings to non-students as a way to protect students, staff and faculty. The stockbroker was arrested in the OSU library shortly thereafter, based on continuing complaints against him and the 1993 stalking order. The arresting campus security employee served the stockbroker with an exclusion notice purporting to ban him from the entire campus.

OSU's campus security manager later sent the stock broker a second exclusion notice because another OSU student had filed a complaint about the stockbroker. The complaining student obtained a temporary stalking protective order from a state court, and law enforcement officers cooperated with OSU security services in the distribution of a safety alert flier depicting the stockbroker. OSU's security manager later denied the stockbroker's requests to return to campus for three specific events. State police cited him for criminal trespass in violation of the exclusion order, and he sued the security manager and others in a federal court asserting civil rights violations under 42 U.S.C. § 1983. The court dismissed the case.

On appeal, the stockbroker alleged that the OSU campus was an open public forum and that the second exclusion order violated his constitutional right to due process. The Ninth Circuit noted that "[w]hile the OSU campus may be open to the public, it does not follow that the University must allow all members of the public onto its premises regardless of their conduct." Even without rules and regulations explicitly allowing officials to exclude persons for conduct, it was reasonable to infer this authority from OSU's exclusion policy. **The U.S. Supreme Court has recognized that educational administrators need flexibility to carry out their educational missions.** Any individual right to use the campus had to be balanced against the university's right to protect its students. OSU acted reasonably in temporarily excluding the stockbroker from its campus, and he was not entitled to due process protections. The court affirmed the judgment for OSU officials. *Souders v. Lucero*, 196 F.3d 1040 (9th Cir. 1999). [OR]

III. BREACH OF CONTRACT

Colleges and universities can be liable for breach of contract even where they have immunity from lawsuits for negligence or other torts.

◆ *A state university could be sued for breach of contract, but not for an intentional tort.*

The dealer for a piano manufacturer entered into a contract with a North Carolina university to loan the university a number of pianos in exchange for the right to service the university's other pianos. When the contract ended, the dealer and the manufacturer sued the university for breach of contract, conversion and property damage, claiming that the university returned the pianos in damaged condition and that the university improperly retained 14 pianos. The university sought to dismiss the lawsuit on grounds of sovereign immunity. The North Carolina Court of Appeals noted that the state's tort claims act allows state entities to be sued for negligence. However, conversion is an intentional tort (wrongfully depriving another of it property) and that action had to be dismissed. The breach of contract action, on the other hand, could continue because **when the university entered into the contract, it impliedly agreed to be sued for damages if it breached the contract.** Also, the property damage claim was a breach of contract claim that could proceed. The court remanded the case. *Kawai America Corp. v. University of North Carolina at Chapel Hill*, 567 S.E.2d 215 (N.C. App. 2002). [NC]

♦ *A public college was shielded from liability by the state tort immunity act.*
An employee at an Illinois public college worked under a series of one-year contracts. He complained to college officials that his supervisor subjected him to physical and verbal abuse that caused him physical and psychological problems. When the supervisor gave him a negative evaluation, his contract was not renewed. He then sued the college for breach of contract, battery and intentional infliction of emotional distress. He also sued the supervisor. A jury returned a verdict in his favor, but the Appellate Court of Illinois reversed in part. The court found that **the Illinois Tort Immunity Act shielded the college from liability for the battery and emotional distress claims**. Also, the college was not liable for breach of contract. Here, the college had to provide three months' notice of non-renewal to avoid a breach. The court held that it did so by postmarking the notice on March 31–the last day it could provide notice. Even though the employee did not receive the notice until early April, it was deemed timely because it was postmarked in March. Finally, however, the court held that the supervisor could be held liable for battery and emotional distress. *Valentino v. Hilquist*, 2003 WL 168450 (Ill. App. 1/24/03). [IL]

♦ *A university could use alternative energy sources without breaching a contract for purchasing steam energy exclusively from one power company.*
A Pennsylvania university entered into a contract with an energy company to purchase all its current and future steam requirements from the company. Subsequently, the university began renovating older buildings and constructing new ones, some of which used energy sources other than steam. The company sued the university for breach of contract, but the Pennsylvania Court of Common Pleas ruled in the university's favor. **The contract only required the university to purchase its steam requirements from the company; it did not obligate the university to use only steam energy in campus buildings.** As a result, the university did not breach the contract by finding alternative energy sources. *Trigen-Philadelphia Energy Corp. v. Drexel Univ.*, 2002 WL 31320499 (Pa. C.P. 10/8/02). [PA]

♦ *A university was determined to have breached its agreement with a philanthropist; it could not claim that the money was a gift.*
A private California university asked a philanthropist to endow a professional chair at one of its research centers. After a number of conversations and the exchange of several letters, the philanthropist agreed to endow the chair. However, the university later selected an existing faculty member for the chair in violation of the endowment terms and also failed to fund the chair. The philanthropist sued for breach of contract, promissory fraud and misappropriation. A state trial court dismissed the action, finding that no contract existed and that the philanthropist made a gift to the university. The California Court of Appeal reversed, finding that **the contract (partially verbal and partially written) existed**. The letters confirmed the verbal agreement; they did not make up the agreement exclusively. The philanthropist could sue the university. *Glenn v. University of Southern California*, 2002 WL 31022068 (Cal. App. 9/10/02). [CA]

IV. INSURANCE

Colleges and universities possess insurance policies, which provide coverage for both first- and third-party claims. Third-party claims generally involve liability policies and lawsuits against schools for negligence of school employees. Unless an exclusion in the policy specifically exempts a claim from coverage, an insurer may be required to defend and indemnify the school in any lawsuit arising from an injury to a third party. First-party claims generally involve property and casualty policies, and direct claims of loss by the school.

◆ *A liability insurer did not have to defend a university accused of fraud.*

A Florida university failed to disclose in its catalog that its physical therapy program's accreditation status was probationary. When the applicable accrediting organization withdrew the program's certification, the students who had enrolled in the program became ineligible to take the physical therapy licensing examination. They sued the university for breach of contract, fraud in the inducement, and violation of the Florida Deceptive and Unfair Trade Practices Act. The university sought to have its liability insurer defend and indemnify it in the action, but the Florida District Court of Appeal ruled in favor of the insurer. Here, the insurance policy covered any bodily injury caused by an occurrence, and defined "occurrence" as an accident. However, **the students were alleging intentionally fraudulent conduct by the university. Fraud in the inducement could not be accidental.** Thus, the university would have to defend itself in the action. *Barry Univ. v. Fireman's Fund Insurance Co. of Wisconsin*, 845 So.2d 276 (Fla. App. 2003). [FL]

◆ *A medical school could not obtain reimbursement from its insurer for a settlement.*

A Missouri medical school agreed to buy land from an energy company that it intended to convert into a parking lot. Before the sale closed, the school's contractor began working on the site, struck and ruptured an underground storage tank, and caused the release of coal tar wastes. The company sued the school and contractor for negligence and trespass, and the school's insurer initially defended it. It withdrew from the defense after a federal court concluded it had no duty to defend. That decision was later reversed. After a court found that the contractor had not trespassed because it had implied permission to work on the site, a settlement was reached. The school then sued its insurer for indemnification. A federal court ruled in favor of the insurer, and the Eighth Circuit affirmed. Here, the policy excluded environmental contamination claims, and the contractor was found not to have trespassed (the only claims the insurer could have been liable for). Thus, **even though the insurer breached its duty to defend the school, it did not have to indemnify the school for the settlement.** *Royal Insurance Co. of America v. Kirksville College of Osteopathic Medicine*, 304 F.3d 804 (8th Cir. 2002). [MO]

◆ *A university was entitled to insurance coverage for damage that occurred during a flood.*

After a record rainfall, the Red River flooded, and the city of Grand Forks shut down two sanitary sewer lift stations that serviced the University of North Dakota campus. As a result, water entered 22 campus buildings through the sewer system and damaged boiler and machinery equipment. The university's insurer denied coverage on the grounds that the sewer backup actually was caused by flooding, which was excluded by the policy. The university asserted that the damage was caused instead by the sewer backup, and that the policy therefore provided coverage. In the lawsuit that followed, a jury ruled in favor of the university, finding that the flood was not the efficient proximate cause of the damage. (Efficient proximate cause is the predominating cause of the loss, though not necessarily the last act in the chain of events, nor the triggering cause of the loss.) **The jury determined that the sewer backup, not the flood, was the efficient proximate cause of the damage.** The North Dakota Supreme Court affirmed, noting that the jury had properly considered the evidence before finding that the sewer backup caused the loss. Accordingly, the court upheld the jury's award of $3.35 million to the university. *Western National Insurance Co. v. University of North Dakota*, 643 N.W.2d 4 (N.D. 2002). [ND]

◆   *By giving its insurer late notice of an occurrence that could lead to a lawsuit, a university lost coverage.*

Vanderbilt University conducted a study in the 1940s to track the absorption of iron in pregnant women. The women unknowingly ingested a solution containing radioactive iron isotopes. In the 1960s, a follow-up study revealed a higher incidence of cancer among the participants. In 1985, the Department of Energy requested information relating to the study for a congressional hearing. In 1994, the women and their children filed a class action lawsuit against Vanderbilt, which was settled for $10 million in 1998. When Vanderbilt sought insurance to cover the loss, its excess insurer denied coverage because of the late notice. A federal court ruled in favor of the insurer, and the Sixth Circuit Court of Appeals affirmed. **Under the policy, Vanderbilt had to notify the insurer of an "occurrence" as soon as possible.** Here, the occurrence was deemed to have happened in the 1960s when the follow-up study was conducted (or at the very latest, in 1985). By failing to give notice until the lawsuit was filed in 1994, Vanderbilt prejudiced the insurer's ability to defend and thus was not entitled to be reimbursed for the settlement. *United States Fire Insurance Co. v. Vanderbilt Univ.*, 267 F.3d 465 (6th Cir. 2001). [TN]

◆   *An excess insurer had to contribute to the defense costs when a university was sued.*

A Colorado professor sued a university in state court for denial of tenure, wrongful termination, defamation and breach of contract, among other claims. Eighteen months later, she filed a second lawsuit against the university in federal court, but chose not to include the defamation claim. The lawsuits were consolidated in federal court, and a question of insurance coverage then arose—namely, which insurer (primary or excess) had to pay the costs of defending the university. The primary insurer was held to have the responsibility for defending the first lawsuit because of the defamation claim—the only claim it was potentially liable for paying. **The excess insurer**

had to contribute $50,000 to the second lawsuit (where no defamation claim was presented and the primary insurer could not be liable) even though the two cases were consolidated. Here, even though the cases were consolidated and the primary insurer had the primary obligation to defend the lawsuit, the second lawsuit retained its separate identity for purposes of allocating defense costs. *Farmington Casualty Co. v. United Educators Insurance Risk Retention Group, Inc.*, 36 Fed. Appx. 408 (10th Cir. 2002). [CO]

♦ *City University of New York (CUNY) did not have to compensate Carnegie Hall Corporation for damages the hall's insurance company paid after a student fell during a graduation ceremony.*

CUNY's licensing agreement with Carnegie Hall allowed CUNY to use the hall for the 1994 graduation ceremony of the university's technical college. The agreement required CUNY to obtain comprehensive general liability insurance to cover any claims arising out of the event, but CUNY never obtained the required coverage. During the ceremony, a graduating student fell on a staircase and sued Carnegie Hall for failing to keep the staircase in a reasonably safe condition. The hall's insurance company ultimately paid $41,987 in settlement fees and defense costs. Carnegie Hall and the insurance company sued CUNY for reimbursement because the university failed to get insurance coverage, as mandated by the license agreement.

A claims court determined that CUNY owed the hall's insurer compensation and granted pretrial judgment in the plaintiffs' favor, but the New York Supreme Court, Appellate Division, disagreed, holding that neither Carnegie Hall nor the insurer had any basis for recovery against CUNY. Carnegie Hall had no ground to seek damages from CUNY because it did not incur any financial loss–its insurer paid the expenses related to the student's lawsuit. In addition, **the insurer was not entitled to recover settlement and defense costs. It was not a party to the license agreement, and it did not claim to be a third party to the agreement.** Therefore, any basis for recovery was based on its status as the subrogee of Carnegie Hall, but New York's high court previously has ruled that recovery for the breach of a contract requiring the purchase of insurance is limited to the cost of obtaining substitute coverage, and not defense costs. Accordingly, the case was dismissed. *Carnegie Hall Corp. v. City University of New York*, 729 N.Y.S.2d 93 (A.D. 1st Dep't 2001). [NY]

♦ *An insurer could seek reimbursement for a student's medical expenses by joining the student's individual action.*

A University of Tennessee student was permanently injured while participating in a track meet. The student and his parents filed a claim against the university with the Tennessee Claims Commission. The matter was settled between the parties, except for the student's subrogation claim seeking $1,026,666 in reimbursement to his insurer for medical expenses. The Claims Commission denied the subrogation claim because the student did not assert the claim in his pleadings and because his insurer was not joined as a party to the action. Initially, the Tennessee Court of Appeals affirmed the commission's determination and found that the insurer should file its own claim to obtain compensation. The student then notified the Claims Commission that he was joining the insurer to the action, but the commission denied the joinder request as too late. The appellate court reversed the commission's decision. It held that the commission was in error when it struck the student's pleadings regarding joinder of the insurer, even though the pleadings were untimely. The panel noted that **the University of Tennessee was previously advised of the subrogation claim and would not be prejudiced if the claim was included, since the commission had not yet decided whether the insurer was entitled to reimbursement**. The case was remanded for a trial on the merits of the insurer's claim. *Hartman v. University of Tennessee*, 38 S.W.3d 570 (Tenn. App. 2000). [TN]

◆ *Where an insured board member at a private college made misrepresentations to the board of trustees to obtain a personal advantage for his company, and where the college lost $2 million as a result, the college's errors and omissions policy did not provide coverage for the loss.*

A Texas Christian College purchased a "school leaders errors and omissions" policy that insured it against wrongful acts committed by directors and officers of the school. Subsequently, a member of the board of trustees convinced the board to invest $2 million of its endowment funds in a company that accepted accounts receivable as security for short-term loans. However, he did not disclose that the company had a negative net worth, that he was a 49 percent owner of the company, or that he also was a salaried employee of the company. **When the investment failed, the college obtained the board member's resignation, then sued him and his company for misrepresentation of certain facts and for making false statements.** The college obtained a judgment against the board member for $1.8 million and against the company for $2 million. Unable to collect on the judgments, it sought to collect under its errors and omissions policy. The insurer denied coverage under the "fraud or dishonesty" exclusion and the "personal profit or advantage" exclusion.

A Texas federal court held that the two exclusions applied to bar coverage, and the college appealed to the U.S. Court of Appeals, Fifth Circuit. The appellate court affirmed. It noted that **the exclusion for "any claim arising out of the gaining in fact of any personal profit or advantage to which the Insured is not legally entitled" applied to bar coverage**. Here, the board member clearly gained a personal advantage by his company's receipt of the $2 million in endowment funds from the college. Despite the fact that the board member did not ultimately make a profit, he did gain a personal advantage by his wrongful acts. As a result, the insurer had no obligation to pay out under the policy. *Jarvis Christian College v. National Union Fire Insurance Co.*, 197 F.3d 742 (5th Cir. 1999). [TX]

◆ *A public university in Oregon could not deny health insurance coverage to domestic partners of homosexual employees.*

The Oregon Court of Appeals determined that a public health sciences university violated the state constitution's privileges and immunities clause by maintaining **a practice of denying health insurance coverage to the**

domestic partners of its homosexual employees. The case arose after three university nurses applied for insurance coverage for their domestic partners. The benefits manager refused to process the application because the university provided health insurance to spouses, not unmarried partners. After the state employee benefits board upheld the denial of benefits, the nurses sued. The court of appeals stated that Oregon's employment discrimination statute protected the nurses on the basis of their sexual orientation. However, the university did not violate that statute. Rather, the university violated the state constitution's privileges and immunities clause (which requires governmental entities to make benefits available on equal terms to all Oregon citizens). **Because homosexuals cannot marry under Oregon law, the university's health insurance benefits were made available on terms that, for gay and lesbian couples, were a legal impossibility.** *Tanner v. Oregon Health Sciences Univ.*, 971 P.2d 435 (Or. App. 1998). [OR]

V. CIVIL RIGHTS ACTS

◆ *The Supreme Court stated that a Florida university secretary did not have to exhaust her administrative remedies before suing under 42 U.S.C. § 1983.*

A white female secretary worked for a Florida university. She alleged that during her employment there, she had been passed over for employment promotions, even though she was qualified for the positions. She sued the university in a federal court under 42 U.S.C. § 1983, alleging gender and race discrimination. The secretary also claimed that the university actively sought to hire minorities and separated applicant files according to race and gender. A panel of the U.S. Court of Appeals, Fifth Circuit, dismissed the secretary's suit for failure to exhaust her state administrative remedies.

The court then agreed to hear the case *en banc* to determine whether the employee should be required to exhaust her state administrative remedies before she could file a § 1983 claim in federal court. Although the U.S. Supreme Court had on several occasions rejected the argument that a § 1983 action should be dismissed where the plaintiff had not exhausted administrative remedies, the court of appeals held that adequate and appropriate state administrative remedies must be exhausted before a plaintiff could bring a § 1983 action in federal court. The U.S. Supreme Court agreed to hear the case and held that **Congress had intended that § 1983 plaintiffs be able to choose the federal district courts as the forum for civil rights lawsuits.** *Patsy v. Board of Regents*, 457 U.S. 496, 102 S.Ct. 2557, 73 L.Ed.2d 172 (1982). [FL]

◆ *42 U.S.C. § 1981 states that all persons shall have the same right to make and enforce contracts as is enjoyed by white persons. In 1987, the Court ruled that although originally intended to vindicate the rights of former slaves, § 1981 extended to persons of Arab ancestry and others besides American blacks.*

A private college in Pennsylvania denied tenure to a professor it had employed under a one-year nonrenewable contract. The professor was a Muslim who was born in Iraq but was a U.S. citizen. He claimed that the college had refused to grant tenure on the basis of his national origin and religion in violation of state and federal civil rights laws, including § 1981. The professor sued the college in a federal district court, which dismissed many of the claims because they were filed too late to meet local statutes of limitations. The court also dismissed the § 1981 claim, ruling that the act did not extend to the professor. It ruled that § 1981, which forbids racial discrimination in the making and enforcement of any contract, does not reach claims of discrimination based on Arab ancestry. The U.S. Court of Appeals, Third Circuit, reversed. The U.S. Supreme Court affirmed the court of appeals' decision. It noted that **although § 1981 does not use the word "race," the Court has construed the statute to forbid all racial discrimination in the making of private as well as public contracts.** Congress "intended to protect from discrimination identifiable classes of persons who are subjected to intentional discrimination solely because of their ancestry or ethnic characteristics." If the professor could prove that he was subjected to intentional discrimination because he was an Arab, rather than solely because of his place of origin or his religion, the lawsuit could proceed under § 1981. The case was remanded for trial. *St. Francis College v. Al-Khazraji*, 481 U.S. 604, 107 S.Ct. 2022, 97 L.Ed.2d 749 (1987). [PA]

◆ *The NCAA has been held not to be a state actor by the Supreme Court. In a 1988 Nevada case, the Court concluded that the NCAA did not have the power to discipline a school's coach, and thus could not be liable for sanctions imposed against him.*

Following a lengthy investigation of allegedly improper recruiting practices by the University of Nevada, Las Vegas (UNLV), the NCAA found 38 violations, including 10 by the school's head basketball coach. The NCAA proposed a number of sanctions and threatened to impose more if the coach was not suspended. UNLV decided to suspend the coach. Facing an enormous pay cut, the coach sued the NCAA under 42 U.S.C. § 1983 for violating his due process rights. The Nevada Supreme Court held that the NCAA's conduct constituted state action for constitutional purposes. It upheld a Nevada trial court's dismissal of the suspension and award of attorneys' fees. The NCAA appealed to the U.S. Supreme Court.

The Supreme Court held that the NCAA's participation in the events, which led to the suspension, did not constitute state action within the meaning of § 1983. The NCAA was not a state actor on the theory that it misused the power it possessed under state law. UNLV's decision to suspend the coach in compliance with the NCAA's rules and recommendations did not turn the NCAA's conduct into state action. This was because UNLV retained the power to withdraw from the NCAA and establish its own standards. The NCAA could not directly discipline the coach but could threaten to impose additional sanctions against the school. **It was the school's decision and not the NCAA's decision to suspend the coach.** *NCAA v. Tarkanian*, 488 U.S. 179, 109 S.Ct. 454, 102 L.Ed.2d 469 (1988). [NV]

◆ *A university's internal appeal procedure did not amount to binding arbitration so as to bar a civil rights lawsuit.*

A Michigan university graduate student was notified that she was being dismissed from the program. She was allowed an internal hearing challenging the decision, even though this was not part of the university's normal procedure. After a ruling against her, she sued the university for civil rights violations. The university asserted that the internal hearing was essentially binding arbitration that precluded the student from suing. The Michigan Court of Appeals disagreed. It found **no agreement between the parties that the internal appeal would constitute binding arbitration.** The student could proceed with her lawsuit. *Jubert v. Central Michigan Univ.*, 2003 WL 288984 (Mich. App. 2/7/03). [MI]

◆ *A student charged but not convicted of assault could not sue the university for violating his civil rights.*

A black male attended a college that was part of the City University of New York. After a white, female student accused him of assaulting her, two campus security officers removed him from class. They interrogated him, but he denied the accusations and asserted that the female was his girlfriend. The police were called, and an officer took the alleged victim's testimony, noting also that she had contusions on her arms. The black student was arrested and prosecuted for assault, but was acquitted by a jury. He then sued the college and university, along with a number of college officials, security officers and the police officer involved in his arrest. He claimed that his civil rights were violated under 42 U.S.C. § 1983. A New York federal court granted the defendants' motion to dismiss the case, finding that **probable cause existed to arrest the student**, and that the detective acted reasonably after questioning the female student. The same defense was available to the security officers, and the college and university were entitled to Eleventh Amendment immunity. Also, the college's vice president could not be sued because she had no personal involvement in his arrest and prosecution. *Obilo v. City Univ. of New York*, 2003 WL 1809471 (E.D.N.Y. 4/7/03). [NY]

◆ *A university could not claim immunity in a lawsuit over its alleged violation of a settlement agreement under Title VII.*

A teacher in a Wisconsin university's art and design department was denied tenure. She filed a Title VII sex discrimination complaint, alleging that the tenure denial had been in retaliation for her complaints of sexual harassment by department members. The EEOC facilitated a settlement agreement between the parties under which the department agreed to recommend tenure. If the board of regents granted tenure, the university would agree to assign her to a department appropriate to her skills, training and abilities. After the board granted her tenure, she was assigned to teach a special program of studies that was not part of a department. When she complained, the university refused to reassign her. She sued the university for violating the settlement agreement, and it sought to have the lawsuit dismissed on grounds of sovereign immunity. A state court and the Wisconsin Court of Appeals refused to dismiss the case. **The university did not have sovereign immunity under Title VII, and the settlement agreement was part of the Title VII claim.** Therefore, the university did not have sovereign immunity with respect to the settlement agreement. The court remanded the case for a determination of whether the university breached the settlement agreement. *Klein v. Board of Regents, Univ. of Wisconsin*, 666 N.W.2d 67 (Wis. App. 2003). [WI]

VI. VICARIOUS LIABILITY

◆   *A university employee was not entitled to immunity for sexual harassment where his conduct was outside the scope of his employment.*

An employee of the Ohio Department of Surgery Corporation worked with an employee of Ohio State University (OSU). She claimed that the OSU employee subjected her to sexual harassment and created a hostile work environment. She accused him of calling her a "worthless slut," an "ignorant slut," and a "pushy bitch." She sued him and OSU in the Court of Claims, seeking a determination regarding the employee's immunity. The court found that the OSU employee was entitled to immunity because, although his conduct was "boorish," he did not act with malice, in bad faith, or in a wanton or reckless manner. The Court of Appeals of Ohio reversed. A state employee is not entitled to immunity if his conduct is manifestly outside the scope of his employment or official responsibilities, or if he acts with malicious purpose, in bad faith, or in a wanton or reckless manner. From the record, the court concluded that the OSU employee's remarks did not further the interests of the state. Consequently, he was acting "manifestly outside the scope of his employment" and was not entitled to immunity. *Oye v. Ohio State Univ.*, No. 02AP-1362, 2003 WL 22511511 (Ohio App. 2003). [OH]

◆   *A university was not liable for the conduct of a research assistant, who hit a car while driving drunk.*

A research assistant at a California university drove to the home of her supervising professor, with whom she also was romantically involved. Although she intended to work at his house, she discovered that he had been in a car accident and instead went to the hospital. She later brought him back to his house and consumed a bottle of vodka while there. When she drove home in the evening, she crossed the median of a highway and collided with another vehicle. She was charged with driving under the influence. The driver of the other vehicle sued the university for his damages, asserting that it was liable under the doctrine of *respondeat superior*. A state court dismissed the lawsuit, and the California Court of Appeal affirmed. Here, **the research assistant had not been acting within the scope of her employment at the time of the crash**. Thus, the crash was not foreseeable as a part of her work, and the university could not be held vicariously liable for her actions. *Williams v. Regents of the Univ. of California*, 2002 WL 31873790 (Cal. App. 12/26/02). [CA]

◆   *A university could seek contribution from the government after a polio vaccine caused a child to develop polio.*

When a baby received an oral polio vaccine, he had a severe reaction that eventually resulted in paralysis. His parents sued a university, the university hospital and the company that developed the vaccine. A jury ruled in favor of the family, and the Missouri Supreme Court upheld the ruling. Later, other cases involving the vaccine were brought against the United States under the Federal Tort Claims Act, alleging that the National Institute of Health's Division of Biologic Standards negligently issued a license to the company that made the vaccine in violation of "neurovirulence" standards established by government regulations. The university then sued the United States for contribution in a Maryland federal court. The court held that the university could seek contribution from the government because **had the government not negligently approved the vaccine, the baby would never have received the oral vaccine and become paralyzed.** The court then held that the company was not liable for contribution to the university because it did not owe a duty separate and apart from products liability law. *St. Louis Univ. v. United States,* 182 F.Supp.2d 494 (D. Md. 2002). [MD]

◆   *Faculty members who volunteered to serve as advisors to Texas A&M's drama club were still considered university employees.*

A student actor was accidentally stabbed with a bowie knife by another student during the final scene of a performance. The injured student sued the university, the director of the play, the choreographer and the faculty advisors for negligence because Texas A&M prohibits deadly weapons on campus. The trial court held the university liable for the incident, but the court of appeals reversed, finding that Texas A&M could not be legally responsible because the director and choreographer were independent contractors, and the faculty advisors were considered volunteers in their roles as advisors to the drama club. The Texas Supreme Court overturned the appellate decision. It ruled that **although the faculty members were not paid additional compensation for their work as advisors to the drama club, they were still considered employees of the university for the purposes of liability under the state's Tort Claims Act.** Even though the faculty members were not directly paid for their role as advisors and were not required to act as advisors, Texas A&M considered their drama club involvement when calculating their salaries. The court did not address whether the director and choreographer were considered university employees because they settled with the injured student out of court. The university was held liable for the faculty advisors' failure to ensure that the university's no-weapons policy was enforced. *Bishop v. Texas A&M University,* 35 S.W.3d 605 (Tex. 2000). [TX]

◆   *A university was held vicariously liable for acts of hazing committed by upperclassmen who were acting as agents of the university, even though the upperclassmen went beyond what they were authorized to do.*

A five-year veteran of the Navy enrolled in the Military College of Vermont of Norwich University under a Navy ROTC scholarship. He lasted for only 16 days, during which he was subjected to, and observed, repeated instances of hazing by upperclassmen. After withdrawing from school, he sued the university for assault and battery, infliction of emotional distress and negligence, asserting that it was vicariously liable for the actions of the upperclassmen. A jury returned a verdict in the student's favor, awarding him almost $500,000 in compensatory damages and $1.75 million in punitive damages. The Supreme Court of Vermont affirmed the compensatory damage award against the university, but reversed the award of punitive damages, finding no evidence of malice on the university's part. Here, **the university had charged the upperclassmen with "indoctrinating and orienting" the student**. As a result, this was not a simple case of student-on-student hazing for which the university could not be held liable. Because the upperclassmen were acting as agents of the university, it breached its duty of care toward the student. The court also found that the nearly $500,000 in compensatory damages awarded by the jury was not clearly erroneous. *Brueckner v. Norwich Univ.*, 730 A.2d 1086 (Vt. 1999). [VT]

◆ *A university may be liable if it is deliberately indifferent to student-on-student sexual harassment.*

Two female students at the University of Colorado who participated in the Reserve Officer Training Corps (ROTC) program alleged that a fellow student (a higher-ranking cadet in the ROTC program) committed acts that created to a hostile work environment. When they reported the acts to a superior ROTC officer, he retaliated against them by denying them further opportunities in the ROTC program and subjected them to other acts of sexual harassment. They then reported the harassment to university officials and asserted that the university did not take adequate measures to respond to their allegations. They sued the university in federal court under Title IX, where the university maintained that it could not be held liable because ROTC members were not agents of the university and it did not exercise control over them. The court dismissed the case against the university, and the students appealed to the U.S. Court of Appeals, Tenth Circuit. The court of appeals reversed, finding that the lawsuit should not have been dismissed. Here, **the students had adequately pled that the ROTC program was a university-sanctioned program, that they had been harassed by members of that program, and that the university did not take remedial action when notified of the harassment**. The case was remanded for further proceedings. *Morse v. Regents of the Univ. of Colorado*, 154 F.3d 1124 (10th Cir. 1998). [CO]

◆ *Where an Army officer who instructed ROTC students was not an agent of a college, the college could not be liable for any negligence on his part.*

A Georgia college student enrolled in a military science Mountaineering Techniques class injured his ankle while practicing rappelling techniques. He sued the college, asserting that the instructor had negligently instructed him, causing the injury. The college maintained that the instructor had not been negligent and that, even if he had, he was not an agent of the college because he was a full-time Army officer who was assigned to the college to teach ROTC courses. The trial court held that the college had the right and authority to control the details of the sergeant's work, but chose not to do so. Accordingly, the sergeant was an agent of the college, which was potentially liable for the student's injury. The Georgia Court of Appeals reversed. It stated that **under the cross-enrollment agreement for the establishment of ROTC instruction, the college did not have the right to control the time, manner and method of the Army's performance**. Because the Army provided the rappelling tower, uniforms, textbooks, ropes and other equipment, and because the training procedures were the Army's, the instructor was an independent contractor rather than an agent of the college. The student's lawsuit was dismissed. *Armstrong State College v. McGlynn*, 505 S.E.2d 853 (Ga. App. 1998). [GA]

◆   *A university was held vicariously liable for an accidental shooting in the following case.*

Two graduate students at a Louisiana university worked as resident assistants in a dormitory. One of them kept a gun in his room. The other approached a student who was not wearing a shirt in violation of dorm rules, and a verbal altercation ensued. Afterward, the graduate student who had been in the altercation asked the other graduate student if he could borrow the gun. He then returned to continue the argument. At this point, another student happened on the scene and tried to intervene. The gun discharged, hitting him in the thigh. He sued the university and the other three students to recover for his injuries. A jury found the student who had fired the gun 90 percent at fault and the other graduate student 10 percent at fault. The court found the university vicariously liable as the students' employer, and the university appealed. The Court of Appeal of Louisiana affirmed. The trial court reasonably concluded that the resident assistants were acting within the scope of their employment. **Even though the university prohibited the possession of weapons on campus, the accident occurred on the university's premises, during the hours of employment while the resident assistants were on duty.** Further, the student who discharged the gun stated that it was an accident and that he only brought it with him because he felt he needed protection from a student he perceived as threatening. *Emoakemeh v. Southern Univ.*, 654 So.2d 474 (La. App. 1995). [LA]

CHAPTER NINE

School Operations

Page

I. STATE REGULATION

A. Residency

◆ *State residency requirements for favorable tuition rates are subject to the due process right of students to present evidence about their residency.*

Connecticut required nonresidents enrolled in the state's university system to pay tuition and other fees at a higher rate than state residents. It also created an irreversible and irrebuttable statutory presumption that if the legal address of a student, if married, was outside the state at the time of application for admission or, if single, was outside the state at some point during the preceding year, the student remained a nonresident as long as the student remained enrolled in Connecticut schools. Two students, one married, one single, who were both residents of Connecticut, challenged the presumption, claiming that it violated the Fourteenth Amendment's guarantee of due process and equal protection. A three-judge district court panel upheld the students' claim.

The U.S. Supreme Court held that **the Due Process Clause does not permit states to deny a student the opportunity to present evidence that the student is a bona fide resident of the state, and thus entitled to in-state tuition rates**, on the basis of an irrebuttable presumption of nonresidence. Such a presumption is not necessarily true, and the state had reasonable alternatives in making residency determinations. *Vlandis v. Kline*, 412 U.S. 441, 93 S.Ct. 2230, 37 L.Ed.2d 63 (1973). [CT]

◆ *The right to rebut a presumption of nonresidence extends even to aliens with visas living in state.*

The University of Maryland granted "in-state" tuition status only to students domiciled in Maryland, or, if a student was financially dependent on the student's parents, to students whose parents were domiciled in Maryland. The university also could deny in-state status to individuals who did not pay the full spectrum of Maryland state taxes. The university refused to grant in-state status to a number of students, each of whom was dependent on a parent who held a "G-4 visa" (a non-immigrant visa granted to officers and employees of international treaty organizations and members of their immediate family). The university stated that the holder of a G-4 visa could not acquire Maryland domicile because the holder was incapable of showing an essential element of domicile–the intent to live permanently or indefinitely in Maryland. After unsuccessful appeals at the administrative level, the students brought a class action lawsuit in federal court seeking declaratory and injunctive relief. The students alleged that university policy violated the Equal Protection Clause. The district court granted relief, stating that the G-4 visa could not create an irrebuttable presumption of nondomicile. The Court of Appeals affirmed.

On appeal, the Supreme Court refused to decide the matter and certified the question to Maryland's highest court, the Maryland Court of Appeals, for a determination. The Court stated that the case was controlled by the principles announced in *Vlandis v. Kline*, above, that **when a state purports to be concerned with domicile, it must provide an individual with the opportunity to present evidence bearing on that issue.** Federal law allows aliens holding a G-4 visa to acquire domicile in the United States. However, the question of whether such domicile could be acquired in Maryland was a question of state law. Since no controlling precedent had been decided by the state's highest court, the Supreme Court declined to rule and certified the question to the Maryland high court. *Elgin v. Moreno*, 435 U.S. 647, 98 S.Ct. 1338, 55 L.Ed.2d 614 (1978). [MD]

◆ *In the follow-up to* Elgin v. Moreno, *above, the Supreme Court struck down a university policy that imposed additional restrictions on an alien's right to acquire domicile in a state and thus qualify for in-state tuition.*

The University of Maryland's student fee schedule policy denied students whose parents held non-immigrant alien visas (those visas issued to officers or employees of certain international organizations and their families) in-state status, even if they were domiciled in the state, thus denying them preferential fee and tuition schedules. The U.S. Supreme Court found the policy to be in violation of the Supremacy Clause of the U.S. Constitution, which states, "This Constitution, and the laws of the United States which shall be made in Pursuance thereof; and all Treaties made, or which shall be made, under the Authority of the United States, shall be the supreme Law of the Land."

The Court stated that the university's policy conflicted directly with the will of Congress as expressed in the Immigration and Nationality Act of 1952.

In passing the Immigration and Nationality Act, Congress explicitly decided not to bar non-immigrant aliens such as these the right to acquire domicile in the United States. **The university's policy denying these aliens "in-state" status, solely on the basis of their immigration status, amounted to a burden not contemplated by Congress** in admitting them to the United States. Thus, the University of Maryland's student fee schedule, as applied to these aliens, was held to be unconstitutional. *Toll v. Moreno*, 458 U.S. 1, 102 S.Ct. 2977, 73 L.Ed.2d 563 (1982). [MD]

◆ *The University of Maryland's residency policy for tuition purposes, which was based on the source of students' financial support, violated the equal protection rights of bona fide state residents.*

A student born in Maryland moved with his mother to Rhode Island after his parents divorced and his mother remarried. In December 1993, he applied for admission to the University of Maryland at College Park and listed his father's District of Columbia home as his residence. The university considered him a nonresident, based on the source of his financial support, and charged him out-of-state tuition. After his sophomore year, he applied for in-state status and claimed that he was a "financially independent permanent resident." His application and subsequent appeal were both denied, since he failed to establish that he supported himself. The student and his father sued, asserting due process and equal protection violations. The court granted the university's motion for pretrial judgment. The Maryland Court of Appeals reversed. It found that **the university's residency policy failed the rational basis test by favoring some Maryland residents over other state residents** based solely on their source of economic support. *Frankel v. Board of Regents of the Univ. of Maryland System*, 361 Md. 298, 761 A.2d 324 (Md. 2000). [MD]

◆ *A university could adopt a higher standard of proof for students seeking in-state tuition status.*

An applicant to the University of Vermont College of Medicine was born and raised in Massachusetts. However, he moved to Vermont on June 1, 1994 and obtained employment at the university. Two weeks later, he applied for admission to 23 medical schools, listing his father's Florida residence as his permanent address. In September, he applied to the university's College of Medicine, listing his Vermont address as his permanent one. He obtained a Vermont driver's license, registered his car in the state, and filed his income tax returns in the state. The following year, he was accepted for admission to the medical school as an out-of-state student. When he applied for in-state tuition status, his application was denied. He appealed, and the university used a "clear and convincing evidence" standard to determine that the student was not entitled to in-state status. The case reached the Vermont Supreme Court, which ruled in favor of the university. It noted that **although the "preponderance of the evidence" standard is usually appropriate for administrative proceedings, the university was free to adopt the more stringent "clear and convincing evidence" standard**. The student was not entitled to in-state status. *Huddleston v. University of Vermont*, 719 A.2d 415 (Vt. 1998). [VT]

◆ *An applicant at a New Mexico medical school could sue to be placed in the next entering class where the school had used her short length of residency to deny her admission.*

In three successive years, an applicant to the University of New Mexico School of Medicine was rejected for admission. At each of her interviews, **her relatively short length of residency was listed as an obstacle**. The university preferred those who had lived in the state for a longer period of time because it believed they would be more likely to stay in the state and provide medical care to underserved areas. She sued the university and a number of officials for injunctive relief and damages, alleging that the residency policy violated her due process and equal protection rights. A federal court held that the residency policy violated clearly established law concerning the fundamental right to travel and that the university could not consider length of residency in future admissions decisions. The Tenth Circuit Court of Appeals reversed in part, finding that the applicant did not have standing to pursue a claim regarding the determination of residency length in future admissions decisions. However, she could pursue her claims for admission under the *Ex Parte Young* exception to qualified immunity. Under *Ex Parte Young*, 209 U.S. 123 (1908), where there is an ongoing violation of federal law, a party may obtain prospective relief against a government official to prevent the official from continuing to violate the law. Accordingly, **the applicant could seek injunctive relief that would place her in the immediate entering class at the university**. *Buchwald v. University of New Mexico School of Medicine*, 159 F.3d 487 (10th Cir. 1998). [NM]

◆ *Where two students indicated that they were in North Carolina for educational purposes, they were not residents for tuition purposes.*

A North Carolina university residence committee affirmed the university's decision to deny two student applications for state residency for tuition purposes. In both cases, the students indicated that their parents resided outside the state, and that the applicants had recently moved to North Carolina, in part to take advantage of educational opportunities. Both of the applicants held part-time jobs, had recently attended college in other states, obtained North Carolina driver's licenses, and registered to vote. In separate actions, state courts upheld the committee's decisions, and the Court of Appeals of North Carolina affirmed. Under state law, both of the students were presumed to have the same domicile as their parents. **Although state law allowed resident tuition for those individuals establishing legal residence in the state for at least 12 months with a bona fide presence in the state, the law presumed that a person's legal residence was with the person's parents.** Both students had failed to rebut this presumption, and both had indicated that their presence in the state was related to education. Because this supported, rather than rebutted, the presumption that the students were only present in the state for educational purposes, residency tuition had been properly denied. *Norman v. Cameron*, 488 S.E.2d 297 (N.C. App. 1997). [NC]

◆ *Where a non-immigrant student did not seek a change in her status, she could not show that she was a resident for tuition purposes.*

A citizen of Uruguay obtained a non-immigrant student visa. She moved to

Arkansas, where she petitioned a state university for resident status for tuition purposes. The university denied her application, basing its decision on state education department regulations. Under the regulations, a student should be classified as an in-state resident for tuition purposes only if the student establishes legal residence within the state. The regulations further require an applicant to establish a permanent legal home in Arkansas for six continuous months with no present intention of moving outside the state. The student filed a federal district court action against the university and certain officials, seeking injunctive and declaratory relief, plus the amount of nonresident tuition she had paid with interest. The court found that **the student's classification as a non-immigrant student depended upon her intention to retain foreign citizenship. The student had failed to seek any change in her non-immigrant status**, and as a result could not form the requisite intent to become an Arkansas resident. Since she could not meet the intent requirement for state residency, the university officials could not have violated her clearly established rights, and the court granted pretrial judgment to the university and officials. *Hein v. Arkansas State Univ.*, 972 F.Supp. 1175 (E.D. Ark. 1997). [AR]

B. Zoning and Land Use

◆   *A Massachusetts zoning board's density regulation was invalid as applied to a college campus under state law.*

Boston College (BC) applied to the Newton Board of Aldermen for special permits to construct three buildings. It also sought an exemption from the parking requirements of a local zoning ordinance. The purpose of the construction project was to provide additional space for academic functions, faculty offices and dining facilities. The board denied the application and BC sued the board in a state court, alleging violation of the Dover Amendment, a state law barring zoning ordinances that prohibit or restrict the use of land for educational purposes. The court held the board unreasonably applied its dimensional and density regulations to the building project, but was reasonably justified in denying a parking waiver. The parties appealed.

The Court of Appeals of Massachusetts noted that **a municipality could reasonably regulate parking, open spaces, and buildings used for educational purposes**. The floor area ratio density requirement of the local zoning ordinance was invalid as applied to the BC middle campus. The entire middle campus was "nonconforming" under the ordinance, with the practical result that enforcement would require BC to always secure a special permit to construct any building there. **Strict compliance with the density requirement would thwart an "educational use" and was invalid**. The trial court correctly found the denial of a waiver for more parking spaces was unreasonable. The court affirmed the decision. *Trustees of Boston College v. Board of Aldermen of Newton*, 793 N.E.2d 387 (Mass. App. 2003). [MA]

◆   *If a city improperly targeted a private university for designation as a Historic District, it could be liable for an equal protection violation.*

The city of Evanston, Illinois, asked Northwestern University to voluntarily contribute to the cost of city services. Northwestern refused to do so. A group of citizens then formed an association that sought to designate parts of the city and parts of the university as a National Historic District. The Department of the Interior approved the designation over Northwestern's objections. Northwestern then sued the city under 42 U.S.C. § 1983 for violating its constitutional rights, and the city moved for dismissal. The district court granted the motion in part. However, it found that Northwestern could proceed on two causes of action. First, under the "vindictive action equal protection" part of the lawsuit, **Northwestern alleged that the city had an improper motive (hostility to the university) and that it was treated unequally as a result.** This claim had to proceed to trial. Also, Northwestern claimed that the city imposed an unconstitutional condition on its right to be exempt from property taxation under the charter granted to it by the state in 1851. It asserted that an alderman suggested university property could be excluded from the Historic District if the university agreed to surrender its tax-exempt status. This claim also deserved a trial. *Northwestern Univ. v. City of Evanston*, 2002 WL 31027981 (N.D. Ill. 9/11/02). [IL]

◆   *A zoning board could place housing restrictions on a university to preserve a neighborhood's character.*

George Washington University became embroiled in a zoning dispute with the DC Board of Zoning Adjustment over the expansion of university-owned student housing into the "Foggy Bottom" neighborhood. The board conditionally approved the university's long-term campus improvement plan, but set certain housing restrictions and an enrollment cap on the university. A federal court ruled that the enrollment cap could not be enforced, but held that the housing restrictions were acceptable. The U.S. Court of Appeals, DC Circuit, reversed in part, noting that **the zoning board had not violated the university's substantive due process rights by imposing the housing restrictions.** Since students are not a suspect class deserving of heightened protections, the board's zoning regulations would be constitutional if they were rationally related to a legitimate governmental interest. Further, the preservation of Foggy Bottom's residential character was a legitimate governmental interest. The zoning restrictions were constitutional. *George Washington Univ. v. District of Columbia*, 318 F.3d 203 (D.C. Cir. 2003). [DC]

◆   *A university could turn a campus building into a child development center under a zoning approval.*

The DC Board of Zoning Adjustment approved a Georgetown University building as a "mixed-use main campus education/educational support" facility under a campus plan. This approval included "accessory uses" as permissible uses for the building. Subsequently, the university sought to turn the building into a child development center to be used exclusively by the university's faculty, staff and students. A group of residents challenged the issuance of the final permits, but the board held that the childcare center supported the university's mission and was a proper function of the university. Therefore, it was exempted from R-3 zoning restrictions. The DC Court of Appeals upheld the board's decision. **Conversion of the building into a childcare center was** a use consistent with the uses permitted under the "mixed-use" campus plan previously approved. Because the childcare center would be for the exclusive use of the university community, it satisfied the definition of "accessory use." *Georgetown Residents Alliance v. District of Columbia Bd. of Zoning Adjustment*, 816 A.2d 41 (D.C. 2003). [DC]

◆ *A city could require certain landlords of college students to comply with a lodging house ordinance.*

Six owners of condominium units in the city of Worcestor leased the units to students at the College of Holy Cross. Four unrelated students lived in each unit. When the condo owners refused to obtain permits as operators of lodging houses, the city filed complaints against them in housing court. The court found the lodging ordinance unconstitutionally vague, but the Appeals Court of Massachusetts vacated that opinion and found the ordinance valid. Here, **the ordinance clearly defined a lodging house as a "dwelling unit that is rented to four or more persons not constituting a family."** Moreover, the ordinance was rationally related to a legitimate governmental interest: creating quiet neighborhoods and limiting the number of unrelated people living together. The condo owners were subject to the ordinance. *City of Worcestor v. Bonaventura*, 775 N.E.2d 795 (Mass. App. 2002). [MA]

◆ *A Pennsylvania city violated proper procedure when its zoning board created a "student residence overlay district zone" prohibiting more than two students from living together in a dwelling unit.*

Muhlenberg College, a private, nonprofit, liberal arts college located in Allentown, filed suit against the town's zoning board when it created the zone surrounding campus. Since 1986, the college has purchased 37 residential properties and converted them for college-related uses—mainly as housing units for three to four students. The area around Muhlenberg's campus is zoned medium and low residential. In 1997, an amendment to the zoning code was drafted that would prohibit more than two students from living in a single-family or multi-family attached dwelling in the area around the campus. That bill was defeated. However, an identical measure with a quicker effective date was passed by the Allentown City Planning Commission.

A state trial court ruled that the city violated the Pennsylvania Municipalities Planning Code Act and the Codified Ordinances of the City of Allentown when it passed the bill, because it did not present the bill to the commission within the required 30 days before public hearings on the amendment. The city council held a hearing and voted to adopt the bill only 13 days after it was submitted. The board argued that the two bills were so similar that no additional recommendations were required. **The court ruled that the different effective date was enough to require that the bill be submitted 30 days before the hearing.** Because the bill was invalid due to the procedural error, the court refused to rule on the other five issues presented by the university. *Muhlenberg College v. Zoning Hearing Bd. of the City of Allentown*, 760 A.2d 443 (Pa. Cmwlth. 2000). [PA]

◆ *The Maxwell Street Historic Preservation Coalition could not get a temporary restraining order enjoining the University of Illinois at Chicago from demolishing certain structures as part of a campus development project.*

The university presented an expansion proposal to the city of Chicago. The university planned to build athletic fields and construct two student residence halls in a blighted area of Chicago. A member of a preservation group requested that the Maxwell Street Police Station, located within the South Campus Project, not be demolished. The Keeper of the National Register of Historic Places (the Keeper), the Illinois Historic Preservation Agency, the City's Commission on Chicago Landmarks, and the Department of Planning and Development denied the request, based on "the lack of integrity of the area." Nevertheless, the university acknowledged the historic significance of the police station and agreed to preserve it as a historic site. Six years later, the group sought to include another area within the project as a historic site. When the state preservation agency rejected their request, the group appealed to the Keeper and sought a temporary restraining order to enjoin the university from proceeding on the project.

The district court denied the preservation group's motion, finding the National Historic Preservation Act was inapplicable to the university and its project. Here, the university presented evidence that, six years ago, the Illinois Historic Preservation Agency and local agencies had determined that the area did not qualify for protection as a historic landmark. Accordingly, the group could not show that the disputed site was likely to be selected for inclusion on the National Register of Historic Sites. *Maxwell Street Historic Preservation Coalition v. Board of Trustees of Univ. of Illinois*, 2000 WL 1141439 (N.D. Ill. 8/11/00). [IL]

◆ *A nonprofit private music school was entitled to a special zoning exception as a private school.*

The school had been in existence for about 20 years and leased space in a building in the District of Columbia. It operated under a "special exception as a private school" previously granted by the Board of Zoning Adjustment. The school offered individual and classroom music instruction in orchestral instruments, piano, and voice, for students of all ages and abilities. It sponsored recitals in conjunction with public and private schools in the community and was one of only 17 schools in the country accredited as "community music schools" by the National Association of Schools of Music. When it began to outgrow its leased building, it sought to renovate three buildings on a single lot, and to construct an addition to the main building that would house teaching studios, some classrooms, rehearsal facilities, offices and a 300-seat auditorium. The school also proposed to build a 114-space parking lot.

Several neighborhood groups opposed the school's proposals, arguing that the presence of the private school would result in increased traffic and parking problems in the neighborhood, and that the school was not eligible for a special exception because it was not a "private school" within the meaning of the applicable regulation. The zoning board conducted a hearing and granted the requested special exception subject to several conditions, including limits on the number of persons allowed at the school at any given time and on the school's hours of operation. The neighborhood groups sought a reversal of the board's ruling before the District of Columbia Court of Appeals.

On appeal, the neighborhood groups claimed that the school was not a "school" within the dictionary definition of the term and that, even if it was, it was a trade school because it trained future concert professionals for whom music was a livelihood. The court of appeals disagreed. It noted that **the school plainly met the dictionary definition of a "school" as an organized source of education or training as well as a place where instruction was given**. It also was a private school because it was established, conducted and primarily supported by a nongovernmental agency. The court then noted that the school was not a trade school because, although a small percentage of its students might go on to further training, and an even smaller percentage to performing careers, the great majority did not. Accordingly, since the school was not a trade school, it was eligible to be granted a special exception. The zoning board's decision was affirmed. *Neighbors on Upton Street v. District of Columbia Bd. of Zoning Adjustment*, 697 A.2d 3 (D.C. App. 1997). [DC]

◆ *An ordinance that prohibited educational uses of property in a historic district owned by a New York private college was struck down as unconstitutional.*

The private college owned property adjacent to its campus that developed into a distinctive, turn of the century residential neighborhood listed on the National Register of Historic Places. The city adopted a zoning ordinance encompassing the property, which limited property uses and restricted special permit uses to public utility facilities, substations and structures. All other special uses, including educational uses, were foreclosed. The college proposed that the ordinance be amended to allow special permit use for faculty offices, administrative offices and homes for visiting dignitaries and guests of the college. The city's Historic Districts Commission and the New York State Office of Parks, Recreation and Historic Preservation both projected that the proposed amendment would have a deleterious effect on the historic preservation of the property. The college then discontinued its pursuit of an amendment and filed a declaratory judgment action in state court against the city, its mayor and city council, seeking a declaration that the ordinance was unconstitutional. The court granted the college pretrial judgment, and the appellate division affirmed. Appeal was then taken to the Court of Appeals of New York, the state's highest court.

The court noted that **proposed educational uses must be weighed against the interest in historical preservation as well as other legitimate, competing interests to determine how best to serve the public welfare**. Here, depriving the college of the opportunity to have its presumptively beneficial educational use weighed against competing interests, and thereby wholly excluding educational uses from the property, bore no substantial relation to the public welfare. Therefore, it was beyond the city's zoning authority. Moreover, neither the variance nor the amendment process allowed the zoning board to balance a particular applicant's educational use against the public interest in historical preservation. The judgment of the appellate division was affirmed. *Trustees of Union College v. Schenectady City Council*, 667 N.Y.S.2d 978 (N.Y. 1997). [NY]

The U.S. Supreme Court examined the Religious Freedom Restoration Act (RFRA) in *City of Boerne, Texas v. Flores*, 521 U.S. 507, 117 S.Ct. 2157, 138 L.Ed.2d 624 (1997), and found the RFRA to be unconstitutional as applied to state actions. The case involved a building permit for the enlargement of a church. It was denied on the ground that the church building was part of a historical district. The Supreme Court held that the church could not use the RFRA to obtain the permit because the RFRA proscribed state conduct that the Fourteenth Amendment did not even prohibit. However, the Supreme Court did not address the question of whether the RFRA was unconstitutional in all respects. It limited its analysis to state actions. Accordingly, the RFRA still may provide protections against federal actions.

◆ *A religious college was required to pay a development fee in order to build an addition. The fee was not a tax for which the college could claim an exemption because it was not compulsory. It was only applied upon development of property.*

A Catholic private college in California acquired an adjacent tract of land in order to build a postgraduate business school and parking structure. The college intended to move its existing business school to the new building, resulting in no increase in students or faculty. Before construction could begin, the college needed a permit that would not be issued unless the college paid a school development fee. Under state statute, any school district can levy a fee against any commercial, industrial or residential development project for the purpose of funding the construction of school facilities. The only exceptions are facilities used exclusively for religious purposes or facilities owned and occupied by agencies of federal, state, or local government. The college paid the fee under protest and then filed a petition for writ of mandamus in state court. The trial court found for the college, and the school district appealed to the California Court of Appeal, Second District.

The college argued that the development fee qualified as a tax, which it should not be required to pay as a nonprofit, educational institution. The court agreed that the college was exempt from state taxes because of its status, but found that the development fee was not a tax. It was not compulsory, like a tax, but was imposed only when a property owner decided to develop. Furthermore, **the California Supreme Court has held that exemptions from taxes refer only to property taxes**. The court also found that the development was not going to be used exclusively for religious purposes. The college did not fall into any of the exceptions to the statute and therefore it had to pay the development fee. *Loyola Marymount Univ. v. Los Angeles Unified School Dist.*, 53 Cal.Rptr.2d 424 (Cal. App. 2d Dist. 1996). [CA]

◆ *A Connecticut university seeking to resubdivide 13 acres of land into 40 building lots had to show that its development plan would not unreasonably destroy natural resources, and that no feasible and prudent alternatives existed.*

The university-owned land was zoned to permit single-family detached dwellings. The university submitted an application with the city's planning and zoning commission to resubdivide the land into 40 building lots. It also filed for a special permit to excavate and fill the land. The commission approved the university's application. A lawsuit was later filed challenging the approval, and several persons who owned land within a radius of 100 feet of the subject property intervened in the action. Specifically, the intervening landowners alleged 1) that the trees and wildlife on the proposed subdivision were natural resources requiring the commission to consider environmental impact; 2) that the proposed subdivision was a cul-de-sac subject to the 10-lot access rule; and 3) that the commission arbitrarily approved the plan despite several regulatory violations. A state trial court ruled for the university, and an appellate court affirmed. On further appeal, the Supreme Court of Connecticut reversed and remanded the case, holding that **even if the trees and wildlife had no economic value, the commission was obligated to consider whether the proposed development would unreasonably destroy those natural resources, and whether there was any feasible and prudent alternative to the development of the property**. *Paige v. Town Plan & Zoning Comm'n of Town of Fairfield*, 668 A.2d 340 (Conn. 1995). [CT]

C. School Licensing and Regulation Issues

◆   *The Court of Appeal of California held a community college was required to perform an environmental study before moving a campus shooting range.*

The college proposed a new site for a shooting range used for firearms courses offered in its criminal justice programs. It obtained approval by county and city governments, but a report indicated high levels of lead contamination at the new site. A public interest group alleged violation of state Environmental Quality Act requirements for an environmental study. A state superior court disagreed, finding the site change was not a "project" under the Act.

The Court of Appeal of California stated that under the Act, **a "project" is defined as "an activity which may cause either a direct physical change in the environment, or reasonably foreseeable indirect physical change in the environment" by a person or agency receiving public funds**. Even though dismantling and removing the range would be accomplished incrementally, these actions were all part of a single project. The college argued the lead abatement aspect of the move was exempt from the Act, as the cleanup would cost less than $1 million. The court held that while lead abatement was exempt, this did not relieve the college of its responsibility to conduct an initial study of the project. **The decision was reversed and remanded with instructions for an environmental study.** *Association for a Cleaner Environment v. Yosemite Community College Dist.*, 10 Cal.Rptr.3d 560 (Cal. App. 5th Dist. 2004). [CA]

◆   *A university had to disclose faculty booklists to a competitor of the campus bookstore under the New York Freedom of Information Law .*

A bookstore seeking to compete with the on-campus bookstore run by Barnes & Noble attempted to obtain faculty booklists. When informal attempts failed, it got an advisory opinion stating that the lists constituted records under New York's Freedom of Information Law (FOIL), then submitted formal requests to university faculty members and the university's records access officer. A few faculty members responded, but the records officer did not. The following semester, the same result was achieved. The bookstore then sued the university to compel it to comply with the FOIL, and a trial court dismissed the action. The supreme court, appellate division, reversed. **Course syllabi and written booklists constitute "records" under the FOIL because they are held by an agency.** It did not matter that the lists were kept by individual faculty members. Regardless of whether the university required the lists to be turned in to the records office, if they existed and someone requested them, they had to be made available. Here, the records existed, and the records officer was required to make them available. *Mohawk Book Co. Ltd. v. SUNY*, 732 N.Y.S.2d 272 (N.Y.A.D. 2001). [NY]

◆ *New York's Freedom of Information Law required disclosure of animal testing information to a citizen group.*

A citizen group sued the Board of Trustees of the State University of New York under the state's Freedom of Information Law (FOIL) to obtain certain records relating to biomedical research on cats and dogs. Under the Federal Animal Welfare Act, a dealer who provides a research facility with a "random source" dog or cat must furnish the research facility with a certification that includes the name and address of the person, pound or shelter from which the animal was obtained. The citizen group sought access to those certifications under the FOIL, and the records officer at the facility denied the request. A New York appellate court held that the facility was not an "agency" under the FOIL when it maintained the random source certifications because it was doing so to comply with federal law. However, the New York Court of Appeals reversed.

The court held the group was entitled to the research information. It found that **the facility was an "agency" for purposes of the FOIL because the certifications were being kept in connection with the research conducted by the facility, and that research was fulfilling the state university system's statutory mission–a state governmental function.** Since the board of trustees had not shown that the information being sought was subject to any exception, the FOIL required that the information be disclosed. *Citizens for Alternatives to Animal Labs v. Board of Trustees of SUNY*, 703 N.E.2d 1218 (N.Y. 1998). [NY]

◆ *The Michigan Department of Education could deny a license to operate to the owner of a trade school teaching casino gambling.*

A Michigan resident applied to the proprietary school unit of the department of education for a license to operate a private trade school teaching casino gambling. The board denied his application because gaming was considered criminal behavior in Michigan. The applicant appealed to a Michigan trial court. The trial court reversed, and the board of education appealed to the Court of Appeals of Michigan. The court of appeals noted that public policy did not completely prohibit casino gambling as evidenced by the legislature's decision to legalize millionaire parties and to allow casino gambling on Indian reservations.

On further appeal, the Supreme Court of Michigan reversed. It adopted the dissenting opinion from the lower court, which stated that **licensing the proposed school would violate public policy.** If the school were allowed to teach casino gambling, it would be teaching behavior that was currently defined as illegal under Michigan law. *Michigan Gaming Institute v. State Bd. of Educ.*, 547 N.W.2d 882 (Mich. 1996). [MI]

◆   *A corporation that provided review courses for nursing school graduates had to pay an annual renewal licensing fee for each location.*

The corporation offered courses that prepared nursing school graduates for state certification exams. It operated at five different locations in the state. The review courses were held in hotel meeting rooms, college auditoriums or hospital conference rooms. The California legislature modified the Private Postsecondary and Vocational Education Reform Act to increase the annual renewal fee for nondegree granting institutions from $225 to a range of $600 to $1,200, depending on size. The corporation made a single $1,200 payment but refused to make a separate payment for each of its course sites.

A lawsuit arose, and a California trial court found that a separate fee could be charged for each location. The California Court of Appeal, First District, noted that because the corporation's educational sites were 50 miles from corporate headquarters and were held in places such as hotel conference rooms, they were neither branches nor satellites subject to separate annual fees under the act. However, since the legislature provided that each site be inspected by the governing council, the court inferred a legislative intent to require separate annual fees for each site. **As long as the governing council used some "reasonable method" of estimating the administrative costs of the entire program, its annual fee interpretation was reasonable.** Thus, the court of appeal required the corporation to pay an annual fee for each site. *RN Review for Nurses, Inc. v. State*, 28 Cal.Rptr.2d 354 (Cal. App. 1st Dist. 1994). [CA]

◆   *Rhode Island was not allowed to require approval of all advertising for proprietary schools prior to publication.*

The owner of a Newport proprietary hairdressing school challenged the regulations governing proprietary schools in Rhode Island, which established a screening system for school advertising. The regulations required all advertising to be approved prior to publication by the Board of Governors of Higher Education. The school filed suit claiming the regulations constituted prior restraint and were overbroad in violation of the First Amendment. The federal district court held for the school.

The court found that **restrictions on commercial speech must satisfy a three-part test**. First, the commercial speech must concern a lawful activity and not be misleading or fraudulent. Second, the government's interest in restricting speech must be substantial. Third, the regulation must directly advance a government interest, and any restrictions must be narrowly tailored to advance that interest. Because the regulations required the approval of all advertisements regardless of their aim or purpose, they failed this final part. *Berger v. Rhode Island Bd. of Governors of Higher Educ.*, 832 F.Supp. 515 (D.R.I. 1993). [RI]

◆   *A New York appellate court upheld the denial of a license to a school that had operated illegally.*

A New York private school that had received a warning for improper conduct from the New York Secretary of Education sought to open another facility. The school began operations at an unlicensed facility and enticed students to enroll with promises of employment. Both of these practices are illegal, but they continued despite orders to desist. Finally, the secretary denied the school a license to operate. The New York Supreme Court, Appellate Division, held that **the secretary may lawfully deny a private for-profit school a license to operate if the secretary has good cause**. The secretary's decision should not be overturned unless it is arbitrary and capricious. The first issue questioned whether the school had received due process. The school in this case had been given an opportunity to refute the authority's findings, and that opportunity was held to be adequate to satisfy the requirements of due process. The court then observed that the school's conduct was clearly unlawful. The license denial was reinstated. *Blake Business School, Inc. v. Sobol*, 575 N.Y.S.2d 955 (A.D. 3d Dept. 1991). [NY]

◆   *A board for community colleges should have provided an occupational school with a hearing prior to terminating the school's license.*

A private Colorado occupational school was licensed to do business by the State Board for Community Colleges and Occupational Educations. A new statute revised licensing requirements, and the school was required to renew its license. The board's vice president rejected the school's application because it had not employed an independent accountant or utilized accepted accounting procedures as required by the new statute. The school filed a 42 U.S.C. § 1983 action in a Colorado district court against the vice president and the board. It alleged that both had failed to provide a hearing prior to terminating the school's license and had failed to provide an impartial tribunal.

The school sought damages and injunctive relief requiring the board to restore its license. A trial court determined that neither the board nor its vice president could be sued under 42 U.S.C. § 1983 and dismissed the case. The Colorado Court of Appeals found that the board was a state regulatory body that was entitled to immunity from suits for damages. Next, the court determined that **the vice president's failure to grant the school a pre-deprivation hearing was not a clear violation of its constitutional rights**. The vice president therefore had immunity on the claim for damages under § 1983. However, the board's refusal to grant the school a pre-deprivation hearing potentially violated its statutory rights. On remand, the school could sue for injunctive relief. *National Camera, Inc. v. Sanchez*, 832 P.2d 960 (Colo. App. 1991). [CO]

◆   *Because a cease and desist order amounted to a license revocation, the board that issued the order should have provided procedural safeguards to the school.*

A corporation operated an association of career schools in Florida. These schools were licensed by the Board of Independent Postsecondary Vocational Trade and Business Schools (board). The board became concerned with the school's advertisement practices and issued the school a cease and desist order that prohibited further advertisement, enrollment of students, or acceptance of further tuition payments. The school contended that the board had in effect revoked the school's license without following the required procedural safeguards. The school appealed directly to the District Court of Appeal of Florida, which noted that the board had the discretion to take the actions included in the cease and desist order. However, other Florida legislation deals directly with revoking or limiting a school's license, and mandates compliance with specific procedural safeguards in the event of an emergency suspension. The school argued that these procedures should be followed because the cease and desist order had the same effect as revoking the school's license. The court agreed. It then held that **the board had not set out specific facts showing the necessity of actions, published an evaluation of the fairness of the action, or provided a prompt hearing**. The court quashed the cease and desist order. *Allied Educ. Corp. v. State, Dep't of Educ.*, 573 So.2d 959 (Fla. App. 1st Dist. 1991). [FL]

◆ *The state of Florida could not prevent a consulting firm's education division from using the word "college" in its name, even though the division did not offer college credit or degrees.*

A division of a management consulting firm maintained classroom facilities and conducted seminars on quality improvement. However, the division, which was called Quality College, did not offer instruction leading to college credit or any academic degree. In July 1985, the Florida State Board of Independent Colleges notified Quality that it could not use the term "college" in its name without prior express authority from the board. The case reached the Florida District Court of Appeal, which observed that the issue was whether the board correctly denied Quality the use of the name "college." The board had interpreted a state statute to mean that only degree-granting institutions that were accredited, licensed, or exempt were eligible to use the word "college." The court ruled that the board's interpretation was wrong. **The board's interpretation prohibited the use of "college" by any other person or entity for any other purpose (such as "Kiddie College" for preschools).** The board's decision was reversed, and Quality College was allowed to retain its name. *Phillip Crosby Associates Inc. v. State Bd. of Independent Colleges.*, 506 So.2d 490 (Fla. App. 5th Dist. 1987). [FL]

◆ *New York City was not allowed to ban a private educational institution's distribution of free magazines via news racks because the proposed ban arbitrarily singled out certain kinds of publications.*

A private institution that offered short, nonaccredited courses in New York City sought to distribute its magazine free of charge by way of news racks placed on city sidewalks. The city contended that the news racks were unsightly, unsanitary and unsafe. It also asserted that the magazine was "commercial speech," which is entitled to a lesser degree of First Amendment protection, and that the ban on all commercial speech through sidewalk news racks was constitutional. The New York Court of Appeals observed that the city's arguments missed the central point in the case: **"a government official or employee may not exercise complete and unregulated discretion, in the absence of duly enacted guidelines, ... to decide which publications may be distributed via [news racks]."** Here, the city's action against the institution was taken without the benefit of any regulatory guidelines. The city's action therefore violated the First Amendment, which requires that government action regulating "speech" be undertaken pursuant to clear guidelines that leave little room for arbitrary decisions. The decision to ban the sidewalk magazine news racks was illegal. *City of New York v. American School Publications*, 509 N.E.2d 311 (N.Y. 1987). [NY]

◆ *A state tuition refund rule was held to be constitutional such that a school could be denied a license renewal for failing to comply with the rule.*

A Florida correspondence school offered courses of instruction for home study with optional training at its Florida training school. Florida Department of Education rules required a tuition refund policy identical to or more liberal than the refund policy recognized by the U.S. Office of Education. Sanctions for failure to comply with the rule included nonrenewal of licensing. The school operated in several states, maintaining 44 field offices.

The field offices utilized 22 separate contract forms to comply with various state regulations while minimizing the tuition refund to dropout students. In each case, the minimum refund corresponded to student domicile state law rather than Florida law. The Florida Department of Education notified the school that it intended to deny its license renewal application for failure to comply with the state tuition refund rule. The District Court of Appeal rejected the school's argument that the refund rule burdened interstate commerce, because **the rule put nonresident students in the same position as resident students concerning tuition refunds.** Since the rule did not burden out-of-state students but placed them on exactly the same footing as Florida students with respect to refunds of prepaid enrollment charges, it was clear that there was no discrimination. Students would no longer be subject to different tuition refunds depending upon their state's law. *Associated Schools v. Department of Educ.*, 522 So.2d 426 (Fla. App. 1st Dist. 1988). [FL]

D. Teacher Certification

◆ *A teacher who had been denied and later granted permanent certification could sue the state department of education for her costs and other incidental monetary damages.*

A student received her undergraduate education at a convent school in Lebanon and subsequently passed the National Teachers Exam. She then obtained a Master of Arts degree from Brooklyn College and began working for the completion of a second Master of Arts degree to teach English as a second language. The New York City Board of Education's Board of Examiners granted her a temporary per diem teaching certificate after accepting her credentials. Two years later, when the Board of Examiners was disbanded, the state Education Department became responsible for evaluating teacher credentials. The teacher's temporary license and substitute teacher certificate were renewed for two successive years. When she applied for permanent certification, the department denied her application for failure to submit evidence of a completed baccalaureate degree. As a result, she lost her job with the New York City Board of Education in its bilingual program. She commenced an administrative proceeding to obtain reinstatement, a credit for seniority status, back pay, health insurance costs and other appropriate relief.

The hearing resulted in her permanent certification and reinstatement by the Board of Education. She then brought a motion for an order granting the relief that she had originally sought–seniority status, back pay, medical insurance and attorneys' fees. The court found that it lacked jurisdiction to consider those claims against the state, and the teacher appealed to the Supreme Court, Appellate Division, which concluded that the lower court should not have dismissed the teacher's remaining claims. Since **the main thrust of the lawsuit had been the review of the department's determination that her convent education was not the equivalent of a baccalaureate degree, and the monetary relief was incidental**, the lower court could hear the entire case. The court remanded the case for a determination of those incidental damages detailed in the petition. *Awad v. State Educ. Dep't of New York*, 658 N.Y.S.2d 755 (A.D. 3d Dept. 1997). [NY]

E. Delegation of Police Power

◆   *An Indiana appellate court held that delegating police power to a private religious university did not violate the Establishment Clause.*

Valparaiso University, an independent institution owned and operated by the Lutheran University Association, operated a police department whose officers were appointed by the governing board of the university. After a university police officer arrested and charged a law student with driving while intoxicated, the student sought to suppress the evidence against him by claiming that the exercise of police power by a religious institution was unconstitutional, that the officer had not undergone the required training of officers employed by the state, and that there had been no reasonable suspicion or probable cause to pull him over. The case reached the Court of Appeals of Indiana, which held that **although the university was religiously affiliated, it was not a religious institution within the meaning of the First Amendment**. It was characterized by a high degree of academic freedom and did not subordinate secular education to religious doctrine. **Accordingly, delegating police power to the university did not violate the Establishment Clause.** Further, because the university was not a political subdivision of the state, the officer was not required to undergo the same training as police officers in Indiana. Finally, there was probable cause for the stop. Accordingly, the evidence against the student was admissible, and his conviction was upheld. *Myers v. State*, 714 N.E.2d 276 (Ind. App. 1999). [IN]

◆   *However, the Supreme Court of North Carolina found that police power could not be delegated to a religious university.*

A North Carolina Baptist University operated a police force consisting of a captain and eight full-time officers. Pursuant to a North Carolina statute, the university's police officers were commissioned as state police officers by the attorney general. When one of the officers spotted a student weaving across the center line of a highway near the university, he arrested the student for driving while impaired. The student later filed suit in state court, alleging that the statute authorizing commission of university police officers as state police officers was unconstitutional, and seeking dismissal of the charge against him. The case reached the Supreme Court of North Carolina, which noted that the statute violated the Establishment Clause. The court noted that **a state cannot delegate an important discretionary governmental power to a religious institution or share such power with a religious institution**. Because police power is an important discretionary governmental power, and because the Baptist university was a religious institution, the state's delegation of its police power to the university was unconstitutional. *State v. Pendleton*, 451 S.E.2d 274 (N.C. 1993). [NC]

F. Term Paper Services

◆ *One of the nation's largest private universities was unsuccessful in its attempt to hold a number of term paper writing services liable for violating state and federal laws.*

Boston University sought to prevent enterprises that it characterized as "term paper mills" from assisting and encouraging student fraud and cheating on term papers. In 1981, the university obtained a permanent order from a state court against various term paper services. However, it claimed that many students continued to purchase term papers from the services and submit them as their own work in order to fulfill class requirements. In 1997, the university organized a sting operation to investigate term paper research and writing services, at least one of which was a party to the 1981 action. After obtaining information that at least one of the services offered a student information on how to alter papers to avoid detection and concluding that many services continued to sell papers to Boston University students, the university commenced a federal district court action alleging interference with its educational policies in violation of RICO. The services responded with counterclaims against the university for RICO violations and abuse of process. The Commonwealth of Massachusetts intervened in the case to address their challenge to the constitutionality of a state law prohibiting the sale of term papers and research materials for submission as original work for academic credit. The services moved for pretrial judgment.

The court rejected the university's RICO claim because it failed to show that a number of distinct entities were engaging in racketeering activities. The services were not distinct entities from their individual owners. It also **refused to apply a Massachusetts criminal statute that prohibits the sale of term papers if the seller has knowledge that they will be submitted for academic credit as original work**. The law created no private right of action to accompany its criminal sanctions. Because the university's remaining claims could not be aggregated to meet the minimum required amount of $75,000 in controversy for federal jurisdiction, the court refused to consider the state law claims for unfair or deceptive acts or practices in commercial relationships between businesses. The only commercial relationship between the university and the services had been the sting operation, which involved only small payments for term papers. The court awarded judgment to the services. *Trustees of Boston Univ. v. ASM Communications, Inc.*, 33 F.Supp.2d 66 (D. Mass. 1998). [MA]

G. Desegregation

◆ *Where a state perpetuates policies and practices that can be traced to a segregative system and that have segregative effects, the policies will be considered unconstitutional unless there is sound educational justification for them and it is not practical to eliminate them.*

Mississippi maintained a dual system of public education at the university level–one set of universities for whites, and another set for blacks. In 1981, the State Board of Trustees issued "Mission Statements" to remedy this, classifying the three flagship historically white institutions (HWI) as "comprehensive" universities, redesignating one of the historically black institutions (HBI) as an "urban" university and characterizing the rest as "regional" institutions. However, the universities remained racially identifiable. A federal court found that state policies need merely be racially neutral, developed in good faith, and not contribute to the racial identifiability of each institution. It held that Mississippi was currently fulfilling its duty to desegregate. The U.S. Court of Appeals, Fifth Circuit, affirmed. The U.S. Supreme Court granted review.

The Supreme Court held that the district court had applied the wrong legal standard in ruling that Mississippi had brought itself into compliance with the Equal Protection Clause. **If a state perpetuates policies and practices traceable to its prior dual system that continue to have segregative effects, and such policies are without sound educational justification and can be practicably eliminated, the policies violate the Equal Protection Clause.** This is true even if the state has abolished the legal requirement that the races be separated and has established neutral policies. The proper inquiry is whether existing racial identifiability is attributable to the state. Applying the proper standard, several surviving aspects of Mississippi's prior dual system were constitutionally suspect. First, the use of higher minimum ACT composite scores at the HWIs, along with the state's refusal to consider high school grade performance was suspect. Second, the unnecessary duplication of programs at HBIs and HWIs was suspect. Third, the mission statements' reflection of previous policies to perpetuate racial separation was suspect. Finally, the state's policy of operating eight universities had to be examined to determine if it was educationally justifiable. *U.S. v. Fordice*, 505 U.S. 717, 112 S.Ct. 2727, 120 L.Ed.2d 575 (1992). [MS]

On remand, a Mississippi federal court **entered a remedial decree prohibiting the state from maintaining remnants of the prior segregated system** and mandating specific relief in areas of admissions and funding. However, the court refused to order the relief requested by the complaining parties, which would significantly increase the number of African-Americans accepted for regular admission at state universities. The complaining parties claimed that the district court order's reliance on a summer remedial program to boost African-American admissions was inappropriate, and the parties appealed to the U.S. Court of Appeals, Fifth Circuit. The court agreed with the complaining parties that the district court's order affirming the elimination of many remedial courses had to be reconsidered, along with its finding that use of college entrance scores as a criterion for scholarships was not traceable to the illegal system of segregation. The court remanded for clarification the status of a proposal to merge two universities to eliminate unnecessary program duplication, as well as questions of increasing the other-race presence at two HBIs and issues of accreditation and funding. The court affirmed many aspects of the district court decision as consistent with the *Fordice* decision, significantly affirming its decision to maintain admissions standards that ensured educational soundness. *Ayers v. Fordice*, 111 F.3d 1183 (5th Cir. 1997). [MS]

H. Financial Aid

◆ *The Supreme Court stated that federal assistance may be based on compliance with federal laws. Thus, a statute mandating compliance with the Selective Service System's requirements as a prerequisite to federal aid did not violate the Fifth Amendment's protection from self-incrimination since no student is compelled to apply for federal aid.*

Section 12(f) of the Military Selective Service Act denied federal financial assistance under Title IV of the Higher Education Act to male students between the ages of 18 and 26 who failed to register for the draft. Applicants for assistance were required to file a statement with their institutions attesting to their compliance with the Selective Service Act. A group of students who had not registered for the draft sued the selective service system to enjoin enforcement of § 12(f). A federal district court held that the act was a bill of attainder (a law that imposes a penalty on a group of people without a trial) because it singled out an identifiable group that would be ineligible for Title IV aid based on their failure to register. The court also held that the compliance requirement violated the Fifth Amendment.

On appeal, the Supreme Court rejected the claims that the law was a bill of attainder and upheld the law. **The law clearly gave non-registrants 30 days after receiving notice of ineligibility for federal financial aid to register for the draft and thereby qualify for aid.** Furthermore, the bill of attainder prohibition in the Constitution applies only to statutes that inflict punishments on specified groups or individuals such as "all Communists." The Court also held that the denial of aid based on these requirements was not "punishment." The Court stated that **if students wish to further their education at the expense of their country, they cannot expect the benefits without accepting their fair share of governmental responsibility**. Finally, the law did not violate the Fifth Amendment because there was nothing forcing students to apply for federal aid. *Selective Service System v. Minnesota Public Interest Research Group*, 468 U.S. 841, 104 S.Ct. 3348, 82 L.Ed.2d 632 (1984). [MN]

◆ *Three students who did not have to register for the draft still had to provide information about why they were exempt in order to qualify for aid.*

Three Boston University theology students, who were exempt from Selective Service registration either because of age or gender, refused to answer questions about their draft registration status on their applications for federal financial aid. They objected to providing information about their exempt status because of religious principles. They were refused federal financial assistance and sued the university, asserting that their religious freedom and free exercise rights had been violated. A federal court prohibited the denial of aid to the students, and the case reached the U.S. Court of Appeals, First Circuit. The appellate court held that although the Department of Education's regulations were broader than the statute on which they were based, they were not unconstitutional. **Even though the department had other means to acquire the information it sought, the burden on the applicants to state that they were female or of a certain age (and thus exempt) was minimal.** Also, the information being sought was not of a religious nature. Thus, the government's interest outweighed the applicants' interest and required the lower court's decision to be reversed and remanded. *Alexander v. Trustees of Boston Univ.,* 766 F.2d 630 (1st Cir. 1985). [MA]

II. PROCEDURAL AND FINANCIAL ISSUES

◆ *In 1982, the Supreme Court ruled that a Pennsylvania taxpayer group lacked standing to challenge a governmental conveyance of surplus property to a private religious college. The Court ruled that the group could show no injury to itself or any of its members as a result of the conveyance.*

Congress enacted the Federal Property and Administrative Services Act, 40 U.S.C. § 471 *et seq.,* to dispose of surplus property and authorize its transfer to public or private entities. This statute authorized the education secretary to dispose of surplus real property for schools. The secretary was permitted to take into account any benefit accruing to the U.S. from any new use of the transferred property. In 1973, the Secretary of Defense and General Services Administration declared a Pennsylvania army hospital site surplus property. In 1976, the secretary conveyed part of the property to a Christian college.

Although the appraised value of the property was $577,500, the secretary computed a 100 percent public benefit allowance, permitting the college to acquire the property for no cost. **A taxpayer group advocating the separation of church from state learned of the conveyance and sued the college and federal government**, claiming that the conveyance violated the Establishment Clause. The court dismissed the complaint, ruling that the taxpayers lacked standing under the Supreme Court's decision in *Flast v. Cohen.* The U.S. Court of Appeals, Third Circuit, reversed the district court's decision, and the Supreme Court agreed to hear an appeal by the college and federal government.

The Court stated that Article II of the Constitution limited the judicial power of courts to cases and controversies. Litigants were entitled to bring a lawsuit only by showing some actual or threatened injury. Without such a showing, lawsuits were to be dismissed for lack of standing. In this case, the taxpayers had alleged injury from deprivation of fair and constitutional use of their tax dollars. This allegation was insufficient to confer standing in federal courts. Under *Flast,* taxpayers were proper parties only to allege the unconstitutionality of congressional actions under the Taxing and Spending Clause and were required to show that the action went beyond the powers delegated to Congress. **Courts were not available to taxpayers to vent generalized grievances of government conduct or spending.** The complained-of statute arose under the Property Clause, and therefore the taxpayers had no standing to complain about the property transfer. The Court reversed the court of appeals' decision. *Valley Forge Christian College v. Americans United for Separation of Church and State*, 454 U.S. 464, 102 S.Ct. 752, 70 L.Ed.2d 700 (1982). [PA]

◆ *A student sought a final court order mandating admission to law school, but by the time the case reached the Supreme Court it was the eve of the student's graduation. The Court dismissed the case as moot.*

A student applied for admission to a state-operated law school in Washington. The size of the incoming class was limited, and the school accepted less than 10 percent of those who applied. The student was among those rejected. **He sued the school, claiming that its policy of giving favorable status to certain minority students in admission decisions discriminated against him** on the basis of his race in violation of the Equal Protection Clause of the Fourteenth Amendment. The student brought suit on behalf of himself and not as the representative of any class. He sought an injunction ordering the school to admit him as a member of the first-year class. A Washington state trial court agreed with his claim and granted the requested relief. The student entered the school and began his legal studies. The Washington Supreme Court reversed and held that the admissions policy did not violate the Constitution. By this time, the student was in his second year.

The student petitioned the U.S. Supreme Court for review and received a stay of the Washington Supreme Court's judgment pending the final disposition of the U.S. Supreme Court. When the case was finally argued before the Court, the student was in his final quarter of law school and the Court determined that the question was moot. The Court stated that since the student had only brought the action on his own behalf and already had been granted the relief he had sought, the controversy between the school and himself was at an end. Furthermore, there was no immediate danger that the student might be subjected to the "gauntlet" of law school admissions again. The Court dismissed the case. *DeFunis v. Odegaard*, 416 U.S. 312, 94 S.Ct.1704, 40 L.Ed.2d 164 (1974). [WA]

◆ *In 1989, the U.S. Supreme Court ruled that a choice of law clause in a university contractor's construction contract superseded arbitration rights found in the Federal Arbitration Act. This was because the parties had intended to incorporate state arbitration rules into the contract. As state law controlled, the Court refused to set aside the judgment of the California courts.*

An electrical contractor contracted with a California university to install conduits. The contract contained a clause in which the parties agreed to arbitrate disputes relating to the contract. The contract also contained a choice-of-law clause that stated that it would be governed by the law of the place of the project's location. A dispute arose concerning overtime compensation, and the contractor made a formal request for arbitration. The university sued the contractor in a California trial court for fraud and breach of contract. **The contractor claimed that it was entitled to arbitration under the contract and the Federal Arbitration Act (FAA).** The court granted the university's motion to stay arbitration under a California statute that permits a stay when arbitration is the subject of pending court action. The contractor appealed to the California Court of Appeal, which affirmed the trial court's decision. The court of appeal acknowledged that although the contract affected interstate commerce, the California statute applied because of the contractual choice-of-law clause. The California Supreme Court denied the contractor's petition for discretionary review, but the U.S. Supreme Court agreed to hear its appeal.

On appeal, the contractor reiterated its argument that the court of appeal's ruling on the choice-of-law clause deprived it of its federally guaranteed right to arbitration under the FAA. The Supreme Court ruled that **the FAA did not confer a general right to compel arbitration. Rather, it guaranteed the right to arbitrate according to the manner provided for in the parties' contract.** The court of appeal had correctly found that the contract incorporated California law. The FAA was not undermined by the state law that permitted a stay of arbitration. The Court affirmed the court of appeal's decision for the university. *Volt Information Sciences v. Board of Trustees of Leland Stanford Junior Univ.*, 489 U.S. 468, 109 S.Ct. 1248, 103 L.Ed.2d 488 (1989). [CA]

◆ *The Supreme Court of Illinois upheld a jury verdict reducing a damage award to Chicago City Colleges in an accounting malpractice case.*

A treasurer of the board of trustees for the City Colleges of Chicago created a "financial emergency" for the colleges by engaging in a securities scheme dependent upon falling interest rates. The board alleged two accounting firms breached their duty to detect and notify it of the treasurer's risky investments during separate time periods in which the firms served as the board's auditor. The board sued the accounting firms in a state court for professional negligence and breach of contract. The firm of Arthur Anderson settled with the board, but the Coopers & Lybrand firm did not, and the case proceeded to a trial. A jury returned a verdict of $23 million for the board. The verdict was reduced by 45 percent, based on the board's comparative negligence. Both parties appealed.

A state appellate court upheld the verdict, and Coopers appealed. **The state supreme court held the board's failure to discover bad investments made by the treasurer could not be asserted as a defense** by Coopers. However, it refused to disturb the jury verdict, which had found the board 45 percent negligent based on its own conduct. Arthur Anderson and Coopers were jointly and severally liable for the harm to the colleges. Any one of the three audits performed by the firms could have uncovered the harm. Coopers was entitled to credit the full amount of the board's settlement with Anderson against the amount of the judgment. *Board of Trustees of Community College Dist. 508 v. Coopers & Lybrand*, 803 N.E.2d 460 (Ill. 2003). [IL]

◆ *A state court must decide whether the University of Utah can prohibit students, faculty and staff from carrying concealed weapons on campus.*

Utah residents can apply for concealed weapon permits. The University of Utah prohibits most students, faculty and staff members from possessing or carrying firearms on campus. When the state attorney general issued an advisory opinion that stated in a footnote that the university's policy was invalid and should not be enforced, the university sued the attorney general in federal court for an order allowing it to uphold the policy. It asserted that the First and Fourteenth Amendments allowed it to enact the firearms policy as part of its commitment to ensuring academic freedom. It also asserted that the Utah Constitution permitted it to enact the policy in order **to protect campus order and discipline, and to promote an environment consistent with the educational process**. The attorney general sought to have the lawsuit dismissed. The U.S. District Court of the District of Utah refused to consider the federal claims, and remanded the case to state court for a decision on the legality of the policy under the Utah Constitution. *University of Utah v. Shurtleff*, 252 F.Supp.2d 1264 (D. Utah 2003). [UT]

◆   *A university was liable for attorneys' fees where it sued for a declaratory judgment and lost.*

Three University of Indiana students working on a project at a geological field station in Montana left for a rafting trip in a university-owned vehicle. They took along the boyfriend of one of the students. En route, the student driving the vehicle lost control, causing an accident in which two students and the boyfriend were killed. Lawsuits ensued. In one, the university sought a declaratory judgment regarding whether it had to indemnify the student driver. A Montana trial court ruled in favor of the student's estate, but refused to award it costs and attorneys' fees. The Supreme Court of Montana reversed. It noted that nothing in the Declaratory Judgment Act precluded an award of attorneys' fees where necessary to provide meaningful relief. It remanded for a determination of the proper amount to be awarded. *Trustees of Indiana Univ. v. Buxbaum*, 69 P.3d 663 (Mont. 2003). [MT]

◆   *A university's bus service was not entitled to a credit for fuel taxes for its campus bus service.*

An Ohio public university owned a campus bus service that provided free transportation within the university campus. It also transported disabled students to and from the airport, and serviced the city of Kent and neighboring townships. However, it did not operate under a contract with the city or any other regional transit authority. When it applied for reimbursement of motor vehicle fuel taxes, claiming eligibility for the credits because its buses were transit buses, the tax commissioner and the Board of Tax Appeals ruled that its buses did not meet the statutory definition of "transit buses." The Supreme Court of Ohio upheld that determination. Here, even though the buses benefited non-students as well as students, **the bus service did not meet the requirement that it be operated by or for a municipal corporation**. The bus service was not entitled to the tax reimbursement. *Campus Bus Service v. Zaino*, 786 N.E.2d 889 (Ohio 2003). [OH]

◆   *The University of Connecticut's suit against the state Department of Public Utility Control survived a motion to dismiss by establishing that the school was adversely affected by an administrative decision.*

In 1989, Charter Communications of Northeast Connecticut entered into a 10-year contract with the university to provide cable services to its campus, using the university's conduits to bring in cable wires both outside and inside campus buildings. Over the 10-year period, the conduits became either full or clogged in several buildings. After unsuccessful negotiations to renew the arrangement, the contractual relationship between the parties terminated when the contract expired. Subsequently, Charter filed a request with the state Department of Public Utility Control, (DPUC) seeking a declaratory ruling regarding its rights to provide cable services to the campus. The DPUC determined that Charter had a right to access the university's buildings and to provide cable services. When the university appealed, Charter moved to dismiss the action.

The court denied the motion. In appealing an administrative decision, the university had to establish that it was "aggrieved." Here, the school demonstrated a specific personal and legal interest that was adversely affected by the DPUC decision. The university argued that permitting Charter's wires to remain in place clogged its conduits. Moreover, the university asserted that a portion of the $750,000 used to create HUSKYvision, its own cable system, was spent because of the presence of Charter's wires in its conduits. **This evidence was sufficient for the court to conclude that the university showed it was aggrieved, and Charter's motion to dismiss was denied.** *University of Connecticut v. Department of Public Utility Control*, 2000 WL 1409799 (Conn. Super. 9/13/00). [CT]

III. ACCREDITATION

Regional and other accrediting institutions have been sued by private schools upon withdrawal of accreditation. The general rules emerging from such cases establish that: 1) actions of accrediting institutions do not constitute "state action" triggering due process requirements, 2) a school may maintain a breach of contract lawsuit against an accrediting institution if the institution fails to follow its own rules and procedures, and 3) if an accrediting institution's procedures are fair, its decision to revoke accreditation will likely be upheld.

A. Grants of Accreditation

◆ *A federal court refused to force the American Bar Association to provisionally accredit a law school.*

After a religious university acquired a non-accredited law school, it applied for provisional accreditation from the American Bar Association (ABA). The ABA rejected the application. The following year, the university applied again, and again was rejected. A group of graduates, students and instructors then sued the ABA seeking a preliminary injunction to force provisional accreditation. The university also filed a third application for provisional accreditation. A Florida federal district court refused to grant the injunction, finding no evidence that irreparable harm would befall the plaintiffs if the injunction was not granted. While the third application was pending, **graduates still could be admitted to practice in other states, and they could seek a waiver of the 12-month rule on sitting for the Florida Bar Exam** from the state supreme court. *Staver v. American Bar Ass'n*, 169 F.Supp.2d 1372 (M.D. Fla. 2001). [FL]

◆ *Where an accreditation foundation's denial of accreditation was supported by substantial evidence, it did not qualify as arbitrary or unreasonable.*

In 1995, Savannah College of Art & Design sought accreditation for its interior design program from the Foundation for Interior Design Education Research. Although a team of evaluators' report generally praised the program, it recommended the denial of accreditation. The foundation's board of trustees accepted the recommendation. Savannah College appealed, and a second on-site evaluation also recommended denial of accreditation for poor student achievement. Believing it had been treated unfairly, Savannah turned to the foundation's appeals panel, which determined that the denial of accreditation was supported by substantial evidence and consistent with other schools' accreditation reports. After the college threatened legal intervention, the foundation sued for a declaration that its decision to reject accreditation was lawful. In response, the college filed counterclaims against it. A federal court granted pretrial judgment to the foundation and dismissed all of the counterclaims. The school appealed to the Sixth Circuit.

The court of appeals determined that the foundation's denial of accreditation was neither arbitrary nor discriminatory. Savannah College argued that the foundation's method of evaluation deviated from the usual evaluative process and was therefore discriminatory. The court agreed that the process in this case differed, but to the college's favor. The foundation would not normally send a second evaluation team, but it did so in this case to ensure fairness. Savannah's final argument claimed the foundation acted arbitrarily because the college's interior design program closely resembled other accredited programs. The court disagreed, ruling that the foundation's decision was based on substantial evidence. The dismissal of the college's claims was affirmed. *Foundation for Interior Design Education Research v. Savannah College of Art & Design,* 244 F.3d 521 (6th Cir. 2001). [MI]

◆ *After an unsuccessful antitrust action in federal court against the American Bar Association, a law school association and an accredited law school, a nonaccredited law school could not sue the same parties again in state court alleging different claims arising from the same set of operative facts.*

A Massachusetts nonprofit, nontraditional law school applied for American Bar Association (ABA) accreditation. Although the school recognized that its practices were contrary to ABA standards, it sought a waiver for each standard that might bar accreditation. An ABA team visited the school and recommended denial of accreditation. The school then brought an antitrust lawsuit in a federal court against the ABA, a law school association, an ABA-accredited law school in Massachusetts, and several individuals. The court dismissed claims against certain defendants and granted pretrial judgment to the remaining defendants. The U.S. Court of Appeals, Third Circuit, affirmed.

Next, the school filed suit in a state court against the same defendants and three new defendants. The U.S. Court of Appeals, First Circuit, noted that **the school's pending claims, although rooted in Massachusetts law, plainly arose from the same set of operative facts as the antitrust suit. Both suits stemmed from the school's failed efforts to receive ABA accreditation.** Because the school had had an appropriate opportunity to litigate its first set of claims, and conveniently could have brought the second set as part of the same proceeding, the prior antitrust suit satisfied due process concerns and the state court lawsuit was precluded. *Massachusetts School of Law at Andover v. American Bar Ass'n*, 142 F.3d 26 (1st Cir. 1998). [MA]

◆ *An amendment to Oregon law, allowing certain schools in the state to be exempted from requirements that out-of-state schools were not exempted from, was struck down.*

A private Washington university with a branch campus in Oregon was accredited by the Northwest Association of Schools and Colleges (NASC). Following NASC accreditation, the Oregon Office of Educational Policy and Planning (OEPP) continued to review non-Oregon schools every three years. The statute provided that "no school ... shall confer ... any degree ... without first having submitted the requirements for such degree to the [OEPP] and having obtained the approval of the director." However, an amendment exempted Oregon schools in good standing with the NASC from OEPP review. The university filed suit in an Oregon circuit court, seeking a declaration that the statute violated the Commerce Clause. The circuit court held for the university and severed a portion of the amendment. The court of appeals affirmed but invalidated the exemption in its entirety. The Oregon Supreme Court allowed the university's petition for review solely on the issue of remedy.

The university contended that the entire amendment had been improperly invalidated. The supreme court disagreed, ruling that the statute as severed was not capable of being executed in accordance with legislative intent. The legislature had intended both to continue the exemption from OEPP authority for Oregon schools that were members of the NASC and to remove the exemption from OEPP authority for out-of-state schools, even if those schools were NASC members. However, the dominant intent of the amendment was to ensure that Oregon branch campuses of the out-of-state schools had the same level of faculty and facilities as their main campuses. **Because a partial severance would subject these out-of-state schools to lesser scrutiny, the court ordered the amendment severed in its entirety.** The court of appeals' ruling was affirmed. *City Univ. v. Office of Educ. Policy*, 885 P.2d 701 (Or. 1994). [OR]

◆ *Denial of accreditation by an association of schools was not state action that would trigger application of the Constitution.*

The Medical Institute of Minnesota, a private technical school training students for careers as medical and dental assistants, received accreditation from the National Association of Trade and Technical Schools for a five-year period commencing in 1977. In 1983, the institute's application for reaccreditation was denied, and an association hearing panel upheld the denial. The institute then sued the association in federal court, claiming a violation of its constitutional rights. The case reached the U.S. Court of Appeals, Eighth Circuit, which held that the **denial of accreditation was not "state action" that triggered application of the U.S. Constitution. The court also refused to substitute its judgment for the association's with respect to a purely educational matter.** It further noted that although the institute had been given an opportunity to justify its deficiencies, it had been unable to do so. The institute's action could not succeed. *Medical Institute of Minnesota v. NATTS*, 817 F.2d 1310 (8th Cir. 1987). [MN]

B. Claims of Fraud

◆ *A university's failure to gain accreditation for its Master of Social Work program did not violate students' due process rights.*

Governor's State University instituted a Master of Social Work Program in 1997. Three years later, university officials informed graduate students enrolled in the program that the National Council of Social Work Education had denied the university's application for accreditation. As a result, graduates were not permitted to sit for a licensing examination in Illinois. Graduating students discussed the accreditation problem with university officials at a board meeting. Additional students remained outside, protesting. A month later, graduate students were invited to an alumni fundraising dinner. The university limited the number of entrances and exits and permitted the students to picket only in the vestibule area. Instead of attending the dinner, the students peacefully protested the university's actions. Security guards removed the students from the premises and refused to allow them to re-enter the grounds.

A group of students sued the university, its president and trustees in a federal district court for due process and speech rights violations. The court held for the university, and the students appealed to the U.S. Court of Appeals, Seventh Circuit. **The court held the students did not show any arbitrary government action in violation of the Due Process Clause. While the university was responsible for ensuring its programs were accredited, the students had adequate remedies at law to resolve their complaints.** The trustees were not involved in the dinner event, and did not prevent the protesters from attending. The university president did not retaliate against the students for their protests. The actions of university security guards were merely a response to overcrowding. The court held summary judgment was properly entered for the university and its officials. *Galdikas v. Fagan*, 342 F.3d 684 (7th Cir. 2003). [IL]

◆ *A class of students was allowed to sue an accrediting agency for fraud after the agency extended the accreditation of a school without checking to see if the school met the agency's standards.*

A District of Columbia vocational school applied to an accrediting agency for accreditation in 1985. The agency granted the school an accreditation that was to expire in two years. Despite areas of concern, including curriculum, instructional materials, clarity of the school's mission statement and the school's financial status, the agency granted the school a series of automatic extensions until November of 1988. A number of students who had enrolled during this period began to notice that the school did not carry through on all of its promises. The students filed suit against the accrediting agency in the U.S. District Court for the District of Columbia, alleging that the agency was liable for fraud because it extended the accreditation of the school without any knowledge of whether the school met its standards for accreditation. On cross-motions for pretrial judgment, the court determined that **the class of students** had established a *prima facie* **case of fraud** under District of Columbia law. The elements of a cause of action for fraud are 1) a false representation, 2) in reference to a material fact, 3) made with the knowledge of its falsity, 4) with the intent to deceive, and 5) on which action is taken in reliance upon the representation. Here, there were issues of fact that precluded the granting of pretrial judgment for either party. The motions for pretrial judgment were denied. *Armstrong v. Accrediting Council for Continuing Education & Training, Inc.*, 961 F.Supp. 305 (D.D.C. 1997). [DC]

◆ *A fraud claim brought by nursing students against a school that had allegedly misrepresented its accreditation status failed where the students could not show that they relied on the school's misrepresentation.*

A Missouri nursing school graduated its first class of students in 1984. The school was accredited by the Missouri State Board of Nursing. It also was a "candidate for accreditation" with the North Central Association for Colleges and Schools (NCA). The NCA recommended that the school's brochure state that it was a "candidate for accreditation by the NCA." However, the brochure actually stated that the school "has ... been granted [NCA] candidacy for review status" and that "accreditation for [the school] is expected in 1983." In 1981, a letter from the student services coordinator restated the above-quoted information to the class of 1984. However, the students were not apprised of the NCA accreditation status prior to their graduation, and the school was not formally accredited until 1987. This accreditation status did not apply retroactively to the class of 1984. Several members of the class of 1984 filed suit in a Missouri trial court, alleging that the school intentionally misrepresented its accreditation status, which limited their job prospects, advanced education and future earning power. The trial court granted the school's motion for pretrial judgment, and the students appealed to the Missouri Court of Appeals.

The students contended that the school's affirmative statement regarding the likelihood of achieving accreditation legally bound it to disclose all material facts related to its receipt of NCA accreditation. Consequently, they argued, the school's silence on this issue was intentional misrepresentation. The court of appeals rejected the students' appeal. **Although misrepresentation of a material fact by silence may amount to actionable fraud, the students failed to show that they relied on the school's allegedly fraudulent statements in enrolling or remaining enrolled in the program.** Because the students failed to establish the reliance element of fraud, the court refused to address the issue of whether the school had a duty to disclose all material facts related to the anticipated accreditation. The holding of the trial court was affirmed. *Nigro v. Research College of Nursing*, 876 S.W.2d 681 (Mo. App. 1994). [MO]

C. Negligence

◆ *Students were allowed to sue accrediting agencies for negligence in the following case. The Higher Education Act did not preempt their lawsuit.*

An Arizona private technical school made certain positive representations to several prospective students about the school's accreditation status as well as the education, jobs and benefits they would receive during school and after they graduated. Based on these representations, the students obtained loans and enrolled at the school. They could not have obtained the loans if the school had not been accredited. The school went out of business prior to the students' graduation, leaving them with thousands of dollars in student loans to repay. The students filed a negligence lawsuit against the accrediting agencies in a U.S. district court, **alleging that they had negligently accredited and failed to monitor the school**. The court ruled that the Higher Education Act (HEA) preempted the students' negligence lawsuit and held for the agencies. The students appealed to the Ninth Circuit. The court of appeals noted that the HEA did not expressly preempt state common law tort claims against accreditors. It also declined to find an implied preemption. Consequently, the HEA did not preempt the students' claims. Rather, state courts had to decide whether to recognize a cause of action for negligent accreditation. *Keams v. Tempe Technical Institute Inc.*, 39 F.3d 222 (9th Cir. 1994). [AZ]

◆   *However, the lawsuit for negligence failed when the U.S. Court of Appeals held that the accrediting agencies did not have a duty to the students.*

In a subsequent case, a group of students, who had taken out federally guaranteed student loans in order to attend the Arizona technical institute, filed suit against the institute and the accrediting agencies in federal district court. They alleged that the agencies negligently accredited and monitored the institute, causing them monetary damages. The district court dismissed their lawsuit for failure to state a claim upon which relief could be granted, and the students appealed to the U.S. Court of Appeals, Ninth Circuit. The court of appeals noted that to establish a cause of action for negligence under Arizona law, **a plaintiff must establish that the defendant has a duty, recognized by law, to conform to a certain standard of conduct**. This duty can be imposed when both the person to whom the duty is owed and the risk are foreseeable to a reasonable person. The students argued that it was foreseeable to the agencies that the negligent performance of their duties would cause the alleged damages. The court disagreed, finding that the students had not sufficiently shown that the agencies had given them false information. It also found no Arizona cases that recognized a duty of care in this type of situation or held that accrediting agencies owe a duty to students attending the institutions that they accredit. The court affirmed the district court's decision. *Keams v. Tempe Technical Institute, Inc.*, 110 F.3d 44 (9th Cir. 1997). [AZ]

D. Withdrawal of Accreditation

◆   *A Texas court upheld provisions of the state education code requiring all private, post-secondary educational institutions to obtain accreditation.*

The Texas Legislature amended the state Higher Education Coordinating Act in 1975 to stem the operation of private post-secondary educational institutions as "degree mills" and to preserve the integrity of post-secondary degrees. New provisions required all private post-secondary educational institutions to obtain a certificate of authority from the Texas Higher Education

Coordinating Board before awarding credits or degrees. HEB Ministries operated three Christian post-secondary educational institutions in Texas. The Board informed HEB it was required to obtain accreditation before issuing credits or degrees. HEB sued the board in a state court, seeking a declaration that the act violated the Establishment and Free Exercise Clauses. The court upheld the law and a $170,000 penalty against HEB, and HEB appealed.

The Court of Appeals of Texas upheld § 61.304 of the state Education Code. Its language was facially neutral and it did not censor any religious subject or philosophy. **The provision had no hidden motivation targeting religious educational institutions and secular. Religious institutions of higher education were treated the same as others.** There was no government inquiry into the religious beliefs of HEB Ministries. There was no evidence to suggest that the legislature intended to thwart any religious sect in drafting the provision. The court upheld the $170,000 fine and imposed another $3,000 penalty on HEB. *HEB Ministries v. Texas Higher Education Coordinating Bd.*, 114 S.W.3d 617 (Tex. App. 2003). [TX]

♦ *A Florida business school was entitled to an injunction to stop an accrediting council from suspending its accreditation where it would suffer irreparable harm if the suspension were allowed and where it was likely to prevail on the merits of the case.*

The school was accredited by a council of independent schools and colleges. The council used a list of criteria in its accreditation decisions. In determining whether to continue accrediting the school, the council conducted an on-site evaluation and found that the school was not in compliance with a number of the listed criteria. Most importantly, less than 50 percent of the school's students had a high school diploma or its equivalent, and the number of students enrolled in nonbusiness programs exceeded the number enrolled in business programs. The school failed to adequately explain its noncompliance, the council suspended its accreditation, and a review board approved this decision. The school filed an emergency motion for injunctive relief in the U.S. District Court for the Southern District of Florida.

The court noted that its review was limited to whether the council's decision was arbitrary and unreasonable or supported by substantial evidence. Although the school had originally reported that most of its students did not have high school diplomas, it later discovered that the report was wrong because of a computer error. Actually, less than 50 percent of its students were without a diploma. The school also argued that it believed its cosmetology and nursing programs qualified as business programs based on language in the council's accreditation manual and the practices of other accrediting agencies. Because the school would not receive federal funding and would be closed if it did not receive accreditation, **the court found that it would suffer irreparable harm. This harm outweighed the harm that the council would suffer.** The court also found that the school showed a substantial likelihood of success on the merits. It granted the preliminary injunction and remanded the case for further proceedings. *Florida College of Business v. Accrediting Council for Independent Colleges and Schools*, 954 F.Supp. 256 (S.D. Fla. 1996). [FL]

◆ *The withdrawal of accreditation by a nonprofit agency was held not to be government action requiring compliance with the Fifth Amendment.*

An Illinois corporation was licensed as a vocational business school by the Illinois Department of Education. The Accrediting Council for Continuing Education and Training is a nonprofit agency recognized by the U.S. Department of Education as a national accrediting agency. The agency accredited the business school for five years but, following subsequent complaints, conducted an on-site examination and revoked the school's accreditation due to financial instability. The school appealed the decision pursuant to agency guidelines, and the matter was reconsidered. However, the withdrawal of accreditation was affirmed. The school appealed to the U.S. District Court for the Northern District of Illinois, alleging a Fifth Amendment due process claim and a violation of common law principles of fundamental fairness.

The school contended that the agency's actions could be attributed to the federal government and therefore required compliance with the Fifth Amendment. The court disagreed. There was not a sufficient nexus between the agency's actions and the federal government. Here, **the agency was a private corporation**. Even if the government promulgated regulations that the agency had to follow and officially recognized the agency, **this was not sufficient state action to require compliance with the U.S. Constitution**. The court also rejected the school's common-law claim. The agency's decision was not arbitrary, unreasonable or unsupported by substantial evidence. To the contrary, the agency had provided for a fair appeals process and had applied objectively fair standards. Here, the school's financial position had "substantially deteriorated," and it might not have been able to complete the instruction of all its enrollees. Accordingly, both the constitutional claim and the common-law claim were dismissed. The agency's decision was affirmed. *Peoria School of Business v. Accrediting Council*, 805 F.Supp. 579 (N.D. Ill. 1992). [IL]

◆ *Where a decision to withdraw accreditation was not arbitrary or capricious, a federal court should not have ordered the agency to continue the accreditation.*

The Commission on Occupational Education Institutions (COEI) is part of the Southern Association of Colleges and Schools (SACS). It was set up to accredit postsecondary, nondegree granting institutions. In March 1988, COEI conducted an on-site inspection of a cosmetology school's campuses to determine whether to reaffirm accreditation. After finding various problems (violations of dual accreditation and of refund and disclosure policies, and failure to submit an annual report for 1986), COEI dropped the school's accreditation. Since this was a prerequisite for the students' receipt of federal financial assistance, the school sued COEI and SACS to stop the disaccreditation. A federal court issued an injunction preventing SACS from withdrawing the school's accreditation for at least one year, and it further ordered SACS to pay the school's attorneys' fees and costs.

During the SACS appeal to the U.S. Court of Appeals, Fifth Circuit, five of the school's six campuses closed. The school voluntarily relinquished SACS accreditation for the other campus. This rendered the validity of the injunction moot. However, the court of appeals found that it had to reach the merits of the case because of the question of attorneys' fees and costs. The court then noted that **there had been clear evidence that the school had been in violation of the dual accreditation policy set by COEI**. The district court had incorrectly found that COEI's policy language was vague. It should have accorded COEI's accreditation decisions greater deference. Thus, the court reversed the district court's award to the school and held that it was not entitled to attorneys' fees and costs. *Wilfred Academy v. Southern Ass'n of Colleges and Schools*, 957 F.2d 210 (5th Cir. 1992). [TX]

◆ *An accrediting agency did not have to accredit a teaching hospital run by the Catholic church, because the hospital did not train future physicians on abortion procedures.*

A teaching hospital followed the guidelines of the Roman Catholic Church. One of the programs offered was in obstetrics and gynecology. This program was cited as deficient by the Accrediting Council for Graduate Medical Education (ACGME) for four reasons. One of those reasons was failure to provide training in abortion, sterilization, and artificial contraception (family planning). This specific deficiency led through probation and hearings to the eventual revocation of the hospital's accreditation. The hospital filed suit in a federal district court, claiming that by forcing a choice between religious principles and accreditation the ACGME violated the hospital's rights guaranteed by the Free Exercise Clause of the First Amendment. The court found the hospital had a sincerely held religious belief that was restricted. However, ACGME had satisfied its burden of showing that it furthered an essential public interest in the least restrictive manner. **Physicians leaving the hospital would be licensed to practice family planning, including abortion, without being trained.** There was no other method by which ACGME could assure the public's interest in safety other than to require the contested training. Also, the procedures followed by ACGME to remove its accreditation fully comported with the Due Process Clause, and its standards of accreditation were fair. Removal of the hospital's accreditation was upheld.

On a motion for reconsideration, and a request for an injunction, the court restated its opinion that the school was unlikely to win at trial. It also held that the accreditation requirements did not irreparably or unnecessarily violate the hospital's First Amendment rights. They allowed residents to get training in family planning with an outside institution. Similarly, a loss of accreditation is not irreparable. The hospital was free to modify its program and reapply for accreditation. Next, the court found that accreditation was ACGME's sole function; restraint of that function would surely result in harm. Finally, the court viewed the accreditation requirements of a residency program as a safeguard of the public's interest, which leaned toward denial of the injunction request. The injunction pending appeal was denied. *St. Agnes Hospital of the City of Baltimore v. Riddick*, 748 F.Supp. 319, 751 F.Supp. 75 (D. Md. 1990). [MD]

IV. CONSTRUCTION AND OUTSIDE CONTRACTS

◆ *A university that did a thorough environmental impact evaluation of a construction project did not have to file an environmental impact statement.*

A New York state university planned five separate campus housing projects, including a 116-unit building for which it filed a full environmental assessment form that was supported by an environmental site assessment report. A lawsuit nevertheless ensued, seeking to compel the university to file an environmental impact statement and seeking a temporary injunction to prevent construction until such statement was filed. The New York Supreme Court, Appellate Division, ruled that the university did not have to file an environmental impact statement because its thorough study of the environmental effects of construction concluded that there would not be an adverse impact on wetlands, cultural resources, groundwater, air quality, solid waste, removal of vegetation, wildlife or open space such that the project should be stopped. **In light of the university's thorough evaluation, the project could proceed.** *Forman v. Trustees of State Univ. of New York*, 757 N.Y.S.2d 180 (A.D. 2003). [NY]

◆ *A university was entitled to money from a contractor who underbid a project and then sought to recoup its losses as additional work.*

The University of Alaska solicited bids for fixing a drainage problem involving an access road and gravel pad surfaces at a research facility. **It accepted the lowest bid, but then experienced problems with the contractor.** The contractor first obtained a one-week extension, then sought approval for extra materials, extra work and the payment of additional money. The university rejected the claims. When the contractor failed to finish the project on time, the ground froze, and it was unable to complete the project. Both the university and the contractor sought financial reimbursement, and a hearing officer determined that the contractor underbid the project, then sought to recover its losses as additional work. However, the university also owed some additional monies to the contractor. The case reached the Supreme Court of Alaska, which largely upheld the hearing officer's determinations. It refused, however, to grant the university liquidated damages because the university had entered into an agreement with the contractor's bonding company regarding the hiring of another contractor to finish the project. *Lakloey, Inc. v. University of Alaska*, 2002 WL 1732561 (Alaska 7/24/02). [AK]

◆ *Fact issues prevented a court from granting pretrial judgment to a university on a breach of contract claim involving an electrical contractor.*

A New York university hired an electrical contractor to perform work on a biomolecular medicine and residential tower. Shortly after the contract was signed, the project fell behind schedule. The electrical contractor blamed the construction manager and inadequate security, which led to vandalism and theft, forcing the electrical contractor to redo some work. Eventually, a lawsuit was filed, with the electrical contractor asserting that the university breached the contract by failing to pay for work performed, and the university asserting that it had to correct and complete work the electrical contractor was supposed to finish. A New York court granted pretrial judgment to the university, but the Supreme Court, Appellate Division, reversed. **Evidence existed indicating that the electrical contractor performed its obligations under the contract.** The court remanded the case for further proceedings. *F. Garofalo Electric Co. v. New York Univ.*, 754 N.Y.S.2d 227 (App. Div. 2002). [NY]

◆ *A coffee shop breached its lease agreement with a university by refusing to pay rent after a competitor opened a shop on campus.*
    An Ohio university entered into a 10-year lease with a coffee shop for one of the sections of its food court. The university agreed that competition between like products among shops would be strongly discouraged. Later, another coffee seller opened a location in the student center, and the coffee shop stopped paying rent. The university sued it for breach of contract, and the coffee shop defended by asserting that the university breached the non-compete agreement of the lease by allowing the competitor onto the university campus. The Ohio Court of Claims ruled in favor of the university, finding that it only had a duty not to allow competitors into the food court. **Since the competitor was not located in the food court with the coffee shop, the university did not breach the non-compete agreement.** The court ordered the coffee shop to pay the university over $37,000 in damages for past-due rent and common area charges. *Kent State Univ. v. University Coffee House, Inc.*, 776 N.E.2d 583 (Ohio Ct. Cl. 2002). [OH]

◆ *A university could not recover from a contractor for an explosion and fire several years after the construction of a power plant.*
    The University of Colorado contracted with a construction company to build a co-generation power facility on its Boulder campus. The contract contained a provision stating that **acceptance of the work would constitute a release of all claims against the company**, and also contained a 12-month warranty period. However, the university purchased an extended five-year warranty from the subcontractor that furnished the gas turbine engines for the facility. After the facility had been in operation for three and a half years, a combination of events caused a backup in one engine, resulting in an explosion and fire. The university sued the contractor and subcontractor for breach of contract, breach of warranty, negligence and strict liability. A state court ruled for the defendants, and the Colorado Court of Appeals affirmed. Here, the contractor's warranty and the release clearly protected it from liability. Also, with respect to the subcontractor, the jury's ruling was not unsupported by the evidence. *Regents of the Univ. of Colorado v. Harbert Construction Co.*, 2001 WL 1381147 (Colo. App. 11/8/01). [CO]

◆ *West Virginia's highest court set forth five factors to be used in determining whether a construction project is a public project.*
    West Virginia University and the West Virginia University Foundation (a private, nonprofit corporation) began planning and developing a layout for the construction of a building to be known as the University Services Center. After a bidding process, a developer agreed to build the center at its own cost and risk. The foundation would then purchase the site and lease the building to the

university. When an affiliation of construction trades sued for a declaration that the proposed construction was a public project governed by state wage and competitive bidding laws, the university and the nonprofit foundation moved for pretrial judgment. A state court granted the motion, finding that the foundation was not a state agency, and its connection to the university did not convert the construction into a public project. The West Virginia Supreme Court of Appeals affirmed. It listed five factors to be used in determining whether a construction project is a public project and held that **the lower court record was not sufficiently developed to determine whether public funds had been used on the project.** Further, the building was now completed, and there was no indication of wage violations. *Affiliated Construction Trades Foundation v. University of West Virginia Bd. of Trustees*, 557 S.E.2d 863 (W. Va. 2001). [WV]

◆ *A university could widen a road through property it did not own where doing so would not interfere with the property owner's rights.*

Georgetown University, as the successor-in-interest to an easement through property owned by a District of Columbia agency, sought to widen the easement based on its rights in an amended deed. The easement was being used as a road that was 12 feet wide, and the university wanted to make the road 14 feet wide. The agency claimed that the university was trying to relocate the easement, and that it did not have the right to do so. Georgetown asserted that it was merely expanding the road, not relocating the easement. A federal court ruled in favor of the university, finding that **the language of the deed clearly allowed Georgetown to expand the road as long as doing so would not interfere with the agency's use of the property.** Here, since the widening of the road would not interfere with the agency's use of the property, the easement could be expanded. *Washington Metropolitan Area Transit Authority v. Georgetown Univ.*, 180 F.Supp.2d 137 (D.D.C. 2001). [DC]

CHAPTER TEN

School Finance

I. PUBLIC ASSISTANCE TO SCHOOLS

Since public schools are financed by a combination of tuition and public grants, finance issues seldom arise in the courts. For the most part, this chapter focuses on the much more common private school finance issues that have reached the courts in recent years.

The Establishment Clause of the First Amendment prohibits Congress from making any law respecting an establishment of religion. It has been construed by the U.S. Supreme Court as prohibiting direct financial assistance by government agencies to religious schools and colleges. In 1997, the Court decided Agostini v. Felton, *521 U.S. 203, 117 S.Ct. 1997, 138 L.Ed.2d 391, an important private school finance case in which the Court abandoned the presumption that the presence of public employees on parochial school grounds creates a symbolic union between church and state that violates the Establishment Clause. Under* Agostini, *government assistance to private schools must not result in government indoctrination or endorsement of religion. The recipients of government assistance must not be defined by reference to their religion, and the assistance must not create excessive entanglement between church and state.*

A. Federal Funding

◆ *The Supreme Court held that the receipt of Higher Education Facilities Act funds by four religious colleges did not violate the Establishment Clause.*

The Higher Education Facilities Act of 1963 contained an exclusion for any facility used for sectarian instruction or as a place of religious worship or any facility that is used primarily as part of a school divinity department. Federal education officials had powers to enforce the statute for a 20-year time period during which they could seek to recover funds from violators. A group of Connecticut taxpayers filed a federal district court action against government officials and four religious colleges that received Higher Education Facilities Act funds, seeking an order against the release of funds to sectarian institutions that used federal funds to construct libraries and other facilities. The court held the act did not have the effect of promoting religion.

The U.S. Supreme Court reviewed the case and held that the statute had been carefully drafted to ensure that no federal funds were disbursed to support the sectarian aspects of these institutions. **The four colleges named as defendants in this case had not violated any of the restrictions in the statute, as they had placed no religious symbols in facilities constructed with the use of federal funds, and had not used the facilities for any religious purposes.** There was no evidence that any of the colleges maintained a predominantly religious atmosphere, and although each of them was affiliated with the Catholic Church, none excluded non-Catholics from admissions or faculty appointments, and none of them required attendance at religious services. The receipt of funds by the colleges did not violate the Establishment Clause. The Court held, however, that the 20-year limit on federal oversight created the potential for religious use of the facilities after the 20 years expired. Because of the risk of use of the facilities for advancing religion, the court invalidated this portion of the legislation. *Tilton v. Richardson*, 403 U.S. 672, 91 S.Ct. 2091, 29 L.Ed.2d 790 (1971). [CT]

◆ *A government agency could seek a refund of grant money to equalize the amounts spent by it and by the university foundation awarded the grant.*

A nonprofit foundation for a California university submitted a project proposal designed to retrain defense engineers for positions in small businesses or manufacturing. The estimated cost of the program was $1,179,544, and the foundation sought $593,166 from a federal grant program administered by the National Science Foundation (NSF). The NSF awarded the foundation $550,000 under a three-year grant that required the foundation to essentially match the grant funds, and to maintain detailed accounting records of all costs as well as of the matching funds. When the NSF later suspected that the foundation was not meeting its financial obligations, an audit was conducted, and a recommendation was made that the NSF should seek a refund of approximately $140,000. The foundation sued to prevent the NSF from obtaining a refund, but a Virginia federal court ruled in favor of the NSF. The Fourth Circuit affirmed, finding that **the foundation had breached the terms of the grant regarding its obligation to fund or obtain funding for approximately half the costs of the program.** The foundation also had improperly stated certain amounts paid to the engineers as matching funds. As a result, the lower court had properly required the foundation to refund part of the grant money to the NSF. *California State Univ. Fullerton Foundation v. National Science Foundation*, 26 Fed. Appx. 263 (4th Cir. 2002). [VA]

◆ *A fired professor was not entitled to be paid her salary out of grant funds the university received.*

An immunologist at an Illinois university received a grant from the National Science Foundation based on her research. She was later fired by the university and sued it for discrimination. She also filed a motion for injunctive relief, asking the university to pay her grant salary. An Illinois federal court denied her request because she failed to demonstrate that she was entitled to the grant money. Here, **the NSF Grant Policy Manual gave the grantee (the university) full responsibility over the project and permitted it to remove the principal investigator**. The grantee could then continue the project under the direction of another principal investigator. Since the NSF was not the party responsible for paying the immunologist's salary, she failed to show that she was entitled to compensation under the grant. *Nanda v. Board of Trustees of Univ. of Illinois*, 2002 WL 398516 (N.D. Ill. 3/15/02). [IL]

◆ *The U.S. Court of Appeals, Second Circuit, upheld federal regulations published under Title IV of the Higher Education Act as representing a reasonable interpretation of the statute.*

Title IV of the Higher Education Act, 20 U.S.C. § 1091b(a), requires college and post-secondary vocational training schools that receive federal funds for student financial aid programs to establish a fair and equitable policy for refunding unearned tuition and other costs when a student receiving such aid fails to enter or prematurely leaves the intended program. Subsection (b) declares that an institution's refund policy shall be considered fair and equitable if the refund is at least the largest of the amounts provided under state law, the institution's nationally recognized accrediting agency formula, or the statutorily described formula for pro rata refunds.

A regulation issued by the Secretary of Education (found at 34 CFR § 668.22(b)(4)) provided that schools had to deduct "any unpaid charges owed by the student for the period of enrollment for which the student has been charged." Former regulations had put the risk of student nonpayment on the government. A coalition of vocational training schools in New York sought a federal district court injunction against the operation of the regulation. The court granted the injunction, but the U.S. Court of Appeals, Second Circuit, vacated the injunction and stated that **§ 668.22(b)(4) represented a reasonable interpretation of the statute**. The statute set a minimum refund amount but did not bar the secretary from asking for a larger amount. *Coalition of New York State Career Schools Inc. v. Riley*, 129 F.3d 276 (2d Cir. 1997). [NY]

◆ *A federal district court upheld regulations under 1992 amendments to the Higher Education Act as rationally related to legitimate government interests.*

The amendments added a new eligibility requirement so that proprietary institutions had to derive at least 15 percent of their revenues from non-Title

VII Funds in order to be eligible for participation in Title VII programs. This was intended to attract students based upon the quality of an institution's programs, rather than its offer of federal student financial assistance. The Department of Education proposed regulations that interpreted "revenue" to mean funds received by the institution from tuition and fees plus funds from other activities necessary to the education and training offered by the institution. It further determined that the revenue calculation pursuant to the formula promulgated by the department was to use a cash-based accounting system and was to go into effect about 60 days later. Several private Puerto Rico institutions that relied heavily on Title VII funds sued to prevent implementation of the regulations.

The court determined that the department's interpretation of revenue reflected the demand for the institutions' educational services and was not arbitrary or capricious. Further, the department complied with the Administrative Procedure Act by publishing a notice of proposed rule-making and providing interested parties 60 days to respond. Nothing in the law required the department to extend the notice period. Because institutions that cannot meet statutory requirements do not have property or liberty rights under the Fifth Amendment, the regulations did not constitute a taking of these interests. The court also noted that **Congress had a legitimate interest in providing better education by tightening the eligibility requirements for Title VII funds**. Consequently, the **regulations were rationally related to legitimate government interests and did not violate the Equal Protection Clause** of the Fourteenth Amendment. The court denied the institutions' request for an injunction. *Ponce Paramedical College v. U.S. Dep't of Educ.*, 858 F.Supp. 303 (D.P.R. 1994). [PR]

B. State Funding

For more than a generation, courts have analyzed Establishment Clause cases under the framework established by the U.S. Supreme Court in Lemon v. Kurtzman. *In recent years, the test has been criticized by legal experts and by members of the Court itself. Nonetheless, the three-part* Lemon *test remains an important one for assessing the validity of government programs under the Establishment Clause and is still routinely applied by the courts.*

◆ In *Lemon v. Kurtzman,* the Court invalidated Rhode Island and Pennsylvania statutes that provided state money to finance the operation of parochial schools. The Rhode Island statute provided a 15 percent salary supplement to parochial school teachers who taught nonreligious subjects using public school teaching materials. The Pennsylvania statute authorized payment of state funds to parochial schools to help defray the cost of teachers' salaries, textbooks and other instructional materials. Reimbursement was limited, however, to the costs of secular subjects, which also were taught in the public schools. The Supreme Court evaluated the Rhode Island and Pennsylvania programs using its **three-part test: First, the statute must have a secular legislative purpose; second, its principal or primary effect must be one that neither advances nor inhibits religion, finally; the statute must not foster "an excessive government entanglement with religion."** Applying this test to the two state programs in question, the Court held that the legislative purpose of the programs was a legitimate, secular concern with maintaining high educational standards in both public and private schools.

The Court did not reach the second inquiry because it held that the state programs failed under the third inquiry. The Rhode Island salary supplement program excessively entangled the state with religion because of the highly religious nature of the Catholic schools that were the primary beneficiaries of the program. The teachers who received the salary supplements provided instruction in classrooms and buildings containing religious symbols such as crucifixes. In such an atmosphere, even a person dedicated to remaining religiously neutral probably would allow some religious content to creep into the ostensibly secular instruction. Similar defects were found in the Pennsylvania program. The Court also observed that in order to ensure that the state-funded parochial school teachers did not inject religious dogma into their instruction, the state would be forced to extensively monitor the parochial school classrooms. This would result in excessive state entanglement with religion. Consequently, **the salary supplement programs were held to violate the Establishment Clause of the First Amendment**. *Lemon v. Kurtzman*, 403 U.S. 602, 91 S.Ct. 2105, 29 L.Ed.2d 745 (1971). [RI, PA]

◆ *In* Hunt v. McNair, *the Supreme Court upheld a South Carolina plan that allowed both private and public colleges to use the state's authority to borrow money at low interest rates.*

Hunt v. McNair involved a Baptist college that used state funding to finance the construction of a dining hall. The college had no religious test for either its faculty or students, and the student body was only about 60 percent Baptist, the same percentage found in the surrounding community. The Supreme Court found that the college was not "pervaded by religion." **Unlike the situation commonly found in K-12 parochial schools, religiously affiliated colleges and universities are often not dominated by a religious atmosphere.** The Court concluded that both **the purpose and effect of the state's borrowing program was secular and was therefore constitutional**. The argument that aid to one (secular) portion of a religious institution makes it free to spend more money on religious pursuits was rejected as unpersuasive and irrelevant. If that were the case, the Court noted, police and fire protection for religious schools would have to be cut off as well. *Hunt v. McNair*, 413 U.S. 734, 93 S.Ct. 2868, 37 L.Ed.2d 923 (1973). [SC]

◆ *The Supreme Court held that the "secular side" of a college could be distinguished from sectarian programs, making it permissible for a state to provide funding to a religiously affiliated college, where the assistance goes only to a college's secular side.*

The state of Maryland enacted a program that authorized annual, noncategorical grants to religiously affiliated colleges. The program was challenged by taxpayers who alleged that state money was being put to religious uses by the schools, which had wide discretion in spending the funds. The Supreme Court began its analysis of the Maryland program with the following observation: "*Hunt [v. McNair]* requires (1) that no state aid at all go to institutions that are so "pervasively sectarian" that secular activities cannot be separated from sectarian ones, and (2) that if secular activities can be separated out, they alone may be funded."

The colleges involved in this case were not found to be pervasively sectarian even though they were affiliated with the Catholic Church. The Court held that the "secular side" of the colleges could be separated from the sectarian and found that **state aid had only gone to the colleges' secular side**. It was admittedly somewhat difficult to ensure that the colleges and the Maryland Council for Higher Education would take care to avoid spending state funds on religious activities, but the Court expressed its belief that those entities would spend the money in good faith and avoid violating the First Amendment. *Roemer v. Board of Public Works*, 426 U.S. 736, 96 S.Ct. 2337, 49 L.Ed.2d 179 (1976). [MD]

◆ *A city development board could issue tax-exempt bonds to a sectarian university for a building project.*

A Christian university began a renovation project and sought $15 million in low-interest loans from the Industrial Development Board for Nashville, Tennessee. The board approved the loan and issued tax-exempt bonds to the university. A group of taxpayers sued, asserting that the bond issuance impermissibly benefited a religious university in violation of the Establishment Clause. A federal court ruled that the university was so pervasively sectarian that no state aid could go to it. The Sixth Circuit Court of Appeals reversed, noting that **the tax-exempt bonds did not violate the Establishment Clause**. First, public funds were not used to issue the bonds; the university had to arrange for private financing, and bond purchasers only had recourse against the university. Second, the bonds were issued in a neutral manner to nonprofit organizations. And third, the bonds advanced the secular objective of promoting economic development. The university was entitled to receive the tax-exempt bonds. *Steele v. Industrial Development Bd. of Metropolitan Government of Nashville*, 301 F.3d 401 (6th Cir. 2002). [TN]

◆ *A Wisconsin program allowing unrestricted telecommunications access grants to sectarian schools and colleges violated the Establishment Clause.*

A 1997 Wisconsin law created the Technology for Education Achievement (TEACH) Board, which administered the Education Telecommunications Access program. The TEACH board approved access for data lines and video links under a heavily subsidized program in which both public and private schools participated. A taxpayer group objected to the program on constitutional grounds because $58,873 of the program's annual total of over $1.9 million was awarded to nine religiously affiliated Wisconsin schools and private colleges. The taxpayers sued state education officials, including the TEACH board, challenging the program as unconstitutional. The court held that the program as a whole did not violate the Constitution, but found that unrestricted cash grants to private, sectarian schools violated the Establishment Clause's prohibition on state support of religion.

The parties appealed unfavorable aspects of the decision to the Seventh Circuit. The taxpayers dismissed their appeal concerning the constitutionality of the full program in view of the U.S. Supreme Court's intervening decision in *Mitchell v. Helms*, 530 U.S. 793 (2000). In *Mitchell*, the Supreme Court upheld the constitutionality of a state-aid program that helped parochial schools acquire computers, televisions, and laboratory equipment. The Seventh Circuit proceeded to the question of grants to religious schools, noting that **the Wisconsin law violated the third *Agostini* criteria, because in the absence of any restriction on the expenditure of public funds by the schools, the expenditures had a primary effect that advanced religion**. The subsidies could easily be used for maintenance, chapels, religious instruction, or connection time to view religious Web sites. The law did not bar schools from using the grants for these and other constitutionally impermissible purposes. Because direct aid from the government to a sectarian institution in any form is invalid, the court affirmed the district court's finding that the direct subsidies to religious schools were unconstitutional. *Freedom From Religion Foundation Inc. v. Bugher*, 249 F.3d 606 (7th Cir. 2001). [WI]

◆   *The Fourth Circuit determined a college operated by the Seventh-Day Adventist Church was eligible for state aid for secular programs.*

Maryland's Joseph A. Selinger program gives public aid to private colleges in the state. Qualifying colleges receive direct payments from the state to be used for secular purposes. In 1990, Columbia Union College applied for Selinger funds, but the Maryland Higher Education Commission denied the application because it believed the college was too sectarian. A few years later, the school sought reconsideration of its application in view of *Rosenberger v. Rector and Visitors of the University of Virginia*, 515 U.S. 819 (1995), which emphasized the importance of neutral criteria in determining eligibility for public aid. The commission continued to reject the school's application. In 1996, Columbia Union applied for Selinger aid to specifically fund its math, computer science, clinical laboratory science, respiratory care and nursing programs, but again the request was denied. The school sued, alleging constitutional and statutory violations. The district court applied the reasoning in *Roemer* to find that Columbia Union was not "pervasively sectarian." Therefore, it was eligible for Selinger funds.

The commission appealed, arguing that the district court wrongly concluded the school was not pervasively sectarian. Columbia Union countered that whether an institution is pervasively sectarian is no longer relevant when determining an institution's eligibility for public aid, in light of *Mitchell v. Helms*, 530 U.S. 793 (2000). In *Mitchell*, the Supreme Court upheld the constitutionality of a state-aid program that helped parochial schools acquire computers, televisions, and laboratory equipment. The Supreme Court used the test outlined in *Agostini v. Felton*, 521 U.S. 203 (1997), examining whether the program had a secular purpose and whether it had the primary effect of inhibiting or advancing religion. Using these cases, the court ruled that **giving Selinger funds to Columbia Union had a secular purpose and did not advance religion because the aid had to be used for secular purposes**. Although the college had a mandatory worship policy, it applied only to a minority of students. Also, the college's traditional liberal arts classes were not taught with the primary objective of religious indoctrination. Although the

Seventh-day Adventist Church had a strong influence over college affairs, and the college preferred to hire and admit members of that faith, these factors by themselves were not enough to make the college pervasively sectarian. *Columbia Union College v. Oliver*, 254 F.3d 496 (4th Cir. 2001). [MD]

◆ *The Virginia Supreme Court held that a Christian school could raise funds for new facilities through the issuance of revenue bonds under a state program without violating the U.S. or Virginia Constitutions.*

Regent University is a private Christian university that applied for assistance under the Educational Facilities Authority Act, seeking financing for various construction projects including new classrooms, administrative space, a communication and arts complex, and an events center. The Virginia College Building Authority (VCBA) approved the application and issued the requested revenue bonds. As a result, members of Americans United for Separation of Church and State, an advocacy group, challenged VCBA's action. A state trial court held that Regent was ineligible for participation in the VCBA program because it is a "pervasively sectarian institution and because its primary purpose is 'religious training'."

The Virginia Supreme Court reversed. Even though Regent was "pervasively sectarian" both in policy and practice, the court focused on the secular purpose of the university and found that its receipt of bonds did not violate the Establishment Clause of the First Amendment. The court distinguished seminaries, which educate students for religious vocations, from church-related colleges, which offer various degrees for secular vocations. Here, the school offered over 20 different graduate degrees in the areas of business, education and journalism. It also was approved by the Southern Association of Colleges and Schools to award masters' and doctoral degrees, and its law school was accredited by the American Bar Association. Because the bond proceeds did not involve governmental aid (the bonds were purchased by private investors who chose to invest in VCBA bonds), the university was eligible to participate in the bond program. **Since no taxpayer dollars flowed into the bonds, VCBA's approval of Regent's application did not involve "excessive government entanglement with religion."** Further, the VCBA program could not reasonably be viewed as an endorsement of religion. *Virginia College Building Authority v. Lynn*, 260 Va. 608, 538 S.E.2d 682 (Va. 2000). [VA]

◆ *However, in 1991, the Supreme Court of Virginia held that a university with a pervasively religious mission could not receive the proceeds of a city bond issue without violating the Establishment Clauses of the U.S. and Virginia Constitutions.*

Liberty University is a private, sectarian institution that is closely related to a local Baptist church. It required all of its students and faculty to comply with clearly spelled out religious requirements. The Lynchburg, Virginia, city council and Industrial Development Authority (IDA) approved the issuance of up to $60 million of Educational Facilities Revenue Bonds in order to assist Liberty University in building and developing academic and administrative facilities in Lynchburg. The validity of the bond issue with respect to both the

U.S. and Virginia Constitutions came under question. The IDA filed an action to answer those questions. A Virginia trial court validated the bond issue, and a group of opposing taxpayers appealed to the Supreme Court of Virginia.

The main issue was whether the bond issuance violated the Establishment Clauses of the U.S. or Virginia Constitutions. The First Amendment states, "Congress shall make no law respecting the establishment of religion." The court turned to a number of decisions in which the U.S. Supreme Court has allowed comparable arrangements for other church-related schools. Those decisions involved schools that imposed no religious requirements for admission or employment, or religious requirements for students or faculty while affiliated with the school. The court contrasted Liberty's policies and found the bond issuance unconstitutional. Liberty had published policies requiring specific church attendance six times per week. Academic freedom also was limited. **The court found Liberty to be "a religious mission" with a "pervasive aim [of] equipping young people for evangelistic ministry." Because of this pervasiveness, the bond issue could only have the effect of establishing religion.** The trial court judgment was reversed. *Habel v. Industrial Development Authority*, 400 S.E.2d 516 (Va. 1991). [VA]

◆   *The Wisconsin Court of Appeals held that a lower court would have to hold a trial to determine whether a private religious college could constitutionally receive state aid. It could not otherwise determine crucial issues such as whether the college was "pervasively sectarian."*

Wisconsin legislators provided a $100,000 grant to a private religiously affiliated college for the establishment of an "international center." The college was a nonprofit organization that was required by its articles of incorporation to be run "within the context of theology, philosophy, [and] other teachings and doctrines of the Roman Catholic Church." Also, a religious organization was the sole shareholder of the college and had complete power to appoint its board of directors and amend or repeal its articles of incorporation. The grant did not further specify the legislature's purpose or whether the activities held in the center would be religious or secular. An assembly of opposed citizens filed suit in a state court against the governor. They sought to reverse the grant and argued that it violated the First Amendment of the U.S. Constitution as well as Article 1, § 18 of the Wisconsin Constitution.

The trial court found that the grant was unconstitutional on its face and granted the citizens judgment on the pleadings. The state appealed to **the Wisconsin Court of Appeals, which held that whether the purpose of the grant was permissible would need to be determined at trial**. The citizens argued that the college was "pervasively sectarian," such that no state aid would be constitutional. It based that argument on the school's control structure. The school asserted that, despite its legal structure, the day-to-day management was done by a board of trustees, of which no more than 30 percent could be members of the religious organization. A trial would resolve these issues. *Freedom from Religion Foundation, Inc. v. Thompson*, 476 N.W.2d 318 (Wis. App. 1991). [WI]

II. PUBLIC ASSISTANCE TO STUDENTS

The U.S. Supreme Court held in Grove City College v. Bell, *below, that private schools whose students receive federal funds are deemed to be recipients of federal assistance. Therefore, even a college with an unbending policy of rejecting all forms of government assistance was required to comply with federal laws because its students received federal grants and loans.*

A. School Funding Issues

◆   *In* Grove City College v. Bell, *the U.S. Supreme Court held that a private college was a recipient of federal financial assistance, and thus subject to Title IX of the Education Amendments of 1972, because its students received federal grants.*

A private college, which had an "unbending policy" of refusing all forms of government assistance in order to remain independent of governmental restrictions, was asked by the Department of Education (DOE) to supply "assurance of compliance" with Title IX, which the college refused to do on the ground that it was receiving no federal funding. The DOE disagreed, saying that because the school enrolled large numbers of students receiving federal Basic Educational Opportunity Grants (BEOGs), it was receiving financial assistance for purposes of Title IX. The DOE then cut off student financial assistance based on the college's failure to execute the assurance of compliance. Four students and the college brought suit challenging the termination of financial assistance. **The Supreme Court held that the college was a recipient of federal financial assistance and was thus subject to the statute prohibiting sex discrimination. This was so despite the fact that only some of the college's students received BEOGs and even though the college did not receive any direct federal financial assistance.** Thus, the college was obliged to submit assurance of compliance, but only with regard to the administration of its financial aid program, in order for students to continue to receive federal aid. *Grove City College v. Bell*, 465 U.S. 555, 104 S.Ct. 1211, 79 L.Ed.2d 516 (1984). [PA]

◆   *A private university system in Puerto Rico lost its appeal seeking review of the U.S. Department of Education's determination that the university system did not meet the eligibility requirements for student financial assistance programs under Title IV of the Higher Education Act.*

In 1991 and 1992, the DOE found the university system, Sistema Universitario Ana G. Mendez, was not eligible for Title IV programs dealing with Pell grant programs. As a result of the DOE's finding, **the university system was responsible for refunding to the federal government $1,712,540 in student grant funds** that were dispersed from 1989 to 1991. The secretary of education's determination was based on the fact that the university system failed to license its additional campuses. When filling out its Title IV application forms, the university system did not report these campuses under the "additional locations" section. It also failed to obtain prior approval from the Puerto Rico Commission on Higher Education for most of the satellite locations. The university system filed an administrative challenge, but a DOE administrative law judge affirmed its $1.7 million liability. The university system appealed to a federal district court, which reversed the administrative decision, finding the satellite campuses were licensed. However, it also found that the certifications did not necessarily constitute legal authorization under the Higher Education Act. On remand, the DOE determined that the certifications did not constitute legal authorization. The district court affirmed.

The university system then asked the U.S. Court of Appeals for the First Circuit to determine whether the Higher Education Act gives the secretary of education the final word on whether a university program is legally authorized by a state under the act and is therefore eligible for Title IV funding. The First Circuit held that **the Higher Education Act does not explicitly give either the secretary of education or the states the exclusive right to determine "legal authorization."** However, the court reasoned that it is not impermissible or unreasonable to allow the secretary to make that determination. The DOE's finding of liability was affirmed. *Sistema Universitario Ana G. Mendez v. Riley*, 234 F.3d 772 (1st Cir. 2000). [PR]

◆   *In the following case, the U.S. Court of Appeals, Ninth Circuit, held that the Higher Education Act does not confer upon educational institutions a private right of action to sue loan guarantors. However, a school, which serviced loans for a large number of minority students, had stated a claim against Arizona's designated federal loan guarantor under 42 U.S.C. § 1981.*

The federal government appointed a private corporation as Arizona's designated guarantor of federally funded and mandated student loan programs. The corporation then terminated a private business school's participation in the Arizona loan guaranty program. The school, which serviced a large number of minority students, filed a race discrimination claim against the corporation in federal court, alleging violations of the Equal Protection Clause pursuant to 42 U.S.C. §§ 1981 and 1983. It also alleged that the corporation terminated its participation in the program without a hearing in violation of the Due Process Clause of the Fifth and Fourteenth Amendments. The district court dismissed both of the claims, and the school appealed to the U.S. Court of Appeals, Ninth Circuit.

The court of appeals held that **the Higher Education Act (HEA) does not confer upon educational institutions a private right of action to sue loan guarantors.** Congress intended review by the secretary pursuant to the requirements of the Administrative Procedure Act to be the exclusive means for ensuring a lender's compliance with the statutes and regulations. The court also dismissed the school's constitutional claim pursuant to 42 U.S.C. § 1983, ruling that the corporation did not act "under color of state law" as the statute required. Specifically, there was no nexus between the state and the challenged termination, the corporation had no sovereign powers, the HEA expressly provided for private guarantors, and the state did not compel the offensive action. However, the court of appeals reversed the district court dismissal of the constitutional claim pursuant to 42 U.S.C. § 1981. The students here were improperly being prevented from attending a private school. **Because the corporation's alleged discrimination could arguably destroy the school's business and property, the school stated a claim under § 1981.** The trial court ruling was affirmed in part and reversed in part. *Parks School of Business, Inc. v. Symington*, 51 F.3d 1480 (9th Cir. 1995). [AZ]

◆   *A federal district court upheld the inspector general's ability to subpoena documents in student loan cases.*

A private Delaware school was one of the nation's largest recipients of Pell Grants and Stafford Loans. The school underwent what was intended to be a routine audit by the Inspector General. The audit was necessary because there were $54 million in Stafford Loans (federally guaranteed student loans) in default. This represented 46 percent of the total amount outstanding from students who had received loans to attend this school. Concurrent with the audit, an investigation began, involving the FBI and the inspector general. After the audit was completed, the FBI seized documents and computer files as part of a further investigation. This seizure was ruled unlawful, and the record of the brief investigation was destroyed. After the records were returned to the school, the inspector general served a subpoena in an attempt to review the documents and files. The school then sued to oppose the subpoena.

The issue in this case involved determining what the inspector general was authorized to subpoena. The school stated that there were so many documents and files called for that it would be unduly burdensome for the school to comply. Additionally, the school objected to some of the specific information requested. The court found that **all of the information asked for in the subpoena was in fact obligatory for the school to maintain and make available to the inspector general**. The school was bound to such duty because of the agreement any school must enter with the Department of Education if the school wishes to become an "eligible school" to receive Pell Grants and Stafford Loans. The court ruled that the school could not object to either the amount or scope of documents requested in the subpoena. The court enforced the subpoena and ordered the school to produce the documents and files. *U.S. v. Teeven*, 745 F.Supp. 220 (D. Del. 1990). [DE]

B.   Grants and Loans for Religious Schools

◆   *The U.S. Supreme Court approved of the state of Washington's choice to exclude devotional theology candidates from a state scholarship program.*

Washington law created the Promise Scholarship Program, which made state funds available to qualified students for their educational costs. To be eligible, students had to meet certain performance standards and income limits, and enroll at least half-time in an eligible postsecondary institution in the state. The program excluded scholarships for theology majors, but students who attended religiously-affiliated schools could still obtain scholarships so long as they did not major in theology and the institution was accredited. A student who received a Promise Scholarship enrolled as a double major in pastoral ministries and business at a private Christian college. A college financial aid administrator advised him he could not use the scholarship to pursue a devotional theology degree and could only receive program funds by certifying he would not pursue a theology degree. The student sued state officials in a federal district court for violating the Free Exercise, Establishment, Speech and

Equal Protection Clauses. The court awarded summary judgment to the state, but the Ninth Circuit reversed the decision.

The U.S. Supreme Court held **the program was not a state expression of disfavor against religion**, as the student argued. The program did not impose civil or criminal sanctions on any type of religious service or rite. **There was no Free Exercise Clause violation, as the program did not require students to choose between their religious beliefs and a government benefit.** The state had only chosen not to fund a distinct category of instruction. The training of ministers was essentially a religious endeavor that could be treated differently than training for other callings. There was no evidence of state hostility toward religion. **The program permitted funding recipients to attend pervasively religious schools, and nothing in its text or the state constitution suggested anti-religious bias.** The state interest in denying funds to theology majors was substantial, and the program placed only a minor burden on recipients. The Court reversed the judgment. *Locke v. Davey*, 124 S.Ct. 1307 (U.S. 2004). [WA]

◆   *In 1986, the U.S. Supreme Court held that the First Amendment to the U.S. Constitution did not prevent the state of Washington from providing financial assistance directly to an individual with a disability attending a Christian college. However, the Supreme Court of Washington then held on remand that the assistance violated the state constitution.*

A visually impaired Washington student sought vocational rehabilitative services from the Washington Commission for the Blind pursuant to state law. The law provided that individuals with visual disabilities were eligible for educational assistance to enable them to "overcome vocational handicaps and to obtain the maximum degree of self-support and self-care." However, because the plaintiff was a student at a Christian college intending to pursue a career of service in the church, the Commission for the Blind denied him assistance. The Washington Supreme Court upheld this decision on the ground that the First Amendment to the U.S. Constitution prohibited state funding of a student's education at a religious college. The U.S. Supreme Court took a less restrictive view of the First Amendment and reversed the Washington court. The operation of Washington's program was such that the Commission for the Blind paid money directly to students, who could then attend the schools of their choice. **The fact that the student in this case chose to attend a religious college did not constitute state support of religion because "the decision to support religious education is made by the individual, not the state."** The First Amendment was therefore not offended. *Witters v. Washington Dep't of Services. for the Blind*, 474 U.S. 481, 106 S.Ct. 748, 88 L.Ed.2d 846 (1986). [WA]

On remand, the Washington Supreme Court reconsidered the matter under the **Washington State Constitution, which is far stricter in its prohibition on the expenditure of public funds for religious instruction than is the U.S. Constitution. Vocational assistance funds for the student's religious education violated the state constitution because public money would be used for religious instruction.** The court rejected the student's argument that the restriction on public expenditures would violate his right to free exercise of religion. The court determined that the commission's action was constitutional under the Free Exercise Clause because there was no infringement of the student's constitutional rights. Finally, denial of the funds to the student did not violate the Fourteenth Amendment's Equal Protection Clause because the commission had a policy of denying any student's religious vocational funding. The classification was directly related to the state's interest in ensuring the separation between church and state as required by both state and federal constitutions. The court reaffirmed its denial of the student's tuition. *Witters v. State Comm'n for the Blind,* 771 P.2d 1119 (Wash. 1989). [WA]

◆ *The Court of Appeals of Minnesota upheld the Minnesota Post-Secondary Enrollment Options Act (PSEOA), holding that the state constitution does not prohibit government assistance for religiously oriented institutions.*

The PSEOA allowed 11th and 12th grade students enrolled in public schools to take secondary or post-secondary courses for credit at eligible public and private colleges and universities. The state reimbursed participating students for the lesser of the actual cost of tuition and related expenses or an amount derived from a formula representing the school district's actual basic revenue. The Minnesota Federation of Teachers filed a federal district court action against state education officials and 15 private institutions, seeking to enjoin state funding of the private schools under the act. The teachers' federation asserted that the PSEOA violated the Establishment Clauses of the state and federal constitutions. The court granted pretrial judgment to the state and colleges for claims arising under the U.S. Constitution and dismissed the state law claims without prejudice. The federation commenced a new action in state court based on the state law claims, and the court granted pretrial judgment to the officials and colleges.

The federation appealed to the Court of Appeals of Minnesota, which found that **the state constitution does not prohibit government assistance in the form of an indirect or incidental benefit to a religiously oriented institution, even if it is pervasively sectarian.** Even though payments were made directly to the colleges under PSEOA, the students decided which school they would attend, and the statute was neutral on its face. The benefit to the institution was incidental, because only some costs were reimbursed. **The PSEOA did not violate the Minnesota Constitution.** However, the court reversed and remanded the pretrial judgment order concerning the status of Bethel College to consider its alleged sectarian nature, as there was an absence of information in the record concerning its use of funds. *Minnesota Federation of Teachers v. Mammenga,* 485 N.W.2d 305 (Minn. App. 1992). [MN]

On remand, the trial court again entered pretrial judgment against the federation, and it appealed to the court of appeals. The court applied a two-part analysis in determining whether the state assistance constituted a prohibited benefit or support of Bethel College. **The assistance would be permissible where the public benefit was indirect and incidental, and the school was not pervasively sectarian.** In this case, the benefit to the private school was indirect and incidental because it had been designed to benefit high school students, not private colleges. Students had the choice to attend either a public or a private college under PSEOA. Bethel College separated PSEOA reimbursements from its other funds to ensure that state benefits were used only for nonsectarian purposes. The PSEOA did not violate the Establishment

Clause of the Minnesota Constitution, and the court affirmed the trial court judgment. *Minnesota Federation of Teachers v. Mammenga*, 500 N.W.2d 136 (Minn. App. 1993). [MN]

C. State Funding

◆   *The U.S. Supreme Court held that the government may show a violation of Title IV of the Higher Education Act without proving specific intent to injure or defraud by a defendant.*

A private, nonprofit technical school in Indiana participated in the Guaranteed Student Loan (GSL) program authorized by Title IV of the Higher Education Act. The program required the school to make refunds to the lender if a student withdrew from school during a term. If the school failed to refund loans to the lender, the student–and if the student defaulted, the government–would be liable for the full amount of the loan. The treasurer of the school conferred with the school's owners and initiated a practice of not making GSL refunds. As a result, the school owed $139,649 in refunds.

After the school lost its accreditation, a federal grand jury indicted the treasurer for "knowingly and willfully misapplying" federally insured student loan funds in violation of 20 U.S.C. § 1097(a). A federal district court dismissed the indictment because it lacked an allegation that the treasurer intended to injure or defraud the U.S. The Seventh Circuit reinstated the prosecution, and the U.S. Supreme Court affirmed the decision. The Court held § 1097(a) did not require the specific intent to injure or defraud. **If the government can prove the defendant misapplied Title IV funds knowingly and willfully, that is sufficient to show a violation of § 1097(a).** *Bates v. U.S.*, 522 U.S. 23, 118 S.Ct. 285, 139 L.Ed.2d 215 (1997). [IN]

◆   *A university properly revoked a student's financial aid award where the student had accumulated too many credits to be eligible.*

During an eight-year period, a student at Cleveland State University accumulated 250 credit hours. In the spring 2001 semester, he applied for financial aid for the summer semester so he could take a physics course. The university awarded him $500 contingent on his satisfaction of the eligibility requirements for receiving financial aid. However, after reviewing the student's academic records, the university realized that **his 250 credit hours made him ineligible for financial aid** (available only to students who had attempted no more than 192 credit hours). The university attempted to collect the $500 plus a late charge of $15 from the student, bringing proceedings against him. The student then sued to terminate the collection proceedings, but the Ohio Court of Claims ruled against him. Here, the student was clearly aware of the financial aid-eligibility requirements, and the university never misled him. The university was entitled to collect the money owed. *Revay v. Cleveland State Univ.*, 2003 WL 149715 (Ohio Ct. Cl. 1/7/03). [OH]

◆   *A federal court upheld a U.S. Department of Education classification of prisoner-students, finding federal law allowed distinctions among students.*

An accredited for-profit vocational-technical school in Texas entered into an agreement with certain privately operated prison facilities to provide training programs for prisoners. The prisoners were not obligated to provide funding; however, the school received compensation by having the prisoners obtain federal Pell Grants based on the amounts it normally charged nonprisoner students, with an adjustment for the shorter prison programs. The school received a total of about $8.1 million. The U.S. Department of Education determined that because the prisoner students were under no obligation to pay tuition, there was no tuition "charge" that could be offset by a Pell Grant. Also, the school could not include "expenses" since the prisoners did not pay for books or other materials, and the state of Texas paid for their living arrangements. Thus, the school was required to reimburse the Department. The school sued the Department, and the case reached the U.S. Court of Appeals, Fifth Circuit.

The Higher Education Act (HEA) defines the tuition and fees component of a student's "cost of attendance" as those "normally charged" at the institution. The Department determined that for prisoner students, to whom the school was required to provide classes free of charge, the tuition "normally charged" was zero. Thus, the school was not entitled to receive reimbursement for tuition in the form of a Pell Grant. The court upheld the Department's subclassification of the prisoner students, finding that the HEA plainly allowed distinctions between groups of students who are normally charged different amounts. **The court held that the school had reasonably and detrimentally relied on the Department's previous interpretation, which indicated that tuition and fee waivers did not affect the "cost of attendance" for Pell Grant purposes, and did not require the school to reimburse the tuition portion of the awards.** However, the school remained liable for reimbursement of the expense allowance portion of the awards. Because the students incurred no expenses, the school was never entitled, nor could it ever have believed it was entitled, to make awards based on those amounts. *Microcomputer Technology Institute v. Riley,* 139 F.3d 1044 (5th Cir. 1998). [TX]

◆ *A federal district court refused to dismiss a complaint against the operator of three Pennsylvania vocational schools that was brought by students alleging fraudulent activity under the federal Racketeer Influenced and Corrupt Organizations Act (RICO).*

A Pennsylvania corporation operating three vocational schools admitted two students without high school diplomas or their equivalent. The students obtained federally guaranteed student loans (GSLs) and enrolled in a course to become medical assistants. One student withdrew after six weeks, and another completed her course work. The school closed before she could receive any placement services. Federal statutes mandate that schools certify to the Department of Education that students admitted without high school diplomas or their equivalent have the "ability to benefit" from the school's courses prior to receipt of any GSLs. The students sued the school owner in a Pennsylvania federal court under RICO, claiming that the owner had fraudulently certified to the DOE that his schools complied with these requirements when, in fact, these schools were using artificially low cut-off scores on the entrance examinations and thereby qualifying students who did not have the ability to benefit from the school's courses.

The students argued that the school's conduct amounted to a pattern of racketeering in violation of RICO. The school argued that the students' injury was not "by reason of" the allegedly fraudulent conduct and, for this reason, it was not liable under RICO. **The court held that the students stated a RICO claim, ruling that the school's allegedly fraudulent certification of the students, which had allowed them to take out federally guaranteed loans, could have proximately caused their injuries** (their indebtedness). The students were directly injured, and the court rejected the school's motion for pretrial judgment. *Rodriguez v. McKinney*, 878 F.Supp. 744 (E.D. Pa. 1995). [PA]

◆ *The New York Supreme Court, Appellate Division, held that the state could review a nonpublic educational institution's certification of a student's eligibility for a state grant.*

A New York private college accepted and certified a group of students who had previously attended a local community college as eligible for state Supplemental Tuition Assistance Program (STAP) grants. The STAP grants provided tuition assistance to New York students whose educational deficits were so great that they would not be considered admissible to a college-level program. The state denied the college's request for STAP award and a New York trial court affirmed the denial. On appeal by the college, the appellate division court held that **the state had both the authority and the obligation to review a nonpublic educational institution's certification of a student's eligibility for a STAP grant.** The regulatory scheme did not contemplate awards to students with successful college experience who had previously received funds pursuant to the Tuition Assistance Program. The appellate court affirmed the trial court's denial of STAP funds. *Touro College v. Nolan*, 620 N.Y.S.2d 558 (A.D. 3d Dept. 1994). [NY]

◆ *A university could not maintain a race-based scholarship program where past discrimination did not justify it.*

The University of Maryland maintained a merit scholarship program open only to African-American students. It alleged that the program redressed prior constitutional violations against African-American students by the university, which had formerly been segregated by law. A student of Hispanic descent attempted to obtain a scholarship under the program, but was denied on the basis of his race. He filed a lawsuit against the university and a number of its officials in the U.S. District Court for the District of Maryland. The court granted summary judgment to the university, and the student won reversal from the U.S. Court of Appeals, Fourth Circuit. On remand, the parties again filed cross motions for summary judgment, and the district court again awarded summary judgment to the university.

The case was again appealed to the court of appeals. It determined that the district court had improperly found a basis in the evidence for its conclusion that a remedial plan of action was necessary. It also had erroneously determined that the scholarship program was narrowly tailored to meet the goal of remedying past discrimination. The court had misconstrued statistical evidence presented by the parties and had erroneously found a connection between past discrimination and present conditions at the university. **The reasons stated by the university for maintaining the race-based scholarship–underrepresentation of African-American students, low retention and graduation rates and a negative perception among African-American students–were legally insufficient.** The court reversed the summary judgment order for the university and awarded summary judgment to the student. *Podberesky v. Kirwan*, 38 F.3d 147 (4th Cir. 1994). [MD]

◆   *Students who belonged to tribes that were not federally recognized sued the Bureau of Indian Affairs for an order awarding them higher education grants.*

A Bureau of Indian Affairs (BIA) regulation authorized funds for higher education grants and loans to students of one-quarter or more degree of Native American blood who enrolled at accredited institutions of higher education. However, this regulation was struck down as invalid in a 1986 decision by the U.S. Court of Appeals, Ninth Circuit. The BIA then adopted a rule requiring students to be members of a federally recognized tribe to be eligible for funds. Two students, who were both five-sixteenths Wintun Indian, were denied higher education grants because the tribe they belonged to was not federally recognized. The BIA's decision was affirmed by the U.S. District Court for the Eastern District of California, and the students appealed to the Ninth Circuit.

The court found that the BIA had violated federal administrative law requirements to publish proposed rules in the *Federal Register* when announcing new criteria for student loans and grants. Accordingly, it could not use the eligibility criteria it had relied on since the 1986 Ninth Circuit decision. Although the students prevailed on this question, **the court determined that without a properly published regulation, there could be no basis for an order directing the BIA to award higher education grants to the students** as they had requested. The court encouraged the BIA to adopt criteria consistent with federal law tending to exempt the California Indian population from federal recognition requirements. The court reversed the district court decision concerning the validity of the BIA's current criteria and affirmed the denial of injunctive relief. *Malone v. Bureau of Indian Affairs*, 38 F.3d 433 (9th Cir. 1994). [CA]

D. Student Default

◆   *A student with overdue loans could not sue to forgive the debt under FERPA or the HEA.*

A student at a private university in Illinois received a master's degree in history, completed the classwork but not the student-teaching requirement in the university's School of Education, and completed his first year at the university's law school. When he became liable to repay his student loans ($80,000), he could not do so and sued the university under the Family Educational Rights and Privacy Act (FERPA)and the Higher Education Act (HEA). His claim under FERPA was that the university failed to provide him with recommendation letters necessary for him to find employment. The university insisted that he first waive any right to view the content of the letters. His claim under the HEA was that the university issued him loans in excess of his ability to repay them, or that the university failed to obtain employment for him. An Illinois federal court dismissed his claims, and the Seventh Circuit affirmed. FERPA and the HEA are funding statutes with certain conditions attached to government money. **Enforcement of each statute is provided by the government.** As a result, the student could not sue the university for violating either act. *Slovinec v. DePaul Univ.*, 332 F.3d 1068 (7th Cir. 2003). [IL]

◆ *A federal district court allowed a Wisconsin student to recover interest and collection fees paid that were not authorized by the federal Fair Debt Collection Practices Act (FDCPA).*

A student enrolled in a Wisconsin private college. Prior to enrollment she was not shown the college handbook, which contained information regarding payment of tuition and charges for interest and collection fees. The handbook also stated that outstanding balances were subject to an 18 percent annual service charge. The student failed to make timely payments, and the debt was turned over to a collection agency. The college assessed interest charges and a collection fee of 33 percent of the account total. The student made over 60 payments to the college, substantially diminishing the amount owed. However, the debt collector demanded payment in full and sent the student a threatening letter. The student filed a lawsuit against the private college and the debt collection agency, alleging violations of the FDCPA and the Wisconsin Consumer Act.

The court held that the **defendants' attempt to collect the collection fees violated the FDCPA**. The student was entitled to recover interest and collection fees paid that were not authorized by law. The private college also was liable for violations of federal and state law. Holding creditors like the college liable for acts of collection agencies they use on a regular basis advanced purposes of fair debt collection statutes: to protect consumers from abusive, unfair or unconscionable collection practices. *Patzka v. Viterbo College*, 917 F.Supp. 654 (W.D. Wis. 1996). [WI]

◆ *A student who defaulted on his student loans was unable to avoid liability under the Higher Education Technical Amendments, which eliminated a six-year statute of limitations on actions under prior law.*

A borrower defaulted on several student loans. These loans were assigned to the U.S. Department of Education on November 30, 1976 and on August 20, 1984. After the department sought to collect the defaulted student loans, the borrower filed suit in a U.S. district court alleging that the department's action was barred by the statute of limitations. The district court granted summary judgment to the department, and the borrower appealed to the U.S. Court of Appeals, Ninth Circuit. The court of appeals noted that the Higher Education Act, as modified by the Consolidated Omnibus Budget Reconciliation Act, provided for a six-year statute of limitations, commencing from the date the loan was assigned to the department. However, **the Higher Education Technical Amendments of 1991 (HETA) eliminated the six-year statute of** limitations and revived all actions that would otherwise have been time-barred. Consequently, the HETA revived all student loan collection actions against the borrower. *U.S. v. Phillips*, 20 F.3d 1005 (9th Cir. 1994). [CA]

◆ *A federal district court rejected a student's due process claims arising from alleged inadequate notice that his loans were in default based on evidence that he knew that his payments were delinquent.*

A student attending a university in Washington, D.C. participated in the Guaranteed Student Loan Program (GSLP) and signed two promissory notes. The student dropped below half-time in January 1990 and graduated in May 1990. He became delinquent after missing his first loan payment in August 1990. However, the student then enrolled in a Texas law school and received a deferment until December 1990. When the student entered the repayment period in January 1991, both the loan servicing agency and the guaranty agency repeatedly and unsuccessfully attempted to contact him. When contact was finally made with the student in June 1991, he was sent a loan deferment form that he failed to return. In July 1991, the guaranty agency paid the amount in default and commenced collection procedures against the student. The student filed suit in a U.S. district court alleging that he received inadequate notice that his loans were in default. The guaranty agency counterclaimed for the amount in default.

The student contended that he was denied procedural due process because the guaranty agency had failed to give him adequate notice of the due date of his first payment. The court disagreed, noting that he was advised of his default status in June 1991. Further, the student had the burden to request a deferment. Here, the student already was delinquent at the time of his first deferment, and he then resumed that delinquent status upon his January 1991 repayment period. Since the student was aware that he was delinquent, and that he could obtain a deferment, he had received adequate notice. **The court held that the student was liable for the promissory notes and entered judgment for the guaranty agency.** *Stone v. United Student Aid Funds, Inc.,* 818 F.Supp. 254 (S.D. Ind. 1993). [IN]

◆ *Because the real purpose of National Health Service Corps (NHSC) scholarships is to encourage health professionals to serve internships, and not to provide financial assistance to students, a federal district court allowed the collection of treble damages against a medical student who defaulted on his obligation to the corps.*

A Texas medical student financed a majority of his education through an NHSC scholarship. The scholarship provided "reasonable educational expenses and a monthly stipend" in exchange for service in the corps in a location where there are not enough health professionals. A student serves one year in the corps for each year he or she receives scholarship funds. If a student fails to fulfill his or her obligation, he or she must pay triple the amount disbursed. In the student's final year, his professional plans changed, and he elected not to extend the scholarship contract. No scholarship funds were paid to him during his final year. After he graduated, the Department of Health and Human Services twice sent him a request for deferment so that he could complete his residency program before fulfilling his obligation in the corps. The student did not respond, and he became liable for $159,369, the trebled scholarship amount plus interest. The United States sued the student, and the case reached the Ninth Circuit.

The court rejected the student's argument that in order to be subject to treble damages one must receive scholarship funds for the entire four years. Rather, scholarship obligations were incurred in "single, one year units." **The student could not escape the previously incurred obligations for each year that he had received the funds.** If treble damages were not assessed, the scholarship could be transformed into a standard loan as long as the student withdrew from the corps before the final year of medical school. This was not the purpose of the scholarship. **The real purpose was to "overcome a geographic maldistribution of health professionals."** Thus, in order to effectuate congressional intent, the court imposed treble damages plus interest. *U.S. v. Williams*, 994 F.2d 646 (9th Cir. 1993). [TX]

III. PRIVATE SCHOOL TAXATION

The U.S. Supreme Court has infrequently considered federal income tax cases involving private schools. In Bob Jones Univ. v. U.S., *461 U.S. 574, 103 S.Ct. 2017, 76 L.Ed.2d 157 (1983), it held that private schools must comply with the strong federal interest against race discrimination and that federal tax exempt status can be denied to schools maintaining discriminatory policies. More recently, in* Camps Newfound/Owatonna, Inc. v. Town of Harrison, Maine, *520 U.S. 564, 117 S.Ct. 1590, 137 L.Ed.2d 852 (1997), the Court found no reason why nonprofit status should exempt a private entity from laws regulating commerce, including local property tax laws.*

A. Federal Income Taxation

◆   *The U.S. government's strong public policy against racial discrimination was held sufficient to deny tax-exempt status to an otherwise qualified private college.*

Section 501(c)(3) of the Internal Revenue Code (IRC) provides that "corporations ... organized and operated exclusively for religious, charitable ... or educational purposes" are entitled to tax-exempt status. The Internal Revenue Service routinely granted tax exemption under IRC § 501(c)(3) to private schools regardless of whether they had racially discriminatory admissions policies. In 1970, however, the IRS concluded it could no longer grant tax-exempt status to racially discriminatory private schools because such schools were not "charitable" within the meaning of § 501(c)(3). In *Bob Jones Univ. v. United States*, two private colleges whose racial admissions policies were allegedly rooted in their interpretations of the Bible sued to prevent the IRS from interpreting the federal tax laws in this manner. The Supreme Court rejected the colleges' challenge and upheld the IRS's interpretation.

The Court's ruling was based on a strong federal public policy against racial discrimination in education. **Because the colleges were operating in** violation of that public policy, the colleges could not be considered "charitable" under § 501(c)(3). Thus, they were ineligible for tax exemption. The Court held that in order to fall under the exemption of § 501(c)(3) an institution must be in harmony with the public interest. It also held that the denial of an exemption did not impermissibly burden Bob Jones' alleged religious interest in practicing racial discrimination. *Bob Jones Univ. v. United States*, 461 U.S. 574, 103 S.Ct. 2017, 76 L.Ed.2d 157 (1983). [SC]

B. State and Local Taxation

◆ *Office space leased by a bank from a university was exempt from property taxation because it was used for a "school purpose."*

The University of Delaware contracted with a bank to develop a student student identification card that could also be used as a debit card for services. The university provided office space to the bank for the project. The local land use department discontinued the university's property tax exemption for the space and assessed taxes on it. A county board of assessment review upheld the assessment, but its decision was reversed by a state superior court, which found the space was used for a school purpose under state law.

The Supreme Court of Delaware noted the term "school purpose" was undefined by 9 Del. C. § 8105. Under that section, college or school property used for educational or school purposes was not subject to taxation. The court rejected the county's argument that § 8105 must be read narrowly. Statutes exempting educational institutions from taxation are generally "construed more liberally than other tax exempting statutes." The trial court had correctly determined the bank served a "school purpose." **The court held "school purposes" included use of school-owned property that contributed to the legitimate welfare, convenience, and/or safety of the school community or its members.** The judgment was affirmed. *New Castle County Dep't of Land Use v. University of Delaware*, 842 A.2d 1201 (Del. 2004). [DE]

◆ *A North Carolina court denied tax-exempt status to a restaurant that claimed to be an institution of higher learning.*

A taxpayer purchased a restaurant and named it the University for the Study of Human Goodness and Creative Group Work. He applied for tax-exempt status as an educational institution, describing the restaurant as a learning laboratory with a three-member faculty and a one-year program with four curriculum tracks. The university was not accredited by any organization, and a local tax review board denied the application. The North Carolina Property Tax Commission also denied the taxpayer's appeal.

The Court of Appeals of North Carolina credited the board's findings that **the restaurant lacked the characteristics typical of an educational institution. It had no formal curriculum and did not issue academic grades. It appeared the restaurant was operated predominantly as a business** with a substantial amount of patronage. The North Carolina Supreme Court had previously held that a spiritual center was not entitled to tax-exempt status because mediation did not qualify as a learning activity. In another case, a day care center was denied tax-exempt status because it was not a "traditional school and not 'wholly and exclusively' used for educational purpose." Based on the evidence and case law, the court upheld the commission's decision. *Matter of Univ. for Study of Human Goodness and Creative Group Work*, 582 S.E.2d 645 (N.C. App. 2003). [NC]

◆ *A city was allowed to proceed in its lawsuit against a Catholic university for back taxes.*

The city of Scranton and its school district sued the University of Scranton, a Roman Catholic institution, for payment of back business privilege and/or mercantile taxes since 1995. The city asserted that the university gained income in those years from the sale of books and food, from parking lot revenue and from other sources. Since those income-generating activities took place in the city, the university ought to have to pay mercantile taxes. The university sought to dismiss the suit, **asserting that it was a charitable institution under the state's Purely Public Charity Act**, and the court of common pleas agreed. However, the Pennsylvania Commonwealth Court reversed, finding issues that required the lawsuit to proceed. As a result, the university had to answer the city's complaint. *School Dist. of City of Scranton v. University of Scranton*, 2002 WL 876980 (Pa. Cmwlth. 5/8/02). [PA]

◆ *Land used by a seminary for recreational purposes and as a buffer zone was exempt from taxation.*

A North Carolina county reviewed several parcels of land owned by a seminary and determined that they were not eligible for tax exemptions because they were not used for educational or religious purposes. After the state property tax commission held that exemptions applied to three parcels, the county appealed. The North Carolina Court of Appeals affirmed the decision in favor of the seminary. **Although the land was used essentially for recreational purposes, and as a buffer between the campus and commercial development surrounding the campus, it served to provide and maintain a relaxed campus atmosphere.** Further, the seminary's attempt to rezone one of the parcels for commercial development so that it could sell the land for a profit was a planned future use, which did not change the present exempted use of the land. *In the Matter of Southeastern Baptist Theological Seminary*, 135 N.C.App. 247, 520 S.E.2d 302 (N.C. App. 1999). [NC]

◆ *An office building owned by teaching doctors of Midwestern University did not qualify for real estate tax exemptions.*

The primary activities taking place at the property constituted billing, collection, data processing, accounting, administration, management, payroll and related functions for the physician group. When a state court held that the physician group did not qualify for the "charitable purposes" or "school" exemptions under Illinois law, appeal reached the Appellate Court of Illinois. **Under Illinois law, a property entitled to an exemption must be used exclusively for charitable purposes and owned by a charitable organization.** Here, the group failed to meet either requirement. The Appellate Court did not allow the group to use its relationship with the university to cast itself as a charitable organization. No patient care, medical research or instructional classes took place on the property. *Midwest Physician Group, Ltd. v. Department of Revenue of Illinois*, 711 N.E.2d 381 (Ill. App. 1st Dist. 1999). [IL]

◆   *A university could not claim tax-exempt status for a parking garage or parts of a building leased to for-profit companies.*

A university owned a four-story building with an attached parking garage, and leased space to five tenants. Two tenants were nonprofit organizations, and the other three tenants were for-profit companies. The Board of Tax Appeals found that the building and the land under it were exempt from taxation, but the garage and land under it were not. The Cleveland Board of Education filed a notice of appeal, wanting the whole property to be taxed.

The Supreme Court of Ohio affirmed the Board of Tax Appeals decisions regarding the tax exemption for the space leased by the two non-profit organizations, and the non-tax-exempt status of the garage and the land under it. It reversed exemptions given to the university for the space held by the for-profit tenants and vacant areas in the building. **The garage did not qualify for tax-exempt status because it was not an essential and integral part of the university's or nonprofit tenants' charitable and/or educational activities.** *Case Western Reserve Univ. v. Tracy*, 84 Ohio St.3d 316, 703 N.E.2d 1240 (1999). [OH]

◆   *The Commonwealth Court of Pennsylvania held a college was entitled to exemption from real estate taxes because it was maintained as a public charity.*

A Pennsylvania educational institution founded by the Presbyterian Church in the 18th century developed into a nonsectarian, private, coeducational four-year college. Students were admitted based on academic qualifications and irrespective of sex, race, color, creed or national origin. No criterion based on financial need was established as a condition of enrollment, but if a student was unable to pay the tuition he or she would not be allowed to complete his or her education. The college's board of trustees served without compensation, and the salaries of the college's employees were not excessive. Nearly 80 percent of the students received financial aid, and the college regularly had an operating loss, although the market value of its endowment fund was over $50 million. The state board of assessment denied the college's application for a real estate exemption. On appeal by the college, a Pennsylvania trial court affirmed the board's decision. The college appealed.

The Commonwealth Court of Pennsylvania held that the college qualified as a purely public charity. It advanced a charitable purpose, donated a substantial portion of its services, and benefited a substantial and indefinite class of persons who were legitimate subjects of charity. For example, the college offered a program to academically underprivileged youth, awarded substantial grants based on academic and financial need to students, enrollment was open, and students were admitted pursuant to a nondiscriminatory admissions policy based on merit. The court also held that the college relieved the government of some of its burdens and operated free from the private profit motive. **Because the college was founded and was maintained as a purely public charity, it was entitled to a real estate tax exemption.** The commonwealth court reversed the trial court judgment. *City of Washington v. Board of Assessment*, 666 A.2d 352 (Pa. Cmwlth. 1995). [PA]

◆ *The Court of Appeal of Louisiana held that state law does not require private colleges to substantiate their tax-exempt status except as set forth by the state legislature.*

A Louisiana church operated a private university that offered a variety of secular undergraduate and graduate programs. The Louisiana Board of Regents notified the university that it had failed to complete and submit the required licensure application and was therefore in violation of state law. Consequently, it sought to close the school. **Although degree-granting institutions were generally required to be registered and licensed by the board, institutions granted a tax exemption under the Internal Revenue Code were exempted from these requirements.** Previously such private universities were required to supply only basic information to obtain a license. The state attorney general filed suit in a Louisiana trial court, seeking to enjoin the church's operation of the university based on its noncompliance with the board's procedural requirements. The trial court found that because the Internal Revenue Code does not require churches to obtain recognition of their exempt status, the board was prohibited from requiring the organization to do so. It denied the state's request for injunctive relief, and the state appealed.

The Court of Appeal of Louisiana affirmed the decision, noting that the state legislature chose to defer to federal law in this procedural area. Federal law, pursuant to the Internal Revenue Code, granted churches automatic exempt status without the necessity of paperwork. Absent a contrary directive from the state legislature, the court refused to read additional requirements into the law. *Ieyoub v. World Christian Church*, 649 So.2d 771 (La. App. 1st Cir. 1994). [LA]

◆ *The Commonwealth Court of Pennsylvania held that property owned by the private college in the following two cases was tax exempt because the college was a public charity under state law and the property was regularly used for the purposes of the college.*

A Pennsylvania nonprofit private college owned a house occupied by its grounds crew leader. The college charged the grounds crew leader a discounted rent that averaged about 70 percent of the fair market value. In exchange for the discount, the grounds crew leader agreed to be available on a 24-hour basis to respond to emergencies and nighttime calls. He was allegedly called to campus after-hours six times in both 1991 and 1992 for snow and ice removal and to remove fallen tree limbs. The Delaware County Board of Assessment Appeals determined that the house was not exempt from property taxes. On appeal by the college, a Pennsylvania trial court reversed, finding the house exempt from taxation. A local public school district appealed the finding to the Commonwealth Court of Pennsylvania.

Article VIII of the **Pennsylvania Constitution provides that the general assembly can exempt real property of public charities "regularly used for the purposes of the institution."** Section 204 of the General County Assessment Law exempts all college property "necessary for the occupancy and enjoyment of the same." The commonwealth court stated that the college need not prove that the property was absolutely necessary to its needs for the exemption to apply. Rather, it was required to show only that it had a reasonable need for the property. Here, emergency personnel were essential to the college community. The grounds crew leader was able to respond much quicker to an emergency than personnel who were living off campus. The college properly chose to forego the additional rental revenues to provide these needed services. Further, the alleged infrequency of emergency situations did not render the house incidental to the college's purposes. **Because emergency services were directly related to the proper functions of the college, the trial court did not err in concluding that the house was tax exempt.** *In Re Swarthmore College*, 645 A.2d 470 (Pa. Cmwlth. 1994). [PA]

The college also owned a large house designed for entertaining. The college's vice president for alumni development lived in the house rent-free and was not charged for utilities. The house was used for meetings, special events, receptions and to entertain potential donors from whom one-third of the college's yearly income was derived. The Delaware County Board of Assessment Appeals determined that the house was not exempt from property taxes. The Commonwealth Court of Pennsylvania stated that the **college was not required to prove that the property was absolutely necessary to its needs for the exemption to apply. Rather, it was required to show only that it had a reasonable necessity for the property.** Here, the vice president was required to live in the house, use it to cultivate personal relationships with donors, and utilize it for numerous college functions. These uses were directly related to the proper functions of the college. Consequently, the vice president's house was tax-exempt. *In re Swarthmore College*, 643 A.2d 1152 (Pa. Cmwlth. 1994). [PA]

◆   *The Supreme Court of Iowa upheld tax-exempt status for property owned by a private university because it was used solely for the university's purpose of providing Catholic education for its students.*

A private Catholic university in Iowa was organized for charitable, scientific, religious, and educational purposes. The university acquired property adjacent to the campus and converted it into a child care center. The purpose of the child care center was to enable parents of preschool-age children to attend the university. Priority admission to the center was given to students, then to faculty, then to the general public. The university vice president, a Catholic priest, also was provided rent-free housing at a location apart from the central campus of the university. This property also served as an office and conference center for the school. The university sought an exemption from general property taxation for both parcels. The district court held that the child care facility was exempt but that the university vice president's residence was not exempt. The university appealed to the Supreme Court of Iowa.

The supreme court noted the statutory requirements for exemption. First, the **property must be used by literary, scientific, charitable, benevolent, agricultural or religious institutions and must not be operated for profit.** Because the child care facility was nonprofit and the university had a religious affiliation, these requirements were satisfied. Next, the property must be used "solely for its appropriate object." Here, the child care facility was properly used to enable students to attend the university and to enable university employees to further their goal of educating the students. The court also noted that the university vice president was a priest, and was therefore "necessary" to further the stated purposes of the university. Consequently, **both the child care facility and the rent-free housing were solely for the university's object of providing an education based on the Catholic religion.** Both properties were exempt from general property taxation. The holding of the district court was affirmed in part and reversed in part. *St. Ambrose Univ. v. Board of Review*, 503 N.W.2d 406 (Iowa 1993). [IA]

◆ *The Court of Appeals of Washington held that property owned by a religious order was of an educational nature as that term was defined in Washington law. The college was therefore entitled to exempt the property from state property taxation.*

An order of Benedictine monks established a small liberal arts college in Washington in the late 1800s. The religious order maintained the college in that same location since its inception. In 1985, the Washington Department of Revenue denied the college's application to exempt certain portions of its campus from real property taxation. After several unsuccessful administrative appeals, the college appealed to a Washington trial court.

The land in question was an undeveloped and unmaintained area of the campus that served essentially as a buffer zone. The students and faculty were free to utilize the property for recreational purposes, but the property was also occasionally used for classes. Additionally, religion students periodically entered the property to meditate. The trial court reversed the administrative decisions and determined that the property was entitled to be exempted from real property taxation. The department appealed the adverse decision to the Court of Appeals of Washington.

On appeal, the department conceded that the property was smaller in size than the maximum acreage permitted by statute (to still be eligible for an exemption), and that the property in question incidentally furthered an educational purpose. However, it contended that the exemption was unwarranted because the property was essentially unused, empty land that was not reasonably necessary for achievement of the educational, athletic or social programs of the college. The court found that the utilization of the property was of an educational nature as that term was defined in Washington law.

The purposes of a religious educational institution could be better carried out in a pleasant atmosphere that was conducive to the contemplation of nature than it could be in a crowded urban setting. The court found it significant that several state colleges and universities also were surrounded by green belts and buffer zones. **Since the property had been and continued to be an integral part of the college campus, the application for tax exemption should not have been denied. The court affirmed the trial court's decision in favor of the college.** *St. Martin's College v. State Dep't of Revenue*, 841 P.2d 803 (Wash. App. Div. 2 1992). [WA]

IV. PRIVATE ASSISTANCE TO SCHOOLS

◆ *The Court of Appeals of Kentucky denied a claim to property by a college under a property owner's will.*

A Kentucky property owner bequeathed property to a relative. However, the will stated that if the relative died without children, the property was to pass to the relative's younger sister and her heirs. The will also provided Georgetown College would receive the proceeds from the sale of 71 acres of farmland, to be used to fund a permanent endowment at the college. Any additional money would be paid to the college for the endowment fund. Both the relative and her sister died without children. A state court distributed $1.3 million from the estate in three equal shares to the sister's heirs, finding the college was only covered under a specific item in the will. The state appeals court rejected the college's argument that the devises to the sisters were substitutional. **When the property owner died, the court explained, the interest in her property vested in the sister's heirs. The college's reasoning would lead to a finding that the property owner had died without heirs.** As this result was disfavored, the court affirmed the judgment for the heirs. *Georgetown College v. Alexander*, Nos. 2002-CA-000651-MR, 2002-CA-000735-MR, 2003 WL 22025156 (Ky. App. 2003). [KY]

Generally, when private parties donate money to schools, they have to be careful to specify how that money will be used or the schools will be able to put the money into their general operating funds.

◆ *A university had to identify donors to its new arena who purchased luxury suites.*

Fresno State University built a new $103 million arena primarily with private donations and created a nonprofit association to operate it. The association leased the arena's luxury suites to interested donors. Prices for the suites ranged from $45,000 to $63,000 per year (with terms of 5, 7 or 10 years). The association promised some of the donors they would remain anonymous. However, when a newspaper sought documents containing the names of the donors who obtained leases, the university and association sought to withhold the information on the grounds that disclosure would cause a decrease in future donations. A state court determined that the documents were public records under the California Public Records Act and thus had to be disclosed. The California Court of Appeal affirmed, noting that **the purchase of luxury suites was more a business transaction than a traditional donation**. People making such a purchase have placed themselves in public view and have a diminished expectation of privacy. Further, because the arena was financed with $8 million in public funds, there was a legitimate public interest in the fairness of the transactions. *California State Univ. v. Superior Court*, 108 Cal.Rptr.2d 870 (Cal. App. 5th Dist. 2001). [CA]

◆ *A university hospital named as an alternate beneficiary could not get money bequeathed to another institution even though a condition of the will was illegal.*

A doctor associated with the Keswick Home in Baltimore provided for four annuitants in his will and, after the death of the last of them, directed that the remainder of his estate (nearly $29 million) go to the Keswick Home for the acquisition or construction of a new building in his name for "white patients who need[ed] physical rehabilitation." If Keswick found the bequest unacceptable, the money was to pass to the University of Maryland Hospital to be used for physical rehabilitation. A lawsuit developed over the funds, with the university hospital arguing that the illegal racial restriction required the money to be awarded to it. A trial court agreed, but the Maryland Court of Appeals reversed. It excised the illegal condition attached to the will and awarded the money to Keswick. *Home for Incurables of Baltimore City v. University of Maryland Medical System Corp.*, 797 A.2d 746 (Md. 2002). [MD]

APPENDIX A

UNITED STATES CONSTITUTION

Provisions of Interest to Higher Educators

ARTICLE I

Section 1. All legislative Powers herein granted shall be vested in a Congress of the United States, which shall consist of a Senate and House of Representatives.

* * *

Section 8. The Congress shall have Power To lay and collect Taxes, Duties, Imposts and Excises, to pay the Debts and provide for the common Defence and general Welfare of the United States; but all Duties, Imposts and Excises shall be uniform throughout the United States;

To borrow money on the credit of the United States;

To regulate Commerce with foreign Nations, and among the several States, and with the Indian Tribes;

To establish an uniform Rule of Naturalization, and uniform Laws on the subject of Bankruptcies throughout the United States;

* * *

To promote the Progress of Science and useful Arts, by securing for limited Times to Authors and Inventors the exclusive Right to their respective Writings and Discoveries;

* * *

To make all Laws which shall be necessary and proper for carrying into Execution for the foregoing Powers, and all other Powers vested by this Constitution in the Government of the United States, or in any Department or Officer thereof.

* * *

Section 9. * * * No Bill of Attainder or ex post facto Law shall be passed.

* * *

495

Section 10. No State shall * * * pass any Bill of Attainder, ex post facto Law, or Law impairing the Obligation of Contracts, or grant any Title of Nobility.

ARTICLE II

Section 1. The executive Power shall be vested in a President of the United States of America. * * *

ARTICLE III

Section 1. The judicial Power of the United States, shall be vested in one supreme Court, and in such inferior Courts as the Congress may from time to time ordain and establish. The Judges, both of the supreme and inferior courts, shall hold their Offices during good Behaviour, and shall, at stated Times, receive for their Services a Compensation, which shall not be diminished during their Continuance in Office.

Section 2. The judicial Power shall extend to all Cases, in Law and Equity, arising under this Constitution, the Laws of the United States, and Treaties made, or which shall be made, under their Authority; - to all Cases affecting Ambassadors, other public Ministers and Consuls; - to all Cases of admiralty and maritime Jurisdiction, - to Controversies to which the United States shall be a party; - to Controversies between two or more States; - between a State and Citizens of another State; - between Citizens of different States; - between Citizens of the same State claiming Lands under the Grants of different States, and between a State, or the Citizens thereof, and foreign States, Citizens or Subjects.

* * *

ARTICLE IV

Section 1. Full Faith and Credit shall be given in each State to the public Acts, Records and judicial Proceedings of every other State. * * *

Section 2. The Citizens of each State shall be entitled to all Privileges and Immunities of Citizens in the several States.

* * *

Section 4. The United States shall guarantee to every State in this Union a Republican Form of Government, and shall protect each of them against Invasion; and on Application of the Legislature, or of the Executive (when the Legislature cannot be convened) against domestic Violence.

ARTICLE V

The Congress, whenever two thirds of both Houses shall deem it necessary, shall propose Amendments to this Constitution, or, on the Application of the Legislatures of two thirds of the several States, shall call a Convention for proposing Amendments, which, in either Case, shall be valid to all Intents and Purposes, as part of this Constitution, when ratified by the Legislatures of three fourths of the several States, or by Conventions in three fourths thereof, as the one or the other Mode of Ratification may be proposed by the Congress; Provided that no Amendment which may be made prior to the Year One thousand eight hundred and eight shall in any Manner affect the first and fourth Clauses in the Ninth Section of the first Article; and that no State, without its Consent, shall be deprived of its equal Suffrage in the Senate.

ARTICLE VI

* * *

This Constitution, and the Laws of the United States which shall be made in Pursuance thereof; and all Treaties made, or which shall be made, under the Authority of the United States, shall be the supreme Law of the Land; and the Judges in every State shall be bound thereby, any Thing in the Constitution or Laws of any State to the Contrary notwithstanding.

The Senators and Representatives before mentioned, and the Members of the several State Legislatures, and all executive and judicial Officers, both of the United States and of the several States, shall be bound by Oath or Affirmation, to support this Constitution; but no religious Test shall ever be required as a Qualification to any Office or public Trust under the United States.

* * *

AMENDMENT I

Congress shall make no law respecting an establishment of religion, or prohibiting the free exercise thereof; or abridging the freedom of speech, or of the press; or the right of the people peaceably to assemble, and to petition the Government for a redress of grievances.

* * *

AMENDMENT IV

The right of the people to be secure in their persons, houses, papers, and effects, against unreasonable searches and seizures, shall not be violated, and no Warrants shall issue, but upon probable cause, supported by Oath or affirmation, and particularly describing the place to be searched, and the persons or things to be seized.

AMENDMENT V

No person shall be held to answer for a capital, or otherwise infamous crime, unless on a presentment or indictment of a Grand Jury, except in cases arising in the land or naval forces, or in the Militia, when in actual service in time of War or public danger; nor shall any person be subject for the same offence to be twice put in jeopardy of life or limb; nor shall be compelled in any criminal case to be a witness against himself, nor be deprived of life, liberty, or property, without due process of law; nor shall private property be taken for public use, without just compensation.

AMENDMENT VI

In all criminal prosecutions, the accused shall enjoy the right to a speedy and public trial, by an impartial jury of the State and district wherein the crime shall have been committed, which district shall have been previously ascertained by law, and to be informed of the nature and cause of the accusation; to be confronted with the witnesses against him; to have compulsory process for obtaining witnesses in his favor, and to have the Assistance of Counsel for his defense.

AMENDMENT VII

In Suits at common law, where the value in controversy shall exceed twenty dollars, the right of trial by jury shall be preserved, and no fact tried by jury, shall be otherwise re-examined in any Court of the United States, than according to the rules of the common law.

AMENDMENT VIII

Excessive bail shall not be required, nor excessive fines imposed, nor cruel and unusual punishments inflicted.

AMENDMENT IX

The enumeration in the Constitution, of certain rights, shall not be construed to deny or disparage others retained by the people.

AMENDMENT X

The powers not delegated to the United States by the Constitution, nor prohibited by it to the States, are reserved to the States respectively, or to the people.

AMENDMENT XI

The Judicial power of the United States shall not be construed to extend to any suit in law or equity, commenced or prosecuted against one of the United States by Citizens of another State, or by Citizens or Subjects of any Foreign State.

* * *

AMENDMENT XIII

Section 1. Neither slavery nor involuntary servitude, except as a punishment for crime whereof the party shall have been duly convicted, shall exist within the United States, or any place subject to their jurisdiction.

Section 2. Congress shall have power to enforce this article by appropriate legislation.

AMENDMENT XIV

Section 1. All persons born or naturalized in the United States, and subject to the jurisdiction thereof, are citizens of the United States and of the State wherein they reside. No State shall make or enforce any law which shall abridge the privileges or immunities of citizens of the United States; nor shall any State deprive any person of life, liberty, or property, without due process of law; nor deny to any person within its jurisdiction the equal protection of the laws.

* * *

Section 5. The Congress shall have power to enforce, by appropriate legislation, the provisions of this article.

APPENDIX B

Subject Matter Table of United States Supreme Court
Cases Affecting Higher Education

Note: Please see the Table of Cases (located at the front of this volume) for Supreme Court cases reported in this Volume.

Academic Freedom
> *Univ. of Pennsylvania v. EEOC*, 493 U.S. 182, 110 S.Ct. 577, 107 L.Ed.2d 571 (1990).
> *Epperson v. Arkansas*, 393 U.S. 97, 89 S.Ct. 266, 21 L.Ed.2d 228 (1968).
> *Sweezy v. New Hampshire*, 354 U.S. 234, 77 S.Ct. 1203, 1 L.Ed.2d 1311 (1957).
> *Meyer v. Nebraska*, 262 U.S. 390, 43 S.Ct. 625, 67 L.Ed.2d 1042 (1923).

Arbitration
> *Volt Information Sciences v. Bd. of Trustees of Stanford Univ.*, 489 U.S. 468, 109 S.Ct. 1248, 103 L.Ed.2d. 488 (1989).

Athletics
> *NCAA v. Tarkanian*, 488 U.S. 179, 109 S.Ct. 454, 102 L.Ed.2d 469 (1988).
> *NCAA v. Smith*, 525 U.S. 459, 119 S.Ct. 924, 142 L.Ed.2d 929 (1999).

Attorney's Fees
> *Webb v. Board of Education*, 471 U.S. 234, 105 S.Ct. 1923, 85 L.Ed.2d 233 (1985).
> *Smith v. Robinson*, 468 U.S. 992, 104 S.Ct. 3457, 82 L.Ed.2d 746 (1984).

Civil Rights
> *Farrar v. Hobby*, 506 U.S. 103, 113 S.Ct. 566, 121 L.Ed.2d 494 (1992).
> *St. Francis College v. Al-Khazraji*, 481 U.S. 604, 107 S.Ct. 2022, 97 L.Ed.2d 749 (1987).
> *Grove City College v. Bell*, 465 U.S. 555, 104 S.Ct. 1211, 79 L.Ed.2d 516 (1984).
> *Rendell-Baker v. Kohn*, 457 U.S. 830, 102 S.Ct. 2764, 73 L.Ed.2d 418 (1982).

Collective Bargaining
> *Central State Univ. v. American Ass'n of Univ. Professors, Central State Univ. Chapter*, 526 U.S. 124, 119 S.Ct. 1162, 143 L.Ed.2d 227 (1999).

Compulsory Attendance
> *Wisconsin v. Yoder*, 406 U.S. 205, 92 S.Ct. 526, 32 L.Ed.2d 15 (1972).
> *Pierce v. Society of Sisters*, 268 U.S. 510, 45 S.Ct. 571, 69 L.Ed. 1070 (1925).

Continuing Education

Austin ISD v. U.S., 443 U.S. 915, 99 S.Ct. 3106, 61 L.Ed.2d 879 (1979).
Harrah ISD v. Martin, 440 U.S. 194, 99 S.Ct. 1062, 59 L.Ed.2d 248 (1979).

Corporal Punishment

Ingraham v. Wright, 430 U.S. 651, 97 S.Ct. 1401, 51 L.Ed.2d 711 (1977).

Court Intervention in School Affairs

Epperson v. Arkansas, 393 U.S. 97, 89 S.Ct. 266, 21 L.Ed.2d 228 (1968).

Criminal Activity

Bates v. U.S., 522 U.S. 23, 118 S.Ct. 285, 139 L.Ed.2d 215 (1997).

Desegregation

U.S. v. Fordice, 505 U.S. 717, 112 S.Ct. 2727, 120 L.Ed.2d 575 (1992).
Freeman v. Pitts, 503 U.S. 467, 112 S.Ct. 1430, 118 L.Ed.2d 108 (1992).

Disabled Students

Florence County School Dist. Four v. Carter, 510 U.S. 7, 114 S.Ct. 361, 126 L.Ed.2d 284 (1993).
Zobrest v. Catalina Foothills School Dist., 509 U.S. 1, 113 S.Ct. 2462, 125 L.Ed.2d 1 (1993).
Dellmuth v. Muth, 491 U.S. 223, 109 S.Ct. 2397, 105 L.Ed.2d 181 (1989).
Honig v. Doe, 484 U.S. 305, 108 S.Ct. 592, 98 L.Ed.2d 686 (1988).
City of Cleburne, Texas v. Cleburne Living Center, 473 U.S. 432, 105 S.Ct. 3249, 87 L.Ed.2d 313 (1985).
Honig v. Students of Cal. School for the Blind, 471 U.S. 148, 105 S.Ct. 1820, 85 L.Ed.2d 114 (1985).
Burlington School Committee v. Department of Education, 471 U.S. 359, 105 S.Ct. 1996, 85 L.Ed.2d 385 (1985).
Smith v. Robinson, 468 U.S. 992, 104 S.Ct. 3457, 82 L.Ed.2d 746 (1984).
Irving Independent School District v. Tatro, 468 U.S. 883, 104 S.Ct. 3371, 82 L.Ed.2d 664 (1984).
Board of Education v. Rowley, 458 U.S. 176, 102 S.Ct. 3034, 73 L.Ed.2d 690 (1982).
University of Texas v. Camenisch, 451 U.S. 390, 101 S.Ct. 1830, 68 L.Ed.2d 175 (1981).
Pennhurst State School and Hosp. v. Halderman, 451 U.S. 1, 101 S.Ct. 1531, 67 L.Ed.2d 694 (1981).
Southeastern Community College v. Davis, 442 U.S. 397, 99 S.Ct. 2361, 60 L.Ed.2d 980 (1979).

Discrimination, Generally

Edelman v. Lynchburg College, 532 U.S. 106, 122 S.Ct. 1145, 152 L.Ed.2d 188 (2002).

Raygor v. Regents of Univ. of Minnesota, 534 U.S. 533, 122 S.Ct. 999, 152 L.Ed.2d 27 (2002).

Alexander et al. v. Sandoval, 531 U.S. 1049, 121 S.Ct. 1511, 141 L.Ed.2d 517 (2001).

Board of Trustees of the University of Alabama v. Garrett, 531 U.S. 356, 121 S.Ct. 955, 148 L.Ed.2d 866 (2001).

Kimel v. Florida Board of Regents, 528 U.S. 62, 120 S.Ct. 631, 145 L.Ed.2d 522 (2000).

Texas v. Lesage, 528 U.S. 18, 120 S.Ct. 467, 145 L.Ed.2d 347 (1999).

Lane v. Pena, 518 U.S. 187, 116 S.Ct. 2092, 135 L.Ed.2d 486 (1996).

Jett v. Dallas Indep. School Dist., 491 U.S. 701, 109 S.Ct. 2702, 105 L.Ed.2d 598 (1989).

Carnegie-Mellon Univ. v. Cohill, 484 U.S. 343, 108 S.Ct. 614, 98 L.Ed.2d 720 (1988).

School Board of Nassau County v. Arline, 480 U.S. 273, 107 S.Ct. 1123, 94 L.Ed.2d 307 (1987).

Hazelwood School Dist. v. U.S., 433 U.S. 299, 97 S.Ct. 2736, 53 L.Ed.2d 768 (1977).

DeFunis v. Odegaard, 416 U.S. 312, 94 S.Ct. 1704, 40 L.Ed.2d 164 (1974).

Due Process

Gilbert v. Homar, 520 U.S. 924, 117 S.Ct. 1807, 138 L.Ed.2d 120 (1997).

Univ. of Tennessee v. Elliot, 478 U.S. 788, 106 S.Ct. 3220, 92 L.Ed.2d 635 (1986).

Memphis Community School Dist. v. Stachura, 477 U.S. 299, 106 S.Ct. 2537, 91 L.Ed.2d 249 (1986).

Cleveland Bd. of Educ. v. Loudermill, 470 U.S. 532, 105 S.Ct. 1487, 84 L.Ed.2d 494 (1985).

Perry v. Sindermann, 408 U.S. 593, 92 S.Ct. 2694, 33 L.Ed.2d 570 (1972).

Board of Regents v. Roth, 408 U.S. 564, 92 S.Ct. 2701, 33 L.Ed.2d 548 (1972).

Employment

Corp. of the Presiding Bishop of the Church of Jesus Christ of Latter-Day Saints v. Amos, 483 U.S. 327, 107 S.Ct. 2862, 97 L.Ed.2d 273 (1987).

Franklin & Marshall College v. EEOC, 476 U.S. 1163, 106 S.Ct. 2288, 90 L.Ed.2d 729 (1986).

NLRB v. Catholic Bishop of Chicago, 440 U.S. 490, 99 S.Ct. 1313, 59 L.Ed.2d 533 (1979).

Federal Aid

Traynor v. Turnage, 485 U.S. 535, 108 S.Ct. 1372, 99 L.Ed.2d 618 (1988).

Selective Service System v. MPIRG, 468 U.S. 841, 104 S.Ct. 3348, 82

L.Ed.2d 632 (1984).

Bell v. New Jersey and Pennsylvania, 461 U.S. 773, 103 S.Ct. 2187, 76 L.Ed.2d 312 (1984).

Grove City College v. Bell, 465 U.S. 555, 104 S.Ct. 1211, 79 L.Ed.2d 516 (1984).

Valley Forge Christian College v. Americans United for Separation of Church and State, 454 U.S. 464, 102 S.Ct. 752, 70 L.Ed.2d 700 (1982).

Board of Education v. Harris, 444 U.S. 130, 100 S.Ct. 363, 62 L.Ed.2d 275 (1979).

Wheeler v. Barrera, 417 U.S. 402, 94 S.Ct. 2274, 41 L.Ed.2d 159 (1974).

Tilton v. Richardson, 403 U.S. 672, 91 S.Ct. 2091, 29 L.Ed.2d 790 (1971).

Freedom of Religion

City of Boerne, Texas v. Flores, 521 U.S. 507, 117 S.Ct. 2157, 138 L.Ed.2d 624 (1997).

Edwards v. Aguillard, 482 U.S. 578, 107 S.Ct. 2573, 96 L.Ed.2d 510 (1987).

Ansonia Board of Education v. Philbrook, 499 U.S. 60, 107 S.Ct. 367, 93 L.Ed.2d 305 (1986).

Freedom of Speech

Bd. of Regents of Univ. of Wisconsin System v. Southworth, 529 U.S. 217, 120 S.Ct. 1346, 146 L.Ed.2d 193 (2000).

Bd. of Educ. of Westside Com. Sch. v. Mergens, 496 U.S. 226, 110 S.Ct. 2356, 110 L.Ed.2d 191 (1990).

Bd. of Trustees of the State Univ. of New York v. Fox, 492 U.S. 469, 109 S.Ct. 3028, 106 L.Ed.2d 388 (1989).

Hazelwood School Dist. v. Kuhlmeier, 484 U.S. 261, 108 S.Ct. 562, 98 L.Ed.2d 592 (1988).

Rankin v. McPherson, 483 U.S. 378, 107 S.Ct. 2891, 97 L.Ed.2d 315 (1987).

Bethel School District v. Fraser, 478 U.S. 675, 106 S.Ct. 3159, 92 L.Ed.2d 549 (1986).

Wayte v. U.S., 470 U.S. 598, 105 S.Ct. 1524, 84 L.Ed.2d 547 (1985).

Connick v. Myers, 461 U.S. 138, 103 S.Ct. 1684, 75 L.Ed.2d 708 (1983).

Board of Education v. Pico, 457 U.S. 853, 102 S.Ct. 2799, 73 L.Ed.2d 435 (1982).

Givhan v. Western Line Consolidated School District, 439 U.S. 410, 99 S.Ct. 693, 58 L.Ed.2d 619 (1979).

Mt. Healthy City School v. Doyle, 429 U.S. 274, 97 S.Ct. 568, 50 L.Ed.2d 471 (1977).

Papish v. Board of Curators, 410 U.S. 667, 93 S.Ct. 1197, 35 L.Ed.2d 618 (1973).

Grayned v. City of Rockford, 408 U.S. 104, 92 S.Ct. 2294, 33 L.Ed.2d 222 (1972).

Police Dep't v. Mosley, 408 U.S. 92, 92 S.Ct. 2286, 33 L.Ed.2d 212 (1972).

Tinker v. Des Moines, 393 U.S. 503, 89 S.Ct. 733, 21 L.Ed.2d 733 (1969).

Pickering v. Board of Education, 391 U.S. 563, 88 S.Ct. 1731, 20 L.Ed.2d 811 (1968).

Whitehill v. Elkins, 389 U.S. 54, 88 S.Ct. 184, 19 L.Ed.2d 228 (1967).

Keyishian v. Board of Regents, 385 U.S. 589, 87 S.Ct. 675, 17 L.Ed.2d 629 (1967).

Elfbrandt v. Russell, 384 U.S. 11, 86 S.Ct. 1238, 16 L.Ed.2d 321 (1965).

Baggett v. Bullitt, 377 U.S. 360, 84 S.Ct. 1316, 12 L.Ed.2d 377 (1963).

Cramp v. Board of Public Instruction of Orange County, 368 U.S. 278, 82 S.Ct. 275, 7 L.Ed.2d 285 (1961).

Shelton v. Tucker, 364 U.S. 479, 81 S.Ct. 247, 5 L.Ed.2d 231 (1960).

Slochower v. Board of Education, 350 U.S. 551, 76 S.Ct. 637, 100 L.Ed. 692 (1955).

Adler v. Bd. of Educ., 342 U.S. 485, 72 S.Ct. 380, 96 L.Ed. 517 (1952).

Intellectual Property

New York Times Co. Inc. v. Tasini, 533 U.S. 483, 121 S.Ct. 2381, 150 L.Ed.2d 500 (2001).

Florida Prepaid Postsecondary Educ. Expense Bd. v. College Savings Bank, 527 U.S. 627, 119 S.Ct. 2199, 144 L.Ed.2d 575 (1999).

College Savings Bank v. Florida Prepaid Postsecondary Educ. Expense Bd., 527 U.S. 666, 119 S.Ct. 2219, 144 L.Ed.2d 605 (1999).

Labor Relations

Lehnert v. Ferris Faculty Ass'n, 500 U.S. 507, 111 S.Ct. 1950, 114 L.Ed.2d 572 (1991).

Fort Stewart Schools v. Federal Labor Relations Authority, 495 U.S. 641, 110 S.Ct. 2043, 109 L.Ed.2d 659 (1990).

Minnesota State Board for Community Colleges v. Knight, 465 U.S. 271, 104 S.Ct. 1058, 79 L.Ed.2d 299 (1984).

NLRB v. Yeshiva University, 444 U.S. 672, 100 S.Ct. 856, 63 L.Ed.2d 115 (1980).

NLRB v. Catholic Bishop of Chicago, 440 U.S. 490, 99 S.Ct. 1313, 59 L.Ed.2d 533 (1979).

Abood v. Detroit Bd. of Educ., 431 U.S. 209, 97 S.Ct. 1782, 52 L.Ed.2d 261 (1977).

Maternity Leave

Richmond Unified School Dist. v. Berg, 434 U.S. 158, 98 S.Ct. 623, 54 L.Ed.2d 375 (1977).

Cleveland Board of Education v. La Fleur, 414 U.S. 632, 94 S.Ct. 791, 39 L.Ed.2d 52 (1974).

Cohen v. Chesterfield, 414 U.S. 632, 94 S.Ct. 791, 39 L.Ed.2d 52 (1974).

Private School Funding

Agostini v. Felton, 521 U.S. 203, 117 S.Ct. 1997, 138 L.Ed.2d 391 (1997).

Bd. of Educ. of Kiryas Joel Village School Dist. v. Grumet, 512 U.S. 687, 114 S.Ct. 2481, 129 L.Ed.2d 546 (1994).

Witters v. Washington Department of Services for the Blind, 474 U.S. 481, 106 S.Ct. 748, 88 L.Ed.2d 846 (1986).

Aguilar v. Felton, 473 U.S. 402, 105 S.Ct. 3232, 87 L.Ed.2d 290 (1985).

Grand Rapids School District v. Ball, 473 U.S. 373, 105 S.Ct. 3216, 87 L.Ed.2d 267 (1985).

Mueller v. Allen, 463 U.S. 388, 103 S.Ct. 3062, 77 L.Ed.2d 721 (1983).

Valley Forge Christian College v. Americans United for Separation of Church and State, 454 U.S. 464, 102 S.Ct. 752, 70 L.Ed.2d 700 (1982).

Committee for Public Education and Religious Liberty v. Regan, 444 U.S. 646, 100 S.Ct. 840, 63 L.Ed.2d 94 (1980).

New York v. Cathedral Academy, 434 U.S. 125, 98 S.Ct. 340, 54 L.Ed.2d 346 (1977).

Wolman v. Walter, 433 U.S. 229, 97 S.Ct. 2593, 53 L.Ed.2d 714 (1977).

Roemer v. Board of Public Works, 426 U.S. 736, 96 S.Ct. 2337, 49 L.Ed.2d 179 (1976).

Meek v. Pittenger, 421 U.S. 349, 95 S.Ct. 1753, 44 L.Ed.2d 217 (1975).

Wheeler v. Barrera, 417 U.S. 402, 94 S.Ct. 2274, 41 L.Ed.2d 159 (1974).

Sloan v. Lemon, 413 U.S. 825, 93 S.Ct. 2982, 37 L.Ed.2d 939 (1973).

Committee for Public Education and Religious Liberty v. Nyquist, 413 U.S. 756, 93 S.Ct. 2955, 37 L.Ed.2d 948 (1973).

Hunt v. McNair, 413 U.S. 734, 93 S.Ct. 2868, 37 L.Ed.2d 923 (1973).

Levitt v. Committee for Public Education and Religious Liberty, 413 U.S. 472, 93 S.Ct. 2814, 37 L.Ed.2d 736 (1973).

Early v. Di Censo, 403 U.S. 602, 91 S.Ct. 2105, 29 L.Ed.2d 745 (1971).

Lemon v. Kurtzman, 403 U.S. 602, 91 S.Ct. 2105, 29 L.Ed.2d 745 (1971).

Flast v. Cohen, 392 U.S. 83, 88 S.Ct. 1942, 20 L.Ed.2d 947 (1968).

Racial Discrimination

Grutter v. Bollinger, 123 S.Ct. 2325 (2003).

Gratz v. Bollinger, 123 S.Ct. 2411 (2003).

St. Francis College v. Al-Khazraji, 481 U.S. 604, 107 S.Ct. 2022, 97 L.Ed.2d 749 (1987).

City of Pleasant Grove v. United States, 479 U.S. 462, 107 S.Ct. 794, 93 L.Ed.2d 866 (1987).

Wygant v. Jackson Board of Education, 476 U.S. 267, 106 S.Ct. 1842, 90 L.Ed.2d 260 (1986).

Regents of the University of California v. Bakke, 438 U.S. 265, 98 S.Ct. 2733, 57 L.Ed.2d 750 (1978).

Runyon v. McCrary, 427 U.S. 160, 96 S.Ct. 2586, 49 L.Ed.2d 415 (1976).

Lau v. Nichols, 414 U.S. 563, 94 S.Ct. 786, 39 L.Ed.2d 1 (1974).

Norwood v. Harrison, 413 U.S. 455, 93 S.Ct. 2804, 37 L.Ed.2d 723 (1973).

Recognition of Student Organizations

Bender v. Williamsport Area School District, 475 U.S. 534, 106 S.Ct. 1326, 89 L.Ed.2d 501 (1986).

Healy v. James, 408 U.S. 169, 92 S.Ct. 2338, 33 L.Ed.2d 266 (1972).

Release Time

Zorach v. Clauson, 343 U.S. 306, 72 S.Ct. 679, 96 L.Ed. 954 (1952).

McCollum v. Board of Education, 333 U.S. 203, 68 S.Ct. 461, 92 L.Ed. 649 (1948).

Religious Activities in Public Schools

Rosenberger v. Rector and Visitors of Univ. of Virginia, 515 U.S. 819, 115 S.Ct. 2510, 132 L.Ed.2d 700 (1995).

Lamb's Chapel v. Center Moriches Union Free School District, 508 U.S. 384, 113 S.Ct. 2141, 124 L.Ed.2d 352 (1993).

Lee v. Weisman, 505 U.S. 577, 112 S.Ct. 2649, 120 L.Ed.2d 467 (1992).

Karcher v. May, 484 U.S. 72, 108 S.Ct. 388, 98 L.Ed.2d 327 (1987).

Wallace v. Jaffree, 472 U.S. 38, 105 S.Ct. 2479, 96 L.Ed.2d 29 (1985).

Widmar v. Vincent, 454 U.S. 263, 102 S.Ct. 269, 70 L.Ed.2d 400 (1981).

Stone v. Graham, 449 U.S. 39, 101 S.Ct. 192, 66 L.Ed.2d 199 (1980).

Chamberlin v. Dade County Board of Public Instruction, 377 U.S. 402, 84 S.Ct. 1272, 12 L.Ed.2d 407 (1964).

Abington School District v. Schempp, 374 U.S. 203, 83 S.Ct. 1560, 10 L.Ed.2d 844 (1963).

Residency

Martinez v. Bynum, 461 U.S. 321 103 S.Ct. 1838, 75 L.Ed.2d 879 (1983).

Toll v. Moreno, 458 U.S. 1, 102 S.Ct. 2977, 73 L.Ed.2d 563 (1982).

Elgin v. Moreno, 435 U.S. 647, 98 S.Ct. 1338, 55 L.Ed.2d 614 (1978).

Vlandis v. Kline, 412 U.S. 441, 93 S.Ct. 2230, 37 L.Ed.2d 63 (1973).

School Liability

Gebser v. Lago Vista Indep. School Dist., 524 U.S. 274, 118 S.Ct. 1989, 141 L.Ed.2d 277 (1998).

Regents of Univ. of California v. Doe, 519 U.S. 425, 117 S.Ct. 900, 137 L.Ed.2d 55 (1997).

Sex Discrimination & Harassment

United States (Brzonkala) v. Morrison, 529 U.S. 1062, 120 S.Ct. 1740, 144 L.Ed.2d 658 (2000).

Davis v. Monroe County Bd. of Educ., 526 U.S. 629, 119 S.Ct. 1661, 143 L.Ed.2d 839 (1999).

U.S. v. Virginia, 518 U.S. 515, 116 S.Ct. 2264, 135 L.Ed.2d 735 (1996).

Franklin v. Gwinnett County Public Schools, 503 U.S. 60, 112 S.Ct. 1028, 117 L.Ed.2d 208 (1992).

Ohio Civil Rights Commission v. Dayton Christian Schools, 477 U.S. 619, 106 S.Ct. 2718, 91 L.Ed.2d 512 (1986).

Mississippi University for Women v. Hogan, 458 U.S. 718, 102 S.Ct. 3331, 73 L.Ed.2d 1090 (1982).

Cannon v. Univ. of Chicago, 441 U.S. 677, 99 S.Ct. 1946, 60 L.Ed.2d 560 (1979).

Trustees of Keene State College v. Sweeney, 439 U.S. 24, 99 S.Ct. 295, 58 L.Ed.2d 216 (1978).

Student Privacy

Owasso Indep. School Dist. No. I-011 v. Falvo, 534 U.S. 426, 122 S.Ct. 934, 151 L.Ed.2d 896 (2002).

Gonzaga University v. Doe, 536 U.S. 273, 122 S.Ct. 2268, 153 L.Ed.2d 309 (2002).

Student Searches

Vernonia School District 47J v. Acton, 515 U.S. 646, 115 S.Ct. 2386, 132 L.Ed.2d 564 (1995).

New Jersey v. T.L.O., 469 U.S. 325, 105 S.Ct. 733, 83 L.Ed.2d 720 (1985).

Student Suspensions

Regents v. Ewing, 474 U.S. 214, 106 S.Ct. 507, 88 L.Ed.2d 523 (1985).

Board of Education v. McCluskey, 458 U.S. 966, 103 S.Ct. 3469, 73 L.Ed.2d 1273 (1982).

Carey v. Piphus, 435 U.S. 247, 98 S.Ct. 1042, 55 L.Ed.2d 252 (1978).

Bd. of Curators v. Horowitz, 435 U.S. 78, 98 S.Ct. 948, 55 L.Ed.2d 124 (1978).

Wood v. Strickland, 420 U.S. 308, 95 S.Ct. 992, 43 L.Ed.2d 214 (1975).

Goss v. Lopez, 419 U.S. 565, 95 S.Ct. 729, 42 L.Ed.2d 725 (1975).

Taxation

Camps Newfound/Owatonna, Inc. v. Town of Harrison, Maine, 520 U.S. 564, 117 S.Ct. 1590, 137 L.Ed.2d 852 (1997).

Allen v. Wright, 468 U.S. 737, 104 S.Ct. 3315, 82 L.Ed.2d 556 (1984).

Bob Jones University v. United States, 461 U.S. 574, 103 S.Ct. 2017, 76 L.Ed.2d 157 (1983).

Mueller v. Allen, 463 U.S. 388, 103 S.Ct. 3062, 77 L.Ed.2d 721 (1983).

Ramah Navajo School Bd. v. Bureau of Revenue, 458 U.S. 832, 102 S.Ct. 3394, 73 L.Ed.2d 1174 (1982).

California v. Grace Brethren Church, 457 U.S. 393, 102 S.Ct. 2498, 73 L.Ed.2d 93 (1982).

Gordon v. Lance, 403 U.S. 1, 91 S.Ct. 1889, 29 L.Ed.2d 273 (1971).

Askew v. Hargrave, 401 U.S. 476, 91 S.Ct. 856, 28 L.Ed.2d 196 (1971).

Doremus v. Bd. of Educ., 342 U.S. 429, 72 S.Ct. 394, 96 L.Ed. 475 (1952).

Teacher Termination

Patsy v. Bd. of Regents, 457 U.S. 496, 102 S.Ct. 2557, 73 L.Ed.2d 172 (1982).

Chardon v. Fernandez, 454 U.S. 6, 102 S.Ct. 28, 70 L.Ed.2d 6 (1981).

Delaware State College v. Ricks, 449 U.S. 250, 101 S.Ct. 498, 66 L.Ed.2d 431 (1980).

Beilan v. Board of Public Education, 357 U.S. 399, 78 S.Ct. 1317, 2 L.Ed.2d 1414 (1958).

Textbooks

Norwood v. Harrison, 413 U.S. 455, 93 S.Ct. 2804, 37 L.Ed.2d 723 (1973).

Board of Education v. Allen, 392 U.S. 236, 88 S.Ct. 1923, 20 L.Ed.2d 1060 (1968).

Cochran v. Louisiana State Board of Education, 281 U.S. 370, 50 S.Ct. 335, 74 L.Ed.2d 1929 (1930).

Transportation

Kadrmas v. Dickinson Pub. Schools, 487 U.S. 450, 108 S.Ct. 2481, 101 L.Ed.2d 399 (1988).

Wolman v. Walter, 433 U.S. 229, 97 S.Ct. 2593, 53 L.Ed.2d 714 (1977).

Everson v. Board of Education, 330 U.S. 1, 67 S.Ct. 504, 91 L.Ed. 711 (1947).

Weapons

U.S. v. Lopez, 514 U.S. 549, 115 S.Ct. 1624, 131 L.Ed.2d 626 (1995).

The Judicial System

In order to allow you to determine the relative importance of a judicial decision, the cases included in ***Higher Education Law in America*** identify the particular court from which a decision has been issued. For example, a case decided by a state supreme court generally will be of greater significance than a state circuit court case. Hence a basic knowledge of the structure of our judicial system is important to an understanding of higher education law.

Almost all the reports in this volume are taken from appellate court decisions. Although most education law decisions occur at trial court and administrative levels, appellate court decisions have the effect of binding lower courts and administrators so that appellate court decisions have the effect of law within their court systems.

State and federal court systems generally function independently of each other. Each court system applies its own law according to statutes and the determinations of its highest court. However, judges at all levels often consider opinions from other court systems to settle issues that are new or arise under unique fact situations. Similarly, lawyers look at the opinions of many courts to locate authority that supports their clients' cases.

Once a lawsuit is filed in a particular court system, that system retains the matter until its conclusion. Unsuccessful parties at the administrative or trial court level generally have the right to appeal unfavorable determinations of law to appellate courts within the system. When federal law issues or Constitutional grounds are present, lawsuits may be appropriately filed in the federal court system. In those cases, the lawsuit is filed initially in the federal district court for that area.

On rare occasions, the U.S. Supreme Court considers appeals from the highest courts of the states if a distinct federal question exists and at least four justices agree on the question's importance. The federal courts occasionally send cases to state courts for application of state law. These situations are infrequent and, in general, the state and federal court systems should be considered separate from each other.

The most common system, used by nearly all states and also the federal judiciary, is as follows: a legal action is commenced in district court (sometimes called trial court, county court, common pleas court or superior court) where a decision is initially reached. The case may then be appealed to the court of appeals (or appellate court), and in turn this decision may be appealed to the supreme court.

Several states, however, do not have a court of appeals; lower court decisions are appealed directly to the state's supreme court. Additionally, some states have labeled their courts in a nonstandard fashion.

In Maryland, the highest state court is called the Court of Appeals. In the state of New York, the trial court is called the Supreme Court. Decisions of this court may be appealed to the Supreme Court, Appellate Division. The highest court in New York is the Court of Appeals. Pennsylvania has perhaps the most complex court system. The lowest state court is the Court of Common Pleas. Depending on the circumstances of the case, appeals may be taken to either the Commonwealth Court or the Superior Court. In certain instances the Commonwealth Court functions as a trial court as well as an appellate court. The Superior Court, however, is strictly an intermediate appellate court. The highest court in Pennsylvania is the Supreme Court.

While supreme court decisions are generally regarded as the last word in legal matters, it is important to remember that trial and appeals court decisions also create important legal precedents. For the hierarchy of typical state and federal court systems, please see the diagram below.

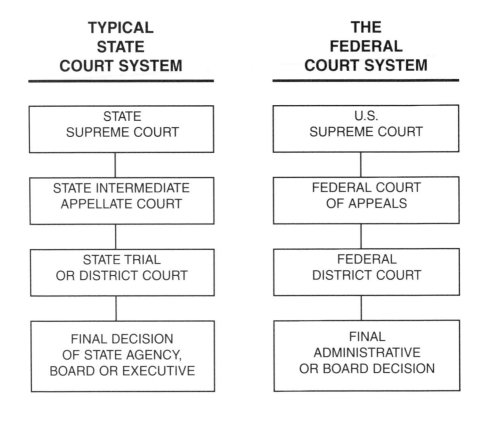

TYPICAL STATE COURT SYSTEM	THE FEDERAL COURT SYSTEM
STATE SUPREME COURT	U.S. SUPREME COURT
STATE INTERMEDIATE APPELLATE COURT	FEDERAL COURT OF APPEALS
STATE TRIAL OR DISTRICT COURT	FEDERAL DISTRICT COURT
FINAL DECISION OF STATE AGENCY, BOARD OR EXECUTIVE	FINAL ADMINISTRATIVE OR BOARD DECISION

Federal courts of appeals hear appeals from the district courts that are located in their circuits. Below is a list of states matched to the federal circuits in which they are located.

First Circuit — Puerto Rico, Maine, New Hampshire, Massachusetts, Rhode Island

Second Circuit — New York, Vermont, Connecticut

Third Circuit — Pennsylvania, New Jersey, Delaware, Virgin Islands

Fourth Circuit — West Virginia, Maryland, Virginia, North Carolina, South Carolina

Fifth Circuit — Texas, Louisiana, Mississippi

Sixth Circuit — Ohio, Kentucky, Tennessee, Michigan

Seventh Circuit — Wisconsin, Indiana, Illinois

Eighth Circuit — North Dakota, South Dakota, Nebraska, Arkansas, Missouri, Iowa, Minnesota

Ninth Circuit — Alaska, Washington, Oregon, California, Hawaii, Arizona, Nevada, Idaho, Montana, Northern Mariana Islands, Guam

Tenth Circuit — Wyoming, Utah, Colorado, Kansas, Oklahoma, New Mexico

Eleventh Circuit — Alabama, Georgia, Florida

District of Columbia — Hears cases from the U.S. District Court for Circuit the District of Columbia.

Federal Circuit — Sitting in Washington, D.C., the U.S. Court of Appeals, Federal Circuit hears patent and trade appeals and certain appeals on claims brought against the federal government and its agencies.

How to Read a Case Citation

Generally, court decisions can be located in case reporters at law school or governmental law libraries. Some cases also can be located on the Internet through legal Web sites or official court Web sites.

Each case summary contains the citation, or legal reference, to the full text of the case. The diagram below illustrates how to read a case citation.

case name (parties) case reporter name and series court location

Gupta v. Florida Bd. of Regents, 212 F.3d 571 (11th Cir. 2000).

volume number   first page   year of decision

Some cases may have two or three reporter names such as U.S. Supreme Court cases and cases reported in regional case reporters as well as state case reporters. For example, a U.S. Supreme Court case usually contains three case reporter citations.

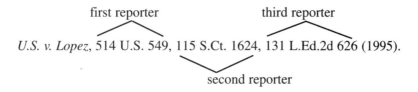

first reporter   third reporter

U.S. v. Lopez, 514 U.S. 549, 115 S.Ct. 1624, 131 L.Ed.2d 626 (1995).

second reporter

The citations are still read in the same manner as if only one citation has been listed.

Occasionally, a case may contain a citation that does not reference a case reporter. For example, a citation may contain a reference such as:

case name   year of decision   first page   year of decision

Thorpe v. Alsaeed, No. 01-99-00549, 2002 WL 567617 (Texas App. 2000).

court file number   WESTLAW[1]   court location

The court file number indicates the specific number assigned to a case by the particular court system deciding the case. In our example, the Texas Court of Appeals has assigned the case of *Thorpe v. Alsaeed* the case number of "No. 01-99-00549,"

---

[1] WESTLAW® is a computerized database of court cases available for a fee.

which will serve as the reference number for the case and any matter relating to the case. Locating a case on theInternet generally requires either the case name and date of the decision, and/or the court file number.

Below, we have listed the full names of the regional reporters. As mentioned previously, many states have individual state reporters. The names of those reporters may be obtained from a reference law librarian.

P. **Pacific Reporter**
Alaska, Arizona, California, Colorado, Hawaii, Idaho, Kansas, Montana, Nevada, New Mexico, Oklahoma, Oregon, Utah, Washington, Wyoming

A. **Atlantic Reporter**
Connecticut, Delaware, District of Columbia, Maine, Maryland, New Hampshire, New Jersey, Pennsylvania, Rhode Island, Vermont

N.E. **Northeastern Reporter**
Illinois, Indiana, Massachusetts, New York, Ohio

N.W. **Northwestern Reporter**
Iowa, Michigan, Minnesota, Nebraska, North Dakota, South Dakota, Wisconsin

S. **Southern Reporter**
Alabama, Florida, Louisiana, Mississippi

S.E. **Southeastern Reporter**
Georgia, North Carolina, South Carolina, Virginia, West Virginia

S.W. **Southwestern Reporter**
Arkansas, Kentucky, Missouri, Tennessee, Texas

F. **Federal Reporter**
The thirteen federal judicial circuits courts of appeals decisions. *See, The Judicial System, p. 511* for specific state circuits.

F.Supp. **Federal Supplement**
The thirteen federal judicial circuits district court decisions. *See, The Judicial System, p. 511* for specific state circuits.

Fed.Appx. **Federal Appendix**
Contains unpublished decisions of the U.S. Circuit Courts of Appeal.

U.S. **United States Reports**
S.Ct. **Supreme Court Reporter** ⟩ U.S. Supreme Court Decisions
L.Ed. **Lawyers' Edition**

GLOSSARY

Ad Valorem Tax - In general usage, a tax on property measured by the property's value.

Age Discrimination in Employment Act (ADEA) - The ADEA, 29 U.S.C. § 621 *et seq.*, is part of the Fair Labor Standards Act. It prohibits discrimination against persons who are at least 40 years old, and applies to employers that have 20 or more employees and that affect interstate commerce.

Americans with Disabilities Act (ADA) - The ADA, 42 U.S.C. § 12101 *et seq.*, went into effect on July 26, 1992. Among other things, it prohibits discrimination against a qualified individual with a disability because of that person's disability with respect to job application procedures, the hiring, advancement or discharge of employees, employee compensation, job training, and other terms, conditions and privileges of employment. The act also prohibits discrimination against otherwise qualified individuals with respect to the services, programs or activities of a public entity. Further, any entity that operates a place of public accommodation (including private schools) may not discriminate against individuals with disabilities.

Bill of Attainder - A bill of attainder is a law that inflicts punishment on a particular group of individuals without a trial. Such acts are prohibited by Article I, Section 9 of the Constitution.

Bona fide - Latin term meaning "good faith." Generally used to note a party's lack of bad intent or fraudulent purpose.

Claim Preclusion - (see Res Judicata).

Class Action Suit - Federal Rule of Civil Procedure 23 allows members of a class to sue as representatives on behalf of the whole class provided that the class is so large that joinder of all parties is impractical, there are questions of law or fact common to the class, the claims or defenses of the representatives are typical of the claims or defenses of the class, and the representative parties will adequately protect the interests of the class. In addition, there must be some danger of inconsistent verdicts or adjudications if the class action were prosecuted as separate actions. Most states also allow class actions under the same or similar circumstances.

Collateral Estoppel - Also known as issue preclusion. The idea that once an issue has been litigated, it may not be re-tried. Similar to the doctrine of *Res Judicata* (see below).

Due Process Clause - The clauses of the Fifth and Fourteenth Amendments to the Constitution which guarantee the citizens of the United States "due process of law" (see below). The Fifth Amendment's Due Process Clause applies to the federal government, and the Fourteenth Amendment's Due Process Clause applies to the states.

Due Process of Law - The idea of "fair play" in the government's application of law to its citizens, guaranteed by the Fifth and Fourteenth Amendments. Substantive due process is just plain *fairness*, and procedural due process is accorded when the government utilizes adequate procedural safeguards for the protection of an individual's liberty or property interests.

Employee Retirement Income Security Act (ERISA) - Federal legislation that sets uniform standards for employee pension benefit plans and employee welfare benefit plans. It is codified at 29 U.S.C. § 1001 *et seq.*

Enjoin - (see Injunction).

Equal Pay Act - Federal legislation that is part of the Fair Labor Standards Act. It applies to discrimination in wages that is based on gender. For race discrimination, employees paid unequally must utilize Title VII or 42 U.S.C. § 1981. Unlike many labor statutes, there is no minimum number of employees necessary to invoke the act's protection.

Equal Protection Clause - The clause of the Fourteenth Amendment that prohibits a state from denying any person within its jurisdiction equal protection of its laws. Also, the Due Process Clause of the Fifth Amendment that pertains to the federal government. This has been interpreted by the Supreme Court to grant equal protection even though there is no explicit grant in the Constitution.

Establishment Clause - The clause of the First Amendment that prohibits Congress from making "any law respecting an establishment of religion." This clause has been interpreted as creating a "wall of separation" between church and state. The test now used to determine whether government action violates the Establishment Clause, referred to as the *Lemon* test, asks whether the action has a secular purpose, whether its primary effect promotes or inhibits religion, and whether it requires excessive entanglement between church and state.

Ex Post Facto Law - A law that punishes as criminal any action that was not a crime at the time it was performed. Prohibited by Article I, Section 9, of the Constitution.

Exclusionary Rule - Constitutional limitation on the introduction of evidence that states that evidence derived from a constitutional violation must be excluded from trial.

Fair Labor Standards Act (FLSA) - Federal legislation that mandates the payment of minimum wages and overtime compensation to covered employees. The overtime provisions require employers to pay at least time-and-one-half to employees who work more than 40 hours per week.

Federal Tort Claims Act - Federal legislation that determines the circumstances under which the United States waives its sovereign immunity (see below) and agrees to be sued in court for money damages. The government retains its immunity in cases of intentional torts committed by its employees or agents, and where the tort is the result of a "discretionary function" of a federal employee or agency. Many states have similar acts.

42 U.S.C. §§ 1981, 1983 - Section 1983 of the federal Civil Rights Act prohibits any person acting under color of state law from depriving any other person of rights protected by the Constitution or by federal laws. A vast majority of lawsuits claiming constitutional violations are brought under § 1983. Section 1981 provides that all persons enjoy the same right to make and enforce contracts as "white citizens." Section 1981 applies to employment contracts. Further, unlike § 1983, § 1981 applies even to private actors. It is not limited to those acting under color of state law. These sections do not apply to the federal government, though the government may be sued directly under the Constitution for any violations.

Free Exercise Clause - The clause of the First Amendment that prohibits Congress from interfering with citizens' rights to the free exercise of their religion. Through the Fourteenth Amendment, it also has been made applicable to the states and their sub-entities. The Supreme Court has held that laws of general applicability that have an incidental effect on persons' free exercise rights are not violative of the Free Exercise Clause.

Incorporation Doctrine - By its own terms, the Bill of Rights applies only to the federal government. The Incorporation Doctrine states that the Fourteenth Amendment makes the Bill of Rights applicable to the states.

Individuals with Disabilities Education Act (IDEA) - 1990 amendment to the Education of the Handicapped Act (EHA) that renames the act and expands the group of children to whom special education services must be given.

Injunction - An equitable remedy (see Remedies) wherein a court orders a party to do or refrain from doing some particular action.

Issue Preclusion - (see Collateral Estoppel).

Jurisdiction - The power of a court to determine cases and controversies. The Supreme Court's jurisdiction extends to cases arising under the Constitution and under federal law. Federal courts have the power to hear cases where there is diversity of citizenship or where a federal question is involved.

Labor Management Relations Act (LMRA) - Federal labor law that preempts state law with respect to controversies involving collective bargaining agreements. The most important provision of the LMRA is § 301, which is codified at 29 U.S.C. § 185.

Mill - In property tax usage, one-tenth of a cent.

National Labor Relations Act (NLRA) - Federal legislation that guarantees to employees the right to form and participate in labor organizations. It prohibits employers from interfering with employees in the exercise of their rights under the NLRA.

Negligence per se - Negligence on its face. Usually, the violation of an ordinance or statute will be treated as negligence per se because no careful person would have been guilty of it.

Occupational Safety and Health Act (OSHA) - Federal legislation that requires employers to provide a safe workplace. Employers have both general and specific duties under OSHA. The general duty is to provide a workplace that is free from recognized hazards that are likely to result in serious physical harm. The specific duty is to conform to the health and safety standards promulgated by the Secretary of Labor.

Overbroad - A government action is overbroad if, in an attempt to alleviate a specific evil, it impermissibly prohibits or chills a protected action. For example, attempting to deal with street litter by prohibiting the distribution of leaflets or handbills.

Per Curiam - Latin phrase meaning "by the court." Used in court reports to note an opinion written by the court rather than by a single judge or justice.

Preemption Doctrine - Doctrine that states that when federal and state law attempt to regulate the same subject matter, federal law prevents the state law from operating. Based on the Supremacy Clause of Article VI, Clause 2, of the Constitution.

Prior Restraint - Restraining a publication before it is distributed. In general, constitutional law doctrine prohibits government from exercising prior restraint.

Pro Se - A party appearing in court, without the benefit of an attorney, is said to be appearing pro se.

Remand - The act of an appellate court in returning a case to the court from which it came for further action.

Remedies - There are two general categories of remedies, or relief: legal remedies, which consist of money damages, and equitable remedies, which consist of a court mandate that a specific action be prohibited or required. For example, a claim for compensatory and punitive damages seeks a legal remedy; a claim for an injunction seeks an equitable remedy. Equitable remedies are generally unavailable unless legal remedies are inadequate to address the harm.

Res Judicata - The judicial notion that a claim or action may not be tried twice or re-litigated, or that all causes of action arising out of the same set of operative facts should be tried at one time. Also known as claim preclusion.

Section 504 of the Rehabilitation Act of 1973 - Section 504 applies to public or private institutions receiving federal financial assistance. It requires that, in the employment context, an otherwise qualified individual cannot be denied employment based on his or her handicap. An otherwise qualified individual is one who can perform the "essential functions" of the job with "reasonable accommodation."

Section 1981 & Section 1983 - (see 42 U.S.C. §§ 1981, 1983).

Sovereign Immunity - The idea that the government cannot be sued without its consent. It stems from the English notion that the "King could do no wrong." This immunity from suit has been abrogated in most states and by the federal government through legislative acts known as "tort claims acts."

Standing - The judicial doctrine that states that in order to maintain a lawsuit a party must have some real interest at stake in the outcome of the trial.

Statute of Limitations - A statute of limitation provides the time period in which a specific cause of action may be brought.

Summary Judgment - Also referred to as pretrial judgment. Similar to a dismissal. Where there is no genuine issue as to any material fact and all that remains is a question of law, a judge can rule in favor of one party or the other. In general, summary judgment is used to dispose of claims that do not support a legally recognized claim.

Supremacy Clause - Clause in Article VI of the Constitution that states that federal legislation is the supreme law of the land. This clause is used to support the Preemption Doctrine (see above).

Title VI, Civil Rights Act of 1964 (Title VI) - Title VI prohibits racial discrimination in federally funded programs. This extends to admissions, financial aid, and virtually every aspect of the federally assisted programs in which private schools are involved. Codified at 42 U.S.C. § 2000d.

Title VII, Civil Rights Act of 1964 (Title VII) - Title VII prohibits discrimination in employment based upon race, color, sex, national origin, or religion. It applies to any employer having 15 or more employees. Under Title VII, where an employer intentionally discriminates, employees may obtain money damages unless the claim is for race discrimination. For those claims, monetary relief is available under 42 U.S.C. § 1981.

Title IX - Enacted as part of the Education Amendments of 1972, Title IX prohibits sexual discrimination in any private school program or activity receiving federal financial assistance. Codified at 20 U.S.C. § 1981 *et seq.*

U.S. Equal Employment Opportunity Commission (EEOC) - The EEOC is the government entity that is empowered to enforce Title VII (see above) through investigation and/or lawsuits. Private individuals alleging discrimination must pursue administrative remedies within the EEOC before they are allowed to file suit under Title VII.

Vacate - The act of annulling the judgment of a court either by an appellate court or by the court itself. The Supreme Court generally will vacate a lower court's judgment without deciding the case itself, and remand the case to the lower court for further consideration in light of some recent controlling decision.

Void-for-Vagueness Doctrine - A judicial doctrine based on the Fourteenth Amendment's Due Process Clause. In order for a law that regulates speech, or any criminal statute, to pass muster under the doctrine, the law must make clear what actions are prohibited or made criminal. Under the principles of the Due Process Clause, people of average intelligence should not have to guess at the meaning of a law.

Writ of Certiorari - The device used by the Supreme Court to transfer cases from the appellate court's docket to its own. Since the Supreme Court's appellate jurisdiction is largely discretionary, it need only issue such a writ when it desires to rule in the case.

INDEX